STRIVING for INCLUSIVE DEVELOPMENT

FROM PANGKOR TO A MODERN MALAYSIAN STATE

SULTAN NAZRIN SHAH

OXFORD
UNIVERSITY PRESS

OXFORD
UNIVERSITY PRESS

Oxford New York
Auckland Cape Town Dar es Salaam Hong Kong
Karachi Kuala Lumpur Madrid Melbourne Mexico City
Nairobi New Delhi Shanghai Taipei Toronto

First published 2019

ISBN 978 983 47 2976 9

Perpustakaan Negara Malaysia Cataloguing-in-Publication Data

Sultan Nazrin Shah
STRIVING for INCLUSIVE DEVELOPMENT: FROM PANGKOR TO A MODERN MALAYSIAN STATE / SULTAN NAZRIN SHAH.
ISBN 978-983-47-2976-9 (hardback)
1. Economics--Malaysia.
2. Economics--Malaysia--History.
3. Malaysia--Economic conditions.
I. Title.
330.9595

Impression: 10 9 8 7 6 5 4 3 2

Text set in 10.5 point ITC Cheltenham Std by
Chitra Computers, India
Printed by Percetakan Jiwabaru Sdn. Bhd., Selangor Darul Ehsan
Published by Oxford Fajar Sdn. Bhd. (008974-T)
under licence from Oxford University Press,
4 Jalan Pemaju U1/15, Seksyen U1
40150 Shah Alam
Selangor Darul Ehsan, Malaysia

For

Azlan and Nazira

Sejambak melati ayahanda suntingkan,
Buat anakanda pewaris watan,
Sejarah negara ayahanda paparkan,
Moga anakanda jadikan pedoman.

About the Author

Sultan Nazrin Shah is the Ruler of Perak, and the Deputy *Yang di-Pertuan Agong* of Malaysia.

He is Chancellor of the University of Malaya. He is an Honorary Fellow of Worcester College, Oxford, and of Magdalene College and St Edmund's College, both Cambridge.

He is the author of *Charting the Economy: Early 20th Century Malaya and Contemporary Malaysian Contrasts*.

Sultan Nazrin Shah has a PhD in Political Economy and Government from Harvard University.

Contents

PART 3 EXPANDING AND DIVERSIFYING THE ECONOMY

PART 5 CREATING AN INCLUSIVE AND SUSTAINABLE FUTURE

Boxes

Figures

Box Figures

Tables

Box Tables

Maps

Abbreviations

1MDB	1Malaysia Development Berhad
ASEAN	Association of Southeast Asian Nations
BAFIA	Banking and Financial Institutions Act
CIAM	Central Indian Association of Malaya
CPM	Communist Party of Malaya
CV	Coefficient of variation
EPU	Economic Planning Unit
EU	European Union
FAMA	Federal Agricultural Marketing Authority
FDI	Foreign direct investment
FELCRA	Federal Land Consolidation and Rehabilitation Authority
FELDA	Federal Land Development Authority
GDP	Gross domestic product
GLC	Government-linked company
GLIC	Government-linked investment company
GLEs	Government-linked entities
GNI	Gross national income
GNP	Gross national product
HDI	Human Development Index
HEI	Higher Education Institution
HICOM	Heavy Industries Corporation of Malaysia
HIS	Household income survey
ICT	Information and communications technology
IIUM	International Islamic University Malaysia
ILO	International Labour Organization
IMF	International Monetary Fund
INCEIF	International Centre for Education in Islamic Finance
ISIC	International Standard Industrial Classification
KRI	Khazanah Research Institute
LINUS	Literacy and Numeracy Screening
LNG	Liquefied natural gas
MARA	Majlis Amanah Rakyat
MCA	Malayan Chinese Association
MCP	Malayan Communist Party
MIC	Malayan Indian Congress
MP	Malaysia Plan
MTUC	Malayan Trade Union Council
NAP	National Agricultural Policy

NDP	National Development Policy
NEAC	National Economic Advisory Council
NECC	National Economic Consultative Committee
NEP	New Economic Policy
NIE	Newly industrialized economy
NKEA	National key economic areas
NVP	National Vision Policy
OECD	Organisation for Economic Co-operation and Development
OPEC	Organization of the Petroleum Exporting Countries
OPP	Outline Perspective Plan
PADU	Education Performance and Delivery Unit
PEMANDU	Performance Management and Delivery Unit
PERNAS	Perbadanan Nasional Berhad
PES	Post-enumeration survey
Petronas	Petroliam Nasional Berhad
PISA	Programme for International Student Assessment
PMFTU	Pan Malayan Federation of Trade Unions
PMGLU	Pan Malayan General Labour Union
PNB	Permodalan Nasional Berhad
PPP	Purchasing-power parity
PWT	Penn World Tables
R&D	Research and development
RIDA	Rural Industrial Development Authority
RISDA	Rubber Industry Smallholders Development Authority
SABK	Sekolah Agama Bantuan Kerajaan (Government-aided Religious School)
SDG	Sustainable Development Goal
SITC	Standard International Trade Classification
SMEs	Small- and medium-sized enterprises
SMKA	Sekolah Menengah Kebangsaan Agama (National Islamic Secondary School)
SNA	System of National Accounts
STEM	Science, technology, engineering, and mathematics
TFP	Total factor productivity
TFR	Total fertility rate
TIMSS	Trends in International Mathematics and Science Study
TPA	Tin Producers Association
TRIPS	Trade-Related Intellectual Property System
TVET	Technical and Vocational Education and Training
UiTM	Universiti Teknologi MARA (MARA University of Technology)
UK	United Kingdom
UMNO	United Malays National Organisation
UNDP	United Nations Development Programme
US	United States

Preface

In my book *Charting the Economy*, published in 2017, I presented a new set of estimates for Malaya's gross domestic product (GDP) in the first four decades of the 20th century. This was a period during which Malaya was under British colonial administration. I also made some comparisons of the dynamics of colonial economic growth with that of post-independence Malaysia. The GDP estimates in that book arose from the research that I undertook during my doctoral studies at Harvard, and which I have continued since through my 'Economic History of Malaya' project—see www.ehm.my.

This publication, *Striving for Inclusive Development: From Pangkor to a Modern Malaysian State*, presents the results of my continuing research. It is based on comprehensive analysis of primary economic and social data, extensive study of archival documents, and an in-depth review of the extant colonial and contemporary economic literature. The analysis reveals the impressive progress Malaysia has made, while also illuminating the challenges that remain. Faced with the possibility of the country falling into the 'middle-income trap', a new approach is now needed to realize the goal of transforming Malaysia into a more prosperous, resilient, and cohesive nation.

I continue to be intellectually indebted to many people and institutions for generously sharing ideas, insights, and information, without which this book would not have come to fruition. Although they are too numerous to mention individually, it gives me great pleasure to acknowledge all those who have supported and enthusiastically encouraged my research.

I would like to recognize the continuing support of Azirah Hashim, Executive Director of the Asia–Europe Institute of the University of Malaya, for hosting the Economic History of Malaya project. My appreciation also goes to the Department of Statistics–Malaysia, especially for the outstanding support given by Chief Statistician Mohd Uzir Mahidin and his staff, as well as to the Ministry of Education–Malaysia, and the staff of the National Archives of Malaysia, Singapore, and the United Kingdom.

I would particularly like to thank the distinguished professionals who graciously reviewed and made helpful comments on earlier drafts of individual chapters. These are Ibrahim Ahmad Bajunid, Karl Bek-Nielsen, Isahak Haron, Kalimullah Hassan, (the late) Khoo Kay Kim, Kim Young Eun, Lim Lin Lean, Mohamed Jawhar Hassan, Sulaiman Mahbob, Anthony Milner, Noor Azlan Ghazali, Shad Saleem Faruqi, Richard Smethurst, Tan Eu Chye, Thillainathan Ramasamy, and Larry Wong.

I have benefited enormously from fruitful discussions over many years with Afifi al-Akiti, Annuar Zaini, Chandra Muzaffar, Jemilah Mahmood, Jomo Kwame Sundaram, Lee Oi Hian, Lin See-Yan, Mohd Azumi, Mohamad Othman Zainal Azim, Mohd Zahidi Zainuddin, Munir Majid, Muthiah Alagappa, Nordin Kardi, Dwight Perkins, Rajah Rasiah, (the late) Shaharil Talib, M. Shanmughalingam, Visu Sinnadurai, John Thomas, C. Peter Timmer, Wan Mohd Zahid Noordin, Steven Wong, Zainal Adzam, and many others, whose ideas have enriched my thinking about Malaysia's past and present development.

It also gives me great pleasure to acknowledge the continued leadership vision provided by Richard Leete, manager of the Economic History of Malaya project. The project has received valuable technical inputs from David Demery, Frank Harrigan, and C. Peter Timmer. I have also received helpful support from several research assistants who have worked with the project, including Chan Kar Ee, Cheng Fan Soon, Noor Ismawati Mohd Jaafar, Angela Lee, Vincent C. S. Lim, Sharon Ng, Sonia Persson, and Rabbi Royan.

In any single book covering some 150 years of the country's economic history, there are bound to be omissions, as well as some important topics that deserve to have been covered in greater detail. I hope that the findings presented here will help inspire further research to fill such gaps. I also hope that the lessons learned from our history will encourage us to strive for greater inclusivity of national institutions, and fairer economic and social policies that will improve the welfare and well-being of all Malaysians.

Sultan Nazrin Shah
Istana Iskandariah

Introduction

This book traces the evolution of what is now Malaysia from a far-flung colonial trading outpost at the time of the Pangkor Engagement in 1874 to a modern, diversified economy. It is divided into five parts, in 10 chapters, which chronicle the events and the transformations—as well as the people—that marked and shaped this journey.

Part 1, *Forming a Nation and a Mosaic Population*, comprises two introductory chapters that focus on how Malaysia and its institutions were formed, and how its population grew.

Chapter 1 outlines the historical evolution of the separate geographical entities of the Malay peninsula over the past 150 years, their changing governance, and how they eventually came together to form Malaysia. It describes the institutions that the British progressively established during their lengthy rule, primarily if not exclusively in order to consolidate their economic and strategic interests. These included political and administrative structures, a legal and security system, and economic policies intended to facilitate investment, trade, and fiscal stability. However, World War II shattered the illusion of British protection of the Malay states, and of Sabah and Sarawak. The post-war proposal to create a Malayan Union with centralized government control and common citizenship aroused widespread opposition among the Malays and led to an upsurge in nationalism. In Britain, too, after the war, there was growing acceptance of the need for a new focus on Malaya's 'development', and for a managed transition to independence.

Chapter 2 begins with an overview of the history of Malayan population census-taking, and of how colonial administrators introduced an ethnicity-based classification that served to separate different communities. It assesses how colonial immigration policy responded to meeting the labour-force needs of the peninsula's growing extractive economy, and the huge impact that migration had on population growth and ethnic composition. Migrants settled in and around tin-mining areas, estate plantations, and the steadily growing towns located in the west coast states. The northern and east coast states attracted far fewer migrants and remained populated predominantly by peninsula-born Malays. At independence in 1957, occupational segregation and segmented settlement patterns were a legacy of colonial immigration policy: they had become institutionalized, and ethnicity had become closely identified with a person's economic function. After 1957, immigration was initially curtailed, but since the 1980s a much more liberal policy has been adopted, with new waves of Asian foreign labour entering Malaysia to meet shortages of lower-skilled workers. Yet, in the other direction, there have been persistent outflows of the more highly skilled Malaysians, weakening the country's human capital base.

Part 2, *Enhancing Human Well-being*, traces the development of the country's segmented education and health systems, and the steps taken by colonial and Malaysian governments to build human capital and advance well-being.

Chapter 3 reviews the nature of Malaya's highly segmented education system, where few children—almost all of them from privileged families—had opportunities beyond the basic primary level. During late colonialism, and especially after independence, the fundamentals of the education system began to change, with progressively expanded opportunities that eventually provided much greater access to all levels of education. A more integrated school system gradually emerged to help support nation building and to meet the country's changing human resource needs. Yet six decades after independence—and despite hugely positive trends in education indicators—the *quality* (rather than the *quantity*) of education has not reached the originally expected standards, an issue experienced by many developing countries. The education system is not responding well enough to the needs of the labour market, nor is it ensuring a successful transition for all from school to decent work.

Chapter 4 examines how Malaya's health policy evolved to support colonial economic development. As infectious diseases took a heavy toll on migrant workers and threatened to decimate the labour force, improved sanitation and health services became imperative. But most measures were implemented in urban areas, and so had little impact on the bulk of the rural population. Only after World War II, with heavy investment in expanding the health infrastructure, improving nutrition, controlling infectious diseases, and adopting disease-prevention and health-promotion measures, was there real progress in health care for the rural population. Health outcomes improved spectacularly, with dramatic gains in life expectancy at birth, consolidating the conditions for a fertility transition and subsequently a demographic dividend which would go on to support economic growth.

Part 3, *Expanding and Diversifying the Economy*, presents the book's core economic analysis. It starts with a discussion of the establishment of institutions and the expansion of the trade in tin and rubber in the colonial period, and proceeds to an evaluation of economic performance since independence.

Chapter 5 begins in the late 19th century, when most of the world's tin was mined in the Federated Malay States. The first two decades of the 20th century then saw Malaya become the world's leading producer of rubber as demand soared, largely as a result of the advent of the mass production of automobiles in the United States. Malaya's economy was ravaged, however, by the Great Depression of the 1930s, when rubber and tin prices collapsed. In the absence of social safety nets, many people suffered great hardship during these years. By the early 1950s, the colonial administration had more or less rebuilt the pre–World War II commodity-exporting economy following the destruction of economic activities during the Japanese occupation. From independence through to 1969, much of the colonial legacy remained. However, while the economy sustained solid growth during these years, the rewards were not evenly felt, with the rural population, and Malays in particular, remaining distanced from the modern sector and enjoying little benefit.

Dissecting the factors underlying post-independence economic growth, Chapter 6 focuses on the increase in productivity, and considers the effects that structural change and the demographic transition have had on Malaysia's economy. Although economic growth compared favourably with that in most other developing countries in the 1950s, Malaysia has not performed as well as the Republic of Korea, Singapore, and Taiwan. The reasons for this are explored, with deficits in human capital identified as a key part of the answer. This chapter also considers the extent to which Malaysia's development is sustainable by looking at development through the lens of the accumulation of 'genuine wealth'—the country's portfolio of natural, human, and manufactured capital.

Chapter 7 continues the story of economic development since 1970. The 1970s saw the emergence of an interventionist state and the start of redistributive policies and aggressive affirmative action intended to sever the colonial association of ethnicity with economic function. The two decades of the New Economic Policy (1971–1990) saw rapid growth and modernization of the economy, and significant social rebalancing in economic terms. Growth accelerated in the first part of the 1990s, appearing to vindicate the policy redirection that followed the commodity crisis of the mid 1980s; but there were signs of overheating and growing economic imbalances in these years, which contributed to vulnerabilities in the economy, and eventually led to severe corrections during the Asian financial crisis. Nonetheless, at the dawn of the new millennium, real incomes were far higher than they had been in 1990 and solid economic growth continued through to 2008, when Malaysia's economy again stalled as the global financial crisis and Great Recession hit. At the start of the current decade, the economy was again growing, even if concerns were being voiced about slowing economic momentum, institutional weaknesses, and the risks of becoming caught in the 'middle-income trap'.

Part 4, *Achieving Growth with Equity*, turns to the processes by which the transition from a predominantly agricultural economy to a modern one led to a huge reduction in poverty, and to more equitable income distribution.

Chapter 8 analyses, at the commodity and state level, the role of agriculture in the country's structural transformation and in the enormous reduction in absolute poverty. After 1970, structural transformation accelerated in nearly all states, and rural Malays found higher-paid jobs in urban areas. The productivity of farmers who remained behind rose nearly as fast as that of workers in urban areas, so that the gap between rural and urban labour productivity started to narrow. Fast-rising incomes in rural and urban areas led to a rapid decrease in poverty. By our present decade, absolute poverty has been virtually eliminated, a transformation essentially driven by economic growth and the diversification of agriculture.

Chapter 9 begins with an analysis of consumption inequality in colonial Malaya, where Europeans—and a tiny minority of other communities who were living a high-status European lifestyle—were vastly better off than the masses. Indeed, differentials in private consumption expenditure *widened* during the first four decades of the 20th century. 'Growth with equity' became the primary policy objective after independence, with the New Economic Policy heralding the start of the government's more interventionist role in managing the economy and pursuing affirmative social objectives. Standards of living improved sharply from the 1970s onwards, and real average household income more than doubled between 1995 and 2016. A sizeable middle class, which includes members of all communities, has emerged. The country has also made some progress towards a more equitable distribution of income among ethnic groups. Even so, while the income share of the bottom 20 per cent of individuals has improved in recent years, it remains unacceptably low.

Part 5, *Creating an Inclusive and Sustainable Future*, concludes this book-length inquiry with a forward-looking assessment of some of the central challenges facing Malaysia today. It underlines the fact that the country has made impressive development progress since the end of colonial rule, and that all communities have played an important role. But the time is now ripe for Malaysians to evaluate their circumstances afresh and make key choices about future directions.

Map of
PERAK
MALAY PENINSULA
Note.
The actual Boundary of this State in-land is not yet determined.
TERRITORY
QUEDAH
PROVINCE WELLESLEY
SALANGORE
Muda
Muda River
Malakoff Estates (Sugar)
Logan's Estates
Alma Estates (Sugar, Tapioca, Tea)
Pry Estates (Sugar & Rice Mill)
Pº Tikus
Pry R.
Pº Jerejak
Pº Kra
Krean R.
Krean Estates (Sugar)
S. Krean
S. Salamah
Jawe Simpit
S. Lemo
Campong Raya
Bagan Samah
North Mound
Mosque
Kurow River
Permatang Boolooh
South Mound
Gunong Hijau
Tin Mines
Matang
Gunong Pondok
Gapis
Roadway
Gula R.
Silensing R.
Teluk Kartang
Bukit Berapit
Bukit Gantang
LAROOT RIVER
Gunong Bubo
Qualla Trong
Juru Mas R.
Tingie River
Qualla Juromas
Hut R.
Elephant Track to Blanja
Bruas R.
Pº Tallong
Teluk Sagah
False Bukit Sigaree
Pathway to Blanja
Dinding River
Kota Siam
Rajah Itam R.
Pulo Pangkor
Little Dinding
Gajah Mati R.
Ayer Tawa R.
Teluk Batu
Pulo Katta
Likior
SAND BANK
Pº Sambilang
Katun
PERAK RIVER
T. Sajaga
Kota Stia
Brimbang Payang
S. Kling
Teluk S.Nebong
Teluk S.Booloo
Salamah
Sagah Galah
Perak River
Prek
Kotah Lamah
Papan R.
Campong Boyah
Tallang
Qualla Kangsa
Saiyong
S.Chumoh
Sengang
S. Jeliang
Tipus
Chankat Dungla
Blanja
Sadang
Iyang
Botah
Teluk Campong
Lamboh Gajah
Pº Tiga
Passir Sala
Bt. Tengah
Bandar Baru
Kotah Lumut
Rajah Lela
Durian Sabatang
Batu Rabit
Plus R.
APPROXIMATE BOUNDARY
Epu
Kinta
Raya R.
Gopin Tin Mines
Campar R.
Kinta R.
Batang Padang R.
Tin Mines
Bidor River
Bidor
Songkei R.
Songkei
River Sipong
Bagan Lipas
Bagan Passir
Sapa
Bernam
Slim R.
Slim
Qualla Slim
Simpang Tajah
BERNAM RIVER
Bernam River
Chengkat Lela

Adapted from:
Tinsley Brothers (ed.),
Map of Perak Malay Peninsula,
London, 1874

Courtesy of:
HRH Sultan Sharafuddin Idris Shah
and Dato' Richard Curtis

PART 1

FORMING A NATION AND A MOSAIC POPULATION

Chapter 1

From British Intervention to Independence

Starting from 1786, when the island of Penang became the first of three settlements in the Strait of Melaka to come under the control of the British East India Company, the Malay peninsula became a sphere of increasing British influence up until the Japanese occupation in 1941. With the receding regional influence of the Dutch, direct—and indirect—British control over the territories of the Malay peninsula was progressively extended after the signing of the Pangkor Engagement in 1874. By the start of World War I, Malay rulers of all the peninsula's states had accepted British protection.[1] These states, together with Penang, Melaka, and Singapore, were collectively referred to as British Malaya, which comprised three loosely integrated entities: the Straits Settlements, the Federated Malay States, and the Unfederated Malay States. While the Straits Settlements were administered directly as a crown colony, the territories that made up the other two entities were protected Malay states, and remained nominally under the sovereignty of their rulers who retained certain rights, including the ability to ratify laws and to decide on Islamic matters.

In the early decades of the 20th century there was little sense, if any, of a national identity among the diverse peoples living in British Malaya. It was essentially a collection of political entities brought together by the colonialists, and not a sovereign state managed for national development. It was a vast, resource-rich, and underpopulated territory, and most of its inhabitants were transient economic migrants from impoverished rural farming communities in the Malay archipelago and elsewhere in Asia. They were lured to the peninsula by the promise of the extraordinary expansion of commercial agriculture that was taking place—principally in rubber

1 Each of the peninsula's nine Malay states was ruled by a monarch whose title was historically defined. Sultan (the Arabic term for ruler) tended to replace raja (ruler in Sanskrit) when Islam came to the peninsula. In Negeri Sembilan, the monarch was traditionally titled *Yang di-Pertuan Besar* (literally, 'he who is made lord'). In some states the ruler's title has changed over time, and minor royals also sometimes use the title of raja.

production—as well as by the earlier prosperity created by the lucrative but volatile tin industry.

Colonial policies guaranteed that British Malaya was, and remained, socially and economically divided. They resulted in a fluctuating numerical balance between the three main population groups—broadly categorized by the British as Malays, Chinese, and Indians—which was contingent on the ebbs and flows of migrant workers. These policies also created a divide within each group between the small elite class, educated in English-medium schools in the main towns, and the large rural majority who received only rudimentary education in their vernaculars. In addition, colonial policies led to huge geographical imbalances in economic development as public and private investments were channelled to those states where enormous profits could be earned from the extractive industries.

The Japanese occupation irreversibly weakened British colonial dominance and challenged the prevailing social and political order. After the Japanese surrendered in August 1945 and British rule was restored, a period of military administration followed until March 1946 during which the British government attempted to impose a new centralized Malayan Union. Vehement Malay resistance to the Union, however, led instead to the creation of the Federation of Malaya on 1 February 1948, which marked the beginning of a decade-long transition to *Merdeka* (independence) in August 1957. With the achievement of political independence, the Federation of Malaya became a self-governing parliamentary democracy.

Sabah (formerly North Borneo) and Sarawak (controlled by the British Brooke family until 1941) on the island of Borneo followed a different path. These two states, separated from the east coast of the Malay peninsula by more than 500 kilometres of the South China Sea, were larger in land area and even more sparsely populated than the peninsula. They were also less developed economically. They both became British-protected states in 1888 through an agreement between the British government and the British North Borneo Company which administered North Borneo. They became British colonies much later, in 1946, and continued to be administered separately both from the peninsula's Malay states and from each other. In September 1963, they merged with the Federation of Malaya (and temporarily with Singapore) to form Malaysia.

This introductory chapter outlines the historical evolution of the separate geographical entities of the Malay peninsula over the past 150 years or so, their changing governance structures, and how the various parts eventually came together to form Malaysia. It describes the institutions and arrangements that the British progressively established during their lengthy rule to consolidate their vital economic and strategic interests. These included political and administrative structures, a colonial legal and justice system, and economic policies intended to promote fiscal stability and to facilitate investment, trade, and, ultimately, the unimpeded flow of resources to London, the metropolitan capital. Some of these institutions were essentially colonial and specific to Malaya, while others were modelled on those which already existed in Great Britain. They were designed to support a capitalist, extractive economy.

Although they were established primarily to serve the political and economic interests of the British, the institutions and systems that took root during colonial rule were highly resilient and provided strong foundations for the post-colonial development of Malaysia.

The Straits Settlements of Penang, Melaka, and Singapore

Between 1825 and 1867, the Straits Settlements—comprising the three strategically located commercial ports of Penang, Melaka, and Singapore, situated on the west and south coasts of the Malay peninsula (Map 1.1, panel a)[2]—were ruled from British India as a single administrative unit. These three settlements were initially under the authority of the East India Company, headquartered in Calcutta, and later under that of the government of India.[3] In 1867, after a decade of petitioning from their European merchant population to the Colonial Office in London, the three settlements were separated from India and combined to form a single administrative area known as the British Crown Colony of the Straits Settlements, administered by the Colonial Office.[4]

As well as dominating trade with India, the East India Company had a large and lucrative network of trading posts throughout Asia, which were integrated into wider trading systems. These were defended using the Company's vast

---

2 The Straits Settlements also included Christmas Island (from 1900), the Cocos Keeling Islands (from 1903), and the Dindings territory (from 1826 until its retrocession to the state of Perak in 1935). The Dindings, presently the Manjung District in Perak, comprising Pangkor Island, Lumut, and Sitiawan, was initially ceded to the British by Perak as part of the 1826 Burney Treaty, although it was not taken up by them until 1874, when the transfer was confirmed through Article XI of the Pangkor Engagement (Box 1.1).

3 The British East India Company, like the Dutch East India Company, was founded in the first decade of the 17th century. They were both large and risky ventures under the protection of government-licensed monopolies. If they made money, they could be tapped for revenue in return for the renewal of their charters. The two companies fought several wars with each other during the second half of the 17th century to seize control of the main sea routes out of western Europe. Initially, the Dutch controlled the East Indies and the spice trade, and the British the trade in Indian textiles (Ferguson, 2002).

4 The main factor that held up the transfer was concern about the possible drain on British government resources that would be required to support the garrison in the Straits Settlements.

military and naval resources, with the backing of the British government.[5] The Straits Settlements were initially used to bolster and protect the East India Company's lucrative trading route to China and other destinations in Asia. The bulk of the world's trade to eastern Asia at that time passed through the narrow Strait of Melaka.

After signing treaties with the Dutch and the Siamese, the Company gradually extended its influence over the peninsula's Malay states through trade and treaties. The Malay rulers of these states regarded the East India Company as the arbiter of local politics and appealed for its help in settling internal and external disputes. The Company, for its part, sought deeper British commercial penetration (Thio, 1969).

In the 19th century, the settlements of Penang, Melaka, and Singapore were, to varying degrees, trading-port towns, each surrounded by a moderately sized rural area. Their small, diverse, and cosmopolitan populations grew rapidly as their economies prospered (Chapter 2). Their differing occupational composition—for example, their numbers of shopkeepers, traders and warehousemen, boatmen and fishermen, cooks, hack-carriage runners, and others—reflected their varying economic activities.

Each of the three settlements had free port status, meaning that shipping and cargo could enter and leave without taxes being levied. Eventually, they were to serve as footholds for British expansion into, and control of, the peninsula's resource-rich Malay states. The settlements benefited greatly in economic terms when the Malay states came under British protection—especially Singapore, which was a flourishing southern port for the ever-growing trade in commodity exports and Western and Asian imports.

Penang

Penang island in the north of the Malay peninsula was the first settlement to be secured by the British. The island's history is closely associated with the East India Company's efforts to obtain a footing in the peninsula's Malay states and to set up a commercial and naval depot midway between its base in India and its trading interests in China. Penang's central location gave it a strategic geographical advantage, while its policy of tax exemption on trade was an additional benefit. The island became a centre for trading in opium from India to China, in various goods with Java, in rice from Siam, and in imports such as cotton manufactures and arms from Great Britain.

5 From 1788, based on legislation drawn up by the British Parliament, governors general of the East India Company were appointed directly by the Crown, the first being Earl Cornwallis. The Indian Mutiny of 1857 forced the British to rule India in a vastly different way and the Company was wound up, ending the anomaly of a corporation governing a sub-continent. The former governor general became a viceroy, and ultimate authority was vested in the secretary of state for India in London (Ferguson, 2002).

Around the 1760s, the East India Company had become aware of the high value of trade in the Malay archipelago from which the Company was excluded by its Dutch counterpart. It was Francis Light, a shipmaster from the Company who had had considerable dealings with the northern Malay state of Kedah, who suggested occupying the island of Penang, which was part of Kedah. He sought and obtained approval from the governor general of the Company, and opened negotiations with Sultan Abdullah. As he was seeking protection from attack by Siam, Sultan Abdullah agreed to sign a treaty ceding Penang on condition that the Company would come to his aid if Kedah was threatened militarily. The Company did not agree to this condition, however, and the sultan refused to sign. Light landed in Penang on 15 July 1786 with 'troops, stores and guns, and hoisted the British flag on 11 August 1786', renaming it Prince of Wales Island (Swettenham, 1906, p. 34). The sultan subsequently attempted to drive the Company out of Penang, but he was repelled and eventually forced to sign a treaty ceding the territory in 1790.

Perai—a narrow rural hinterland opposite the island of Penang on the mainland—also came under the jurisdiction of the East India Company in 1800. Renamed Province Wellesley, it was an important source of Penang's expanding exports of commodities, and securing it also ensured control of the harbour and the island's food supply (Winstedt, 1962). It was more populous than Penang, with internal communications facilitated by rivers. Province Wellesley's two staple goods were rice, cultivated by the Malays, and sugar cane, mainly controlled by European enterprise. In the early 19th century, there were 11 extensive sugar plantations in that territory, funded with European capital and run by European managers and engineers, and employing mainly Chinese workers (Cameron, 1865). As well as growing sugar, most of the sugar plantations operated milling machines that produced raw sugar and distilled rum for export. There was also some small-scale growing and trading of tapioca, coconuts, coffee, and tobacco.

Melaka

The port of Melaka was at the centre of a flourishing sultanate during the 15th century until it was conquered by the Portuguese in 1511. In 1641, with the support of the Johor sultanate, the Dutch drove the Portuguese out of Melaka and made it the headquarters of their enterprise in the Malay peninsula. They opened trading stations in Perak, Selangor, and other Malay states where tin was bought and commodities bartered. The East India Company took control of Melaka from the Dutch in 1795 during the Napoleonic wars. Although Melaka was then handed back to the Dutch in 1818 through the Treaty of Vienna, it became a British possession once again in 1824 through the Anglo-Dutch Treaty, which divided the Malay archipelago into a northern British zone and a southern Dutch zone. In exchange for Melaka, the British gave Bencoolen in west Sumatra to the Dutch.

By this time, the population of Melaka was also engaged in agricultural production, mainly of tapioca and rice, as well as open-cast tin mining.[6] The occupation of Penang by the East India Company, and later the establishment of a British trading station in Singapore, led to the dwindling importance of Melaka as a commercial trading port. By the late 19th century, Melaka had 'drifted out of the stream of endeavour, away from the struggle of riches and greatness' (Swettenham, 1906, p. 10). It had become commercially and strategically unimportant.

Singapore

The island of Singapore, with its highly favourable trading location adjoining the southern coast of Johor at the end of the Malay peninsula, became a British possession through a treaty signed in 1819 by Stamford Raffles on behalf of the East India Company, and by Sultan Hussein and Temenggong Abdul Rahman of Johor. Through this and a series of subsequent treaties, by 1824 the British were given the right to settle on the island. The East India Company had been searching for a good location in which to establish a British settlement to continue to counter Dutch influence and to support the extension of trade in the Malay archipelago. Singapore was a prized locale, situated on major shipping routes, and would in time become the pre-eminent trading and commercial hub of the peninsula.

Singapore grew rapidly from this point onwards. The bulk of its commerce was with Southeast Asian ports for which the island was ideally located (Webster, 1998). It also became a major destination for British, Indian, and Chinese goods. Singapore's revenues, at first derived largely from duties on the sale of opium and liquor, and to a lesser extent from stamp duties, came to exceed those of Penang and Melaka by a significant degree. Trade expanded further in the 1860s following the construction of wharves, docks, and warehouses on what later became known as Keppel Harbour. The opening of the Suez Canal in 1869 greatly increased East–West trade and passenger travel by considerably lessening journey distances and shortening shipment times.[7] A further major boost for Singapore's trade came with the phenomenal growth of the peninsula's exports of tin and rubber in the late 19th and early 20th centuries.

---

6 Melaka was the only one of the Straits Settlements that was on the peninsula and not an island.

7 In 1867, the passage from London to Singapore around the Cape of Good Hope took 116 days, whereas in 1870 a steamship made the voyage from Glasgow to Singapore through the Suez Canal in 42 days (Drake, 2018).

Map 1.1 Straits Settlements, Federated and Unfederated Malay States, and Malaysia[a]

a. Straits Settlements circa 1826[b]

b. Straits Settlements, Federated Malay States, and Unfederated Malay States—British Malaya circa 1914

c. Malaysia 1965 to present

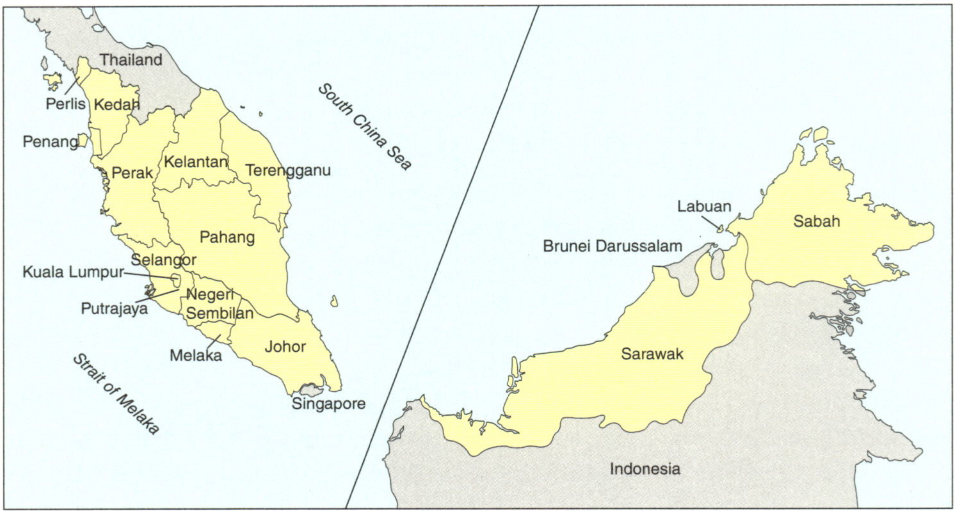

Note: [a] Country boundaries are approximate and are intended for illustrative purposes only.
[b] See footnote 2.

Governance of the Straits Settlements

Singapore replaced Penang as the administrative centre of the Straits Settlements in 1832. After their separation from British India in 1867, the settlements were headed by a British governor who reported to the secretary of state for the colonies. The governor was based in Singapore, while Melaka and Penang were supervised by lieutenant governors. The governor had executive powers, and could direct policies and appoint judges and justices of the peace. He was assisted by an Advisory Executive Council, which included the resident councillors of Penang and Melaka, as well as nominated unofficial members from local communities. A Legislative Council, vested with the power to make laws, was formed in 1867, and in 1887 a Municipal Council was established to administer town areas separately from rural districts (Makepeace et al., 1921; Hairudin Harun, 1990).[8] With some adjustments, this model of colonial governance was later adopted in the Federated Malay States.

The Pangkor Engagement, 1874

The rapid growth of commercial tin production that took place in the 1860s and even earlier had attracted an influx of labour to the tin-producing states of Perak, Selangor, and Negeri Sembilan. The new mines, generally established on land owned by local Malay chiefs, were funded mainly by wealthy Chinese businessmen based in the Straits Settlements. In the early 1870s, violent disputes broke out over the control of these mines between rival Chinese factions, which were formed around dialect groups and clan membership. Penang, where each faction had supporters among the Chinese merchants, was overwhelmed by large numbers of Chinese escaping the violence, especially from Larut in Perak, where the most serious fighting took place.[9] This situation threatened the stability and security necessary for trade.

As the disturbances in Perak (as well as in Selangor) began to affect the economic interests and security of the British and other communities, there were renewed calls by powerful sections of the Straits Settlements' trading community for the British government to change its long-standing policy of 'non-interference in the Malay states' and to take action to restore order.[10] As noted by Northcote Parkinson (1964, p. xvi), 'The people who mattered in the Straits Settlements were resolved to establish British influence over the Malay states, thus opening for themselves a new field of investment and trade'. This was particularly the case in relation to tin production and

---

8 Among the departments and authorities that already existed, or were formed in the following decades, were the treasury (1855), the land office (1855), public works (1859), the supreme court (1868), the Chinese Protectorate (1877), and the Indian immigration department (1879).

9 Serious incidents also took place in Selangor, where a government vessel was attacked by pirates in the mouth of the Selangor river, and tin-mining companies were badly affected by the ongoing civil disturbances (Swettenham, 1906). Sungai Ujong, the area on which Melaka's commercial prosperity depended, experienced unrest as well.

10 In July 1873, a petition from 248 Chinese traders arrived in London to deliver the news that the west coast, from Province Wellesley to Melaka, was in a state of anarchy. This was one of the factors that prompted the Earl of Kimberley, then Colonial Secretary, to intervene in the Malay states.

commercial agriculture. A Straits Settlements Association was established in London to pressure the Colonial Office into extending British influence over the Malay states. Given the impacts of broader developments on trade in the Straits Settlements, including increased competition resulting from the opening of the Suez Canal, European and Chinese merchants in the Straits Settlements were eager to create fresh business opportunities for themselves and to develop the resources of the Malay states (Cowan, 1951).

Associated with the business rivalries and violent civil disturbances, there was also a serious dispute at this time among a divided royal court about the succession to the Perak throne following the death of Sultan Ali in May 1871 (Swettenham, 1906; Sadka, 1968; Gullick, 1992). Power struggles and violent conflict were common in royal succession bids in 19th-century Malaya, especially as trade and industry grew, and Malay clans bitterly contested the rights to collect revenues from tin-mining concessions (Khoo, 1972). The competing claimants to the Perak throne were backed by the rival Chinese clans involved in the Larut mining disputes. Harry Ord, Governor of the Straits Settlements (1867–1873), had previously tried to resolve the dispute without success, and its prolongation provided another reason for the British government to reconsider its non-interference policy. Despite his concern to prevent disorder from spreading to the Straits Settlements and to provide favourable conditions for the expansion of trade, Ord failed in his attempts to persuade the Colonial Office to intervene.

The instructions of the Earl of Kimberley, then British Colonial Secretary, to Andrew Clarke, the incoming Governor of the Straits Settlements, on 20 September 1873 were what eventually provided the basis for British intervention. Sadka (1968) maintains that while imperial policy and strategy did play a part in prompting British intervention, it was the local administrators, motivated by economic interests, who pushed most strongly for this. Kimberley's instructions were seen as both highly beneficial to British economic interests, and closely aligned with those of the mercantile community in the Straits Settlements.[11] They included the following key passage:

> I have to request that you will carefully ascertain, as far as you are able, the actual condition of affairs in each State, and that you will report to me whether there are, in your opinion, any steps which can properly be taken by the Colonial Government to promote the restoration of peace and order, and to secure protection to trade and commerce with the native territories. I should wish you especially to consider whether it would be advisable to appoint a British Officer to reside in any of the States. Such an appointment could, of course, only be made with the full consent

11 Macintyre (1961) and Winstedt (1962) contend that Kimberley's decision was also influenced by concern that, without British intervention, the peninsula's Malay states would put themselves under the protection of some other European power—possibly Germany—which was also staking claims in the region.

> of the Native Government, and the expenses connected with it would have to be defrayed by the Government of the Straits Settlements. (Swettenham, 1906, p. 175)

At the end of 1873, Raja Muda Abdullah of Perak requested that Governor Clarke prepare a mutually beneficial treaty with the British government. His letter inviting the colonial administration to 'pacify' Perak and appoint a Resident provided the basis for the British to intervene more formally in protecting and expanding their economic interests through the Pangkor Engagement (Parkinson, 1964).[12] The treaty was signed and sealed on 20 January 1874 by the British government and Perak's hereditary Malay leaders (Box 1.1).

Box 1.1 The Pangkor Engagement, 20 January 1874

Whereas, a state of anarchy exists in the Kingdom of Perak owing to the want of settled government in the Country, and no efficient power exists for the protection of the people and for securing to them the fruits of their industry, and,

Whereas, large numbers of Chinese are employed and large sums of money invested in Tin mining in Perak by British subjects and others residing in Her Majesty's Possessions, and the said mines and property are not adequately protected, and piracy, murder and arson are rife in the said country, whereby British trade and interests greatly suffer, and the peace and good order of the neighbouring British Settlements are sometimes menaced, and,

Whereas, certain Chiefs for the time being of the said Kingdom of Perak have stated their inability to cope with the present difficulties, and together with those interested in the industry of the country have requested assistance, and,

Whereas, Her Majesty's Government is bound by Treaty Stipulations to protect the said Kingdom and to assist its rulers, now,

His Excellency Sir Andrew Clarke, K.C.M.G., C.B., Governor of the Colony of the Straits Settlements, in compliance with the said request, and with a view of assisting the said rulers and of effecting a permanent settlement of affairs in Perak, has proposed the following Articles of arrangements as mutually beneficial to the Independent Rulers of Perak, their subjects, the subjects of Her Majesty, and others residing in or trading with Perak, that is to say:-

I That the Rajah Muda Abdullah be recognised as the Sultan of Perak.

II That the Rajah Bandahara Ismail, now Acting Sultan, be allowed to retain the title of Sultan Muda with a pension and a certain small Territory assigned to him.

III That all the other nominations of great Officers made at the time the Rajah Bandahara Ismail received the regalia be confirmed.

IV That the power given to the Orang Kayah Mantri over Larut by the late Sultan be confirmed.

12 According to Winstedt (1962), Raja Muda Abdullah's letter was instigated by W. H. Read, a prominent Singapore merchant.

V That all Revenues be collected and all appointments made in the name of the Sultan.

VI That the Sultan receive and provide a suitable residence for a British Officer to be called Resident, who shall be accredited to his Court, and whose advice must be asked and acted upon on all questions other than those touching Malay Religion and Custom.

VII That the Governor of Larut shall have attached to him as Assistant Resident, a British Officer acting under the Resident of Perak, with similar power and subordinate only to the said Resident.

VIII That the cost of these Residents with their Establishments be determined by the Government of the Straits Settlements and be a first charge on the Revenues of Perak.

IX That a Civil List regulating the income to be received by the Sultan, by the Bandahara, by the Mantri, and by the other Officers be the next charge on the said Revenue.

X That the collection and control of all Revenues and the general administration of the country be regulated under the advice of these Residents.

XI That the Treaty under which the Pulo Dinding and the islands of Pangkor were ceded to Great Britain having been misunderstood and it being desirable to readjust the same, so as to carry into effect the intention of the Framers thereof, it is hereby declared that the Boundaries of the said Territory so ceded shall be rectified as follows, that is to say:- From Bukit Sigari, as laid down in the Chart Sheet No. 1 Straits of Malacca, a tracing of which is annexed 1, marked A, in a straight line to the sea, thence along the sea coast to the South, to Pulo Katta on the West, and from Pulo Katta a line running North East about five miles, and thence North to Bukit Sigari.

XII That the Southern watershed of the Krean River, that is to say, the portion of land draining into that River from the South be declared British Territory, as a rectification of the Southern Boundary of Province Wellesley. Such Boundary to be marked out by Commissioners; one named by the Government of the Straits Settlements, and the other by the Sultan of Perak.

XIII That on the cessation of the present disturbances in Perak and the re-establishment of peace and amity among the contending factions in that Country, immediate measures under the control and supervision of one or more British Officers shall be taken for restoring as far as practicable the occupation of the Mines, and the possession of Machinery, &c., as held previous to the commencement of these disturbances, and for the payment of compensation for damages, the decision of such officers shall be final in such case.

XIV The Mantri of Larut engages to acknowledge as a debt due by him to the Government of the Straits Settlements, the charges and expenses incurred by this investigation, as well as charges and expenses to which the Colony of the Straits Settlements and Great Britain have been put or may be put by their efforts to secure the tranquillity of Perak and the safety of trade.

Source: Allen et al, 1981.

With the Pangkor Engagement, the period of indirect rule of the peninsula's Malay states began. The Engagement provided for the appointment of a British Resident to 'advise' the Sultan of Perak in all matters affecting the general administration of the state, including maintaining peace and security, overseeing the collection of revenue from taxes, and encouraging economic development. It provided the basis for developing the institutions, systems, and infrastructure that would support the exploitation of natural resources. Moreover, it marked an important step towards integrating the economies of the Straits Settlements with those of the peninsula's west coast Malay states.

The Residential system—a core feature of the Pangkor Engagement—involved British control over all aspects of the state's administration, other than those touching on Islam and Malay custom. Leaving the important matters relating to *agama* (religion) and *adat* (custom) to the sultan and religious scholars helped to maintain continuity. Residents were instructed not to interfere with the 'minor details' of government, but to focus instead on the maintenance of peace and security; the initiation of a sound system of taxation; and the supervision of the collection of revenues so as to pay for the cost of British officers, and whatever establishments might be necessary to support them (Swettenham, 1906).

Although the Pangkor Engagement led to a resolution of the disputes in the mines and to the appointment of Raja Muda Abdullah as the Sultan of Perak, there was immediate (and later violent) resistance by some of the competing sections of Perak's royalty and their followers, as well as by the chiefs in other states. This was in part because the Engagement, while securing the position of the sultan, undermined traditional Malay institutions, structures, and administrative and financial systems (Gullick, 2004).[13] Local chiefs were disempowered and could no longer collect and spend revenue as they pleased. The sudden transition towards a centralized system of revenue collection also severely curtailed the existing modes of wealth acquisition utilized by other members of the Malay royalty.[14] Article nine of the Pangkor Engagement provided for a civil list that sought to compensate the local chiefs for their loss of revenue and power by providing for generous pensions and allowances, as well as appointments to office in the administration. But it was only implemented after the arrival of Hugh Low, the third Resident

13 Until the period of colonial rule, each of the peninsula's Malay states had its own unique features of governance, with the sultans ruling but not governing. The royal court officials generally comprised a *Bendahara* (prime minister), a *Bendahari* (treasurer), a *Temenggong* (security chief), and a *Mantri* (secretary). In the west coast states, district chiefs, nominally appointed by the sultans, provided executive leadership with responsibility for revenue collection, administration, defence, and justice (Gullick, 2004). Values, ceremonial traditions, hereditary titles, and ranks also played a part in maintaining the prevailing social order (Milner, 1982). Milner conceptualizes the polity of the pre-colonial Malay world in terms of the *kerajaan* system, which literally means the 'condition of having a raja'.

14 The ending of the traditional system of debt slavery in which members of the aristocracy could treat and inherit lower-class people as property was also a matter of frustration to some (Sadka, 1954). Debt slavery was formally abolished on 1 January 1884.

of Perak, in 1887 (Sadka, 1954). Political resistance to the Engagement was eventually crushed, but not before it had led to the murder of Perak's first British Resident, James W. W. Birch, on 2 November 1875 at Pasir Salak on the Perak River (Swettenham, 1906).

Treaty arrangements similar to those of the Pangkor Engagement were reached in the following months and years with the Malay rulers in Selangor, Negeri Sembilan (where there had also been civil wars over the rights to tin-mining royalties),[15] and Pahang.[16] The Malay rulers in each of these states accepted a British-appointed Resident on the basis of assurances about their protection and the maintenance of their sovereignty and rule. This process strengthened the indirect political rule of the British over the peninsula, and with it their ability to exploit the abundant natural resources of these four states. At the same time, it led to the enhanced security of the sultans, who no longer had to fear rivalries from powerful local chiefs, and it also increased their prestige and wealth through the small shares they held in the rising revenues generated by their states' booming economies.

By recognizing the ruler's sovereignty over his people and his control over religion and Malay custom, the British ensured that critical aspects of the traditional local power structure and culture remained untouched. The Residents were supported by the agency of the Malay rulers, whose authority over their subjects was indispensable in strengthening colonial rule. According to Milner (1982), the role of the sultan, or raja, was as much political as it was moral and religious. From the raja the Malays derived their sense of identity and position in life, and service to him was seen as the gateway to social and spiritual advancement. Capitalizing on this bond between ruler and subjects, the British were thus able to establish dominance over the indigenous population using their relationship with the Malay rulers.

The Federated Malay States and Their Governance

By 1896, the three neighbouring west coast states of Negeri Sembilan, Selangor, and Perak, along with the east coast state of Pahang, had been combined through the Treaty of Federation to form a single administrative

15 Owing both to the complicated political and clan organizations in the nine districts of Negeri Sembilan and to the disputes, the establishment of British influence and control over this state was a gradual process, beginning with the district of Sungai Ujong in 1889, and then extending to all other districts by 1895.

16 After the state came under British protection, civil war broke out in 1891–1895 in Pahang. Sultan Ahmad and the British Resident, Hugh Clifford, were confronted with challenges from rebellious chiefs over customary revenue collection and debt slavery similar to those that had been encountered in Perak by the ill-fated Birch. As in Perak, the rebels were eventually suppressed with the help of British forces (Linehan, 1936; Winstedt, 1962).

unit designated the Federated Malay States, which was overseen by a Resident General[17] (Map 1.1, panel b).

The union into a federation of the four states, where the bulk of Malaya's commercial and extractive industries were centred and where railways had been built to facilitate exports, served to strengthen and streamline British political and legislative control. It also undoubtedly helped to coordinate and promote colonial economic objectives. Over time it would accentuate the imbalance in the pace of economic and social development between these states and the Unfederated Malay States (with the exception of Johor). The ostensible justification for the federation was that it would create policy and regulatory consistency, that the richer states of Perak and Selangor would help the less-developed states of Negeri Sembilan and Pahang[18] (although there was no common treasury), and that the Resident General would be able to advocate directly on behalf of the sultans (Swettenham, 1906).

Kuala Lumpur in Selangor, already a flourishing tin-mining town, was designated as the administrative capital which gave further momentum to its development. The British Residents remained in charge in each state, while key departments were placed under one federal head based in the new capital. A Federal Council was established in 1909, headed by a British High Commissioner and assisted by the Resident General, with the British government retaining responsibility for defence and foreign affairs (Gullick, 1981). The Governor of the Straits Settlements also served as the British High Commissioner of the Federated Malay States, which effectively ensured his control over the state Residents and the four sultans. He supervised state budgets, and ran the Federal Council that passed all legislation and approved the estimates of expenditure and revenue. The council was an extension of the political and legislative authority of the Governor/High Commissioner.[19]

The Resident General assumed de facto control of the four states through the centralized government and civil service based in Kuala Lumpur.[20] This arrangement provided a simplified form of unified governance that diluted the powers and prestige of the individual sultans, who served as heads of the State Councils in their respective states. Their powers had already been diminished by the introduction of the Torrens system of land registration. This regulated procedures for the registration of land titles, replacing Islamic

17 Frank Swettenham, the architect of the federation, became its first Resident General before becoming the Governor of the Straits Settlements in 1901, when he succeeded his brother James Swettenham.

18 At that time, Pahang was the least economically important state, being indebted and inaccessible. It was reachable by sea for only about half of the year, and by land only with great difficulty (Parkinson, 1964).

19 The first meeting of the Federal Council of the Federated Malay States was held on 11 December 1909. Membership comprised the British High Commissioner, the Sultans of Selangor and Perak, the *Yang di-Pertuan Besar* of Negeri Sembilan, the Regent of Pahang, the Resident General, the four state Residents, and five others with business interests (Robson, 2001).

20 In 1911, the post of Resident General was renamed Chief Secretary of the Federation, diminishing the legislative powers of the Federated Malay States (Kaur, 2001).

land law, and making possible the allocation of land for commercial plantation and other agricultural activities (see below and Chapter 5).

The rulers in the four states acted on all matters other than those affecting Islam and Malay custom[21] according to 'advice' from the British Resident. Although the individual states remained under the nominal rule of the sultans, all royal decisions were subject to review by the State Councils, which were first established in Selangor and Perak in 1877. These councils comprised the Resident, local chiefs, and representatives of the Chinese community nominated by the sultan. The functions of these councils were mainly related to legislative issues, and included review of all capital punishment sentences.

As economic development progressed rapidly in the Federated Malay States, so too did the scope and size of the government administration. Government policy was not to tax trade or to levy high rents to finance the fiscal budget, but to rely instead on taxes placed on the consumption of opium, tobacco, and liquor; on a small export duty on tin and rubber; and on fees for issuing licences. Over time, the importance of the customs duty on tin came to exceed that of the excise duty on opium, such that by 1937 tin export duties accounted for 24 per cent of the total revenues of the Federated Malay States (Straits Settlements and Federated Malay States, 1939). Court and police structures were established in each of the Federated Malay States, along with departments for mining, plantations, medical services, public works, treasury, museums, and a Chinese Protectorate. Centralized departments for agriculture and education were set up subsequently, as were sanitary boards to provide sanitation, drainage, and water supply, and to regulate buildings, markets, and slaughterhouses.

The Unfederated Malay States and Their Governance

In 1909, the remaining five peninsular Malay states were grouped together to form the Unfederated Malay States. This entity comprised Kelantan and Terengganu in the east, Kedah and Perlis[22] in the north, and Johor in the south. All of these states—although Kedah and Johor to a lesser extent—were predominantly Malay and heavily rural, and the vast majority of their populations were engaged in traditional agriculture and fishing. Up until the end of the first decade of the 20th century, with the exception of Johor, these states had close governance relations with Siam.

---

21 As noted by Gullick (2001, p. 70), 'No one had a precise idea of the extent of "Malay customs" in which the Resident might not interfere, but any reform of a traditional monarchy was bound to alter its customs'.

22 This state was part of Kedah until 1841.

Great Britain, through the East India Company, had signed a secret treaty known as the Burney Treaty with the Kingdom of Siam in 1826.[23] The British acknowledged Kedah, Terengganu, and Kelantan as Siamese dependencies, and Siam accepted British ownership of Penang and Province Wellesley, and allowed the East India Company to trade freely in Terengganu and Kelantan. Siam itself maintained its independence, balancing the competing interests of the British (with possessions in neighbouring Burma and the Malay peninsula) with those of the French (with possessions in neighbouring Indo-China).

Kelantan and Terengganu

In 1897, another secret convention was signed between Siam and Great Britain. The British recognized Siamese political suzerainty over Kelantan and Terengganu, and gained the power to veto the establishment of foreign enterprises or military installations in these two states (Klein, 1969). The death of Kelantan's ruler, Sultan Ahmad, in 1889, had sparked a protracted period of intense competition among the state's ruling class and rivalry among the sultan's sons for political power. Siam had taken advantage of this chaotic situation to make inroads into matters of revenue, land, and justice (Shaharil Talib, 1995).

By the beginning of the 20th century, the British were also recognizing the potential of these states for trade and mining concessions. In 1900, the Duff Syndicate (which became the Duff Development Company in 1903), with the support of large British agency houses operating in Southeast Asia, had mobilized start-up capital of £10,000 to prospect for mineral wealth in Kelantan and Terengganu (Archive document, FO 69/224, 1900). The Raja of Kelantan, keen to reduce Siamese interference in his state, gave approval for the Syndicate to invest in mining, timber, and other lucrative rights, and granted large land concessions in specified districts. The Duff Development Company became increasingly active in Kelantan but did not extend into Terengganu (Robert, 1972).[24] By 1906, with the mining concessions not showing commercial promise and with the great rubber boom underway, the Company turned to rubber planting in Kelantan and sub-leased some of the large tracts of land it had been granted to other commercial companies (Tate, 1996).

At a meeting in Singapore in February 1902, Swettenham, the Governor of the Straits Settlements, pressured Siam's King Chulalongkorn to dispose of Kelantan and Terengganu and to accept British Residents for them, as in the Federated Malay States, arguing that these states had become a 'danger to Siam' (Klein, 1969, p. 122). The king resisted disposing of the territories,

23 The rulers of Kedah, Terengganu, and Kelantan were not present at the signing.

24 As compensation for the concessions, the rajas would be given shares and would receive a small duty on receipts and exports.

but reluctantly accepted the British plan, which led to an agreement later that year for a British Advisor (tasked with modernizing the administration) to be appointed by the Siamese government to support the Sultans of Kelantan and Terengganu (FO 93/95/16, 1902). This strengthened British influence in these two states without appearing to be in violation of earlier treaties (Kobkua, 1984). It marked a turning point in British intervention in these states' internal affairs and led inexorably to the 1909 Anglo-Siamese Treaty, which transferred suzerainty to the British and, in effect, defined a new international boundary between Siam and British Malaya (Andaya and Andaya, 2017).

From 1903 to 1909, the Kelantan ruling class, guided by the British Advisor, remodelled the state's government, establishing a state treasury and creating new posts for superintendents of justice and of rural administration (FO 881/8305, 1904; Shaharil Talib, 1995). Members of the ruling class were excluded from salaried positions and a few Malays from Singapore were recruited to fill selected posts, including district officers, thereby diminishing the status of traditional chiefs. The first British-government-appointed Advisor, who arrived in 1909, was content to carry on with the existing administration.

Primarily because of the resistance of its ruler, a Siamese-appointed British Advisor was not sent to Terengganu (Chan, 1965). In 1909, the state admitted a British Agent with limited powers; it only accepted a British-government-appointed Advisor when its finances could not meet the obligations of its reform measures, and it was thus forced to request a loan from the Straits Settlements in 1911 (Andaya and Andaya, 2017). The outbreak of World War I delayed the Advisor's arrival until 1919, however. The administrative structure in Terengganu included a State Council, as well as ministers and offices of the state secretary, treasurer, and commissioner of lands. But the British found that there was an absence of departmental systems, a lack of resources to improve the administration, and a problematic division of power between the territorial chiefs. It took until 1924 to convert the traditional administration into a more modern one that was, nevertheless, built on the foundations of the old system (Shaharil Talib, 1984; Gullick, 1992).

Kedah and Perlis

By the late 19th century, Siam's influence over Kedah was diminishing. Kedah's strong commercial ties with Penang meant that it was more developed than either Kelantan or Terengganu. In 1904, however, with recurring financial problems and its credit line with Penang exhausted, Kedah requested a loan from Siam to repay its debts. This request was granted on the condition that the state accept a British subject as a Siamese financial advisor who would reorganize the state's finances. The advisor arrived in Kedah in 1905.[25] This

25 Two years later, an advisor was also placed in Perlis.

arrangement allowed the advisor to work with Raja Muda Abdul Aziz and a few leading members of his court, bringing to an end the ruler's improvident control of the government. The State Council became the key governing body with responsibility for state finances and the right to levy taxes (Khoo and Mohd Taib Osman, 2011). District officers and assistant district officers were appointed to collect revenue; administer the land; supervise and encourage agriculture, public works, health care, and education; and supervise the *penghulu*, or village chiefs (Gullick, 1992).

Through the Anglo-Siamese Treaty of 1909, Siam also gave up its claim to Kedah and Perlis, which then formally came under British control.[26] The British Advisor appointed in 1909 regarded Kedah's central administration as adequately organized. A few British officials were brought in to strengthen the land, police, and public works departments.

Johor

Johor, the largest in size among the Unfederated Malay States, accepted a treaty of protection with the British government in 1885, and in 1914 yielded to British pressure to accept a resident British Advisor. Despite accepting protectorate status, Johor chose to remain outside the Federated Malay States. Having benefited greatly in economic terms from its proximity to Singapore, and with a more ethnically diverse population than the other Unfederated Malay States, Johor was comparable in its level of development to the Federated Malay States. The enterprise of wealthy Chinese in Singapore, who owned large plantations in Johor where they initially cultivated pepper and gambier (from which a valuable dye was extracted), had helped the state to reach this level of development. The economy continued to prosper in the early decades of the 20th century due to highly profitable agricultural exports, which by then consisted mainly of rubber, pineapple, and copra. Palm oil was also an important export by the late 1930s (CO 852/95/6, 1937).

Johor became the first state in the Malay peninsula to have a formal written constitution, promulgated in 1895. The constitution circumscribed the powers of the ruler, and upheld the rule of law. The ruler surrendered his powers on certain matters to the State Council. Of particular note is Article 15 of the constitution which barred the ruler and his heirs from handing over the state to any European power. Sultan Abu Bakar, ruler from 1862 to 1895, played an instrumental role in establishing an efficient and well-organized system of administration, which contributed to the building of schools, hospitals, police stations, mosques, and courthouses (Tunku Shahriman Tunku Sulaiman, 2004).

---

26 The north-east Malay sultanate of Pattani remained as Siamese territory.

Administration of the Unfederated Malay States

The Unfederated Malay States were much more autonomous than the Federated Malay States, with their rulers enjoying some political discretion and retaining greater control over state affairs. These states were not administered centrally or collectively (Heussler, 1981). They were less important commercially from the perspective of the British, and their traditional Malay system of government was allowed to continue. The sultans appointed *menteries* and, in outlying areas, district chiefs, who were typically members of the royal family who had local connections but were loyal to the ruler. The main duties of the local administrators were to collect taxes and maintain law and order. The district chiefs used traditional powers to requisition labour for public works (Gullick, 1992). Each state had its own judiciary and supreme court, although the constitution of the courts varied from state to state (Rudner, 1976). Malay remained the language of administration.

While these states accepted British Advisors in their administration, they did not accept the centralized political structure of the Federated Malay States.[27] They were willing to adopt the land system of the Federated Malay States, the collection of land rents, and the imposition of new taxes on agricultural crops and forest produce, which were seen as likely to result in improvements in their public services. The British Advisors, with the support of the rulers, promoted the emergence of a professional cadre of local Malay administrators for the civil service, and places were allocated for the sons and younger kinsmen of the rulers at the Malay College in Kuala Kangsar, Perak, which was established in 1905 (Gullick, 1992). The states gradually moved from an aristocratic system of administration in which power and high office were granted according to birth and status towards a meritocratic system based on ability and achievement.

Administration of British Malaya, 1900–1945

Through a series of treaties, by the early 20th century the British had progressively gained political and administrative control over the nine Malay sultanates on the peninsula. The overall governance structure of British administration in Malaya is summarized in Figure 1.1. Both the Federated Malay States with their British Residents, and the Unfederated Malay States with their British Advisors, were under British protection, while the Straits Settlements were directly administered as a British colony. In practice, despite differences in their respective sovereignties, the three territories known collectively as British Malaya became ever more administratively, socially,

27 Plans put forward from time to time by the British to unite the Unfederated Malay States with the Federated Malay States were rejected by the sultans.

and economically interconnected as the century progressed.[28] Singapore gradually became the real centre of decision-making for British Malaya, with its governor—who from the late 1920s also served as the High Commissioner for the Federated and Unfederated Malay States—implementing Colonial Office policies.

Figure 1.1 **British governance of Malaya, early 20th century**

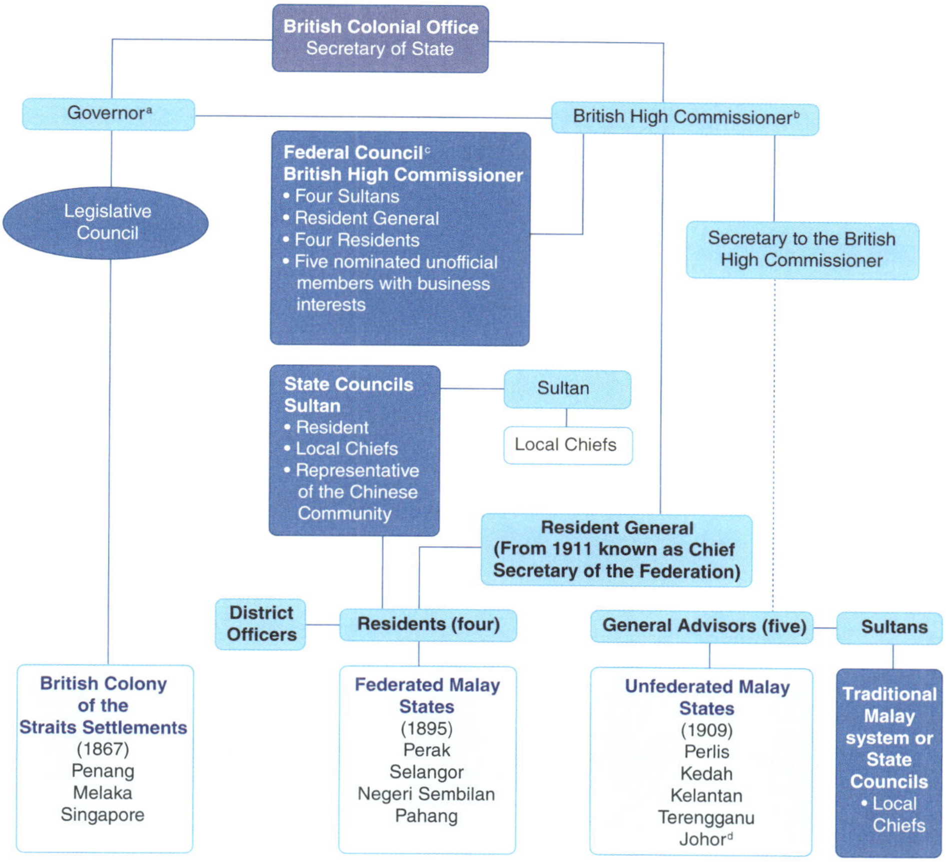

Notes:

[a] The Governor of the Straits Settlements, who was assisted by an Advisory Executive Council, had power to veto Bills of the Legislative Council.

[b] The Governor of the Straits Settlements in Singapore served as the *ex officio* British High Commissioner for the Federated Malay States.

[c] This is the Federal Council as originally composed in 1909.[29]

[d] Johor became a British Protectorate in 1885 and accepted a British Advisor in 1914.

---

28 The economic context that lay behind the evolution of these administrative arrangements is set out in Chapter 5.

29 In 1926, it was decided that the Malay rulers would be replaced in the Federal Council by their representatives. Members of the traditional Malay elite, who were now also senior civil servants, were chosen. However, their positions in the Federal Council differed from those of British officials as they were considered unofficial members representing Malay interests (Puthucheary, 1978).

Malayan Civil Service

The British built a strong administrative service to implement the government's economic and social policy objectives, including matters relating to land and immigration. They established a Civil Service as an elite first tier, and in 1910 the Malay Administrative Service as a second tier. The civil services of the Straits Settlements and the Federated Malay States were merged in 1920 to become the Malayan Civil Service (Heussler, 1981; Sandhu and Wheatley, 1989). Administrative and recruitment procedures were standardized and centralized, which allowed for mobility of officers across the Malay states and the settlements (United Nations Department of Economic and Social Affairs, 2005).

Aristocratic Malays were admitted into the civil service under the Malay Administrative Service, which marked the beginning of the modern Malay administration. The traditional Malay elite had lost some power and control due to the imposition of colonial rule. The British gave them government positions with personal allowances and pensions in order to preserve the existing social order, as well as to recognize the status of the indigenous elite, and to placate them. The Malay officers also acted as a bridge between the *rakyat* (people) and the British (Khasnor Johan, 1984).

At first, the intake of Malays into both tiers of the Malayan Civil Service was low due to a widespread inability to speak English, and most senior and mid-level positions were filled by British expatriates. In time, English-educated Malay graduates of the Malay College did increasingly join its senior and middle echelons, while graduates of all races from the English-medium schools were recruited for clerical and specialist positions in the Malay Administrative Service (Chapter 3). By the 1930s, Malays accounted for about 10 per cent of the Malayan Civil Service (Heussler, 1981). The lower grades were filled mainly by Indian migrants, while the Chinese occupied most of the technical and specialized positions.

Malays were preferred by the British for the higher-level civil service positions because this helped to consolidate control and to maintain close connections with the Malay rulers. In the Federated Malay States, seven out of ten government posts were reserved for Malays, a practice that was later enshrined in the Constitution of the Federation of Malaya. The number of Malays in the Malay Administrative Service increased, and avenues for promotion to the more senior Malayan Civil Service opened up. However, by late 1941, when the Japanese invasion began, there was a growing sense of frustration among non-Malays with this pro-Malay government service recruitment policy (Turnbull, 1974).

District Offices

Before British colonial rule, the hierarchy of state administration generally comprised the *penghulu* (village chiefs), the district chiefs, and, above them, the sultan. States were divided into districts, which were usually centred on an estuary or section of a river. District chiefs raised revenue by levying tolls on the traffic along the waterways of their districts.

After the Pangkor Engagement, the British took over the functions previously performed by the district chiefs, including the collection of revenue. The districts in each state were generally administered by British district officers working closely with local Malay officials. Before the 1930s, each of the three British entities had its own administration, and potential district officers, who were required to be proficient in the Malay language, had to apply directly for a position. In the 1930s, a unified Colonial Service was created, managed by the Colonial Office, and district officers became civil servants of both their particular territories and the Colonial Service.

The district officer was an administrator, a delegate of the Resident.[30] He was the link between the professional and technical services of the colonial government and the people, and was responsible for all government activities in his district (Jeffries, 2015). He served, first, as the land officer, and was also initially the magistrate. He represented the treasury, the police, the mines department, and the education department, and was required to implement new regulations issued in the *Government Gazette* (Robson, 2001). He was accompanied by an assistant district officer, often a local, who had the same responsibilities with slightly less authority. In addition, the *penghulu* was generally recognized as the district officer's right-hand man, and provided the link with the local community. Matters concerning Malay customary law were handled either by the local *kadi* (religious official) or by the *hakim* (judge) (Blake, 1990).

Land in the Malay peninsula was abundant, and historically came under the domain of the sultans, whose subjects were entitled to cultivate and occupy it. Starting from 1879, the colonial administration progressively introduced individual land ownership to facilitate the development of commercial agriculture. The administration of land was modelled on the Torrens system practised in Australia—which meant the alienation and registration of land for private ownership and security of tenure.[31] Each state capital had a central office for the registration of titles that administered grants for large

30 Raja Sir Chulan, Raja di-Hilir of Perak—the second son of Sultan Abdullah—was the first Malay district officer in Upper Perak, serving until 1911. He then became a member of the State Council. In 1924, he became the first Malay unofficial member of the Federal Council, while serving concurrently on the State Council of Perak between 1907 and 1933 (Robson, 2001).

31 The Torrens land registration system was also applied in North Borneo and Sarawak.

land parcels, while each district had its own land office that administered grants for parcels of land of less than four hectares (Voon, 1978).[32]

Administration during the Japanese Occupation, 1941–1945

Throughout the Japanese occupation, the civil administration of Malaya remained in the hands of the pre-war bureaucracy, but with the Japanese military administration in control of all senior positions.[33] At the local level, the principal change was the appointment of Malays to fill district officer positions, which had previously been held by British expatriates, with preference being given to members of the aristocracy. The district officers continued to perform the same functions as before—controlling district land offices, serving as sub-treasurers, and inspecting and reporting on local conditions. Malays in government service were required to sign a statutory declaration of allegiance to the Imperial Nipponese Government (Kratoska, 2018). The Japanese also abolished the dual form of government of British Malaya, administering the Straits Settlements and all of the Malay states under one central government based in Singapore, with Malay administrative assistance (Puthucheary, 1978).

Administration of North Borneo and Sarawak

The British North Borneo Chartered Company was established in 1881, from which time it administered a territory on Borneo island that had been ceded to it by the Sultans of Brunei and Sulu. According to its charter, the Company had to respect native rights and customs as well as religious freedom. Trade monopolies were forbidden, moreover, and the Company's governor had to be approved by the British secretary of state (Jones, 1966). North Borneo was made a British Protectorate in 1888 although it was still administered by the Company, which also began administering the strategically located island of Labuan from 1889 until it became part of the Straits Settlements in 1907 (Durand and Curtis, 2013).[34]

The Company's Court of Directors in London delegated authority to a governor residing in Sandakan, the capital of North Borneo (Kahin, 1947).

32 The significance of issues around land, and its ownership and use, is discussed further in Chapter 5.

33 The Japanese Military Administration established a Special Military Court presided over by a Japanese judge to try civilians charged with offences under the Japanese Maintenance of Public Peace and Order Law.

34 Between 1890 and 1905, Labuan was administered by the British North Borneo Company, after which the governor of the Straits Settlements was also made the governor of Labuan. On 1 January 1907, Labuan was annexed to the Settlement of Singapore, and on 1 December 1912 it was constituted as a separate settlement within the Straits Settlements. On 15 July 1946, Labuan was incorporated into North Borneo.

The governor was advised by a Legislative Council which comprised the government secretary, the chief justice, the commandant, the financial controller, the Residents, and the principal medical officer (Kahin, 1947). There were five Residents—one each in Sandakan, the east coast and the west coast, and two in the interior (CO 874/1012, 1925). Under each Resident were district officers recruited from London who were responsible for the administration of their districts, for the maintenance of law and order, for the collection of land revenues, and for the settlement of disputes, including labour disputes (Rutter, 1922).

Initially, the Chartered Company was an entirely administrative body and did not trade directly (Reece, 2011). Early revenues for the Company were derived from quit rent, export duties on jungle produce and timber, tobacco duties, import duties, and land sales, among other sources (Rutter, 1922). With funding sourced almost entirely from private capital, North Borneo developed steadily but slowly. From around 1920, the Company's transformation into a governing-cum-trading concern was envisaged in order to provide the capital that was needed for more substantial development.

Sarawak, which also became a British Protectorate in 1888, was governed for three generations by the Brooke family (Runciman, 1992). The Sultan of Brunei had appointed James Brooke, a British adventurer, as Raja and Governor of Sarawak in 1841 as a reward for his help in calming a rebellion of the Sarawak Malays against Brunei. Over the next six decades, Sarawak's territory was gradually enlarged with additional grants of land ceded by the sultan, and the River Lawas area purchased from the North Borneo Chartered Company in 1905. Trade expanded, especially in the early 20th century, in oil, gold, and coal, as well as in agricultural commodities (Ooi, 1997).

The Brookes were assisted in the administration of Sarawak by a few British officials, with Residents eventually appointed to each of the territory's five divisions. In a governing structure similar to that in North Borneo, the Residents were assisted by district officers in each of the divisions. A Supreme Council was established in 1855 comprising the British Resident of the first division and the treasurer, as well as four Sarawak Malay *Datus* (the highest title after Raja) (Reinhardt, 1970). The council advised on policy matters and had legislative powers. In 1865, a State Council was established to address matters of national welfare. It included members of the Supreme Council, the Residents, the treasurer, the commandant, the principal medical officer, and the leading native chiefs from the state. Compared with North Borneo, native officers played a more significant role in Sarawak's administration.

Following their liberation from the Japanese, North Borneo and Sarawak came under 17 years of direct British colonial rule, which marked a period of growth spurred by rehabilitation efforts and progressive development policies.[35] They continued to be administered separately from the Malay states on the peninsula and from Singapore, as well as from each other. It was partly for this reason that, even by the start of the 1960s, these two underpopulated, land-abundant, and natural-resource-rich states were a world away from Malaya's political awakening. Like the peninsula, both states were ethnically diverse, but they had a different mix of communities as indigenous groups constituted a much greater, and Malays a much smaller, share of their populations (Chapter 2). Both states had substantial populations of migrant Chinese, who had been arriving since the 19th century, attracted by the opportunities in mineral resource extraction, commercial agriculture, and trade.

From Fragmentation to the Federation of Malaysia, 1945–1963

Decolonization to *Merdeka*, 1945–1957

After the Japanese surrender on 15 August 1945, the Colonial Office made plans for Malaya's socio-economic rehabilitation, political reconstruction, and progression towards self-government. In the years immediately after World War II, there was strong momentum worldwide for decolonization, and a growing recognition of the right to self-government of colonized peoples.[36] This period also marked a fundamental break from Malaya's colonial past and was an important milestone in shaping the political independence that was to follow just 12 years later.

A more enlightened perspective towards the colonies was emerging in the United Kingdom, especially with the election of a Labour government in 1945 and the advent of the welfare state. The great economic and social hardships experienced by the Malayan people during the period of Japanese occupation had put acute stresses on traditional coping mechanisms. In the years leading up to independence, the colonial government came to play a more active role in promoting the development and social welfare of the people. Driven in part by Fabian ideals in Britain, expanded social policies were viewed as essential to the legitimization of the new colonial institutional and economic model. The scope of the Colonial Development and Welfare Act 1945 was expanded,

---

35 Raja Charles Vyner Brooke returned to Sarawak on 15 April 1946, and resumed power briefly until 1 July 1946.

36 The Atlantic Charter had been drafted by the US and the UK in 1941, and defined Allied goals for the post-war world. It was followed on 1 January 1942 by the Declaration of the United Nations, which laid the foundations for the United Nations Charter of 1945. The Charter championed 'respect for the principle of equal rights and self-determination of peoples', and helped to change public policy and opinion about colonization (United Nations, 2019, p. 37).

as were the resources allocated for technical assistance (British Information Services, 1960). But such policies were still always intended to be limited, with the emphasis on helping communities to help themselves rather than on providing large-scale, state-funded welfare programmes.

Malayan Union

Plans for the future of Malaya were being worked out in London even during the Japanese occupation. British authorities considered the existing decentralized administrative arrangements of the Federated Malay States, the Unfederated Malay States, and the Straits Settlements to be complex, inconvenient, and unsuited for the post-war international environment. They preferred a strong central government and national institutions that would support the political and economic development of the entire country.

The secretary of state for the colonies set out the proposed future constitutional policy for Malaya in January 1944 in a War Cabinet Secret Paper (CO 273/675/11, 1945). Despite earlier assurances given by the British government to the Malay rulers about maintaining the independence of the Malay states, these plans entailed a union of the nine Malay states and the settlements of Penang and Melaka. A separate government was proposed for Singapore. As the majority of its population was Chinese, its inclusion was seen as likely to provoke negative sentiment among Malays towards the proposal.

With this policy decision made, the Colonial Office began to prepare arguments for its justification. These arguments included the need to create Malayan nationalism, and to foster a national outlook among the area's different communities; a belated recognition of the crucial role of the 'immigrant races' in Malaya's past and future economic development; and the inefficiency of the existing decentralized administration in which each state enacted its own legislation through the Federal and State Councils, and the Legislative Council of the Straits Settlements. The proposed Malayan Union would have a single central legislature.

The Secret Paper contended that a unified Malay monarchy would not be acceptable to the non-Malay communities with substantial interests in the country. It proposed that only the British government could provide the common link that would draw the separate communities together, promote a sense of shared interest, and enable the development of common institutions. It argued that a continuation of the British government's pro-Malay policy—'Malaya for the Malays'—would inevitably lead to political unrest (CO 273/675/11, 1945). In January 1946, a government White Paper was issued to parliament by the secretary of state for the colonies. It stated that 'all those who have made the country their homeland should have the opportunity of a due share in the country's political and cultural institutions' (Secretary of State for the Colonies, 1946, p. 1). The White Paper set out the rationale and arrangements for the future constitution of the Malayan Union and Singapore.

On 1 April 1946, following a short period of military administration, the British government attempted to impose the Malayan Union. The process began in September 1945 with the dispatch of Brigadier H. C. Willian to Malaya to interview each of the sultans. His discussions had three main purposes: examining the conduct of the royal family and government servants during the Japanese occupation, with the aim of identifying and punishing collaborators; explaining the role of the military administration; and briefing the Malay rulers on the proposed Malayan Union treaty arrangements (CO 273/675/12, 1945). A key objective of Willian's was to prepare the ground and establish tactics for the upcoming mission of Harold MacMichael, special representative of the British government, who visited Malaya from October 1945 to January 1946. During his visit, MacMichael induced formal agreements with each of the rulers of the nine Malay states, which seemingly paved the way for the imposition of the Union (MacMichael, 1946).[37]

The Union was intended to create a strong and united country with a centralized government and central legislature, and to be the final step before the full transfer of political power to the people of Malaya. The Straits Settlements were dissolved, and Melaka and Penang were grouped with the Federated and Unfederated Malay States as part of the Union. Singapore was excluded, and on 1 April 1946 it became a separate British colony. However, strident criticism and fierce opposition to this externally imposed unified system of administration among the Malay rulers and the urban aristocratic elite began almost immediately (Lau, 1991; Rais Yatim, 2007).

This opposition was due mainly to the plan to grant Malayan Union citizenship to all communities living in Malaya, based on the principle of *jus soli* (Latin for 'right of the soil', meaning citizenship due to place of birth), or on their having resided in Malaya for ten of the past 15 years, or having five continuous years of residence.[38] Citizenship of the Malayan Union would carry with it eligibility for public and administrative service. These proposals

37 These agreements, which diminished the power of the sultans, would succeed earlier treaties signed with the rulers over the previous 70 years, starting with the 1874 Pangkor Engagement.

38 Tan Cheng Lock, later to become the first president of the Malayan Chinese Association (MCA), had campaigned for equal citizenship rights for those Chinese who claimed Malaya as their homeland. He also drew attention to the considerable amount of anti-Chinese propaganda that had been circulating in Malaya (CO 537/1565, 1946).

gave rise to fears among Malays of political domination by non-Malays, and of the erosion of their special rights.[39] Opposition to the Union was also generated because it took away the sultans' legal rights of state sovereignty, and because it submerged the identities of the individual states (CO 537/2143, 1947).

The proposed Union galvanized Malays into radical political action for the first time, leading to the formation of the United Malays National Organisation (UMNO) in 1946 (Mohamed Nordin Sopiee, 1974). A nationwide grassroots campaign was organized opposing the Union, which focused on the potential loss of Malay political power and its consequences. As Azlan Tajuddin (2012, p. 103) put it, 'a contagion of Malay ire quickly spread across the Malay peninsula, sending a stern message to those complicit with the Union proposal to beware of the consequences of their actions'. In the face of this strong opposition, and given the risks of internal political destabilization, the Union proposal was abandoned. The Japanese occupation had stirred pro-Malay nationalist sentiments, and had also displaced hundreds of thousands of Chinese, who now presented a strategic and political threat. The communities were even more divided than before, and had become suspicious of each other's intentions.

Federation of Malaya

Having failed to impose the Malayan Union (it was never formally fully promulgated), the British negotiated a new Federation of Malaya Agreement with the sultans and political leaders.[40] In an important step towards self-government, on 1 February 1948 the Malayan Union was replaced by the Federation of Malaya, again comprising the 11 peninsular states and excluding Singapore.[41] The federation's constitution created a strong central government responsible for most of Malaya's internal and external affairs. The Malay rulers were given an important role in its administration through the Federal Legislative Council and Executive Council, which were presided over by the British High Commissioner. While the principle of a centralized government was retained, considerable power was to be exercised by the sultans at the state level, with their traditional rights, powers, and dignity protected. Through separate state agreements made with the individual Malay rulers, the states retained control over land matters, which ensured

39 The effect of the long phase of Chinese and Indian migration flows on ethnic balance had become extremely sensitive politically, and Malays, particularly in the Unfederated Malay States, feared the potential loss of their political power, given the delicate population balance (Chapter 2).

40 The Malayan Agreement was heavily influenced by a working committee consisting of representatives of the British government, the Malay rulers, and UMNO (CO 537/2143, 1947).

41 A formal commitment to Malaya's eventual full independence was made by the British prime minister to parliament in March 1949. Gerald Templer, the British High Commissioner, was instructed to make political progress towards that outcome, without endangering Britain's substantial financial investments in Malaya (Stockwell, 1984).

them revenue from the sale or rental of state land, as well as income from mining and forestry activities.

The Federation of Malaya Agreement 1948 also contained a crucial provision whereby the British High Commissioner, in exercising his executive authority, was given the responsibility, among others, of 'safeguarding the special position of the Malays, and of the legitimate interests of other communities' (CO 537/2143, 1947; Federation of Malaya, 1948, p. 12). A new proposal in the Agreement also made it more difficult for Chinese and Indians to acquire citizenship than had been proposed in the Union, to their evident alarm.

Towards *Merdeka*

The decade between the agreement of 1948 and *Merdeka* on 31 August 1957 was marked by considerable internal turbulence and political tension. There was also a serious security threat from the Communist Party of Malaya (CPM), which led to strikes in industries vital to an economy struggling to recover from war damage as well as other civil disturbances. As the CPM's actions became more violent, and with business interests increasingly affected, an Emergency was declared (Box 1.2).[42] Issues relating to citizenship, education, and other matters were bitterly contested. The political role of the civil service was greatly expanded, and Malays were increasingly emboldened to protect themselves against the perceived encroachments of the other races without relying on the British (Puthucheary, 1978).[43]

Box 1.2 The CPM and the Malayan Emergency, 1948–1960

The CPM, a mostly locally organized Chinese movement (but also including some Malays and others), was formally established in 1930 at the time of the Great Depression (Too, 1990). The CPM established general labour unions in urban areas through which it aimed to promote the interests of workers, and to attain political power. Towards these ends, it sought to disrupt the tin and rubber industries, as well as the ports, by instigating strikes and rallies among low-paid workers. In reaction to strong pressure from British business interests, the government's initial response was to tighten already harsh labour laws and to declare strikes illegal, rather than to accommodate the CPM in a political negotiating process (Jesudason, 1989; Andaya and Andaya, 2017).

42 The Malayan Security Service, established in 1945 and responsible for obtaining intelligence information on subversive organizations in British Malaya, was disbanded in 1948 when it allegedly failed to forewarn the colonial authorities of the capabilities and intentions of the CPM. The breakdown in security intelligence-gathering was resolved when the Singapore and Malayan Special Branch became fully operational in 1952 (Comber, 2003).

43 The British concept of the political neutrality of the civil service was necessary for parliamentary government in independent Malaya. Provisions were made to allow civil servants to resign to contest the 1955 federal elections. Out of the 103 Malay candidates, 53 were ex-civil servants (Puthucheary, 1978).

The CPM rejected the legitimacy of the colonial government and started an insurgency to achieve an independent communist-led nation. It had limited support among rural Malays. Its recruits were mainly poor migrant rural Chinese squatters, many of whom had settled illegally as smallholder farmers during economic recessions and, being unable to acquire title to land because of the colonial land administration policy, now faced eviction. The creation of the Federation of Malaya on 1 February 1948, and in particular the proposed conditions for achieving citizenship, further alarmed the impoverished Chinese who lived outside the administrative framework of Malayan society. Many had suffered cruelty during the Japanese occupation and had previously sided with the British against the Japanese.[44]

Fearing a popular uprising as the CPM became increasingly violent—with attacks on British security forces and administration, derailment of trains, and disruptions to production in plantations and mines—the government declared a state of Emergency in June 1948. It was initially limited to parts of Perak and Johor, but was later extended to the entire peninsula. The Emergency empowered the government to arrest communist sympathizers and detain them without trial.

The CPM did enjoy some advantages at first, as sections of the local population, suffering from poverty and insecurity, sympathized with their aims. To curb the perceived support from rural Chinese, the Briggs Plan was introduced in 1950. This extreme and harsh initiative, devised by the Director of Emergency Operations, General Harold Briggs, resettled the rural Chinese involuntarily in so-called New Villages, with land allocated to support their agricultural activities. By the early 1950s, some 500 villages had been established, of which one-third were in Perak.[45] These villages were surrounded by wire fences, and curfews were imposed to curtail night-time movements. As the majority of villages were located on the fringes of cities and towns, this had the effect of making the Chinese a predominantly urban community, and changing the composition of rural areas (Ross-Larson, 1980) (Chapter 2).

The CPM was brutally suppressed, and the war against it was won through the interaction of several factors. These included the mastery of jungle warfare by the British security forces; the resettlement of rural Chinese in New Villages; an improved intelligence organization; and an efficient internal security command and control system, which was operated mainly by Malays. A robust socio-economic development programme, introduced by the British High Commissioner Gerald Templer and continued by the Malayan government, also played a significant part by winning the support of the local population (Box 5.8, Chapter 5). With the grievances of its supporters being addressed in this way, the CPM was further isolated (Sunderland, 1964). The Emergency was officially declared over in July 1960. However, the insurgency had had the effect of worsening relations between the different communities, and of strengthening the Malay nationalism that had already gained momentum owing to the Malayan Union proposals (Myrdal, 1968).

44 According to Khoo (2017), during the Japanese occupation the British had covertly supported the communists, then the Malayan People's Anti-Japanese Army, as this force was perceived to be the most organized anti-Japanese movement.

45 By the 1970 census, there were 465 New Villages with a total population of more than one million (EPU, 1976).

The number of federal government servants increased rapidly as the end of British rule approached. With a new nation-state on the horizon, the functions of government were expanded to cope with the evolving internal and external environment. In the years leading up to *Merdeka*, the 'Malayanization' of the public service gathered pace, and the number of British expatriate officers gradually diminished. By 1956, public servants numbered 107,000, of whom 61,000 were Malays, 29,000 Indians, 13,000 Chinese, and the rest Eurasians. The Malay rulers tended to oppose non-Malays working in state jobs that involved administering Malays directly. Most Chinese and Indians found opportunities for careers in the higher echelons of the Straits Settlements' government (Sunderland, 1964; Rudner, 1976; Heussler, 1981).

Due to perceived potential threats to their economic interests in a soon-to-be independent Malaya, Chinese and Indian business leaders formed their own political organizations: the MCA and the Malayan Indian Congress (MIC). These parties, with encouragement from the British, then joined with UMNO to form the Alliance for the first federal elections to the Federal Legislative Council, which were held in 1955.[46] Compromises on the most contentious issues then became achievable.

Following approval by the British government and the Malay rulers, an independent constitutional commission was established in March 1956, headed by Lord Reid, to prepare recommendations for a self-governing and independent Federation of Malaya within the Commonwealth. Its terms of reference arose out of a London Constitutional Conference held earlier in 1956, which took into account the Federation of Malaya Agreement. These recommendations were then agreed by the Conference of Rulers (CO 889/8, 1957). Their Highnesses the Rulers, representatives of political parties, and other groups took part in an extensive consultation process organized by the commission to ensure that different interests were considered. After much political bargaining, the draft constitution was presented to and agreed by the British Parliament in June 1957, and ratified by the Malayan Legislative Council.

On 31 August 1957, the independence of the Federation of Malaya was proclaimed. Tunku Abdul Rahman became the first prime minister and formed his first cabinet, which comprised seven Malays, two Chinese, and one Indian (Puthucheary, 1978).[47] The country moved from British colonial control to parliamentary democracy within a new sovereign state.[48]

---

46 The Alliance won 51 out of 52 seats in the Legislative Council and 80 per cent of the total votes cast.

47 Tunku Abdul Rahman initiated Malaya's membership of the United Nations and the British Commonwealth, and later initiated the Association of Southeast Asia, a grouping of Malaya, Thailand, and the Philippines. This was the precursor to the Association of Southeast Asian Nations (ASEAN), which now includes ten nation states in the region.

48 The evolving institutional landscape associated with independence is discussed in Chapter 5.

Malaya to Malaysia, 1957–1963

A 'Grand Design' or 'Greater Malaysia Plan' in which there would be some form of association between the Federation of Malaya, the three Borneo territories of North Borneo, Sarawak, and Brunei, and Singapore, was under consideration by the British government and Tunku Abdul Rahman from around 1960. However, there was no agreement on the most suitable arrangement for bringing all of these entities together.[49] The British government felt that some form of association among these territories was consistent with its strategic and commercial interests in the area, given that it still had constitutional responsibility for Singapore and the Borneo territories, and was in the process of guiding them to full self-government within the Commonwealth. It regarded the formation of a larger group under the leadership of the Federation of Malaya as beneficial to regional political stability and prosperity, as this would provide greater strength and security than could be achieved by each territory individually. This was particularly the case against the current backdrop of the threats of communist subversion and external aggression. The British government also feared that Singapore could become a communist state and form a direct alliance with China (FCO 141/17152, 1961).

Ethnic balance once again became an issue of explicit public and political discussion, as delicate and complex negotiations over the formation of the Federation of Malaysia gained momentum in the early 1960s. From the perspective of Malaya, bringing the vast, sparsely populated territories of North Borneo, Sarawak, and Brunei into the proposed federation would provide a reassuring ethnic and political balance to the largely Chinese population of Singapore.[50] Conversely, the special status of the Borneo states would be assured by the presence of Singapore, which was also to have a different status from the peninsular states in the new federation.

In January 1962, the Cobbold Commission was appointed as an outcome of the negotiations between the government of the Federation of Malaya and the British government to explore the views of the communities in North Borneo and Sarawak on the proposed merger. This commission recommended that 'in view of the special circumstances which apply to the Borneo territories, autonomy and safeguards should be given in certain matters which are not enjoyed by the other states' (Cobbold Commission, 1962, p. 46). Some of the political leaders of these two states, and a significant share of the population,

49 For a detailed discussion of the merits and implications of the various combinations of territorial association that were considered under the Grand Design, see the discussion papers and correspondence contained in FCO 141/17151, 1960 and FCO 141/17152, 1961.

50 Tunku Abdul Rahman had previously felt that Malaya's interests would be better served by keeping Singapore separate, as this would make it easier to insulate Malaya from any serious political deterioration in Singapore (for instance by closing the causeway). In addition, the British were keen to maintain the unrestricted use of their naval bases in Singapore (FCO 141/17151, 1960).

opposed joining the federation, preferring instead full independence (Kitingan and Ongkili, 1989; Leigh, 1974 and 2018). Another possibility considered by the Colonial Office was that North Borneo, Sarawak, and Brunei be merged into a single state (FCO 141/17151, 1960). The merger was proposed because of the security concerns stemming from the perceived communist threat in the Southeast Asian region, and was also expedient for Britain, as it was consistent with its decolonization policy.[51]

After lengthy negotiations, the Federation of Malaysia was formed on 16 September 1963, with Sabah, Sarawak, and Singapore as the three new component states (Map 1.1, panel c). The Malaysia Agreement, with an annex bill, was signed in London on 9 July 1963 between the UK, the Federation of Malaya, North Borneo, Sarawak, and Singapore (United Nations, 1970).[52] Sabah and Sarawak became the largest member states in size, although they lagged behind those on the peninsula socio-economically. They retained greater control over immigration, education, and the civil service than the peninsular states. Brunei was meant to have joined the new Federation of Malaysia, but withdrew from negotiations because of disagreements, particularly concerning the position of its sultan in the new federation, and the control of its oil production and oil revenues.

Almost immediately upon the formation of Malaysia, multiple disagreements arose between Tunku Abdul Rahman and Lee Kuan Yew, secretary general of Singapore's People's Action Party. The problems included differing views on the appropriateness of the participation of that party in the 1964 peninsular elections; differences inside and outside the federal parliament over economic and financial issues; challenges to the constitutionally guaranteed rights of Malays; and the call by Lee Kuan Yew for a 'Malaysian Malaysia' that would be a multiracial meritocracy 'where everybody will have his place: equal; language, culture, religion' (Lee, 2011, p. 219). Early in 1965, the People's Action Party announced the formation of an association with political parties from other states in opposition to the Alliance (the ruling parties in the federation), as part of an attempt to create such a Malaysian Malaysia. After a series of meetings failed to sort out these various issues, 'a separation agreement' was signed, and on 9 August 1965 Singapore was allowed to separate and became an independent nation.[53]

51 Indonesia opposed the creation of the Federation of Malaysia and launched a series of cross-border military raids into Borneo in 1962–1966. During the confrontation between Indonesia and Malaysia, the Malaysian Army was supported by Commonwealth forces from New Zealand and Australia under British command. Further challenges came from the Philippines, which made a claim to Sabah.

52 The Federation of Malaya, and the new states of Sabah, Sarawak, and Singapore, were all to be equal partners in the Federation of Malaysia. However, in 1976 the federation's constitution was amended such that the statuses of Sabah and Sarawak changed and they became states in the federation on a par with the 11 states in the peninsula, although still with some special rights.

53 The Constitution of the Federation of Malaysia, which had been amended to restructure Malaysia's legislative, judicial, executive, and administrative powers in 1963, was further amended when Singapore left the federation.

Maintaining Law and Order

The Military

Before colonial rule, the Malay rulers and other royals had struggled to maintain a semblance of order in the face of wars, disturbances, and disputes over lands and property, sometimes signing treaties with the East India Company in exchange for support. For the British, the maintenance of external and internal peace and security was essential for the expansion of trade and commerce, for encouraging private investment in the peninsula's natural resources, and for ensuring credibility with the Malay rulers.

Territorial rivalry among European powers for the control of Southeast Asian lands and their adjoining seas meant that securing their defence was a high priority. In the early stages of British rule, defence was maintained through the presence of British military and naval forces. Heavily armed ships and garrisons, stationed under various treaty arrangements, served to protect the trading ports, and acted as powerful symbols of British strength (Morrah, 1963). Troops from the British Indian army, including Europeans and Indians (mainly Sikhs, Pathans, and Punjabis), maintained by the government of the Straits Settlements, were stationed in Singapore and Penang from as early as 1859.

Following the Pangkor Engagement, and subsequently the formation of the Federated Malay States, local paramilitary and policing arrangements were extended to individual states. This typically involved a force comprising mainly Indians, as well as some Malays, under British command. These detachments were strengthened as trade and commerce grew. Locally recruited regiments were also expected to form part of Singapore's garrison in emergencies. In 1885, Sultan Abu Bakar of Johor established the *Askar Timbalan Setia Negeri* (state auxiliary force), later renamed the Johor Military Force, a small body that fulfilled the state's obligation under treaty arrangements for the joint defence of Johor and the Straits Settlements (Tunku Shahriman Tunku Sulaiman, 2004; Abdul Rahim Ramli, 2018).

The Malay States Guides had been formed as a paramilitary force in 1896 and stationed in Perak (with infantry bases in Taiping), as well as in Kuala Lumpur, and Kuala Lipis in Pahang. At the outbreak of World War I, the Guides were transferred to Singapore to perform garrison duties when the British battalion stationed there was called back to Europe. This reduced the number of regular troops by about half, to around a thousand (Abdul Karim Bagoo, 1962; Nadzan Haron, 1990). The Malay States Guides saw active service in Aden during World War I. The Guides were disbanded in 1919, however, and replaced by a battalion of the Burma Rifles on loan from India.

In 1912, Sultan Idris of Perak proposed to the Federal Council that the Federated Malay States should offer a first-class ship to support the UK's war efforts, leaving the British admiralty to decide on the type of vessel. The proposal was accepted, and HMS Malaya was built at a cost of $2,300,000. This ship was ready for the Battle of Jutland in 1916 (Robson, 2001, p. 112). A temporary tax was also collected in the Straits Settlements and the Federated Malay States to support the imperial government's war efforts.

The Malayan Army was not established until 1933, when the Malay Regiment Bill of 1933 was passed by the Federal Council. This was a full two decades after it was first proposed by the *Yang di-Pertuan Besar* of Negeri Sembilan who was expressing a widely held desire among the Malay rulers and their subjects for Malays to play a greater role in the protection of their homeland (Dol Ramli, 1963). The reluctance of the colonial administration to establish a locally recruited force in part reflected concerns about its cost. There was also a hesitancy to arm the Malays as memories of the disorder and violence in Perak, Pahang, and elsewhere—which had required the intervention of the British—were still relatively fresh. Thus, the proposal was shelved during World War I.

The growing expense of maintaining the Burma Rifles, especially in the context of the Great Depression, helped to change the cost equation, and continued pressure from the Malay rulers eventually paid off. The new force was initially set up as a small 'experimental company', but after a successful trial period was confirmed as the Malay Regiment in 1935. Its development continued during the 1930s with investment in infrastructure, equipment, and training, and expansion to full battalion strength. The regiment was further expanded following the outbreak of World War II with a second battalion created in March 1941. The two battalions fought alongside British troops against the Japanese army during the invasion of 1941 and early 1942.

Naval and air support were added to the infantry units as part of the establishment of the Malayan Armed Forces. The Royal Malaysian Navy grew out of the Straits Settlements Naval Volunteer Force, established in 1934 and based in Singapore under British command. A Penang division was established in 1938, and the volunteer reserve force received training and equipment from the Royal Navy. Recruitment for a 'Malay section' of the Royal Navy then started in 1939 as part of war preparations, but these efforts were cut short by the Japanese invasion, and the unit was disbanded by the British after the war ended. The Malayan Naval Force was then re-established in 1948 to support action against the communist insurgency.

A Straits Settlements Volunteer Air Force was also set up in 1936 in order to assist the British in defending the Straits Settlements. The force was strengthened in 1940, becoming the Malayan Volunteer Air Force, in anticipation of the threat from the Japanese Empire. This force was, however, destroyed by the Japanese in 1942. In 1950, the Malayan Auxiliary Air Force was established in Singapore to assist in the defence of the country during the Emergency. Local technicians were recruited who worked under the supervision of the Royal Air Force (RAF). Post *Merdeka*, the Malayan government recognized the importance of having its own air force to reduce dependence on the RAF. This led to the passing of the Air Force Ordinance in 1958 to allow the establishment of the Royal Malayan Air Force. The initial scope of the air force was to provide communication services between the various federal forces, and to assist the RAF and the Royal Australian Air Force (RAAF) against the CPM. Upon the formation of Malaysia in 1963, it was renamed the Royal Malaysian Air Force.

All three branches of the armed forces were heavily involved in responding to the Emergency, along with the police. The Malay Regiment was trained and equipped to carry out counter-insurgency operations. It had increased to seven battalions by 1955, and was renamed the Royal Malay Regiment in 1958. The naval forces played a key role transporting personnel, food, and equipment to river mouths, as well as disrupting supplies to the insurgents through coastal patrols. The Malayan Air Force supported the work of the RAF and the RAAF, which contributed significantly to the counter-insurgency efforts through their intelligence-gathering operations.

The Police

During colonial rule, armed police forces were established to maintain law and order, and were organized along military lines. They were first put in place in the Straits Settlements, where the police force exercised a civilian function based on the Police Force Ordinance of 1871. Using the Straits Settlements' model, police forces were later established in Perak, Selangor, Negeri Sembilan, and Pahang, although they were at first constrained in size by the limited resources allocated for public safety and security in these states.

In 1896, the four state police forces were merged to form the Police Force of the Federated Malay States. By the turn of the century, the force was over 2,300 strong comprising mainly Indians and Malays, with a British Police Commissioner and senior officers (Swettenham, 1906). Indian police officers were deployed for guard and town duties and to oversee Chinese communities, and Malays were posted to stations in coastal areas and rural districts. The 1924 Police Force Enactment further refined the roles, functions, and responsibilities in the four states' forces. The police forces of the Unfederated Malay States followed, with some delay, along a similar path.

The forces of the Straits Settlements, the Federated Malay States, and the Unfederated Malay States were combined in 1946 as the Malayan Union Police Force, renamed the Federation of Malaya Police Force upon the formation of the Federation of Malaya in 1948. Led initially by British officers, the force was intended to be commanded and staffed by nationals, a goal that was achieved through Malayanization during the 1950s. The Special Branch and Police Field Force played a critical role in state-building, and also provided vital support during the Emergency (Zakaria Haji Ahmad, 1977). A Jungle Company was formed, along with seven units of the Police Field Force, all of which were equipped and trained specifically in internal security. A key objective of their operations was to prevent supplies from reaching the insurgents through roadblocks and inspections. The wives of police personnel were brought in to assist with searches of female suspects, and in 1955 the first unit of policewomen was officially formed.

In 1963, the forces of all the states, including Sabah and Sarawak (and temporarily Singapore), were combined into one single organization as the Royal Malaysian Police. Headquartered in Kuala Lumpur, units were divided into functional specializations—paramilitary, intelligence, criminal investigation, and public safety. The functions and duties of all the various branches were then set out in the Police Act of 1967.

The Justice System

Before British rule of the Malay peninsula, as noted by Shad Saleem Faruqi (2019, p 30):

> custom was the dominant source of law in Malaya. For the Malay community, custom referred to the composite, indigenous Malay adat enriched by Hindu and Buddhist elements and overlaid with principles of the Syafie school of Islamic law. Though Malay adat (custom) and the Syariah (Islamic law) are distinct, the Malays often see them as synonymous. That is why Malay custom is enforced in Syariah courts ... As colonialism took root, common law became the dominant law of Malaya and Malay adat and Islam were relegated to personal matters.[54]

The British set up a legal system aimed at establishing certainty and uniformity, and maintained detailed records of all legal and judicial proceedings. They introduced courts of law where all classes and nationalities were treated alike (Swettenham, 1906). These courts were initially presided over by British magistrates, assisted by Malay magistrates. The introduction of English law in

54 While Shad Saleem Faruqi here describes the general sway of Malay custom over legal matters in the peninsula prior to British rule, it should nevertheless be noted that custom was accompanied by the codification of some laws in some Malay states. During the reign of Sultan Muzaffar Shah of Melaka (d. 1456), laws were compiled into the *Hukum Kanun* legal tradition for the sake of promoting the administration of justice. Between the fifteenth and nineteenth centuries, various Digests and Codes were codified—among them, the *Undang-Undang Melaka* or *Risalut Hukum Kanun* (1523), *Undang Laut Melaka*, *Pahang Digest* (1596), *Kedah Digest* (1605), *Johor Digest*, and the famous *Ninety-Nine Laws of Perak* (Wu, 1999, p. 3).

the Malay peninsula came in phases—beginning first in the Straits Settlements, then in the Federated Malay States, followed by the Unfederated Malay States. The general principle in the implementation of English law was that it is the 'law of general application', but exceptions or modifications were allowed for personal law matters of religion, manners, and custom (Wan Arfah Hamzah and Ramy Bulan, 2003, p. 153).

In the Straits Settlements, the formal implementation of English law began with the first Charter of Justice of 1807, which established a Court of Judicature in Penang. The court had jurisdiction over all civil, criminal, and religious matters, subject to local conditions and circumstances. In 1826, the second Charter of Justice united the Courts of Judicature for Penang, Melaka, and Singapore. A third Charter of Justice, introduced in 1855, reorganized the Court of Judicature into two divisions, the first of which had jurisdiction over Singapore and Melaka, and the second over Penang and Province Wellesley. The Supreme Court of the Straits Settlements was established in 1868 and reconstituted in 1873. English commercial law was introduced in the Civil Law Ordinance of 1878.[55]

Before the formation of the Federated Malay States, the judicial system was decentralized. Each state had a Magistrates' Court, with appeals to the Ruler in Council. Shortly after the formation of the Federated Malay States, the Court of the Judicial Commissioner was established as the highest court.[56] These arrangements were superseded by the establishment of the Supreme Court by state legislation, and later by the Courts Enactment of 1918, which established a federal Supreme Court, consisting of, among others, a Court of Appeal and Courts of a Judicial Commissioner (Abdul Hamid Omar, 1994). This legislation also created the post of Chief Judicial Commissioner to try death penalty cases and hear appeals from the Courts of the Senior Magistrates. The Chief Judicial Commissioner also had powers to admit persons as advocates and solicitors of the Supreme Court. Final appeals could be made to the Judicial Committee of the Privy Council in London, the highest court of appeal for the British Empire (Sinnadurai, 1990). English common law and rules of equity were not formally introduced until the Civil Law Enactment of 1937 came into force in the Federated Malay States.[57]

In the Unfederated Malay States, each state retained its own judiciary and Supreme Court. In 1921, Johor became the first unfederated state to make provision for appeals to the Judicial Committee of the Privy Council. Under the Malayan Union Order in Council of 1946, the judicial systems of the Straits Settlements (excluding Singapore), the Federated Malay States,

55 Other laws enacted were the Evidence Ordinance, Criminal Procedure Code, Civil Procedure Code, Penal Code, and the Contract Act, all modelled on similar legislation from India (Zaki Tun Azmi, 2011).

56 Courts of a *Kadi*, Assistant *Kadi*, and *Penghulu* were also established with jurisdiction over Muslim matters.

57 This was subsequently extended to the Unfederated Malay States in 1951, and this Enactment continues to be applicable in the form of the Federation of Malaya's Civil Law Ordinance 1956, revised in 1972 (Hooker, 1984).

and the Unfederated Malay States were unified. A Supreme Court, including a High Court and Court of Appeal, with civil and criminal jurisdiction, was established.

The introduction of the British legal system provided legal pluralism in that civil courts became a parallel court system to the *syariah* courts. In the Federated Malay States and the Unfederated Malay States the position of Islam and Malay custom was left unaffected. The coexistence of Islamic and customary laws under the *syariah* court system was common, especially in family matters such as marriage, divorce, and inheritance of property (Ahmad Ibrahim, 1965; Zakaria Haji Ahmad, 2006).

In North Borneo and Sarawak, early legal disputes were resolved by the British administrators acting as adjudicators. The Courts Order of 1922 established a more formal court structure which comprised five courts: the Supreme Court, the Residents' Courts, District Courts, Magistrates' Courts, and Native Courts—provided under Charter granted to the British North Borneo Company in 1881 for the administration of justice by the Company to the people of Borneo. The Order in Council 1951 combined the judiciaries of North Borneo, Sarawak, and Brunei until the formation of Malaysia in 1963, when the federal Civil Law Act 1956 was extended to apply to all Malaysian states.[58]

The native courts in Sabah and Sarawak continued to operate even after the formation of Malaysia. These had long been an important component of the court structure, particularly in Sabah. Native courts have dealt with native matters ever since. The three-system court structure in Sabah and Sarawak (civil, native, and *syariah*) thus differs from that in the other states of the federation, where there are two court systems in parallel (civil and *syariah*).[59]

The Tax System

Before British intervention, taxation was administered by the Malay chieftains with substantial revenues being allocated to the sultan. As colonial control extended over the peninsula, revenue collection and state expenditure were increasingly controlled by British-appointed administrators (Ooi, 2012; Sultan Nazrin Shah, 2017). British policy held that colonial governments should finance themselves from revenues collected locally. Taxes on opium, tobacco, and liquor—consumed predominantly by Chinese—were collected through revenue farms (also called tax farms), which were given exclusive

58 The judiciary at that time consisted of the High Court and the Court of Appeal.

59 More formalized courts to deal with *syariah* matters were established in the early 1990s, and the Native Court Ordinance was introduced in 1992.

distribution rights over these items. The British auctioned these rights to private individuals. Rents were paid directly to the colonial administrators, obviating the need for investment in bureaucratic infrastructure and administration (Trocki, 2002).

Expenditure on opium was high in the Straits Settlements and in most of the Malay states, and substantial excise duties were earned from it (Sultan Nazrin Shah, 2017). Opium remained a significant component of revenue up to the 1930s, when the Straits Settlements government began to discourage its use in the face of pressure on the Colonial Office from the United States (Manderson, 1996).[60] In Kedah, for example, revenues from opium made up over 40 per cent of total revenues in 1919. After 1920, rapid growth in other revenues, especially customs duties and other indirect taxes, helped to reduce reliance on opium receipts. By the 1930s, the opium monopoly accounted for around 12 per cent of Kedah's revenue (Lim, 1967).

Outside the Straits Settlements, which were free ports, taxes on trade became an even greater source of revenue. In the Federated Malay States, export and import taxes together accounted for 52 per cent of total government revenue in 1937 (Straits Settlements and Federated Malay States, 1939). This heavy reliance on export duties on tin and rubber meant that state revenues were subject to the volatility of the trade in these commodities, however. At the same time, the tax burden was inequitably distributed, with tin and rubber exporters paying heavy duties, and the merchant and professional classes paying nothing.

In the late 1930s, following the loss of the sizeable revenue from opium taxes, an attempt by the British administration to introduce income tax foundered in the face of fierce opposition from the European and Chinese business communities (Thompson, 1943), even though income tax was already being levied in several neighbouring Asian countries (Booth, 2016).[61]

After World War II, the Colonial Office determined that taxes should finance post-war rehabilitation,[62] and income tax was viewed as the only practicable method to raise sufficient revenue to meet the rehabilitation and development goals (Rudner, 1994). Many businesses, struggling after the war, were still opposed to its introduction, and took the view that there should be 'no taxation without representation'. Nevertheless, the British governor vetoed a decision against the tax by the Legislative Council, which was dominated by business interests, and income tax was introduced in Malaya on 1 January 1948. Legislation for the introduction of income tax was also

60 The British adopted a policy of total prohibition of opium smoking throughout its colonies in November 1943. This was implemented on reoccupation after World War II (CO 865/54, 1943–1944).

61 An earlier attempt to introduce income tax in the Straits Settlements had been made in 1910, but was withdrawn in the face of strong business opposition. However, in 1917 a system of income tax was adopted there to help finance British expenditure in World War I. The tax ceased in 1919 (Loo and McKerchar, 2014).

62 The British military administration was entrusted with revising the tax policies.

passed in North Borneo and Sarawak in 1948 and 1949 respectively, but lack of administrative capacity caused delays in its introduction (CO 825/90, 1950).

The Financial System

As trade and commerce grew from the mid 19th century, British agency houses such as Guthrie and Company, Edward Boustead and Company, and Sime Darby played an increasingly important role helping to promote Malayan commodities among potential European investors and to raise capital on the London stock market (Sultan Nazrin Shah, 2017; Drake, 2018). Several major British banks, such as Chartered Bank and the Hong Kong and Shanghai Banking Corporation, established branches in the Straits Settlements at first, and later in the tin and rubber commercial centres of the peninsula. While branches were initially exchange banks rather than deposit and loan institutions, they provided the agency houses and other customers with a broad range of financial services. These included creating demand deposits, and increasing the money supply by issuing bank notes (Wong, 2004) (Chapter 5).

In the late 19th century, the silver dollar was the main currency used in local and regional trade. Mexican and Japanese silver dollars were in general circulation and were widely used in trade with China, while the British pound, minted as a silver dollar, and the Hong Kong dollar, in the form of a silver coin, were also accepted as legal tender (King, 1957; Drake, 1969; Pridmore, 1975). As it became less manageable to conduct trade using coins, bank notes issued by exchange banks came to be accepted, on condition that they were fully backed by bullion or silver dollars. Fluctuations in the value of the silver dollar were a major concern, however (Drake, 2018).[63]

Such exchange rate variability affected trade, and in 1902 a Straits Settlements Currency Committee was appointed to look into the matter. The committee recommended that in order to protect against silver price fluctuations, the dollar should be changed from a silver standard to a gold standard, and a firm rate of exchange between the dollar and sterling should be fixed.

New Straits Settlements Dollar

The Straits dollar was introduced in 1903 after the establishment of a currency board under the 1897 Currency Ordinance (Box 1.3). The newly created Board of Commissioners of Currency, modelled on that of Hong Kong, was committed to converting Straits dollars to sterling at the set exchange rate. This was initially placed at par; but in January 1906, the government decreed

63 The value of the silver dollar varied between a low of 3 shillings and ¼ pence in 1889 and a high of 3 shillings and 6 pence in 1891.

that currency commissioners could issue notes in exchange for gold at the rate of £7 sterling for Straits$60, or 2 shillings and 4 pence for Straits$1. This stable rate was maintained until 1939.

These currency and banking arrangements, dominated by British banks, lasted for more than 60 years, providing currency for local circulation with full convertibility of the Straits dollar into pounds sterling (Drake, 2018). Any issuance of the local currency (Straits dollars) required the Board to acquire reserve currency (sterling) of at least the same value. Domestic currency in Malaya then expanded or contracted as the supply of the reserve currency expanded or contracted, while interest rates on the Straits dollar adjusted automatically to changes in sterling interest rates.

Box 1.3 Currency board

The principal features of a currency board system are its predictability and rules-based structure. A stable exchange rate had particular benefits for Malaya's plantation crop exporters, as it allowed them to proceed with their business plans with far greater certainty about the future convertibility of their export earnings. Stability was also important for foreign investors—including British banks—in relation to the repatriation of their profits, and may therefore have helped to maximize capital inflows (Huff, 2002).

Another feature of currency board arrangements is that they remove from the authorities any discretionary power to affect the supply of money or interest rates, and thereby to use monetary policy to influence economic activity or the general level of prices. The adoption of a currency board by the colonial administration thus reflected a political preference for exchange rate predictability over monetary autonomy.

Although the currency board fixed the nominal exchange rate (the parity at which the Straits dollar could be converted to sterling), the real exchange rate (the nominal rate adjusted for differential inflation between Malaya and its trading partners) remained susceptible to changes in the stock of Straits dollars in circulation, and to changes in the general level of prices. Therefore, other things being equal, a balance-of-payments surplus that added to sterling reserves and to the stock of Straits dollars would have boosted domestic prices and supported an appreciation in the real exchange rate.

Malaya established its own central bank in 1959, which issued its first Malaysian currency in 1967. That put an end to the currency board arrangement and to the Malayan dollar. This currency was split, with Malaysia, Singapore, and Brunei all issuing their own currencies. The issuing of a Malaysian currency also marked the end of the sterling exchange standard for Malaysia, as well as for Singapore (Lee, 1990).

Before the exchange rate of the new Straits dollar could be fixed to sterling—a currency on the gold standard—the face value of the Straits dollar had to be decoupled from its intrinsic silver value. In order to do this, sufficient amounts of the new dollar were circulated and its export was banned, while other foreign currencies were withdrawn and their import prohibited (King, 1957; Drake, 1969; Lee, 1990). The exchange rate had to be fixed at a sufficient margin above the bullion value so that the dollar coins would not be melted down. The price of silver continued to rise, however, and the dollar coin had to be re-minted twice, each time to a lower weight and/or fineness.

When Britain left the gold standard in 1931, the Straits dollar remained on the sterling exchange standard. In 1938, the Malay states became jointly responsible for the currency through the Board of Commissioners of Currency, Malaya, and in 1939, the Straits dollar was replaced at par by the Malayan dollar (Drake, 1969).

Conclusions

From 1867 onwards, after the British Colony of the Straits Settlements of Penang, Melaka, and Singapore was established, the territories of the Malay peninsula came under increasingly centralized colonial control up to the start of World War II. After the end of the Japanese occupation in 1945, the country experienced a turbulent journey: from British military rule through the Malayan Union and the Federation of Malaya, to *Merdeka*, and then further, to the formation of Malaysia in 1963 following the merger with Sabah and Sarawak, and with Singapore until its separation in 1965.

Malaya's institutions were established in connection with the evolution of the different territories, and were designed above all to promote colonial economic objectives. These institutions served to consolidate British rule over the people, and to supply a steady flow of workers to support economic activities (Chapter 2). They had the effect of stratifying society, in part through segmented education and health provisions (Chapters 3 and 4). At the same time, they helped to provide the security of property and stability of financial arrangements that were necessary to facilitate unfettered imperial investment, and the free flow of trade and capital required for the success of the colonial administration's commercial ventures (Chapter 5).

The legacy of these colonial structures and institutions, and of the colonial 'divide and rule' policy, has reverberated long after independence, as the remainder of this book demonstrates—in Malaysia's population structure (the rest of Part 1), in the education and health of its people (Part 2), in its economy (Part 3), and in relation to economic inequality (Part 4). The next chapter describes the massive changes in the country's population, notably regarding ethnic composition and geographical distribution, that have taken place since the second half of the 19th century, and explores some of the key economic, social, and political factors driving these changes.

Chapter 2

Population and Migration

Perhaps even more so than in any other Asian country, population change has played a pivotal role in the economic, social, and political development of Malaysia. The nature of this development has in turn powerfully influenced the country's demographic dynamics. In the mid 19th century, the resource-rich Malay peninsula, undeveloped beyond the narrow coastal trading and transhipment enclaves of the Straits Settlements, and consisting predominantly of dense jungle, was very sparsely populated. It was inhabited by only around half to three-quarters of a million people, although this figure had already grown steadily from the late 18th century.[1]

Malaysia today is a multi-ethnic, multicultural, multireligous, and multilingual society, and this diverse character stems largely from key policy decisions that were made by the British colonial administration in the late 19th century and during the first half of the 20th century. As in other parts of the British Empire, the creation of a wage economy and the inward migration of low-cost labour were encouraged and supported in order to promote British commercial interests. Migrants to British Malaya—mainly of Chinese, South Indian, and Javanese origin—were generally enterprising and resourceful, and were essential to the spectacular rates of economic growth that occurred, as well as to population growth. Immigration regulations were tightened during the Great Depression in the early 1930s, however, owing to the high levels of unemployed migrant workers, and also to emerging concerns about ethnic balance. Labour migration virtually ceased as a result until about two decades after independence.

There has been sustained population growth in the period since independence too, but this has been driven primarily by 'natural increase',

1 The mid 19th century population estimates for British Malaya are taken from the work of Newbold (Myrdal, 1968, pp. 1, 396), and Dodge (1980), who provide a comprehensive review of early population numbers.

the difference between births and deaths. Since around 1980, rising levels of Asian labour migration, facilitated by the government in order to sustain its economic growth targets, have again been experienced. Over the same period there has been a continuing brain drain, with high levels of net emigration of generally young, highly skilled, and professional Malaysians leaving for Singapore and for Western countries.

The plural society that evolved as a result of the development of the colonial economy on the peninsula consisted primarily of Malays, Chinese, and Indians. There was also a small elite group of Europeans, mainly from Britain, who enjoyed a markedly higher standard of living.[2] Each population group was itself heterogeneous, with its own subcultural differences. The main ethnic groups did not share a sense of common identity or solidarity, and there were few 'bridges' that existed between them. The educational and occupational demarcations that were contrived by the colonial authorities, and readily embraced by the main ethnic groups, perpetuated these divides, while language, religion, and customs proved further social barriers. Successive post-colonial governments have struggled to overcome the legacy of this colonial-era social and economic segmentation.

This chapter begins with an overview of the history of Malayan population census-taking, and of how individuals and groups have been classified in these censuses. This is followed by a review of how colonial immigration policy responded to the labour force needs of the growing extractive economy on the peninsula, including the recruitment mechanisms that were introduced and the employment patterns of the different migration streams. The third section assesses the substantial impact that migration had on population growth and ethnic composition from the mid 19th century up to independence. The fourth section examines post-independence population policy and population dynamics, and assesses the impact of these on population growth and ethnic composition. The final section assesses how changes in population movements over almost 12 decades (1901–2017), arising from the changing patterns of economic development, have affected the country's levels of urbanization and the spatial distribution of the population at the state level.

2 As the British considered their rule to be based in part on the respect that the local population had for them, it was important for all British, and other Europeans, to enjoy a high standard of living, and not just those at the commanding heights of society (Butcher, 1979).

Counting and Classifying the People

A census is the primary source of statistical information on the size, spatial distribution, and socio-economic characteristics of the population of a country. Census information is crucial for understanding and governing a geographical area or country, and for guiding public and private policy decisions on a wide range of social and economic matters. Because of the large scale of population censuses and the high costs involved, they are generally conducted only every 10 years, with similar topics canvassed from one census to the next.

Censuses in the Malay peninsula began during the British administration as part of colonial policy. They were generally conducted in the same years as in Britain and in other British colonies, and employed similar methods and principles (Box 2.1). Early-19th-century censuses were essentially statistical summaries of the population because of the challenges of collecting more detailed data, such as information on age and occupation from a largely illiterate population. Those conducted since the start of the 20th century have collected a much wider range of statistical information, which provides the indispensable empirical basis for the analysis in this chapter.

Box 2.1 **Frequency and geographical coverage of censuses**

Malaysia's history of census-taking is inextricably linked to the varied evolution of its different component political entities—the Straits Settlements, the Federated Malay States, the Unfederated Malay States, North Borneo (Sabah), and Sarawak.

Census-taking began in the Straits Settlements—the first Malayan territories to come under British colonial rule—in the mid 19th century; in the Federated Malay States and in North Borneo in 1891; in the Unfederated Malay States in 1911; and in Sarawak in 1939 (Box Table 2.1).

The first unified census of British Malaya was conducted in 1921. Thereafter, Malaya-wide censuses have been held decennially, apart from in 1941, when the census was postponed because of the Japanese occupation. Population data collection was severely disrupted during this period, and many official administrative records were destroyed.[3] Decennial censuses were resumed in 1947, and have been held regularly since.

---

3 Some population estimates were made during the Japanese occupation for the purpose of food rationing. The Japanese estimated the population of British Malaya, including Singapore, at 5.7 million in 1945, a figure that is in line with the estimate from the 1947 census of 5.8 million (Kratoska, 2018).

Box Table 2.1 History of census-taking in Malaya/Malaysia and constituent entities since 1850

Census year	Straits Settlements	Federated Malay States	Unfederated Malay States[a]	British Malaya	North Borneo (Sabah)	Sarawak	Federation of Malaya[b]	Malaysia
1850–1852[c]	✓							
1860	✓							
1871	✓							
1881	✓							
1891	✓	✓			✓			
1901	✓	✓			✓			
1911	✓	✓	✓		✓			
1921				✓	✓			
1931				✓	✓			
1939						✓		
1947						✓	✓	
1951					✓			
1957							✓	
1960					✓	✓		
1970								✓
1980								✓
1991								✓
2000								✓
2010								✓

Notes:
[a] A census of Kedah was held in 1901 and a census of Perlis in 1905, under the direction of the Siamese government (Cavendish, 1911).
[b] The 1947 census covered Malaya, comprising the Federation of Malaya and the colony of Singapore.
[c] Singapore (1850), Penang (1851), and Melaka (1852).

How Population Classification Has Evolved

Many censuses include questions that aim to obtain information on an individual's race or ethnicity; these terms are often used interchangeably, although they carry subtly different connotations. Over time, various terms with different meanings such as race, ethnicity, and community—the last defined as a group bound by a common language, religion, and customs—have been used to arrive at a classification in Malayan censuses, with fluidity in the conceptual boundaries of the definitions of these terms (Hirschman, 1987).[4]

4 The pioneering article in tracing this evolution of census ethnic classifications is that of Hirschman (1987). Annex Table 2.1 updates that work by taking into account the three most recent censuses.

Thus, while racial identity is usually considered as involuntary and immutable, there is some flexibility for individuals to choose the ethnic group with which they most closely identify. Population censuses emphasize this personal, self-selected aspect of ethnicity, which is defined as what the individual declares rather than by any objective or external measurement.[5]

Malayan, and later Malaysian, census information relating to race or ethnicity has always been published at two levels, comprising both a broad classification of a small number of major categories and a more detailed classification of subcategories, reflecting the wide diversity of ethnic groups subsumed within each major category (as described below). Historically, the classification of the different population groups into major categories was carried out by the colonial census commissioners. Since independence, this task has been led by a committee chaired by the chief secretary to the government.

The categorization of the racial mosaic of Malaysia's people is vitally important, as it forms the basis for the cross-classification of a wide range of population data on which socio-economic policy and planning decisions are based, including those concerning eligibility for various entitlements.[6] It has become the prism through which many of the country's political, social, and economic outcomes can be understood. Yet despite such crucial ramifications, there is a level of arbitrariness involved in the classification of people by race and ethnicity in this way. The British imposed a race-based paradigm to categorize the different peoples across the British Empire (Milner et al., 2014). In Malaya, and in North Borneo and Sarawak, the colonial institutionalization of a racial classification in policy implementation in areas such as education, land, and employment can be interpreted as part of the colonial strategy of 'divide and rule'.

Using the template of earlier colonial censuses, the first Malaya-wide census of 1921 employed the concept of 'race' in an attempt to achieve a purely ethnographic classification; it categorized people into groups according to common physical characteristics. Race was used in the absence of any more

5 The view of the United Nations, as set out in its 'Principles and Recommendations for Population and Housing Censuses', is that 'because the ethnocultural composition of a country can vary widely from country to country and due to the diversity in the approach and the various criteria for establishing ethnicity, it is recognized that there is no single definition or classification that could be recommended that would be applicable to all countries' (United Nations Department of Economic and Social Affairs Statistics Division [UN DESA], 2017, p. 205). Measurement of ethnicity may be highly sensitive, and can be carried out using either one single criterion or multiple criteria, including ethnic ancestry or origin, ethnic identity, cultural origins, nationality, race, colour, minority status, tribe, language, and religion.

6 Even during the colonial era, in the interpretation of the Malay Reservation Enactments (the first of which was for the Federated Malay States in 1913, as mentioned in Chapter 5), the category of 'Malay' was defined in different ways in several states when determining entitlement. The term 'Malay' in these enactments generally meant 'a person belonging to the Malayan race who habitually speaks the Malay language or any Malayan language and professes the Moslim religion' (Voon, 1977, p. 496). But in practice, the definition was not standard across all states: an individual of Arab descent was a Malay in Kedah but not in Johor; a person of Siamese descent was a Malay in Kelantan, but not in Negeri Sembilan (Shamsul and Athi, 2015).

appropriate term to cover a complex set of ideas, of which biological race was itself only one element (Vlieland, 1932). For the 1931 census, however, the term 'race' was broadened to comprise a combination of geographical and ethnographic origin, political allegiance, and racial and social affinities and sympathies.

Since 1980, the term 'ethnic group' has been used in the population censuses to define people who are bound together by a common language or dialect, religion, and customs.[7]

Major Categories of Ethnic Classification

Tracing the evolution of census ethnic classification reveals the changes in perceptions of ethnicity from official administrative and political perspectives, as the major ethnic categories and subcategories used have varied over time. The major categories remained the same for the first three censuses of the 20th century, comprising the six categories of Malays, Chinese, Indians, Europeans, Eurasians, and Others. This classification of the major groups was changed for the 1957 census, which was conducted a few months before independence. Europeans and Eurasians, previously separate major categories, were both subsumed under Others (Fell, 1960). This continued in subsequent censuses, with the major categories becoming Malaysians, Chinese, Indians, and Others. They were then changed again in 1991 to Malays, Other *Bumiputera*, Chinese, Indians, Others, and Non-Malaysian Citizens.

While the term 'Malay' was used in the first Malayan-wide census in 1921, the term 'Malaysian' was employed in 1931, 1947, and 1957. Both uses included three subcategories, namely Malays, Aborigines (*Orang Asli*, Box 2.3), and Indonesian. In the first census held after independence, in 1970, Malay replaced Malaysian in the major ethnic group classification, and this continued in 1980. Since 1991, the term '*Bumiputera*' has been used, which includes Malays and 'Other *Bumiputera*', a group that consists of the aborigines and other natives of Sabah and Sarawak (Box 2.2).

Changing Classifications of Ethnic Subcategories

The number of ethnic subcategories within the major categories has also varied between censuses, as has the allocation of these subcategories to the major categories. There has been much greater consistency and stability in the classification of Chinese by subgroup (identified by clan or language group) than in the classification of Malays and Indians (Annex Table 2.1).

7 Before 1991, censuses classified ethnic group (or race) for the total population. Since then, ethnic classification has been restricted to Malaysian citizens only.

In the 1911 census, Malays were defined to include Malays and 'allied races' of the Malay archipelago. The allied races were predominantly people who were born in the different islands that became Indonesia. Thus, those identified as Menangkabau and Rawa (tribes from West Sumatra) were included as Malays (Pountney, 1911). In the 1921 census, Jambi (a tribe from east central Sumatra), which had been a separate subcategory in 1911, was also classified under Malays, which was now defined to include 'all Peninsula Malays and all Sumatran Malays except Achinese, Korinchi and Mendeling' (Nathan, 1922, p. 72). Banjarese from South Kalimantan were included as Malays in the 1901 census, but subsequently and up to 1947 they were shown as a separate subcategory.

The efforts by the census administrators to distinguish between the indigenous Malays of the peninsula and immigrant Malays from elsewhere in the archipelago became increasingly complex. The 1931 and 1947 censuses had many more Indonesian subcategories, and those born outside Malaya, whether in Java, Sumatra, or other parts of the archipelago, were not treated as Malays, but classified within these separate Indonesian subcategories under 'Other Malaysians'. Their children and later descendants, however, were treated as Malays (Box 2.2).

Box 2.2 The Malays—*Bumiputera* or 'Sons of the Soil'

Before the mid 19th century, the population living on the Malay peninsula consisted overwhelmingly of Malays and aboriginal tribes. The largest concentrations were in the east coast states of Terengganu and Kelantan, and the northern state of Kedah (Dodge, 1980). Migration of archipelagan Malays, mainly from Java, Sumatra, and Sulawesi in the Dutch East Indies, increased sharply after the Pangkor Engagement. They tended to settle primarily in the west coast states and in Johor, where the growing employment opportunities were located.[8] They helped to increase the size of the peninsula's population, but at a lower rate than the Chinese and Indians.

The first generation of Malay migrants clustered together, and did preserve their own identity. However, distinctions disappeared for their descendants, with most local-born migrant offspring referring to themselves simply as Malay. This shifting self-identity was made possible by the Malays' perception of the peninsula as their native land; by the use of Malay as a common language; by the shared religion of Islam; and by the tendency of the colonial administrators to group Malays together in the population censuses and for other administrative purposes.

8 In 1911 almost half of the population of Malays on the peninsula was concentrated in the four northern and east coast Unfederated Malay States. By independence this figure had fallen to 40 per cent.

The Malays were mainly rice growers, planters of coconuts and various other crops, and coastal fishermen. The British adopted a policy of 'minimum interference' towards the peninsula's indigenous Malays, and sought to maintain them in their traditional social order, rural subsistence occupations, village communities, and cultural milieu. In each state, or *negeri*, the ruling classes, led by the sultan, continued to exercise control over the lives of their subjects, the *rakyat* (Nonini, 1992).

The British helped to perpetuate the economic and social divides that existed between the Malay rulers and aristocratic elite, and the rest of the Malay population, in part through state Land Reservation Enactments, which encouraged the non-elites to remain as farmers, especially of *padi*. While high-quality education was provided for the Malay aristocracy, giving them access to federal and state government jobs, only rudimentary basic education was available to the majority of rural Malays. This was in an attempt to ensure that they remained contented with subsistence agriculture and stayed outside the growing wage economy (although some did have agricultural smallholdings). Migrant Malay labour was also used, particularly for the felling of trees and the clearing of land for estate plantations.

In the towns in the west coast states, as the first three 20th-century population censuses show, there were also significant numbers of Malays engaged in a variety of non-agricultural occupations, such as government service, transport and communications, and petty trading. In the northern and east coast states, most Malays were engaged in farming and fishing, although the production of handloom textiles—*songket* and *batik* weaving (Box 5.6 in Chapter 5)—and traditional mat-making, mainly by women, were important industries.

Indonesians as a subcategory were listed under Malaysians in the 1957 census, and then under Malays in the 1970 and 1980 censuses. In subsequent censuses, Indonesians reporting themselves as Malaysian citizens have been classified under the category of Others, while Indonesians who are non-Malaysian citizens have been classified under the Non-Malaysian Citizens category without any further ethnic breakdown. The treatment in the censuses of the aboriginal tribes (*Orang Asli*) living in the Malay peninsula has also changed over time (Box 2.3).

The subcategories included under Indians also differ from one census to another, with certain subcategories classified at some times as Others, and at other times as Indians. Nepalese or Gurkhas, for example, were classified under Indians in the 1921 and 1931 censuses, but since 1947 have been classified under Others. In all the censuses held between 1901 and 1957, Sri Lankan Tamils, Sinhalese, and Other Sri Lankans were classified under Others, but since 1970 they have been classified under Indians. Pakistanis (including Bangladeshis), who in 1957 were classified under Others, were classified under the Indian category in the censuses between 1970 and 2000, but in 2010 were again included under Others.

These changes in classification or nomenclature, and in how the subcategories are allocated to the major categories, must be taken into account in comparisons of measures of the size, growth, and composition of the population by ethnic group over time.

Box 2.3 *Orang Asli*, the peninsula's original inhabitants

The earliest inhabitants of the Malay peninsula were hunting and gathering tribes, who were collectively grouped in the early-20th-century population censuses as the *Sakai*, or aboriginal races, and after independence as the *Orang Asli* (the original people). They have maintained their distinct identities and traditional ways of life, living mainly in forests or on the fringes of forests.

Of the peninsula's three broad groups of *Orang Asli*, the Negrito, who live in jungle interiors, are considered the earliest migrant settlers and the most traditional. The Senoi are the biggest group and are shifting cultivators who live communally. The proto-Malay, or Jakun, are the most advanced, cultivating traditional crops and living as families in villages. Within each of these three broad groups are different tribes who speak their own dialects and have different cultures, beliefs, and customs (Nik Haslinda Nik Hussain, 2007).

The early decennial population censuses made separate arrangements through the network of district offices to try to enumerate the aborigines despite their nomadic style of living which made them less accessible and greatly complicated the process of completing accurate counts (Wilkinson, 1912; Winstedt, 1922).[9] The aborigines have tended to increase their permanent or semi-permanent settlements over time, with some intermarriage, making them easier to count. Those who have converted to Islam would have been counted as Malay thereafter. These factors make it impossible to interpret changes in the size of the aboriginal population as enumerated in the sequence of censuses, and the numbers recorded for them should be taken as minimum estimates (Box Table 2.2). At independence, there were an estimated 41,400 aborigines, with the biggest concentrations in Pahang (39 per cent), Perak (32 per cent), Selangor (10 per cent), and Kelantan (10 per cent).

Box Table 2.2 Aboriginal population in Malaya

1911	1921	1931	1947	1957
30,100	32,400	31,900	34,700	41,400

Sources of data: Del Tufo (1949); Fell (1960).

Until around the end of the colonial period, the aborigines had relatively limited contact with other communities and took care of their own social and economic needs. They became more prominent during the Japanese occupation after being

9 In the early-20th-century censuses the *Orang Asli* were a subcategory within the main category of Malays. In the 1931 census they formed a subcategory under Other Malaysians, and in the 1947 census they were once again classified as Malays. In 1957 they were classified under Malaysians, while in the 1970 and 1980 censuses they were classified as Malays. Since 1991 they have been classified as Other *Bumiputera*.

enlisted by the communists to support the resistance movement. They were then recruited by both the colonial government and the communists during the Emergency of 1948–1960 (Chapters 1 and 5), because of their unique understanding of the dense and deep jungle terrain (Leary, 1989). Some unsuccessful attempts were made to resettle them.

The post of Protector of Aborigines was established in 1939 with the objective of ensuring that the aborigines enjoyed the same social and economic rights as other communities, and provisions for their protection are enshrined in the constitution. The 1967 Aborigines (Amendment) Peoples Act defined who the *Orang Asli* are, set out who is responsible for their general administration and welfare, and established the aim of integrating and assimilating them into the main national community (Department of *Orang Asli* Affairs, 1972). Since 2011, the *Jabatan Kemajuan Orang Asli* has had the responsibility within the government of implementing various programmes to support the *Orang Asli*. However, they remain politically, socially, and economically marginalized (Gomes, 2015).

A Century of Migration to 1957

Substantial and unrestricted migration into the Malay peninsula began around the 1850s and lasted until the Great Depression, after which increasingly strict controls were imposed. The Pangkor Engagement of 1874, which gave fresh impetus to trade and investment in tin mining and plantations, encouraged a sharp rise in immigration to levels far beyond those of previous decades. The states where Malaya's abundant natural resources were located, and which were targeted for large-scale commercial exploitation, could not meet the growing demand for labour, nor was there sufficient labour, ready for wage employment, available from other parts of the peninsula.

The establishment of supportive institutions and an open immigration policy to facilitate population movements from labour-surplus countries were both essential in order to meet British economic objectives. Through these means, the colonial administrators encouraged private British and other European investment in trading and agriculture, construction work, tin mines, and, later, rubber plantations. The colonial government created an enabling environment by establishing institutions that would ensure public safety and security, property rights, and the rule of law, and would facilitate the operations of commercial banks and capital markets, while also providing the necessary physical infrastructure. With all these elements falling into place, there was a massive increase in the demand for workers across a broad range of occupations, but especially in estate agriculture, mining, public works, and infrastructure.

Until around 1910, many, or even most, of the foreign workers who came to the Malay peninsula were indentured labourers.[10] The tradition of unfree labour, already well established by the mercantilists before the British arrived in the Straits Settlements, was adopted by the British as an effective means of organizing the large-scale movement of labour that was necessary.[11]

Chinese migrants who came by the most direct sea route arrived from the north across the South China Sea, in steamers that landed first in Singapore and then in Penang. Indians were transported from the west via the Bay of Bengal across the Indian Ocean, and their first port of arrival was Penang. By the first decade of the 20th century, these steamships also went on to Port Swettenham and Singapore. Migrants from the Dutch East Indies arrived through multiple entry points. Unlike the migration of the Chinese, which was initially only loosely controlled, the movement of Indians was highly regulated by British India, as was that of the Javanese by the Dutch East Indies government.

The densely populated agricultural areas of southern China, southern India, and central Java offered a huge potential supply of low-cost, unskilled labour. Around 1900, the combined population of these countries was close to 800 million, vastly outnumbering the 1.7 million people living in the Malay peninsula. The desire to escape from abject poverty and hunger, and the lack of local opportunities for wage employment, were powerful common factors that drove migrants from all of these places towards Malaya and the opportunities it offered. The increasing monetization of economies across Asia also meant that migrants could earn and save money from their employment in Malaya to improve not only their own lives, but also those of their families back home. Most migrants saw themselves as sojourners rather than permanent settlers.

As well as being determined by demand from Malaya, the size of annual flows also reflected local agricultural conditions in migrants' source areas. Chinese migration thus tended to be lower when harvests in south China were bountiful, the price of rice was low, and real incomes were high; and vice versa (Campbell, 1923).

With the widespread retrenchments and severe social dislocations caused by the Great Depression, the colonial government began to regulate the entry of foreign workers on the basis of political, social, and economic

10 Interesting accounts of labour migration of the different communities into Malaya from the early 19th century until 1920 are given by Jackson (1961), who was employed by the Malayan Civil Service at the Chinese Secretariat and the Labour Department. For the Chinese community, accounts are given by Blythe (1947), who also joined the Malayan Civil Service and was the Protector of Chinese between 1926 and 1936 before becoming the Colonial Secretary.

11 The indenture system often implied compulsion. As Myrdal notes (1968, p. 969), 'even when workers from distant places were recruited on a basis that preserved some elements of "voluntariness", the process of settling them down to steady work was accomplished in ways that severely restricted their freedom of movement'.

needs.[12] These restrictions remained in place until the Japanese occupation and were then further tightened after the war.[13] Fresh immigration almost came to an end at this point, except in 1952 and 1953, when there was a net inflow of Indians, partly in response to a temporary boom in the rubber sector triggered by the Korean war (Fell, 1960; Sandhu, 1969). Given the growing numbers of Malays who were entering the labour force, higher rates of natural increase, and increasing tensions around ethnic balance, the colonial government further restricted immigration in 1953; and then from 1959 the Malayan government more or less entirely curtailed it.

Measurement of net migration flows is subject to severe limitations until the end of the third decade of the 20th century, when the system of collecting migration statistics was overhauled (Del Tufo, 1949). Complete data on all the flows into and out of the Malay states are in any case unavailable, as no records were kept of movements across land borders. The primary data sources on migration into and out of Malaya are the 'examined-on-board' records of vessels arriving in, and departing from, the ports of Singapore and Penang. Official records were kept by the Chinese Protectorate in Singapore of arriving sea-passengers, including those in transit to Penang or to other countries, as well as of departures to China. Meanwhile, Indians were recorded in the annual reports on arrivals and departures of the Immigration Department.[14] The net migration figures derived from these records are unreliable, however. For a more accurate assessment of the extent of foreign migration and its impact on the peninsula's population, it is better to rely on changes over time in the population stock as recorded in the censuses.

The next three subsections review the distinct patterns among the three major groups of migrants—Chinese, Indians, and Javanese.

Chinese Migration

Background

People had been migrating to the Malay peninsula from China in fairly small numbers for generations (as they had to a lesser extent from India).[15] Many of the earliest Chinese arrivals—prominent among whom were the *Peranakan*

---

12 These restrictions were imposed using the Immigration Restriction Ordinance enacted in 1928. In 1929, the last year of unrestricted immigration, the number of Chinese adult males entering the Colony was 195,600. This fell to 152,000 in 1930, and to just 50,000 in 1931 (Straits Settlements, 1932).

13 The Immigration Ordinance 68 of 1952, which came into effect on 1 August 1953 with the Immigration Prohibition of Entry Order of 1953, controlled the entry of all persons into the Federation of Malaya, whether British subjects, British-protected persons, or aliens (Federation of Malaya, 1953–1955).

14 The Annual Reports of the Protector of Chinese, 1881 to 1932, and the Annual Reports of the Immigration Department, 1933 to 1938.

15 The earliest Chinese settlers came to the Melaka sultanate in the 15th century (Yen, 2000).

or *Baba-Nonya*—went to the Straits Settlements.[16] Under British colonialism, however, Chinese migrants came in increasing numbers during the 19th century and the first 40 years of the 20th century. They were initially engaged mainly in trade and commerce, but later expanded into mining and agriculture.

During the latter part of the 19th century and into the 20th century, the British became increasingly dependent on this migration to implement their ambitious economic expansion plans (Box 2.4).[17] Migrants supported activities at the ports, cleared jungles, and, crucially, provided the expanding mining and plantation sectors with the almost limitless low-cost labour supply on which they depended. Chinese migrants, who were drawn first to the busy trading enclaves of Penang and Singapore, increasingly spread out to the emerging new towns of Ipoh, Taiping, Kuala Lumpur, and Seremban, located around the tin mines in the thriving west coast states. Demand for Chinese labourers grew dramatically during the tin-mining boom of the late 19th century in what was then still a Chinese-controlled industry.

Most Chinese migrants came to Malaya with the intention of returning home to China in a few years rather than settling permanently; and many did return, albeit with diminished savings due to gambling, opium smoking, and other habits. Many others died in Malaya after contracting infectious diseases, such as malaria and tuberculosis, which were widely prevalent (Chapter 4).

The migrants were recruited from a number of different provinces and districts within China, and spoke different dialects and subdialects. The strong kinship and protective ties that existed within each of the Chinese communities served to maintain cohesion and promoted a strong sense of cultural identity. Hokkiens (Amoys), who came from Fujian and Xiamen, were the largest Chinese population group in Malaya. They had a long association with trade in the Straits Settlements, and would sponsor family members to come and work as shopkeepers or in their business enterprises (Lee and Tan, 2000). The Cantonese, who originated from Guangdong and eastern Guangxi, were the next largest group, prominent as traders and among the earliest tin miners. Hakkas (Khehs), the third largest Chinese community, came from Guangdong, Fujian, and other provinces, and were also frequently employed in the tin industry.[18] Teochews were the next largest group, with many coming to Malaya from Chaozhou. They worked mainly as agricultural labourers, at

16 The Straits Chinese, predominantly *Peranakan* or *Baba-Nonya*, were well established by the end of the 19th century. They were clearly differentiated from the subsequent flows of Chinese migrant workers in terms of culture, language, and inter-ethnic marriage with Malays (Khoo, 2017).

17 Tin had been mined on the peninsula for some time, with lampan mining undertaken by Malays in Perak, Pahang, Selangor, and Sungai Ujong well before the huge increase in Chinese mining from around the mid 1820s. Much of the early expansion was encouraged by local Malay chiefs through the '*Kapitan Cina*', as it provided a source of revenue for them. It was financed by wealthy Chinese in the Straits Settlements.

18 Unlike other Han Chinese groups, the Hakkas are not named after a geographical area, but are usually identified as those who speak the Hakka language or share some Hakka ancestry.

first on sugar plantations and later on rubber plantations. Hailams originated from Hainan and were usually taken on as rubber plantation labourers or in services, including as domestic servants (Vlieland, 1932; Tan, 2000).

Box 2.4 Recruitment and regulation of Chinese migrants

Until the first decade of the 20th century, most Chinese labour migrants were recruited as indentured labourers under a 'credit-ticket' system, with only a small proportion paying for their own voyages and entering as free workers. Although this system evolved during the 19th and early 20th centuries, its main features remained largely unchanged.

Chinese labour brokers—*Kheh-Thau* or headmen—located in China's southeastern coastal provinces of Kwangtung and Fukien, and in Hong Kong after its colonization in 1847, recruited groups of workers from rural districts and paid for their passage to Malaya. These labour brokers worked with counterparts in Singapore and Penang to whom the labourers were assigned, with the first labour broker paid by the second.

Housekeepers of lodgings at the Chinese ports would arrange the passage of workers with the agents of the largely British- or German-owned steamers, with the *Kheh-Thau* paying the master of the steamer for his workers (Campbell, 1923). The workers were then transported to Singapore, taking about a week to arrive. This transport of migrants was highly profitable as there was considerable demand for workers not just from Malaya but also from Sumatra and Borneo, and from the British colonies in the Caribbean.

Although the Chinese authorities and the intermediate ports of call under British control did inspect the ships, the regulations did little to protect the migrants, who were often shockingly exploited at all stages. The credit-ticket system was subject to serious abuses, including deceitful recruitment methods, trafficking of labourers, overcrowded ships, mistreatment and oppression, and exploitation by secret societies. Early attempts by the British to introduce legislation to reduce these abuses and to establish holding depots for lodging the workers on arrival at Singapore were stymied by local business interests (Blythe, 1947).

Upon the arrival of the *sinkheh* (new recruits) in Singapore, the second labour broker sold them on to the labour agents of wealthy Chinese or European mine or plantation owners at the highest price he could get. The migrants would then enter into an indenture for a year or more, on completion of which they became free to leave and work elsewhere. The agents thus acted as intermediaries between the labourers and the business owners. The labourers' wages were paid to the agents, who charged a commission for their services, and deducted any credit that had been extended to the men. In many mines, labourers were not paid until the extracted ore had been smelted and sold, usually every six months. Employers provided food and provisions, and deducted the costs from wages (Loh, 1988).

The social organization of migrant Chinese communities revolved around membership of powerful secret societies or *hoey*, a brotherhood arrangement based on dialect groups, kinship lines, and territorial boundaries. Recognizing the positive role played by secret societies, colonial administrators had enlisted *hoey* leaders as the intermediaries through which their indirect rule of the Chinese migrants could be sustained. Between 1845 and 1885, however, there was a series of violent clashes and riots between the rival societies, and in 1887 the first Protector of Chinese for the Straits Settlements and Secretary for Chinese Affairs of the Federated Malay States, W. A. Pickering, was assassinated by a secret society.[19] The secret societies were increasingly seen as undermining British economic interests, and with the backing of the Governor of the Straits Settlements, Cecil Clementi Smith, a new policy of suppression was introduced. Under the provisions of the Societies Ordinance of 1889, societies of more than 10 members were deemed illegal unless they had obtained official approval and were registered with the government (Comber, 1955 and 1957). Although the 1889 ordinance was a serious blow to the secret societies, their activities continued illegally.

An ordinance passed in 1880 and sanctioned by the Chinese government incorporated regulatory reforms aimed at the protection of migrants (Blythe, 1947). Depots for the reception and safety of new arrivals were established and regulated; one such depot for housing newly arrived Chinese labourers was built in 1890 at the south end of Petaling Street, Kuala Lumpur. A system of written contracts between employers and employed was put in place. Migrants could be landed only at the main ports, and the Protector would board their ships to examine the status of the migrants on arrival and explain their rights. The aim was to bring new arrivals into direct contact with the government immediately, to demonstrate its power both to protect—and to control—them (Jackson, 1961).

The surge in rubber prices, expansion of plantations, and shortages of labour all contributed to growing pressure for further labour reforms, which were then introduced to increase the number of independent Chinese labourers. But the two systems of Chinese labour—free and indentured—could not easily coexist, and the various reforms culminated in June 1914 in the abolition of the Chinese indentured immigration system.

In April 1933, the Aliens Immigration Restriction Ordinance came into effect, which fixed a monthly quota for new immigrants. Those already in Malaya received a Certificate of Admission, which allowed them to leave and return outside the quota. At first, the quota system was applied only to males, which resulted in an influx of an estimated 190,000 Cantonese women between 1934 and 1938, most of whom joined the labour force (Blythe, 1947). In May 1938, this concession was ended.

Chinese Migrant Employment

From the second half of the 19th century and into the first half of the 20th, Chinese dominated the labour force of the tin mines; they also worked on

19 A Protector of Chinese Immigration in Singapore and an Assistant Protector of Chinese in Penang were appointed under the Straits Settlements Chinese Immigration Ordinance of 1877, and as part of the post-Pangkor Chinese Protectorate established in Perak in 1883. Protectorate offices were later established in all other states, and were mandated to carry out inspections at places of work. W. A. Pickering, the first Protector, had considered it imperative to recognize the secret societies, and for the colonial administration to train staff who were competent in the Chinese language in order to control them.

plantations of gambier, pepper, sugar cane, nutmeg, and tapioca; and they operated revenue farms—places licensed and regulated by the government to sell opium and alcohol. They were also engaged in many other occupations, including in commerce and as retail shopkeepers, artisans, contractors, and financiers. Some worked as gold miners in Raub in Pahang, some as coal miners in Batu Arang in Selangor, and others as iron miners in Terengganu and Johor. In time, they came to dominate the secondary industries of rice and oil milling, coconut oil refining, and pineapple canning (Tai Yuen, 2013). Other prominent groups were brickmakers, phosphate workers, wharf labourers, woodcutters, actors and actresses, barbers, carpenters, masons, sawyers, shoemakers, painters, and teachers.

Take the Kinta Valley in Perak as an example. With the discovery of rich tin deposits the Chinese population there increased rapidly, rising from 45,000 in 1889 to 123,000 in 1901, and reaching 185,000 in 1911; about one-fifth were women (Loh, 1988). The use of labour-intensive tin-mining methods (open-cast mining by hand and *Dulang* washing) was decreasing, however. In 1920, just 36 per cent of ore was mined using European technology-intensive methods and 64 per cent using Chinese labour-intensive methods. By 1930, these shares had virtually reversed to 63 per cent and 37 per cent respectively (Purcell, 1965). As the mines became increasingly European-owned and more capital-intensive, particularly with the introduction of dredges, Indians and Malays were also employed. However, many of the higher-paying ancillary technical operations in the increasingly mechanized mines were still carried out by Chinese workers. Even so, by 1931 just 62,000 Chinese men and 9,000 Chinese women worked in the tin industry in the Federated Malay States. Meanwhile, although the Chinese were traditionally less prominent in the rubber sector, the 1931 census recorded that 84,000 Chinese men and 16,000 Chinese women were employed in the industry in this year.

During the Emergency in the 1950s, because of the threat from the communist insurgency, a large proportion of rural Chinese were compulsorily resettled in New Villages (Box 1.2 in Chapter 1 and Box 5.8 in Chapter 5). They were mostly workers (along with their families) who had been retrenched from the mines, as well as Chinese who had fled in fear of their safety during the Japanese occupation. Many had turned to market gardening of groundnuts, tapioca cultivation, or other agricultural and livestock activities, conducted illegally on non-alienated land (Loh, 1988).

By the 1980s, the vast majority of the 340,000 Chinese living in the Kinta Valley no longer depended on the mining industry, which by then was run by corporations and was heavily mechanized. It employed only 17,000 people, or one-sixth of the number employed in the 1910s. By 1991, this had declined further to 5,600, and by 2010 had fallen to half this number. The Chinese in the

Kinta Valley, now roughly equal numbers of males and females, live in family units with children born and bred in Malaysia.

Indian Migration

Background

The growing demand for Indian workers, at first in the Straits Settlements and later in the Malay states, was closely linked to the expansion of commercial agriculture—initially sugar, coffee, and tapioca plantations (some double-cropped)—and later to the rubber plantation boom. The plantations were primarily owned, organized, and managed by Europeans, mainly British. As well as considerable capital investment, the opening up of the forest frontier to large estate rubber plantations required the recruitment of many low-cost, unskilled, and compliant labourers. Planting, tapping, and weeding, as well as processing the rubber and bringing it to the export market, were all labour-intensive. So, too, was the construction of enabling infrastructure by the government, such as roads, railways, and ports; and there was an increasing demand for unskilled work in the growing public sector. As local labour was in short supply, these needs were met primarily by migrants.

Indian migration to the Malay peninsula began with the early traders, or *Chuliahs* as they were called at the time. Engaged in commerce and as labourers, they first came to Penang with the British East India Company when the settlement was founded in the late 18th century.[20] The traders typically lived on the island for only a few months to trade, then went back to India once they had sold their goods. Migrant labourers stayed much longer before returning. In the first half of the 19th century, the Indian population grew slowly, first in Penang island and later in adjoining Province Wellesley.

Although large numbers of Chinese workers had already migrated to the Straits Settlements in the first half of the 19th century, and further supply was readily available, Indian labourers were considered more suitable for plantation work. This was mainly because they were prepared to accept lower wages and were also considered to be more submissive. Moreover, immigration of Indians and of other nationalities was seen by some British officials as a means to counterbalance the influence of the large numbers of Chinese migrants (Sandhu, 1969).

Indian estate migrants were predominantly Tamils, along with smaller numbers of Telegus and Malayalees, all from southern India. A smaller and more highly skilled group of Indian workers, originating mainly from northern

20 Sandhu (1969) provides an account of earlier Indian contact with the Malay peninsula in pre-British Malaya.

India, made their way to Malaya on vessels from Calcutta. This higher-caste group—mainly Sikhs and other Punjabis—were often free migrants travelling at their own expense.

As a community, Indians were even more heterogeneous than Chinese, differing considerably in language, religion—the community comprised Hindus, Muslims, and Sikhs—as well as in customs and diet. These differences mirrored the Indian caste system and tended to keep the subgroups apart.

Tamil labourers were transported by a weekly steamer service under contract with the British India Steamship Navigation Company (Box 2.5). They arrived at Penang, which was the first port of disembarkation for Perak, and some went on to Port Swettenham. Passengers were quarantined upon landing at Pulau Jerajak—the biggest of the many islands in the immediate vicinity of Penang island—for observation and in order to identify any infectious diseases, such as cholera, plague, and smallpox.

Box 2.5 Recruitment and regulation of Indian migrants

Until 1867, the Straits Settlements were governed as part of British India, which meant that Indian labour laws applied to the recruitment of Tamil workers. The government of India passed laws in the late 1850s to regulate the migration of Indian nationals and to ensure their safety on the seas and their basic well-being. These laws also prohibited Indian migration to the peninsula's Malay states, a measure that stayed in force until 1883, limiting the mobility of non-indentured workers.

At first, Indian workers were recruited mainly as indentured labourers—they became free labourers only after completing their contracts and repaying their advances. New regulations incorporated in the Straits Settlements Ordinance 1 of 1876[21] and then the India Act 5 of 1877 governed Indian migration of indentured labour to the Straits Settlements until 1884. The legislation compelled migrants to use specified Indian ports and established a Protector of Emigrants appointed by the government in Madras. Recruitment could take place only through licensed migration agents, who were required to establish holding depots at each port. Migration had to be voluntary. As demand for Indian workers and the wages offered to them both increased, so too did the 'desertion' rates of indentured labourers. While this was a breach of contract and could lead to punishment in the courts, in practice many deserters were not apprehended.

In 1884, the earlier legislation was repealed and replaced with new measures to improve migrant protection. All restrictions on the migration of non-indentured labourers to Malaya were removed.

21 This Ordinance is also referred to as the Indian Immigrants Protection Ordinance.

Employers who wanted to recruit Tamils would engage a labour-recruiting agency in Madras or Negapatam to gather labourers, arrange their passage to Penang, and deliver them to an embarkation depot at their home port. Under the control of the Straits Settlements Indian Immigration Department, which was headquartered in Penang, all labourers had to be brought to the depot to be medically examined and prescribed fit for work in Malaya.

Once an immigrant vessel arrived in Penang, it was boarded by an Indian Immigration Department official who made sure that the indentured passengers signed contracts and were taken to a holding depot before being handed over to the employers' agents. Each disembarking indentured labourer signed his own contract, with a copy sent to his employer, a copy in Tamil retained by the labourer, and a record of the contract kept by the Department.

The demand for Indian labourers was high and there was competition from other British colonies, such as Burma and Ceylon, where the sea passage costs were cheaper and where migrant labourers were offered higher wages and more attractive conditions, such as shorter contracts.[22] Faced with continuing labour shortages, in 1887 the Straits Settlements government began granting subsidies to steamers to secure cheaper fares that would incentivize migration.

By the late 1890s, the *kangani* system of recruitment was becoming increasingly popular. A *kangani* served both as a labour recruiter and as the estate foreman managing the people he recruited. An employer would sponsor a *kangani* to go to India himself to recruit the required number of workers, advancing his pay and expenses. The *kangani* paid the workers' fares and later collected refunds from them.

As the growth of acreage under rubber surged at the end of the 19th century, the Malayan government recognized that access to low-cost Indian labour was essential to ensure the continued expansion of the sector, and made strong representations to the Indian government to support increased migration. This led to legislative reforms and new measures to try to stimulate supply, including advertising campaigns in southern Indian newspapers (Sandhu, 1969).

In 1907, following a recommendation of the Resident General of the Federated Malay States who had visited India, an Indian Immigration Committee was set up to centralize recruitment measures.[23] The Committee was chaired by the controller of labour of the Federated Malay States and comprised public and private sector members. From then on, all southern Indian migrant labour was recruited under the Committee's supervision, and a government officer was appointed to serve as a migration agent in India.

The first meeting of the Immigration Committee decided that all employers should meet the cost of their imported Indian labour through a tax system, and that steamers would charge a fixed rate for passage. In 1908, an Indian Immigration Fund

22 There was also demand for Indian workers in more distant British colonies, such as Fiji in the Pacific and various locations in the West Indies.

23 The Straits Settlements government codified the functions of the Indian Immigration Fund and the Tamil Fund Immigration Ordinance in 1907, with several amendments in the following years.

was established by the Committee, with revenues collected from employers based on the number of Indian labourers they engaged.[24] All employers of Indian labourers were required to share the costs of hiring them. The aims of these changes were to avoid large deductions from labourers' wages for recruiting expenses, to attract more labourers with the prospect of competitive wages, and to prevent unscrupulous practices by recruiters in India, as well as exploitation on estates (Jackson, 1961).

The Immigration Fund was not part of regular government revenue, and was administered solely in the interest of employers of Indian labour. The government was the largest contributor. It also paid for the cost of improving and maintaining the departure depots in Madras and Negapatam, and the arrival and quarantine depots in Penang and Port Swettenham. Additionally, it subsidized the British-owned steamship company that transported the migrants.[25]

These measures led to a significant expansion in licensed *kangani*-recruited labourers. The exploitative indentured labour system had outlived its purpose, and with opposition to it from sections of the British and Indian governments, it ceased to operate in 1910 and was outlawed in 1914. The new system of assisted migration was a success, leading to a huge jump in annual arrivals.[26]

Indian Migrant Employment

Most Indian labourers worked on rubber plantations. In the early period, they were almost all male, but as the 20th century progressed, male labourers increasingly began to bring their wives with them as there was work for women on the estates. The migrant population was at first largely transitory, with recorded annual departures equalling about half of the number of arrivals. Although some Tamil labourers did stay for more than three years, estate managers were always struggling with high labour turnover.

Low wages, indebtedness, poor social status, rural seclusion, and high labour turnover tended to keep most Indian estate workers socially isolated for much of the first half of the 20th century. They were mainly uneducated and endured harsh living conditions. While accommodation standards were regulated in theory and subject to government inspections, housing and living conditions were often unhygienic, insalubrious, and spartan. There was

24 Employers paid the annual assessment, and in return received the railway fares of labourers from home to port and the passages of labourers by steamer to Penang or Port Swettenham. They also received a rebate for each *kangani*-recruited labourer and for each free labourer. The scheme was expanded in 1914 to pay for the local costs of migrants travelling to their place of employment.

25 Madras became Chennai in 1966, and Port Swettenham became Port Klang in 1972.

26 Immigration was stopped on 1 August 1930 and as a consequence the number of tickets on steamers fell short of the guarantee made by the Immigration Committee. In 1931, a total of Straits$1,278,000 was spent on Indian repatriation from the Indian Immigration Fund. Half this sum was recoverable from the various government administrations, with the Federated Malay States' share being Straits$435,000 (Federated Malay States, 1932).

constant concern about the poor health of workers, and very high rates of morbidity and mortality, especially among new arrivals (Chapter 4).[27]

Beyond the plantations, a smaller number of Indians were employed by the colonial government, mainly in the Public Works Department, the Federated Malay States Railways, and the sanitary boards, and also as clerical workers in the lower ranks of the colonial bureaucracy. One socially exclusive Indian community was the Tamil Chettiars, who came to play an important role in providing capital and credit across Malayan society (Suppiah and Raja, 2016). Other Indians came as English-speaking teachers and as health workers. In addition to their long-standing service in the Malayan garrison of the British military, many Indians, especially Sikhs, were also recruited to the police force and as security guards. Some Indians, meanwhile, migrated to Malaya for commercial reasons, especially in the retail trade.

Javanese Migration

Open territorial boundaries and lack of border controls have long enabled the cross-border movements of people in the Malay archipelago. For several centuries and especially in the first half of the 20th century, migration flows of Javanese from the densely populated island of Java into the west coast states of the Malay peninsula and the Straits Settlements were sizeable. Migration of people from other islands of the Dutch East Indies was also considerable, particularly from among the Menangkabau in Sumatra, the Boyanese on the island of Bawean, the Banjarese in south Kalimantan, and, to a lesser extent, the Bugis of south Sulawesi. Ethnically, linguistically, and culturally similar to Malays, they were all readily accepted as settlers and provided a valuable source of labour supply.

The Javanese were the largest group from among the allied races of the archipelago migrating to the peninsula: in 1947, they accounted for 62 per cent of the 304,000 allied-race individuals.[28] They included persons with government permits who had been recruited in Java under indentured contract by licensed agents; those with local contracts who had become free labourers; and members of gangs who worked together under their own contractors.[29]

Many Javanese workers arrived in the peninsula through arrangements with the government of the Dutch East Indies. In 1887, however, the Dutch

27 An interesting account of the organizational structure, community systems, and the working and family life of Indians on a large European-owned west coast rubber estate from an anthropological perspective is given in Jain (1970).

28 If the Boyanese—from the island of Bawean, which is close to Java—are included as Javanese, this share increases to 69 per cent (Del Tufo, 1949).

29 One early specialization of gangs of Javanese workers, who generally preferred irregular jobs to routine estate activities, was in digging and repairing drainage systems on plantations (Jain, 1970).

government imposed strict conditions on Javanese labour migration. By agreement between the British and Dutch colonial governments, the terms of Javanese migration came to be regulated by the Dutch Indian Labour Protection Enactment 1908 of the Straits Settlements. This enactment sought to limit the period of contract indenture and to protect workers from maltreatment. A year later, a similar enactment was passed in the Federated Malay States. Employers were allowed to deduct a maximum of Straits$2 a month from the labourers' pay to recoup advances. Recruitment of Javanese was more costly than that of Indians (Jackson, 1961).

Estate managers who wanted to recruit labourers from the Dutch East Indies first had to make application to the Governor General of the Dutch East Indies through intermediaries in Penang or Singapore. After they had obtained permits, they relied on professional labour recruiters licensed by the Dutch East Indies government. These recruiters frequently lured labourers on false expectations of the living and working conditions in Malaya (Saw, 1988). Breach of contract—for example, through disobedience or desertion—could result in a fine or imprisonment.

It is extremely difficult to quantify migration flows from the different areas of the Dutch East Indies to the Malay peninsula because of the paucity of data, especially on outflows, and because of the porous nature of the peninsula's borders, which enabled movement through many entry and exit points without any record. The censuses, which enumerate the population by race and country of birth, are the best source of primary data. Even these data have limitations, however, because many of the allied races came to identify themselves as Malays in the censuses, especially those originating in Sumatra or born on the peninsula.

The number of Javanese rose from 68,000 in 1911 to 94,000 in 1921, reaching 188,000 in 1947, or some 8.3 per cent of the Malayan population. There were big increases in Perak and Selangor over this period, but the biggest concentration of Javanese migrants was in Johor, with around 80,000 in 1947. The Johor state government encouraged Javanese immigration, and an estimated 30,000 Javanese were already living in the state as early as 1894, making up about a third of its Malayan population. Roughly 10,000 of them were engaged in planting cocoa, gambier, and other crops (Tate, 1996). They worked in the three west coast districts of Muar, Batu Pahat, and Kukob (Kukup), areas that were readily accessible by ferry from the Dutch East Indies and where a large proportion of the land was cultivated in smallholdings. Later, they were employed on rubber estates or as *padi* cultivators, and many acquired rubber smallholdings of their own. As land was abundant and the population sparse at that time, land acquisition was uncomplicated (Tunku Shamsul Bahrin, 1967).

Of the other streams of Malay-allied races who migrated to the peninsula from the Dutch East Indies, the biggest group was the Menangkabau from Sumatra. Since many peninsular Malays were themselves descended from inhabitants of the east coast of Sumatra, the Menangkabau assimilated easily. Many of them, who were 'ethnographically indistinguishable' from Malays, would have identified themselves as such in population censuses and would have been enumerated as Malays (Del Tufo, 1949, p. 72). Thus the Sumatrans' recorded share of the allied races declined from 14 per cent in 1931 to 9 per cent in 1947. Another large group of migrants was the Banjarese, who made up about one-fifth of the allied races in the 1947 census. The south Sulawesi Bugis had also long been present on the peninsula, but in much smaller numbers.

The settlement patterns of the different communities from the Dutch East Indies varied, with particular groups clustering together. The Javanese have traditionally been heavily concentrated in Johor, Selangor, and Perak, as well as in Singapore; the Banjarese in Perak; the Sumatrans in Selangor and Perak; the Boyanese in Singapore; and the Bugis in Johor. These migrant communities tended to be more gender-balanced than the early Chinese or Indians, the vast majority of whom were male. Indeed, gender imbalance due to those skewed inflows was a cause of growing concern to the authorities.

The next section focuses on the impact of migration flows on the growth, ethnic composition, and sex ratio of the population from the late 19th century to independence.

Population Growth, 1871–1957

From the 1870s to *Merdeka*, Malaya's population growth was closely correlated with its pattern of economic development. Spurred by strong but volatile economic growth, migration was the dominant driver of population growth. Inflows of migrant labour helped to propel the peninsula's transition from a trading outpost to the world's leading producer of tin, and later, of natural rubber.

Impact of Migration on the Population of the Straits Settlements and Federated Malay States, 1871–1911

Malaya's population grew very rapidly in the last quarter of the 19th century and the first decade of the 20th, fuelled entirely by immigration flows, mainly into the Straits Settlements and the Federated Malay States. Much of the late-19th-century population growth stemmed from the expansion of commercial trading activities, as well as sugar and coffee plantations.

The early population censuses between 1871 and 1911, which were not Malaya-wide (Box Table 2.1), show the speed of growth in the population of the Straits Settlements, especially Singapore (Table 2.1). Natural increase would have been zero or even negative during this period because of high mortality rates. The bulk of this growth was due to inflows of Chinese migrant workers, whose share of the Straits Settlements' population grew from 34 per cent in 1871 to 52 per cent in 1911, when they overtook Malays to become the largest population group (Figure 2.1). The growth of the Straits Settlements' Indian population was numerically more modest.

Table 2.1 **By 1911, Singapore's population had overtaken Penang's as the largest among the Straits Settlements**

Settlement	Population (thousands)					Annual growth (%)
	1871	1881	1891	1901	1911	1871–1911
Penang	133.2	190.6	235.6	248.2	278.0	1.8
Melaka	77.8	93.6	92.2	95.5	124.1	1.2
Singapore	97.1	139.2	184.6	228.6	312.0	2.9
Straits Settlements	*308.1*	*423.4*	*512.3*	*572.2*	*714.1*	*2.1*

Sources of data: Straits Settlements Census Reports (various years).

Figure 2.1 **By 1911, the Chinese had become the largest ethnic group in the Straits Settlements**

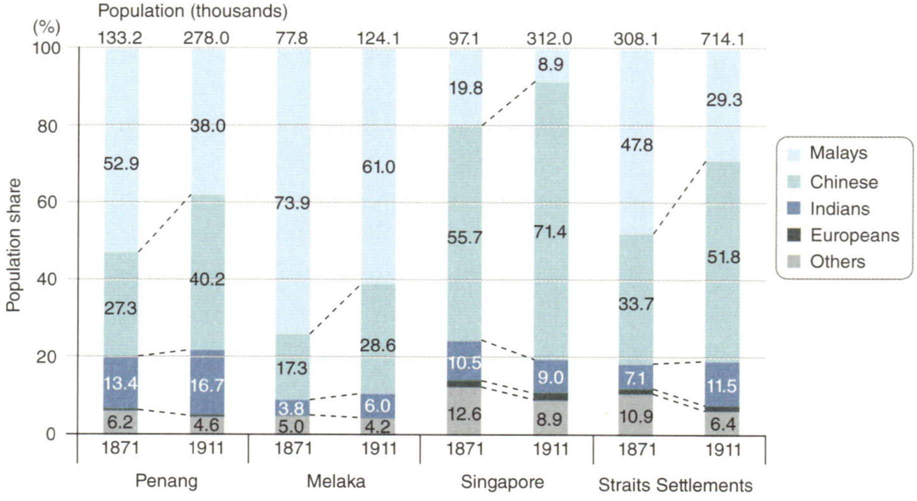

Sources of data: Straits Settlements Census Reports (various years).

Tin mining was growing rapidly during these decades in response to surging international demand (Chapter 5). This period also witnessed the spectacular growth of the natural rubber industry, which at the time was concentrated in the Federated Malay States. As mentioned, there was also substantial government investment in infrastructure, such as railways and roads, in order to support these industries.

With their rising economic prosperity, the populations of Selangor and Perak experienced the fastest growth (Table 2.2). Between 1891 and 1911, Selangor's population more than tripled, surging by 6.4 per cent a year, while Perak's more than doubled, rising by 4.2 per cent a year. During these 20 years, the ethnic composition of the Federated Malay States changed dramatically. In 1891, the Malay share was 55 per cent, but this had fallen to only 41 per cent by 1911. Of the migrant communities, Indians grew the fastest, with their share of the population rising from only 5 per cent in 1891 to 17 per cent in 1911 (Table 2.2).[30]

Table 2.2 Selangor's and Perak's populations grew the fastest with economic prosperity, and the share of Indians surged during the plantation boom

State	Population (thousands)			Annual growth (%) 1891–1911
	1891	1901	1911	
Perak	214.3	329.7	494.1	4.2
Selangor	81.6	168.8	294.0	6.4
Negeri Sembilan	65.2	96.0	130.2	3.5
Pahang	57.4	84.1	118.7	3.6
Federated Malay States	*418.5*	*680.1*	*1,037.0*	*4.5*

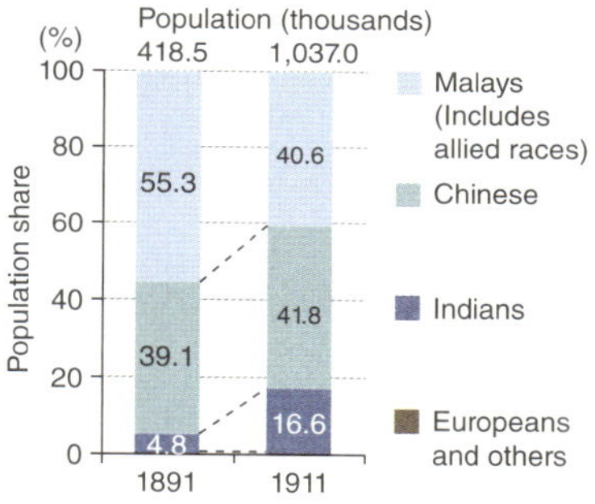

Sources of data: Federated Malay States Census Reports (various years).

Impact of Migration on the Peninsula's Growth and Ethnic Composition, 1901–1957

The censuses reveal just how rapidly the population of the peninsula grew during the first half of the 20th century, from only 1.7 million in 1901 to 6.3 million in 1957, an average annual growth rate of 2.3 per cent (Table 2.3).[31] This

30 The 1911 census showed that 63 per cent of the population of the Federated Malay States was foreign-born, with the share of foreign-born among Chinese and Indians being 92 per cent and 93 per cent respectively (Pountney, 1911).

31 Note that error in population census coverage, often caused by a small proportion of people being missed in the enumeration, is almost certain to have affected the Malayan censuses, as has been common across the world since modern censuses began over 200 years ago (Glass, 1973). Coverage error is usually corrected through a post-enumeration survey. The first of these surveys was conducted by the Department of Statistics–Malaysia only after independence; it evaluated the 1970 census data for Peninsular Malaysia. Subsequent post-enumeration surveys have covered the whole of Malaysia.

growth was due mainly to net inflows of migrants, with the natural increase remaining small throughout much of this period, although rising gradually. Growth rates fluctuated sharply, however, as the demand for labour migrants changed according to the prices of rubber and tin, and in response to other external events (Sultan Nazrin Shah, 2017).

Table 2.3 **In 1957, Malaya's population was nearly four times as large as in 1901**

Census year	Malays	Chinese	Indians	Others	Total
	Population (thousands)				
1901	1,088.9	508.5	107.7	28.6	1,733.7
1911	1,369.0	693.2	239.2	37.7	2,339.0
1921	1,568.6	855.9	439.2	43.1	2,906.7
1931	1,863.9	1,284.9	572.6	66.4	3,787.8
1947	2,427.8	1,884.5	530.6	65.1	4,908.1
1957	3,125.5	2,333.8	696.2	123.3	6,278.8
	Annual growth rate (%)				
1901–1957	1.9	2.7	3.3	2.6	2.3
	Distribution (%)				
1901	62.8	29.3	6.2	1.6	100
1911	58.5	29.6	10.2	1.6	100
1921	54.0	29.4	15.1	1.5	100
1931	49.2	33.9	15.1	1.8	100
1947	49.5	38.4	10.8	1.3	100
1957	49.8	37.2	11.1	2.0	100

Sources of data: Innes (1901); Hare (1902); Marriott (1911a and 1911b); Pountney (1911); Cavendish (1911); Nathan (1922); Vlieland (1932); Del Tufo (1949); Fell (1960).

The high population growth rates in the years preceding World War I were stimulated by an economic upturn as the price of rubber rose sharply during 1910–1912 (Jackson, 1961). As rubber prices surged, planting greatly expanded, with new forest areas opened up.[32] Immigration rose quickly in 1911–1913, then levelled out somewhat with the outbreak of World War I, when it was temporarily restricted. In 1925, Malaya's rubber industry recovered from the post–World War I downturn. The price of rubber started

32 107,200 acres were opened for rubber in the Federated Malay States in 1911, more than double the area cleared in the previous year (Federated Malay States, 1911). As rubber planting became increasingly profitable, large-scale estate cultivation of tapioca and sugar diminished.

the year at 67 cents per pound, rose steadily to Straits$1.74 per pound by the middle of July, and reached its highest point of Straits$1.80 per pound in November. This spurred another round of opening up new areas of forest for rubber planting. In 1926, new planting in Malayan estates increased by 70 per cent from 1925, with a further increase in 1927 (Barlow, 1978). As the sector boomed, the demand for labour expanded, and population growth was thus exceptionally high in 1926 and 1927, at just under 5 per cent (Chapter 5).[33]

The Great Depression had a devastating impact on Malaya's economy, mainly because of the calamitous fall in the price of rubber. The rubber industry by then employed one-third of the working population; so this price collapse, combined with relatively low tin prices, led to widespread unemployment and considerable emigration of Chinese and Indians. In 1931–1933, net emigration was around 400,000, and the population contracted (Del Tufo, 1949). These outflows were at least in part involuntary and were underwritten by the colonial administration.

The Japanese occupation also had a profound effect on the size of the population. Growth was close to zero as live births were depressed, while deaths surged (Del Tufo, 1949). Many married couples were separated; for example, some 79,000 Indian males from rubber plantations in Selangor, Perak, and Negeri Sembilan were forcibly recruited by the Japanese to work on the Siam–Burma railway. The decline in the provision of health services, along with malnutrition, led to increased death rates, especially among infants and young children. There was also a high, but unknown, number of deaths from air raids and summary executions (Del Tufo, 1949). The country's high population growth rate resumed after the war, by this time reflecting rising rates of natural increase due to rapidly declining death rates, along with high and fairly constant birth rates.

The substantial inflows of foreign workers from China and India, and to a lesser extent from the Dutch East Indies, not only had an impact on population growth, but also markedly affected Malaya's ethnic composition. There were, in addition, much smaller inflows of Europeans, mainly British (who numbered between 15,000 and 19,000 over the period 1921–1947), and of Ceylonese, Siamese, Arabs, and Japanese (Box 2.6); but these had only a marginal impact on ethnic balance.

33 Chinese immigration was 349,000 in 1926 and reached a record of 359,000 in 1927; immigration of Indians in these peak years was 175,000 and 156,000 respectively (Straits Settlements, 1926, p. 43 and 1927, p. 55–56).

Box 2.6 The Japanese diaspora in colonial Malaya

Expansionist Japanese colonial and economic aspirations in British Malaya were evident well before the 1941 invasion. Having initially entered the fishing industry, the Japanese became increasingly involved in the exploitation of the peninsula's natural resources, investing in the plantation and mining sectors. Following the post–World War I ban on the import of German goods, the Japanese saw Malaya as a potential market for their own manufactures (Khoo, 1999).

The Japanese invested in rubber plantations as part of the huge growth of the rubber industry in the first decade of the 20th century, and by the end of the second decade they owned 13 estates, five of which were in the Kota Tinggi district of Johor. Their production was mainly for the Japanese market.

The Japanese also moved into mining, but in contrast to the British focus on tin, it was the potential of iron, manganese, and bauxite for military use that attracted their investments (Shaharil Talib, 1996). By 1931, they held a monopoly over iron ore mining—mainly in Terengganu, and to a lesser extent in Johor and Kelantan—producing some 2 million tons annually during the 1930s (Yuen, 1974 and 1978). The output of their plantations and mines was exported to Japan, and made significant contributions to state revenues through export taxes.[34]

The Japanese population in Malaya grew from around 1,500 in 1901 to a peak of nearly 7,000 in 1921. Almost half the Japanese lived in Singapore, mainly as traders and shopkeepers, where they established a Japanese school with the assistance of their government. The next highest concentrations were in Selangor, Perak, and Negeri Sembilan. The census reports of 1911 and 1921 showed that there were more females than males, reflecting the many Japanese women who had been trafficked to Singapore, avoiding immigration controls, to work in brothels.

At the end of World War II, there were some 125,000 Japanese military personnel in Malaya, who were either relocated to internment camps or employed as labourers for rehabilitation work (Kratoska, 2018). The number of Japanese had dwindled to around 250 by 1947, however, and the assets of Japanese companies in Malaya were auctioned, with the proceeds going to the War Damage Fund (Yoshimura, 2002).

The Chinese in Malaya periodically expressed strong anti-Japanese sentiment, with sporadic protests and riots in Singapore and Penang and tensions over the employment of Chinese labourers by Japanese companies. In 1919, the Chinese organized a boycott of Japanese goods, refused to unload cargo from Japanese ships, and looted and burned their businesses. The British imposed martial law to quell the disturbances. Similar hostile actions followed the Japanese attack on Manchuria in 1931 and their invasion of China in 1937–1941 (Koh and Kyoko, 1984).

---

34 Kratoska alludes to the covert activities conducted by the Japanese in British Malaya, including the use of Japanese business holdings in Johor and Singapore as vantage points to observe the construction of British naval bases and coastal defences, and the use of Japanese fishing fleets for surveying Malayan coastal towns (Kratoska, 2018).

Despite the significant net migration from the Malay archipelago in the first three decades of the 20th century, Malays, including allied races, accounted for just 49 per cent of Malaya's population in 1931 compared with 63 per cent in 1901 (Table 2.3).

The Chinese share of the population was around 29 per cent during the first two decades of the 20th century. A substantial rise in the number of Chinese occurred between 1921 and 1931, increasing their share of the population to 34 per cent. It had reached 38 per cent by 1947, and then stabilized over the following decade (Table 2.3).[35] The share of Indians rose very sharply from 1901 to 1921, from just 6 per cent to 15 per cent, as rubber planting expanded and migrant inflows were at their highest. It peaked at 15.1 per cent in 1931.

The Great Depression of the 1930s saw net emigration of Chinese and Indians, although this was somewhat offset by renewed net immigration after the Malayan economy recovered in 1937 and 1938. An increase in demand for labour from the plantation sector resulted in net immigration in 1937 of about 181,000 Chinese and 90,000 Indians; this combined figure was the highest for any single year in pre–World War II Malaya (Tregonning, 1964).[36] Despite this, there was a sharp decline in the share of Indians to 10.8 per cent in 1947 (Table 2.3). This was attributable in part to a steep increase in mortality, especially among infants and children, due to malnutrition during the Japanese occupation (Del Tufo, 1949), as well as forced recruitment of Indian males to work on the Siamese Death Railway (Sandhu, 1969).

The peninsula's ethnic composition remained delicately balanced up to independence. In 1957, Malays had a 49.8 per cent share of the population of the Federation of Malaya, while Chinese had 37.2 per cent, Indians 11.1 per cent, and Others 2.0 per cent (Table 2.3). These figures reflected trends that had emerged since 1871, notably labour migration up to World War II and natural increase subsequently.

Impact of Migration on the Sex Ratio of the Peninsula's Population

The very large inflows of male labour migrants from the 1880s to the early 1930s conspicuously altered the population's sex ratio. Not including the Unfederated Malay States, in 1901 there were 214 males for every

35 Of the total Chinese and Indians enumerated in Malaya's 1931 census, 69 per cent and 79 per cent respectively were foreign-born. The corresponding figures in the 1947 census were 37 per cent and 50 per cent, reflecting the increasing permanency of the migrant communities (Vlieland, 1932; Del Tufo, 1949).

36 Annual Report on the Social and Economic Progress of the People of the Federated Malay States for 1937, p. 59, and Annual Report on the Social and Economic Progress of the People of the Straits Settlements, 1937, p. 11–12.

100 females.[37] Whereas the sex ratio for the Malays was similar to that expected of a settled population, the ratios of Chinese and Indians exhibited huge disparities: in 1901, there were 646 Chinese males and 292 Indian males for every 100 females of the same community (Table 2.4). Until the late 1930s, inflows of Chinese workers, and to a lesser extent of Indian workers, tended to be predominantly made up of young males. They were either single or, if married, had left their wives behind.[38] The intention of most of these economic migrants was simply to save as much money as possible before returning to their families in their homelands, although very high mortality on estates and in mines meant that many never did return (Smith, 1952). Owing to restrictions and cultural inhibitions, there was also considerable reluctance among Chinese females to migrate until well into the 20th century (Eng, 1986).

Table 2.4 Sex ratios of the peninsula's migrant communities were heavily imbalanced until after independence

	Ethnic group (males per 100 females)			
	Malays	Chinese	Indians	Total
1901[a]	106	646	292	214
1911[b]	107	468	310	192
1921	104	282	236	154
1931	103	206	194	142
1947	99	123	146	112
1957	99	108	134	106
1970	99	101	113	101
1980	99	101	106	100

Notes: [a] Excludes the Unfederated Malay States.
[b] Excludes Kelantan and Terengganu.

The number of female arrivals from China did not even exceed 10 per cent of the number of males in the first decade of the 20th century. In the second, the share increased to 14 per cent in 1915, and then rose dramatically to 31 per cent by 1919, a rate not seen at any point in the following decade (Straits Settlements, 1920 and 1932). In the 1930s and 1940s, the Chinese sex ratio became much more evenly balanced because the government restricted male migration, while introducing schemes to encourage existing migrants to bring

37 In a normal population unaffected by sex-selective migration or sex-selective mortality (owing to war, for example), a population's sex ratio is determined by the sex ratio at birth and differential age-specific mortality rates. In most populations, the sex ratio at birth is around 106 males for every 100 females, but at almost every age male mortality rates are higher than those of females, such that the sex ratio becomes progressively more balanced, and at older ages there are more females than males.

38 The sexual needs of these single males were catered for through a large number of organized brothels, with a flourishing trade in the trafficking of young women for this purpose.

their wives and settle in the peninsula.[39] The result was that the net inflows of Chinese female migrants rose much faster than those of males. By 1957, as natural increase became the dominant factor in the growth of the Chinese population, its characteristics approached those of a settled population, with a sex ratio of 108 males to 100 females.

By contrast, the Indian population's sex ratio, while never as imbalanced as that of the Chinese, took far longer to approach that of a settled population. After the 1920s, the Malayan and Indian governments attempted to address this. For example, the Indian government passed the Indian Emigration Act 1922 and Indian Emigration Rules, which stipulated that there should be at least one female for every 1.5 males assisted to emigrate as labourers (Sandhu, 1969). For its part, the Malayan government reduced the assessment paid to the Indian Immigration Fund on female workers, and increased the commission to *kanganis* for female recruits and for married men accompanied by their wives.

Population Policy After 1957

Until the 1940s, net immigration was the main driver of the peninsula's population growth. Population policy and supportive legislation were driven by British economic interests. At various times during the colonial era, government attention was focused on encouraging immigration to meet labour shortages, on controlling migrant labour flows in periods of economic reversal, and on reducing the gender imbalance. At independence, with the population becoming more settled, immigration strictly controlled, and natural increase the major contributor to demographic growth, government attention began to shift towards ethnic balance and reproduction rates (Chapter 4).

Ethnic Balance and the 1969 Riots

The impact of the long phase of Chinese and Indian migration flows on ethnic balance had become extremely sensitive politically in the run-up to independence (Chapter 1). As part of the pre-independence bargaining which began in the late 1940s, Chinese and Indians living in the peninsula had been offered full citizenship and therefore most were also enfranchised. This caused dismay among some Malays, who were concerned about their potential loss of political power, given the peninsula's delicately balanced ethnic composition.

39 In 1938, this exemption was cancelled, and instead a monthly immigration quota of 500 alien women was proclaimed, effective from 1 May 1938 (Straits Settlements and Federated Malay States, Report on the Immigration Department, 1938, p. 61).

Ethnic balance was again a critical issue in the negotiations over the formation of Malaysia in the early 1960s. The peninsula was the dominant entity in terms of population size, having 69 per cent of the total population of the proposed Federation of Malaysia. Singapore would make up the bulk of the remainder, with 18 per cent of the total, while Sabah and Sarawak had a combined share of 13 per cent.

Significantly, the inclusion of Singapore in the federation would reverse the dominance of Malays, from 43.5 per cent Malays and 35.7 per cent Chinese without Singapore, to 42.9 per cent Chinese and 38.2 per cent Malays with it (Leete, 2011). As neither group would constitute the absolute majority in either combination, Indians and indigenous groups would potentially hold the 'balance of power'. Despite this, Malaysia was established in September 1963, uniting the Federation of Malaya, Singapore, Sabah, and Sarawak. However, the country's demographic character changed again in September 1965 when Singapore separated and became an independent nation.

The political significance of this substantial shift in ethnic balance became all too apparent when ethnic riots erupted in May 1969, after which the country's prospects of recovering its interracial cooperation were described as 'gloomy' (Archive document FCO 24/485, 1969). While many factors contributed to the riots, a key aspect was the heightening of ethnic tensions following elections in which the opposition parties had performed far better than expected (Chapter 5). With deteriorating ethnic relations following Singapore's departure from the federation, and high and rising levels of inequality (Chapter 9), the situation became increasingly tense. While the Malays feared that they were losing political control to the non-Malays, especially to the higher-income Chinese, the Chinese in turn felt that they were second-class citizens in comparison with the Malays.

The ethnic riots demonstrated the complexity for the newly independent nation of managing a multi-ethnic society against the backdrop of people's differing and rising expectations. Two days after the riots broke out, a state of Emergency was declared on 15 May 1969, parliament was suspended (until February 1971), and a National Operations Council (NOC) was formed, chaired by Tun Abdul Razak.[40] The riots led to the formulation and launch of the New Economic Policy (NEP) in 1971, which then provided a framework for the ethnicity-based economic and social policies of the next two decades and beyond—in education, employment, housing, the award of business contracts, and equity ownership. The NEP represented an aggressive form of affirmative action in support of Malays and other indigenous communities, implemented both through the distribution of

40 In September 1970, Tun Abdul Razak succeeded Tunku Abdul Rahman to become Malaysia's second prime minister.

the benefits of economic growth and through the processes and institutions that support growth (see the 'Urbanization' subsection, and Chapter 7).[41] In the same year, Malaysia's constitution was amended to support these additional special privileges for the Malays and other *Bumiputera* of Sabah and Sarawak, as well as to prevent public questioning of the new provisions.

A 70 Million Policy

In 1981, prime minister Dr Mahathir Mohamad announced that Malaysia should aim and plan for a population of 70 million by 2100. The population was just 14 million at the time. The policy, in support of the broader 'Look East' strategy (Chapter 6), came during a period of substantial public investment in heavy industries, which was justified in part through calls for a much larger domestic market. The 70 million policy was a radical U-turn, given that much of the previous two decades had been spent establishing and expanding a national family planning programme to reduce what was viewed as over-rapid population growth (Chapter 4). The prevailing view was that slower population growth was essential to support economic development, increase modern-sector employment opportunities, improve living standards, and reduce poverty (Leete, 2011).

In 1984, the Economic Planning Unit of the Prime Minister's Department developed a demographic-economic model which confirmed that while a 70 million population target could be achieved in the long-term future, a gradual rather than rapid movement towards it was preferable if the economy were to optimize welfare gains—whether measured by gross domestic product (GDP) per worker, GDP per capita, or household income per capita. The model also provided evidence to support the view that further pro-natalist policies were unnecessary for achieving a population of 70 million.

The 70 million policy was not referenced in the Mid-Term Review of the Fifth Malaysia Plan, 1986–1990 (MP5), or in later plans. Formulated at a time of economic recession as a result of the collapse in commodity prices, this review in fact noted that population growth in Malaysia was the highest among all countries in the Association of Southeast Asian Nations (ASEAN), and was substantially above that of other newly industrialized economies (NIEs). Population policy has since become more tacit, and has focused again on allowing lower-skilled foreign workers to enter Malaysia through special entry visas.

41 The publication of Dr Mahathir Mohamad's controversial book *The Malay Dilemma* (1970), which argued the case for Malay political dominance and the need for affirmative action to balance Chinese economic dominance, may well have influenced the radical reforms proposed to the NOC, the content of the NEP and its subsequent implementation.

Lower-skilled and Higher-skilled Emigration, 1957–2017

Immigration regulations, which had been progressively tightened from the 1930s, were further restricted by the Immigration Ordinance of 1959.[42] Officially, only those with professional and specialist qualifications, and those whose admission was certified as being in the national economic interest, were permitted to enter for work. However, the historical cross-border movements of communities with strong cultural, ethnic, and linguistic ties to population groups in Malaysia continued. These were mainly flows from southern Thailand to the northern peninsular states, from the southern Philippines to Sabah, and from Indonesia to various Malaysian states. While immigration was strictly controlled, there is some evidence that there was net emigration from Peninsular Malaysia between 1957 and 1970, especially among Chinese leaving for Singapore and other countries, although the size of the flows is difficult to quantify (Hirschman, 1975).

From the early 1980s to the present, the social and economic importance of net immigration has again become increasingly apparent, alongside the continued net emigration of Malaysians with higher skills. As labour shortages began to emerge in the early 1980s, employers once more sought to recruit foreign workers from neighbouring countries. This generated a renewed upturn of lower-skilled foreign labour migrants, both legal and illegal, entering Malaysia to help sustain high economic growth rates.

This upwards trend has been interrupted only by the Asian financial crisis of 1997–1999 and the Great Recession of 2008–2009, in both of which periods the Malaysian economy went into recession. Consequently, restrictions were put on entry and many foreign workers were repatriated. As nationals have become increasingly reluctant to take lower-skilled jobs in agriculture, construction, manufacturing, and basic services, foreign workers have been sourced from both traditional and new lower-income labour-surplus countries in South and Southeast Asia, including Indonesia, Bangladesh, Nepal, Pakistan, the Philippines, Myanmar, and Viet Nam.

As Malaysia's economy has expanded, the labour-intensive sectors have become increasingly reliant on these inflows of unskilled and semi-skilled foreign workers. The number of foreign workers surged from just 136,000 in 1982 to 2.2 million in 2016, with their share of the labour force increasing over this period from just 2.6 per cent to 16 per cent (Figure 2.2). The country's agricultural sector has become particularly dependent on foreign workers, who accounted for some 37 per cent of its workforce in 2016. Foreign labour

---

42 Immigration Ordinance, 1959 No. 12 (Federation of Malaya, 1960).

also accounts for more than one-fifth of the workforce in construction and in manufacturing.

Figure 2.2 **The sharp rise in foreign workers in Malaysia since the early 1990s has been heavily concentrated in particular sectors**

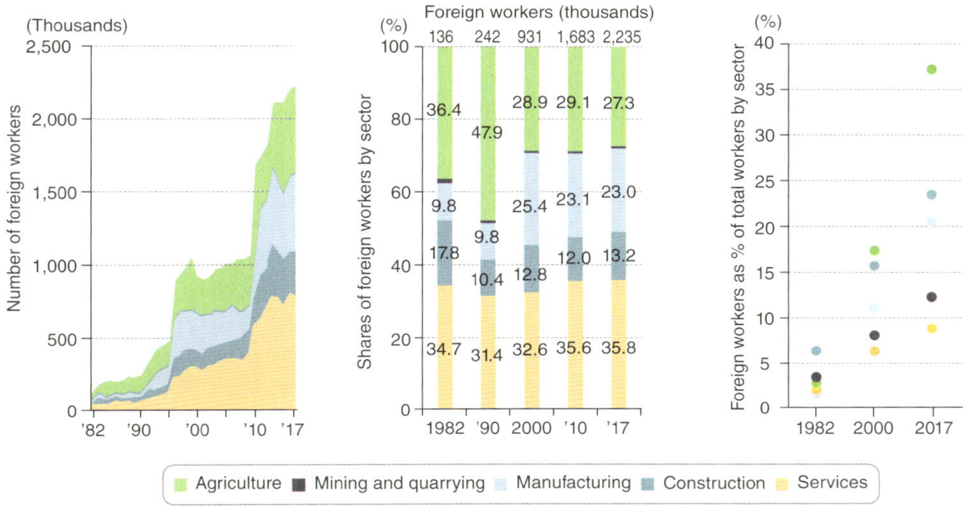

Sources of data: Department of Statistics–Malaysia (various years).
Notes:
Data are from the Labour Force Survey based on households, and relate to those aged 15–64 years; they differ from the number of foreign workers counted on the basis of work permits/visit passes (legal migrants).
Industry data of Labour Force Surveys 1982–2000 are classified according to the *Malaysia Industrial Classification, (Updated) 1972*; those for 2001–2009 according to the *International Standard Industrial Classification of All Economic Activities (ISIC) Revision 3*; and those for 2010–2016 according to *ISIC Revision 4*.

With growing numbers of unskilled and semi-skilled foreign migrants entering Malaysia—many of them undocumented—policy guidelines governing the entry of migrant workers were gradually put into place from about the mid 1980s. These included setting out permissible sectors, source countries, recruitment procedures, and the rights and responsibilities of foreign workers. The Ministry of Human Resources was made responsible for all matters relating to their employment and welfare (Azizah Kassim et al., 2014).[43] Annual levies on foreign workers were introduced, differing according to sector and skill level, with the aim of controlling the size of the inflows.

43 In 1991, a Cabinet Committee on Foreign Workers was established with a mandate to set policy on labour immigration and to monitor its implementation. With increasing inflows of undocumented migrants, its mission was expanded in 2005 to include illegal immigration, and it was renamed the Cabinet Committee on Foreign Workers and Illegal Immigrants. The Committee is chaired by the deputy prime minister, and includes representatives from 13 ministries.

These have failed to have a significant impact on recruitment, however, mainly because of the large cost differentials between local and foreign workers in terms of wages and benefits, and also because some employers have simply deducted the levies from workers' wages. Attempts to increase levies have been derailed by opposition from employers.

Since independence, Indonesians have formed the major component of Malaysia's foreign workforce. A key feature of immigration policy has been the 'dominant presence of a race paradigm, subsumed under security considerations' (Azizah Kassim, 2014, p. 162). Recruitment of migrant workers was initially mainly limited to those from Indonesia and the southern Philippines, as it was believed that their cultural similarities would not affect the existing ethnic balance or contribute to any interethnic conflict. However, after serious disturbances among Indonesian workers in 2001 and early 2002 at detention centres and at a textile factory in Nilai, Negeri Sembilan, there was growing concern that an overdependence on migrant workers from a single country carried security risks. A decision was made to diversify the countries from which migrant workers were sourced, leading to a striking change in the composition of foreign workers. While in 2000 Indonesians accounted for 75 per cent of foreign workers, by 2017 their share had fallen to around 40 per cent (Figure 2.3).

Figure 2.3 Share of Indonesian workers among all foreign workers in Malaysia is declining

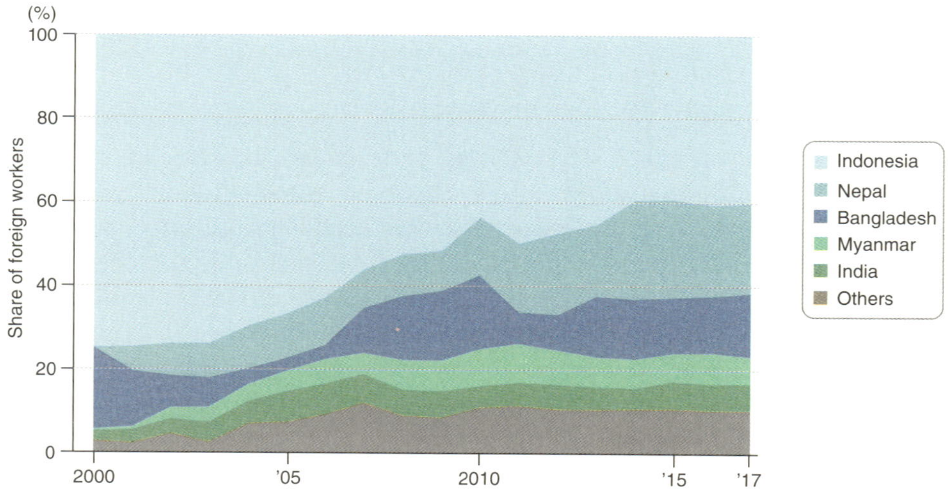

Sources of data: Unpublished data supplied by Department of Statistics–Malaysia; Ministry of Home Affairs–Malaysia (2019).

At the same time, there have been continued net outflows, mainly of skilled and highly skilled Malaysian Chinese, and to a lesser extent of members of higher-skilled groups in other communities. Malaysia's diaspora has grown markedly since 1990, from 563,000 to 1.9 million as of 2017 (Table 2.5), and it is global. The main destination countries are Singapore, Australia, the US, the UK, Brunei, and Canada, with a growing number heading to Singapore. In 2011–2015, 80 per cent of the net outflow of migrants went to Singapore compared with 68 per cent in 2006–2010 and 61 per cent in 2001–2005. The emigrant population continues to increase, although the rate is slowing. Tighter immigration policies, such as those imposed by the UK in 2008, have contributed to this slower pace, although these policies are likely to have restricted the emigration of lower-skilled workers to those countries more than higher-skilled ones.

For every ten skilled Malaysians, one has chosen to leave the country in recent years, which is twice the world average (World Bank, 2011a). In 2010, this brain drain—defined as the emigration of individuals aged 25 and over with at least a tertiary-level degree—represented about one-third of the total Malaysian-born diaspora. Given the increasing trend towards higher education, and the growing difficulties faced by the young and educated in finding suitable employment at home, this figure could well climb further.

Table 2.5 Singapore is the main destination for Malaysians living abroad

Destination country	Number of Malaysians living abroad (thousands)					
	1990	1995	2000	2005	2010	2017
Singapore	195.1	431.9	710.4	818.3	971.8	1,158.9
Australia	72.1	80.8	84.7	101.4	129.9	164.5
US	33.8	42.2	50.7	55.8	62.6	70.7
UK	42.8	45.1	48.2	55.3	66.9	65.3
Brunei	40.3	42.8	45.3	46.3	47.3	51.0
Canada	15.5	18.2	21.3	21.5	22.4	26.0
New Zealand	8.7	11.6	11.2	13.9	15.6	17.4
Hong Kong	10.2	11.4	12.6	13.8	15.0	15.5
India	12.3	13.8	15.2	14.0	12.9	12.3
World	*562.6*	*863.5*	*1,203.5*	*1,380.2*	*1,606.6*	*1,855.6*

Source of data: United Nations Department of Economic and Social Affairs (2018).
Notes:
Bangladesh also featured among the top 10 countries, but it is assumed the data captured the country of last residence rather than the country of birth.
The figures represent the international migrant stock and may include some students and other Malaysians who may not be long-term permanent residents overseas.

In an attempt to counter the rising emigration of highly educated Malaysians, in January 2011 the government established a new agency, TalentCorp, to try to stem the outflows and to attract skilled and professional Malaysians who had migrated abroad to return.[44] However, TalentCorp lacked the mandate to tackle the deeply rooted institutional reasons for the outflows, and by 2017 it had facilitated fewer than 5,000 returnees (Chapter 7).

Population Growth and Changing Ethnic Composition, 1957–2017

Since independence, Malaysia's population has more than tripled, growing from 9.0 million in 1963 to 18.1 million in 1990 and to 32 million in 2017, with an average annual growth rate of 2.3 per cent—a relatively high figure compared with Europe, North America, and East Asia. Although still small relative to its Southeast Asian neighbours Indonesia, the Philippines, Myanmar, Thailand, and Viet Nam, Malaysia's population is now almost six times larger than Singapore's and 7.4 million higher than Australia's. In contrast to the colonial period, natural increase has replaced international migration as the main driver of population growth, although there have been significant net inflows of foreign workers since the 1980s.

During these six decades or so, population growth rates among the main ethnic communities in the peninsula have been highly uneven, with the Malay and other *Bumiputera* growth rates the highest, and Chinese the lowest. Between 1957 and 2017, the average annual population growth rate was 2.7 per cent for Malays and other *Bumiputera*, 1.5 per cent for Chinese, and 1.7 per cent for Indians, reflecting varying fertility levels among the communities as well as net emigration of Chinese.

These differential ethnic growth rates have changed the balance of the ethnic composition of the peninsula (Figure 2.4). The Malay and other *Bumiputera* share of the population rose from 49.8 per cent in 1957 to 66.3 per cent in 2017, while the Chinese and Indian shares declined over the same period to 24.5 per cent and 8.5 per cent respectively from 37.2 per cent and 11.1 per cent. The peninsula's ethnic distribution in 2017 was in fact similar to what it had been over 100 years previously, in 1900.

44 The Returning Expert Programme, under which skilled Malaysians were actively encouraged to come home, was introduced in January 2001, and was later revised and placed within the purview of TalentCorp in April 2011.

Figure 2.4 **Different growth rates have led to big swings in the ethnic composition of the peninsula's population over 12 decades**

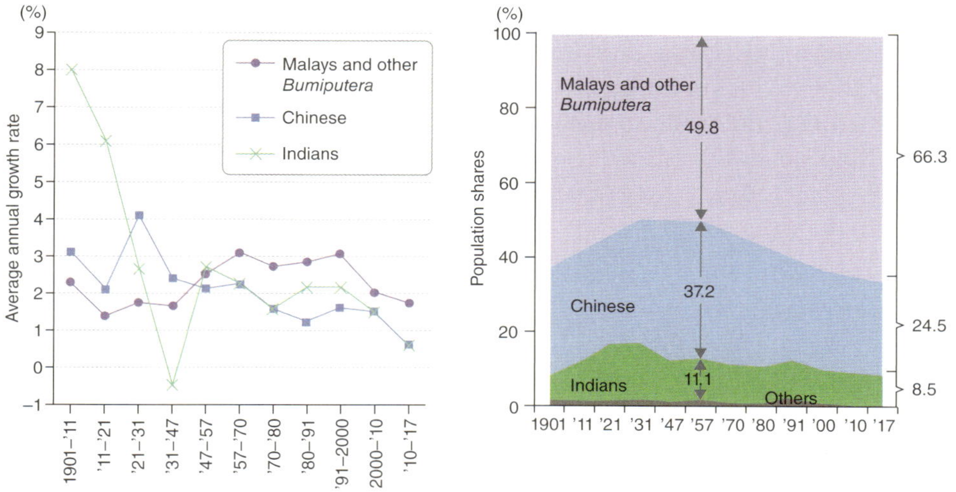

Sources of data: Innes (1901); Hare (1902); Marriott (1911a and 1911b); Pountney (1911); Cavendish (1911); Nathan (1922); Vlieland (1932); Del Tufo (1949); Fell (1960); Chander (1977); Khoo (1983); Khoo (1995); Shaari Abdul Rahman (2001); Wan Ramlah Wan Abdul Raof (2011); Department of Statistics–Malaysia (2018a).

Sabah and Sarawak, 1963–2017

At the end of British rule in 1963, Sabah and Sarawak were even more sparsely populated than the peninsula and their small populations were overwhelmingly rural. Both states have since experienced sustained economic growth and development, such that whereas in 1963 their working populations were predominantly engaged in agriculture, by 2016 less than one-third of the labour force was engaged in agriculture, forestry, and fishing (Department of Statistics–Malaysia, 2016c).

Sabah's economy grew strongly in the 1950s and 1960s as the price of rubber rose and as other natural resource industries, particularly timber, also enjoyed growing prosperity. Sabah's timber boom and the planting of new export crops—especially oil palm and cocoa—on both estates and smallholdings led to rapid economic expansion. This growth was fuelled by large migrant inflows, attracted by the new plantations, timber production, construction, and smallholder farms (Jones, 1966).

Sabah's population has surged as a result, rising from just 549,000 in 1963 to more than 4 million in 2017 (Table 2.6). While high rates of natural increase have been a factor, this striking growth stems mainly from phenomenal rates of labour migration, both legally—of Indonesians from Sulawesi and Kalimantan, and Filipinos—as well as illegally, with immigrants entering across the state's long and porous border with Indonesia, and refugees arriving from the southern Philippines. Foreign labour has helped to meet shortages in the state's vast oil palm plantations, and to a lesser degree in construction, and has supported Sabah's economic development; but it has put pressure on health and education services, and has raised social, political, and security concerns, including concerns related to the sensitive issue of the state's ethnic balance.

Since 1960, Sarawak's population has grown far more slowly than that of Sabah—though it has nevertheless trebled from 857,000 in 1963 to 2.8 million in 2017 (Table 2.6). Unlike Sabah's, Sarawak's population growth has been far less affected by migration: the state is much less accessible to the southern Philippines and north Sulawesi, which curtails undocumented migration, and immigration policy has been more strictly enforced. Foreign workers thus account for a smaller fraction of the state's labour force, although the share has increased somewhat since 1990 owing to increasing economic diversification away from rubber and timber into oil palm plantations, as well as into manufacturing.

Table 2.6 Malaysia's population is now three and a half times as high as it was in 1963, while Sabah's population is seven times as high

	Peninsular Malaysia	Sabah (including Labuan)	Sarawak	Malaysia
	Numbers (thousands)			
1963	7,614.2	549.3	857.1	9,020.7
1970	9,146.7	697.9	1,037.0	10,881.5
1980[a]	11,473.0	1,055.1	1,351.1	13,879.2
1990[a]	14,626.9	1,787.6	1,687.8	18,102.4
2000[a]	18,743.8	2,679.6	2,071.5	23,494.9
2010[a]	22,753.3	3,348.2	2,487.1	28,588.6
2017[a]	25,302.7	3,953.5	2,766.3	32,022.6

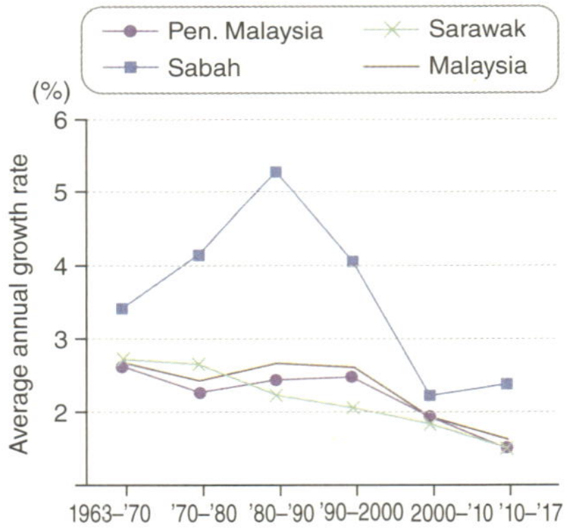

Source of data: Department of Statistics–Malaysia (2001 and 2018a).
Note: [a] Revised on the basis of the Post-enumeration Surveys of the 1980, 1991, 2000, and 2010 population censuses.

Sabah and Sarawak are ethnically diverse, with a different mix of communities from that of the peninsula. In particular, there is no significant presence of Indians in either state. Indigenous people, who form many distinct groups in both states, are dominant. These communities have different characteristics, subcultures, dialects/languages, and religions (Ongkili, 1985; Hood Salleh, 2006). While some groups are mainly Christian, others are mainly Muslim, and some do not adhere to any organized religion.

The ethnic composition of Sabah and Sarawak has changed in various ways since the formation of Malaysia. However, because of major revisions in census practices for categorizing citizens and non-citizens, especially in the classification of Indonesians, quantifying these changes from the data is challenging. At the time of Sabah's 1960 census, the Kadazan/Dusun were the largest community, accounting for about one-third of the population (Table 2.7). By 2010, their share had declined to just 24.1 per cent. The Chinese were the next largest group in 1960 and their share also fell over the same period, from 23 per cent to 13 per cent, largely due to low fertility rates.

Table 2.7 Ethnic composition in Sabah and Sarawak has changed markedly since 1960

Community	Percentage		
Sabah and the Federal Territory of Labuan	**1960**	**1991**	**2010**
Malay	0.4	8.9	9.0
Kadazan/Dusun	32.0	24.5	24.1
Bajau	13.1	15.2	19.1
Murut	4.9	3.9	4.3
Other Indigenous	20.0	19.3	28.4
Indonesian	5.5	10.2	n/a
Chinese	23.0	15.6	12.8
Others[a]	1.3	2.5	2.4
Malaysian citizens (%)	100.0	100.0	100.0
Malaysian citizens (thousands)	n/a	(1,398.9)[b]	(2,391.7)[b]
Non-Malaysians (thousands)	n/a	(464.8)[b]	(901.9)[b]
Total population (thousands)	454.4	(1,863.7)[b]	(3,293.6)[b]
Sarawak			
Malay	17.4	21.2	24.1
Iban	31.9	29.8	30.3
Bidayuh	7.7	8.3	8.4
Melanau	6.0	5.7	5.2
Other Indigenous	5.1	6.1	6.6
Chinese	30.8	28.0	24.5
Others[a]	1.1	0.9	0.7
Malaysian citizens (%)	100.0	100.0	100.0
Malaysian citizens (thousands)	n/a	(1,700.0)[b]	(2,354.0)[b]
Non-Malaysians (thousands)	n/a	(18.4)[b]	(117.1)[b]
Total population (thousands)	744.5	(1,718.4)[b]	(2,471.1)[b]

Sources of data: Computed from Jones (1962a, 1962b); Khoo (1995); Wan Ramlah Wan Abdul Raof (2011).

[a] Before 1991, the category Others comprised mainly Indians and others, such as Europeans, but for 1991 it also included Filipinos.

[b] Revised on the basis of the Post-enumeration Surveys of the 1991 and 2010 population censuses.

In Sarawak in 1960, the two biggest groups were rural Ibans and urban Chinese, each of which accounted for slightly less than one-third of the population (Table 2.7). By 2010, their shares had fallen to 30 per cent and 25 per cent respectively. There has been a significant increase in the proportion of Malays in both states—in Sabah from less than 1 per cent to 9 per cent, and in Sarawak from 17 per cent to 24 per cent. These increases mainly reflect changes in the way some people choose to identify themselves in the censuses, however. To a smaller degree, they are also the result of migration of Malays from the peninsula.

A Century of Spatial Redistribution, 1901–2017

Urbanization

Economic growth and urbanization are normally closely associated with the structural transformation of an economy (Chapters 6 and 8). As food and commercial crop production per farmer rises, progressively fewer farmers are needed to work in agriculture. Attracted by the prospects of higher-paid modern-sector jobs, farmers and their families migrate to cities and towns. The growth of urban areas in colonial Malaya, however, was due primarily to the inflows of foreign workers, and it was only after independence that there was substantial migration from rural to urban areas.

In the late 19th century and the first half of the 20th century, the growing urban population reflected the settlement patterns of foreign workers in the small number of existing towns and the newly emerging ones (Figure 2.5).[45] Immigrant settlement and employment opportunities were heavily concentrated in the cosmopolitan towns, the formation and growth of which were closely linked to the development of tin, rubber, infrastructure, commerce, services, and government administration. New migrant settlements required further rounds of investment in infrastructure and services, which further boosted the drive to urbanization. Urban growth was highest, however, in the decade 1947–1957 because of the relocation of mainly Chinese rural families into towns and New Villages during the Emergency (Fell, 1960).

45 The definition of what constitutes an urban area has changed over time. Until the 1947 census, urban areas were defined as towns or large villages of a gazetted administrative area with a population of 1,000 or more. In the 1957 census, it was felt that this overstated the degree of urbanization, and the definition was changed to gazetted administrative areas with a population of 10,000 or more (Fell, 1960). In the 1991 census, the definition was modified again to cover gazetted areas, together with adjoining built-up areas contiguous to a gazetted area, with a combined population of 10,000 or more, and with at least 60 per cent of their population engaged in non-agricultural activities (Khoo, 1995). Urban areas thus gradually came to include reclassified rural localities.

Nevertheless, at independence in 1957, Malaya's population was still predominantly rural and the majority of workers were still engaged in agriculture. Just over a quarter of the population lived in towns. Kuala Lumpur, the administrative capital, and George Town, the centre of Penang's commercial activities, were the largest of these, with Ipoh, the leading tin-mining and business centre in Perak, the next biggest. A feature of the composition of the urban population at that time, reflecting the segmented employment patterns of the colonial era, was the relative over-representation of Chinese and Indian communities (45 per cent and 31 per cent of the total respectively), and under-representation of Malays (11 per cent) (Fell, 1960).

In the early post-independence years the rate of urbanization grew slowly. In the peninsula it increased from 26 per cent in 1957 to just 29 per cent in 1970, as smaller towns grew and became classified as urban (Hirschman, 1975). With the progressive structural transformation of the economy and the associated shift in employment from agriculture towards manufacturing and modern service industries, the pace of growth quickened. By 1980, the urban proportion had risen to 37 per cent (Figure 2.5).

Figure 2.5 **A century of increasing urbanization affected all states**

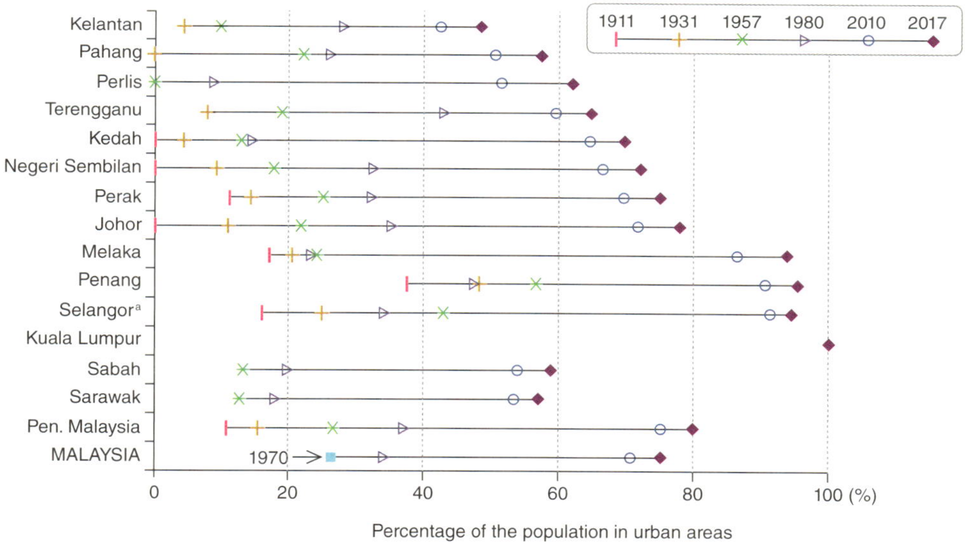

Sources of data: Fell (1960); Khoo (1983); Wan Ramlah Wan Abdul Raof (2011); Department of Statistics–Malaysia (2017c).

Notes:

[a] Selangor includes Kuala Lumpur for 1911, 1931, and 1957.

In the early decades of the 20th century, although only some states had gazetted areas with population concentrations of over 10,000, they all had small towns with population concentrations of between 1,000 and 10,000.

The proportion of Malaysia's population living in urban areas, especially in large urban centres with more than 150,000 people, more than doubled after 1980, reaching 75.5 per cent by 2017.[46] The average annual rate of urban population growth peaked between 1980 and 1991 at 5.9 per cent. The increase in higher-paying jobs in manufacturing, modern services, and government administration all contributed to this process, along with NEP measures that encouraged rural Malays to move to towns and suburban areas. Although economic development programmes remained focused at first on the established urban centres along the west coast, they later spread to include the comparatively less-developed and poorer east coast and northern states.

The NEP had the aim, among other objectives, of reducing the existing social, economic, and spatial inequalities among the three main ethnic communities, in part through measures that supported greater Malay urbanization. Measures included support for urban-based higher education and the provision of low-cost urban housing, as well as the expansion of modern-sector employment, particularly in the public sector and also, geographically, within free-trade zones. In 2010, as shares of each community's population, the Chinese were 91 per cent urban, Indians 89 per cent, and Malays and other *Bumiputera* 63 per cent. Malaysia's urban areas, especially the biggest cities and metropolitan towns, have gradually become more cosmopolitan and ethnically diverse, and have developed the character and features of vibrant global cities.

With the focus on a more geographically balanced pattern of economic development, urbanization has occurred throughout Malaysia to such a degree that by 2017 more than half of the population in 12 of the country's 13 states was classified as urban. Kelantan was the exception, with only 48.7 per cent of its population classified as urban dwellers. Penang (94.6 per cent) has now overtaken Selangor (93.7 per cent) as the most urbanized state, with Melaka (93.4 per cent) rapidly catching up.[47] Particularly notable has been the evolution of Kuala Lumpur (the Klang Valley metropolis) into a mega-urban region spreading over a large part of Selangor. At least one large city or big town is located in each of Malaysia's states, giving most rural dwellers ready access to a range of modern urban services.

Distribution by States

The country's population distribution has long been highly uneven, with settlement patterns determined by the location of opportunities for profit or

---

46 The number of large urban centres in Malaysia increased from just nine in 1980 to 32 in 2010, accounting for 56 per cent and 63 per cent of the total urban population respectively (Abdul Rahman Hasan and Nair, 2014).

47 Selangor and Johor are the states with the largest number of urban centres (Abdul Rahman Hasan and Nair, 2014).

employment. At the beginning of the 20th century, four states—Perak (19 per cent), Penang (14.3 per cent), Kelantan (13.1 per cent), and Kedah (11.2 per cent)—together accounted for 57.6 per cent of the peninsula's population. Population concentrations were along the coast and river banks.

At independence, the distribution had changed dramatically, reflecting the pattern of economic development and related migrant labour settlement (Map 2.1). International migrants, who arrived at the peninsula's western seaports, settled mainly in Penang, in and around the mining towns in the west coast states, and in Johor. These states were all well connected through a commercial railway system and road network, as well as through their seaports. The state of Selangor, where the administrative capital of Kuala Lumpur was located, had grown the most by independence, increasing its population share from 10 per cent in 1901 to 16 per cent in 1957. This continued to be lower than the share of Perak, which had about one-fifth of the total. The southern state of Johor was another growth area, with its population share nearly doubling from 8 per cent in 1901 to 15 per cent by 1957.

Pahang, the peninsula's largest state by land area, had one of the smallest population shares throughout this period. Interestingly, and reflecting their uneven secular pattern of development, the population shares of the east coast states of Kelantan and Terengganu fell sharply over this period. Relatively few international migrants were attracted to the less accessible and less developed northern and east coast states.

Map 2.2 shows how Malaysia's population distribution continued to change over the period 1970–2017 as a result of interstate migration, international migration, and demographic dynamics.

A conspicuous feature is the substantial growth in the combined share of the population of Selangor and Kuala Lumpur—the Klang Valley metropolis—which grew from 15.6 per cent in 1970 to 19.9 per cent in 1991, and reached 25.8 per cent in 2017. Commercial, industrial, and service activities have increasingly been located in the metropolis so as to achieve scale and specialization—the economies of agglomeration. The Klang Valley's population is culturally diverse, and its cities and suburbs have become more closely connected through networks of super-highways and mass rapid transit systems. They have become enclaves of high-paid employment for professional and technical workers, and have spawned a market for lower-paid service workers. They have also seen the emergence of a new stratum of very low-paid workers; and there is a growing disparity between the abundance of opportunities here compared with those in other parts of the country. This settlement pattern is consistent with the worldwide rise of dominant metropolitan cities associated with globalization (Collier, 2018).

Map 2.1 The share of Malaya's population in the west coast states and Johor increased sharply between 1901 and 1957

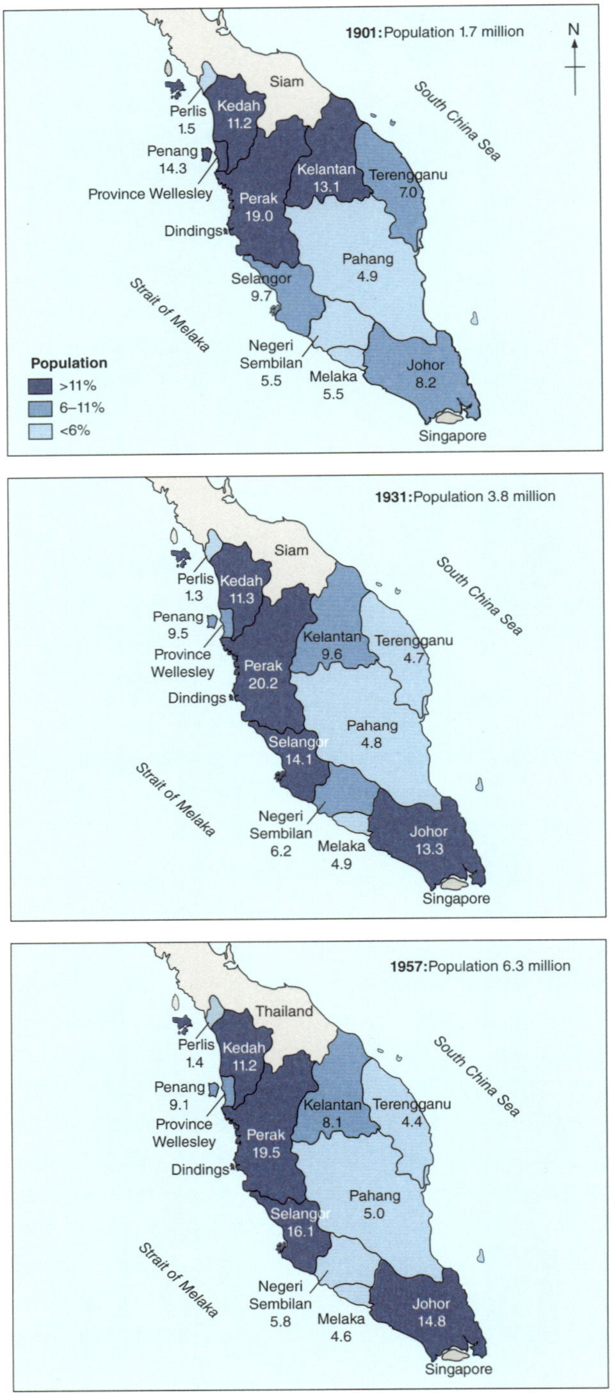

Sources of data: Innes (1901); Hare (1902); Vlieland (1932); Fell (1960).

Map 2.2 Selangor and Sabah saw spectacular growth in their shares in Malaysia's population between 1970 and 2017

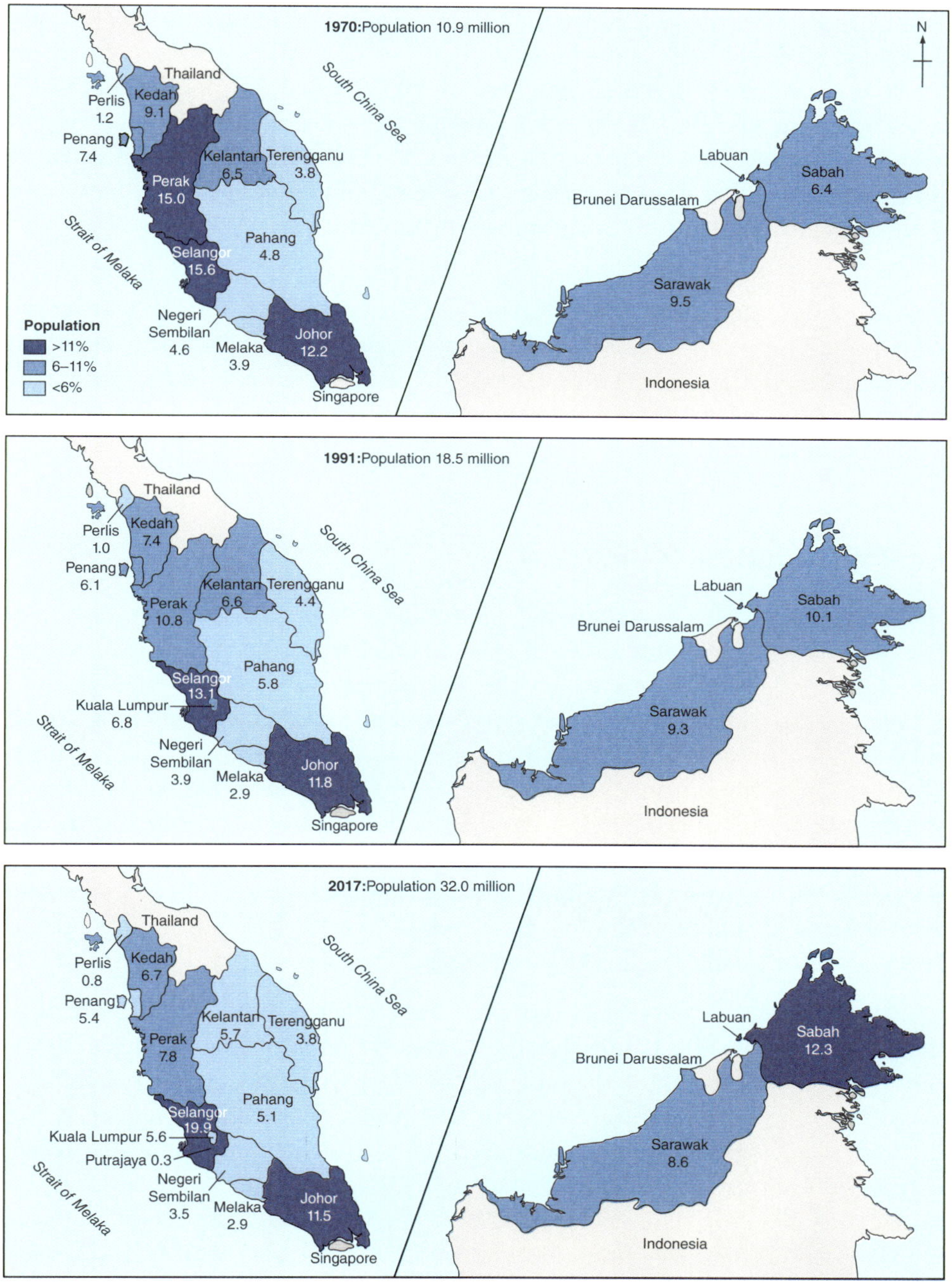

Source of data: Department of Statistics–Malaysia (2018a).
Note: Data for Labuan added to Sabah.

There has been significant and continued emigration from Perak and Melaka principally to Selangor and Kuala Lumpur. The outflows from Perak reflect the running down of its once-flourishing tin-mining industry and its lack of any major new industries until quite recently. Perak's population share almost halved from 15 per cent in 1970 to just 7.8 per cent in 2017. High levels of emigration have also taken place from the least developed east coast states, especially from Kelantan. Migrants from these states travel predominantly into Pahang, which was the main beneficiary of new land development resettlement programmes (Chapter 8).

The extremely high population growth rate experienced in the formerly sparsely populated state of Sabah has been the major factor in the shift in the distribution between Peninsular Malaysia and Sabah and Sarawak. These two less-developed states, which constitute 60 per cent of Malaysia's land area, accounted for just over 21 per cent of the country's population in 2017, up from 16 per cent in 1970.

Conclusions

Decennial population censuses, conducted by the British as they progressively established control over Malaya from the mid 19th century, provide invaluable estimates of the peninsula's population size and its ethnic, occupational, and spatial composition. Before censuses were held, there were only rough guestimates of the populations of individual states. The census administrators introduced an ethnicity-based classification of the people, which initially helped to distinguish between the indigenous and peninsula-born population, and migrants from elsewhere. With increasing proportions of each community being peninsula-born, this distinction became less useful. But ethnicity-based classification has continued and has served administrative and policy purposes.

Malaya's rapid economic growth and development could not have happened without the input of migrant workers. From the mid 19th century until World War II, population growth in the peninsula stemmed from the large net inflows of migrant workers who came to meet the needs of the expanding colonial economy. Migrants settled in and around tin-mining areas, estate plantations, and the steadily growing towns located in the west coast states and in Johor. The northern and east coast states attracted far fewer migrants and remained populated predominantly by peninsula-born Malays. The highest population growth rates occurred during periods of comparative prosperity for the two major industries of tin and rubber—periods when there were increasing prices, production levels, and wages.

At independence, occupational segregation and segmented settlement patterns were a prominent legacy of British colonial immigration policy, and ethnicity had become closely associated with both economic function and geographical location. In the absence of measures to promote social, economic, and cultural integration, these patterns proved unsustainable and were undoubtedly a major contributing factor to the growing ethnic tensions that culminated in the riots of 1969.

After independence, net immigration was curtailed through several new regulations that progressively restricted the entry of new migrants. Since the 1980s, however, a much more liberal policy has been adopted, and new waves of Asian foreign labour have entered Malaysia in response to the shortage of lower-skilled workers. These have come mainly from Indonesia, but also from other lower-income, labour-surplus Asian countries. Malaysia's population of documented foreign workers is now around 2.2 million, most of whom have limited education. They are employed in low-skilled assembly-based industries, construction, low-end services, and agriculture. In addition, there is a large but indeterminate number of undocumented migrants.

These large inflows of low-skilled foreign labour are likely to have depressed wages, and have disincentivized employers from introducing measures to enhance labour productivity—such as more highly mechanized methods of production—as well as from investing in skills in support of the country's aspiration to become a high-income economy (Chapter 7). At the same time, the desired transition to skill-intensive, technology-driven, and higher-value-added employment has not taken place quickly enough to enable any significant reduction in dependence on foreign workers.

There has also been a persistent net outflow of higher-skilled Malaysians, especially Malaysian Chinese. This brain drain is further diluting the country's human capital base and undermining Malaysia's aspiration to become a high-income nation. This dynamic is closely related to affirmative action measures in education and employment, which engender a sense of social injustice among the non-Malays (World Bank, 2011a).

Malaysia's population has become increasingly concentrated in its major cities and suburbs, consistent with the experience of other countries at a similar stage of economic development. While such trends create greater modern-sector employment opportunities and are associated with higher standards of living and well-being, they also bring new challenges for urban governance. These range from worsening problems of urban poverty, traffic congestion, and emissions of pollutants to growing demands for affordable housing, better public safety and security, and other services.

At this point, approaching the end of the second decade of the 21st century, there is no longer a fine balance in the ethnic composition of Malaysia's population of some 32 million as there was at the end of the colonial era, when Malays accounted for just under half of the country's inhabitants. All communities have benefited substantially from the country's sustained economic growth and development, and economic power is now more evenly spread. Yet increased inclusiveness among the population remains elusive.

Part 2 will now review the steps taken by colonial and Malaysian governments to advance the education (Chapter 3) and health (Chapter 4) of the population, and to reduce geographical and ethnic disparities in these two key areas of well-being. The story is generally one of success, although significant problems remain.

Annex Table 2.1 History of ethnic sub-classifications used in Malayan/Malaysian population censuses

Malays	Chinese	Indians
Federated Malay States 1901		
Malay	Cantonese	Tamil
Aborigine	Hokkien	Bengali
Achinese	Hainanese	Burmese
Boyanese	Hakka	Parsee
Bugis	Straits-born	
Dayak	Teochew	
Javanese	Kwongsai	
Jawi-Pekan	Others	
Manilamen		
Federated Malay States 1911		
Malay	Hokkien	Tamil
Javanese	Cantonese	Telegu
Sakai (Aborigine)	Hakka	Malayali
Banjarese	Teochew Kheh	Punjabi
Boyanese	Hainanese	Bengali
Mendeling	Kwongsai	Hindustani
Krinchi	Hokchiu	Gujerati
Jambi	Henghua	Maharatta
Achinese	Hokchia	Burmese
Bugis	Teochew	Afghan
Others	Others	Others
Malaya 1921		
Malay	Hokkien	Tamil
Javanese	Cantonese	Telegu
Boyanese	Hakka	Malayali
Achinese	Teochew	Punjabi
Mendeling	Hainanese	Bengali
Korinchi	Kwongsai	Hindustani
Banjarese	Hokchiu	Pathan
Bornean Races	Henghua	Gujerati
Bugis	Hokchia	Maharatta
Sakai (Aborigine)	Northern Provinces	Burmese
Others	Others	Gurkha
		Others

Malaysians		Chinese	Indians
Malaya 1931			
Malays		Hokkien	Tamil
Other Malaysians		Cantonese	Telegu
Javanese	Riau Lingga	Hakka	Malayali
Boyanese	Banjarese	Teochew	Punjabi, etc.
Achinese	Other Dutch Borneo	Hainanese	United Provinces
Batak	Bugis	Kwongsai	Burmese
Menangkabau	Other Dutch East Indies	Hokchiu	Bengal
Korinchi	Dayak	Hokchia	Bombay
Jambi	Sakai (Aborigine)	Others	Bihar and Orissa
Palembang	Settled & Nomadic		Nepal
Other Sumatra	Others		Others
Malaya 1947			
Indigenous Malaysians	Other Malaysians	Hokkien	Tamil
Malay proper	Indonesians	Cantonese	Telegu
Aborigine (Settled)	Sundanese	Hakka	Malayali
Biduanda, Mantera & other Jakun	Javanese	Teochew	Other South Indian
Negrito	Boyanese	Hainanese	Sikh
Other aborigine	Achinese	Kwongsai	Bengali
Aborigine (Nomadic)	Menangkabau	Hokchiu	Gujerati
Negrito	Korinchi	Henghua	Maharatti
Jakun	Jambi	Hokchia	Marwari
Semai (Semak, Senoi)	Palembangan	Others	Pathan
Sisek (Besisi)	Other Sumatran		Punjabi
Semelai	Riau Lingga Malay		Rajput
Temiar	Banjarese		Sindhi
Others	Dayak		Others
	Other Borneo		
	Bugis		
	Other Indonesian		
Malaya 1957			
Malays		Hokkien	Indian Tamil
Indonesian		Cantonese	Telegu
Aborigine		Hakka	Malayali
Negrito		Teochew	Others
Jakun		Hainanese	

Malaysians		**Chinese**	**Indians**
Semai		Kwongsai	
Semelai		Hokchiu	
Temiar		Henghua	
Other Aborigine		Hokchia	
		Others	

Malays		**Chinese**	**Indians**
Malaysia 1970			
Malay		Hokkien	Indian Tamil
Indonesian	Indigenous Sabah	Cantonese	Telegu
Orang Asli	Kadazan/Kwijau	Hakka	Malayali
Negrito	Murut	Teochew	Punjabi
Jakun	Bajau/Illanun	Hainanese	Pakistani
Semai	Lotud	Kwongsai	Sri Lankan Tamil
Semelai	Rungus	Hokchiu	Other Sri Lankan
Temiar	Tambanuo	Henghua	Others
Others	Dumpas	Hockchia	
Other Malay	Maragang	Others	
Indigenous Sarawak	Paitan		
Melanau	Idahan		
Sea Dayak	Minokok		
Land Dayak	Rumanau		
Bisayah	Mangka'ak		
Kadayan	Orang Sungei		
Kelabit	Brunei		
Kenyah	Kadayan		
Murut	Bisaya		
Punan	Tidong		
Others	Sino-native		
	Others		

Malaysia 1980			
Malay		Hokkien	Indian Tamil
Indonesian		Cantonese	Telegu
Orang Asli	Pribumi (Sabah)	Hakka	Malayali
Negrito	Kadazan	Teochew	Sikh
Jakun	Kwijau	Hainanese	Other Punjabi
Semai	Murut	Kwongsai	Pakistani
Semelai	Bajau	Hokchiu	Bangladeshi
Temiar	Illanun	Henghua	Sri Lankan Tamil
Indigenous (Sarawak)	Lotud	Hokchia	Other Sri Lankan
Melanau	Rungus	Others	Others

Malays		Chinese	Indians
Sea Dayak	Tambanuo		
Land Dayak	Dumpas		
Bisayah	Maragang		
Kadayan	Paitan		
Kenyah	Idahan		
Kelabit	Minokok		
Murut	Rumanau		
Punan	Mangka'ak		
Others	Sulu		
Other Malay	Orang Sungei		
	Brunei		
	Kedayan		
	Bisaya		
	Tidong		
	Others		
	Sino-native		
	Native of Philippines		
	Cocos Islander		

Bumiputera		Chinese	Indians
Malaysia 1991			
Malay		Hokkien	Indian Tamil
Other *Bumiputera*		Cantonese	Telegu
Negrito	Mangkaak	Hakka	Malayali
Senoi	Minokok	Teochew	Punjabi/Sikh
Proto Malay	Maragang	Hainanese	Sri Lankan Tamil
Dusun	Paitan	Kwongsai	Singhalese
Kadazan	Rumanau	Foochow/Hokchiu	Pakistani
Kwijau	Lotud	Henghua	Bangladeshi
Bajau	Cocos Islander	Hokchia	Others
Iranun/Illanun	Other Indigenous (Sabah)	Others	
Murut (Sabah)	Iban/Sea Dayak		
Orang Sungei	Bidayuh/Land Dayak		
Sulu/Suluk	Melanau		
Bisaya (Sabah/ Sarawak)	Kenyah		
Rungus	Kayan		
Sino-native	Lun Bawang/Murut (Sarawak)		

Bumiputera		**Chinese**	**Indians**
Kadayan (Sabah/ Sarawak)	Penan		
Tidong	Kajang		
Tambanuo	Kelabit		
Idahan	Other Indigenous (Sarawak)		
Dumpas			
Malaysia 2000			
Malay		Hokkien	Indian Tamil
Other *Bumiputera*		Cantonese	Telegu
Negrito	Idahan	Hakka	Malayali
Senoi	Dumpas	Teochew	Punjabi/Sikh
Proto Malay	Maragang	Hainanese	Sri Lankan Tamil
Dusun	Paitan	Kwongsai	Singhalese
Kadazan	Rumanau	Foochow/Hokchiu	Pakistani
Kwijau	Lotud	Henghua	Bangladeshi
Mangkaak	Cocos Islander	Hokchia	Others
Bajau	Other Indigenous (Sabah)	Others	
Iranun	Iban/Sea Dayak		
Murut (Sabah)	Bidayuh/Land Dayak		
Orang Sungei	Melanau		
Sulu/Suluk	Kenyah		
Bisaya (Sabah/ Sarawak)	Kayan		
Rungus	Lun Bawang/Murut (Sarawak)		
Sino-native	Penan		
Kadayan (Sabah/ Sarawak)	Kajang		
Tidong	Kelabit		
Minokok	Other Indigenous (Sarawak)		
Tambanuo			
Malaysia 2010			
Malay		Foochow	Indian Muslim/ Malabari
Other *Bumiputera*	Sarawak *Bumiputera*	Hainanese	Malayali
Orang Asli	Bidayuh	Henghua	Punjabi
Negrito	Bisayah	Hokchia	Sikh

Bumiputera		**Chinese**	**Indians**
Senoi	Bukitan	Hokchiu	Sinhala
Melayu Asli	Iban	Hokkien	Indian Tamil
Sabah *Bumiputera*	Kadayan	Cantonese	Sri Lankan Tamil
Bajau	Kajang	Hakka	Telugu
Balabak/Molbog	Kanowit	Kwongsai	Others
Bisaya/Bisayah	Kayan	Teochew	
Bulongan	Kejaman	Others	
Dusun	Kalabit		
Idahan/Ida'an	Kenyah		
Iranun/Ilanun	Lahanan		
Kadayan/Kedayan	Lisum		
Kadazan	Lugat		
Lundayuh/ Lundayeh	Lun Bawang/Murut Sarawak		
Murut	Melanau		
Orang Sungai	Penan		
Rungus	Punan		
Suluk	Sabup		
Tidung	Sekapan		
Other Sabah *Bumiputera*	Sian		
	Sipeng		
	Tabun		
	Tagal		
	Tanjong		
	Ukit		
	Other Sarawak *Bumiputera*		

North Borneo (Sabah) and Sarawak pre-1970 censuses

Indigenous groups, Malays and others		**Chinese**	**Indians**
North Borneo 1901			
Indigenous groups, Malays and others			
Dusun	Brunei		
Murut	Sulu		
Bajau	Malay		
Orang Padas	Others		

Indigenous groups, Malays and others		Chinese	Indians
North Borneo 1911			
Indigenous groups, Malays and others			
Dusun	Sulu		Indian
Murut	Tidong		Pakistani
Bajau/Illanun	Native of Sarawak		Ceylonese
Brunei	Malay		
Kedayan	Indonesians		
Orang Sungei	Native of Philippines		
Bisaya	Others		
North Borneo 1921 and 1931			
Indigenous groups, Malays and others			
Dusun/Kwijau	Sulu	Hakka	Indian
Murut	Tidong	Cantonese	Pakistani
Bajau/Illanun	Native of Sarawak	Hokkien	Ceylonese
Brunei	Malay	Teochew	
Kedayan	Indonesians	Hailam	
Orang Sungei	Native of Philippines	Others	
Bisaya	Others		
North Borneo 1951			
Indigenous groups, Malays and others			
Dusun/Kwijau	Sulu	Hakka	Indian
Murut	Tidong	Cantonese	Pakistani
Bajau/Illanun	Sino-native	Hokkien	Ceylonese
Brunei	Malay	Teochew	
Kedayan	Indonesians	Hailam	
Orang Sungei	Native of Philippines	Others	
Bisaya	Others		
North Borneo 1960			
Indigenous groups, Malays and others			
Dusun/Kwijau	Tidong	Hakka	Indian
Murut	Sino-native	Cantonese	Pakistani
Bajau/Illanun	Malay	Hokkien	Ceylonese
Brunei	Native of Sarawak	Teochew	
Kedayan	Indonesians	Hailam	
Orang Sungei	Native of Philippines	Others	
Bisaya	Cocos Islander		
Sulu	Others		

Malays, Indigenous groups and others			Chinese	Indians
Sarawak 1939, 1947, and 1960				
Malays, Indigenous groups and others				
Malay	Sea Dayak	Kedayan	Cantonese	Indian
Beliun	Balau	Kayan	Foochow	Pakistani
Narum	Batang Ai	Kenyah	Hakka	Ceylonese
Seru	Batu Blah	Badang	Henghua	
Melanau	Iban	Barawan	Hokkien	
Bintulu	Lemanak	Long Kiput	Hailam	
Bukitan	Maloh	Lelak	Teochew	
Kajaman	Milikin	Lirong	Others	
Kanowit	Saribas	Murik		
Lahanan	Sebuyau	Nyamok		
Lisum	Skrang	Sebob		
Lugat	Tanjong	Kelabit		
Matu	Ulu Ai	Sabun		
Rejang	Undup	Tabun		
Seduan	Land Dayak	Murut		
Sekapan	Jagoi	Tagal		
Segalang	Salakan	Punan		
		Penan		
Sian	Taup	Others		
Sipeng	Bisaya	Indonesians		
Tatau	Belait			
Ukit	Bukit			
	Tutong			

Sources of data:
Hare (1902); Pountney (1911); Nathan (1922); Vlieland (1932); Del Tufo (1949); Fell (1960); Chander (1977); Khoo (1983); Khoo (1995); Shaari Abdul Rahman (2001); Wan Ramlah Wan Abdul Raof (2011).

Note: The classification scheme used in the censuses up to 1980 was for the total population irrespective of citizenship, while that for subsequent censuses was for Malaysian citizens only.

KEDAH
KUALA MUDA
PROVINCE
WELLESLEY
PENANG
NORTH CHANNEL
SOUTH CHANNEL
BUTTERWORTH
STATE OF KELANTAN
FEDERATED MALAY STATES
STATE OF PERAK
UPPER PERAK DISTRICT
SELAMA DISTRICT
KRIAN DISTRICT
LARUT DISTRICT
TAIPING
KUALA KANGSAR DISTRICT
MATANG DISTRICT
IPOH
KINTA DISTRICT
DINDINGS
Pulau Pangkor
LOWER PERAK DISTRICT
BATANG PADANG DISTRICT
K Perak
Sembilan Islands
Kuala Bernam
River Bernam
SERAU
TELOM
TENOM
KECHAU
ULU JELEI
KUALA LIPIS
LIPIS DISTRICT
SULU PAHANG
RAUB DISTRICT
Bentong
TEMERLOH DISTRICT
STATE OF SELANGOR
KUALA SELANGOR DISTRICT
ULU SELANGOR DISTRICT
KUALA LUMPUR
KLANG DISTRICT
ULU LANGAT DISTRICT
KUALA LANGAT DISTRICT
STATE OF JELEBU DISTRICT
KUALA PILAH
NEGRI SEMBILAN
SEREMBAN DISTRICT
SEREMBAN
COAST DISTRICT
TAMPIN DIST
Cape Rachado
MALACCA
STRAITS OF MALACCA
A MAP OF
THE BRITISH TERRITORIES & BRITISH PROTECTORATES
THE MALAY PENINSULA
TO ACCOMPANY THE GUIDE BOOK TO
THE FEDERATED MALAY STATES
By C. W. HARRISON, Esq. Malay Civil Service
1911
EXPLANATION
Scale

Adapted from:
C.W. Harrison,
Map of the British Territories & British Protectorates in the Malay Peninsula, London, 1911

Courtesy of:
HRH Sultan Sharafuddin Idris Shah and Dato' Richard Curtis

PART 2

ENHANCING HUMAN WELL-BEING

Chapter 3

Building Human Capital

Education is vitally important for individual well-being, human development, and broader societal progress. Education also contributes to better health which, in turn, opens up a lifetime of opportunities. In colonial Malaya, illiteracy was widespread, with most children in rural and urban areas receiving only a few years of basic education. Since World War II, however, education has been recognized as essential to national prosperity.

There are important linkages between education, human capital, and economic prosperity.[1] A better-educated workforce has an enhanced ability to assimilate ideas and knowledge, which in turn raises productivity and the ability to compete internationally, as well as promoting innovation. Labour and capital inputs—the traditional factors of production—alone cannot fully explain the growth of income per capita over time, or the differences in economic performance between countries. It is the *quality* of these factors that counts in the structural transformation of an economy. The quality of labour is mediated and strengthened through education and training, which support the absorption of ideas and the application of new technologies. Earnings and education are, of course, closely associated. On average, earnings increase with higher levels of education. Education is thus a means of improving both individual welfare and national development.

The processes of globalization have made countries more economically integrated, more interdependent, and more competitive with one another. This increased integration and competition have reinforced the notion that investments in human capital—through education and training, as well as lifelong learning—are fundamental for productivity improvements, management of technological change, and creative innovations that are so critical for sustaining economic growth. Such investments have been a priority of Malaysian planners and policymakers since the 1950s, as seen in successive national development plans and the sustained high levels of government spending on education.

1 Human capital is made up of three interrelated components: health, nutrition, and education. The focus in this chapter is on education.

The economic and social benefits of education do not accrue automatically, however. They require an appropriate policy environment that enables human capital to develop optimally (Barro and Lee, 1994; World Bank, 2018a). If an education system is not well managed, it cannot be expected to deliver the intended outcomes. Indeed, economic and social differences between groups may even be exacerbated by poorly designed or ineffectively implemented education policies. If they are not given the opportunities to use their skills at home, the most talented citizens of a country may well move to other countries where their skills are better valued. Like capital, labour is highly mobile, and the most gifted individuals are in high demand globally.

This chapter describes and assesses the evolution of education in Malaysia from colonial times to the present. It does so primarily through the prism of human capital (Box 3.1), although it is recognized that other perspectives on education could also be employed.[2] It considers the way in which education has served as a channel to build human capacities and capabilities, and to contribute to social and economic development. Thus far, there have been only a handful of scholarly studies of the history of Malayan and Malaysian education.[3] Other writers have analysed particular aspects of the country's education system, from how it has changed to the various levels of education that have developed. This chapter brings together the various sources to trace the spread of education as the means of building the country's human capital from the time of the Pangkor Engagement (1874) to the present. It considers the successes and lessons learned during this process, as well as the challenges still to be overcome.

This chapter has six sections. The first section provides an overview of how a rudimentary and ethnically segregated system of schooling evolved under British colonial rule. This is followed by a review of the sometimes contentious and radical education reforms of the post–World War II transition from late colonialism to independence—the *national awakening* period. This section provides the context for the subsequent analysis of the post-independence era, and helps to bring out key institutional, structural, and policy issues.

Within the framework of six decades of Malaysia's development plans, which articulated the broad policy directions for human capital development, the next section explains how education policy attempted to integrate and unify the country's sharply divided ethnic communities, while accommodating ethnic preferences and differences. It considers how education policy

2 Education encompasses a broad range of ideals and goals of which the development of economic or productive capabilities is just one, albeit important, aspect.

3 The key historical works in this area are Kennedy (1962), Lim (1967), and Awang Had Salleh (1994).

sought to meet the rising expectations of, and resolve tensions among, all communities, especially after the launch of the New Economic Policy (NEP) in 1971. The fourth section describes how Malaysia responded to the growing demand for tertiary education by expanding public sector institutions, and, later, encouraging the private sector to play an increasing role as a provider of higher education.

The penultimate section assesses the outcomes of the various education reforms, measured according to multiple indicators, including education expenditure, literacy rates, educational attainment, and the supply of and demand for human capital. The final section reviews how well the country's education system has performed in meeting the needs of a growing and rapidly diversifying economy, and considers the challenges that it faces in the context of both intense global competition and new sources of growth—an environment markedly different from that encountered by previous generations.

Box 3.1 Human capital theory and its application to Malaysia

Discussions of human capital began to feature prominently in economics in the 1960s, spurred by the studies of Nobel Prize winners Theodore W. Schultz and Gary S. Becker. At a time when direct expenditures on education were counted as *consumption* expenditure, Schultz (1960 and 1961) proposed the notion of education as an *investment* and, therefore, as a form of human capital (since the knowledge and skills obtained from education become part of the person receiving it). Schultz advocated for public policy measures to incentivize investment in human beings based on his findings which showed that additions to human capital better explain the differences in economic growth between countries than the accumulation of land, hours worked, or reproducible capital. Building on Schultz's work, Becker demonstrated the positive effects of on-the-job training and formal education on earnings and productivity, and the private and social gains of secondary- and college-level education (Becker, 1993).

Human capital has since become a central focus of economics and neoclassical growth theories. Mankiw et al. (1992) adapted the Solow–Swan growth model (Box 5.2 in Chapter 5) and concluded that the inclusion of human capital as a factor of the production function accounted for a significant portion of cross-country differences in income per capita. Many econometric studies have sought to quantify the contribution of growth in human capital to economic growth. However, in those studies where the quantity of education is used to measure human capital, the results have varied. Recent studies have turned to using indicators measuring the quality of education, such as the results of international education assessments. These have shown a consistent link between human capital and economic growth, with the quality of education having a greater positive impact on economic growth than its quantity (Hanushek and Woessmann, 2007).

With human capital widely accepted as a significant factor contributing to economic growth and as inextricably linked to education, there are significant policy implications for growth and development. Public investments in human capital through education generally take place over a longer period than investments in physical capital (Langelett, 2002). The free provision of schooling requires public-sector expenditure for a decade or more to complete the investment.

When faced with the choice of extending education beyond the compulsory level, an individual will need to compare the costs and benefits of staying in school. Consider an individual's decision to engage in an additional year of schooling. The main cost would be the loss of earnings during the extra schooling year—the opportunity cost. The return, meanwhile, would be the extra income the individual could expect to receive because of the additional schooling. The rate of return to schooling (Box 3.6) is the additional income expressed as a return on earnings forgone. These returns assume that schooling is free—that there are no direct costs of education.

As the structural adjustment of Malaysia's economy gathered momentum, from agriculture to manufacturing and services, greater emphasis was placed on a more holistic approach to education and on equipping people with the knowledge and skills required for modern-sector employment. The country's first comprehensive human capital study, the National Human Resources Development Plan, was completed in the late 1980s, and led to strengthened labour market mechanisms. The supply of education and training opportunities has continuously expanded, including through the provision of alternative pathways to post-secondary education. Recognizing both the economic and social benefits of increases in human capital, public policy has also been used to influence the cost side of investment in post-secondary education through scholarships and low-interest loans.

Ethnically Segmented Education in Colonial Malaya

Although our starting point is the 1870s, the history of education in the Malay peninsula began even earlier. Elements of an education system were already operating in the Straits Settlements as well as in other parts of the peninsula by this decade, in the form of Christian missionary and Chinese schools.[4] Historical records also point to the presence of a local apprenticeship-based education system in which Malay boys were mentored by their fathers or other experienced village elders in the development of the skills necessary for their agricultural pursuits and other economic activities, as well as in arts and crafts.[5] There were also the *sekolah pondok* and *kampung madrasah* religious

4 There were also early but unsuccessful attempts to open Tamil schools in the Straits Settlements. These were only revived in the 1870s, and then extended to Perak and Negeri Sembilan in 1900 (Andaya and Andaya, 2017).

5 Memorandum of the Sultan Idris Training College and Malay Vernacular Education (Archive document CO 273/576/16, 1931).

schools, particularly prevalent in the northern and east coast states close to the border with Siam, where mainly Malay boys from around the age of nine learned about Islam through a process of rote learning of Arabic characters and reading the Koran.[6]

The prevailing economic philosophy in pre-independence Malaya was that of laissez-faire (Chapter 5). The primary interest of the colonial power was to facilitate the extraction of natural resources from Malayan soil in an environment of relative peace and security. The provision of education was thus viewed more as a marginal social service than as an investment in the future of the people (Rudner, 1977; Hirschman, 1979).

Instead of developing according to a planned education policy designed to create a unified and common cultural identity, the evolution of Malaya's education system followed a pattern of cultural pluralism (Sultan Nazrin Shah, 2017). Under the colonial laissez-faire approach, the education system of each community was left to grow separately, at its own pace, in its own direction, and under its own management. Some commentators view this process as a deliberate feature of the 'divide and rule' policy employed by the British, subtly keeping the different ethnic groups apart in order to help minimize any potential combined resistance to colonial rule. Some have argued further that the lack of educational provision reflected the British concern that an overeducated population could be detrimental to their political interests, based on experiences in the Indian subcontinent (Rosnani Hashim, 1994).

Opportunities for schooling and employment were not provided equally to the distinct and highly segmented groups in Malayan society. The Chinese were left largely to fend for themselves in this as in all spheres of their lives (Lim, 1967). From the perspective of the British colonial administration, there were limited benefits to be gained from investing in the education of a transitory migrant population, the members of which were expected to return to their countries of origin; this was another self-interested motivation behind the philosophy of 'benign neglect'.

As described in Chapter 1, the geographical entities of the Malay peninsula were administered separately until after the end of World War II. The education systems of each evolved at different paces according to the speed at which these entities developed. Schools in the more economically developed Straits Settlements, the Federated Malay States, and Johor progressed much faster and further than those in the other Unfederated Malay States, due to differences in government expenditure which, in turn, reflected vast disparities in state revenues.

6 Hinduism, Buddhism, Islam, and Christianity, through their well-funded trading, migrant, and missionary networks, have all played a role historically in the spread and content of religiously infused education and schooling throughout the Malay archipelago and beyond (Harper, 2017).

Five distinct school types emerged that represented the cultures and languages of the dominant communities in the peninsula: Malay, Chinese, and Indian vernacular schools, English-medium schools, and Islamic schools.[7] This set-up formed the institutional framework of primary education that would continue, in its essential features, up to the present.

Malay Vernacular Schools

Malay schools, initially mainly for boys from around the age of seven, were a creation of the British and were built, financed, and managed by the colonial government. As described by George Maxwell, Chief Secretary of the Federated Malay States from 1921 to 1926, 'Malay vernacular schools were started by the government (never by the missionaries), they were the "Cinderellas" of the family. The buildings were incomparably inferior, the teachers were untrained and badly paid, and the highest school standard went little beyond the rudiments of teaching, writing and arithmetic' (CO 273/574/8, 1931, p. 6). Maxwell believed that it was important to recognize the cultural value of Malay vernacular education even though an education in English was the route to more highly paid employment. Malay was also the lingua franca throughout the peninsula and in the state councils and government departments (Swettenham, 1906).[8]

Malay schools, under the Director of Education, were located in rural villages as part of the government's paternalistic policy of not disturbing rural Malay society and culture (Hirschman, 1979). They served to reinforce traditional structures and the colonial-imposed occupational division of labour. They were the training ground for small-scale farmers and agriculturalists who would remain attached to their land, loyal to their ruler, and unwavering in their religious belief. Each state and settlement progressively acquired its own inspector of schools who had oversight of these Malay vernacular institutions.

The schools taught basic literacy and numeracy, the Koran, and some Malay literature. The curriculum had an agricultural bias consistent with the economic activities of the Malays.[9] After four to five years of this primary education, the most able students could apply to enter any government English-

7 In 1927, there were 1,241 schools registered in the Federated Malay States of which 479 were Malay vernacular, 340 Tamil vernacular, 353 Chinese vernacular, and just 63 English-medium schools, along with a few others (CO 717/61/6, 1928). By 1935, there were 1,474 schools of which 547 were Malay vernacular, 401 Tamil vernacular, 394 Chinese vernacular, and 128 English-medium schools (CO 717/119/1, 1936–1938).

8 From the late 19th century onwards, many government offices, as well as the courts and police stations, gradually employed Chinese and Tamil writers and interpreters (Swettenham, 1906).

9 In 1925, there were also some 200 Malay vernacular girls' schools, focused initially on the Malay crafts of embroidery, basketry, and weaving. Due to the lack of female teachers, reading, writing, and arithmetic were taught by part-time untrained male teachers.

medium school for which they were exempt from fees, with scholarships available for up to seven years.[10] This provided them with an opportunity for modern-sector employment and upward mobility. Although rural Malay families were initially reluctant to send their daughters to Malay vernacular schools, these schools gradually gained acceptance once their value in terms of opening up opportunities was recognized, and there were enough teachers willing to go out to the villages.[11]

The number of Malay schools in the Federated Malay States increased from 130 at the end of the 19th century to 400 in 1920, with another 357 in the Unfederated Malay States by this year, together catering to 46,000 students in total between the ages of five and 15 (Mehmet, 2011). Compared with the English-medium schools, the teachers, most of whom were pupil-teachers (the most able students served as teachers), were inadequately trained and paid. As Maxwell noted, 'every Malay school child must feel ashamed of his school, as he passes the English School', a feeling he attributed to the fact that every English school had a European master, while every Malay school did not (CO 273/574/8, 1931, p. 10). The low policy priority of Malay education meant that insufficient resources were allocated for the establishment of training institutes for Malay teachers.

The rudimentary nature of Malay vernacular education reflected, above all, the British policy of 'minimum interference' as articulated by Swettenham, and was intended to maintain the existing highly stratified social order. It ensured that the overwhelming majority of Malays remained as subsistence farmers, lacking the skills to participate in the emerging modern economy. Providing a more comprehensive education, especially in English, was thought to be dangerous, in part because it was believed that it could lead to political activism (Stevenson, 1975).

Chinese Vernacular Schools

From as early as the end of the 18th century, and beginning in the Straits Settlements, the Chinese community began to build a peninsula-wide network of urban and rural primary schools (Tan, L.E., 2000). A few of these Chinese

10 Due to the growing employment opportunities in the towns resulting from the expansion of colonial government administration and commerce, many Malay boys left school to become clerks before completing the full seven years of English secondary schooling.

11 The first college for Malay teachers was opened in Singapore in 1878. In 1901 a new training college for Malay vernacular teachers was opened in Melaka, followed in 1913 by another in Matang, Perak. These colleges provided two-year training courses. In 1922, the elite residential Sultan Idris Training College was opened in Tanjong Malim, Perak, offering a three-year training course for students intending to become Malay vernacular schoolteachers. The medium of instruction was Malay and most of the annual intake of some 130 students came from the Straits Settlements and the Federated Malay States (CO 273/576/16, 1931).

schools also taught secondary-level classes, which for most of the colonial era were accessible and affordable only to a small minority. The growth of Chinese schools was particularly marked in the 1920s and 1930s, mainly because of the increasing number of Chinese children being born in Malaya, as the community's sex ratio was becoming more balanced (Chapter 2). The Chinese were quick to perceive that the education of their children was a route to upward social mobility and higher-paying employment.

Chinese vernacular schools were of two types: Confucian schools, which were established earlier and were run as private institutions; and public schools, which came into existence just before the 1911 revolution in China and became the dominant type (CO 717/60/15, 1928). These schools were financed, managed, and operated by the Chinese community, and had little connection to the colonial administration. Chinese public schools were maintained through voluntary subscriptions from the Chinese community, including substantial donations from affluent traders, as well as through the payment of fees, which were lower than those for English-medium schools.[12] They were run on a non-profit basis and faced financial difficulties during economic downturns.

The schools were China-centric, using Mandarin as their medium of instruction (although other Chinese dialects had also been used in the 19th century), and their teachers and teaching resources came from China. As China considered all overseas Chinese schools to be part of its education system, they were susceptible to its political thought and prevailing policies (Andaya and Andaya, 2017).[13] The Chinese schools were thus highly nationalistic and guarded their independence jealously. Until the early 1930s, only a small number accepted government assistance, and the government had little control over them (CO 273/579/1, 1932). However, in 1935, with growing concerns about the spread of communist political ideology by the mainland's Chinese Communist Party and an increasing recognition that many Chinese would probably settle permanently in Malaya, the colonial government authorized the Education Department to introduce sizeable subsidies for Chinese schools and to initiate a teacher-training programme.

---

12 The extent of the network of Chinese schools can be gleaned from the fact that in the Straits Settlements in 1929 there were 332 Chinese schools with some 24,000 pupils compared with 213 Malay schools with 20,000 pupils (CO 273/574/8, 1931). There was also a similar number of children attending English schools. An increasing recognition of the importance of schooling, coupled with the growing school-age population in all communities, meant that the number of all vernacular schools grew rapidly until the Japanese occupation.

13 This close affinity with China spilled over into Chinese riots and other acts of civil unrest in the peninsula, such as periodic anti-Japanese riots and boycotts of the unloading of Japanese goods, for instance during the 1931 invasion of Manchuria.

Indian Vernacular Schools

The education of the children of Indian rubber plantation workers began in the early 20th century and gradually spread to many estates.[14] The Labour Code of 1923 provided for a school to be established on every estate with ten or more children of school age, after which the number of estates on which schools were maintained increased rapidly, rising from 227 in 1923 to 303 in 1924 (Federated Malay States, 1925).

Some estate owners at first tried hard to make these schools ineffective, apparently due to the cost, and despite the availability of government grants (Sandhu, 1969). Others, however, maintained efficient schools, with the managers taking a genuine interest in the pupils and their progress. Until World War II, these schools—usually just simple sheds—did not have qualified teachers and the teaching was carried out by estate clerks or the estate labour manager (*kangani*). Only in 1937 was a Tamil-speaking official inspector of schools appointed and a programme for training Tamil teachers initiated (Andaya and Andaya, 2017). Teaching materials were imported from India and the teaching was focused on India.

Attendance was not mandatory and the schools were often badly managed by committees overseen by estate managers. The medium of instruction was usually Tamil or else one of the other Indian languages, such as Telugu or Malayalam, which were of little value for prospective employment in either the government or the commercial sector. This ensured that the children of rubber estate workers remained on the estates, providing plantation companies with the unlimited supply of low-cost labour that they needed. The estates had no secondary schools. For more than 70 per cent of Indian children, estate-based education was the only form of education available (Tan, 2001). Of those Indian children who lived in more urban areas and were of higher economic status, many attended English schools, which were managed by religious organizations, by trustees, or by the government.

English-medium Schools

English education in the Malay states grew out of the efforts of Christian missionary groups. These groups began establishing mission schools in the Straits Settlements in the early 19th century, just as they were doing throughout the British Empire. The Penang Free School, established in 1816, was the first English-medium school in the Malay peninsula and was open to

---

14 From around 1912, the annual supplement to the Federated Malay States' Report on the Work of the Labour Department provided statistics on the number of Tamil schools, the average enrolment, and how they were funded (Federated Malay States, 1913).

children of all communities and all religions.[15] The colonial government later supported these endeavours, providing resources and facilities to expand the number of English-medium schools, which were located predominantly in the towns of the west coast states.

These schools were of a much higher standard than the vernacular schools and were attended from the age of six onwards by a select group of boys and girls of all nationalities, not only Europeans and Eurasians.[16] In 1937, government expenditure on English education accounted for 71 per cent of the total expenditure on education in the Straits Settlements, and 48 per cent of the total in the Federated Malay States, amounts that were in both cases disproportionate compared with the number of pupils (Lim, 1967).[17] This had been the pattern of education spending during most of the pre–World War II years, and only started to change towards the end of the 1930s when the government began providing grants to Chinese schools.

As noted above, the disproportionately high expenditure on English schools, and to a far lesser extent on Malay schools, compared with the schools of the other communities reflected in part the view that the Chinese and Indians were only transient residents of Malaya who would in time return home to China or India (Chapter 2).[18] The government did, however, provide some limited funding for Tamil schools. Support for English-medium schools, which were located in urban centres and offered the possibility of secondary education, was seen as most important, as these schools were intended to produce clerical staff and junior administrators to support the colonial administration. Tuition fees were charged by these schools, however, which served as an insurmountable barrier to entry for children from poorer families.

Unlike the vernacular education streams, English-medium schools taught music, art, and drama as part of the curriculum. Education in English through to secondary level provided students with a route to further education, available in Singapore at Raffles College for the sciences and humanities, and at the King Edward VII College of Medicine, as well as at British and foreign

---

15 In 1818, the evangelical Anglo-Chinese College was founded in Melaka, and in 1823 the Singapore Institution Free School (later renamed Raffles Institution after its founder Stamford Raffles) was set up.

16 About half of the students at English-medium government schools were Chinese, while roughly 30 per cent were Indians and some 15 per cent were Malay. Most of the Malay students had spent at least four years at a Malay vernacular school and gained exemption from school fees. They joined the English-medium schools at around age 11 and were put through two years of intensive training in oral and written English.

17 In 1937, 41.5 per cent of the Federated Malay States' education expenditure went to Malay schools, with 4.2 per cent going to Tamil schools, and 6 per cent to Chinese schools (Lim, 1967).

18 Among the better-known schools that received some government funding were the Anglo-Chinese School in Penang (established in 1891), the Methodist Boys School in Kuala Lumpur (1897), the Convent School in Kuala Lumpur (1899), and the St. John's Institution in Kuala Lumpur (1904). The Malacca High School was established in 1878 from what used to be the Malacca Free School. The Victoria Institution was founded in 1894 from a fund created to celebrate Queen Victoria's Jubilee (Kennedy, 1962, p. 263).

universities. An alternative path was to obtain technical and trade skills.[19] An English-medium education was a passport to a better-paying job and was the only avenue for social mobility (Hirschman, 1979). It also helped to bridge the cultural gaps among the elites of each of the different communities.

The British approach to education thus generated a segmented system of four dominant school types, with each inculcating its own values and imbuing its students with a distinct sense of identity and direction.[20] By 1938, there were 788 Malay schools, 654 Chinese schools, 607 Tamil schools, and 221 English-medium schools (Ong et al., 2014). Although fewer in number, the students graduating from the English-medium schools had markedly better job opportunities, as English was the language of the colonial government and of international commerce.

Islamic Schools

Before independence, as well as attending vernacular and secular English-medium schools, Malays and other members of the Islamic faith could also access a religious education through traditional *pondok* and *madrasah* schools.

Pondok schools were most prominent in the east coast states of Kelantan and Terengganu, as well as in Kedah, having been introduced from Pattani in Siam in the early 19th century. These schools were often residential institutions where boys went to study the Koran. The schools aimed to provide a deeper spiritual understanding of Islamic teaching and practice, with lessons conducted by village *ulama* (persons learned in religion). The scope of subjects taught varied from one school to another and evolved over time. The most able students were prepared for jobs in Islamic courts, religious schools, and mosques. *Pondok* schools were later opened in other states in the peninsula by *pondok* graduates from Kelantan and Terengganu (Stevenson, 1975; Mohd Zahirwan Halim Zainal Abidin et al., 2017). Some *pondok* schools converted to the *madrasah* system of education (Abdul Halim Tamuri and Che Pee Saad, 2008.)

Madrasahs, which often admitted girls as well as boys, were more Arabic in orientation than *pondok* schools, especially as they initially taught using translated Arabic texts. *Madrasah* schools spread in the early 20th century and provided a somewhat broader education that was more attuned to the

19 Before World War II, there were four trade schools in British Malaya: one each in Kuala Lumpur and in Ipoh, training youths to become general fitters and motor mechanics; and one each in Bagan Serai and Rembau, offering training in carpentry (CO 717/101/1, 1933).

20 In 1926, the distinguished educationalist O. T. Dussek remarked of the education system: 'No thought appears to have been given either to the needs of the country or the state of intellectual development, or to the social culture attained by the inhabitants' (CO 717/53/14, 1926, p. 1).

emerging capitalist economy. Beyond the standard core curricula, some secular subjects, such as mathematics, were included. *Madrasahs* provided students with certificates upon graduation, which were recognized by some Middle Eastern universities, and gave them wider employment options (Muhamad Ali, 2016).

North Borneo and Sarawak

In the first half of the 20th century, North Borneo and Sarawak were administered separately from the peninsula's Malay states, and their education systems developed more slowly. Education in these sparsely populated, vast, and ethnically diverse states was provided mainly by Christian missionaries, Chinese communities, Malay-Muslim religious authorities, and the government. The missionary English-medium schools and the Chinese schools typically charged fees.

In Sarawak, education had always been a low priority for the Brooke administration, which was in favour of preserving the customs and traditions of each community (Ooi, 1990). Malay schools were gradually established in the towns, with the primary aim of providing a pool of Malay workers for government administration. The first government-funded Malay school was opened in 1883 by Charles Brooke. This was followed by the Government Lay School in 1903, which aimed to educate each major ethnic group (excluding the non-Malay indigenous communities) in its own mother tongue. In 1919, all lay schools were converted to Malay schools, with admission being restricted to male Muslims. In 1930, the first government Malay girls' school was established. Before the establishment of Malay vernacular schools, religious education was conducted in mosques, *suraus*, or the homes of religious teachers.

Nevertheless, mission schools and Chinese schools remained the largest education providers in Sarawak throughout the Brooke era. Education for the non-Malay indigenous communities was left to the missionaries, and mission schools received a relatively high proportion of the total grants-in-aid from the government. In the first quarter of the 20th century, despite financial difficulties, Chinese schools grew rapidly. In 1939, a combined total of 219 mission and Chinese schools, some of which provided secondary education, made up 85 per cent of the schools in Sarawak, while government schools, which provided only primary education, accounted for the remaining 15 per cent (Ong et al., 2014).

Education was also neglected in North Borneo. In 1938, only 2 per cent of total government expenditure in the state was spent on education, most of which went towards supporting Malay vernacular primary schools. About 24 per cent was directed in the form of grants-in-aid to mission schools, which had the largest enrolment of students, particularly from among the non-Chinese community (Kahin, 1947). Secondary education was provided only by a few Chinese schools and one or two mission schools.

After the end of the Japanese occupation, there was increasing demand for education in both states. In Sarawak, mission schools and Chinese schools continued to be at the forefront of primary and secondary education, as the British administration could not cope with the demand. The Malay communities began to establish their own *sekolah rakyat* or 'people's schools', and between 1947 and 1954 the number of such schools rose from eight to 54 (Ong et al., 2014). By 1947, the colonial government had also built around 17 schools for the indigenous communities. In 1948, the first local authority school was set up in Kuching, and in 1957, the first government secondary school was established in Miri. In the post-war years, similar developments in the provision of schooling were also seen in North Borneo.

Nonetheless, decades of ethnic segregation in Sabah and Sarawak's education system had created vast disparities in education levels among the different ethnic groups and between urban and rural areas. In 1960, the overwhelming majority of the populations of both states remained illiterate: just 26 per cent of Sabah's population and 27 per cent of Sarawak's aged ten and over were literate. After the formation of the Federation of Malaysia in 1963, education in the two states became the responsibility of the federal government, although they retained their own education policies and administration.

Higher Education in Colonial Malaya

In the first half of the 20th century, there were no secondary Malay schools. Although the elite Malay-medium Sultan Idris Training College[21] provided some vocational secondary education for male students, its main function was to train teachers for Malay schools throughout the Federated Malay States and the Straits Settlements. It also served as the centre for Malay literary translation activities. For cultural reasons, until the 1930s there was no similar establishment for training Malay female schoolteachers, and no attempt was made to set up government-funded training colleges for Chinese and Tamil vernacular schoolteachers.

The founding of the Malay College in Kuala Kangsar in January 1905 was an important milestone in Malaya's human capital development. Administered along the lines of an English public school, the college offered high-quality secondary-level education. Its primary objective was to produce a pool of administrative talent drawn from sons of the Malay aristocracy and elite, who

21 The college was founded in 1922, and located in Tanjong Malim, Perak.

would support the senior echelons of the expanding Malayan Civil Service and share in its colonial culture and values.[22] This promoted the separate development of the children of the Malay aristocracy, although the college did later begin to enrol talented Malay students from a broader spectrum of families and from outside the Malay elite.

English was the exclusive medium of instruction at the college, which was referred to as the 'Eton of Malaya, the products of which could play cricket and quote Shakespeare in Oxford accents' (Barber, 2008). At first, its graduates all went on to join the ranks of the Malayan Administrative Service when this was established in 1910. This practice continued until 1921, after which admission to the service was extended to other schools (Tilman, 1968). Much later, the college expanded its vocational offerings so as to prepare students for the professions as well as for senior government administrative posts.

The new post-war outlook in the era of decolonization, with the more enlightened perspective of the British government towards rising local aspirations in its colonies, was finally enough to overcome the pre-war colonial diffidence about establishing a university in Malaya. The University of Malaya was formed in 1948 through the consolidation of Singapore's Raffles College and the King Edward VII College of Medicine, the only two colleges of higher education in the peninsula before the war (Koay, 2018). The establishment of Malaya's first university, based on a recommendation of the 1948 Carr-Saunders Commission Report, was aimed at uniting the elites of the different communities of the peninsula and enhancing the national image (Carr-Saunders, 1948).[23] Located in Singapore, the university met the needs of English-educated students from both the Federation of Malaya and Singapore itself.[24] In 1959, after Singapore had gained full internal self-governance, two University of Malaya divisions were created, one in Singapore and the other in Kuala Lumpur. In January 1962, they both became completely autonomous as the University of Singapore and the University of Malaya. Graduates of Chinese-language secondary schools could attend Nanyang University, set up in Singapore in 1956 on the eve of Malaya's independence through private voluntary funding from the Chinese community (Tan, L.E., 2000).

22 While recruitment to the higher administrative grades of the Malayan Civil Service was exclusively from the Malay elite, appointments to the clerical, technical, and professional grades, which also had specific educational criteria as part of the selection process, were primarily of non-Malays (Silcock and Fisk, 1963).

23 The Carr-Saunders Commission Report was prepared in 1947 at a time of high tension resulting from the imposition of the Malayan Union. In a follow-up mission in 1949, as the university was taking shape, and with 62 per cent of its 650 students coming from the Federation of Malaya, Carr-Saunders noted the urgency of adhering to the Commission's earlier recommendation of relocating the institution to the north-west of Johor Bahru. This proposal was abandoned in 1954, however, due to financial considerations as noted in the Report of the Joint Committee on the Future of University of Malaya (Singapore, 1954).

24 By 1948, the Straits Settlements had been dissolved, and Singapore was not part of the 11 states that formed the Federation of Malaya. Universities were viewed as important for 'imbuing elites of emerging nations with a "British view of the world," and to prepare them for postcolonial membership of the Commonwealth' (cited in Koay, 2017, p. 41).

Modernization of Education Policy

Education Policy After the Japanese Occupation

The Japanese occupation was a bleak yet significant period for education in the peninsula. The development of the education system that was being implemented in the pre-war period was interrupted. All schools were closed and institutions of higher education ceased to function. There was subsequently a revival of Malay vernacular education during the occupation, although this was modified to include the Japanese language as a compulsory subject. Schools were also used for propaganda.[25] Most Chinese schools remained closed. In order to train teachers in Japanese, a small Japanese-language institute was established in Johor Bahru. Another, the Institute for the Development of Malaya, was set up in Melaka and ran six-month courses on Japanese language, culture, and army training. A small number of young men who were selected to become teachers were also sent to Hiroshima to learn Japanese.

After the occupation ended, and driven by the more enlightened perspective of the newly elected Labour government in the UK, the colonial government took a keen interest in reviewing and reconstructing the education system. The Malayan Agreement of 1948 (Chapter 1) explicitly called for education and training of the Malay residents 'so as to fit them to take a full share in the economic progress, social welfare and government of the state and of the federation' (CO 537/2143, 1947, p. 333).

In an important and comprehensive memorandum on the post-war direction of education policy for the Malayan Union and Singapore, the then Director of Education, Harold Cheeseman, identified many constraints in the existing system (CO 273/676/6, 1946). These included the lack of a unified policy for Malaya as a whole up to college or university standard, with associated administrative weaknesses;[26] the absence of local committees' interest in, or control of, the English and vernacular schools maintained by the government; a lack of liaison between, or pooling of experience among, the three vernacular branches and the English-medium schools, which all formed separate units; an 'alien' outlook, or lack of Malayan outlook, especially among teachers in Chinese and Indian schools, most of whom came from China and India; insufficient funding for Chinese and even more so for Indian schools;

25 Education in Sarawak suffered a similar fate during this period. Malay and Chinese vernacular schools were initially closed, but a few were reopened and had to teach the Japanese language and disseminate propaganda.

26 Cheeseman also argued that if one accepts the principle that it is the duty of the state to provide some education for all of its children irrespective of race or mother tongue, then the argument that a particular state needs a different policy because of its large Malay population is untenable (CO 273/676/6, 1946).

a neglect of the vernaculars in English schools, so that some Chinese and Indian pupils—who, unlike most Malays, came to these schools directly—left school unable to read and write in their own languages; and the neglect of science and technical subjects in the curriculum.

Cheeseman suggested that a reconstructed Malayan education system should gradually include: a compulsory and free period of six years of primary education for every child aged six to 11, irrespective of ethnicity, in schools in one of the four main languages under the direction of the government following an approved syllabus, and staffed by teachers with prescribed qualifications; the teaching of English in every school; the establishment of English and Malay secondary schools; and the introduction of vocational education, based on the 1938 Report on Vocational Education. Cheeseman's report emphasized that teachers in all four types of school should be born and educated in Malaya. Post-primary education would remain neither compulsory nor free. The Cheeseman Plan called for a more coordinated, higher-quality, and uniform vernacular school system, and for the establishment of an education system that would serve the needs of Malaya by 'creating citizens with Malayan interests, a Malayan background and a Malayan outlook' (CO 273/676/6, 1946, p. 20).

The plan was not implemented, however, mainly due to issues of timing. The Education Department was stretched by the reconstruction of damaged schools, while the attention of most British administrators and Malayans was focused on the political crisis brought about by the imposition of the Malayan Union in 1946 (Awang Had Salleh, 1994).

Although the plan did not come to fruition, it was an attempt to launch a process of review and reform of the existing fragmented education system, which could not contribute to the development of a national outlook among students from the different ethnic groups or to a sense of common identity. The plan marked a turning point, as it was the first time that the serious weaknesses of the pre-war education system were officially recognized, and the need to introduce some element of commonality into the system was acknowledged. This was especially warranted given the formation of the Federation of Malaya in 1948.

By the end of the decade, despite limited financial and human resources, and the high level of expenditure on security necessitated by the Emergency, progress had been made in the rehabilitation and repair of schools, and efforts to provide free primary schooling for all children were making headway. In August 1949, the number of children at school in Malaya was 576,000 compared with just 263,000 in 1941 (CO 825/90, 1950).

Education Policy towards *Merdeka*

During the decade-long phase of decolonization from 1948 to *Merdeka* in 1957, a series of reviews of the Malayan education system was conducted with the aim of developing a comprehensive plan that would lead to a unified national education system. The colonial administration began to put greater emphasis on multiethnic schools as a means of encouraging national social integration, and on the promotion of English as a common language. These policies were sensitive and potentially threatening to all the communities, but particularly to the Chinese, who saw them as imperialistic and against their legitimate rights (Tan, L.E., 2000). The issues surrounding education reform were highly charged, especially in the turbulent and tense post–World War II environment, and during the mid 1950s they became a central focus of the discussions of the Alliance, the emerging coalition of political parties that represented the political interests of the three main ethnic communities in Malaya.

The first of the reviews, the Holgate Report of 1949, proposed that English be used as a medium of instruction in all schools in order to unify the people through a common language, but this was rejected by the Federal Legislative Council. The Barnes Report of 1950 then recommended the use of both Malay and English as media of instruction at the primary level, with Chinese and Tamil taught only as subjects. It also called for an end to separate vernacular schools. At the secondary level, English would be the only medium of instruction. These recommendations were not well received by the Chinese community, however, which wanted to maintain its cultural and linguistic heritage and identity, in part by continuing its vernacular schools.

In the same year, the Fenn-Wu Report argued in favour of the various communities being allowed to maintain their own schools with their own languages and cultures, and suggested that the status of Chinese vernacular schools should remain unchanged. The report also proposed that Malay and English should be taught as subjects in these schools, which would be integrated into the national education system.

The Education Ordinance of 1952 followed the recommendations of the Barnes Report, and failed to take into account the concerns of the Chinese and Indian communities that their languages would no longer be the media of instruction in their schools. Attempts to achieve any consensus among the communities over a framework for a national education system aimed at promoting national integration thus faced great difficulties, with the issues of language and curriculum proving the most emotive. These sensitive and divisive issues meant that reform efforts were continually challenged by Chinese educationists, Malay nationalists, or both. Education became highly politicized, with consequences for its quality.

By contrast, in multiethnic Singapore, despite its Chinese majority population, the government decided to make English the common language in all schools soon after independence. It was recognized that English was the language of international commerce and also, increasingly, the lingua franca of intellectual inquiry, research, and knowledge. The adoption of the English language has helped to integrate Singapore's citizens of various ethnic backgrounds and to link the country closely with the international trading system. The local languages of all the main communities were also made available within the schooling system. This decision to make English the common language in schools was 'not up for debate' (Mukherjee and Wong, 2011, p. 134).

Coming in the wake of the 1955 Federation of Malaya general election, which was won convincingly by the Alliance, the Razak Report of 1956 supported making Malay the national language. It recommended that English and Malay should both be compulsory at primary level, but that Malay should be the main medium of instruction. All schools, irrespective of language medium, should adopt a common curriculum. If 15 or more parents requested instruction in Chinese or Tamil at a primary school, then these should also be made available and funded by the government. The Malay-medium schools were to be called national schools, while schools where English, Mandarin, or Tamil was the medium of instruction were to be termed national-type schools.

The Razak Report proposed that there should be just one type of national secondary school with a centralized examination system conducted in Malay, the country's official language. Chinese secondary schools using Mandarin as the medium of instruction could continue to operate, but only if they conformed with the centralized final examination system and fulfilled the requirement to teach Malay and English as compulsory subjects.

Post-independence Education Policy Reforms

Although the Razak Report recommended that Malay should become the national language and the primary medium of instruction in schools, the use of other languages was preserved, and the important role of English for employment and higher education was recognized. The Federal Legislative Council accepted the report's recommendations, which became the main elements of the 1957 Education Ordinance, despite fears among non-Malays over the diminution of Mandarin and Tamil at secondary level. The issue of the language used for examinations in secondary schools remained particularly controversial among the Chinese.

Established after the 1959 general election, the Rahman Talib Committee maintained the role of Malay as the national language, extended the school-leaving age from 12 to 15,[27] and recommended the creation of two types of secondary school: national schools with Malay as the medium of instruction and national-type English-medium schools. Both types would have a common curriculum and examination system, and would receive public funding. Schools that did not comply with these recommendations would not receive state funds and would become private independent schools outside the national system.[28] Other recommendations included the expansion of vocational education for students who did not gain entry to the secondary academic stream, to enable them to follow courses such as carpentry, agriculture, and domestic science.

The Razak and Rahman Talib recommendations became the foundation of the 1961 Education Act, which formed the basis of all subsequent education policy and programme development up to 1995, when new legislation was enacted. With the adoption of these recommendations, the status of Malay as the primary medium of instruction in schools became entrenched, notwithstanding the use of other languages in national-type schools.

Rudner (1977) argues that, despite these reforms to secondary education, the approach adopted did not depart from the academically oriented, grammar-school-style education system inherited from the British. In his view, the obsession with this tradition circumscribed the development of post-primary institutions, and restricted the ability of schools to meet the needs of a modern economy. It also explains why, in line with colonial practice, an arbitrary pass rate of 30 per cent was set between primary and secondary education, and a vocational extension programme (subordinate to the academic stream) was created to absorb the less academically inclined.

The continued implementation of this grammar-school approach led to a labour-market mismatch by the early 1960s, with increasing demand for middle- and upper-level professional and technical human resources set against a large pool of semi-educated and unemployed school leavers. This challenge was highlighted in the First Malaysia Plan (MP1), 1966–1970 (Table 3.1), which noted that, despite the expanded higher-secondary school enrolment and output, the acute shortage of high-skilled human resources had become a major constraint for development in the peninsula. Skill shortages were also observed in Sabah and Sarawak.

MP1 recognized that effective training of professional and upper-level individuals had a longer gestation period and required more systematic

27 This aimed to provide a minimum of nine years of education for every child.

28 Despite reservations, 54 out of the 70 Chinese secondary schools adopted the official policy, with only 16 becoming self-funding independent secondary schools.

planning. In the Plan, the role of education was reoriented to incorporate a focus on meeting the needs of the economy (EPU, 1966).[29] To address the strong and growing demand for secondary-education-level skills in Sabah and Sarawak, it provided for an expansion of secondary school places in both states, where at the time only around 20 per cent of children of secondary school age were in school.

Further education reforms were introduced as a result in 1965 and subsequently, which removed the bar between primary and lower-secondary schooling, and introduced a three-year lower-secondary education that combined academic, technical, and craft subjects. Upper-secondary education was still selective, but was expanded to include technical and vocational streams, as well as arts and science. A similar form of streaming was introduced at the sixth form (pre-university) level. These changes were incorporated to help align the education system more effectively with the country's human resource requirements (Rudner, 1977).

Despite the presence of the vocational technical stream, the overwhelming majority of secondary school students (98 per cent) continued to enrol in the academic stream. After changes to the curriculum in 1987, the proportion entering the vocational stream did increase sharply, but from a small base (Tzannatos and Johnes, 1997). Up to the present, most students have continued to follow an academic path, even as the economy has undergone a major structural transformation from dependence on agriculture towards a broader industrial base, and despite the government's concomitant recognition of the critical role of technical and vocational education and training (TVET) in meeting the demands of industry and contributing to economic growth.

The introduction of the NEP in 1971 following the ethnic clashes in the aftermath of the May 1969 elections was a watershed, both in Malaysia's economic development and in its education policy. The NEP increased the use of affirmative action, for instance, by introducing education quotas to lift the economic and social development of Malay and other indigenous communities (*Bumiputera*). This approach was grounded in the view held by some Malays that their limited opportunities under colonial rule had been largely the product of the inequities of the British education system (Ismail Mohd Salleh and Meyanathan, 1993).

All English-medium schools were gradually converted to Malay-medium instruction by 1976, and by 1982 all former English-medium secondary schools in Peninsular Malaysia had been converted to national schools (Solomon, 1988).[30] Chinese and Indian primary schools were allowed to

29 The role of education in promoting national integration was also still enshrined in MP1.

30 One impact of this policy change was to reduce the numbers enrolled in English primary schools and to increase enrolment in Chinese primary schools.

continue as vernacular schools, but they had to follow a common curriculum, with public secondary schooling in Malay only. In 1977, the Education Act was extended to Sarawak, and the transition to Malay instruction throughout the entire school system was completed in both Sabah and Sarawak by 1985 (Dumanig et al., 2012).

Planning and Human Capital Development

Against the backdrop of a young population and a rapidly increasing number of school-age children, increased access to primary and secondary education, especially in rural areas, became a national development priority immediately after the adoption of the First Five-Year Plan of the Federation of Malaya in 1956. Education policy, at first based on the recommendations of the Razak Report, was a central focus of Malaysia's development planning and the sector has continued to receive a fairly high share of the budget.[31] The five-year plans have served as vehicles for articulating education policies from MP1 to the current MP11 (Table 3.1).

Table 3.1 **Malaysia's education policy objectives have evolved over the last half century**

Plan period	Policy objectives
First Malaysia Plan (MP1), 1966–1970	▪ Promote national unity; ▪ Meet expanding needs for places for primary and secondary education; ▪ Meet needs for specialized training in agriculture, commerce, and industry; ▪ Extend basic education to include three years of secondary education; ▪ Establish upper-secondary vocational schools.
Second Malaysia Plan (MP2), 1971–1975	▪ Consolidate the education system to promote national integration and unity; ▪ Introduce *Bahasa Malaysia* as the main medium of instruction in Peninsular Malaysia's schools; ▪ Provide nine (instead of six) years of compulsory education for every child; ▪ Improve content and teaching methods to enhance quality of education; ▪ Ensure greater access to educational opportunities for rural children and the poor, and set up rural residential schools (ten pilot schools); ▪ Gear education and training programmes to meeting manpower needs; ▪ Improve quality of education towards modern science and technology.

31 It has been said that one of the wisest decisions of Tunku Abdul Rahman, Malaysia's first prime minister, was 'to build schools instead of barracks and train teachers instead of soldiers. Malaysia's subsequent remarkable economic transformation owes much to that earlier prescient move' (Mohammad Bakri Musa, 2003, p. 30).

Plan period	Policy objectives
Third Malaysia Plan (MP3), 1976–1980	▪ Maintain education as a major vehicle for national integration and unity; ▪ Meet national manpower needs, especially in science and technology; ▪ Continue with *Bahasa Malaysia* as the main medium of instruction in primary schools and in secondary schools by 1980, and use English as a second language; ▪ Reduce the gap in educational opportunities between rural and urban children.
Fourth Malaysia Plan (MP4), 1981–1985	▪ Meet the country's manpower requirements; ▪ Achieve the NEP objectives; ▪ Nurture national unity through education; ▪ Fully adopt *Bahasa Malaysia* as the medium of instruction at secondary level by 1982 in the peninsula and Sabah, and by 1990 in Sarawak, and adopt it at tertiary level with English remaining the second language.
Fifth Malaysia Plan (MP5), 1986–1990	▪ Continue emphasis on education for national integration and unity; ▪ Meet manpower requirements; ▪ Introduce a new curriculum to produce balanced individuals with moral values, knowledge, and strong skills.
Sixth Malaysia Plan (MP6), 1991–1995	▪ Ensure access and better quality of education for all; ▪ Increase the role of the education system to mould better Malaysians and equip them with knowledge and skills necessary to achieve Vision 2020.
Seventh Malaysia Plan (MP7), 1996–2000	▪ Increase capacity, especially of science and technology and of professional manpower; ▪ Strengthen research and development (R&D) capabilities within higher learning institutions, including collaboration with local and foreign institutions; ▪ Encourage private sector participation in education; ▪ Strengthen use of *Bahasa Malaysia* as a medium of instruction, while improving competency in English.
Eighth Malaysia Plan (MP8), 2001–2005	▪ Expand supply of highly skilled and knowledgeable manpower to support a knowledge-based economy; ▪ Increase accessibility to high-quality education and training to enhance income-generation capabilities and quality of life; ▪ Improve the quality of the education and training delivery system to ensure that manpower supply is in line with technological change and market demand; ▪ Increase supply of science and technology manpower; ▪ Intensify efforts to develop and promote Malaysia as a regional centre of educational excellence.
Ninth Malaysia Plan (MP9), 2006–2010	▪ Make comprehensive improvements to the education delivery system; ▪ Create universities of international standing by raising quality; ▪ Establish a Malaysian Qualifications Framework for quality assurance for TVET; ▪ Bridge the performance gap between urban and rural schools; ▪ Strengthen national schools to become schools of choice of all Malaysians to achieve national unity; ▪ Establish a National Innovation Council.

Plan period	Policy objectives
Tenth Malaysia Plan (MP10), 2011–2015	▪ Revamp the education system to raise student outcomes; ▪ Emphasize increasing enrolment and quality of pre-school education with public–private partnerships; ▪ Strengthen proficiency in English; ▪ Enhance teacher training; ▪ Increase competency of graduates of higher learning institutions for greater employability.
Eleventh Malaysia Plan (MP11), 2016–2020	▪ Shift TVET delivery from vocational and technical schools to vocational colleges; ▪ Implement the Higher Education Blueprint, 2015–2025, with a focus on accelerating access and quality to improve student outcomes; ▪ Enhance governance and stakeholder partnership for better school support; ▪ Raise the quality of graduates and strengthen research for innovation; ▪ Strengthen the governance of higher education institutions (HEIs) and ensure their financial sustainability; ▪ Strengthen school curricula to build 21st-century skills, including a third language, and focus on developing critical, creative, and innovative skills.

Source: Economic Planning Unit–Malaysia (2018a).

Note: The source cited above provides access to the series of Malaysia Five-Year Development Plans and their Mid-term Reviews.

What has remained strikingly common is the consistency with which the unifying and integrative roles of education are written into almost all national plans, and are linked to the politically sensitive role of Malay as the medium of instruction in national schools. Another common theme is the emphasis on meeting the needs of the labour market through manpower planning, which is increasingly coordinated with the expected outputs of schools (academic and technical/vocational), institutions of higher learning, polytechnics, and other manpower-supplying institutions. A third recurring theme is the importance of science, mathematics, and technology for national industrialization efforts, and particularly for export-oriented industrialization.[32] With Vision 2020,[33] the Multimedia Super Corridor, and the increasing demand for high-skilled, professional manpower with expertise in science, mathematics, computing, and information technology, there has been growing recognition of the importance of fostering a science and technology culture, and of ensuring effective teaching of science, technology, engineering, and mathematics (STEM). The extent to which these planning priorities have been realized in practice is considered below.

A trend which can be discerned in more recent plans is the subtle push for greater competency in English without de-emphasizing the role of Malay as the medium of instruction in all schools and educational institutions. In 1996, the Private Higher Educational Institutions Act allowed the use of English as

32 This is first mentioned in MP2.

33 This was launched in 1991 with the vision that Malaysia would become a high-income country by the year 2020.

the medium of instruction in twinning programmes and branch campuses of foreign universities allied with Vision 2020. In MP7, an increasing role was given to the private sector, although by this point it was already highly involved in secondary and post-secondary education provision. There are consistent references to the quality of education in all aspects of educational development in all the five-year plans.

The process of transitioning to a knowledge-based, technology-driven economy requires forward-looking policies and institutions which can build high-quality human resource capacities to absorb global knowledge flows and contribute to new sources of productivity gains. Towards the end of the 20th century, there was a growing acknowledgement of the sharp digital divide that existed between schools in rural and urban areas stemming from poor information and communications technology (ICT) infrastructure, and from a lack of experienced teachers in rural areas, particularly the more remote ones.

Like many other countries, Malaysia began to invest heavily in ICT in schools.[34] In 1999, a nationwide public–private Smart School Initiative was introduced, initially piloted in 88 schools, spreading to 8,454 schools by 2009, and with plans eventually to reach all schools. This initiative aimed to improve the quality of teaching and learning in primary and secondary schools by incorporating ICT into teaching and management. As an evaluation showed, however, some schools, especially those in rural areas, had insufficient computer facilities and inadequate broadband connectivity; timely maintenance was missing; and teachers lacked ICT capacities (Lee and Thah, 2017). A decade after the programme was launched, just 1 per cent of schools had achieved a 'highest' approval ranking.

In summary, the evolution of Malaysia's education objectives spanned three overlapping phases.

In the early post-independence phase, the primary objective was to build national identity and increase access, especially for disadvantaged rural Malays. The principles of *Rukunegara*, the national value system formulated in 1970, were embodied in educational teaching.[35]

In the second phase, beginning in 1971 with the introduction of affirmative action, the focus was on extending the NEP objectives to the education sector through quotas and scholarships for higher education for Malays and other *Bumiputera*. The aims were to redress historical disadvantages and economic

34 While technology can be useful in delivering education and training on a large scale, Dzulkifli Abdul Razak et al. (2019) caution against a technology-centric education system which treats individuals only as human capital to be invested in for gain, and not as human beings to be nurtured.

35 The *Rukunegara* sought to create a shared sense of Malaysian national identity, proclaiming Malaysia as a united, just, and progressive nation, with a plural society of diverse cultures and religions, and with fundamental freedoms guaranteed to all citizens (Department of Information–Malaysia, 2004).

and spatial disparities, and to restructure society to eliminate the connection between occupation and ethnicity. This period also marked the strengthening of Islamic schooling (Box 3.2).

Box 3.2 The post-independence rise of Islamic schooling

After independence, the new national education system began to include Islamic religious classes for Muslim students, especially following the implementation of the recommendations of the 1960 Rahman Talib Report, which had called for the incorporation of Islamic religious knowledge into the curricula of government primary and secondary schools.

With a resurgence in Islamic consciousness in the 1970s, there were calls for Malaysia's education system to be more closely aligned with Islamic principles, and the government adopted several reforms. In 1977, national religious secondary schools—*Sekolah Menengah Kebangsaan Agama* (SMKA)—were introduced for high achievers in the primary school evaluation examination. These schools offered Arabic language and higher Islamic religious knowledge, beginning in the first year of secondary school. During the 1980s, further measures were introduced to strengthen the Islamic content of primary and secondary schools (Rosnani Hashim, 1994; Ahmad Fauzi Abdul Hamid, 2010).[36] In 2010, government-aided religious schools—*Sekolah Agama Bantuan Kerajaan* (SABK)—accounted for less than 1 per cent of primary students and for about 4 per cent of secondary religious schools. Many graduates from religious secondary schools go to Middle Eastern universities, including Cairo's Al Azhar University, and they generate a large number of *ulama*.

The private primary and secondary religious schools sector has also expanded. While national religious schools fall under the jurisdiction of the Ministry of Education, receive federal funding, and use a combination of the national curriculum and a religious curriculum, private religious schools come under the jurisdiction of state religious authorities and tend to place more emphasis on a religious curriculum. One indicator of the growing demand for religious schooling has been the huge rise since the 1990s in the number of privately run *tahfiz* schools, which aim (among other things) to teach students to memorize all the verses of the Koran. There were an estimated 1,200 of these schools by 2015.

In the third phase, which started in the 1990s and has continued ever since, the role of education, especially post-secondary, has been viewed as critical for developing the skilled human resources necessary for a knowledge-based and high-income country. A defining feature has been the liberalization and

36 In 1982, partly in response to the pressures for increased Islamic teaching, Dr Mahathir Mohamad proposed the establishment of the International Islamic University Malaysia (IIUM); it opened in 1983. IIUM graduates communicate in English and Arabic, and the university's multidisciplinary subject matter makes them readily employable. Later, in 2006, with the growing national and international importance of Islamic finance, the government established the International Centre for Education in Islamic Finance (INCEIF), which offers masters and doctorate programmes.

corporatization of higher education. The social equity objective of facilitating access to higher education for students from disadvantaged socio-economic backgrounds was introduced more recently in the Malaysia Education Blueprint 2013–2025.

Emergence of the Private Sector and Liberalization of Higher Education

From the 1970s onwards, Malaysia's higher education sector experienced substantial growth in enrolment and graduate numbers, as well as in the number and type of institutions offering tertiary qualifications. At a time when the country's population was growing rapidly, the size of each new cohort reaching tertiary-education age was larger than the preceding one, raising demand even without an increase in the rate of tertiary enrolment. To meet this growing demand, there was a rapid expansion of public higher education institutions (HEIs), along with a liberalization of higher education to allow private providers into the sector. Multiple tertiary pathways and choices thus became available to Malaysian youth: public universities, polytechnics, and community colleges, as well as private colleges and universities, including 11 international branch campuses of foreign universities, such as Nottingham University (UK) and Monash University (Australia).

In recognition of the need for a diverse range of skills, including essential mid-level professional skills, the country has also increasingly provided post-secondary TVET pathways to employment opportunities: in other words, non-academic pathways to skilled employment. From the late 1990s onwards, there has been a considerable expansion of polytechnics, with 36 established as of 2018. These offer three-year diploma courses in a wide range of subjects, including engineering, commerce, design, and tourism. As part of this extension of educational opportunities to those unable to enter university, since around 2000 the government has opened a network of community colleges across the country, which provide three-year diploma and shorter certificate courses. There were about 100 community colleges in existence by 2018. These provide alternative education and training for secondary-school leavers, as well as the opportunity for a second chance for those who have left the formal education system. Their students are mainly Malays and other *Bumiputera*.[37]

---

37 Malaysia's community colleges provide technical and vocational education at certificate and diploma levels in subjects such as agriculture, building, business, electrical engineering, health science, and ICT.

The growth of public sector tertiary institutions that began in the 1970s was intended to accommodate the rising number of Malay and other *Bumiputera* secondary-school leavers, as well as to meet the broader human resource needs of the economy. As part of the NEP's affirmative action policy of trying to increase the quantity of human capital of Malays, a quota system was introduced to regulate entry to universities, replacing the meritocratic criteria that had previously applied. The aim was to align the share in higher education of the different ethnic groups with their distribution in the population, as Malays were historically under-represented at the university level. In practice, however, the Malay quotas for public HEIs exceeded their relative share in the population (Lee and Nagaraj, 2012).[38] University entry requirements for Malays were also relaxed, overriding consideration of outcome standards (Ruslan Khalid, 2013). As a result, many Malay students were given places in prestigious courses that were not necessarily well matched to their interests and talents, while non-Malays often had to settle for courses that were their second choice. Many of the Malay students were from lower-income families, and scholarships were readily available to finance their studies, especially for courses in scientific or professional fields.

The success of these policies in meeting their numerical targets led to chronic shortages of places at local public institutions, especially in high-demand courses; the supply of places simply could not keep up with the very-fast-growing demand from all communities. Increasing numbers of non-Malay secondary school graduates seeking post-secondary opportunities began to feel excluded from the public HEIs. A growing number of non-Malays therefore started to seek post-secondary qualifications abroad. The shortage of supply in public sector colleges and universities spurred a boom in private post-secondary education. Stimulated by the huge unmet demand arising from the sharp increase in secondary school graduates, and by the limited capacity of public sector institutions, local entrepreneurs perceived an investment opportunity and established colleges offering higher education programmes. This major expansion of private sector tertiary institutions at degree and diploma levels began in the late 1980s, and by the mid 1990s several hundred had been established.

The liberalization of higher education through the private sector has helped to reduce government expenditure on higher education and stem the outflow of foreign exchange on overseas students. It has also contributed to Malaysia becoming an international education hub, which now attracts large

38 In 2002, public university quotas were supposed to be replaced by a merit-based entrance policy, but implementation of the change has not been apparent. Lee, H.G. (2013) estimates that enrolment in public universities in 2005 was 82 per cent Malay and other *Bumiputera*, 13 per cent Chinese, and 3 per cent Indian; these figures include Universiti Teknologi MARA (UiTM), which was exclusively for Malays and other *Bumiputera* (Perkins et al., 2017).

numbers of foreign students. Legislation regulating private HEIs was first introduced in an amendment to the Universities and University Colleges Act in 1995, and then more extensively set out in the Private Higher Institutions Act in 1996 and in other supplementary laws.[39] These laws provided the regulatory framework under which all colleges have to be registered, and made their curricula subject to the scrutiny of the Ministry of Higher Education.[40] It also provided the means for public universities to become corporatized. English language was allowed as a medium of instruction in private HEIs.

Once the legislation was in place, the number of private universities grew very quickly, including campuses of foreign universities from 1999. The government encouraged several government-linked companies to establish private universities, in some cases building on the training institutes that had been part of their operations for many years.[41]

With growth in both the number and proportion of students entering higher education, the existing system expanded outwards by constructing new universities, hiring new faculty members, and encouraging the entry of private higher education providers. The escalating demand for faculty staff to serve the growing number of public and private universities, moreover, meant that the system also expanded upwards through the introduction of graduate programmes to prepare additional qualified staff (Chapman and Chien, 2014). These programmes in turn led to a growing number of post-graduate research centres, with further benefits for the country. In order to meet NEP affirmative action targets, the recruitment and promotion of Malays were prioritized in the new administrative and academic positions. While these expansions of the system were commendable, the pace at which they were implemented may have compromised the quality of faculty. As noted by Perkins et al. (2017, p. 62), 'Malaysia must also greatly improve the quality of its tertiary education if knowledge-based growth is to ever occur. The NEP mechanisms have weakened the incentives for universities to upgrade themselves'.

The opening up of more places at private universities and colleges provided increased opportunities for non-Malay students to pursue their higher education locally instead of taking the far more costly option of studying abroad. Enrolment in private HEIs has now come to exceed that

39 MP6 directed government agencies to continue facilitating the private sector in establishing education and training institutions, based on the rationale that this would help to drive private participation in economic development and reduce the outflow of foreign exchange.

40 The Ministry of Education and Ministry of Higher Education were merged in 2013 to ensure seamless planning and policy implementation from pre-school through to higher education and beyond.

41 Among the government-linked companies' universities were Multimedia University (1996), Universiti Teknologi Petronas (1997), and Universiti Tenaga Nasional (1999). Political parties in the ruling coalition also established universities, such as UMNO's Universiti Tun Abdul Razak (1997) and the Malayan Chinese Association's Universiti Tunku Abdul Rahman (2002).

in public institutions. While the latter increased from 370,000 to 652,000 students between 2002 and 2016, the former rose from 295,000 to 695,000 over the same period (Ministry of Higher Education–Malaysia, 2018). Non-Malay students are in the majority at private HEIs, many of which are English-medium, with Malay students still predominant at the public HEIs, which are mostly Malay-medium. This divide poses a further challenge to the higher education system (Leete, 2007; Lee, 2013),[42] but is something that the country aims to overcome (Box 3.3).

Box 3.3 Higher Education Blueprint, 2015–2025

The Blueprint seeks to:

- Increase *access* to and enrolment in higher education, collaboratively with industry;
- Strengthen the *quality* of graduates, institutions, and the system itself;
- Improve *equity* through increased enrolment and completion rates for disadvantaged students;
- Ensure *unity* by creating among students a sense of shared values, aspirations, and experiences through a better mix of ethnicities in university enrolment; and
- Maximize *efficiency* of investments in higher education.

The Blueprint envisages the transformation of higher education through ten steps:

- Developing more holistic, entrepreneurial, and balanced graduates;
- Encouraging higher learning institutions to pursue different forms of institutional excellence, diversify career pathways for their talent, and recruit and develop new talent;
- Increasing public awareness of lifelong learning, including the establishment of pathways for re-entry into the education system;
- Strengthening technical and vocational education, including through intensified industry involvement in curriculum design and delivery;
- Increasing the financial sustainability of public higher learning institutions, for instance, by linking funding to performance and targeting government investment;
- Empowering governance through greater decentralization of decision-making to higher learning institutions in return for accountability against a set of agreed outcomes;
- Strengthening the innovation ecosystem through focusing on creating scale and growth in a few select strategic research areas;
- Enhancing the appeal of higher learning institutions to attract more international students;

42 Malay students rely mostly on government loans to support their higher education, whereas non-Malay students rely mostly on their parents or other relatives, or on self-financing (Khazanah Research Institute, 2018).

- Increasing the potential for online learning and establishing national e-learning platforms; and
- Transforming higher education delivery.

Source: Ministry of Education–Malaysia (2015).

Educational Inputs, Impacts, and Outcomes

Education Expenditure

Expenditure on education is an important indicator for assessing the extent of national commitment to, and prioritizing of, human capital objectives. Although the level of education expenditure is not necessarily correlated directly with learning outcomes—as efficiency of spending is also important—it is a useful way of assessing the impacts and outcomes of Malaysia's educational investments and reforms. As Figure 3.1 shows, in terms of inputs, much has been invested to support policy reforms and to improve the education system. Annual government spending on education as a share of GDP has been consistently high over the past four decades at around 5 to 6 per cent, while per capita expenditure on education has also risen considerably from just over RM850 in 2000 to RM1,800 in 2015. A significant proportion of public expenditure on education is for teachers' remuneration.

Figure 3.1 **Malaysia's expenditure on education has been generally high, although since 2000 it has been declining as a percentage of the development budget**[a]

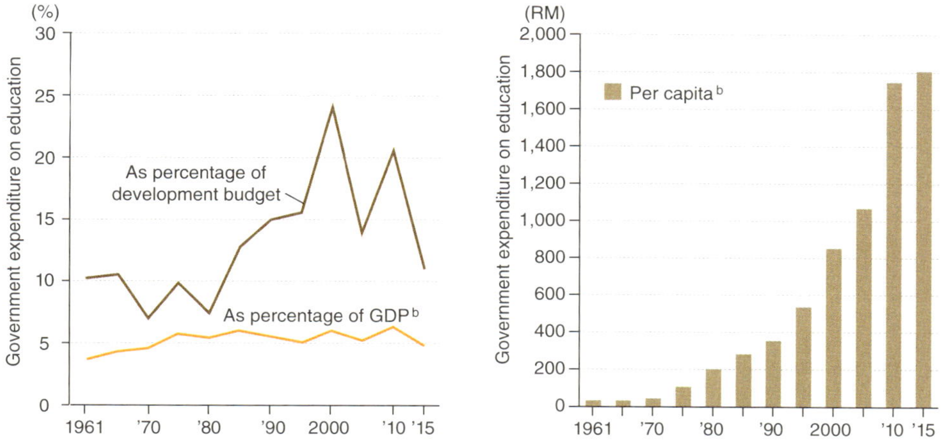

Sources of data: Ministry of Finance–Malaysia (various years).
Notes: [a] Three-year average figures centred on the given years.
[b] Includes operating and development spending.

Universal Literacy

At its most basic level, the purpose of education is to create literate individuals; this is the first step on the road to human capital formation. Once someone is literate, she or he can move on to the larger goals of education. The expansion of schools after the end of World War II and the broadening of educational opportunities had already helped to improve literacy rates prior to *Merdeka*, and at independence half the population aged ten and over were literate. By 1970, literacy rates were approaching two-thirds, and they continued to rise in successive decades, such that by 2010 more than 95 per cent of the population was literate. Illiteracy is now confined to a small proportion of the older generations who did not receive any education when they were of school age, as well as some of the new migrant workers.

The colonial education system had resulted in substantial differences in literacy rates between the main communities, with literacy among Malays lagging far behind the other ethnic groups (Figure 3.2). By 1970, however, the gap had almost closed, and among those aged 15–24 Malays had the highest literacy rates. Over time there has been a convergence in literacy rates, with all communities achieving almost universal literacy, and with parity between males and females.

Figure 3.2 **Ethnic differentials in literacy levels have disappeared**

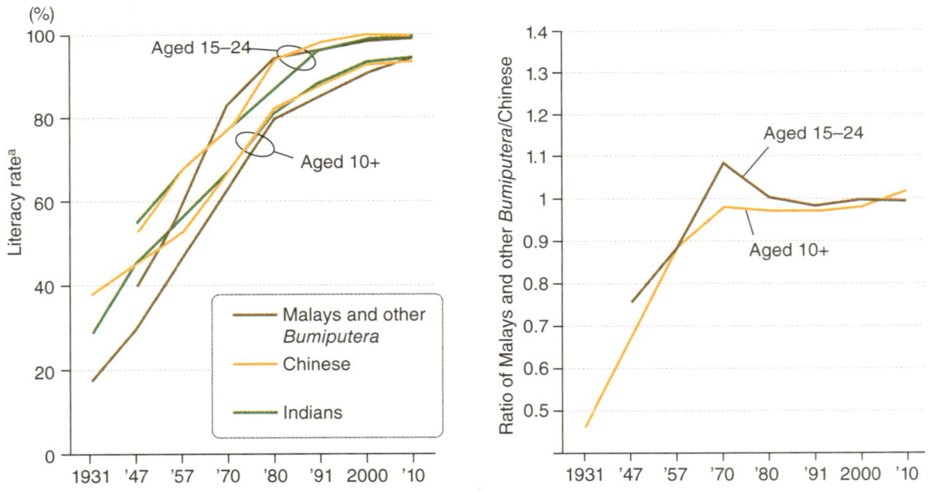

Sources of data: Vlieland (1932); Del Tufo (1949); Fell (1960); Chander (1977); Khoo (1983); Khoo (1995); Shaari Abdul Rahman (2002); Haji Abdul Rahman bin Hasan (2013).

Notes: [a] Data for 1931 and 1947 are for Malaya.
Data for 1957, 1970, and 1980 are for Peninsular Malaysia.

The large spatial disparities in literacy rates—with the east coast states and Sabah and Sarawak lagging behind due to their slower development—have progressively narrowed. Literacy rates have greatly improved across all states, although there are still small variations between them. Even in Sabah and Sarawak, where access to education continues to trail that in other states, and where the opportunities for the older generations to attend school were very limited, literacy was around 90 per cent by 2010 (89 per cent in Sarawak and 93 per cent in Sabah) (Figure 3.3).

Figure 3.3 **Historical sharp divides in literacy rates between states have narrowed**

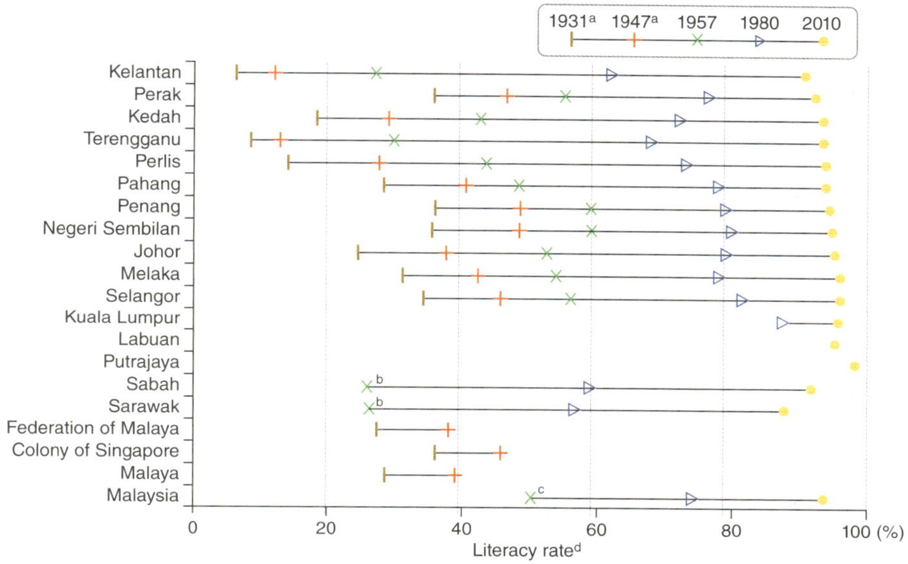

Sources of data: Vlieland (1932); Del Tufo (1949); Fell (1960); Khoo (1983); Haji Abdul Rahman bin Hasan (2013).

Notes: [a] Aged 15+.
[b] 1960 data.
[c] Data are for Peninsular Malaysia.
[d] Data before 2010 include non-Malaysian citizens.

A key objective of the NEP was to improve equity and eradicate absolute poverty, as measured by the national poverty line income. One of the strategies for achieving this goal was to increase free access to state-provided education at all levels, especially among the rural population.[43] By the early 21st century, Malaysia had almost eradicated absolute poverty, an achievement strongly associated with the country's progress in building human capital. As Figure 3.4 shows, there is a close correspondence by state between poverty rates and literacy rates, used as a proxy for educational attainment: states with the highest literacy rates are those that have made the most progress in reducing poverty. While higher educational attainment opens up possibilities for higher-income modern-sector employment, however, the inverse is also true (Box 3.4). Progress in ending poverty has been slowest in the more rural

43 To encourage children from poor rural families to attend school, the government provided assistance, such as scholarships and grants for textbooks and meals.

states of Sabah and Sarawak, as well as in those along the peninsula's east coast, where both economic development and the spread of educational opportunities have lagged behind.

Figure 3.4 As literacy rates increased, poverty rates declined

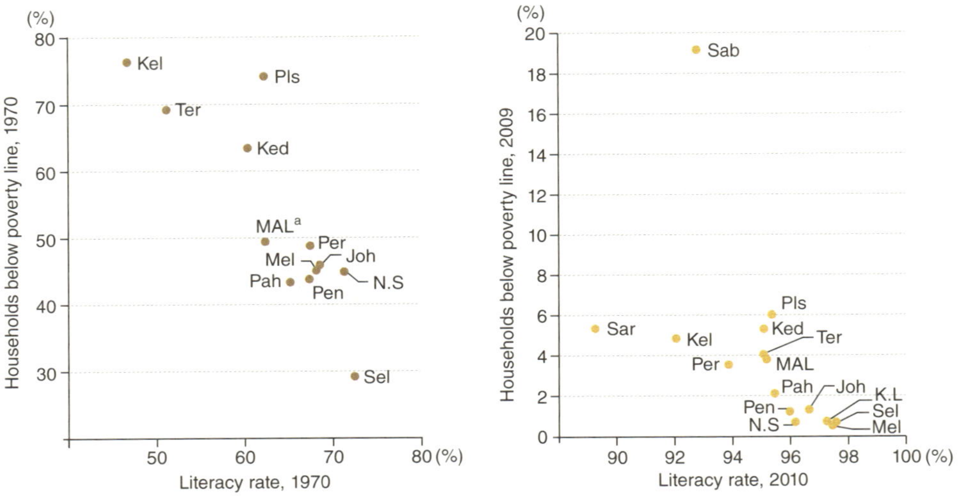

Joh = Johor	Mel = Melaka	Pen = Penang	Sab = Sabah	Ter = Terengganu
Ked = Kedah	N.S = Negeri Sembilan	Per = Perak	Sar = Sarawak	K.L = Kuala Lumpur
Kel = Kelantan	Pah = Pahang	Pls = Perlis	Sel = Selangor	MAL = MALAYSIA

Sources of data: For poverty rates, Economic Planning Unit–Malaysia (2018b). For literacy rates, Chander (1977); Haji Abdul Rahman bin Hasan (2013).

Note: [a] Data for 1970 are for Peninsular Malaysia.

Box 3.4 Low educational attainment is detrimental to household income

Education is a powerful determinant of employment and income, and of other life-influencing outcomes. Malaysia's overall level of educational attainment has improved hugely over the past two decades, as shown by data from Household Income Surveys in 1995 and 2016. By 2016, 15 per cent of the population lived in households where the head had only primary schooling or less compared with 54 per cent in 1995 (Box Table 3.1). In 2016, some 27 per cent of individuals lived in a household whose head had received tertiary schooling: two decades earlier, the figure was just 6 per cent.

In 1995, ranked by their household's 'equivalized income', 77 per cent of individuals in the bottom 20 per cent of the income distribution lived in households where the head had only primary schooling or less, while only 25 per cent of the top 20 per cent lived in such households (Box 9.4 in Chapter 9).[44] Very few individuals in the bottom 20 per cent had a household head with schooling beyond secondary level, whereas 23 per cent in the top 20 per cent lived in households headed by an individual with tertiary education (Chapter 9).

Greater access to education since 1995 has not diminished the significance of educational attainment in determining household income. In 2016, just under a third of the bottom 20 per cent lived in a household where the head had only basic schooling (primary or less), while close to two-thirds were members of households whose head had secondary schooling. Fewer than 5 per cent of the bottom 20 per cent had a household head with schooling beyond secondary level. By contrast, nearly two-thirds of the top 20 per cent were in households where the head had tertiary schooling. Educational attainment of the head of household is thus an important driver of income inequality.

Box Table 3.1 Households with the lowest educational attainments also have the lowest incomes

Education of head of household	Equivalized income rank			
	Bottom 20%	Middle 40%	Top 20%	All Individuals
1995				
No schooling	25.4	13.2	6.0	14.2
Primary	52.0	42.2	18.6	39.5
Secondary	22.4	41.9	52.5	40.1
Tertiary	0.3	2.7	22.9	6.2
2016				
No schooling	6.8	1.8	0.5	2.6
Primary	24.7	12.0	3.0	12.8
Secondary	63.6	64.1	33.2	57.8
Tertiary	4.9	22.0	63.4	26.9

Sources of data: Computed from unpublished data from the Household Income Surveys of 1995 and 2016 conducted by the Department of Statistics–Malaysia.

44 All individuals in the 1995 and 2016 Household Income Surveys received an 'equivalized income'—the total income of their household divided by the number of 'equivalent' adults in the household (Chapter 9).

Increasing Enrolment at All Education Levels

One important result of the sustained high level of expenditure on education is the impressive increase in school enrolment rates that can be seen at all levels of education (Figure 3.5). As early as 1970, primary enrolment rates had reached 88 per cent, and by the 1980s almost universal access to primary education had been achieved. Completion rates in primary education have also soared, reaching 99 per cent in 2014 for both girls and boys (United Nations Development Programme, 2015). With high and increasing primary school enrolment and completion rates, enrolment rates at lower- and upper-secondary levels have also increased sharply. Secondary school completion rates have improved across all states, increasing overall from 85.7 per cent in 2000 to 90 per cent in 2014; females have higher secondary school completion rates than males.

Figure 3.5 **Malaysian enrolment rates at all levels have risen**

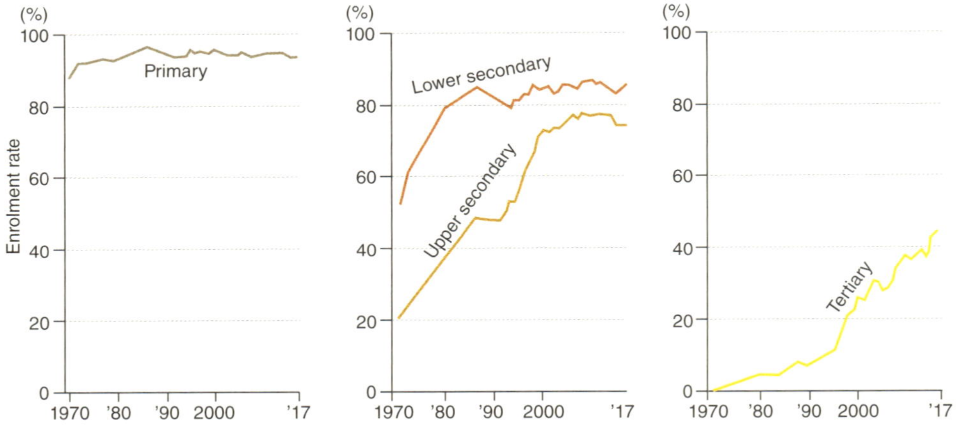

Sources of data: Data for primary and secondary levels, and tertiary up to 1978, are from Ministry of Education–Malaysia (various years between 1970 and 2017). Tertiary data after 1978 are from the United Nations Educational, Scientific and Cultural Organization (2018c).

Notes: Primary refers to schooling for 6–11-year-olds; lower secondary for 12–14-year-olds; and upper secondary for 15–16-year-olds. Tertiary includes study in private educational institutions and study abroad.

Enrolment in tertiary education has also surged, especially since the liberalization of HEIs during the 1990s. Malaysia's gross tertiary enrolment rate rose from just 7 per cent in 1990 to 26 per cent in 2000, and reached 44 per cent in 2016 (Figure 3.5). Although this is a very welcome shift, there is still considerable scope for improving tertiary enrolment rates, especially among lower-income groups. The country's tertiary enrolment remains well below the average for countries in the Organisation for Economic Co-operation and Development (OECD) which is 72.8 per cent, and also below that for the newly industrializing economies (NIEs) (Figure 3.6 and Box 3.5).[45]

Box 3.5 Achieving high human development

Human development is a multidimensional concept with three measurable dimensions: to have the capacity to live a long and healthy life; to be educated and knowledgeable; and to have access to assets, decent employment, and income. Being well educated and knowledgeable is thus a key component of human development.

Malaysia's progress in human development as measured through the Human Development Index (HDI) of the United Nations Development Programme (UNDP) was rapid in the 1980s and 1990s, when it moved from 'medium' to 'high' human development. Progress has slowed in the 21st century, however, although the country graduated to 'very high' human development in 2017 (Box Figure 3.1). In 2017, Malaysia was ranked 57th of 189 countries compared with 59th of 173 countries in 2000. Improving its educational outcomes will help the country progress to even higher levels of human development.

Box Figure 3.1 Malaysia's progress in human development benchmarked against the average of the world's top five countries

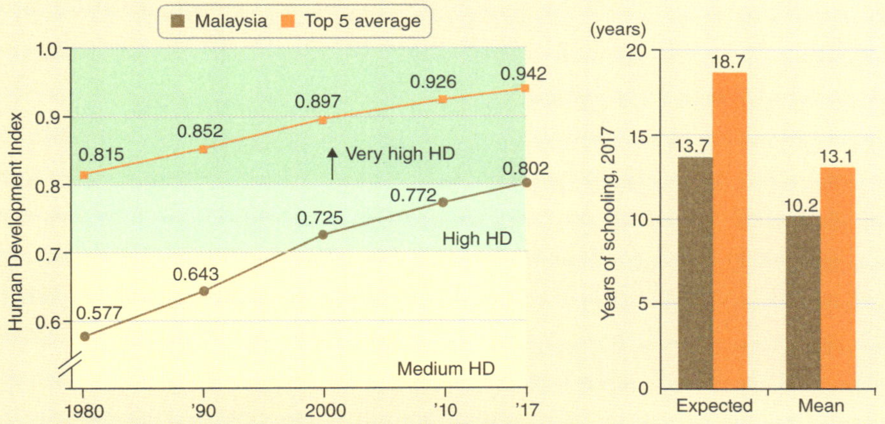

Source of data: United Nations Development Programme (2018).
Note: The top five HDI countries in 2017 were (in descending order) Norway, Switzerland, Australia, Ireland, and Germany.

45 The figures for tertiary enrolment exclude the many Malaysian students studying abroad.

Figure 3.6 Malaysia's tertiary gross enrolment rates still lag behind those in many OECD countries and the NIEs

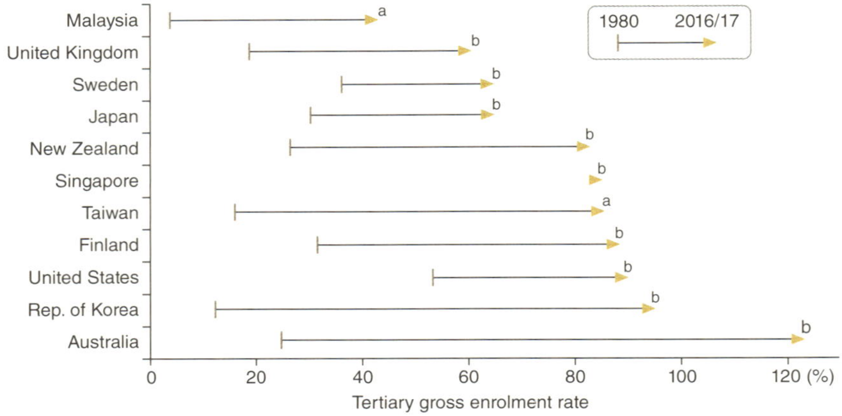

Sources of data: United Nations Educational, Scientific and Cultural Organization (2018c). Ministry of Education–Taiwan (2018).

Notes: [a] Data are for 2017.
[b] Data are for 2016.

Improving Pupil–Teacher Ratios

Rising enrolment rates have been accompanied by significant improvements in the delivery of education, as indicated by steep declines in the number of pupils per teacher at both primary and secondary levels since 1970 (Table 3.2). At independence, there were 29 students for every teacher at primary level and 26 at secondary level, whereas by 2017 the figures were 12 and 11 respectively, with some variation between urban and rural areas. These pupil–teacher ratios, which are associated with high recurrent public education expenditure, compare well with international benchmarks, and are lower than the average across OECD countries, which in 2016 were 16 for primary schools and 14 for secondary schools (World Bank, 2018a). The quality of teachers is also critical to the success of an education system, and this aspect is assessed below through various outcome indicators.

Table 3.2 Malaysia's pupil–teacher ratios continue to improve

	Primary	Secondary
1957[a]	28.9	25.5
1970[a]	31.5	25.3
1980	27.3	22.5
1990	20.4	18.8
2000	19.0	17.6
2010	12.6	13.7
2017	11.6	11.2

Sources of data: Department of Statistics–Malaysia (Social Statistics Bulletin, various years between 1957 and 2018).

Note: [a] Peninsular Malaysia only.

Rising Educational Attainment

Educational attainment—the highest level of schooling completed by an individual—is a useful indicator of human capital, although it says little about the quality of the education received. Malaysians have become much more educated, in keeping with national policy objectives and the massive expansion of public and private higher education. Between 1991 and 2010, the share of the population with only primary education fell sharply, and the share of those attaining secondary and tertiary levels increased (Figure 3.7). While educational attainment has increased for all of Malaysia's communities, particularly notable has been the rise in the share of Malays and other *Bumiputera* with tertiary qualifications, from 9 per cent to 13 per cent over the same period. With the continued expansion of tertiary opportunities, this trend is likely to continue, and will help to further expand the Malay and other *Bumiputera* middle class.

A technology-driven knowledge economy requires a high share of graduates in science and mathematics, ICT, and other technical subjects, whether these qualifications have been acquired through vocational, professional, or academic routes. However, a survey conducted by the Khazanah Research Institute (2018) in 2017–2018 found that just 32 per cent of Malaysian tertiary students, and an even lower proportion among female tertiary students, are enrolled in science, technology, engineering, and mathematics courses. Between 2004 and 2016, Malaysia increased its share of tertiary graduates with engineering, manufacturing, and construction qualifications, but its share of natural science graduates remained small, and was lower than its international comparators (Figure 3.8). The share of graduates with degrees in education increased markedly, however, and was higher by 2016 than in all benchmark countries.

Figure 3.7 Educational attainment levels have risen for all communities

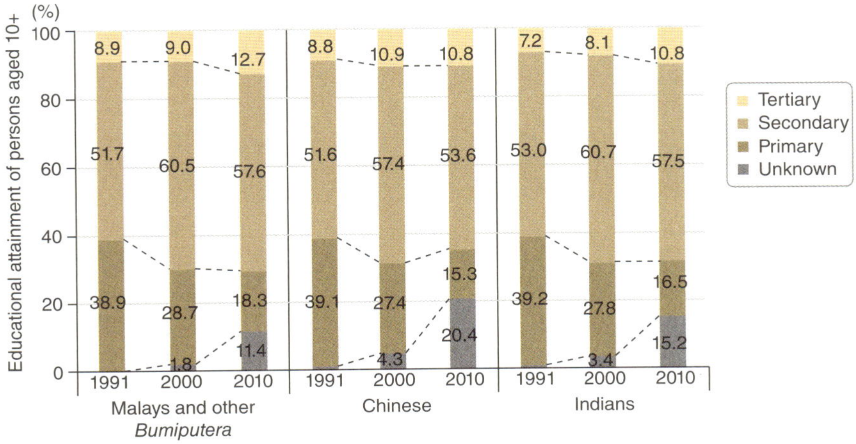

Sources of data: Khoo (1995); Shaari Abdul Rahman (2002); Haji Abdul Rahman bin Hasan (2013).
Note: For 2010, the high percentage in the 'unknown' category is a result of the fact that many people were reluctant to reveal their educational attainment in the 2010 census.

Figure 3.8 **Malaysia's share of tertiary natural science graduates lags behind many OECD countries**

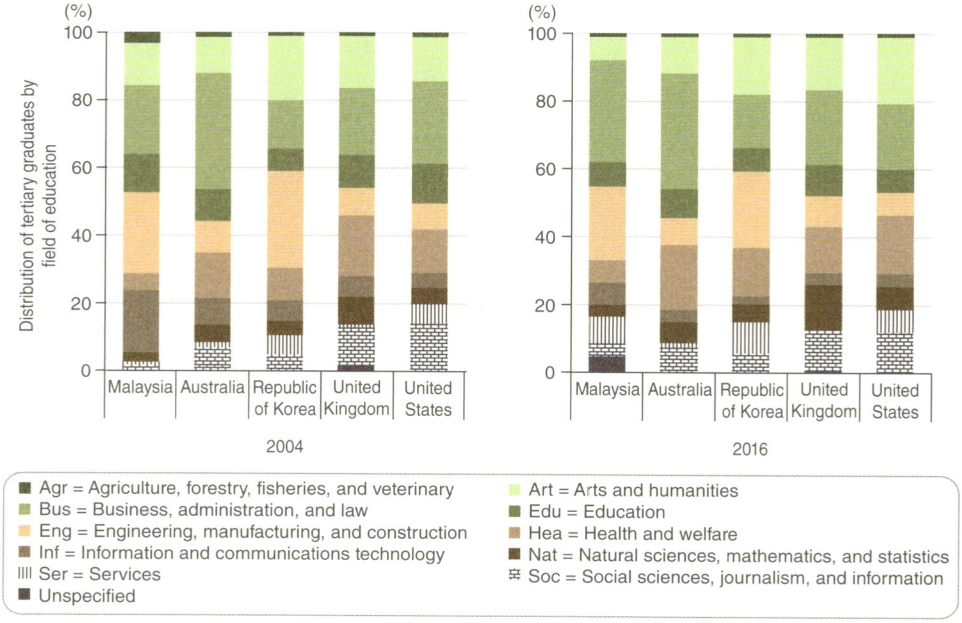

Source of data: United Nations Educational, Scientific and Cultural Organization (2018b).

Supply of and Demand for Human Capital

With higher educational attainment, the human capital of Malaysia's labour force has deepened. In 2017, 55.8 per cent of the employed had a secondary education, up from 35.5 per cent in 1982 (Table 3.3). The share of employed Malaysians with a tertiary education increased nearly four times over the same period, from just 6.1 per cent to 28.3 per cent, consistent with the strong growth in tertiary institutions and tertiary enrolment rates.

Table 3.3 **Shares of Malaysia's labour force with secondary and tertiary education are increasing**

	No formal education	Primary	Secondary	Tertiary	Total (%)
1982	15.8	42.6	35.5	6.1	100
1990	9.8	34.6	46.8	8.8	100
2000	5.6	25.3	54.7	14.4	100
2010	3.7	17.9	55.0	23.4	100
2016	2.7	14.7	55.1	27.5	100
2017	2.6	13.3	55.8	28.3	100

Sources: Department of Statistics–Malaysia (various years).

On the demand side, the transition to a knowledge-based, diversified economy requires greater numbers of higher-skilled workers and smaller numbers of lower-skilled workers. However, the low-skill intensity of employment increased in most industries between 2002 and 2007 (National Economic Advisory Council (NEAC), 2010). The electrical and electronics sector, for example, which has traditionally been the major contributor to output growth in manufacturing, has experienced one of the biggest declines in high-skilled labour. The share of highly skilled workers nationally was only 25 per cent in 2007, lower than in Singapore, Taiwan, and the Republic of Korea (Table 3.4). This may suggest that workers have not been competing to upgrade their skills in order to gain wage premiums, or that firms have not been prepared to pay for skills upgrading, preferring instead to use low-cost, low-skilled foreign workers (NEAC, 2010).

Table 3.4 Skill level of Malaysia's labour force remains behind that of the NIEs

	Skill level of labour (%) in 2007		
	Highly skilled	Lower skilled	Total
Malaysia	25	75	100
Singapore	49	51	100
Taiwan	67	33	100
Republic of Korea	65	35	100

Source: National Economic Advisory Council (2010).

Challenges in Human Capital Development

From the evidence presented above, it is apparent that, by any measure, Malaysia has made excellent progress in increasing educational access and attainment. With improvements made in these areas, questions then arise about the quality of the education that is offered, about how innovative the country is, and about how effective the education system has been in promoting employability and in ensuring that supply meets demand for labour in the rapidly changing world of work. These questions are addressed in the following sections. In addition, the emigration of higher-skilled individuals from Malaysia—which has a bearing on quality, innovation, and the human capital base—is also considered (Chapters 2 and 7).

Performance in International Assessments

The Malaysia Education Blueprint 2013–2025 (Ministry of Education–Malaysia, 2013) noted that the education system has come under increased public scrutiny in recent years. Parents' expectations have risen, and employers have begun to question the ability of the system to adequately prepare Malaysian students for the challenges of the 21st century. The Blueprint sets a target for students to perform better than the global average by 2025, and for Malaysia by this time to be among the top third of countries that take part in international test assessments, which measure quality dimensions of national education.

Malaysia's performance in the series of Trends in International Mathematics and Science Study (TIMSS)[46] reveals a worrying trend. Malaysian students performed at a similar level to Australian students in the 1999 and 2003 assessments, but their performance plummeted in the following two assessments, recovering only moderately in 2015 (Figure 3.9). Girls performed significantly better than boys in both subjects in each year. In 2015, Malaysia's performance lagged markedly behind high-income countries in the region, such as Australia, Japan, the Republic of Korea, and Singapore, although it did perform marginally better than Thailand.

Figure 3.9 Malaysia's TIMSS scores are below those of regional high-income countries

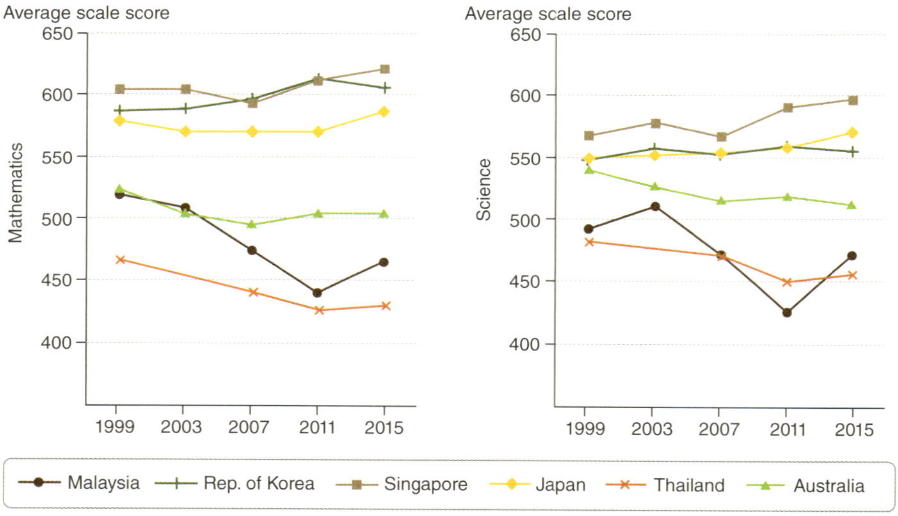

Source of data: International Association for the Evaluation of Educational Achievement (2018).
Note: Scores around 625 represent the 'advanced benchmark', around 550 the 'high benchmark', around 475 the 'intermediate benchmark', and around 400 the 'low benchmark'.

46 TIMSS, run by Boston College's International Association for the Evaluation of Educational Achievement, and managed in the United States by the National Center for Education Statistics (part of the US Department of Education), measures trends in mathematics and science achievement of fourth- and eighth-grade students (10-year-olds and 14-year-olds) in a diverse range of participating countries. Launched in 1995, TIMSS is conducted every four years, with 2015 the sixth in the series. Malaysia has participated in each assessment since 1999.

Malaysia has taken part in the three-yearly Programme for International Student Assessment (PISA) since 2009.[47] Results in 2009 showed that Malaysian students ranked in the bottom third of the 74 participating countries, well below the OECD averages. Fewer than half of Malaysian students met the minimum proficiency level in mathematics, science, and reading.[48] By the 2015 PISA, Malaysia's scores had improved moderately, narrowing the gap with the average OECD scores (Figure 3.10).[49] However, the country's overall ranking did not materially change.

Figure 3.10 **Malaysia's PISA scores in mathematics, science, and reading are well below OECD averages**

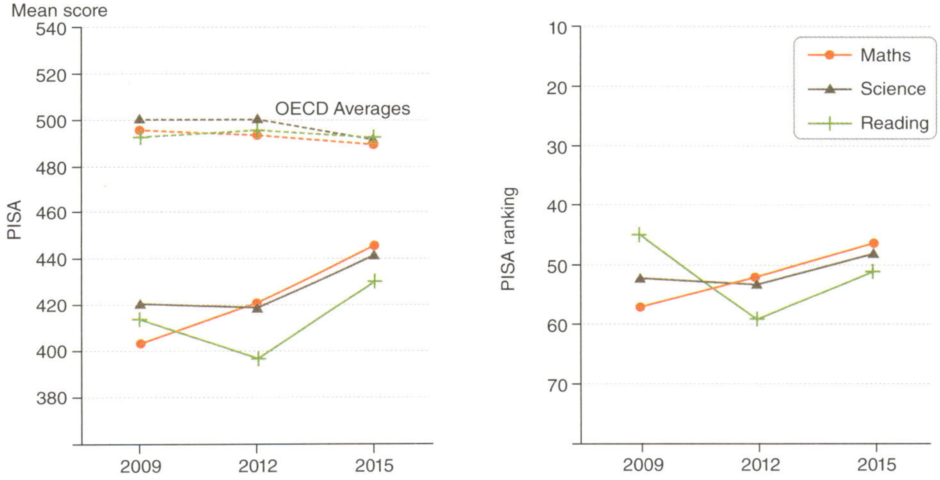

Sources of data: Organisation for Economic Co-operation and Development (2014 and 2016).

Malaysian students are clearly underperforming in these three critical areas of learning. Although secondary school enrolment is high, schooling is not being converted into the higher levels of human capital necessary for the fulfilment of the country's economic aspirations. Between 2012 and 2015, Malaysia did overtake the lower-income Thailand in all three proficiency tests, but its scores remain below those of the less-developed Viet Nam and are considerably lower than higher-income Singapore (Figure 3.11).

47 PISA was launched in 2000 by the OECD to assess the achievements and the application of key knowledge and skills by 15-year-olds. PISA assesses whether students who are approaching the end of compulsory education have the basic knowledge and skills in mathematics, science, and reading necessary for effective participation in contemporary society.

48 A difference of 38 points on the PISA scale is equivalent to one year of schooling. A comparison of scores shows that 15-year-olds in Singapore, the Republic of Korea, Hong Kong, and Shanghai are performing as though they have had three or more years more schooling than 15-year-olds in Malaysia.

49 The OECD notes, however, a need for caution in interpreting Malaysia's 2015 results: 'In Malaysia, the PISA assessment was conducted in accordance with the operational standards and guidelines of the OECD. However, the weighted response rate among the initially sampled Malaysian schools (51 per cent) falls well short of the standard PISA response rate of 85 per cent. The results may not be comparable to those of other countries or to results for Malaysia from previous years' (OECD, 2016, p. 304).

Figure 3.11 **Malaysia's PISA scores and rankings are well below those of Singapore and Viet Nam**

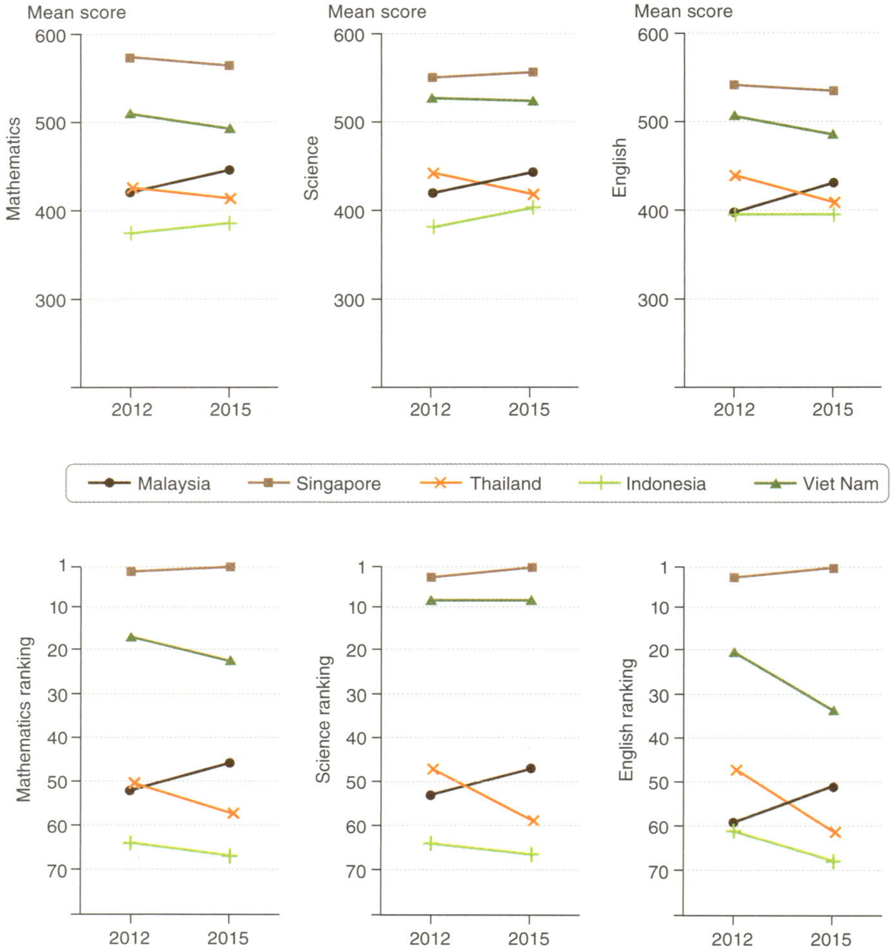

Source of data: Organisation for Economic Co-operation and Development (2014 and 2016).

Why Did Malaysia's Performance Decline in International Assessments?

It is useful to explore the reasons for the sharp decline in Malaysia's TIMSS score after 1999 and 2003 (when Malaysian students performed well in mathematics and science), as well as for its weak performances in PISA 2009, 2012, and 2015.

One explanation is the abrupt switch in the medium of instruction for the teaching of mathematics and science from Malay to English in national primary and secondary schools in 2003. A study conducted in 2007 showed that the sudden switch of language had negative effects on students' performance, with most pupils unable to understand concepts and procedures cognitively in English (Isahak Haron, 2015).[50]

As part of the language change, a computer-aided instruction manual was designed to help teachers conduct mathematics and science lessons in English. Large sums were invested in supplying schools with computers to facilitate the teaching and learning of these subjects in the English language. However, many teachers were not sufficiently proficient in English to explain the concepts and procedures effectively. This issue particularly affected Malay and other *Bumiputera* students—around 300,000 students per annual cohort—who attended national primary and secondary schools. Chinese students attending vernacular schools were less affected as Mandarin was maintained as the medium of instruction (Isahak Haron, 2015).

The cumulative effect of poor learning and performance in mathematics and science at primary and lower-secondary levels can be seen in the sharp decline in the percentage of pupils qualified to take the science stream at Form 4 and 5 levels (ages 16 and 17). This had dropped from 43 per cent in 2003 to only 20 per cent in 2015, falling far short of the stated target of a 60:40 ratio for the science and arts streams (Isahak Haron, 2015).

The decline in standards of mathematics and science at secondary level has also affected tertiary enrolments in these subjects. A lower proportion of Malay and other *Bumiputera* students were choosing either the 'pure' science fields (physics, mathematics, and chemistry) or engineering studies, and those who did were less prepared for these fields of study than non-Malay students. Recognizing the negative impact of teaching these subjects in a language other than the pupils' national language, since 2010 the Ministry of Education has gradually reverted to the use of Malay for the teaching of mathematics and science.

In an analysis of the 2009 and 2012 PISA scores, the World Bank found that even the top 5 per cent of Malaysian students were comparable only to *average* pupils from the Republic of Korea or Japan. It concluded that despite similar enrolment rates, these quality gaps meant that more schooling was not translating into higher levels of human capital (World Bank, 2013). This is a cause for concern because it is educational achievement measured by the level of cognitive skill, rather than school attainment measured by years of schooling, that contributes most to economic growth (Hanushek, 2013).

In summary, it appears that Malaysian students' cognitive skills—such as knowledge recall, the application of knowledge in problem solving, and

---

50 Cognitive skills include reasoning, problem solving, learning ability, and speed of information processing. Non-cognitive skills include integrity, motivation, persistence, and teamwork.

the ability to use reasoning to work through problems—have not improved over the past two decades, and may even have deteriorated. The country's performance in international student assessments is below what might be expected given its level of expenditure on education, and is significantly lower than that of the high-income economies with which Malaysia aspires to compete in driving forward innovation and technological change.

Improving the Quality of Education

In 2009, the government established an Education Performance and Delivery Unit (PADU) to implement and monitor a national Literacy and Numeracy Screening programme (LINUS) aimed at primary school students.[51] Previous attempts to reform the system had not brought about the desired outcomes. Students were graduating with diplomas certifying that they had completed more years of schooling, but the education they received gave them only limited mastery of English, critical thinking, or analytical reasoning abilities, and was inconsistent with the quality needed for Malaysia to reach high-income status. The extent to which LINUS has helped to improve standards is unclear because the programme did not allow implementers to specify treatment and control groups. Moreover, it was not launched in isolation. A curriculum review conducted in 2011, for example, resulted in the introduction of the Primary School Standard Curriculum, which may also have contributed to literacy improvements (World Bank, 2018c).

One of the best tests of educational quality is found in the workplace (Chapter 7). In 2007, more than 40 per cent of firms reported that job applicants with tertiary qualifications lacked the skills necessary to meet the requirements of job vacancies for skilled production workers. The waiting time to fill these positions was reported at four weeks, which affected business operations and growth (OECD, 2013). Another survey on graduate employability conducted in 2008 showed that almost 25 per cent of graduates remained unemployed for six months after completing their studies, while about 30 per cent of those who found jobs were working in roles involving lower skill requirements than they had trained for (NEAC, 2010). A study on the supply of, and demand for, talent in the electrical and electronics sector by Ipsos Business Consulting (2012) showed that only 57 per cent of the demand for skilled workers in this sector in 2012–2014 could be met, with the lack of skill among graduates cited as one of the main reasons for the shortfall.

51 Improving the quality of education was a key priority of Malaysia's 2009 National Transformation Programme. PADU, working closely with the Ministry of Education, adopted a similar programme methodology as was used by Malaysia's now disbanded Performance and Management Delivery Unit (PEMANDU), which was under the Prime Minister's Office. PADU aimed to achieve the LINUS objectives through, for example, strengthening coordination and collaboration among stakeholders at central, state, district, and school levels; training teachers using professional facilitators; and introducing tailor-made training and screening materials (World Bank, 2017).

The unemployment rate among young Malaysian graduates was 16.6 per cent in 2016 compared with 9.3 per cent among young people without tertiary education. Paradoxically, while employers were reporting challenges in finding skilled Malaysians, the unemployment rate among new graduates was rising. The disproportionate share of graduates among the unemployed suggests a mismatch between the skills being produced and the skills in demand, pointing to inefficiencies in the skill delivery system in responding to labour market signals (World Bank, 2013).

Despite the consistent emphasis in Malaysia's development plans on the need to improve the quality of education, this important outcome seems to remain elusive. How can the education system produce more innovative students with the requisite analytical skills? Comparisons with benchmark countries suggest that there is a need to improve inputs, including government policy and practices for standards, as well as to increase the efficiency of resource use, develop the curriculum, and boost the capacity of the education workforce. The quality of teachers, especially of those teaching science and mathematics in rural and semi-rural areas—long a target of reform—is a key constraint. While primary and secondary pupil–teacher ratios have improved considerably (Table 3.2), helped in recent years by declining numbers of new school entrants, the recruitment of teachers from among high-quality graduates with skills in science, mathematics, and English remains an ongoing challenge, particularly against the backdrop of the compelling social and economic case for continuing to encourage higher enrolment in tertiary education (Box 3.6).

Box 3.6 High rates of return to schooling

The skills acquired at school are influential throughout the course of life, and are reflected in both non-monetary and monetary returns to schooling for individuals. Non-monetary returns include healthier decisions about the timing of marriage, better parenting, more positive attitudes towards health, and greater civic participation. Monetary—or economic—returns to education are also important for individuals and for governments in making decisions on the length of schooling. For example, both individuals and governments will need to consider by how much income can be expected to rise as a result of one additional year of formal schooling.

The following returns to schooling estimates, based on the individual records in Malaysia's 2004 and 2016 Household Income Surveys, are obtained from an income equation estimated by Heckman's 'maximum likelihood method', which corrects for sample selection bias (Heckman, 1979).[52] The income of individuals is assumed to be a function of work experience (and its square to allow for a non-linear effect) and the

52 The decision to work or 'selection' equation had the following determinants: age, age-squared, years of education, number of children in the household, the individual's marital status, and other household income.

level of schooling. The returns to schooling at different levels are obtained through the inclusion of dummy (0/1) variables for lower-secondary schooling (Forms 1–3), upper-secondary schooling (Forms 4 and 5), Form 6, and tertiary education. Primary schooling is universal, so only the rates of returns for schooling above this level are estimated. Primary schooling is assumed to cover the first six years of schooling. Lower-secondary schooling covers a further three years of education, upper-secondary another two years, Form 6 an additional two years, and tertiary education three more years.

Box Table 3.2 presents the results of the analysis. The rates of return are all statistically significant (the null hypothesis that they are zero is rejected) and they are also significantly different from each other. The returns are based on the assumption that education is free and that students earn nothing while at school. The return to the individual is the income earned as a result of one more year of schooling expressed as a percentage of the opportunity cost of the schooling—the income forgone during the extra schooling.

The rates of return to schooling at upper-secondary level are all above those at lower-secondary level. The returns from completing two further years in Form 6 are below those for Forms 4 and 5. The returns to tertiary schooling are the highest of all for males. For females, whereas in 2004 the gains were greatest for those with upper-secondary education, in 2016 they were much the same for those with tertiary and upper-secondary education. This pattern held in analysis for the different ethnic communities. The results support a decision to continue in education beyond secondary level, although the returns will vary markedly depending on the course of study. They are consistent with international experience that more educated individuals earn higher wages.

Education can therefore be taken as an investment of earnings forgone—the opportunity cost of not starting work earlier.

Box Table 3.2 Rates of return to schooling are beneficial to males and females

Level of schooling	Marginal returns (2004)		Marginal returns (2016)	
	Males	Females	Males	Females
Lower secondary (Forms 1–3)	9.511 (0.456)	8.856 (0.807)	2.001 (0.411)	7.404 (0.709)
Upper secondary (Forms 4–5)	14.607 (0.569)	18.802 (0.964)	12.145 (0.438)	23.024 (0.803)
Form 6	10.949 (1.284)	6.654 (0.146)	8.892 (0.839)	11.969 (0.853)
Tertiary	20.904 (0.952)	14.470 (1.032)	19.390 (0.580)	22.795 (0.564)
Sample size	46,550	47,274	108,629	111,493

Source of data: Derived from unpublished data from the Household Income Surveys of 2004 and 2016, supplied by the Department of Statistics–Malaysia.

Note: Numbers in ( ) are robust standard errors.

The Challenge of Innovation

Innovation—an important driver of economic growth—has traditionally been defined in terms of the successful exploitation of new ideas (World Bank, 2010). In an innovation-led economy, competitiveness depends on how science, technology, and engineering are integrated into the production process. More recently, there has been a growing recognition that innovation goes beyond R&D to encompass new processes in production, new marketing methods, and new organizational methods in business practices, workplace organization, and external relations (OECD/Eurostat, 2005).

Innovation may contribute to economic growth in three different ways: through technological progress, through investment in intangible capital, and through increases in multifactor productivity.[53] These three components combined are estimated to account for about half of economic growth in OECD countries over the period 1995–2013 (OECD, 2015). As well as driving growth directly in this way, Stiglitz and Greenwald (2015) contend that a learning or innovative society can also increase the rate of growth over a sustained period beyond what could be achieved with a one-time increase in allocative efficiency or an increase in the savings rate.

While innovation is critical to long-term output growth, it is also susceptible to market failure. The high costs of R&D and certain other fixed expenditures, the lack of insurance for risky investments, and imperfect design protection systems are all deterrents to investment in innovation (Greenhalgh and Rogers, 2010). Market structure is another factor that helps to determine whether innovation succeeds or fails, with some scholars arguing in favour of more monopolistic and oligopolistic structures, and others for greater competition. While there is general acceptance of the role of intellectual property rights in incentivizing innovation, moreover, some view the World Trade Organization's Agreement on Trade-Related Aspects of Intellectual Property Rights (TRIPS), which governs all member economies, as serving to impede knowledge diffusion, and to disadvantage developing economies (Baker et al., 2017).

So, how innovative is Malaysia? Answers to this question are mixed. The Report of the New Economic Model for Malaysia, Part 1 (NEAC, 2010) suggests that sluggish economic growth was a result of insufficient innovation and creativity, among other factors. The implication is that, despite government intentions and programme interventions to create a science and technology culture and societal orientation, Malaysians are still not innovative and creative enough. Indeed, the country's productivity growth has been modest (Chapter 6), and it scores unsatisfactorily on various science and technology

53 Multifactor productivity includes non-technological innovation, spillover effects, and efficiency improvements. See Chapter 6 for an analysis of Malaysia's total factor productivity growth.

indicators, including research output, researchers per capita, expenditure on R&D as a share of GDP, and quality of human capital.

Using the overall rankings given in the Global Innovation Index for the years 2010 to 2014, Rasiah and Yap (2015) conclude that Malaysia's innovation performance did stand out in some ways compared with its fellow middle-income countries. This was particularly true in the area of innovation inputs and outputs, business financing of innovation, and market and business sophistication. The country had not performed so well in other areas, however, including innovation efficiency, linkages between government R&D institutions and private firms, and the commercialization of research results. These weaknesses have made Malaysia a net importer of foreign technology and services, as reflected in the chronic intellectual property deficit in royalty and licensing fees and payments (Rasiah, 2018 and 2019).

In a review of innovation in Malaysia, the OECD commended recent policy efforts to promote innovation-led growth, but also highlighted several key weaknesses. These included the skills mismatch and shortcomings in education, low R&D and innovation capacity in domestic firms and small and medium-sized enterprises, and disparities in research capacity and performance in public research institutes and universities (OECD, 2017).

Concerns about the quality of the country's human capital pervade all analyses of Malaysia's lack of an innovation culture. The country has reached the point in its economic development where it must innovate rapidly and widely in order to continue to grow. The question is whether it has sufficient capacity and the high-quality human capital needed to achieve the necessary level of innovation, especially given the long-running net emigration of talented individuals.

The education system requires further reform in order to gear it more effectively towards training students in the necessary cognitive and non-cognitive skills, while also imparting other hard skills and knowledge. Advanced cognitive skills such as complex problem-solving, sociobehavioural skills such as teamwork, and adaptability skills that include reasoning and self-efficacy are some of the main types of skills needed to succeed in a world of increasing innovation (World Bank, 2019). In its 2016 review of innovation policy, the OECD (2017) suggests that the quality of Malaysia's universities needs to improve so that they can contribute to research and innovation, and produce skilled graduates who will better meet the needs of industry. The evidence shows that, while the number of researchers and R&D outputs have both increased impressively, this has not translated into high-quality innovative products with global impact.

University rankings, based on academic research and a broad range of other criteria, are a widely used measure of institutional excellence. The

University of Malaya—the country's oldest university—has risen in some rankings in recent years, indicating institutional improvements of the kind the OECD is targeting. For example, the university has steadily improved its position in the overall Quacquarelli Symonds ranking from 151 in 2014/2015 to 87 in 2018/2019, and it has risen in the area of academic performance over the same period from 276 to 234. By comparison, the university's position was in the range of 301–350 in the Times Higher Education rankings, and in the range of 301–400 in the Academic Ranking of World Universities in 2018. In the Times Higher Education Emerging Economies University rankings, the university improved its position from 27th out of 378 universities in 2018 to 18th out of 444 universities in 2019.

Higher rankings serve to enhance national and international prestige, and therefore help to attract higher-quality students and faculty, which in turn can lead to better academic performance and research outputs. However, Dzulkifli Abdul Razak et al. (2019) have articulated concerns that ranking systems may be opaque and unrepresentative, often rewarding research excellence while not fully recognizing the equally significant activities of teaching and learning, and community engagement. Rankings remain important indicators of institutional success, but they may not always tell the whole story.

Lee and Nagaraj (2012) note that public expenditure per student in higher education is greater in Malaysia than in Singapore—although the trend has reversed since 2012 when measured in purchasing parity terms.[54] Public expenditure on higher education as a share of total public spending on education in Malaysia continues to exceed that in Singapore. Even so, the National University of Singapore and the Nanyang Technological University are among the top universities in all the ranking lists, suggesting that Malaysia should expect better returns on its investment in education.

The Brain Drain

A technology-driven, diversified economy has to recruit and retain top-quality talent (NEAC, 2010). Yet Malaysia has continued to suffer a net outflow of highly educated Malaysians for multiple reasons, including the shortcomings of the education system (Chapters 2 and 7). This cumulative brain drain was estimated at somewhere between 280,000 and 455,000 in 2010 (Foo, 2011; World Bank, 2011a), and had almost certainly increased to around 500,000 by 2015 if it is assumed that nearly one-third of Malaysians living abroad have received tertiary level education (Chapter 2). The country's talent loss

54 Based on data on government expenditure on tertiary education in purchasing power parity obtained from UNESCO, and the numbers of students in tertiary education obtained from the Department of Statistics–Malaysia and the Department of Statistics–Singapore.

represents a very large proportion of its tertiary-educated labour force, while the skill selectivity of these emigrants magnifies the human capital impact.

In 2015, among all of Malaysia's skilled emigrants, including talented medical and university professionals, more than four-fifths were living in Singapore, Australia, the UK, and the US. Singapore is the destination for almost half of Malaysia's total brain drain.[55] Its proximity to Malaysia, its similarities in culture and climate, and its higher real incomes, along with attractive non-financial aspects of living and working, are major pull factors for both low- and high-skilled workers.

Data from the United Nations Educational, Scientific and Cultural Organization's Global Flow in Tertiary-level Students suggest that Malaysia's brain drain to the US and UK has increased since 2010, while that to Australia has declined. The number of Malaysian students studying in the US and the UK grew by about 5–6 per cent each year between 2011 and 2015 (Figure 3.12). Many Malaysians develop attachments and set down roots in their host countries during their student years, with a strong likelihood of staying on after they complete their studies.

Figure 3.12 **The number of Malaysian tertiary students studying overseas is increasing (selected countries)**

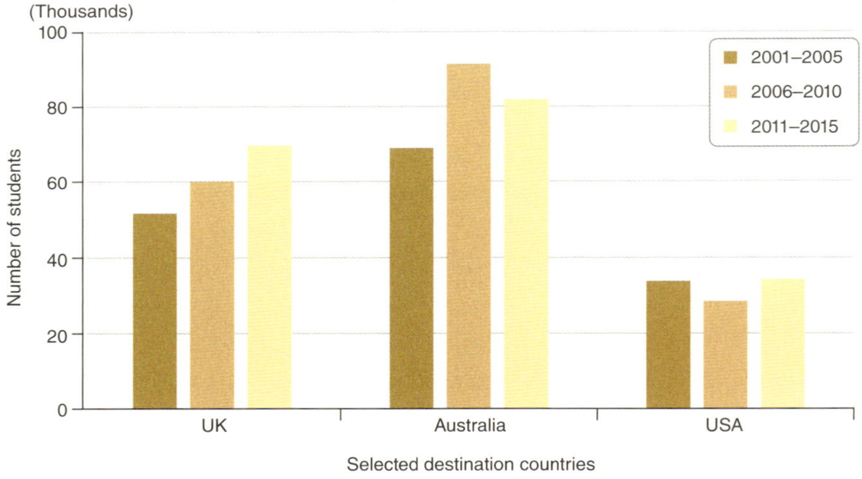

Source of data: United Nations Educational, Scientific and Cultural Organization (2018a).

Although emigration is a worldwide phenomenon and is an important source of remittances for many countries, it is probable that in Malaysia's case this huge loss of talent has held back national development aspirations.

55 Reflecting the talent loss from Malaysia to Singapore, in 2005 some 10.8 per cent of faculty at the National University of Singapore were from Malaysia, although this was down from 12.8 per cent in 1997 (Mukherjee and Wong, 2011).

Conclusions

Before World War II, the education system in the Malay peninsula was, like the occupational structure, highly segmented. It was largely rudimentary, with different management systems and curricula for different types of schools. Mirroring the spatial pattern of uneven economic development on the peninsula, access to education progressed fastest in the Straits Settlements, followed by the Federated Malay States, and was least advanced in the Unfederated Malay States, as well as in Sabah and Sarawak. Except for children from elite and privileged families, there were few educational opportunities beyond basic primary level. The colonial government did not prioritize education in support of development. It provided funds for English-medium schools for the elite, limited resources for Malay vernacular schools, and minimal support for Indian and Chinese schools, thus leaving most of the population illiterate.

During the period of gradual decolonization after the end of World War II, and especially after independence, Malaysia's education system began to undergo fundamental changes. Educational opportunities progressively expanded, eventually offering wide access to all levels of education. A more integrated school system gradually emerged, with the Malay language serving as a unifying medium of instruction until the end of secondary level. The aims of education policy were to support nation-building, ensure equity, and meet the country's changing human resource needs to drive economic growth. Even as progress was being made, however, the continued segmentation of primary schooling between national schools and national-type schools (Chinese and Tamil) served to reinforce ethnic and cultural identities, and to perpetuate the segregation that had characterized colonial Malaya.

Malaysia has established an increasingly diversified base of higher education and training institutions, which provides multiple post-secondary pathways for students with different abilities and interests, and which aims to cater for the changing needs of the economy and the labour market. An *equitable* higher education system, however, also needs to ensure that all qualified students have access to higher learning opportunities, and that all are effectively supported to make a successful transition from school to gainful employment. Equally, universities and colleges must ensure that students who are admitted are able to follow the curriculum and graduate. Affirmative action policies that were designed to rectify historical injustices and to restructure society, while successful in increasing the access of Malays and other *Bumiputera* to higher levels of education through a quota system and scholarships, and in creating a new middle class (Chapter 9), have also had serious negative impacts for talented non-Malay students and academics.

One such impact is the brain drain. Many non-Malays, crowded out of public universities, have left the country to study abroad, often never returning to work in Malaysia, resulting in an unaffordable loss of talent. The more relaxed standards of entry qualifications may well have affected the quality of graduate output. The country must improve its productivity, and the issue of educational quality is central to that objective.

Despite highly positive trends in indicators of literacy, educational attainment, and enrolment in the six decades since independence, the quality of education has not reached the expected or desired standards as measured by international student assessments and by labour market outcomes. Malaysia lags behind its international comparators despite the government's substantial and sustained spending on education, especially at higher levels. High-quality education is vital for building human capital, which is in turn the bedrock of innovation, and policy appraisals have led to new reform initiatives and renewed commitment in this area. The imperative of educating schoolchildren more effectively in cognitive and non-cognitive skills to boost productivity and innovation is now widely recognized—if not as yet widely implemented—and this area will remain a high priority in education policy, including through partnerships with the private sector.

The policy of increasing private sector involvement in higher education, while helping to equalize ethnic pathways towards post-secondary qualifications, build a larger stock of higher-quality human capital, and reduce government expenditure, must be very carefully managed. The risk is that a newly segmented system of higher education will become entrenched: for the majority of Malays, a scholarship-supported public sector and private universities owned by government-linked companies, often with Malay as the medium of instruction; and for non-Malays, fee-paying private universities with English as the medium of instruction. Such a system is unlikely to support labour market objectives. Neither will it help to promote national solidarity nor strengthen inclusiveness among the country's diverse ethnic communities.

In health and demographic outcomes, too, despite the huge advances made in the post–World War II period, some differences remain between rural and urban areas, and among ethnic groups. These issues are now analysed in Chapter 4.

Chapter 4

Increasing Well-being

Malaysia has been transformed from an impoverished, highly unequal, and disease-ridden society to a relatively healthy one with an upper-middle-income economy. During the colonial era, most people were illiterate and lived in insanitary conditions in rural areas without basic amenities. Early measures undertaken by the colonial government to improve health were confined to urban areas, and were motivated mainly by the devastating impact of infectious diseases on the labour force and the disruption this caused to the economy.

After decades of neglect of the population's well-being, massive investments were made in physical and social infrastructure, as well as in education and health.[1] This radical transformation started in the late colonial period, gathered pace in the 1950s and 1960s, and accelerated further in the 1970s. This development was in line with the country's rapid economic progression from rural subsistence and estate agriculture to modern urban services and manufacturing employment. With the expansion of public health services in urban and rural areas, people began living much longer and the diseases of poverty, such as malaria and tuberculosis, which were prevalent in the past, have gradually been replaced by diseases of affluence, such as cardiovascular diseases and cancers, which are now the leading causes of ill health and death.

In the decades before World War II, epidemics were common and public health measures were limited. Infant and child mortality rates were very high—with perhaps 20–25 per cent of babies dying in their first year—and families had many children to compensate. After World War II, as socio-economic conditions and health services improved, and levels of urbanization steadily increased, mortality rates tumbled. The chances of child survival

1 In this chapter the concept of well-being is defined simply in terms of health and prosperity. It is recognized, however, that well-being has several elements and can be more broadly defined in terms of multiple indicators, including safety and security, voice and freedoms, social capital, and happiness (see Stiglitz et al., 2010, and Deaton, 2013).

grew, and family size started to decline towards the lower levels of more industrialized countries. Better-educated mothers, with fewer children to take care of, increasingly found greater job opportunities outside the home, and contributed directly to the country's rapid economic growth.

How did Malaysia's health and fertility transitions come about? How did these transitions improve the well-being of the country's people? And what were their economic implications for employment—in particular for female labour force participation, workplace productivity, and higher earnings?

This chapter examines these trends and questions, taking into account the links between health and fertility, and Malaysia's demographic transition. It shows that significant changes in public policy, with huge investments in sanitation and health, along with improvements in living standards, led to sharp and sustained gains in human well-being.

The first of four sections examines how Malaya's health policy evolved in response to the needs of colonial economic development, and how this widened the existing gaps in well-being between those living in towns and those living in rural areas. The second section reviews the changes in health policy after independence and examines how these led to dramatic reductions in mortality rates.

The third section provides an overview of Malaysia's demographic transition, and assesses the two-way relationship between changes in fertility and female labour force participation, as well as the impact of fertility decline on the population's well-being. The final section shows how the country's fertility transition has shifted the population's age composition, and considers the opportunities this has created for the economy to benefit from a demographic dividend (Chapter 6).

Health and Development in Colonial Malaya

Until around the middle of the 20th century, the majority of Malaya's rural population were impoverished landless *padi* farmers, agricultural labourers, and fishermen, producing barely enough to meet their basic needs. Although the colonial economy grew rapidly from around 1880 up to 1930, the benefits of this growth were enjoyed disproportionately by the British agency houses and the local capitalist class (Chapter 5).

Those in rural areas experienced very few changes in living standards or available technologies, and were largely bypassed by this economic development. Education was minimal, social protection non-existent, and life for most people was very insecure, with high vulnerability to undernourishment, deprivation, and largely unavoidable infectious diseases (Box 4.1). Inadequate diet took a heavy toll, especially on the very young, and life was short, with high rates of morbidity. Rural households were caught in a cycle of poverty from which British colonial policies offered no escape. A demographic trap also operated (Sachs, 2005) in which families had many children to compensate for the high mortality rates, but could not invest sufficiently in their nutrition and health. In this way, the high fertility rates in one generation impoverished the children of the next, creating vicious cycles of poverty.

Urban areas had a very different experience which was also challenging in its own way. Towns at the centre of commerce and industry grew rapidly, with large inflows of migrant workers from China, India, and the Dutch East Indies. These migrant workers were brought in to support colonial economic development, especially of tin mines and rubber plantations, and to build rail and road infrastructure (Chapter 2). Many of these new migrants settled at first in makeshift shelters on town fringes, where clean water, safe sanitation, and health-care facilities were either minimal or non-existent. Serious infectious diseases, especially malaria and tuberculosis, spread quickly in these overcrowded, poorly ventilated, and insanitary housing conditions. International migration also brought with it the cross-border transmission of diseases. Large numbers of migrant workers died before they could return home.

Most people in the peninsula relied on traditional medicine to address ailments and sicknesses. Such medicine was based on folklore, beliefs, and customs, combining a number of Hindu and Islamic practices and traditional Arab treatments (Abdul Majid Ismail, 1974; Gullick, 1987).[2] The early Chinese and Indian migrants had their own ethnic medicines and medical practitioners. Traditional medicine contributed to the health care of the Malay and migrant populations without burdening the British administration with additional costs.[3] As the Straits Settlements of Penang, Melaka, and Singapore came under British colonial control, small medical centres were established, based on concepts of Western medicine, primarily to provide medical treatment for Europeans.

After the Pangkor Engagement in 1874, the accelerated growth of the tin and rubber industries, along with infrastructure development, were the key

---

2 This traditional medicine has been described as a blend of ancient folklore, Hindu mythology, Muslim orthodoxy, and Arabic pharmacopoeia (Abdul Majid Ismail, 1974). Largely Malay, the practitioners consisted of the *pawang* (priest or religious healer), the *bomoh* (medicine man), the *bidan* (midwife), and the *mudim* (barber-surgeon).

3 Later, when Western medicine began to take hold, Malays were at first reluctant to seek treatment in hospitals, although medicines were provided to the *penghulu* (village chiefs) to distribute to the villagers, including vaccinations for smallpox.

drivers of colonial health policy. Large areas of jungle were opened up for these new activities, exacerbating vulnerability to malaria by multiplying the number of mosquito breeding grounds close to human settlements. In the late 19th and early 20th centuries, the incidence of malaria and beriberi soared, causing very high death rates of migrant workers.[4] The loss of these workers, who dominated the labour force, began to seriously undermine the project to expand the Malayan economy. A more interventionist colonial health strategy became imperative.

This strategy essentially comprised introducing sanitary boards under the municipal authorities to improve disease prevention; establishing a network of hospitals and public health programmes under the Medical Department; encouraging medical research into the causes of infectious diseases; and training doctors and other health personnel.

Box 4.1 Infectious and non-infectious diseases in colonial Malaya

Colonial economic expansion in Malaya was accompanied by the massive opening up of land, especially for plantations and tin mines. Much of this land was thick equatorial jungle, often with many swamps. The influx of migrant labour put great strains on living and health conditions in the rapidly growing towns and estates, many of which lacked sanitation and sewage facilities, creating conditions conducive to the spread of infectious diseases.

Malaria: Caused by a protozoan parasite and transmitted by the Anopheles mosquito, malaria was the most devastating infectious disease and affected individuals of all ages. The entire Malay peninsula was intensely malarial. Deaths from malaria rose steeply due to the start of new economic activities, such as the clearing of jungle lands for rubber cultivation. Malaria alone accounted for about 30 per cent of hospital cases between 1900 and 1940 (Manderson, 1996), and was the leading cause of death among migrants.[5]

As the breeding grounds of the Anopheles mosquito—swamps, marshes, and watercourses—were found in rural and urban areas alike, malaria control measures were undertaken in both settings, initially in Klang and Port Swettenham (Watson, 1921). These mainly comprised environmental measures to reduce the risk of transmission, such as draining and filling up swampy grounds, and oiling stagnant water pools. Drainage was handled by the urban sanitary boards, along with sanitation and hygiene, while the Malaria Advisory Board focused on overall environmental control.

---

4 In the early months after Port Swettenham (now Port Klang) was opened in September 1901, 'malaria had so disorganised the working of the port that ships refused to call at it, crews refused to join ships which did call at it, and the Governor, Sir Frank Swettenham ordered its closure by telegram' (Archive document CO 865/54, 1943–1944, p. 40).

5 Apart from hospital records, there are no reliable data on annual numbers of deaths by cause. Deaths in rural areas, especially of infants and young children, were seriously under-reported, and of those that were registered, the causes of death were often missing or vague.

Tuberculosis: An infectious bacterial airborne disease, tuberculosis was widespread in areas where people lived in overcrowded, poorly ventilated, and insanitary housing conditions, but affected all communities. Tamil labourers on rubber estates, where the incidence of malaria was high and where living conditions were insanitary and crowded, were especially susceptible. Tuberculosis also affected Chinese workers, especially opium smokers, who lived in cramped and insanitary conditions, whether in towns or in mining shacks. Early control measures included barring people with tuberculosis from working in occupations related to food handling and personal services, as well as health education campaigns and active case detection.

Beriberi: A non-infectious disease caused by vitamin deficiency, beriberi was associated with a limited diet of polished rice and a lack of vegetables, and was common among Chinese. The high incidence decimated large sections of the workforce.

Hookworm: A parasite that lodges itself in the intestines and then feeds on the blood of the victim resulting in anaemia, hookworm was common among plantation workers, especially where latrine conditions were poor.

Leprosy: Another serious contagious bacterial disease, leprosy mainly affects the skin and peripheral nerves. The number of persons affected by leprosy increased steadily in the early decades of the 20th century; some 4,600 were being treated in leper settlements in 1939 (Archive document CO 273/662/5, 1940).

Other common infectious diseases: These included smallpox and waterborne diseases such as cholera, dysentery, and diarrhoea, and sexually transmitted diseases.

Sanitary Boards

By the late 19th century, it was increasingly recognized that unclean water and other insanitary conditions were responsible for the transmission of common diseases and high mortality rates. The colonial authorities started to introduce sanitary and preventive public health measures, first in the Straits Settlements and later in the Federated Malay States, with the aim of improving public hygiene and maintaining healthy living environments. They educated the public about the importance of clean water, good hygiene, and safe drainage.

Municipal sanitation services were established under the umbrella of municipal councils in the Straits Settlements, and as separate sanitation boards in the Federated Malay States.[6] They progressively introduced services designed to benefit the health of the entire urban population, including safe water supply, drainage maintenance, street cleaning and lighting, and sewage removal. They also required people to keep their residences clean. Sanitary boards helped to improve town governance, and began to tackle the long-standing health and

6 The first sanitary board was approved by the Selangor State Council in 1890, with others being formed a few years later in Perak and elsewhere in the Federated Malay States (Hairudin Harun, 2017).

hygiene issues in towns and large villages. Similar bodies, known as rural boards, were gradually created to run rural areas under district officers (South, 1946; Kennedy, 1962; Yeoh, 1993).

Apart from in Johor, there was very limited progress in implementing any of these sanitation and public health measures in the Unfederated Malay States, where both economic development and investment in health lagged behind. Insanitary conditions and a lack of public health measures resulted in frequent epidemics of smallpox and cholera, which often decimated whole villages (Dodge, 1980). Other common afflictions of the populations of these less-developed states were pneumonia, hookworm, malaria, dysentery, and other waterborne diseases. Death rates were very high at every age, and especially during infancy, which acted as a check on the natural increase of the population—the difference between the birth and death rates.

The Medical Department and the Expansion of Public Health

The Medical Department, first established in Penang in 1826 to cover the Straits Settlements[7] (and, much later, the Federated Malay States), was led by a principal medical officer headquartered in Kuala Lumpur. It had three main branches: Laboratories, Health, and Hospitals. The department's anti-malaria activities were carried out by the Health Branch and a Malaria Advisory Board, and included investigation, prevention, and cure of the disease; educating the public; and auditing employers, who were required by law to protect their workers' health. District-level medical or health officers were supported by their district officers, who, guided by standing orders, coordinated public programmes for health and sanitation that were implemented by mobilizing community resources.[8]

The 1918 influenza pandemic, which caused a sharp increase in mortality in the peninsula, had a major impact on Malaya's health policy. The pandemic reached Southeast Asia in June of that year, spreading rapidly from Singapore and Penang to the rest of the peninsula and North Borneo (Lee et al., 2009). By October, the virus had mutated into a more virulent strain that claimed the lives of an estimated 35,000 people in Malaya. As public health services were overwhelmed, medicines were commonly distributed by village headmen, schoolteachers, and local police. However, both Western medicine and traditional remedies were ineffective. The pandemic hit the Malayan economy hard, bringing work on many rubber estates to a standstill and affecting

7 In 1835, the headquarters of the Medical Department was transferred from Penang to Singapore.

8 By the beginning of the 20th century, vaccinations and immunization programmes for children against smallpox and diphtheria were gradually being introduced, starting in urban areas.

workers in the mines.[9] As a consequence, the following decade would see elevated awareness of the importance of health and medical infrastructure, as well as greater official interest. One response was to move to more centralized (and more international) disease information networks.

In 1920, a new public health policy was announced by the Governor of the Straits Settlements and High Commissioner of the Federated Malay States, Lawrence Guillemard. With the aim of providing a more comprehensive system of health-care delivery, and of implementing more effective coordination, the medical and sanitary services were reorganized under a single authority, the Director of Medical and Sanitary Services, to whom both the curative and preventive branches of the medical service would report (Phua, 1990).

Sexually transmitted diseases, which were widespread, were another major health issue, with the very high male-to-female sex ratio among the migrant population encouraging prostitution.[10] A record of hospital in-patients' deaths by major diseases for the Straits Settlements for 1920–1924 shows that sexually transmitted diseases were a common cause of death (Wellington, 1926). By the 1920s, the governments of the Straits Settlements and the Federated Malay States had established clinics and dispensaries, and offered free hospital treatment, as well as education on the health risks of prostitution.

But it was the high incidence of malaria—the principal cause of early death during the first half of the 20th century—that was the major concern on account of its impact on the labour force (Box 4.2).[11] The public and private sectors joined forces to try to eradicate the disease, including government medical officers, medical officers employed by commercial companies, entomologists, and engineers. The most effective prevention methods at that time were filling in mosquito breeding grounds, building concrete drains, clearing vegetation, and felling trees. 'Composite boards' were set up for organizing and coordinating anti-malaria work, including the Malaria Advisory Board, mosquito destruction boards, sanitary boards, and the Public Health Education Committee (Wellington, 1926, p. 16).

9 In Perak, the pandemic caused at least 10,000 deaths, and perhaps many more, as death certification was poor at the time (Watson, 1919). In Negeri Sembilan, the death toll from influenza exceeded 4,000, and in Selangor, deaths increased by some 7,000 in 1918 compared with 1917 (Lemon, 1919; Broaderick, 1919).

10 Prostitution increased in the Malay peninsula after the arrival of migrants. Tan, L. E. (2001) mentions that young girls were bought, kidnapped, or tricked by syndicates and employers of male workers. In 1889, there were 3,673 registered prostitutes out of a Chinese female population of less than 30,000. Many Japanese prostitutes were also brought to the Straits Settlements. A Contagious Disease Ordinance was passed in the Straits Settlements with the aim of containing prostitution and infectious diseases, but was repealed in 1888 and replaced by the Protection of Women and Girls Ordinance, 1889 (Mudeliar et al., 1983).

11 Malaria deaths surged to epidemic levels in 1926 and 1927 following a rise in normal water levels over large tracts of the Federated Malay States. This was due to abnormal flooding which increased the number of mosquito breeding areas (Federated Malay States, 1927).

The growth of Malaya's public health-care sector was not the result of any colonial vision of social development. Public health-care measures were introduced to address the widespread incidence of contagious diseases, such as malaria and other diseases of poverty, which would otherwise have decimated the population of migrant workers.[12] Concern that ill health could directly weaken the colonial administration and the economy was thus the main driver behind the expansion of public health programmes and facilities for those living in urban areas. The rural population benefited from few such measures.

Box 4.2 Malaria and economic development

Lim (1967) analyses the relationship between disease and economic development for the period 1891–1955, using data on malaria hospital admissions and changes in the area of land planted with rubber in the Federated Malay States.[13] The incidence of malaria went through three phases.

The first phase, from 1870 to 1900, saw rapid growth of the tin industry, early plantation development, and the start of infrastructure development.[14] During this period, the incidence of malaria was relatively high, as the clearing of jungles exposed workers to malaria-carrying mosquitoes. During the second phase, from 1900 to 1940, with the further expansion of economic activities, the rise of the rubber industry, the consolidation of the tin industry, and the extension of railway and road networks, there was an upsurge in malarial incidence. This was positively correlated with the growth of rubber acreage. For the third phase, from 1947 to 1955, when jungle clearing was less intensive, malarial incidence declined. This was also a period when greater efforts were being made by the health authorities to keep malaria under control.

Hospitals, Research, and Training

The last quarter of the 19th century witnessed the appearance of several hospitals intended to provide curative health services to stem the loss of workers from disease outbreaks, especially of malaria and tuberculosis. Hospitals were among the first government buildings constructed, and their

12 Rudimentary health-care infrastructure was first established in the major Straits Settlement towns of Penang, Melaka, and Singapore, including general hospitals, and medical facilities for districts, prisons, and paupers. Funded by philanthropic and public contributions, the early hospitals, like paupers' hospitals and lunatic asylums, served essentially as 'houses of death' and sanctuaries for poor migrants. These health facilities were poorly staffed and the services they provided were very basic (Phua, 1990; Manderson, 1996).

13 The relationship between land clearance and incidence of malaria can be traced back even earlier, as it was during the 1870s that the tin industry started to grow rapidly and the peninsula's jungle hinterlands were first opened up for economic development.

14 Especially the construction of the railway network and cart roads.

upkeep was one of the heaviest charges on state revenue (Swettenham, 1906).[15] As economic activity expanded and as sickness increased—threatening economic development—a broader network of government-sponsored health facilities emerged.

By 1910, Perak had 15 hospitals, Selangor 14, Negeri Sembilan three, and Pahang two. Hospitals were often located in large tin-mining towns. There were also Chinese-funded private hospitals that catered largely to the urban Chinese population.[16] The first urban hospitals primarily for Malays were established in Kuala Kangsar from 1908 (Hairudin Harun, 2017). On rubber estates, plantation owners were made responsible for providing health services to their workers (Box 4.3).

Box 4.3 Health care in Malaya's rubber plantations

The health of plantation workers was critical, given the labour intensity of estate cultivation. The growth and profitability of rubber plantations in the early 20th century were dependent on a steady supply of Tamil labourers from southern India, most of whom came to Malaya to escape drought, famine, and poverty (Hagan and Wells, 2005).

However, their new life as plantation workers was also one of misery (Liew, 2010). Working and living conditions were harsh and unhealthy, resulting in high death rates. A major killer was malaria, which was 'hyper endemic to the Malayan jungle, unlike in southern India, so Tamil migrant workers had little natural immunity to it' (Amrith, 2014, p. 1,569). Plantation workers faced other health risks, such as cholera, diarrhoea, and dysentery, as well as infectious diseases like tuberculosis that arose because of poor sanitation and hygiene, and overcrowded living conditions. Many estates were cramped, lacking potable water, latrines, and rubbish disposal. Workers also suffered from poor nutrition, which complicated existing infections and lowered their resistance (Manderson, 1996). The colonial government did not have experience or knowledge of these infectious diseases, and, as a consequence, huge numbers of workers died (Parmer, 1990).

The onus of caring for the health of plantation workers was put on plantation owners themselves. The Indian Immigration Enactment of 1904 required estates to provide basic welfare and medical facilities for their workers, especially if government hospitals were unavailable nearby. The 1911 Estate Labourers' Ordinance further tightened the legal requirements, specifying stringent sanitary and space criteria (Chang, 2001). It was compulsory to have hospital accommodation (with four beds to every 100 workers), a dresser (or nurse), and essential medicines in stock.

---

15 In 1880, the first hospital was built in Taiping, supported jointly by Chinese mining *towkays* and the new colonial government, with voluntary contributions from mineworkers. About a decade later, the Ipoh Hospital was established. In 1889, a hospital for paupers was set up on the site of the present-day Kuala Lumpur General Hospital.

16 These included the Lam Wah Ee hospital in Penang, and the Tung Shin hospital in Kuala Lumpur. The first private maternity hospital was established in Perak in 1904.

While most estates complied with the legal requirements to provide basic health facilities, these often consisted of only a shack and a compounder (of medicines), although some estates did have slightly better-equipped hospitals. A few estates also employed private medical practitioners to make periodic health inspections of their workers (Liew, 2010).

In 1924, a Commission on Estate Health was appointed, which in 1925 reported that on European-owned estates health measures and services were minimal, and that Asiatic holdings provided no health services at all. Out of 1,304 estates of 100 acres or more, only 167 had hospitals: these were poorly equipped, and in half of them the person in charge had no medical qualifications. Only two of the hospitals had resident doctors, while a third was served by visiting private doctors.

The Commission called for a comprehensive health and medical scheme, and a health board to oversee implementation, to be paid for out of a tax on estates above 25 acres. This was met with strong opposition from the Rubber Growers' Association and Planters' Association of Malaya because of the exemption of smallholdings of 25 acres and below, and of mining properties. As a result, an amended Health Boards Enactment was passed, but its implementation was postponed and later cancelled because of the Great Depression.

In Sarawak, the situation was dismal. Medical care had been neglected. At the end of the Brooke administration in 1941, there were only two hospitals—in Kuching and in Sibu—and these had a combined capacity of only 300 beds (Kaur, 1995). North Borneo fared better and was said to be the 'most well doctored country in the world' in the 1920s, considering its size, population, and transport facilities (CO 874/1012, 1925, p. 13). In 1925, it had a Medical Department with a principal medical officer, four district surgeons, one assistant surgeon, two nurse-matrons, and one nursing sister. There were 15 doctors comprising full-time, part-time, and estate doctors, two government hospitals, and multiple dispensaries servicing out-of-town districts. All estates had their own hospitals, and under the 1936 labour legislation all labourers were entitled to medical care and hospitalization, with the employer bearing the cost.

State hospitals were funded out of state revenues, managed by British government officers, and their medical staff included European and locally recruited medical officers and nurses (Kennedy, 1962). Perak pioneered travelling dispensaries to provide health services for miners. As mines expanded further from the hospitals, European and Chinese owners had to buy ambulance carts to transport workers to them (Khoo and Abdur-Razzaq Lubis, 2005). Yet even by the 1930s the hospitals were far from sanitary, and they were not safe from cross-infection. In 1931, a report highlighted the appalling conditions in the General Hospital in Kuala Lumpur, including those in the wards and operating theatre, and concluded that 'so unsatisfactory did we find conditions to be that we have had to restrain ourselves from saying harder and sterner things' (CO 717/84/5, 1931, p. 27).

At the turn of the 20th century, malaria and beriberi were the greatest health concerns and the biggest constraints on economic development, given the heavy toll they took on the labour force. In 1901, the Institute for Medical Research was opened to improve the health status of the population.[17] Plans for the institute originated in recommendations by Swettenham, then Resident-General of the Federated Malay States, for the establishment of a pathological institute in Malaya to 'carry out scientific and sustained research into the causes, treatment and prevention of such scourges as beriberi and all forms of malarial fevers' (Institute for Medical Research, 2018). Research conducted by the institute played a role in helping to contain and reduce tropical diseases; for example, it established that beriberi was diet-related and could be prevented by replacing polished rice with parboiled rice (Cheah and Ong, 2005).

In 1905, the colonial government established a medical school, initially called the Straits Settlements and Federated Malay States Medical School, and later renamed the King Edward VII College of Medicine. Located in Singapore, this was the only Malayan source of assistant surgeons and general practitioners for the public and private sectors (University of Malaya Editorial Board, 1955). The Chinese business community raised Straits$71,000 towards the cost of its establishment, and the governments of the Straits Settlements and the Federated Malay States provided funds for staff and overheads, as well as grants-in-aid. During the 1920s, the college expanded its medical school and received endowments to support additional chairs, including in midwifery, gynaecology, and dentistry. With a shortage of British or other European doctors, graduates of the King Edward VII College of Medicine, as well as those from similar institutions in India, helped to staff Malaya's hospitals and to conduct the work of the Medical Department (Faridah Abdul Rashid, 2012).[18]

Health Care from World War II to Independence

Despite the improvements that had been made, health conditions and the health sector were hit hard by the Japanese occupation. Public health deteriorated,

17 Under the leadership of Joseph Chamberlain—the secretary of state for the colonies from 1895 to 1903—a public health and tropical medicine policy for the British colonies was established, and programmes in tropical medicine and research were progressively introduced. Schools of hygiene and tropical medicine were founded in London and Liverpool to investigate the causes of tropical diseases and to train public health practitioners to serve in the tropics.

18 In its first 50 years, there were 645 graduates in medicine and surgery (573 males and 72 females), of whom 304 were Chinese, 243 Indians, 51 Eurasians, and 41 Malays, with six identified as 'Others' (University of Malaya Editorial Board, 1955).

anti-malarial work was neglected, hospitals were damaged, and medicines and drugs were in short supply. There was a severe shortage of health-care workers and medical supplies for the large numbers of war casualties among the civilian population. Diseases such as malaria, beriberi, tuberculosis, and cholera, as well as malnutrition were widespread (IBRD, 1955). The Japanese Military Administration took over the management of hospitals, employing Japanese doctors and medicines. They made Singapore's General Hospital the main surgical centre for their troops serving in Southeast Asia.[19] Asian doctors cared for the local population, and suddenly found themselves running hospitals, training younger colleagues in managing severe illnesses, and performing major surgery, as European hospital staff were evacuated (Abdul Majid Ismail, 1974).

After the Japanese surrender, the period of British decolonization saw the repair and reconstruction of war-damaged buildings, while a longer-term programme for the expansion of health and medical services was outlined (CO 927/43/4, 1947). Public expenditure was initially constrained due to the high defence outlays during the Emergency period, but large investments were later made in new health infrastructure and the expansion of health services. With the government playing a more active role in the support of health and social welfare, health-care services were increasingly provided to the impoverished and deprived rural population. Clinics and health services were also provided to the rural Chinese communities who were relocated to New Villages during the Emergency period (Box 1.2 in Chapter 1 and Box 5.8 in Chapter 5).

Preventive services continued to target malaria—by this time through programmes of spraying and surveillance—as well as tuberculosis, through Bacillus Calmette-Guérin vaccination and treatment of cases of pulmonary tuberculosis. The germ theory of disease was becoming better understood, and was gradually put into practice through routine vaccination against a range of diseases. Towards the end of the colonial period, deaths from malaria and tuberculosis, and from other infectious diseases, declined sharply.

After the Federation of Malaya was established in 1948, administrative districts were set up and given responsibility for health matters. Health-care policy was centralized, with the federal government taking over some of the functions that were previously provided by states. The states retained executive authority over the administration of the health services, but funding for these now came from the federal government. Together, the federal and state governments managed

19 The King Edward VII College of Medicine ceased to function, and the Japanese moved the medical college to Melaka where it remained until the end of the occupation. When the College of Medicine and Raffles College merged to become the University of Malaya in 1949, the medical school became the Faculty of Medicine.

to operate reasonably comprehensive public health programmes, with health services provided free of charge.

Impact of Colonial Health Measures

The available statistics are insufficient to accurately quantify changes in health outcomes during the colonial period. It is impossible to measure the extent of gains in life expectancy in the early decades of the 20th century, for example, because of the incompleteness of mortality data, especially for rural areas. Moreover, while measures such as the crude death rate are highly sensitive to changes in age composition, the large inflows of young migrants meant that the population's age structure was very different from that of a 'normal' population. While provisions for the civil registration of births and deaths did exist, there was serious under-reporting until the late 1940s, and even later in North Borneo and Sarawak.[20]

With these caveats, however, it is possible to examine broad trends in infant mortality—a well-recognized indicator of a population's well-being that is sensitive to socio-economic and environmental conditions—in the more urbanized areas of the Straits Settlements where registration levels were the most complete. Because these areas also had better sanitation, health, and medical services, it is highly probable that they correspondingly had significantly lower death rates than the states in the peninsula. Table 4.1 shows the positive impact on infant mortality of the major improvements in living and public health conditions, including immunization campaigns, in the pre-independence period.

Table 4.1 **Infant mortality rates (per 1,000 live births) tumbled in the years leading up to independence**

	Singapore	Penang and Province Wellesley	Melaka
1931	192	134[a]	244
1940	140	118	186
1946	89	90	81
1950	82	86	111
1955	50	70	83

Sources of data: Straits Settlements (1933); Singapore (1947, 1959); Malayan Union (1948); Federation of Malaya (1952); McDonald (1956).
Note: [a] Relates to Penang only.

20 Legislative provision for the civil registration of births and deaths was made as early as 1868—and later amended in 1897—in the Straits Settlements, but registration of deaths outside hospitals was incomplete. Statistics on causes of death were often vague, especially outside the main towns where there were no qualified persons to certify the medical cause of death.

As noted by a World Bank Mission to the Federation of Malaya in 1954:

> the health and medical services of the Federation have been eminently effective in achieving a relatively high level of health. Malaria has been brought under control in large parts of the country and various other endemic and epidemic diseases have been greatly reduced. As a result, Malaya, for centuries one of the unhealthiest places in the tropics, is now one of the healthiest and its death rates compare favourably with those of many countries in sub-tropical climates. (IBRD, 1955, p. 148)

In summary, the colonial period saw the gradual establishment of good sanitation services and a strong urban health infrastructure comprising hospitals, district clinics, and static and mobile dispensaries, as well as the genesis of a rural health service. Access to health and medical services was uneven, however, with bigger and better facilities available only in the state capitals and major towns. Doctors were also heavily concentrated in large urban centres. Health services in many of the rural and poorest states—Kedah, Kelantan, Perlis, and Terengganu, as well as North Borneo and Sarawak—lagged far behind.[21] In 1953, among the peninsula's states, annual government health expenditure ranged from M$14 per capita in Negeri Sembilan to only about M$3.50 in Kelantan (IBRD, 1955).

The colonial legacy was thus one of a wide gulf between the provision of health services to the populations of the main urban areas of the Straits Settlements and the Federated Malay States, and the provision to the majority of the population living in poorer rural areas. One consequence of this strong urban bias was that health indicators for rural Malays lagged markedly behind those for the rest of the population.

Post-independence Health Policies and Their Impact on Well-being

Immediately after independence, while the existing colonial structure of medical and health services was maintained, service delivery was progressively expanded, with a key objective being greater equity. In the 1960s, primary and secondary health care was provided by both the public and private sectors, with rural areas served by a network of government health centres, sub-centres, and clinics. Existing hospitals were expanded and new ones were built, including in Sabah and Sarawak. The national development budget

21 Excluding Johor, health services developed much more slowly in the Unfederated Malay States, with only a small general hospital in each of the state capitals as well as in Sarawak and North Borneo, where most health services were based in towns.

provided generous allocations for training health professionals, and large numbers of young doctors were sent abroad for training and certification, mainly to the UK. The number of doctors, medical technicians, nurses, and midwives increased accordingly.

Health Policy

Extending and improving Malaysia's health-care services and facilities has long been, and remains, a national development priority, with these policy objectives outlined in the successive five-year national development plans (Table 4.2). The key implementation goals can be summarized in four main phases as follows.

The first priority after independence was to make services more accessible, especially in rural areas, with interventions directed primarily at addressing the highly uneven access to health care that existed at this point. Health development for the rural population, much like the development of the education system, was a central component of the NEP. In addition to the direct efforts to increase access to health services, large public investments in rural areas have helped to reduce poverty more broadly, thereby also improving health outcomes. Nevertheless, health inequities linger, and some areas are still short of facilities, especially in Sabah, Sarawak, and Kelantan.

With most infectious diseases having been brought under control through the extensive public health and nutritional programmes, the second phase has involved a growing emphasis on preventive health, and, more recently, on well-being. However, a review of government expenditure and allocation in the Sixth, Seventh, and Eighth Malaysia Plans indicates that even into the first decade of the new millennium, patient care still accounted for 70–80 per cent of total development expenditure on health.

Table 4.2 Key health policy objectives in Malaysia's five-year development plans

Plan period	Policy objectives
First Malaysia Plan (MP1), 1966–1970	▪ Expand and improve health and medical facilities, especially in rural areas; ▪ Control communicable diseases, with improved environmental sanitation and nutritional standards; ▪ Promote family planning.
Second Malaysia Plan (MP2), 1971–1975	▪ Achieve balanced coverage of health and medical services between urban and rural areas and most remote areas; ▪ Improve environmental sanitation and nutritional standards; ▪ Strengthen capacities and services of the Ministry of Health; ▪ Extend family planning services to rural areas.

Plan period	Policy objectives
Third Malaysia Plan (MP3), 1976–1980	▪ Improve the quality of rural health services and extend coverage; ▪ Improve nutritional status and environmental sanitation; ▪ Strengthen staff training to produce more and better health personnel; ▪ Expand the family planning programme.
Fourth Malaysia Plan (MP4), 1981–1985	▪ Expand medical and health programmes for target groups and areas; ▪ Increase emphasis on disease prevention; ▪ Promote healthy living environments; ▪ Introduce food and nutritional programmes in Sabah.
Fifth Malaysia Plan (MP5), 1986–1990	▪ Increase emphasis on preventive care; ▪ Promote greater community involvement in health care; ▪ Move towards a primary health-care approach; ▪ Improve inter-agency coordination, and that between public and private sectors; ▪ Expand access to rural health services to reduce disparities.
Sixth Malaysia Plan (MP6), 1991–1995	▪ Promote health for all by 2000 using the primary health-care approach; ▪ Provide more efficient and equitable access to quality health care, and strengthen district-level services.
Seventh Malaysia Plan (MP7), 1996–2000	▪ Increase emphasis on preventive health care to reduce high expenditure on curative and rehabilitative health care; ▪ Intensify supply of trained health personnel to meet increasing needs; ▪ Expand role of the private sector in provision of health services; ▪ Increase community involvement and cost sharing in health.
Eighth Malaysia Plan (MP8), 2001–2005	▪ Improve accessibility to affordable and high-quality health care; ▪ Expand the wellness programme; ▪ Promote coordination and collaboration between public and private sector providers; ▪ Increase the supply of health personnel; ▪ Enhance research capacity of the health sector; ▪ Develop and institute a health-care financing scheme.
Ninth Malaysia Plan (MP9), 2006–2010	▪ Focus on health promotion and health awareness, and the importance of individuals taking more responsibility for their own health; ▪ Work towards greater integration of health and medical services, including through better use of technology to realize efficiency, equity, access, and quality.
Tenth Malaysia Plan (MP10), 2011–2015	▪ Reform the health system by transforming the delivery system; increasing quality, capacity, and coverage; transitioning towards wellness and disease prevention rather than treatment; and increasing quality of human resources.
Eleventh Malaysia Plan (MP11), 2016–2020	▪ Move towards universal access to high-quality health care, targeting underserved populations; ▪ Strengthen capacity of health facilities and health staff; ▪ Improve health system delivery to increase efficiency and effectiveness; ▪ Increase public sector collaboration with the private sector and non-governmental organizations to increase health awareness.

Source: Economic Planning Unit–Malaysia (2018a).

Thirdly, strengthening human resources in health-care delivery has been a continuing policy priority, in recognition of the fact that the growing needs of Malaysia's population can only be met with an increase in the supply of well-qualified physicians and other health personnel. Economic development and associated changes in the age structure of the population have shifted the burden of disease from diseases of poverty, such as malaria and tuberculosis, to those of affluence, such as cancers and cardiovascular diseases. This transition requires differently qualified health professionals to deal with the increasingly complex and chronic health issues now faced.

One useful health indicator that highlights the extent of progress in the area of human resources is the doctor-to-population ratio (per 100,000 population). In 1957, there were just 14 doctors per 100,000 people, rising to 26 in 1970, and to 40 in 1990 (Figure 4.1). By 2017, there were 180, more than 12 times the number at independence.

Figure 4.1 **Malaysia's ratio of doctors to population has seen a huge improvement since independence**

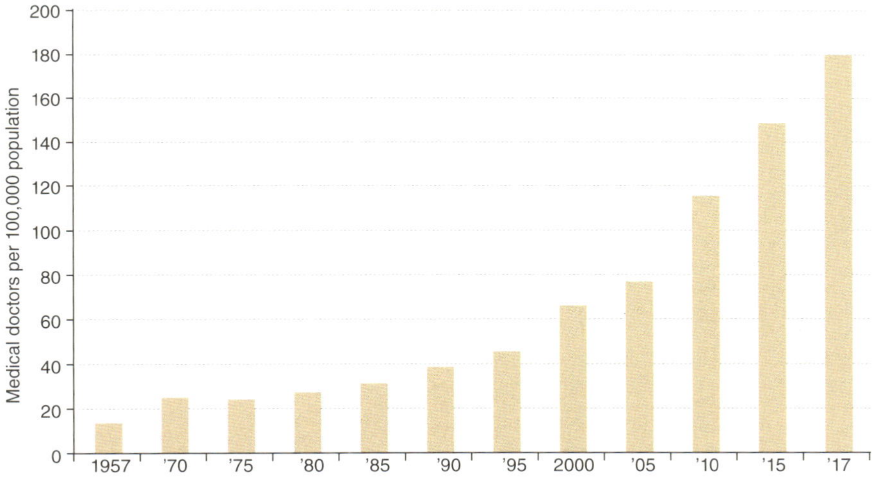

Sources of data: Department of Statistics–Malaysia (various years between 1957 and 2018).
Note: Data for 1957, 1970, and 1975 are for Peninsular Malaysia.

The fourth trend in health policy can be seen in the efforts since the mid 1990s to shift the growing financial burden of health-care costs away from the government. Individuals have been encouraged to take greater responsibility for their own health. There have also been efforts to increase the role of the private sector in health promotion and disease prevention, in response to the fact that private sector health professionals have generally been more engaged in curative work, leaving preventive measures to the public sector. While implementing this policy, however, care has been taken not to exacerbate health inequalities, and to maintain health benefits as an essential public service (Kim and Loayza, 2018).

Apart from during times of severe economic recession, public health expenditure as a share of GDP has been fairly stable at around 1.6 per cent from independence until the year 2000, after which it gradually rose to above 2 per cent. Health-care expenditure as a share of total government expenditure has also been increasing since 2000. Malaysia's public health expenditure as a share of both GDP and government expenditure is still far below that of OECD countries, however.[22] In terms of GDP share, Malaysia's health expenditure is around the average of five of the countries in the Association of Southeast Asian Nations (ASEAN), but in terms of government expenditure share it is below the average (Figure 4.2).

Figure 4.2 **Public health expenditure in Malaysia is markedly below the average of OECD countries, but broadly comparable with five ASEAN countries**

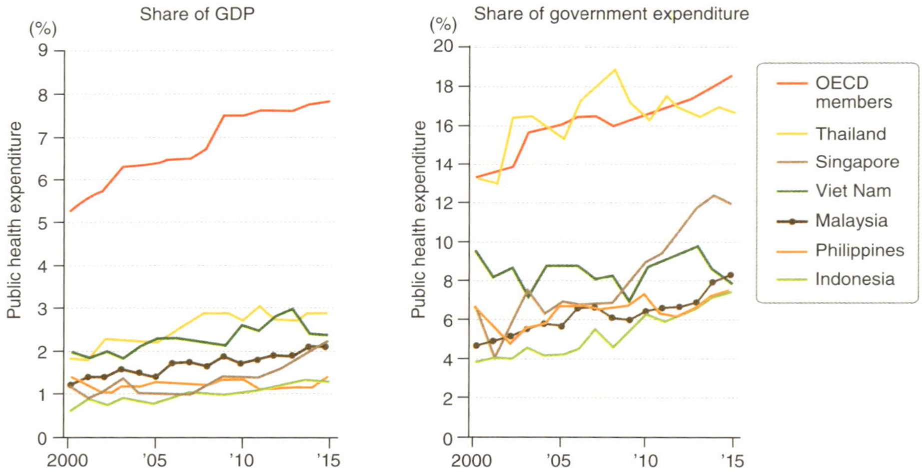

Source of data: World Bank (2018b).

Health Outcomes

The health status of Malaysia's population has improved considerably, largely as a result of the strong policy emphasis on increasing access to health-care services and on ensuring equity in their provision, as well as better education and increasing economic prosperity. At independence, life expectancy at birth was around 57 years compared with around 70 years in the UK and US, whereas by 2017 Malaysians had a life expectancy at birth of 75 years, approaching that of the US (79), but still six years behind the UK (81).

22 One reason for the significantly higher health expenditure in OECD countries is the much older age structures of their populations, as ageing creates a budgetary burden.

Malaysia's epidemiological transition, from high mortality rates due mainly to infectious diseases to lower mortality rates caused by chronic and non-communicable diseases, began in the decade or so before 1957, and gained momentum as the benefits of economic growth became shared more equitably. As material living standards and educational levels have increased, and as health promotion measures have improved, life expectancy at birth has continued to rise (Figure 4.3). While various highly correlated factors affect life expectancy, rising prosperity levels have undoubtedly been key.

Figure 4.3 **Malaysia's life expectancy has increased with rising prosperity**

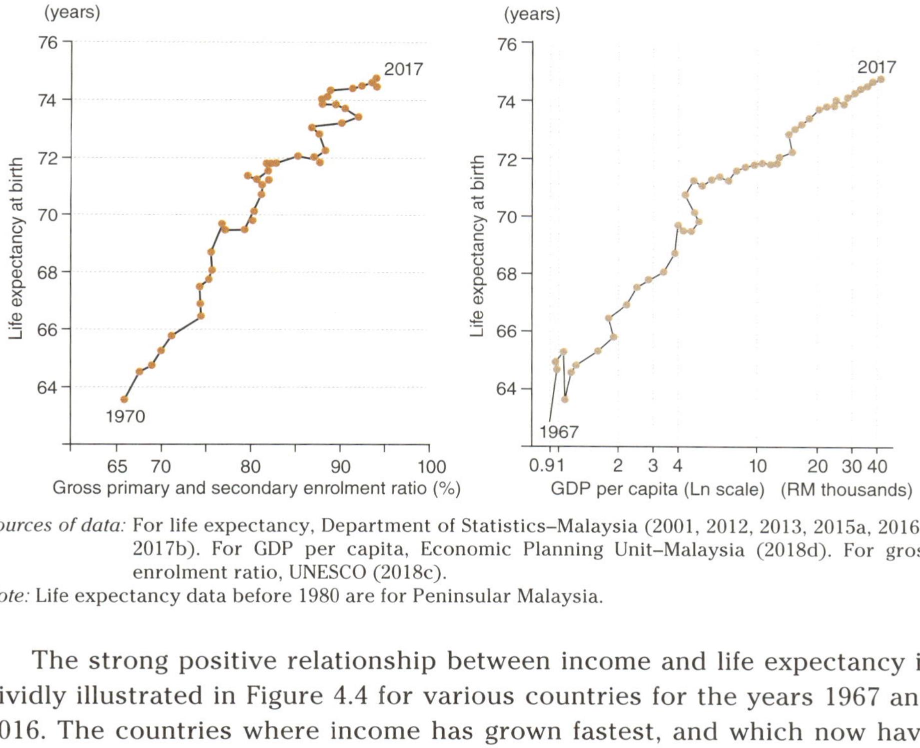

Sources of data: For life expectancy, Department of Statistics–Malaysia (2001, 2012, 2013, 2015a, 2016a, 2017b). For GDP per capita, Economic Planning Unit–Malaysia (2018d). For gross enrolment ratio, UNESCO (2018c).

Note: Life expectancy data before 1980 are for Peninsular Malaysia.

The strong positive relationship between income and life expectancy is vividly illustrated in Figure 4.4 for various countries for the years 1967 and 2016. The countries where income has grown fastest, and which now have the highest incomes, also tend to be those with the highest life expectancies. There are exceptions to this tendency, however; in ASEAN, both Thailand and Viet Nam had higher life expectancies at birth than Malaysia by 2016, despite their lower average income levels. The correlation between income and life expectancy has also tended to weaken as countries approach the current outer limits of life expectancy.

As countries have become wealthier, they have consequently made significant gains in well-being. As noted by Deaton, 'In this age of globalisation, international inequalities in longevity have been shrinking' (Deaton, 2013, p. 127). This tendency is shown in Figure 4.4 in the convergence of life expectancies at birth for different countries that has taken place between

1967 and 2016, although the gap between Malaysia and the leading Asian economies of Japan, the Republic of Korea, and Singapore has widened over this period. The ideas, technological innovations, and treatments that improve health and well-being can be diffused very quickly, supported by economic growth.

Figure 4.4 **The gap between Malaysia's life expectancy at birth and that of Japan, the Republic of Korea, and Singapore has increased, but has narrowed against some other high-income countries**

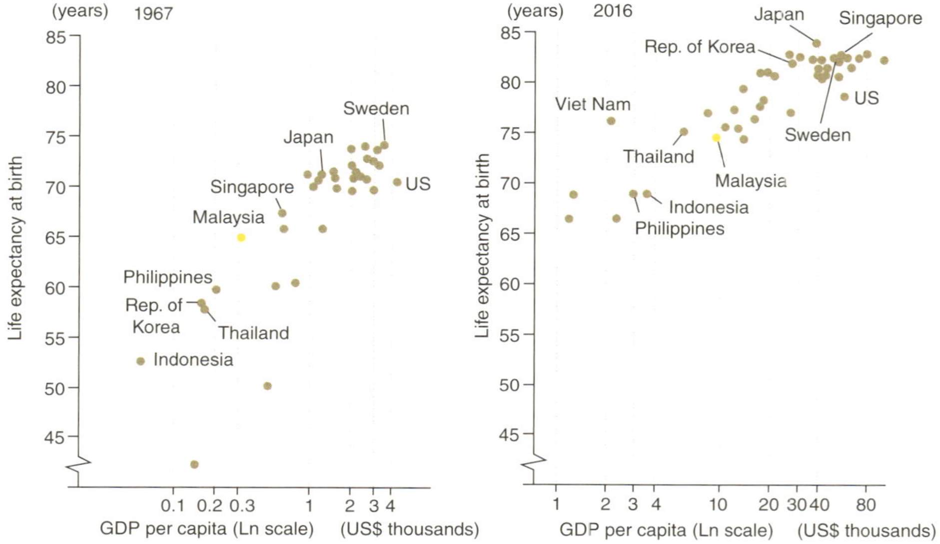

Sources of data: For Malaysia's life expectancy, Department of Statistics–Malaysia (2001, 2017a). For other countries' life expectancies and GDP, World Bank (2018a).
Note: Malaysia's life expectancy data in 1967 are for Peninsular Malaysia.

Increased life expectancy at birth has been driven by rapid declines in infant (under one year old) and under-five child mortality. In 1957, Malaysia's infant mortality rate was 76 per 1,000 births. It had fallen by half to 38 per 1,000 by 1972, then again to around 19 by 1982, and was nine by 1996. By 2000, it had reached just six per 1,000, meaning that less than 1 per cent of babies were dying in their first year of life compared with around 20–25 per cent a century ago. Infant mortality has remained around this level, and further improvements would require inroads to be made into preventing deaths that occur within four weeks of birth. Immunization programmes against diphtheria, pertussis, and tetanus, coupled with other medical advances and improved antenatal care, have undoubtedly been a major factor in this massive improvement in infant survival chances. However, reductions in poverty, with much higher standards of living, better nutrition, and improved levels of education, have also been a significant driver.

While all of Malaysia's ethnic communities have experienced these impressive declines in infant and under-five mortality rates, and while absolute differences between them have narrowed dramatically, inequalities remain, and rates for Chinese are still the lowest (Figure 4.5). This could reflect the more urbanized nature of Chinese communities and the greater access to higher-quality health services that this provides, especially at times of emergency during pregnancy and delivery.

Figure 4.5 **Differentials in infant and under-five mortality have narrowed among the main ethnic communities**

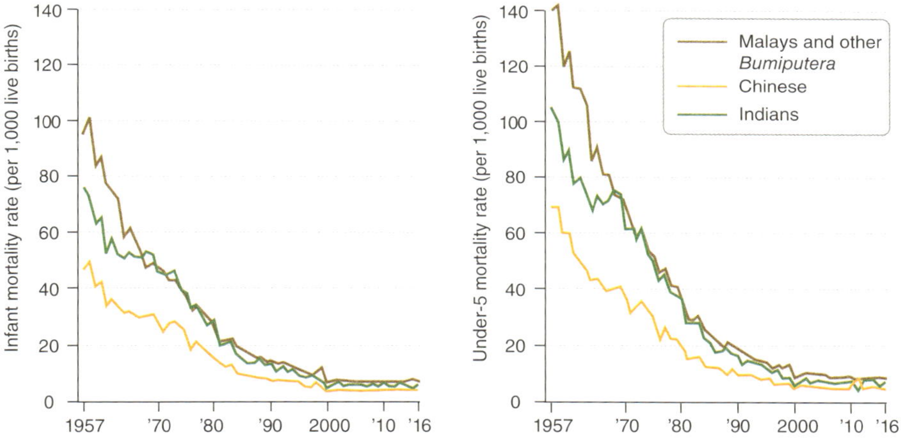

Sources of data: Department of Statistics–Malaysia (1991, 2001, 2012, 2013, 2015a and b, 2016a, 2017b).
Note: Data before 1981 are for Peninsular Malaysia.

The Demographic Transition

In the demographic transition that is often associated with economic development, improvements in living standards are reflected in declines first in mortality and then in fertility, which tend to proceed in a fairly standard manner (Box 4.4).

Box 4.4 Demographic transition theory

Demographic transition theory is based on the experience of Europe, where the population started to increase sharply from the start of the industrial revolution (Coale and Watkins, 1986). Over a period of about 100 years, gradual declines in mortality also took place due to steady increases in living standards, and then finally declines in fertility occurred. This European demographic transition represented a change from a balance of birth and death rates at moderately high levels to a balance at very low levels.

The theory explains how this shift from high mortality and high fertility to low mortality and—with a lag—low fertility occurs, with the lagged fertility response reflecting the greater resistance of fertility to modernizing forces. Historically, this demographic transition has taken place after centuries of relative stability, beginning as the mode of economic and social organization has shifted from rural subsistence farming to urban-based manufacturing employment. The key causal link is between economic development and reductions in mortality and fertility rates (Davis, 1945; Notestein, 1953).

With industrialization, standards of living rise and new ideas about health and hygiene spread. This leads to improved health conditions and a decline in death rates—the epidemiological transition. The result is that population growth accelerates as the combination of falling death rates and constant high birth rates leads to a high rate of natural increase; fertility rates initially remain high due to long-established social practices and institutions.

As societies continue to progress from rural subsistence agriculture towards modern urban employment, and as education levels increase, patterns of family formation slowly adjust to the changing socio-economic conditions. Perceptions about the costs and benefits of large families begin to shift. As the marginal costs of each child rise, the marginal benefits of having additional children decline, and as economic opportunities widen, families start choosing to have fewer children. Thus, after a lag, fertility also declines towards the population replacement level, as people realize that infant and under-five survival rates have risen, and as social norms adjust accordingly to accept lower fertility rates (Jones, 1984).

As a country goes through the demographic transition, and particularly once the fertility transition gets underway, the age composition of the population changes considerably. The share of the population below 15 years of age declines, while the share of those of working age rises. With a lag, and at the final stage of the transition, the proportion of older people begins to increase.[23]

Figure 4.6 shows Malaysia's demographic transition as evidenced by the trends in the crude birth and death rates for the total population and for each

23 See Chapters 6 and 8 for a discussion of the economic consequences of Malaysia's demographic transition.

of the main ethnic communities since 1957.[24] The mortality transition began earlier, probably in the 1930s, but was temporarily interrupted and even reversed during the Great Depression and the Japanese occupation. It then gathered momentum from around the mid 1940s when death rates started to decline rapidly in the decade of decolonization. At independence, the crude death rate had fallen to just 12 per 1,000 population, with the crude birth rate remaining high at around 46 per 1,000 population.

Figure 4.6 All communities have undergone a demographic transition, but this has been most significant among Chinese and Indians

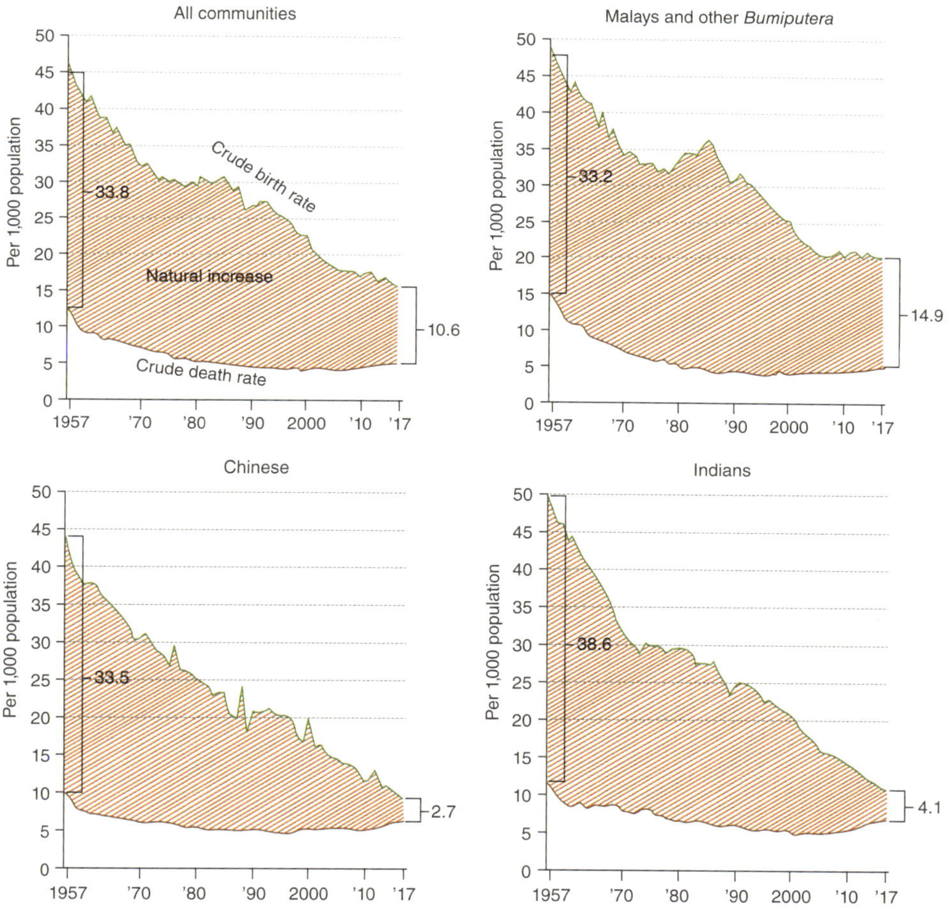

Sources of data: Department of Statistics–Malaysia (1991, 2001, 2012, 2013, 2015a and b, 2016a and 2017b).
Note: Data before 1992 are for Peninsular Malaysia.

24 The crude birth rate represents the number of live births in a given year related to the total mid-year population in the same year; the crude death rate is defined in the same way, with number of deaths as the numerator. The crude birth rate minus the crude death rate gives the crude rate of natural increase of the population.

As seen in the top-left panel, the crude death rate continued its long-term decline from 1957 until around 1990, when it stabilized at a low level. In 1957, the crude birth rate also started a sharp decline from its very high level of 46 births per 1,000 population, and this decline continued until 2017, by which time it had reached just 16 births per 1,000 population. Malaysia's rate of natural increase, which was just over 3.4 per cent in 1957, has now fallen to about 1 per cent.[25]

The timing, speed, and magnitude of the demographic transition have been very different among the various ethnic communities, as shown in the other three panels. The transition has been quickest and deepest for the more urbanized Chinese and Indians. By 2017, their rates of crude natural increase had fallen to only 0.3 and 0.4 per cent respectively, and both are now fast approaching zero or even contraction. The demographic transition of the Malays and other *Bumiputera* has been somewhat slower due to the much more gradual decline in their crude birth rates, which was temporarily reversed in the early 1980s. In 2017, their rate of natural increase, at 1.5 per cent, was more than triple that of Chinese and Indians.

The Fertility Transition and Its Impact on Well-being

The Fertility Transition

Fertility rates depend on many factors. When infant and child mortality are high, couples tend to have many children to compensate for the risk, while as death rates decline, women bear fewer children, confident that more will survive. As socio-economic conditions improve, with the share of the population working in low-productivity agriculture declining and the share living in urban areas increasing, fertility inevitably falls. Large numbers of children are no longer necessary as farm workers, while with urban living, the cost of raising children greatly increases, especially due to education costs and the rising aspiration to possess material goods. As mothers find improved economic opportunities outside the household, the opportunity cost of raising more children also increases. Urban couples thus choose to have fewer children. After independence, Malaysia's socio-economic

25 The crude death rate started a substantial decline from the mid 1940s, falling by half by the late 1950s, and this explains why the country's natural population increase began to rise quickly during the 1950s and 1960s (see for example, Hirschman, 1980; Saw, 1988).

conditions became increasingly conducive to a fertility transition: that is, a progression from women bearing six or seven children on average to having only two or three.

Around the time of independence, the total fertility rate (TFR) per woman—a measure that may be equated with the average number of children that women bear under conditions of constant fertility—was high, at approximately 6.7.[26] This level of childbearing is typical in an agrarian society where marriage takes place at a young age, and where women continue to bear children into their late reproductive years. By 1957, Malaysia's fertility transition had begun and it continued fairly steadily over the next few decades, stalling only slightly in the late 1970s, and reversing temporarily after the announcement of the 70 million policy in the early 1980s (Figure 4.7) (Chapter 2).

As early as MP1 (1966–1970), Malaysia had initiated an anti-natalist population policy. Influenced largely by the advice of foreign advisers, Tunku Abdul Rahman's government had come to view the country's rapid population growth as a threat to the objective of raising per capita income levels, and as a contributor to high youth unemployment and underemployment. The decision was made to promote smaller families, and a target was set to slow annual population growth from 3 per cent to 2 per cent within 20 years. Following earlier efforts by non-governmental organizations that had already had some impact in urban areas, family planning became part of the government's health service delivery system. A National Family Planning Board was established in 1966, and by the early 1970s its programme was reaching both urban and rural areas.

But a gradual softening of the country's anti-natalist population policy was seen in the late 1970s in the context of increasing evidence of labour shortages, particularly in the fast-growing manufacturing and service sectors. Thus, the Mid-Term Review of MP3 (1976–1980) no longer identified population growth as a major development concern, as earlier development plans had, and family planning allocations were underspent. Despite this de-emphasis on family planning and the implementation of the 70 million policy, fertility continued its secular decline. By around 2010, the fertility rate had fallen to the population replacement level of approximately 2.1 children per woman, and by 2017 had fallen below it to only 1.9.

26 The TFR per woman is the average number of children that a woman could expect to bear if the prevailing age-specific fertility levels in a given year were to remain unchanged into the future.

Figure 4.7 **All communities have transitioned from high to low fertility, but at different paces**

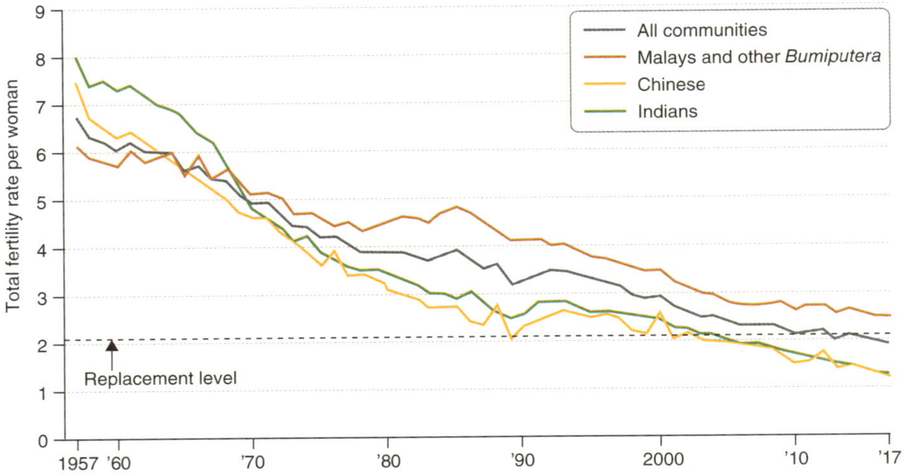

Sources of data: Department of Statistics–Malaysia (1991, 2001, 2012, 2013, 2015a and b, 2016a, 2017b).

This transformation in social behaviour from having large to small families has occurred among each of Malaysia's main ethnic communities at different speeds, with the fertility transition of Malays and other *Bumiputera* more gradual than that of Chinese and Indians (Figure 4.7). At independence, fertility was higher for Chinese and Indians, despite the earlier age at first marriage and earlier start at family formation among Malays and other *Bumiputera*. This may reflect different ethnic patterns of family formation, with Malay women spending far longer periods of time breastfeeding their infants (Leete, 1996), which increases the intervals between births.

The start of the fertility decline for Chinese and Indians in the late 1950s and for Malays some years later, as well as its subsequent continuation, is due in part to the trend towards a later age at first marriage. Changing marriage patterns are associated with rising educational levels and increasing opportunities for modern-sector female employment, reaffirming the importance of socio-economic determinants in explaining fertility transitions (Teh and Chor, 2017). The fertility rates of Chinese and Indian communities in Malaysia display similar patterns to those of other Chinese and Indian communities elsewhere in East and South Asia, and have been below replacement level since around 2000. Chinese and Indian fertility rates appear to be following, albeit with a lag, the trajectory of the very low fertility rate found in Singapore, which has been below replacement level for more than 40 years. By 2017, the TFR for these communities was 1.3 per woman, about half the level of Malays and other *Bumiputera* at 2.5 per woman. That Malay fertility has yet to fall to replacement level, and that the transition has been slower, is partly a result of their lower rate of urbanization.

As Figure 4.8 shows, in common with its ASEAN neighbours, Malaysia has experienced a convergence towards the low mean level of family size among OECD countries, although its transition has been less rapid than that of some countries with similar or even lower levels of economic development. Malaysia's fertility rate has fallen further than that of the Philippines, however, where pro-natalist advocacy by the Catholic Church supports high fertility. Since around 2002, Malaysia's fertility rate has also been below that of Indonesia.

Figure 4.8 International convergence in family size

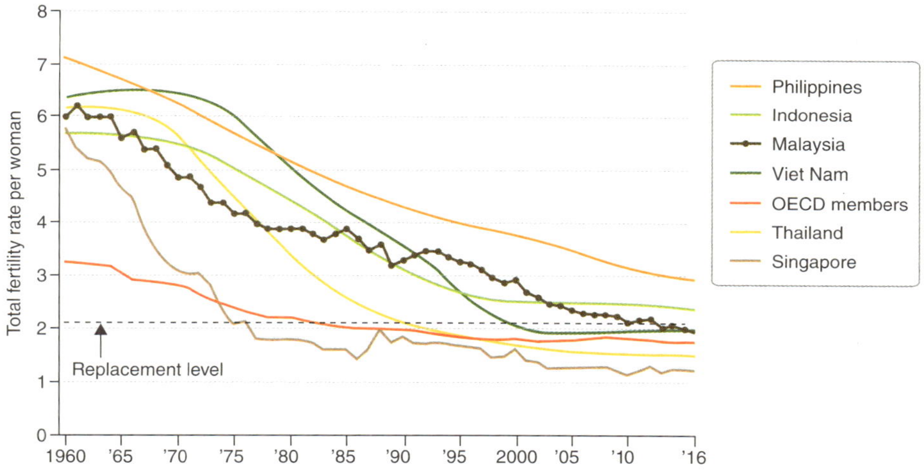

Sources of data: Department of Statistics–Malaysia (1991, 2001, 2012, 2013, 2015a and b, 2016a, 2017b). For OECD and other ASEAN countries: World Bank (2018a).
Note: Data before 1991 are for Peninsular Malaysia.

Changing Family Size and Female Labour Force Participation

The relationship between education, fertility, and female labour force participation rates is complex. Education and fertility are closely connected, and both also affect female labour force participation. Education enables women to engage in modern-sector employment, increasing both their earning power and the opportunity cost of staying at home to raise children. Education also empowers women to make their own marriage and fertility choices, including about whether to access family planning and reproductive health services. Since independence, as discussed in Chapter 3, Malaysian women have become better educated, with increasing participation and attainment levels.

Figure 4.9 Female labour force participation is associated with family size

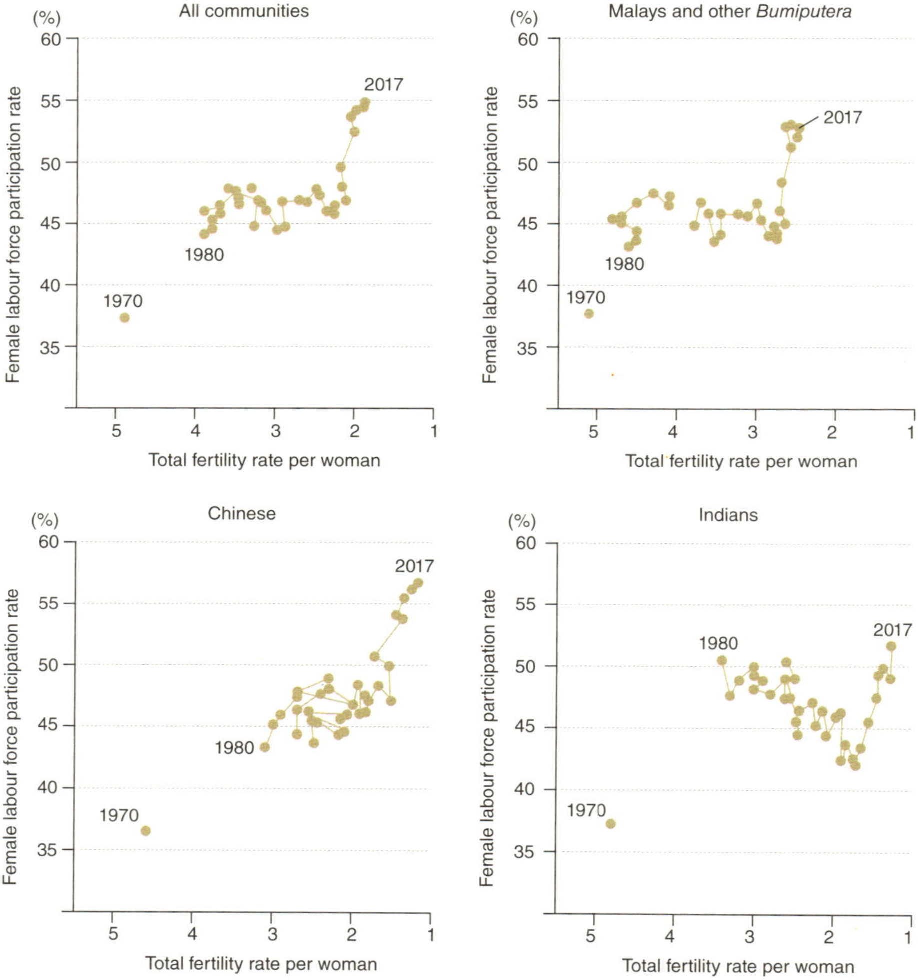

Sources of data: For labour force, Chander (1977); Department of Statistics Malaysia (various years). For TFR, Department of Statistics–Malaysia (2001, 2012, 2013, 2015, 2016a, 2017b).
Note: Labour force data for 1970, and TFR data for 1970–1990, are for Peninsular Malaysia.

Malaysia's transition from high to low fertility has been associated with a sharp rise in female labour force participation (Figure 4.9). Between 1970 and 2016, TFR per woman fell from an average of just under five to less than two, while female labour force participation rose sharply between 1970 and 1990, from 37 per cent to 48 per cent. It stabilized at around this rate from 1990 to 2012, before rising again to 55 per cent in 2017. This pattern can be observed among all ethnic groups, although participation is significantly higher among Malay and Chinese women. For Indian women, the structural transformation of the economy from the 1980s, which included a transition from rural estate agriculture to urban sector employment (Chapter 8), had a depressing effect on their participation, possibly because they lacked the necessary modern skills and were also not readily absorbed into public sector employment (Siti Rohani Yahaya, 2009). Their participation rates have risen only since 2010 (Figure 4.9).

During the 1970s, there was a surge in newly created urban employment opportunities in manufacturing and government administration that attracted women from all communities. However, the subsequent increase in female labour force participation was lower than might have been expected, given the country's sustained economic growth and the resulting increase in demand for labour, and given the experiences of other low-fertility countries. This may be due in part to a lack of part-time jobs and limited child-care facilities.[27] Despite increased labour market participation since independence, the full potential of the women's labour force has yet to be tapped. In 2017, participation was 54.7 per cent, much lower than the OECD average of 63.3 per cent, or Singapore's 68.6 per cent, and far below Sweden's 80.6 per cent, where female employment is incentivized through supportive social policies (World Bank, 2018a). More effective utilization of highly educated women in the labour force has considerable potential to raise productivity and boost economic growth (Barro, 2001). It would also help to reduce the country's growing reliance on migrant workers, especially in certain occupations, unless this is compensated for by increasing numbers of migrant domestic workers.

Changing Family Size and Women's Well-being

Malaysian men and women are living longer, healthier, and more productive lives. With higher educational attainment, women are choosing to marry and to have their first child at a later age than in the past. They are also choosing to have fewer children, with wider spacing of births, and are investing more in each of them. If well-being is defined simply in terms of satisfactory living conditions, then the decline in fertility towards replacement level has been a contributing factor to women's increased well-being. Impressive gains in life

27 The 2014 Fifth Malaysian Population and Family Survey found that a key reason for opting out of paid employment for about one-third of women was responsibility for child care (National Population and Family Development Board–Malaysia, 2014).

expectancy at birth, coupled with increases in material standards of living, are other important factors.

Substantial gains have been made in school enrolment and completion rates for girls (Chapter 3). Gender parity in primary education had been achieved by 1980, and female participation in secondary and tertiary education now exceeds that of males. While better-educated women contribute more to the health, nutrition, and education of their children, educated parents also make better choices about family size and child spacing, with these factors all resulting in improved family well-being.

In economic terms, the contribution from female employment to real GDP has more than trebled in recent years from an average of 4 per cent in 2001–2008 to 14 per cent in 2011–2016 (IMF, 2018).[28] This increased contribution reflects the greater share of women in total employment, especially in managerial positions, as well as the reductions in the gender gap in average years of schooling. But gender gaps still persist, for example, in mean salary levels, as well as in the lower number of females who are themselves employers.

In summary, declining fertility, improved women's health, higher educational attainment, stronger labour market participation—in terms of both rates and skill levels—and higher incomes have all played a role in enhancing Malaysian women's well-being and living standards, as well as those of their families.

Changing Family Size and Impact on the Population's Age Structure

The age composition of Malaysia's population has changed dramatically since the first half of the 20th century. During colonial times, and especially in the early decades of the 20th century, the age and sex compositions of the population were both heavily influenced by the impact of large flows of transient migrant workers, which created a bulge of population at young working age, as well as highly uneven sex ratios. After World War II, with severe restrictions placed on immigration until around the 1980s, the population's age composition began to take on a pattern more typical of a country at the early stages of the demographic transition, in which the population in any

28 Estimates based on a growth accounting framework using human capital formation and drawing on data from surveys on salaries, wages, and employment by sex undertaken by the Department of Statistics–Malaysia (IMF, 2018).

five-year age group, for example, will be smaller than that of the next oldest five-year group.

As fertility declined, the population's age composition began to change (Figure 4.10).[29] The fraction of children aged 0–14 years fell sharply, while the share of the working age population, between the ages of 15 and 59, increased substantially. The time-lagged impact of smaller birth cohorts entering working age meant that the growth rate of the population of children began to slow before that of the working age population. The gradual trend towards population ageing gained momentum after 2000: the share of the population aged 65 and over rose from just 2.8 per cent in 1957 to 6.3 per cent in 2017.

Figure 4.10 **Malaysia's age composition has changed dramatically**

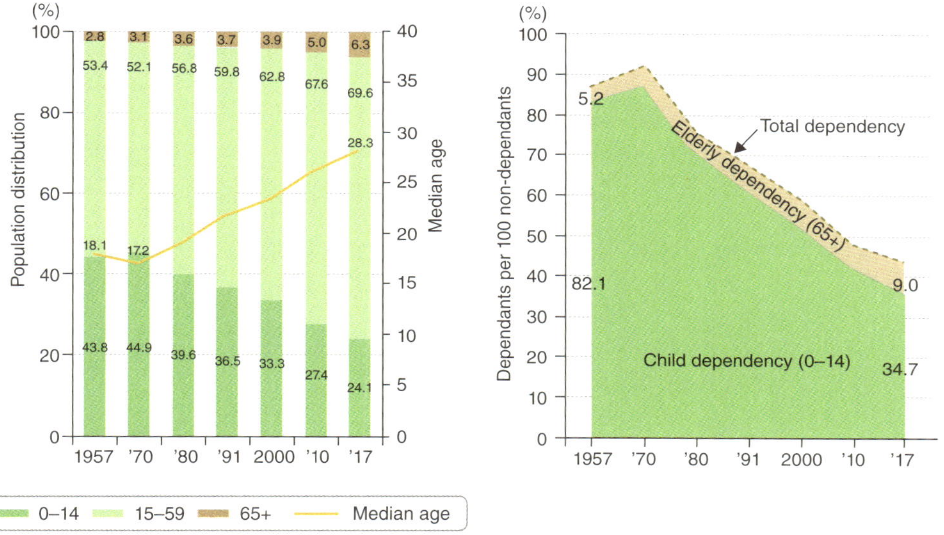

Sources of data: Fell (1960); Chander (1977); Khoo (1983); Khoo (1995); Shaari Abdul Rahman (2001a); Wan Ramlah Wan Abdul Raof (2011); Department of Statistics–Malaysia (2018a).
Note: Data for 1957 are for Peninsular Malaysia.

Malaysia's fertility transition has led to a steep decrease in the child dependency ratio (children aged 0–14 as a share of those of working age), as a larger proportion of the population has moved into and through working age (Figure 4.10). With a time lag, Malaysia's elderly dependency ratio (those aged 65 and over as a share of those of working age) will inevitably continue to rise.

---

29 This reasoning assumes that the population is closed to migration. Of course, as in colonial times, sizeable international migration flows can significantly change the age composition of the population. The one-off impact of the fertility decline on the population's age composition thus relates only to Malaysian citizens.

The Demographic Dividend

A declining dependency ratio can present a 'demographic dividend', which, if exploited effectively, can promote economic growth. When the share of the working population in the total population increases, and dependency ratios decrease (with fewer children, but before an increase in ageing dependants), a window of opportunity opens for increased savings and investment. This is because fewer resources are required for age-related expenditure, such as education and health care.

This window has been open for Malaysia since the 1970s, with labour force growth exceeding that of the total population in each decade subsequently (Figure 4.11). Other things being equal, this reduced dependency ratio should lift output or income relative to the total population. This positive income effect will be magnified if lower fertility rates also encourage higher female participation in the labour force, thus further widening the gap between labour force and population growth rates. Lower fertility rates, and the associated changing age structure of the population, may thus accelerate economic growth.[30]

Figure 4.11 Malaysia's labour force has grown faster than its population

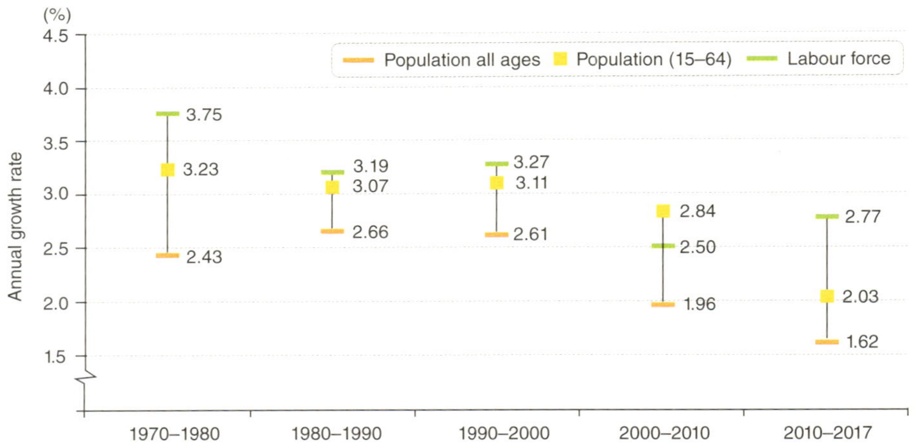

Sources of data: For population data 1970–1990, Department of Statistics–Malaysia (2001), for 1991–2000, Department of Statistics–Malaysia (2014), and for 2017, Department of Statistics–Malaysia (2018a). For labour force data, Department of Statistics–Malaysia, Labour Force Survey Report Malaysia (various years).

Note: Data for 1970–1980 are for Peninsular Malaysia.

30 The positive effects of Malaysia's changing demographic dynamics on its economic growth are explored in Chapter 6.

Conclusions

During early British colonial rule, life in Malaya was short. Infectious diseases were endemic, epidemics were not infrequent, and perhaps a fifth to a quarter of infants died before reaching their first birthday. The rapid spread of infectious diseases, such as cholera, malaria, smallpox, and tuberculosis, took a heavy toll on migrant workers and threatened to decimate the mining and plantation labour force; it was imperative, therefore, to develop improved, expanded, and more effective sanitation and health services. In the towns, sanitary controls were introduced, a health structure created, and public health programmes pursued.

But most of these measures were urban-based and aimed primarily at supporting colonial economic interests. They had little impact on the lives of the bulk of the rural population who continued to live in poverty, suffering nutritional deficiencies and high levels of disease. The benefits of economic growth were monopolized by the British and did not spread much beyond the main urban areas, despite the rapid growth in real GDP per capita from 1900 to 1930. Particularly in the Unfederated Malay States of Kelantan, Terengganu, Kedah, and Perlis, rural dwellers' lack of access to clean water, sanitation, and medical treatment made them highly vulnerable to disease and early death. Only after World War II, in the decade of decolonization, did their situation begin to improve.

After independence, the major thrust of health policy was to improve access to health services for the rural population by extending the network of hospitals and clinics. Health was integrated into national development plans, and substantial investments were made to expand and improve nutrition, health infrastructure, human resources for health, infectious disease control, and health promotion programmes. Health outcomes improved spectacularly as a result, with dramatic declines in infant and child mortality, and increases in life expectancy at birth, to levels approaching those of the world's developed countries. Economic growth and reductions in poverty were perhaps as important in achieving these outcomes as the improved health services.

As infant and child mortality rates declined, as living standards improved, and as access to education and modern-sector jobs expanded, conditions in Malaysia became increasingly conducive to a fertility transition. This transformation from high to low fertility has occurred among each of the main ethnic communities, albeit at varying speeds. With much lower fertility rates and higher educational attainment, there has been a substantial increase in female labour force participation in modern urban-sector employment. This has further boosted incomes and living standards, and has contributed to the significant improvements witnessed over time in the well-being of the population, including women and children.

Steep declines in fertility have greatly changed the age composition of the population. At independence, half the population was aged under 18, whereas by 2017 the median age was 28.3. The share in the population of children below the age of 15 has fallen, while that of the working age population has increased. The reduced support ratios since the 1970s have helped to increase output relative to the total population, creating the conditions for a demographic dividend that has supported Malaysia's economic growth.

Part 3 will now focus on the outcomes of economic growth and development, as well as the reasons for them. Chapter 5 starts by charting the country's economic journey from a commodity-producing tropical outpost of the British empire to a comparatively successful developing economy in charge of its own destiny by the close of the 1960s.

Pulau Langkawi
Perlis
Kangar
Arau
Alor Star
KEDAH
G. Perak 2823 ft
G. Jerai 3978 ft
Baling
Kroh
Georgetown
PENANG
PROVINCE WELLESLEY
Kulim
Selama
Parit Buntar
Bagan Serai
Larut Hills
Port Weld
Taiping
Matang
G. Bubu 5434 ft
Kuala Kangsar
Sungei Siput
PERAK
Ipoh
Batu Gajah
Tronoh
Kampar
P. Talang
P. Pangkor
Lumut
Sembilan Is.
Perak R.
P. Jara
Bagan Datoh
Telok Anson
Tapah
Bidor
G. Batu Puteh 6987
G. Korbu 7160
Merapoh
Chegar Perah
Kuala Lipis
Grik
G. Bintang 6103 ft
Lawin
G. Besar 5725 ft
G. Hulu Temengor 7020 ft
Kota Trunci
Blimbing Range
G. Noring 6194 ft
G. Labo 3948 ft
Belum
KELANTAN
Tumpat
Kota Bharu
Pasir Puteh
Tanah Merah
Kuala Krai
Manek Urai
Bt. Temiang 4082 ft
R. Kelantan
S. Lebir
S. Galas
Gunong Tahan 7186 ft
Perhentian Is.
Great Redang
Little Redang
R. Besut
Kuala Trengganu
P. Kapas
Bt. Chintawaseh 3874 ft
R. Trengganu
TRENGGANU
R. Dungun
Kg. Dungun
Pulau Tenggol
Mandi Angin 4794 ft
S. Tembeling
G. Ulu Bakar
G. Irong 3908 ft
Tanjong Peninjut
Chukai
FEDERATED
MALAY STATES
PAHANG
Jelai
S. Tekai
Tembeling
K. Tek
Benta
G. Tapis 4958 ft
Tanjong Gelang
Kuantan
R. Kuantan
G. Serudom 3462 ft
G. Lerek 3434 ft
G. Benom 6916 ft
Trolak
Slim
Raub
Bentong
Semantan
R. Pahang
Pekan
Pahang River
Chini L.
G. Chini 2099 ft
Temerloh
Mengkarak
Tasek Bera
P. Berhala
K. Merchong
Rompin
Kuala Kubu
B. Tinggi
Batang Berjuntai
Serendah
Kuala Selangor
SELANGOR
G. Nuang 4908 ft
Kuala Lumpur
Batu Caves
G. Hantu 4799 ft
Pt. Swettenham
P. Klang
Klang
Ampang
Kajang
Kuala Klawang
NEGRI SEMBILAN
Mantin
Bahau
Kuala Pilah
Jugra
Banting
Seremban
Sepang
Pt. Dickson
Rembau
G. Tampin 2507 ft
Tampin
C. Rachado
MALACCA
Malacca Town
Batang Malacca
Gemas
Mt. Ophir 4187 ft
Segamat
Kepong
Beremban
G. Besar 3403 ft
Endau
K. Mersing
Bekok
Paloh
Niyor
R. Muar
Bandar Maharani
G. Blumut
Kluang
Bandar Penggaram
JOHORE
Tanjong Tohor
Batu Pahat
Layang Layang
G. Pulai
Benut
Johore Bharu
Tebrau
Kota Tinggi
P. Pisang
Kukup
Pulau Tioman
P. Tinggi
P. Sibu
STRAIT OF MALACCA
CHI
S

Adapted from:
John Bartholomew,
British Malaya,
Edinburgh, 1935–46

Courtesy of:
HRH Sultan Sharafuddin Idris Shah
and Dato' Richard Curtis

PART

3

EXPANDING AND DIVERSIFYING THE ECONOMY

Chapter 5

Economic Growth and Change, 1874–1969

This chapter charts the dramatic economic changes and upheavals that took place during the period 1874–1969. It describes the institutions created to serve the interests of the colonial government and of British business. It documents the rise and fall of the tin industry, and, later, the rubber industry, and charts the economic roller-coaster of the first three decades of the 20th century. It recounts the economic and human devastation of the Great Depression, the physical devastation that occurred during the Japanese occupation, and the challenges of recovery and rehabilitation. It examines the late colonial economic model and the pathway to independence. Following independence in 1957 and the unification of Sabah and Sarawak—and, temporarily, Singapore—with the Federation of Malaya in 1963, Malaysians finally began the process of modernizing and diversifying their own economy, and moulding their own institutions and policies. The story ends in 1969, when political tensions, fuelled by ethnic divisions, erupted into violence, creating pressures for a major policy redirection.

In charting the trajectory of the economy over this extended period, extensive use is made of the author's own estimates of gross domestic product (GDP) covering 1900–1939 (Sultan Nazrin Shah, 2017), and of the estimates from the 2018 update of the Maddison project database which cover 1911–1969 (University of Groningen, 2018). While GDP metrics are essential for analysing economic performance and progress, they have their limitations. One notable shortcoming is that they do not capture the impacts of changes in the terms of trade on real income, which is particularly important when imports and exports are large relative to the size of the economy. The comprehensive data that would be required to make the adjustments necessary to calculate real gross domestic income (GDI)—which takes into account the income effects of terms-of-trade changes—unfortunately do not exist for colonial Malaya. Because of data shortages, it is also not possible to account for the income flows that accrued to non-residents using gross national income (GNI) measures.

To overcome the data limitations of the earlier period, and reach a better understanding of how the welfare of the general population fared during the colonial and immediate post-independence periods, other indicators are used. These include estimates of household consumption, real wage changes, unemployment rates, and other relevant social and economic indicators. However, even data on these aspects, where they are available, are generally sporadic and sparse.[1]

The study of economic growth and development is a centuries-old academic pursuit. Economists have developed a number of theories about how growth occurs, and why it varies by place and period. Some of the earliest perspectives can be traced to Adam Smith's *The Wealth of Nations*, originally published in 1776. Smith (1910) emphasized the role of private property, markets, the division of labour, economic specialization, and exchange in the creation of prosperity. He recognized that these developments in turn depend on the nature of political, legal, and social institutions. David Ricardo, writing in the early 19th century and building on the foundations laid by Smith, was the first to stress the crucial role that capital accumulation plays in advancing a nation's wealth. Ricardo (1911) linked this back to the factors that determine the distribution of income and savings.

These 'classical' perspectives on growth resonate strongly with much of the Malayan experience. More modern perspectives, including those that emphasize the conditions that allow growth to be self-sustaining, also help to shed light on how Malaysia has managed to narrow the income gap between itself and the more advanced countries.

Rather than trying to fit Malaysia's experience into any theoretical straitjacket, however, this chapter offers a broad historical perspective which seeks to trace outcomes (or effects) to their underlying causes. This approach naturally focuses attention on the institutional aspects of development that were unique to Malaysia, which are explored in some depth. Relevant theoretical frameworks are also presented and explained.

This chapter starts with a broad overview of the trajectory of real incomes from 1900 to 1969. The subsequent sections then provide a more in-depth analysis of the evolution of the economy in six successive historical periods: post–Pangkor Engagement, 1874–1899; growth, volatility, and reversals, 1900–1941; Japanese occupation, 1941–1945; recovery, 1946–1949; commodity

1 The first set of national accounts for Malaysia was not produced until the 1960s, and data for earlier periods were not harmonized among the states.

dependence and institutional transformation, 1950–1959; and post-independence, 1960–1969.

Although there were important developments within each of these periods, and particularly before World War II, overall the institutional features of the economy were more or less stable within each period, and a distinct pattern of economic outcomes can be identified.

GDP Growth and GDP Gaps, 1900–1969

Data and Data Sources

Any analysis of economic growth over such an extended historical period will face challenges. A major one in this case, as explained in Chapter 1, is that the territory of what became Malaysia only took final shape in 1965, after Singapore left the federation. Before that, there were not even any consolidated economic accounts available for the territories that became Malaysia.

The process by which national accounts were constructed, from fragmentary and incomplete sub-national data, for the years 1900–1939 is explained elsewhere (Sultan Nazrin Shah, 2017; forthcoming). A much earlier effort to construct GDP estimates for Peninsular Malaysia for the post–World War II period, before national accounts started to be collated by the national statistical office, was made by Bhanoji Rao (1976). He built on estimates made by Benham (1951), the International Bank for Reconstruction and Development (IBRD) (1955), and Lim (1967). Walters is credited with having made the first estimates of national accounts for the Federation of Malaya covering the years 1955–1960 (Harvie, 1960).

Box 5.1 describes the three main data sources for this and the following two chapters.

Box 5.1 GDP data and sources

To patch together a detailed description and analysis of Malaysia's economic development for 1870–2017, extensive use is made of data from different sources. One of the most important is the author's own estimates of expenditure-based GDP in Malaya for 1900–1939 (Sultan Nazrin Shah, 2017). These estimates are calculated in local current prices and in local constant 1914 prices. For the years before 1900, there are limited economic data available other than for trade, as reported by Drabble (2000).

The various constraints mean that some of the analysis unavoidably draws on data that are incomplete and highly fragmented.

The Maddison database for Malaysia provides a continuous series for the years 1911 to 2016, with a short break for the war years from 1943 to 1946. The Maddison database also gives estimates for Malaysia for the years 1820, 1850, and 1870. The Maddison data for the period 1946–1969 are used to extend the Sultan Nazrin Shah series. For the earlier period from 1900 to 1939 the Sultan Nazrin Shah series is used, as it was carefully built up from primary sources and is therefore likely to provide a more accurate picture of the underlying economic dynamics of the peninsula. By contrast, the Maddison data were indirectly imputed and modelled. The strengths and weaknesses of the various estimates and their application in particular years and periods are set out below.

The Maddison database provides estimates of per capita GDP in constant 2011 purchasing power parity (PPP) units (refer to the box note below). Although consistently estimated local prices can be safely used to examine economic performance within a country over time, the use of common prices is necessary for comparisons between countries. Both measures of performance are integral to assessing a country's development.

In Chapter 6, the 2019 release of the Penn World Tables (PWT9.1) is used extensively. The use of this series permits estimation of productivity dynamics, which the Maddison database cannot support. PWT9.1 and the Maddison estimates of per capita income in international PPP units for 1970–2016 are in fact very similar. PWT9.1 gives separate estimates of real PPP output and real PPP expenditure.

As is most appropriate, expenditure measures of GDP are used in the comparisons of real standards of living between Malaysia and selected benchmark countries. The expenditure measures have the advantage that they capture the impact of terms-of-trade changes, which, as mentioned, are particularly important for countries where imports and exports are large relative to GDP. For Malaysia, expenditure measures of GDP average around 2 per cent more than output measures over the period 1955–2014, although the difference ranges considerably from −11 per cent to +19 per cent. In addition to aggregate and component estimates of GDP, the PWT9.1 database provides information on the factor components of GDP: human capital; physical capital; number of persons engaged in employment; labour's share in income; and hours of work. These data can be used to estimate different measures of productivity change.

In the analysis that follows, it is not always possible to use the data in a consistent manner. For the pre-war years, data are generally expressed in local constant prices, with a 1914 base year. For the post-war years through to 1959 and subsequently, data are expressed in the international 2011 PPP dollars that are the backbone of the latest releases of both the Maddison project and the PWT. In Chapter 6, both local constant price data and PPP data (generally PWT9.1) are used, depending on the topic considered. All measures of convergence and cross-country comparisons (Box 5.2) use PPP measures.

Note: PPP units reflect the cost of a given basket of commodities in different countries measured in a common currency (usually US dollars of a given base year). The ratio of the local cost of the set basket in Malaysia to its cost in the US is the PPP conversion factor. If the PPP conversion factor is less than the market exchange rate, Malaysia's real income (in terms of its purchasing power over the set basket) measured in US dollars is greater than that given by a simple conversion of local currency income to US dollars at the prevailing market exchange rate. The use of PPP conversion factors normally raises measured income in low-income countries, because the prices of non-traded goods (which have a large weight in the consumption basket) in low-income countries are cheaper than in high-income countries (the Balassa-Samuelson effect).

Growth of Per Capita GDP

Figure 5.1 shows the logarithm of per capita GDP for the period 1900–1969, with data plotted on two scales. The first of the two series covers 1900–1939 measured in constant 1914 Straits dollars—the units used in the Sultan Nazrin Shah data set. The data refer to per capita GDP of the territories of Malaya, which were under British colonial rule at the time but were not part of a unified or sovereign state.[2] The second series presents estimates from the Maddison project database, measured in constant 2011 PPP-adjusted dollars, for 1911–1969. Although these two series are not directly comparable, the GDP estimates have been converted to logarithmic scales and displayed over intervals that span identical ranges, so that differences in the underlying rates of growth can be visualized. The steeper the slope of a series, the faster the implied rate of growth.

Despite the problems of comparability among these estimates and the missing values for the World War II years, the two series tell a broadly consistent story about the overall direction of per capita GDP over this protracted period. Both sets of estimates suggest that the colonial economy grew strongly until 1930. Starting from a low base in 1900, per capita GDP had doubled by 1917 according to the Sultan Nazrin Shah estimates, and by 1929 had reached its peak of nearly four times its 1900 value. The Maddison data, starting from a base in 1911, show per capita GDP roughly doubling by 1929—again the peak year—and growing at a rate only marginally slower than the doubling speed implied by the alternative estimate.

2 Data are not available for North Borneo and Sarawak for this period.

Figure 5.1 **Per capita income gains fell by more than half after the Great Depression and World War II**

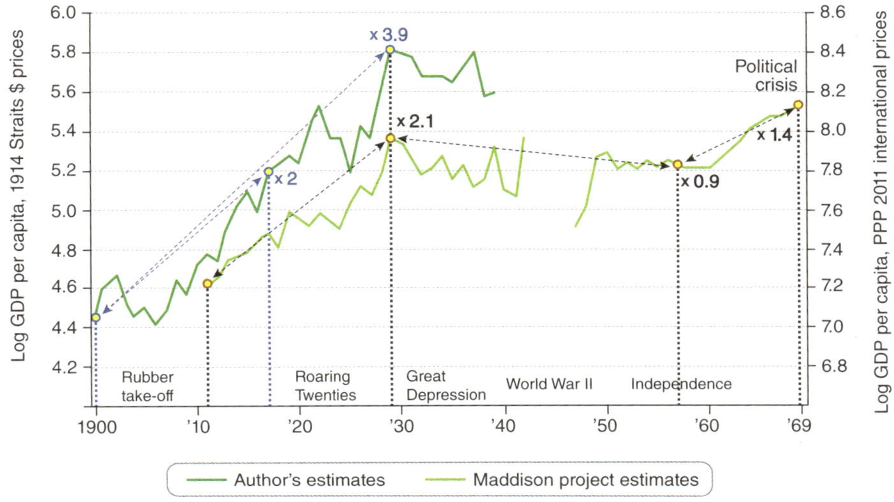

Source of Maddison project estimates: University of Groningen (2018).

Both series also concur that, despite solid underlying trend growth, the colonial economy oscillated wildly in the first three decades of the century. Episodes of rapid growth of per capita GDP were regularly punctuated by sharp reversals. During the period 1911–1929, the Maddison series shows three such reversals, while the Sultan Nazrin Shah series suggests four.[3] For both series, this sawtooth pattern of growth reflects the violent swings in the prices of Malaya's rubber and, to a lesser extent, tin exports, both of which were dependent on demand in the global economy, particularly from the US, where consumer demand for cars and other durable products was growing rapidly. During these years, rubber and tin dominated the landscape of Malaya's economy, accounting for the bulk of exports.

Although the two sources suggest differences in the multiple movements of per capita GDP during the 1930s, both concur that this was a 'lost decade' for the Malayan economy. By 1939, the final year of the Sultan Nazrin Shah series, both data sets show per capita GDP below the peak achieved in 1929. However, the retreat in per capita GDP in the Sultan Nazrin Shah series is more accentuated than in the Maddison series.

3 A reversal is defined as an interval over which per capita income declines from its preceding peak, and may contain more than one year in which per capita GDP contracts.

With the onset of war in Europe, the Maddison data suggest a sharp decline in Malaya's per capita GDP in 1940, and a further decline in 1941, caused by disruption of shipping and supply chains. The Maddison data show a small jump in per capita GDP in 1942, but as this was the first year of Japan's occupation of Malaya and as the occupation is known to have triggered a collapse of the colonial exporting economy (see discussion below), the reliability of this point estimate is questionable. There are no GDP estimates for the years 1943–1946.

Estimates of GDP in the immediate post–World War II period also come from the Maddison project database. These suggest that per capita GDP rebounded quickly from its depressed levels as the British colonial administration focused on reconstruction, rationalization of the different administrative arrangements, and planning for decolonization. The Maddison data peg growth in real per capita GDP at 11 per cent in 1948, accelerating to 29 per cent in 1949, reflecting rapid recovery following the wartime devastation. Estimates made by Bhanoji Rao (1980) also suggest reasonably rapid recovery, although not at the pace implied by the Maddison data, putting growth of real per capita GDP instead at 5.7 per cent in 1948 and 4.4 per cent in 1949.[4]

The sources agree that by the early 1950s the structure of the economy was close to what it had been before the war, and output and exports of rubber and tin had largely recovered. Nevertheless, according to the Maddison estimates, per capita GDP was no higher by this decade than it had been on average in the late 1930s. Three expansionary periods were experienced in the 1950s and two contractions, with per capita income at the end of the decade lower than it had been at the beginning.

At the start of the 1950s the war on the Korean peninsula encouraged commodity stockpiling, which led to soaring rubber and tin prices. The Maddison data show growth of per capita GDP at 1.9 per cent in 1950, while Bhanoji Rao's estimates (1980) suggest an even lower rate of just 0.9 per cent. However, there were sizeable terms-of-trade gains, and Bhanoji Rao's estimates of per capita GNI suggest that this measure grew by an impressive 30.6 per cent in 1950, subsiding to 6.6 per cent in 1951. Subsequently, as rubber and tin prices fell again, real GDP and GNI both retreated. In the mid 1950s,

---

4 In striking contrast, Lim (1967) comments that over this same period, 'the economy was crawling along at a snail's pace' and provides estimates of real aggregate GDP (not real per capita GDP) that put growth for Malaya (excluding Singapore) at 0.8 per cent in 1947 and 0.7 per cent in 1948. It seems likely that the Bhanoji Rao (1980) estimates are the more credible, however, as these were constructed using superior information and a more rigorous methodology, incorporating internal consistency checks. Indeed, Bhanaji Rao (1980) explicitly comments that Lim's (1967, p. 8) estimates are based on simple extrapolation methods.

growing demand in industrial countries again lifted rubber and tin prices, rekindling GDP and GNI growth, but the terms of trade then deteriorated once again resulting in another period of contraction during the second half of the decade. These reversals were then partially offset by a recovery in 1959, but at the end of the 1950s both the Maddison and the Bhanoji Rao (1980) data suggest that real per capita GDP was 4 per cent less than at the start of the decade.[5]

The 1960s saw the advent of sustained gains in per capita GDP.[6] The Maddison data show that per capita income in 1969 was 31 per cent higher than at the start of 1960, in marked contrast to the experience of the 1950s. During the 1960s, commodity dependence began to wane as domestic demand was boosted by rising investment in infrastructure assets. Agriculture diversified and achieved productivity gains as palm oil production picked up pace, and traditional agricultural activities gradually became more commercialized (Chapter 8). This diversification and broadening of the economic base was assisted by the Pioneer Industries Ordinance of 1958, by the expansion of oil production in Sarawak, and by growth in the timber industry, largely in Sabah.

Convergence and Gaps in Per Capita GDP

How did Malaysia perform relative to benchmark countries at the income frontier? The Solow–Swan model of economic growth, which has framed countless empirical investigations into the determinants of economic growth among and within countries, predicts that, under certain conditions, economies with income levels that are initially low will grow faster and catch up with those economies in which income levels are initially high—the 'absolute income convergence' hypothesis (Box 5.2).

Useful insight into comparative economic performance can be gained by tracking movements of per capita GDP in Malaysia relative to those in high-income countries, using the ratio of per capita income in Malaysia to a representative high-income country (or equivalently, the difference in their logarithms). If the ratio of per capita incomes shows a tendency to rise (with Malaysian per capita income in the numerator), this can be considered as evidence of relative income convergence. In Figure 5.2, relative incomes,

5 It is important to note that the change in real per capita GDP over the decade is highly sensitive to the choice of the base year. Using the Maddison database, the comparison is between 1948 and 1959, and per capita GDP rose by 22 per cent; between 1949 and 1959, by contrast, per capita GDP declined by 4 per cent.

6 The only year in which there was no expansion of per capita output is 1967.

measured in PPP units and in per capita terms, are compared using the Maddison data for 1911–1969.[7]

Box 5.2 The Solow–Swan growth model

Taking the rate of growth of the labour force (in terms of population size) as a given, the Solow–Swan model identifies the factors that influence the level of per capita income in an economy in which markets clear to ensure that planned savings equal planned investment. Under these conditions, all variables eventually grow at the same rate as the exogenously determined rate of growth of the labour force, and the level of output per worker is positively related to the savings rate. A one-time improvement in technology raises the level of output per worker, while faster labour force growth and/or a faster rate of capital depreciation lowers the level.

The 'transitional dynamics' of the Solow–Swan model, or its behaviour outside of equilibrium, as an economy develops towards maturity are of particular interest. These dynamics imply that the lower the capital–output ratio is relative to its equilibrium level (the poorer the economy), the faster the growth of the economy will be; meanwhile, growth will slow as the economy approaches its long-run equilibrium level of income. This suggests that low-income countries should grow more quickly than countries with higher incomes, forming the basis of the so-called 'unconditional convergence' hypothesis. These predictions of the Solow–Swan model resonate with the experience of post-independence Malaysia of gradually 'catching up' with the income levels of advanced economies (Figure 5.2). As per capita income levels have risen in Malaysia, their rate of growth has indeed slowly tapered.

However, this property of unconditional (or absolute) convergence is based on the assumption that countries share identical characteristics, differing only in their initial capital–labour ratio. If other fundamental characteristics differ, such as savings rates, depreciation rates, and/or levels of technology, as is likely to be the case in practice, nations will end up with different equilibrium levels of per capita income.

The so-called 'conditional convergence' hypothesis suggests that the potential for lower-income countries to experience faster rates of growth thus depends not only on initial income levels, but also on structural characteristics, and on the choices that are made about policies and institutions. These factors will determine the specific equilibrium that particular countries are moving towards, with those with more favourable conditions and constructive policies able to attain higher equilibrium levels of income than those which face more difficult constraints, or make less judicious choices.

7 There are no estimates before 1911 that would facilitate an extended comparison, and the PWT9.1 data start only in 1955.

Figure 5.2 **Catch-ups, stalls, and reversals on the path to convergence**

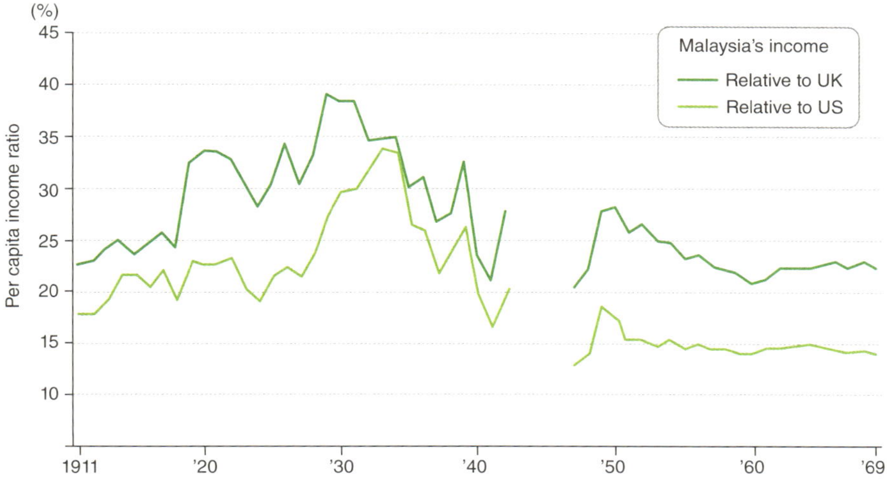

Source of data: University of Groningen (2018).

The figure shows three distinct sub-periods. From 1911 to the onset of the Great Depression in 1930 there was rapid catch-up of per capita GDP with the most advanced countries. The 1930s then saw a rapid reversal of these gains, returning Malaya's economy to where it had been in the early part of the century. The war years seem to have led to further regression, but were followed by reconstruction and sharp recovery. Thereafter, the relative income gap again widens and meanders in a narrow range, showing little sign of convergence. Thus, while the 1960s marked a turning point in that growth became far more sustained and considerably less volatile than in earlier decades, it also appears that since this decade Malaysia has only been keeping pace with economic growth in the US and UK, rather than gaining any ground.

In the following sections, the factors that underpinned economic performance in the six distinct historical periods identified over 1874–1969 are examined.

Post-Pangkor Engagement, 1874–1899

Britain's imperial interests in Malaya expanded significantly in 1874 with the arrival of a British Resident in Perak following the signing of the Pangkor Engagement (Chapter 1). The institutions that would shape the political and economic administration of the territories of Malaya, and leave their imprint even during the formation of Malaysia nearly a century later, began to form in this early period. From this point onwards, the colonization of the peninsula was increasingly formalized, and colonial laissez-faire economic policies—entailing minimum government involvement in, or regulation of, enterprise—were progressively introduced (Box 5.3).

Box 5.3 Laissez-faire economic policy

Laissez-faire (from the French 'allow to do') is an approach restricting the scope of government involvement in economic affairs. Laissez-faire does not imply the total absence of government intervention, but it does mean that there is only limited involvement. In all economies, the government plays some role to a greater or lesser extent, such as in the maintenance of public safety and security, in ensuring property rights, in financing and operating infrastructure, and in the provision of public works and services (including education and health), which may not be provided by private enterprise. This was the case in colonial Malaya.

In this book, the use of the term *laissez-faire* to describe the economic approach during the British colonial period denotes minimal government involvement in the regulation of the economy, and especially in the ownership and control of businesses. The government encouraged free trade, and for much of the period there were only minimal business taxes and no personal income tax. In practice, the colonial government intervened heavily in the interests of British companies, for example, by protecting British companies' interests in exports of tin and rubber, and by supporting the interests of plantation companies over rubber smallholders. The government raised revenues, especially through indirect taxation, to finance its administration, security, and development programmes, such as infrastructure, urban sanitation, and in the social sectors. However, these programmes were primarily in support of its economic objectives.

After World War II, there was a greater leaning towards government activity in a 'mixed' economy, and after 1970 the government was increasingly engaged in planning and managing the economy, with direct government involvement in business. In his 1926 book *The End of Laissez-Faire*, the English economist John Maynard Keynes accepted in principle that a marketplace of free individuals pursuing their own self-interest without government interference has a better chance of improving a society's economic situation than socialist alternatives. However, he argued that markets may not always adjust with sufficient speed to avoid mass unemployment in cyclical downturns, and he proposed that governments should engage in deficit spending during recessions. Keynes's (2009) ideas provided the impetus for governments to take a far greater role in the economy.

Legal, judicial, and administrative systems, as well as monetary and fiscal arrangements, were all put into place, designed to secure property rights and to facilitate investment, trade, and the unimpeded flow of resources to the metropolitan capital.[8] Over time, and with the growing influence of the British in other tin-producing states, these arrangements were gradually extended.

In North Borneo, a territory in which the Colonial Office had less strategic or economic interest than it did in the tin-mining areas of the peninsula, direct administration started from 1881, but was later ceded to the British North Borneo Chartered Company. The company ran the territory for profit, exploiting its rich natural resources, especially timber, with little interest in its diverse indigenous population. From the late 19th century there had been sustained prospecting for oil onshore in North Borneo, particularly in Tawau and the Klias peninsula. While oil was struck, it was not found in large commercial quantities (Worth, 1940). The company opened up the land for commercial agricultural activities, but its efforts were often hampered by difficult geography and by native resentment towards coercive taxation and other measures. Remote decision-making by a board of directors in London who had little experience in matters other than business, incompetent administration on the ground, and a lack of understanding of the culture and traditions of North Borneo's indigenous population, led many ventures to the verge of bankruptcy (Azlan Tajuddin, 2012).

In Sarawak during this period the Colonial Office provided administrative and military support to the Brooke family. A Supreme Council advised Raja James Brooke on major policy decisions, and had legislative powers. In 1867, a General Council was also established as a forum for the chiefs and heads of the various communities to meet the raja on a triennial basis, in order to build rapport between the raja and the leaders of his subjects (Ooi, 1997). Elements of a legal and judicial system were initiated, and these supported the development of modest commercial activity that largely revolved around the production and export of coffee, pepper, sago, and gambier, as well as gold and especially oil.[9] Essentially, however, the territory remained a private fiefdom in which indigenous hierarchies had been co-opted by the Brooke government, and in which day-to-day authority was exercised through the family's appointed British Residents, who presided over each of Sarawak's divisions (Azlan Tajuddin, 2012).

From an economic perspective the Pangkor period was largely dominated by tin. Drabble (2000) calculates that by 1895 tin accounted for 88 per cent

8 For example, the State Council of Perak, which was formed in 1877, quickly passed legislation that introduced concessions and leases on land for which no markets or market value had previously existed. The creation of such proprietary rights on land paved the way for the growth of plantations. Azlan Tajuddin (2012) notes that the largest land concessionaire in the state of Selangor, Hill and Rathbone, was able to obtain 999-year leases for lands totalling more than 10,000 acres.

9 The importance of oil to British interests was such that, as early as the late 1920s, contingency military arrangements were being planned by the Oversea Defence Committee to protect the Miri oilfields in the event of internal disorder or external invasion (Archive document CO 531/21/4, 1927–1930).

of the exports of the recently formed Federated Malay States. As global industrial demand surged, the production of tin grew seven-fold between 1878 and 1894 (Figure 5.3). By the 1890s, Malaya produced more tin than the rest of the world combined, with more than half coming from the Perak mines. Indeed, it was Britain's strategic and commercial interest in securing these tin supplies that had induced the British government to abandon its policy of non-interference and pursue a more direct custodial role over the territories of the peninsula.

Figure 5.3 Perak's tin production was dominant in 1878–1912

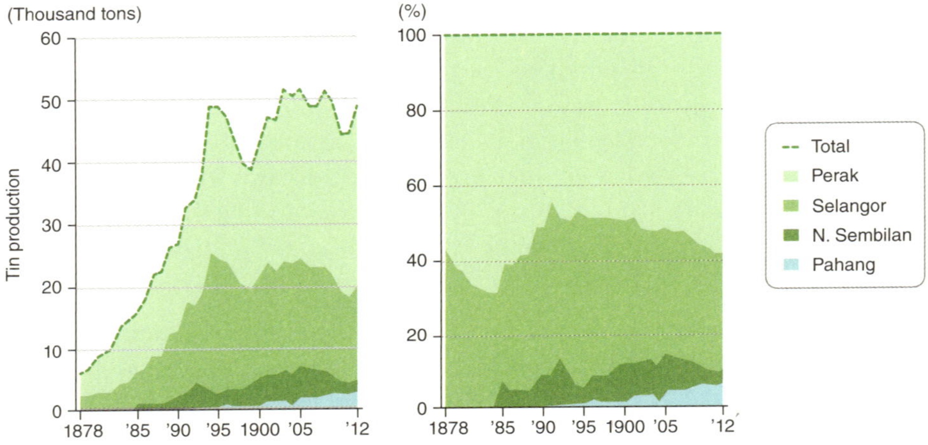

Source of data: Wong (1965, Appendix A).

In the 19th century, tin mining was still exploiting readily accessible ore deposits using relatively simple techniques. It was a highly labour-intensive process, pre-dating mechanization in the form of steam pumps and dredging equipment. The industry was largely the preserve of Chinese, who acquired rights to mine from Malay landowners; sometimes Chinese and Malay rulers established partnerships for the joint development of tin resources (Tai Yuen, 2013). Much of the investment in tin mining came from Chinese entrepreneurs in the Straits Settlements.

There are only very limited economic data available for this period. The Maddison project provides estimates of GDP for 1830 and 1870. To the extent that these are accurate, they suggest very little growth over the intervening period, averaging just 0.2 per cent a year. However, after Pangkor, Drabble's (2000) estimates of export and import flows suggest that the commercial part of the economy was expanding quickly, and that this expansion increased even more spectacularly in the early 20th century due to the rubber industry (Figure 5.4).

Figure 5.4 Malaya's imports and exports grew spectacularly in the half century 1870–1920[a]

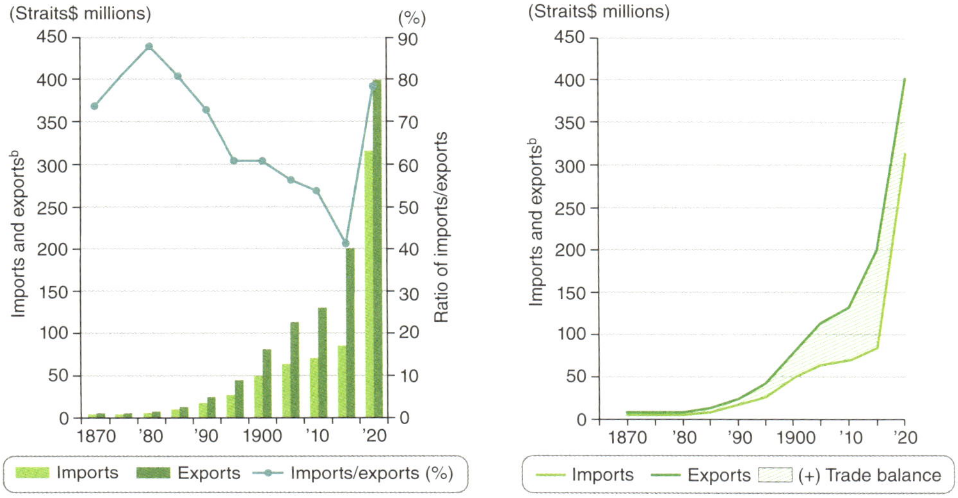

Source of data: Drabble (2000, p. 38).

Notes: [a] Malay peninsula (excluding Straits Settlements).

[b] Imports are taken as exports from Straits Settlement ports to the Malay peninsula; exports, vice versa. Data for Kedah are not available for 1901–1909.

The second half of the 19th century saw the costs of trade fall dramatically as the Suez Canal opened, and steamships replaced sailboats. From 1875 to 1900, the volume of Malaya's exports is estimated to have grown five-fold and by a factor of 13 in value terms. Imports also grew quickly, although not quite at the pace of exports, growing in value by a factor of 10 over the same period. Tin was extracted and exported in such quantities that its revenues more than met needs for imports. Steep gains in the terms of trade, as industrialization in Britain and elsewhere in Europe quickly reduced the costs of manufactured imports such as textiles, helped to widen the trade surplus. Although the benefits of this vigorous growth would certainly have rippled throughout the domestic economy, leakages are also likely to have been significant through outbound remittances of profits and other income.

Growth, Volatility, and Reversals, 1900–1941

This period was marked by notable economic growth, but even more so by economic turbulence (Sultan Nazrin Shah, 2017). At the dawn of the 20th century, a conjunction of constraints on the cultivation of established cash crops (mainly sugar, coffee, and gambier) and a surge in the global price of rubber encouraged rapid expansion of rubber planting. The area under cultivation multiplied quickly, and by 1915 rubber had replaced tin as the major export earner. For the next four decades, the fate of the Malayan economy became tightly bound to the vicissitudes of the global demand for rubber. The Malayan economy boomed during the so-called Roaring Twenties as US motor vehicle production and the demand for rubber tyres grew exponentially. The tin-mining sector also benefited from a new wave of investment during this period, encouraged by higher tin prices and technological advances that lowered the cost of exploiting less accessible ore deposits. However, the country's fortunes sank with the onset of the Great Depression, and the economy languished in the 1930s.

The Rubber Boom, 1900–1929

Rubber trees were introduced to Malaya from Brazil in the 1870s. From a few experimental saplings planted in northern Perak, an industry of prodigious proportions grew, one that was to define and transform the economic fortunes of Malaya for decades to come. Commercial rubber production only began in 1890, but the sector quickly became established as Malaya's major export earner. Rubber demand was initially stimulated by its use for shoes and bicycle tyres, and fast-rising prices at the start of the century fed into the rapid expansion of the acreage under rubber cultivation. There was huge growth during this period, with rubber plantations opening up new frontiers and pushing into the interior of the peninsula. By 1910, real investment in cultivated assets in the Federated Malay States was a staggering 36 times larger than it had been in 1900; this increase was due almost entirely to investment in rubber.

Rubber cultivation was initially undertaken by individual planters moving away from other crops (for instance, coffee), but as both the demand for, and price of, rubber grew massively, large-scale expansion required investment and organizational capabilities beyond the means of individual planters. British merchant houses in the Straits Settlements provided the solution to both challenges. Leveraging their reputations and connections, they coordinated funding through the creation of joint-stock companies in London. Through the provision of shared services across the estates in which they had investments, moreover, the agency houses also helped to overcome operational constraints and lowered costs (Drake, 2018).

The government encouraged investment in rubber through tax breaks, concessions, and secure leases on land, and allowed investors the freedom to recruit low-cost migrant workers, supporting systems which facilitated this process (Chapter 2). The rapid opening up of land for rubber cultivation—

with rubber acreage increasing five-fold between 1905 and 1908 and then doubling between 1909 and 1916—was made possible by the introduction of British land tenure and leasing arrangements under the Land Enactment of 1897.

The rapid expansion encroached on customary land, however, creating stresses in rural Malay society. In response to pressure from Malay rulers concerned about the loss of land, the government modified the land regulations through the Malay Reservation Enactment of 1913, which prevented the further disposal or sale of hereditary Malay *kampung* land to non-Malays and its conversion for large-scale agricultural activities.[10] Nearly 16 per cent of the land area of the Federated Malay States was designated as reserved land. In 1917, the Federated Malay States Rice Lands Enactment further prohibited the planting of rubber on land suitable for wet rice cultivation (Drabble, 2000).

Support for the creation of these reservations was motivated by the government's interest in sustaining domestic food supplies as part of the broader colonial policy of preserving traditional Malay economic and social roles. Limited support for local rice growers was also provided, with the establishment of government milling facilities (intended to break Chinese monopolies), the formation of rural farmer credit cooperatives (intended to help resolve problems of indebtedness), and the reduction of land sales intended to cover debts.[11]

It was the Unfederated Malay States, and Kedah in particular, that formed the 'rice bowl' of colonial Malaya. By the early 1920s, the Unfederated Malay States supplied over 80 per cent of the locally produced rice consumed in British Malaya (Azlan Tajuddin, 2012). However, the lack of support for improving agricultural conditions in these states kept productivity levels low, and limited the potential for the livelihoods of rural Malays to be improved. Reserved lands were not earmarked in these states until the 1930s.[12]

At the macro level, the paltry investment in traditional agriculture contributed to a growing dependence on rice imports, which imposed ever-larger claims on highly volatile export earnings. Only later in the 1920s, when the high price of imported rice began to be felt more keenly in the Federated

---

10 This legislation was initially implemented in the Federated Malay States in 1913, and enacted only later in the Unfederated Malay States, starting with Kelantan in 1930. Malay reservations were areas demarcated for exclusive alienation to, and settlement by, Malays.

11 Rural cooperative credit societies began in the early 1920s when the colonial administration established a Co-operative Societies Department in 1922 to promote the interests of rural Malay farmers and smallholders. Members contributed savings and in return were eligible for low-interest loans. The expansion of the movement suffered due to lack of capacities of various types, however, and was halted with the Great Depression. It was later deemed to have brought no significant improvement to the lives of Malays (CO 717/164/5, 1947).

12 Reserved lands were earmarked in Kelantan in 1930; in Kedah in 1931; in Perlis in 1935; in Johor in 1936; and in Terengganu in 1941.

Malay States, draining both export revenues and government resources, did the colonial authorities pay much attention to lifting the productivity of the *padi* economy (Drabble, 2000).

By the early 20th century, rubber had eclipsed the cultivation of established crops such as sugar and tapioca, which by this point were facing numerous impediments, including lack of land for extension, soil exhaustion, escalating labour costs, and volatile prices. Initially, rubber investments were made in those states where there was abundant suitable land and some existing transport infrastructure, namely Perak, Selangor, Negeri Sembilan, and Johor. Much of the expansion was large scale, funded by the capital investment coordinated by British agency houses in the Straits Settlements, and raised in Britain through joint-stock company structures. There was also significant expansion of smallholding activity by Malay and Chinese producers, who, encouraged by the prospects of high prices and elevated incomes, used family labour to clear land and plant trees.[13]

The substantial growth of demand for motor cars in the US after the adoption of mass assembly methods, and the consequent dramatic fall in manufacturing costs, took the demand for rubber to new levels. World War I further stimulated demand for motorized transport and thus for rubber tyres, and while it also disrupted trade routes to Europe, the opening of the Panama Canal in 1913 and the availability of vessels from Japan brought trade costs down in the Pacific. Although demand boomed, prices retreated from the peak they had reached in 1910 as supply was expanding even more quickly. Despite falling prices, however, rubber production remained highly profitable for Malaya's cultivators, who benefited from first-mover advantage in this burgeoning global trade. By 1915, rubber had overtaken tin as the country's major export earner.

While the rubber industry experienced this phenomenal expansion, the tin industry was undergoing a huge change in structure and ownership. As easily accessible ore deposits were exhausted, new technologies—including hydraulic sluicing, mechanized dredging, and pumping techniques—were adopted to increase the extraction efficiency of hard-to-reach mining deposits. These technologies required heavy capital investments and organizational skills, which British and other European interests could acquire much more easily than smaller Chinese enterprises. British interests in tin mining were supported by the colonial government through the provision of infrastructure, land concessions, and affordable leases on expensive capital equipment. The colonial licensing system, which was used to regulate mining activity, also

13 Malaya's small Chettiar community, besides owning a number of estates, played an important role in providing capital and credit to rubber smallholders (Suppiah and Raja, 2016).

charged high fees, which presented barriers to entry for weakly capitalized Chinese interests. Thus, whereas in 1910 Chinese operators had managed 78 per cent of tin production, by 1935 British firms accounted for 66 per cent (Li, 1982).

The 1920s was a decade of growing international prosperity during which industrial economies that had been geared towards war production were reconfigured to support a boom in peacetime demand, particularly in the US. New technologies (consumer goods and motor vehicles), new methods of mass production, marketing and distribution, the easy availability of consumer credit (with many unregulated banks in the US), and falling prices of consumer goods, all supported vigorous growth of demand and jobs, as well as a surging stock market. The US economy enjoyed a golden age, expanding by 45 per cent over the 1920s despite a serious reversal in 1924.

Rapid growth in demand for final consumer and investment goods fuelled demand for material inputs, including primary commodities. The demand for rubber continued to soar, while the demand for tin also grew rapidly as products canned in tinplate became an integral part of domestic life in the richer economies, and as the industrial demand for alloys containing tin—for use in cables and metal pipes, for example—quickly expanded. Labour productivity in Malaya made substantial advances, with output per worker in the estate rubber sector almost doubling from 1920 to 1930, and tripling in the tin-mining sector. By 1929, Malaya was the world's largest producer of both rubber and tin, accounting for 51.6 per cent and 36.7 per cent of global production respectively (Lim, 1967).

Figure 5.5 **Malaya's share of world rubber production rose as prices fell**

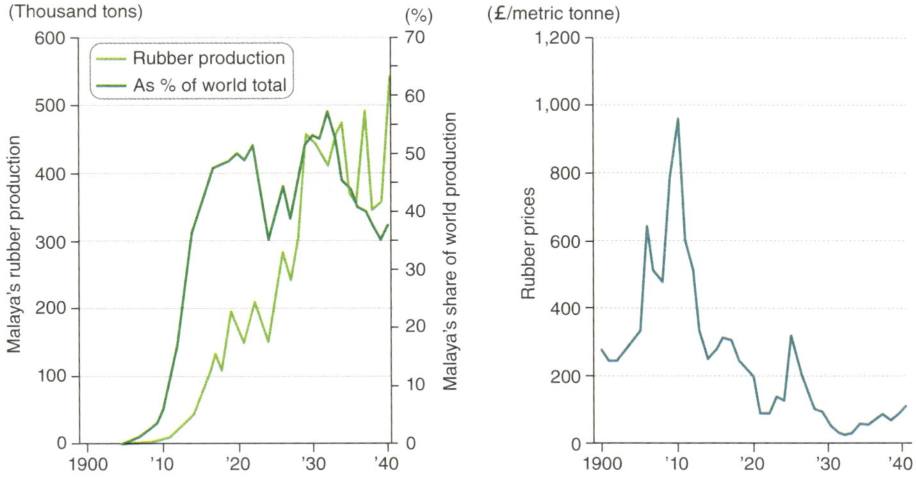

Sources of data: Tate (1996, p. 210); International Rubber Study Group (various years).

The increasing manufacture of synthetic rubber alternatives following World War I, growing supplies from the Dutch East Indies, and booming production in Malaya combined, however, to cause a glut, and prices slumped, reaching a two-decade low in 1920–1922 (Figure 5.5). The European estates favoured restrictions on production as a means of raising prices (and revenues), but smallholders and Asian planters who required steady incomes to service their debts were less keen on this approach.

In 1920, following the post–World War I recession, the London-based Rubber Growers' Association requested that the British government prepare a plan to stabilize rubber prices at a time of rapidly rising production and very low prices (Figure 5.5). In November 1922, the British government adopted the Stevenson Plan, which imposed production and export quotas on both Malaya and Ceylon, aimed at achieving target prices.[14] The plan initially succeeded in stabilizing prices, with output quotas at around 80 per cent of capacity, but its mechanics failed to anticipate a sudden expansion in US demand in 1924 and 1925. This caused prices to jump and prompted another wave of investment by estates and smallholders in the peninsula, as well as in North Borneo and the Dutch East Indies. As prices subsequently fell back, however, and as other unrestricted sources of supply—particularly from the Dutch East Indies—made rapid inroads into the North American market, the British ended the Stevenson Plan in 1928. The Stevenson Plan had serious distributional effects that hurt smallholders by discriminating against them in quota allocations, and by greatly under-assessing their productive potential. This denied smallholders the opportunity for a better livelihood and curtailed expansion opportunities that could have led to cheaper rubber for consumers (Barlow et al., 1994).

This period witnessed a rapid expansion in newer economic activities, including the production of palm oil, iron ore, and, briefly in Sarawak, petroleum. Trading enterprises also prospered, many of them British-owned and often vertically integrated with rubber and tin ventures. There was little by way of an industrial sector, however, beyond some basic tin smelting and rubber processing, cement production, manufacture of consumer foods, and small-scale fabrication and maintenance operations.

During the decades up to around 1930, most manufactured goods, including machinery, were imported from the UK. Generally, only high-weight-to-value products could be profitably produced locally, as the liberal trade regime and high domestic costs made other activities uneconomic. Farming, forestry, fishing, and livestock activities, which coexisted alongside the modern agricultural export economy, remained largely traditional and predominantly the preserve of rural Malays. Deficits in rice production for

14 Drabble (2000) notes that the underlying goal was not so much to support plantation economic interests as to stabilize sterling area reserves in a context where earnings depended heavily on rubber export sales to the US.

domestic needs, swollen by a large migrant population, had to be met by imports as efforts to increase rice cultivation lagged (Chapter 8).

From 1900 to the start of the Great Depression, the experience of the Malayan economy can without doubt be compared to a roller-coaster ride, with periods of very rapid growth followed by equally sharp contractions (Sultan Nazrin Shah, 2017). These oscillations reflected the volatile price movements that were an unremitting feature of the rubber and tin markets, both of which were characterized by highly inelastic supply and demand conditions (Box 5.4).

Box 5.4 Demand for, and prices of, rubber and tin, and their volatility

The demand for, and prices of, rubber and tin during the colonial period were highly volatile and were affected by many factors, including wars—for instance, World War I and the Korean War—which increased demand for materials (and were price positive); large negative demand shocks like the recession of 1922 and the Great Depression (price negative); positive demand shocks, for instance in 1924–1925 (price positive); the availability of substitutes, namely synthetic rubber, after World War I in Russia and after World War II in the US (price negative); technological changes, such as higher-yielding rubber tree varieties, and new tin-mining technologies including steam water pumps and dredges (price negative); mass assembly techniques that increased the demand for cars and other consumer durables (price positive); exhaustion of ore deposits (price positive); and supply quotas, such as those under the Stevenson Plan (temporarily price positive).

Under normal conditions—all other things being equal—producers will find it profitable to increase (or reduce) supply in response to higher (or lower) prices for their output. However, there may be conditions in which the ability of producers to adjust supply in response to a change in price is constrained. When large changes in price induce little response in supply, supply is considered to be 'price inelastic'. Likewise, demand is price inelastic when large changes in price have little influence on demand. For example, the necessities of life (food, clothing, and shelter) are generally price inelastic, whereas the demand for luxury goods (consumer durables and recreational services) may be highly sensitive to price.

Given price-inelastic supply (or demand), any factor that leads to a shift in market demand (or market supply) will have little effect on volume but a large effect on price, as illustrated by Box Figure 5.1. In the left-hand panel, the movement from point A to point B (or B to A) and the large price fall (rise) occurs when there is a negative (positive) shift in market demand for rubber. In the right-hand panel, the impact of a shift in market supply is shown.

While *market* conditions may be characterized by inelastic demand, an *individual* supplier may still face a highly elastic demand curve. Any attempt to set prices above the market-determined level will tend to lead to substitution by other suppliers, and if prices are set below the market level, this will attract increased demand. Of course, setting prices below the market level would make economic sense only if the producer had inventories or spare production capacity that it could bring to market profitably.

Box Figure 5.1 How shocks to rubber and tin supply and demand affect prices

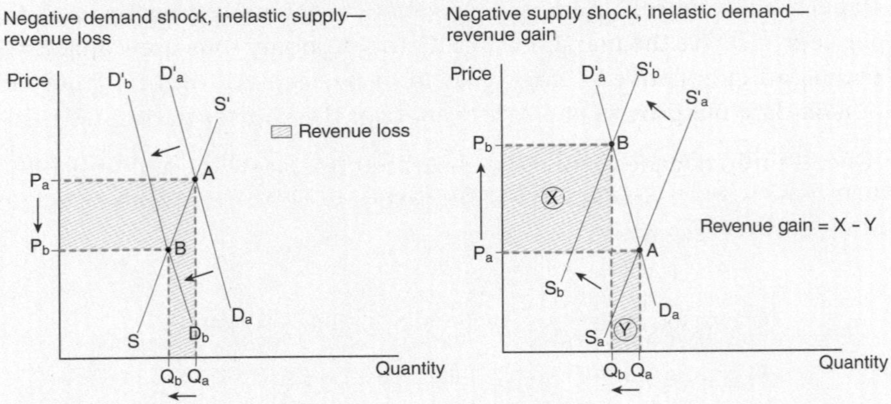

The markets for rubber and tin both have price-inelastic supply and price-inelastic demand—structural features that go a long way to explaining price and revenue volatility. It takes six or seven years after planting for a rubber tree to yield latex, and the productive life of a tree is then about 27 years. Once a tree is planted, provided the price of latex covers the costs of tapping and bringing the latex to market, it will be tapped. While higher prices may encourage investment for longer-term returns, they will have little near-term impact on production. Supply is fixed by the stock of trees planted between six and 33 years ago, and by the limits that nature places on the volume of latex that can be tapped from each tree.

On the demand side, rubber materials and components usually represent only a small part of the total cost of the end product in which they are used. For example, an increase in the price of rubber has only a marginal impact on the final cost of producing a car or on its price. Changes in the price of rubber are, therefore, unlikely to have much influence on producers' decisions regarding the volume of car production. Accordingly, once production decisions about cars are made, demand for rubber parts and components is fixed, largely irrespective of price—demand will be price inelastic.

Similarly for tin, known ore deposits and mining technology limit the extent to which production can adjust to short-run variations in price. If prices rise, it will take time to open new mines. And if prices fall, it will still be profitable to extract ore from existing mines provided that the costs of doing so (the 'variable costs' of a unit of production) are covered by the unit price.

On the demand side, tin is used mainly as an intermediate input into the production of industrial and consumer goods. As tin, like rubber, generally only makes a small contribution to costs, changes in the price of tin will have little influence on decisions about the production of final goods in which it is used. Hence, once upstream production decisions are made, the demand for tin is determined in a way that is largely insensitive to its own price. The market for tin, like the market for rubber, in the colonial period is therefore characterized by price-inelastic supply and price-inelastic demand.

The Sultan Nazrin Shah (2017) estimates indicate that of the 30 years from 1900 to 1929 there were only 12 in which GDP did not either grow or contract by 10 per cent or more.[15] In 14 of these years the economy grew by more than 10 per cent. Despite the marked volatility the economy thus grew apace, with an estimated cumulative average growth of per capita GDP of 4.7 per cent. Maddison data put growth at 4.2 per cent over the shorter period 1911–1929.

Of the three decades, growth accelerated the most quickly from 1920 to 1929. Primed by the voracious global appetite for rubber and tin, and by rapid labour productivity growth, per capita GDP in the 1920s grew at a cumulative average rate of 6.5 per cent, rapidly closing the gap with per capita GDP in the US and the UK (Figure 5.2).[16] The Great Depression marked the end of this remarkable economic roller-coaster ride, and it was decades before GDP regained the heights reached in the late 1920s.

Although per capita GDP is the usual metric used in studies of economic performance and growth, it does have limitations as a barometer of development. For the period of colonial rule in Malaya, it is likely that estimates of per capita GDP growth exaggerate the gains that were made in the living standards of the general population. The Sultan Nazrin Shah (2017) estimates suggest that per capita consumption grew much more slowly than per capita GDP. In the two decades from 1910 to 1929, for example, per capita consumption grew at an average rate of only 0.7 per cent compared with per capita GDP growth of 5.8 per cent.

The most plausible reason for this divergence is that the presence of substantial overseas interests in rubber and tin meant that a high proportion of the returns in each sector leaked out of the local economy, as profits were transferred overseas.[17] Large surpluses were repatriated to the foreign investors who had acquired sizeable stakes in plantation agriculture and in tin-mining ventures, including the British agency trading houses.[18] In the prevailing laissez-faire economy, it was the imperial interests in buttressing the reserves of the greater sterling area and maximizing the returns to

---

15 Note that 'contraction' refers to a decline in real GDP over the previous year, as opposed to 'reversal' (see footnote 3), which is a period during which per capita GDP remains lower than the previous peak level. A reversal can thus contain a number of periods of contraction.

16 Gross domestic income, which accounts for the income effect of changes in the terms of trade, would have grown even more as the price of rubber and tin increased relative to the costs of Malaya's import basket (Sultan Nazrin Shah, 2017).

17 Thoburn (1977) maintains that over the long period from 1900 to the 1970s, there were high retention rates of profits from rubber and tin mining. Yet in 1900–1939 domestic investment rates were generally low, and there is evidence that dividends to shareholders of London's joint-stock companies were extremely high. In Sultan Nazrin Shah's (2017) estimates, the gap between per capita GDP growth and consumption growth cannot be attributed to fast investment growth, and is therefore deemed most likely to reflect the repatriation of profits.

18 The top five British agency houses operating in Malaya at that time were Harrisons and Crosfield, Guthrie, Boustead, Sime Darby, and Cumberbatch.

British shareholders that were paramount, not the welfare of the people of Malaya.

Investments in rubber and tin yielded extraordinarily high rates of return, which were reflected in large dividend payouts. For example, between 1910 and 1920, the returns on capital for Harrisons and Crosfield, one of the largest agency houses managing Malayan rubber plantations, fluctuated between 14 and 33 per cent (Koike, 2017). Many of the companies active in plantation and mining were considered to be domiciled overseas and so paid no local taxes on their profits. Additionally, the colonial administration from time to time repatriated some portion of its financial surpluses to London for particular purposes; they did this, for example, during World War I. It also regularly allocated surpluses to the reserves of the Straits currency board in the form of sterling securities or loans, thereby contributing to sterling area balances.[19]

Although a few local merchants, colonial administrative staff, members of the Malay elite, and rubber smallholders would have seen their standard of living rise, the gains for most migrant workers and for rural Malay communities are likely to have been far more limited. Among the few exceptions would have been those migrants who managed to save money and establish prosperous businesses. For most, though, wage levels were held in check by the continued arrival of newcomers, as well as by the steep wage cuts that would invariably accompany any decline in commodity prices. Moreover, many migrants would also have sent a portion of their earnings back home to support their families, in some cases retaining only what was required to meet their basic needs. For rural Malay communities that were not participating in rubber smallholding activities, the benefits of the commodity boom would have been contingent on real price increases for their traded surpluses of rice, fish, fruit, and other produce.

It thus seems reasonable to conclude that improvements in standards of living for the majority of the population would have been more modest than is suggested by the growth of per capita GDP up to 1930, or by the data on convergence trends with income levels in the US and the UK.

---

19 Resources flowed out of Malaya to the metropolitan capital through three main official channels. First, direct contributions of financial surpluses were made through grants to support specific needs, such as the funding of the war effort during World War I. Second, under the currency board arrangement, issuance of Straits dollars had to be backed at the given parity and the stipulated reserve ratio by sterling reserves, providing a ready market for metropolitan securities and loans. Third, following the collapse of the gold standard and the creation of the greater sterling exchange area, Malaya's dollar trade surpluses were remitted to London and were at the disposal of Britain to finance imports across the entire sterling exchange area.

Volatility in Tin Output and Prices

Tin production and prices fluctuated wildly during the first three decades of the century, especially during the economic downturns of the 1920s (Figure 5.6). Tin prices rose rapidly in the latter years of World War I because of shipping disruptions, but at the same time stocks were accumulating. The accumulated stocks, when combined with a global depression in 1921, reduced the average annual price by more than half compared with 1918.

Figure 5.6 **Malaya's share of world tin production declined as prices fluctuated**

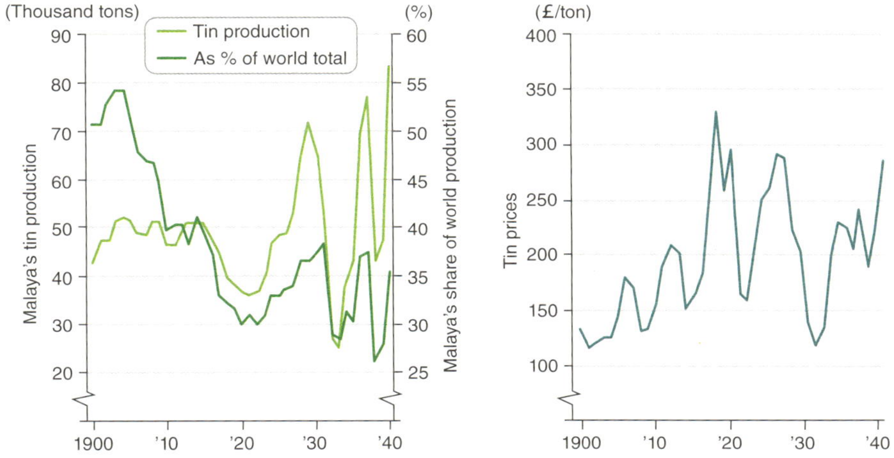

Source of data: Lim (1967, Appendix 2.1).

From December 1920 to February 1921, the government of the Federated Malay States bought and stocked Malayan tin at a minimum price. In 1921, it agreed with the government of the Dutch East Indies to form a pool—the Bandoeng Pool—to withhold tin from the market. From 1921 to June 1923, about 15 per cent of 1920 world production was withheld from the market. As prices strengthened, the tin was gradually released until stocks were exhausted in 1925, by which time world consumption had almost doubled. In 1928, tin was again withheld from the market by large tin-producing corporates to shore up the price. However, these steps were ineffective in supporting higher prices in the face of declining world consumption.

The Great Depression and Its Aftermath, 1930–1941

Any semblance of income convergence with the more advanced economies was shattered by the outcomes of the 1930s, and the Great Depression marks a broken decade during which Malaya fell behind. Per capita income in 1941 is estimated by the Maddison project to have been little different from its 1929 peak, while per capita incomes measured relative to those in the UK and the US had by this point reverted to the ratios seen in 1911.

The main causes of the Great Depression are still debated,[20] but its impact on Malaya was unmistakable. In the US, real GDP collapsed by 39 per cent between 1929 and 1933, and as the US was Malaya's major trading partner, the impact was felt immediately. Per capita GDP in Malaya fell by 13 per cent from 1929 to 1933,[21] and this retreat in per capita GDP would have been even larger had it not been for the repatriation of a sizeable number of unemployed migrant workers.

In the immediate aftermath of the collapse in US demand, Malaya's export volumes remained more or less steady.[22] However, this reflected short-run inelasticity of supply rather than any inherent resilience of the economy. Export prices bore the initial burden of adjustment, with rubber export revenues shrinking by 43.5 per cent from 1929 to 1930. Malaya's terms of trade deteriorated by 35 per cent between 1929 and 1930, and this decline was transmitted quickly to domestic demand (Figure 5.7). In 1930, real investment levels fell by 18 per cent and real per capita consumption by 12 per cent compared with the corresponding levels of 1929. There was also a notable contraction of imports, which were down 14 per cent in real terms. By contrast, government consumption spending rose by 5 per cent, mainly reflecting the additional costs of repatriating unemployed migrant workers (there was virtually no social safety net and no automatic fiscal stabilization mechanism). By 1931, real per capita consumption had fallen by 23.5 per cent from its 1929 level.

---

20 Some maintain that the booming US stock market created credit shortages elsewhere, such as in Germany and Britain, Europe's largest economies, causing their output to fall by mid 1928. Another interpretation (Eichengreen and Temin, 1997; Bernanke and James, 1990) concludes that the gold standard played an important role in triggering the crisis, because countries with a balance-of-payments deficit were forced to deflate, rather than devalue, their currencies. Under the gold standard, the value of each currency was fixed in terms of gold. In order to maintain that fixed exchange rate during deficit periods, countries were forced to increase interest rates to ensure that they did not run out of reserves (Bernanke, 2004). Faced with dwindling reserves, Britain abandoned the gold standard in 1931, while the US chose to raise interest rates and exited only two years later. Banking sector vulnerabilities in the US, including inadequate reserves and the asset price inflation fuelled by rapid credit growth, also played a role. Most agree that the policy response to the Great Depression, which in industrialized countries entailed monetary tightening and fiscal austerity, contributed to its depth and duration. The Great Depression also led to a rise in protectionist trade policies, which were responsible for deepening the crisis (Stiglitz, 2006).

21 Apart from where other sources are specified, the author's estimates in local constant prices are employed in this section to describe the growth dynamics.

22 The level of real GDP did not fall until 1931.

Figure 5.7 **Malaya's terms of trade deteriorated sharply during the Great Depression**

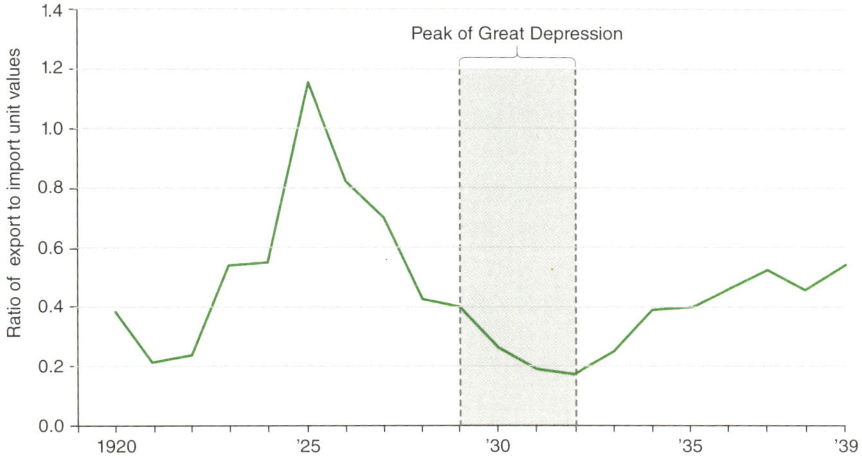

Source of data: Sultan Nazrin Shah (forthcoming).

With the Great Depression's devastating impact on trade, the major British and Dutch rubber producers once again turned to regulatory mechanisms to try to maintain prices. The new International Rubber Regulation Agreement, implemented from 1934 to 1941, was signed by all major rubber-producing countries, covering 98 per cent of the world's planted area. The agreement stipulated production quotas for existing plantings, and new planting was forbidden. It appears to have succeeded in supporting rubber prices. Prices rose slowly up to 1937, dipped in 1938, and then climbed again. As with the Stevenson Plan, however, the interests of smallholders were neglected, and eventually new sources of supply undercut the agreement (McFadyean, 1944; Barlow et al., 1994).

Responding to continued declines in tin prices, the Tin Producers' Association (TPA) was formed in 1930. The TPA stockpiled tin concentrates at smelters and restricted output. Again, these steps were ineffective in supporting higher prices in the face of declining world consumption. The TPA campaigned for formal tin restrictions, and in 1931 an International Tin Cartel started operations.

The International Tin Cartel Agreements—three successive agreements covering 1931–1933, 1934–1936, and 1936–1941—pioneered the use of output controls, and buffer pools and stocks to influence the market (Thoburn, 1994). The agreements sought to achieve price stability while maintaining adequate supplies. Production was regulated by means of output quotas established in relation to a 'standard tonnage' based on 1929 outputs, with some minimum output guarantees for producers. The 1929 output understated Malayan capacity, since in addition to the 105 dredges in operation, there were ten under construction in 1929 and another eight on order (Yip, 1969). Malayan output outside the Federated Malay States was ignored, as was smaller-scale mining capacity, which meant Malayan capacity was about 35 per cent higher than was represented by its standard tonnage. Tin exports were restricted over 1931–1941 as a result of these measures, and this succeeded in raising world tin prices.

The recession inevitably had a devastating effect on workers. Migrant workers were especially hard hit by retrenchments, and many either became small-scale subsistence farmers or were repatriated at the expense of the government (Bhattacharya and Kripalani, 2015). From 1929 to 1932, the total estate labour force of the Federated Malay States tumbled by 47 per cent (Kaur, 2004). At the nadir of the slump in 1932, 790,000 acres—15.5 per cent of the smallholdings' rubber area—went untapped (Lim, 1977). The number of tin mines in operation fell by 17 per cent, and by 1933 the number of workers employed in tin mines had been slashed from 100,000 in 1929 to just 40,000 (Jomo, 1986).

Retrenchment was accompanied by sharp falls in real wages, of 13.6 per cent in 1930 and 10.3 per cent in 1931. Although real wages began to pick up in 1933, they remained well below the levels seen before the onset of the Great Depression. For instance, daily wage rates for Indian males on rubber estates, which were estimated to have been Straits$0.50–0.70 in 1929, had fallen to Straits$0.32–0.40 in 1933 (Kaur, 2004). With the sharp decline in real wages and high unemployment, Malaya's workers were exposed to extreme hardship and destitution.

The depression in economic activity strongly affected public finances. From 1929 to 1932, the declines in export duties earned on rubber and tin reduced the revenue of the Federated Malay States by 47 per cent, from Straits$81.8 million to Straits$43.8 million. Resulting shortfalls were met through the surpluses that the administration had previously accumulated.

Other fragmentary evidence confirms the severity of the impact of the downturn on business. Between 1930 and 1935, the number of local companies registered in the Federated Malay States fell by 42 per cent, while the number established outside the Federated Malay States but operating within the area fell by 29 per cent (Federated Malay States, Annual Reports, various years). The number of people who received bankruptcy orders increased from 26 in 1927 to 123 in 1932 (Federated Malay States, Annual Reports, various years).

Other broader indicators of commercial activities also show sharp declines. Railway goods traffic, for example, fell from 2.6 million tons in 1929 to 0.9 million tons in 1933, while passenger railway travel fell from 14.1 million to 5.5 million over the same period.

Trade flows recovered most quickly from the shock of the Great Depression. Export and import values and import volumes bottomed out in 1932, and followed an uptrend from 1933 onwards (Figure 5.8). Export volumes began to grow one year later. By 1935, the terms of trade had recovered, matching the level seen in 1929; the terms of trade continued to strengthen until the end of the decade. This recovery coincided with a mild increase in global demand, but may also have been influenced by producers' efforts to regulate the supply of rubber. Despite the recovery in trade, the impact of the depression lingered. Total exports during the 1930s were 26 per cent lower than during the 1920s, and total imports were 19 per cent lower.

In 1934, per capita GDP grew for the first time since 1929. While growth continued thereafter, faltering only briefly in 1935, real per capita GDP in pre-war Malaya never regained the level seen in 1929, although it came close in 1937. Real per capita consumption staged a mild recovery in 1933, but it took until 1937 for it to return to its 1929 level. Real investment was harder hit, and contracted until 1936. Despite some recovery thereafter, investment languished below its pre-depression level until 1939, and probably for several years after. Like consumption, real wages took seven years to return to their pre-crisis level.

Figure 5.8 Malaya's trade balance recovered after the Great Depression but was not as large as in the mid 1920s

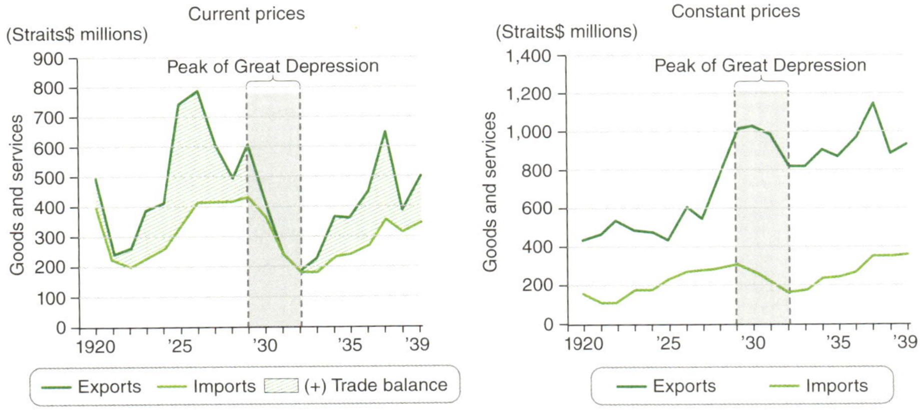

Source of data: Sultan Nazrin Shah (forthcoming).

The economic institutions created by the colonial administration were ill-equipped to respond to such economic shocks. Public financial matters were guided by principles of fiscal conservativism, with spending generally capped by available revenues. Faced with falling revenues in 1932, the administration established a Retrenchment Commission, which implemented a programme to reduce the number of government servants and imposed a 40 per cent cut in administrative costs across the board (Nadaraja, 2016). Despite these measures, budgets fell into deficit. The currency board arrangement, which linked the supply of Straits dollars to sterling reserves, offered no provision for easing monetary conditions to stimulate economic growth in response to the downturn. Indeed, it seems highly likely that there would have been an erosion of reserves and a monetary contraction at this time.

In short, the economy had no coordinated policymaking capability; no macroeconomic, shock-absorbing capabilities; and no stabilization mechanisms. The design of both fiscal and monetary arrangements, which were primarily intended to support colonial enterprise and commerce, actually conspired to aggravate the negative impact of the collapse of external demand and the negative terms-of-trade shock.[23]

Regulatory responses to the Great Depression focused on immigration. With demand for the major exports of rubber and tin in free fall, and with profit margins squeezed, tens of thousands of migrant workers lost their jobs. As the pool of unemployed migrant workers grew, the colonial administration moved to end Malaya's liberal immigration regime, using the Alien Ordinance of 1933 to impose new restrictions on migration (Chapter 2).

Beyond the revision and extension of the protection of reserved lands for Malays in the Federated Malay States (likely to have been motivated in part by colonial concerns over rice deficits given the rising population), and the introduction of new legislation in the Unfederated Malay States, the administration did little to protect the basic needs of the rural population. Although the restrictions imposed on rubber exports and the planting of new rubber did help to prop up prices,[24] they penalized Malay smallholders disproportionately and also discouraged investment in new, more efficient, planting techniques and higher-yielding tree varieties. Those who could diversify their economic activities survived the economic slump best (Harper, 1999).

---

23 Even if Malaya had had capable economic institutions, the prevailing wisdom was that the depression called for restrictive monetary and fiscal policy responses, a perspective that was to be challenged by the rise of Keynesian economic thinking.

24 The International Rubber Regulation was signed in 1934 to restrict exports of rubber from 1934 to 1938; it was later extended to 1944. From 1931 to World War II, four other international agreements were also signed.

A Segmented Economy and People

Malaya's pre-war colonial economy depended on foreign capital; on imported technologies such as dredges for tin mining and medicine for tropical disease control; on imported systems such as legal and judicial mechanisms, and land registration and titling; on foreign migrant workers; and on demand for raw materials from foreign markets. Most goods, including large quantities of rice—the staple food—were imported. Malaya had all the hallmarks of a 'dependent' economy (Box 5.5).

Box 5.5 Colonialism and dependency theories

There are many variants of 'dependency' theory, but all are rooted in a view of political economy that asserts that poor developing nations are dependent on rich countries for capital and markets. One version maintains that rich countries invest in poor countries primarily to extract natural resources and surpluses for their own benefit. Poor countries are unable to control their own domestic economies or the distribution of value from the exploitation of their resources, and remain trapped in a state of backwardness.

One way in which countries may become trapped in dependency is through a long-run deterioration in the terms of trade for primary commodities relative to manufactured goods, leading to successively larger volumes of domestic resources being exchanged for (manufactured) imports (the Prebisch–Singer hypothesis). Malaya did experience a decline in its terms of trade from 1900 to 1939 (Sultan Nazrin Shah, forthcoming).

Although the Prebisch–Singer hypothesis seems to describe one facet of colonial Malaya's trading relationships, there is little evidence that the demand for rubber was income inelastic over this period, or indeed any less elastic than the demand for imported goods. Declining prices for rubber had more to do with new sources of supply than inelastic demand. Moreover, the adverse income impacts were not confined to Malaya, as lower prices narrowed the profit margins of investors in the metropolitan capital and elsewhere.

The main manifestations of dependence in colonial Malaya were in the claims on the profits from the country's rubber, tin, and trading activities that were made by British and other foreign investors, and in the channelling of foreign exchange surpluses after World War II to support the wider sterling pool. Fiscal and monetary arrangements also put the interests of the metropolitan capital first, and provided little scope for independent economic management. The economy of colonial Malaya was dependent, too, on an army of migrant workers from China, India, and the Dutch East Indies. Colonial Malaya lacked the unified functions of the government of a unified state, and depended on colonial direction in virtually all major policy areas.

The economy also had a highly dualistic structure. A traditional peasant agricultural sector coexisted alongside commercial rubber production, tin mining, and a vibrant trading sector. These separate economies could be mapped on to distinct areas of Malaya. The north and east of the peninsula were home to traditional agricultural activities and handicrafts (Box 5.6), while the west had the major plantations and tin-mining operations. Trading activity was concentrated in the Straits Settlements and in the new colonial administrative centres. While Johor benefited from its proximity to Singapore, North Borneo and Sarawak lagged behind.

Box 5.6 The weaving industry in Kelantan and Terengganu

The production of handloom textiles, especially in the state capitals of Kelantan and Terengganu, flourished until the depression years of the 1930s. Weaving centres for *songket* and *batik* were inspired by Arab and Indian traders. The traditional Malay fabric of *songket* is highly labour-intensive, being handwoven from silk or cotton threads, and then embroidered with gold and silver threads to form motifs. *Batik* is made from cotton cloth decorated with motifs applied in wax, which are either hand-drawn or stamped using a copper or wooden stamp. The cloth is then dyed, but the waxed areas resist the dye, creating a pattern. This process can be repeated to create complex multicoloured designs (Jefferies et al., 2015).

The handloom industry was concentrated in Terengganu, and to a lesser extent in Kelantan, and was controlled by Malay merchant middlemen. They purchased raw materials from a few large Singaporean wholesalers, and imported spun silk yarn from China, dyestuffs from the UK, and metallic thread from India. They provided upstream specializations, including the dyeing of silk, construction of looms, and technical common facility services required by the weavers, who worked for wages based on each piece produced. Master weavers were in charge of the production process, the division of labour, and quality control. Specialized skills, like design and setting, were trade secrets applied within the master weavers' homes before the rest of the process was passed on to less skilful workers. Weaving was carried out almost entirely by women.

In 1920, the weaving industry boomed, with imports of raw materials—silk and cotton—at a peak. The export value of textiles in Terengganu also peaked in that year at around 28 per cent of the state's total commodities. The 1921 census records that there were 10,194 weavers in Terengganu and Kelantan, making up 90 per cent of Malaya's total. As competition from imported cotton goods intensified, Terengganu's industry responded by focusing on silk *sarong* production, while Kelantan exploited the availability of cheap textiles by using imported cotton to establish a new industry, the *batik sarong* (Maznah Mohamad, 1996). However, traditionally designed textiles gradually became marginalized in favour of cheaper, mass-produced imported products, and by the mid 1920s both weaver numbers and industry incomes had declined. Following the Great Depression in the 1930s, the weaving industry became less viable.

The colonial Department of Industry and Commerce tried to protect the local textile industry from imported lower-cost machine-made textiles by providing support in marketing and by introducing British dyes and yarns to local weavers. Preferential tariffs were accorded to the industry, allowing raw silk to be imported free of duty, and export duties were raised. These actions also increased British economic interests in the east coast states, opening local markets to British products and allowing Imperial Chemical Industries to build a dye factory in Terengganu (Maznah Mohamad, 1996).

In the years leading up to independence, efforts were made by the Rural Industrial Development Authority (RIDA) to revive the industry, and in 1956 a temporary centre for the dyeing of silk yarn was established. In 1957, there were 4,170 weavers and 3,886 looms in Terengganu and Kelantan (Fisk, 1959). Although the weaving industry had become mostly a peripheral 'spare time' industry with seasonal production—far fewer textiles were produced during *padi* harvesting, for example—it still brought economic benefits, particularly to Terengganu. It provided women, 95 per cent of whom were from low-income households, with a means of supplementing their income. The average monthly income from weaving of about M$16.75 raised household income by around 20 per cent (Fisk, 1959).

Pre-war colonial Malaya was not yet a unified administrative or political entity, and its economy was managed to serve the interests of the metropolitan capital as part of the broader colonial trading system.[25] A centralized administrative system prevailed in the economically advanced Federated Malay States, but each of the Unfederated Malay States was administered separately, as were North Borneo and Sarawak. Within each administrative jurisdiction, separate fiscal systems operated, and the extent and depth of government service provision depended on locally generated revenues. As a consequence, infrastructure provision in the Federated Malay States was far ahead of that in the Unfederated Malay States, with the exception of Johor. North Borneo and Sarawak were again the least developed.

The colonial economy created and cemented social and economic segmentation. Improvements in standards of living were modest, unequally distributed, and highly erratic. Labour conditions, already poor, worsened in the depression years when wage rates in estates and mines were reduced to bare subsistence levels, and large numbers lost their jobs altogether. When the economy began to recover, many employers kept wages at depression levels despite the rising cost of living. The lack of organizational leadership among the labourers amid their growing socio-economic grievances led to external political influences taking up their cause instead. There was increased labour agitation by the Malayan Communist Party (MCP) among Chinese workers, and by the Central Indian Association of Malaya (CIAM)

25 There was, of course, often a paternalistic interest expressed by colonial officials in 'the welfare of the people', particularly in relation to rural Malays, but this interest was subordinate to those of empire and commerce.

among Indian labourers (Leong, 1999). In 1937, the first militant labour strike by Chinese contract labourers took place, followed by a series of organized strikes until 1941. Malayan trade unionism had emerged.

On the eve of the Japanese invasion in late 1941, per capita incomes in Malaya had made little or no headway against those in the US or UK relative to their levels three decades earlier, and were languishing well below their 1929 peak (Figure 5.2).

Japanese Occupation, 1941–1945

The years of Japanese occupation were little short of disastrous for the people of Malaya and its economy. The retreating British armed forces destroyed strategic infrastructure and plant and equipment in compliance with the government's 'scorched earth' policy, and the Japanese plan to build a 'co-prosperity sphere' promoting cultural as well as economic unity in East Asia foundered (Kratoska, 2018, p. 3). Malaya's export-oriented economy was effectively destroyed and replaced by military command and control structures that resulted in widespread shortages and rampant inflation, greatly aggravating the brutal hardships of war.

While Japan's reason for occupying Malaya was partly to secure raw materials, particularly bauxite, to support its war effort, the greater strategic aim was to deny these resources to the Allied forces (Kratoska, 2018). Civilian administrative and economic structures from the British colonial era were demolished and replaced by military structures. Kedah, Kelantan, Terengganu, and Perlis were ceded to Thailand, and the remainder of the peninsula was amalgamated with Sumatra under military rule from Singapore. Controls were introduced, not just on trade (external and internal), but over the location and movement of people and on production activities. Businesses (particularly those owned by Chinese and Indians) were appropriated and placed under Japanese monopoly—*kumai*—ownership, which controlled both prices and supply.[26]

Malaya's trading economy soon buckled. The rubber industry crashed as its capacity far exceeded the needs of Japan's wartime economy. The effects on rubber smallholders were particularly severe, and many cut down their trees and turned to cultivating food crops. With output levels plummeting, rubber estate assets also fell into disrepair. Cumulative shipments from 1942 to 1945 are reported to have been just one-third of the output of a single year

26 Despite these and other constrictions on commerce, the Maddison data for 1942 suggest that per capita GDP expanded modestly that year. Although this could reflect a measurement error, it is also possible that the early efforts by the Japanese to restore industry and to rehabilitate infrastructure and other assets that had been destroyed by the British as they retreated did initially boost economic activity.

prior to the occupation (for instance, 1940). By 1943, tin production was only one-third of its pre-war level and it declined further, facing mounting problems with equipment maintenance and growing shortages of spare parts (Drabble, 2000). British efforts at sabotaging tin-mining assets as they retreated had proven singularly successful. After an initial spell in which the output of iron and coal expanded, both contracted in 1943. Oil production in Borneo fared somewhat better, with exploitation of new fields.

The collapse of the two main export sectors created numerous problems. The loss of tax revenues from exports compelled the authorities to print vast quantities of a new currency to finance spending (the so-called 'banana', an unbacked military scrip currency), which quickly led to hyperinflation. As foreign exchange reserves dwindled, shortages ensued of imported consumer goods, fuel, parts and machinery, and essential supplies such as rice and medicines. Job losses in the rubber and tin-mining sectors worsened unemployment.

Responses by the Japanese authorities aggravated economic and social distress. To counter unemployment, there was forced allocation of labour and resettlement of the population to support Japanese war efforts. This included the deployment of around 80,000 Indian migrants to work on the Burma railway, of whom half may have perished. Compulsory rice procurement and controls on trade created shortages and fuelled black market activity. By 1944, food shortages in urban areas led to a movement of the population back to the countryside, as well as to increasing malnutrition. With a poorly nourished population and shortages of medicine, diseases that were otherwise treatable spread quickly.

In September 1945, the Japanese army surrendered to British forces. While the devastating effects of the occupation were pervasive and widespread, North Borneo seemed to have fared the worst. Tregonning (1965, p. 222) remarks that 'no other part of the British Commonwealth, not even Burma, had been so utterly devastated. In some respects, the country was back to pre-1881 standards'. Maddison data (Figure 5.1) put per capita income in 1946 at just 65 per cent of what it had been in 1939.[27]

Recovery, 1946–1949

The Japanese occupation left little lasting structural impression on Malaya's economy. Although the occupation and associated shortages of imports had stimulated new small-scale manufacturing activities, and even some

27 The volatility of income in the pre-war period makes the selection of a benchmark year somewhat difficult. By 1939, per capita income had almost returned to the levels seen in the pre-depression era, but incomes then fell again in 1940 and 1941 before the start of the occupation.

diversification in the food sector—for example, towards vegetables and tapioca—these activities were highly inefficient. It was not long after the resumption of open trading arrangements that inferior locally produced goods were replaced by higher-quality and lower-cost imports. Perhaps somewhat ironically, the blockage of rubber exports during the occupation accelerated interest in the production of synthetic rubber substitutes in the US, which would later compete with Malaysia's exports.

In 1946–1949, the returning colonial administration focused on economic reconstruction and on rationalizing administrative structures. The goal was to rebuild the pre-war economy, and by about 1949–1950 it was a close facsimile of what it had been in the late 1930s. The successful rehabilitation of the rubber and tin sectors drove this recovery from a lost decade of development.

Yet hunger, destitution, displacement, sickness, communal violence, and widespread economic deprivations met the returning British colonial administration (Harper, 1999). Malaya's economic and societal structures had been severely shaken by the war, as the colonial model of trusteeship and indirect rule from Britain had so utterly failed to protect the country and its people. Territorial, administrative, and societal unification became the principal concern of the post-war colonial government. The segmented nature of the pre-war colonial institutional arrangements was perceived to be inefficient and an impediment to modernization and controlled decolonization.[28] Initial efforts focused on territorial integration and centralization of government through the creation of the Malayan Union in 1946. However, Malay hostility towards the perceived erosion and dilution of their traditional rights and status stymied the new proposed constitution, as discussed in Chapter 1, and eventually an agreement was reached establishing the Federation of Malaya in 1948.

In July 1945, post-war Britain elected a Labour government. When discussing the future economic set-up in Malaya, the new secretary of state for the colonies declared that 'too much money had been taken out of the country in the past and not enough left behind and that this ought to be corrected in the future' (CO 717/149/14, 1946, p. 2). Great fortunes had been made by a few from the profits derived from the export of rubber, tin, and less lucrative products like copra, palm oil, and pineapples. There was a need for a financial policy that would ensure that a larger proportion of profits from the exploitation of the country's natural resources would be retained

28 The post-war Labour government in Britain was committed to independence of the colonies, although no timetable had been set for Malaya. After the failure of the Malayan Union, the agreement forming the federation in 1948 explicitly acknowledged a commitment to independence.

for the benefit of the Malayan people instead of being sent abroad. There was, however, no equivalent of the Marshall Plan[29] for Malaya.

Questions were posed about the long-term viability of a protected subsistence agrarian economy coexisting alongside a capitalist export sector. With the growing use of modern planning concepts and the emerging political concerns about the development of the colonies (echoing the Colonial Welfare and Development Act of 1941), a transition was envisaged towards a mixed agricultural and industrial economy which would provide more inclusive economic opportunities. However, as Harper (1999, p. 58) puts it, 'the British had not come to Southeast Asia to collect butterflies', and the metropolitan capital retained a vital and immediate interest in rehabilitating Malaya's commodity-exporting activities and in managing its reserves and sterling balances (White, 2013).

Financial policies tended to subordinate any concerns about the rehabilitation and reconstruction of the Malayan economy, or the welfare of its people, to imperial interests in the stability of London's capital market and the sterling area, as had been the case in earlier periods (Rudner, 1975). The British Military Authority quickly demonetized the Japanese 'banana' and reintroduced the pre-war currency board arrangements, re-establishing the pre-war parity of 2 shillings and 4 pence to the Malayan dollar.[30] The infusion of vast quantities of Malayan dollars by the British Military Authority (up by over 80 per cent on pre-1942 issuance) not only entailed a massive transfer of real resources to the colonial authorities, but also stoked already rampant inflation and caused a sharp real appreciation of the currency. This resulted in further hardships for wage earners, and raised the costs of the export sector.[31] Moreover, restrictions imposed by the British authorities on Malaya's hard currency imports, which were intended to help offset the gold–dollar deficit of the sterling area—and which extended to the deferment of sterling imports that could be rerouted to hard currency areas—had the effect of slowing the recovery of sectors hobbled by shortages of parts and equipment.

In such circumstances, with competing and pressing demands on expenditure to finance rehabilitation, recovery, and expanded social services

29 This was formally called the European Recovery Program.

30 The motivations for demonetization were also political, intended to demonstrate a reassertion of British control over the territories of Malaya, and to punish profiteers and others (including the Malayan communists) who were thought to be holding large quantities of the scrip. However, the resulting hardships were probably felt much more widely by all consumers (Rudner, 1975).

31 Uncontrolled printing of the 'banana' scrip, combined with supply shortages, had led to hyperinflation, and inflationary expectations had become ingrained. While the demonetization of the 'banana' would have created a transitory squeeze on liquidity, the inflationary impacts of the rapid monetary expansion that accompanied the reintroduction of the Malayan dollar would have been further fanned by these ingrained inflationary expectations and supply bottlenecks.

and subsidies (introduced to combat the escalating costs of living), fiscal policy proved equally unaccommodating. This helped to bring social policy issues to the fore in the immediate post-war years (Chapters 3 and 4). Access to London's capital market was blocked by the Bank of England, and the portion of sterling currency reserves that was invested in interest-bearing assets (namely, in the Currency Fund) fell from a pre-war level of 70 per cent to only 41 per cent by 1947 (Rudner, 1975). The pre-war colonial tax regime, which had depended on indirect taxes, simply could not cope with the growing demands, and in 1948 an income tax was introduced despite passionate opposition from commercial and trading interests. However, it took some time for tax revenues to increase.[32]

Domestic bank credits supported by government guarantees, the drawdown of Malayan government reserves accumulated before the war and deposited in London, and government borrowing from internal Malayan sources (including the issuance of saving certificates to small savers) were all mobilized to bridge the funding gap. As Rudner (1975, p. 343) observes, 'post-war restoration of British rule did not entail a therapeutic inflow of sterling area capital for the economic development of Malaya'. Those resources that were mobilized within Malaya were then allocated disproportionately in favour of British interests. In circumstances where the upheaval of war had put acute stresses on traditional coping mechanisms, however, a more active role for government in support of social welfare was being envisaged. Investments were made in improving and expanding electricity supplies, as well as in rehabilitating the railways.

Rebooting the economy presented an array of challenges. Shortages of labour existed in the rubber sector, while replanting with higher-yielding trees (to allow competition with the emerging synthetic industry) was hindered by a shortage of land. Tin-mining infrastructure and machinery had been seriously damaged during the war and could not be returned to working order overnight. In urban areas, there was still high unemployment among skilled, clerical, and artisanal workers, and an attendant looming threat of social unrest. Despite the 'Grow More Food Programme',[33] domestic production fell short of local needs, and difficulties in shipping imports resulted in rationing.

World War II had disrupted pre-war patterns of settlement. Large-scale migration to the interior of the peninsula had occurred, precipitated by low wages, high unemployment, and fears for safety in the towns. This presented the returning colonial administration with a raft of problems.

32 At first, the revenues captured from taxation were small, accounting for less than 1 per cent of total revenues in 1948. This figure increased to just under 10 per cent in 1949, and rose even higher by the mid 1950s (Lim, 1967).

33 This was an initiative started during the Japanese occupation to encourage people to strive for self-sufficiency by growing their own food.

Squatters—upwards of half a million, many of whom had become settled—occupied land that had once been used for tin mining, rubber cultivation, and timber production, and their presence impeded a frictionless return to pre-war patterns and levels of economic activity. The clearance of large tracts of tropical forest by squatters (and also earlier by the Japanese occupiers) had created a host of environmental and ecological problems, including soil erosion, silting of rivers, and flooding. Ultimately, these manifold post-war stresses and hardships in the interior of Malaya fanned the flames of the communist insurgency, and also influenced the subsequent economic trajectory of the embryonic Malaysian state.

Despite the challenges and the political flux, there was a spurt in post-war economic growth. According to the Maddison database, using 1941 as the base year, per capita GDP had regained its pre-war level by 1949.[34] These data put cumulative average growth of per capita GDP between 1947 and 1950 at 13 per cent. Measured over 1948–1950, per capita GDP growth was even higher, at 15 per cent. Estimates by Bhanoji Rao (1976) also suggest recovery, with per capita GDP growth averaging 3.7 per cent between 1947 and 1950. Despite this progress, however, real incomes in 1950 still languished well below the heights seen at the end of the 1920s.

The rubber industry recovered most quickly, despite difficulties in relation to labour, land, and material supplies, and new competition from synthetic substitutes. By 1947, rubber production had surpassed the level seen in 1940. Output per worker rose sharply, and yields per acre increased due to replanting in the 1930s with higher-yielding species and the enforced rest of trees during the war (Drabble, 2000). Smallholders proved particularly agile and were able to respond to the lifting of pre-war restrictions on exports quite quickly. Rubber output in North Borneo and Sarawak also rebounded.

Tin took longer to recover as mines and machinery needed to be restored to working order, and there was an initial shortage of capital. Financial assistance from the colonial administration aided the process, and British owners benefited disproportionately. New investments created a more technologically advanced tin industry. Between 1947 and 1950, tin production doubled, and by 1950 was over 20 per cent higher than it had been in 1939 (De Micheaux, 2017). In general, economic recovery in North Borneo and Sarawak lagged behind that in the peninsula (Drabble, 2000).

The recovery of rubber and tin production explains much of the post-war spurt in economic growth, but other factors also contributed. Although the Grow More Food programme was beset with problems and has been described as a 'dismal chronicle of failure' (Kratoska, 1988, p. 37), rice production had

34 If peak income attained in 1942 is used instead as the base year, per capita income did not regain this level until 1963.

returned to pre-war levels by 1948. From 1949, the recovery also benefited from favourable movements in the international prices of rubber and tin, as stockpiling was occurring in the context of the growing hostilities on the Korean peninsula. Rubber prices increased four-fold between 1949 and 1951, while tin prices doubled (Stubbs, 1974).

By the early 1950s, the economy was strikingly similar to the pre-war colonial export model, based around rubber and tin. Despite recognition by the colonial administration that a more diversified economy was necessary to support future development, the economic base remained highly concentrated, with 50 per cent of GDP coming from primary industries. The economy remained segmented, and the agricultural sector beyond rubber remained largely unmodernized. Manufacturing still contributed very little to GDP, at only 6 per cent of the total (Bhanoji Rao, 1976).

The generation of solid external trade surpluses also resumed, and these provided crucial support for the balance of payments of the wider sterling pool. Indeed, White (2013) observes that in this period Malaya's rubber US dollar earnings exceeded total UK exports to the US.[35] Domestically, however, government revenues still fell short of outlays and reserves had to be tapped to fund the gap. Drabble (2000) reports that the bulk of claims on the budget were for economic services and for increased military outlays associated with the insurgency and the Emergency that it triggered. Despite the government's increased emphasis on social policy, social programmes made only small claims on the budget, consuming 4–7 per cent of total outlays.

Per capita GDP metrics again offer only a partial view of what was happening to the standard of living of the general populace during this recovery period. According to Bhanoji Rao's estimates (1976), real per capita consumption rose by 8.7 per cent between 1947 and 1949. Although this is still somewhat lower than the 10.4 per cent growth of per capita GDP over the same period, it does reflect the improvements that were occurring. A variety of other indicators also suggest an improvement in standards of living, as death rates fell, school attendance increased rapidly, and ownership of consumer durables—from radios to motorcycles and cars—grew fast. Meat consumption climbed sharply, again suggesting that real incomes were picking up. Deposits in post office savings accounts also rose, another signal that, at least for some, incomes had surpassed the level at which basic needs could be met.[36]

35 In the post-war period Malaya was forced to make payments to support Britain's pool of reserves and, in 1946, also had to increase the amount of sterling reserves backing the Straits dollar from 110 per cent to 115 per cent under the restored currency board arrangements. British business interests would also have repatriated a proportion of profits from their rubber, tin, and trading businesses. Net factor outflows are reported to have been small, however—less than 1 per cent of GDP—possibly because profits were being used to finance reinvestment in the domestic economy (Drabble, 1989, p. 158).

36 See Lim (1967, Appendix 1.2) for details.

These fruits of recovery were not shared equally, however. Reports of labour unrest in the post-war years in the face of low wages, rice rationing, and accelerating food prices point to the continued hardships being experienced by some workers and their families. Organized labour strikes and demonstrations had ceased during the Japanese occupation, but political awareness among the labour class of all communities was growing. When the British re-occupied Malaya, pent-up demands for work and higher wages were unleashed through waves of demonstrations, strikes, and riots, instigated by the MCP.

The post-war resurgence of communist influence had important implications for Malayan trade unionism. In early 1946, the Malayan and Singaporean branches of the MCP's general labour unions were merged under a central organization, the Pan Malayan General Labour Union (PMGLU). The PMGLU represented Chinese and Indian labour, and was the first multiracial labour organization in Malaya (Leong, 1999). Towards the end of 1946 the PMGLU was reorganized as a federation of trade unions, and was renamed the Pan Malayan Federation of Trade Unions (PMFTU). As a result of its countrywide campaigns, by 1947 the number of registered unions had risen and trade union density reached a peak of 21 per cent of the workforce (Wad, 2012). Nonetheless, the efforts made to achieve better cooperation with the government failed. In 1948, following the declaration of Emergency, the PMFTU and its subsidiaries were declared unlawful and subsequently banned.

The Emergency ushered in a new phase in labour relations. Malayan labourers were forced into compliance under strict police supervision and employer control, and estate and mining workers were regrouped. The suppression of trade unionism was condemned internationally, however, including by the World Federation of Trade Unions and the International Labour Organization (ILO), and in 1950 the government relented and allowed the formation of the Malayan Trade Union Council (MTUC).

Commodity Dependence and Institutional Transformation, 1950–1959

The 1950s was a decade in which economic performance was again closely linked to export performance and movements in the terms of trade. Brief periods of rising rubber and tin prices in the early, mid, and late 1950s—due to the Korean War and strong global demand—were interspersed with periods in which prices were more depressed. After the post-war economic recovery and a short growth spurt prompted by soaring commodity prices, and despite the continued rapid growth of the US economy, Malaya's aggregate economy contracted. Economic growth failed to keep pace with underlying population growth, such that average per capita income at the end of the decade was lower than at its start.[37]

This uninspiring economic performance stemmed largely from inherited structural and institutional weaknesses, including a narrow commodity export base vulnerable to the vagaries of international demand; colonial arrangements that drained surpluses for the benefit of the larger sterling area; and a legacy of infrastructure, education, and health deficits. The Emergency, declared in 1948 and lasting through the 1950s, also took its toll.

But this weak economic performance masked deeper changes that would culminate in the birth of the Federation of Malaya in 1957. These included sweeping institutional changes that would leave their lasting imprint on the new nation. From this point on, economic choices began to reflect the interests of the newly emerging local political classes rather than the preferences of the metropolitan capital. Among other key developments were the formation of national institutions and centralization of government functions, which had hitherto been devolved and uncoordinated; steps towards embryonic economic planning and coordination; and efforts towards diversifying the economy and reorienting its trading and investment ties. Subsistence agriculture was starting to make way for cash crops and commercialization, and many young Malays were leaving their *kampung* for better prospects in the towns or for wage labour on plantations. By 1957, Malaya was the most urbanized country in Southeast Asia,[38] and it had built an infrastructure backbone, administrative capabilities, and social services that were comparatively advanced by Asian standards.

The 1950s were a difficult decade for Malaya's rubber industry, however. Synthetic substitutes began to command a larger share of the market and, after an initial upturn in 1949–1951, prices for natural rubber fell sharply and remained low throughout the decade. While natural rubber had over 70 per cent of the total market in 1950, by 1959 its share had fallen to just over 50 per cent and would continue to decline with the growing penetration of synthetic rubber. After peaking at US$0.60 per pound in 1951, natural rubber prices then averaged only US$0.32 per pound until 1959 (Ul Haque, 1972).

37 A World Bank mission in 1955 estimated that GDP at current market prices more than doubled between 1949 and 1951, but then fell back by 23 per cent by 1953 (IBRD, 1955, p. 21). Much of the change in nominal values was attributed to price alterations, but GDP was estimated to have grown in real terms by 20 per cent. The Maddison project data suggest, conversely, that per capita income in real terms fell between 1949 and 1951, and then stagnated between 1951 and 1953. As year-to-year changes may well be affected by measurement errors, as these data highlight, the focus here is more on broad, decadal trends.

38 By 1957, the proportion of people living in urban settlements (of more than 1,000 people) had risen to 42.5 per cent from 26.5 per cent a decade earlier.

By the early 1950s, about half of the trees on rubber estates and two-thirds of those on smallholdings were over 30 years old and beyond their productive years (Drabble, 2000). Replanting with new high-yielding varieties required substantial government finance, particularly for smallholders who lacked the means to support themselves for the seven years before the trees could be tapped. Rubber plantations were also a prime target for communist insurgents during the Emergency years, and in some areas security concerns meant that trees went untapped, as large areas were abandoned (Ho, 2006). The obstacles to rehabilitating the rubber sector, and weak external demand, caused production to stagnate during the 1950s in the peninsula and in North Borneo and Sarawak (Drabble, 2000). The US dollar surplus that rubber exports had previously generated for the sterling pool shrank considerably, and the UK replaced the US as the main market for rubber exports.

Still, Malaya remained the world's foremost tin producer in the 1950s. But once US strategic stockpiling of tin came to an end at the close of the Korean War in July 1953, tin prices began to fall from the highs of 1951 and 1952. With technological advances in metallurgy and uncertainties about future tin demand, an agreement was negotiated among producers and consumers in 1953 that aimed to stabilize prices, although it took until 1956 for this to be put into effect. Prices then stabilized, but at a low level not far above those of the 1930s. Agreements on buffer stocks set limits on production in Malaya and in other producing countries, and until 1957 tin production worldwide was broadly stable. Triggered by a global recession, it then fell by about one-quarter in 1958 and remained at a depressed level in 1959. Malaya's share in global output barely changed, and its production moved up and down in step with global consumption.

The fate of the rubber and tin industries in the 1950s explains much of the variable performance of the wider economy. Gross export receipts accounted for nearly half of GDP and Malaya remained one of the most open economies in the world (Lim, 1967). Rubber and tin accounted for the bulk of exports: an estimated 80 per cent in 1953 (World Bank, 1995). Although the direct contribution of rubber and tin to GDP was estimated at only 25 per cent (World Bank, 1995), with the exception of rice cultivation and other secondary agricultural crops, much activity elsewhere in the economy was also highly dependent on these two sectors. They in turn depended heavily on demand conditions in world markets. For rubber, the impact of shifting demand was felt primarily on prices, given its inelastic supply, while for tin, volumes as well as prices were shaped by external demand conditions.

The patchy growth of the Malayan economy during this decade therefore owed much to global shifts in demand for rubber and tin. The manufacturing sector, although relatively large by Asian standards (ranking behind only

Japan and India in its direct contribution to GDP, at about 10 per cent in 1953), was still dominated by small-scale and family-based businesses concentrated in downstream rubber and tin processing, or in the manufacture of bulky, low-value goods and foodstuffs to serve the domestic market.

Other factors also contributed to anaemic growth, with dependency rates increasing as overall population growth exceeded that of the labour force. Rising natural rates of population growth, combined with the rapid slowdown in migration, meant that there was a growing number of young dependants. For a given level of labour productivity, the falling share of workers in the total population would have diluted per capita GDP. More years of schooling and retirement at earlier ages also lowered the proportion of workers in the total population. Moreover, the movement of workers from lower- to higher-productivity activities was modest (Hirschman, 1971), meaning that any gains from improved labour efficiency would have been limited.

There appear to be no estimates available of the economic impact of the Emergency. The conflict saw the destruction of assets, the dislocation of economic activity, and the departure of businesses and key personnel from the country and of workers from the isolated rubber- and tin-producing areas. The Emergency also raised costs: the tin industry alone spent US$30 million in defending its installations, and a large area under rubber cultivation was abandoned (IBRD, 1955). It also triggered an outflow of capital, mainly from Asian (chiefly Indian) business people who had invested heavily in Malaya, but were scared off by memories of earlier failed investments in Burma (Harper, 1999). Inevitably, the counter-insurgency measures made substantial claims on public resources, with fiscal outlays estimated at US$350 million–375 million in 1953 alone. Part of the military expense of the Emergency was met by sterling transfers from Britain, estimated at just over US$200 million from 1951 to 1953. By 1953, Malaya's net sterling balances had declined, although the accumulated stock was still over US$2 billion (IBRD, 1955).

Change was in the air, however, as independence loomed. The approach of the pre-war colonial administration had already started to give way to a more active government with functions beyond the provision of a narrow range of essential public goods—law and order, security, and basic administration. Government activities expanded to include investment in rural and urban infrastructure; in rural economic development through RIDA (Box 5.7);[39] in other economic assets, including rubber replanting and land development

---

39 In a royal address to parliament, the first *Yang di-Pertuan Agong*, Tuanku Abdul Rahman, stated that the 'Rural Industrial Development Authority will play an important role in the development of rural areas by its programme of training the rural people to improve their standard of living. The Authority will lay particular emphasis on encouraging the establishment of cottage and small industries and the financing of rural trade and industry' (DO 35/9990, 1957–1960, p. 3).

schemes under the Federal Land Development Authority (Chapter 8); in social services, including education and public health; and in pension provision through the Employees Provident Fund (set up in 1951).

Box 5.7 The Rural Industrial Development Authority

In August 1950, the colonial administration established the Rural Industrial Development Authority (RIDA) in response to growing economic and social stresses within the traditional rural economy, and with the intention of buffering security and consolidating rural Malay support.

RIDA sought to improve rural livelihoods at the community level through initiatives to establish cottage industries and rural markets, as well as to boost productivity in agriculture and the fishing industry. Initially it pursued a 'self-help' ethos, but the failure of many schemes, owing partly to the neglect of critical enabling elements in rural supply-chain infrastructure, led to more direct assistance, such as the building of amenities and the provision of credit. RIDA also provided and operated some manufacturing and transport services, and after 1956 it began to offer training courses on trades and on rural development. In 1957, a new RIDA directive resulted in a reduction of its development schemes (financed by grants) as they were assessed to be incompatible with its role in projects and the provision of credit (financed through loans).

RIDA got off to a slow start owing to a lack of human resource capacities, a paucity of viable schemes identified, and the government's focus on the Emergency.[40] In 1951, it spent less than 15 per cent of its Straits$5 million allocation on development projects and schemes, with the bulk of expenditure concentrated in Perlis, Selangor, Kelantan, and Kedah. In the following years implementation expanded, and between 1951 and 1959, RIDA's expenditure on development schemes—for instance, funding roads, bridges, and social amenities—exceeded Straits$13 million (Beaglehole, 1969).

In 1956, the Federal Land Development Authority (FELDA) was created (Box 8.2 in Chapter 8) as the main vehicle for alleviating rural poverty and for resettling the landless poor in agricultural estates. At the end of the 1950s, and with the government's increasing emphasis on rural development, RIDA, which was now tasked with supporting rural Malays through training, loans, and projects, was brought together with FELDA under the newly established Ministry for Rural Development.

Yet mounting financial losses largely from its direct enterprises, a lack of technical expertise in loan administration, and a lack of firm political support led to RIDA's reorganization in the mid 1960s. It was replaced by the Majlis Amanah Rakyat (MARA), whose mandate was to extend assistance, training, and support to Malays and other *Bumiputera* in business and industry. In 1960, RIDA's expenditure on vocational and post-secondary education represented about 13 per cent of federal development expenditure, and with the establishment of MARA, it had jumped to 54 per cent by 1968.

40 At the beginning of 1951, RIDA, chaired by Onn Ja'afar, founding president of UMNO, had just two members of staff, and it only started to implement its projects properly in the second half of 1951 when its staff strength increased to seven (CO 717/208/8 and 9, 1951 and 1952).

While an early assessment of RIDA by the IBRD (1955) suggested that it was bringing significant development benefits, later analysis concluded that the institution had done little to improve rural livelihoods and communities (with migration to the towns continuing), and that it was a failure of the colonial administration's development policy (Harper, 1999).

The Emergency required an expanded role for government, demanding unified functions (administrative, economic, fiscal, and military), and causing the ranks of the police, specialist technocrats, and administrators to grow quickly. While in 1948 the government of Malaya employed 48,000 people, by 1959 this number had nearly tripled to 140,000 (Harper, 1999, p. 539, citing Stubbs, 1974). Large-scale recruitment of young, male Malays into the uniformed services and their migration to urban areas brought large numbers into the wage economy, but also created shortages of labour in the *padi* economy. In this and other ways, the Emergency left an indelible imprint on the physical, economic, social, and institutional development of Malaysia (Box 5.8).

Box 5.8 The development legacy of the Emergency and the New Village programme

The New Village programme was instigated by the British during the Emergency (Box 1.2, Chapter 1). It entailed the forced relocation to new settlements of around a million Chinese, of whom about half were squatters, while the other half had legitimately occupied rural land from which they were now forcibly removed. Within the New Villages, the rule of law was enforced under reward and punishment principles: some 23,000 Chinese were punished by deportation.

Economic and social dislocation resulted from this forced resettlement. Squatters removed at very short notice lost both their jobs and the crops that they had cultivated (CO 717/202/1, 1951). Supplies to towns of fresh foods by Chinese squatters and agriculturalists shrank, and prices escalated. Established communities were wrenched apart. Sanitation was initially poor and health services inadequate in these new, nucleated communities in which people now lived alongside their animals. Disease and illness spread quickly. People were also reluctant to farm the land that had been allocated to them, as much of it was considered unsuitable for cultivation, and the 30-year leases on offer were too short to warrant the necessary investment.

By 1951, what had started as an essentially military tactic began necessarily to evolve into a comprehensive social and economic programme. The introduction of 'aftercare' programmes was essential to 'socialize' the villagers and to create communities that would 'share the benefits of urban living with rural livelihood' (Harper, 1999, p. 182). Education in the villages was instrumental in creating new economic opportunities. Health was also a priority in circumstances where nature and poverty spread illness. However, the demands on resources dwarfed government means, and ultimately voluntary efforts provided by the fledgling Malaysian Chinese Association and organizations such as the Women's Red Cross were crucial in influencing outcomes. The results of many aftercare programmes were mixed and opinions on their impacts vary. Harper's (1999) critical views, for instance, contrast with the more positive perspectives of Dhu Renick Jnr (1965) and Loh (1988).

The villages left a lasting imprint on development. The eventual construction of paved roads between them connected isolated parts of the peninsula to each other and to larger urban centres. Electrification and the provision of basic amenities and facilities followed, helping to expand economic opportunities and improve the quality of life in rural areas, although a survey conducted in 1972 revealed that living conditions in many of the New Villages were still poor (EPU, 1976). The villages also helped the peninsula to urbanize faster, with many of them later evolving into towns, promoting the benefits of larger population concentrations.

The villages brought more workers into the wage economy and out of subsistence, partly because poor land made smallholding difficult. Dhu Renick Jnr (1965) concludes that by bringing isolated and disparate groups into daily touch with government and with each other, the villages, despite their foundation in coercive regulation, helped to foster a sense of community and an attachment to the country. The lessons learned from the Emergency were put to use in scaling up the FELDA programme, including through the establishment in each state of a rural development committee and a state operations room under the Ministry of National and Rural Development. The military operations techniques 'were applied to the civil tasks of creating a coordinated and responsive rural development apparatus' (Harper, 1999, p. 367).

Other important post-independence features of Malaysia's development can be traced to this period. Embryonic planning mechanisms had started in the post-war reconstruction efforts (Box 5.9). These would evolve into five-year economic plans, which later became the instruments for negotiating, distilling, and expressing national development priorities; guiding national resource allocation; and coordinating actions in pursuit of national goals. In preparation for independence, a public investment programme was created and a new economic committee was set up, with a secretariat that would be located in the office of the new prime minister.

Box 5.9 Embryonic planning, 1950–1955 and 1956–1960

The first rudimentary Malayan economic plan—the Draft Development Plan—was formulated for the six years 1950–1955 in compliance with a requirement of the British Colonial Development and Welfare Act for colonies receiving aid (Lee, 1974). The plan, published in three parts, was prepared by the Office of the Finance Secretary (a member of the Federal Executive Council) with the support of its economics department, and approved by the Federal Legislative Council (CO 717/192/7, 1950).

The main goals of the plan were social progress and the rebuilding of the economy, with investment targets for social development, natural resources, and utilities (Federation of Malaya, 1950b). While attention was given to the improvement of living conditions, few resources were allocated to social services, which were considered 'non-productive'. In Rudner's view, the plan was mostly about developing 'productive' economic services, with priority given to capital projects with short gestation periods which could contribute to the UK's balance of payments (Rudner, 1972).

In 1951, the initial investment target of Straits$215 million was revised sharply upwards to Straits$856 million, prompted by buoyant revenues from surging rubber and tin exports due to the Korean War of 1950–1953.[41] There was no detailed costing of projects or a financing plan beyond an intended split between domestic and foreign sources of financing at 25 per cent and 75 per cent respectively.

Ness (1962) suggests that government investment reached about 60 per cent of the target set in the plan, whereas Drabble (2000) proposes a figure of 80 per cent and observes that the majority of funding (more than four-fifths) came from domestic rubber and tin revenues rather than from foreign sources. Investments were targeted primarily at rebuilding infrastructure—including roads and electricity—following the damage suffered during the Japanese occupation, and at the rehabilitation of the rubber sector. Shortages of qualified staff and heavy commitments for defence and internal security restricted implementation by the Public Works Department, however (CO 825/86, 1951).

In North Borneo (1948–1955) and in Sarawak (1947–1956), plans for development and investment were formulated along similar lines as part of post-war reconstruction efforts, but there too project disbursements fell short of planned targets.

The next 'plan', the First Malaya Plan, 1956–1960, was prepared by the Economic Council of the Council of Ministers, which had replaced the Federal Executive Council after the 1955 elections (Federation of Malaya, 1956). While this plan was more detailed than the first, it was essentially an investment plan rather than a comprehensive national development strategy. In setting priorities, it drew on the analysis of the 1955 World Bank mission concerning the challenges facing the peninsula's economy (IBRD, 1955). These challenges included the rapid increase in population and the pressure that this put on land resources; the need for social services, particularly health, education, water supply, and housing; and the need for development of the rural economy (EPU, 2007).

A decision was made to allocate 60 per cent of capital expenditure to the economic sector, 30 per cent to the social sector, and the remaining 10 per cent to the government sector. Funds were also set aside for rehabilitating the rubber industry, where there had been a lack of replanting during the Depression and the Japanese occupation, and for increasing the productivity of the rural subsistence sector. In the middle of the Emergency period, military spending also featured prominently.

41 Development expenditures related to the New Village resettlement programme, including schools, water supplies, roads, and medical and preventive services were not part of the Draft Development Plan, and the allocations to the states for various social sector and infrastructure projects were also not included.

Ness (1962) reports that aggregate investment fell short of the target by just 12 per cent. However, the social sectors lagged behind, with spending on education reaching only 65 per cent of the target and spending on health only 25 per cent. An evaluation of economic performance during 1956–1960 suggested only modest growth in per capita income (a cumulative average of about 0.7 per cent). It estimated that rice production increased by 30 per cent, reflecting government investments in irrigation, particularly in Kedah and Kelantan (Chapter 8). Ness suggests that manufacturing output was up by 25 per cent. The evaluation also showed something of an investment push, with investment rates averaging 12 per cent over the plan period, up from about 7 per cent in earlier years. The bulk of this investment was private. By the end of the 1950s, the improved social outcomes as a result of public investment were becoming increasingly visible (Chapters 3 and 4).

A compromise between the Malay and Chinese political classes cemented the achievement of independence in 1957. For Chinese and others who had migrated to Malaya, and their offspring, the constitution provided access to citizenship and guarantees of economic freedom and security. In return, it enshrined the paramount importance of the rights and privileges of Malays. Although for many national identity was an artifice and still subordinate to ethnicity, the arrival of independence and the new constitution finally gave Malayans the opportunity to distil, articulate, own, and pursue national development goals. While the UK felt reassured by the pro-British perspective of the new Malayan leaders, Malaya's interests would now acquire primacy. Britain's colonial interests were in any event shifting, with the recognition that Malaya's shrinking contribution to the sterling pool had made it increasingly marginal in economic terms (White, 2013).

The process of building the institutional apparatus of a modern state accelerated. The Ministry of Finance was formed in 1957 and the first federal budget was tabled that year, which in the face of a deficit announced increased income taxes, despite protests from the business community (Santasombat, 2017). The creation of Bank Negara as the country's central bank in 1959 was another milestone, even though Malaya remained part of the sterling area and retained its currency board arrangements. The General Economic Committee of the Federal Executive Council had been created in 1956, and in 1961 would become the Economic Planning Unit of the Prime Minister's Department.

The newly independent government sought to diversify the economy. One strategy was the Pioneer Industries Ordinance of 1958, which granted incentives to foreign industrial investors, including tariff protection and guarantees of profit remittance. Much of this investment, sourced largely from

Singapore and Britain, was channelled into import-substituting producer and consumer goods industries. Investment earmarked in the early plans helped to generate demand for construction services and industrial goods. The producer goods sector was the most dynamic part of the economy in the late 1950s, posting double-digit rates of expansion (Drabble, 2000). While primary activities continued to dominate the economic landscape through the 1950s, the share of industrial output rose, albeit from a small base.

The late 1950s also saw Malaya begin to reorient its economic ties and deepen a process of greater economic engagement with Japan and other countries in the region as the system of Commonwealth preferences was liberalized. In 1960, Japan became the first country to which the newly independent Malaya extended 'Most-Favoured Nation' status after trade and commercial links had intensified in the 1950s.

In summary, the 1950s presented a decade of contrasts. The economy was still hostage to international demand for its major exports of rubber and tin, and outcomes fell short, with the income gap with advanced countries widening over the decade. At independence in 1957 real per capita GDP in the newly formed nation state was 14 per cent below what it had been in colonial Malaya in 1929. There were undoubtedly improvements in the general standard of living after the deprivations of World War II, but it is not clear whether living standards had risen much over the longer term.

Yet these aggregate metrics mask the deeper changes in the economic, physical, and institutional complexion of the country, which would greatly influence its trajectory over the decades to come. Critical challenges were also surfacing. A rapidly expanding population was adding to the demand for essential services, as well as to the need for the creation of jobs for the country's growing number of youths. Even after early moves to diversify the economy, Malaysia's economic base remained narrow, with the flow of revenues still dependent on volatile rubber and tin export earnings, both being sectors with limited longer-term prospects. The generation of new resources to support development efforts would thus require greater efforts to promote economic diversification.

Post-independence Economic Priorities, 1960–1969

During the 1960s, the Malaysian economy performed strongly by the standards of its developing country peers. Significant investments were channelled into physical and social infrastructure, and into improvements in rural productivity. Per capita incomes registered respectable gains, and other economic indicators were positive. But these macroeconomic achievements concealed the deeper societal imbalances which would eventually trigger a political crisis in 1969.

The early post-independence years presented Malaysia with the opportunity to chart new directions and to develop policies attuned to its own interests, rather than to those of the metropolitan capital. Several priorities were set. Most immediately, there was a political determination to promote national integration, and to raise the welfare of low-income groups.[42] In practical terms, this meant bridging the rural–urban divide, building viable rural communities, and redressing regional imbalances among the states. A second priority was to create new jobs for the rapidly expanding labour force. Attention was given to energizing the rural economy, but there was also a push for industrialization, with an emphasis on import-substituting manufacturing activities. A third imperative was to strengthen the infrastructure backbone of the country, and to build the assets needed to support longer-term gains in productivity and welfare. In allocating investment, priority was to be given to strengthening rural infrastructure and to helping Sabah and Sarawak to catch up with the infrastructure provision and the level of integration on the peninsula.

Nevertheless, the economic institutions and arrangements that had been put in place during the colonial period, designed largely to serve metropolitan interests, endured. Malaysia stayed within the sterling area and retained the colonial currency board arrangements, leaving no scope for independent management of domestic liquidity. Laissez-faire principles guided trade and investment. Asset ownership structures in the plantation and mining sectors remained largely intact; the dominance of the agency houses was unchallenged; and foreign enterprise and investment continued to be courted and welcomed (Puthucheary, 1960). The principles guiding budgetary policy remained conservative, aimed at limiting claims on resources that would otherwise be available to the private sector. Budget deficits proved difficult to avoid in practice, however, as population expansion continued to increase the demands on the government.

Direct state intervention in the productive sector was limited, and corporatist and commercialization initiatives such as FELDA and MARA were the main instruments for catalyzing rural transformation. Government support for industry focused on infrastructure construction (including serviced industrial land, such as the industrial park at Petaling Jaya) and on investment incentives to encourage import-substituting industrialization.

42 While there is no explicit association of ethnicity with socio-economic status in the wording of the First Malaysia Plan, 1966–1970 (phrasing that was to come later in the New Economic Policy), its detailed description of the groups in society on whom poverty alleviation efforts should focus refers to Malays and other *Bumiputera*, including *padi* cultivators, aborigines in the peninsula, and shifting cultivators in Borneo.

Development planning became increasingly sophisticated in support of infrastructure spending and implementation of the new industrialization strategy. However, its goals were still high-level and indicative, and its main operational instrument was a public investment programme (Box 5.10). Change was coming more slowly to the economy than to the body politic.

Box 5.10 The economic plan, 1961–1965

The Second Malaya Plan, 1961–1965, was prepared before Sabah and Sarawak (and briefly Singapore) joined the federation in 1963 (Federation of Malaya, 1961). It marked a departure from the two earlier embryonic plans, and represented the first comprehensive attempt at national economic planning. It was prepared by the Economic Secretariat of the Prime Minister's Department with participation from other ministries, including Treasury, Commerce, and Rural Development, as well as Bank Negara.[43] The plan's objectives were improving the economic and social well-being of the rural population; raising employment, income, and living standards; and increasing diversification in agriculture and industry (EPU, 2007). It set out its assumptions for key variables, such as world rubber prices, and included targets for overall aggregate growth of the economy and for each of its major sectors.

However, when the plan was being prepared Malaysia had no national income statistics, so the targets were formulated without a reliable baseline. Planned infrastructure investment was the single largest line item, comprising 41 per cent of the total budget, and up by 75 per cent compared with disbursements in 1956–1960. Large outlays were also planned for agriculture, focused on rubber replanting and land development, and for social services—up by 253 per cent compared with disbursements in 1956–1960. It was envisaged that domestic savings would pay for 83 per cent of the intended investment, with shortfalls in public sector savings to be bridged by foreign financing and by a drawdown in accumulated reserves.

Targets for sectoral growth and employment were specified for the plan period. These targets foresaw rapid growth of mining and manufacturing industry (36 per cent) and of construction activity (76 per cent), but also broader growth, including in the agricultural sector (15 per cent). It was hoped that overall economic growth could generate 350,000 new jobs.

The logic embedded in the plan was that accelerated investment would stimulate output growth through the expansion of capacity. Ness (1962) reports that during 1956–1960, Malaysia had achieved an incremental capital–output ratio of 3.2 and had speculated, on that basis, that the output targets for 1961–1965 would be easily exceeded.

A number of other features of the 1961–1965 plan merit comment. First, the plan's goals were now guided by national development aspirations (although its preparation

43 After the 1959 federal elections, the Cabinet took the place of the Council of Ministers, and the Economic Council, chaired by the prime minister, became an important Cabinet committee. In 1962, the Economic Secretariat was reorganized into the Economic Planning Unit (EPU) with more clearly defined powers for planning, and it became an integral part of the Prime Minister's Department (Thillainathan, 2007).

continued to draw on international technical assistance), and security concerns were no longer foremost, as they had been during the Emergency. Second, the logic of the plan flowed from its economic targets to the means of financing them, rather than from an estimate of available resources that would then cap investments, as in 1956–1960. Third, there was broad consistency between the general direction of the plan and the federal budgets, particularly between the statement of goals and the intended allocation of resources. Finally, while the World Bank provided technical assistance, the preparation of the plan was made possible by expanded national technocratic capabilities built by international advisors, including the creation of a specialized planning function within the Prime Minister's Department.

Headline GDP growth accelerated in the 1960s. In per capita terms, the economy grew at a cumulative average rate of 3.5 per cent, according to the Maddison data.[44] At this rate, the Malaysian economy just about kept pace with the US and slightly closed the gap with the UK (Figure 5.2). The volatility of the colonial period and the early 1950s had been overcome, and by the end of the decade real per capita income was higher than at any previous point in the country's turbulent economic history. It was also considerably higher than in neighbouring countries. The Maddison data indicate that at the end of the 1960s per capita income in Malaysia was 53 per cent higher than in Thailand, and 60 per cent above that of the Philippines.

As in the colonial period, advances in headline GDP overstated the actual gains in standards of living. During the 1960s, real per capita consumption (in local prices) grew at a cumulative average rate of 1.7 per cent.[45] By 1969, the share of consumption in GDP (PPP) had fallen to 60 per cent from over 70 per cent at the start of the decade. This increased aggregate savings rate suggests that incomes were rising faster among higher-income households (thus widening household income inequality), as affluent households tend to save more than those living on the margins of subsistence. Higher investment shares in the 1960s absorbed some of this additional saving, with the remainder accounted for by the external current account surplus and net lending abroad.[46]

Malaysia had a broader economic base at the end of the 1960s than at the start. Although rubber and tin remained the principal exports, their share in export revenues declined from a combined 69 per cent in 1960 to 54 per

44 The PWT9.1 estimates are 3.4 per cent. The Second Malaysia Plan (MP2), 1971–1975, reported that average annual per capita growth in the 1960s was 2.8 per cent for output and 2.4 per cent for income.

45 The MP2 also reported an increase in per capita consumption of 1.5 per cent, attributing some of this slower growth to adverse terms-of-trade movements.

46 This is based on current account surpluses recorded in all years apart from 1962–1964, and net lending overseas throughout the decade.

cent by 1970. In volume terms, rubber output increased (at an average annual rate of 5.2 per cent) as the benefits of earlier investments in replanting and higher-yielding trees started to be realized, but rubber prices were depressed throughout the 1960s as the market penetration of synthetics continued. The picture was the reverse for tin. By 1970, production had fallen below the levels of 1960 as older deposits were gradually exhausted, but world prices were much more favourable.

Elsewhere in the primary and mining sectors, production of palm oil (mainly on the peninsula) and timber (largely in Sabah) expanded rapidly, along with some other more minor crops, including tapioca, sugar cane, and cocoa. The production of crude oil from Sarawak also increased markedly, rising by a factor of 15 between 1965 and 1970, and crude oil exports ranked alongside those of palm oil behind the traditional export earners of rubber, tin, and timber.

Diversification was also evident in the rest of the economy, with large public sector investments in infrastructure—particularly in 1961–1965—and with policy support for pioneer industries contributing to a growing share in aggregate economic output for manufacturing and for industry more broadly, including construction (Figure 5.9). The continuing trend towards urbanization, and the rapid growth of the government, employment, and consumption all lifted the share of services. Yet despite these early signs of diversification, Malaysia was still predominantly a primary-goods-exporting economy at the start of the 1970s.

Figure 5.9 **Early progress was made towards economic diversification in 1959–1969**

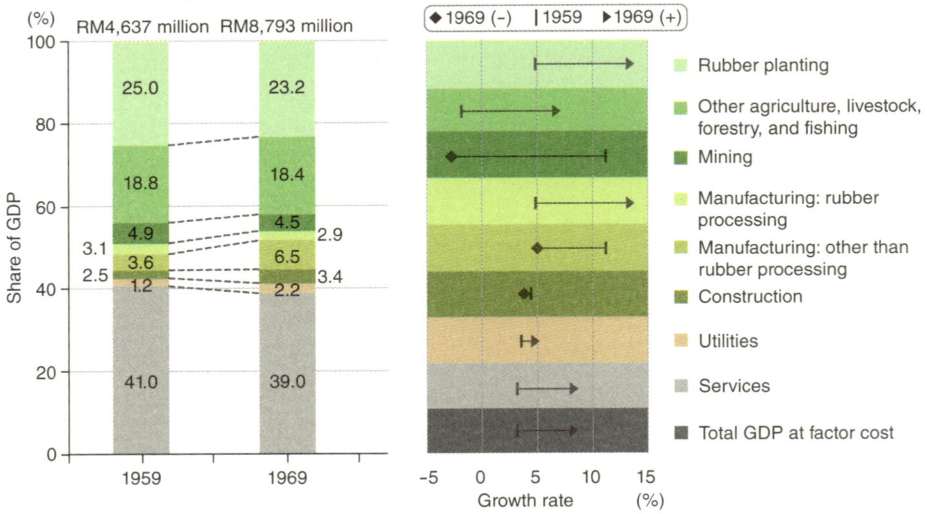

Source of data: Bhanoji Rao (1976).

Economic planning in the 1960s was predicated on the belief that the benefits of economic growth would gradually ripple throughout society, improving the livelihoods of the general population, and providing the funding needed to expand investments in public services such as education and health. But although the plans did explicitly seek to accelerate 'catch-up' by the rural sector and implicitly suggested the aim of equalizing the ethnic distribution of income, they did not set a timeline for these goals. Sizeable allocations were made to rural development and to the social sectors, but spending outcomes in health and education again fell short of plan targets. After a surge of public sector investment in 1961–1965, with an average annual growth rate of 19 per cent in nominal terms, the plan for 1966–1970 placed much more emphasis on the private sector for investing and creating the jobs that would be needed to absorb the growing pool of workers.

Although public sector investment had risen steeply in the first half of the decade (growing by 27.6 per cent between 1961 and 1965), by 1970 the private sector still accounted for 65 per cent of investment. Public sector investment grew by just 1.9 per cent in 1966–1970, whereas private sector investment expanded by 9.6 per cent each year. Aggregate investment rates had risen to around 19 per cent of GDP by the end of the decade,[47] up from about 12 per cent a decade earlier.

The major traditional targets of private sector investment in estate rubber and tin mining had by this time diminished in importance. The replanting of estates had been largely completed, and tin reserves were being depleted. In the primary sector, private sector investments in palm oil, timber, and oil extraction had come to the fore. Accelerated output growth in manufacturing was also being stimulated by growing private sector investment.[48] The share of manufacturing in total output increased to 13 per cent by the end of the decade, a rise of 4.5 per cent from 1960. Although a substantial part of manufacturing was focused on the domestic market, a growing range of manufacturing products started to be exported. While admittedly from a very small base, manufacturing exports began to expand fast, with an average growth rate of 14 per cent a year in the second half of the decade.

47 Reported investment rates in the second plan are expressed as a percentage of gross national product (GNP), and are estimated at around 15–16 per cent of GNP (in current prices) for the period of the MP1, 1966–1970. MP1 reports investment-to-GDP ratios of 19 per cent by 1965 (again in current prices). However, as there are no ratios expressed in GNP units for 1961–1965, and neither are there GDP ratios for 1966–1970, the 19 per cent given is a 'guesstimate'. Nevertheless, there is little doubt that investment ratios in the 1960s were far larger than they had been in the 1950s.

48 In the second half of the decade, MARA started its operations aimed at diversifying the rural economy, providing credit, and investing in a variety of small-scale manufacturing activities and services (such as bus transport and wholesaling services). Although there appear to be no data available on the number of new jobs directly and indirectly generated during this period by the various MARA activities, the diversification efforts it supported would have helped to create new jobs for those previously engaged in estate and smallholder rubber cultivation.

In the service sector, performance was more uneven. Partly due to the efforts of Bank Negara to promote the development of credit markets, as well as the creation of new financial institutions, banking, insurance, and real estate services all rose strongly, at an average rate of 10.8 per cent in 1966–1970. Other sectors, though, were more sluggish. Transport and storage, and wholesale and retail trade grew at about 3 per cent, trailing the overall rate of growth in the economy by some distance.

Despite solid economic expansion and some improvement in living standards, with Sabah and Sarawak growing faster than the peninsula, the economy failed to create new jobs at a rate that kept up with the increasing labour force.[49] In 1970, unemployment in Peninsular Malaysia was estimated at 8 per cent compared with 6.5 per cent in 1965 and 6 per cent in 1960. Estimates for Malaysia overall put unemployment in 1970 at 7.3 per cent, with even higher rates among persons below the age of 25. Although new jobs were created in all sectors of the economy, these were not enough to avoid the emergence of a surplus of workers. Moreover, the headline unemployment rate disguised prevalent underemployment. In 1967, for example, 11 per cent of workers classified as employed were working fewer than 25 hours a week, largely in rural occupations such as single-crop *padi* cultivation and fishing.

In 1961–1965, reflecting the ongoing structural transformation, all sectors other than agriculture created jobs at a rate that exceeded labour force growth. Most of these were in construction, transport, and utilities, which were benefiting from the high levels of public investment in infrastructure. Services and manufacturing also contributed to job creation, with government services posting the second-fastest rate of expansion. In agriculture, rubber estates reduced workers by nearly 20 per cent in the 1960s, but expansion in palm oil and in smallholdings helped to ensure a net creation of jobs, and the average annual growth was 1.7 per cent.

Job growth in the second half of the decade failed to meet its target. The second plan estimated that 461,000 new jobs would be required in 1966–1970 to absorb the anticipated increase in the labour force. The plan assessed that agriculture would provide some 44 per cent of these new jobs in the states of the peninsula, and about 80 per cent in Sabah and Sarawak. Outcomes for agriculture fell far short of these targets, however, largely because of job

49 In 1962–1967, the labour force on the peninsula grew at 2.9 per cent, but employment grew at only 2.7 per cent. A comparable gap is likely to have persisted over the period of MP2. MP2 notes that MP1 greatly underestimated labour force growth. The situation in Sabah was different, with immigration restrictions creating shortages of skilled and unskilled workers.

losses in estate agriculture. Although manufacturing contributed new jobs at a rate exceeding labour force growth, its small share in total employment meant that it accounted for just 15 per cent of the new jobs created.[50] Public services contributed most to job creation.

Labour market mismatches were also apparent. Job growth was fastest among the most educated members of the labour force. Employment of professionals and skilled workers more than doubled during the plan period, but many of the entrants to the labour force lacked the education and skills that jobs demanded. In the public sector, this led to a large number of unfilled vacancies, particularly in health, education, and specialized technical areas such as agricultural research and extension services. Too few Malaysians were qualified to fill these posts. Such mismatches disproportionately affected youths, and in the peninsula more than 64 per cent of the unemployed were in the 15–25 age group. In major towns, youth unemployment reached 27 per cent, exacerbated by the migration of rural youths looking for jobs in the modern, urban sector. While development expenditure grew rapidly over the first half of the 1960s, spending increases then slowed in the second half, probably partly because of the difficulties of absorbing allocations, particularly in education, health care, and social services (Figure 5.10).[51]

In aggregate macroeconomic terms, Malaysia's economy navigated a stable course. While budget deficits emerged in response to high rates of public investment—and the commensurate rise in government consumption that delivery of expanded services entailed—the deficits were modest and were easily financed by private sector surpluses and the reserves accumulated in earlier years. Under currency board arrangements, consumer price inflation remained low, averaging less than 1 per cent over the decade. After a brief period of current account deficits in 1962–1964 as revenues from rubber exports declined, surpluses resumed in the second half of the decade, with trade surpluses more than offsetting large outward income remittances. Strong capital inflows also added to Malaysia's foreign exchange reserves position.

50 Labour force and employment data for this period are patchy and there are apparent inconsistencies in reporting between MP1 and MP2, but broad patterns can be discerned. The assertion made by De Micheaux (2017) that the government was relying on industry to create a large number of jobs appears to be contradicted by the plan documents, which are clear about the limited job creation capacity of manufacturing.

51 MP2, Table 2.4, p. 28.

Figure 5.10 **The 1960s saw rapid growth of government revenue and expenditure**

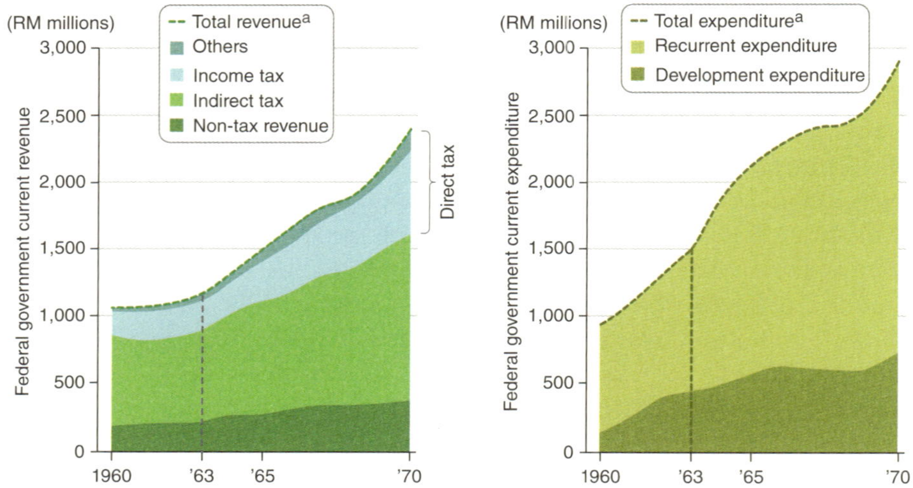

Sources of data: Ministry of Finance–Malaysia (1972, 1973).
Note: [a] 1960–1963, Malaya; from 1964, Malaysia.

Compared with many other developing countries, Malaysia performed strongly in the 1960s. Higher investment rates accelerated growth and increased labour productivity. Government investments in physical and social infrastructure laid the foundations for future growth and promoted welfare. Particularly in the second half of the decade, private investment helped to generate jobs and to diversify income. The economy had become less susceptible to the ups and downs of international movements in rubber and tin prices, with timber, palm oil, and crude oil broadening the export base.

Institutionally, the outlines of a modern state were forming. The government was delivering essential public goods and services, and mobilizing resources to pay for them through taxes, including on the rents accruing from timber and crude oil extraction. Federal government revenue more than doubled between 1960 and 1970, and expenditure also grew rapidly, especially on the growing number of government jobs.[52]

But these achievements masked widening imbalances. One concern was that too few jobs were being created for a rapidly expanding labour force.[53] Youth unemployment, in particular, presented a serious challenge, especially in major towns. Another key issue was that income growth for Malays was lagging behind that for other ethnic groups. In 1957, average incomes for

52 MP2, Table 2.9, p. 39 reports an overall deficit for the public sector, which consolidates the accounts of the federal and state governments with those of the public authorities.

53 Unemployment was prevalent in the peninsula and Sarawak, whereas Sabah faced shortages of labour in key areas.

Malays in Peninsular Malaysia were 53 per cent of the average for Chinese; by 1970, the average income gap had widened, with the ratio at 44 per cent.[54]

Although average incomes had grown steadily during the 1960s, Snodgrass (1980) observes that the incomes for the poorest 40 per cent of the population actually fell, and in 1967 average incomes for Malays were below their 1958 level in nominal terms. The Gini coefficient was 0.513 in 1970, indicating a high level of income inequality (Anand, 1983). Intra-ethnic inequalities were also high and had been growing (Chapter 9).[55] Spatial inequalities remain clearly evident at the territorial level, with real incomes on the peninsula considerably higher than those in Sabah and Sarawak,[56] and with the east coast and rural areas where most Malays lived lagging behind the more urbanized west coast and Johor. In 1970, about half of the population was still living in poverty. This was concentrated mainly among rural Malays and other *Bumiputera* with only weak connections to the emerging modern market economy, as well as the growing cohort of unemployed urban youth.

Underlying these widening disparities was a colonial legacy that had segmented occupations along ethnic lines and confined the majority of Malays to low-income agricultural activities. These historical patterns were coming under increasing pressure from a combination of fast population growth, rising indebtedness, and fragmentation of land. Such circumstances pushed increasing numbers of young Malay men into the towns for work. However, an education system that had failed to equip them for opportunities outside the rural economy meant that they fared little better here, with many trapped in low-income, marginal activities or enduring unemployment. Malays across nearly all occupations had fewer years of schooling than non-Malays, and received markedly lower wages.[57]

---

54 As no data on distribution for Sabah and Sarawak exists until later in the 1970s, the discussion here relates to Peninsular Malaysia.

55 Later research, based on the 1978 First Malaysian Family Life Survey, emphasize that intra-ethnic disparities were pronounced (accounting for 80–90 per cent of inequality) (Da Vanzo and Kusnic, 1980). The authors caution, however, that disparities in broader measures of income (including imputations for own production and consumption, imputed rent, housework, child care, and so on) were less stark than those based on market income alone. Still, these calculations assume that household workers face an infinitely elastic demand for their labour at the prevailing market wage, and that there are unconstrained choices about the substitution of leisure and all economic activity. These assumptions seem problematic for poor households where unemployment may be involuntary.

56 As a result of oil extraction (and, to a lesser extent, of timber exploitation), by 1970 per capita incomes in Sarawak were higher than in any other state, but much of the oil income flowed back to the federal authorities. Income generated by timber exploitation was not widely shared, and thus did not benefit the majority of the population either.

57 Schooling alone cannot explain all of the differences in observed incomes, however. For example, Hirschman (1974) reports that across all occupations, Chinese had a monthly income 2.4 times higher than Malays, but had only 1.7 years more schooling, implying, at face value, a rate of return for one year of additional schooling of a staggering 139 per cent. Among miners and labourers, Malays are reported as having more years of schooling, yet had an average monthly income of only 79 per cent of that of the Chinese. One explanation for these biases is that the quality of education received by Malays, and its relevance to economic needs, was poor.

Widening income inequality was also a function of highly skewed asset ownership. Foreign ownership was prevalent not just in traditional rubber, tin, and trading activities, but also in the emerging manufacturing sector and in oil and gas activities. In all these sectors, business decisions still largely served the interests of overseas shareholders. Domestic ownership of assets was also highly concentrated within the Chinese community and among a small group of privileged Malays. Other than through their relationship to the land, which permitted some diversification of economic activity but generated mainly non-market sources of income, rural Malays had a limited stake in the expanding modern sector, which was the engine for the growing prosperity of the nation. Those Malays finding employment in the civil service and in public and uniformed services fared much better.

The policies of the new government also had their part to play. Although interventions through FELDA and MARA were helping to modernize and diversify the rural economy, the productivity advances that were crucial to agricultural success were at the same time blunting its job creation potential owing to increasing mechanization, for example in estate rubber. And while the 'pioneer industries' approach had been successful in attracting foreign investment into import-substituting activities, its potential was inherently limited. A comparatively small domestic market, with much of the population on a low income, constrained growth and, by extension, job creation as well.

Conclusions

In the late 19th and early 20th centuries, Malaya's position in the regional and international economy was a key factor that contributed to its substantial development. Sparsely populated and undeveloped, but strategically located and with an abundance of natural resources, Malaya matched Britain's criteria for a base in Southeast Asia, and fulfilled its demand for raw materials at a time of rapid industrialization in Europe and the US (Drake, 1979).

During this period, the territories of what is now Malaysia experienced rapid growth of per capita GDP up to about 1930. The economy then collapsed with the onset of the Great Depression, the impacts of which persisted throughout the 1930s. The period from 1941 to 1945 saw the occupation of Malaya, North Borneo, and Sarawak by the military forces of Japan, which caused economic devastation and terrible human hardship. Post-war reconstruction efforts had, by 1950, rehabilitated the pre-war laissez-faire trading economy, and economic momentum was again subject to the vicissitudes of global market conditions for rubber and tin.

In the 1960s, commodity dependence tapered, and the seeds of economic diversification began to germinate. For the first time in three decades, Malaysia's economy kept pace with economic growth at the frontier—the US. Yet, by the end of the 1960s, the gap between per capita GDP in Malaysia and that in the US was larger than it had been in 1911. The gains that were made up to 1929 had been extinguished by the Great Depression, World War II, and a colonial 'development' model that embedded economic and social segmentation and inhibited diversification.

Despite the economic achievements following independence, the 1960s ended in crisis with the declaration of Emergency and dissolution of parliament. The economic marginalization of a large number of Malays, deeply segmented communities, contested identities, and perceived threats to the paramount importance of Malay constitutional rights all contributed to the mounting tensions that came to a head in the ethnic violence of 13 May 1969.

Starting from the assumption that the 1969 crisis was a consequence of Malay economic exclusion,[58] the New Economic Policy framed ethnicity-based, redistributive targets and interventions intended to rebalance opportunities. The Outline Perspective Plan 1971–1990 (EPU, 1971) and the Second Malaysia Plan (MP2) 1971–1975 set out the initial strategy, emphasizing that economic growth would be an essential means of reducing poverty and thereby fostering national unity and social integration (Chapter 7). Before discussing the economic strategies of the 1970s onwards, Chapter 6 explores further the nature and origins of Malaysia's impressive economic growth since independence.

58 This interpretation, by equating ethnicity directly with distribution, disregards the fact that there were wide inequalities within ethnic groups, and that poverty and lack of opportunity were not an exclusively Malay phenomenon (De Micheaux, 2017).

Chapter 6

Growth, Productivity, and Wealth Since Independence

The search for the underlying factors that cause some economies to grow faster than others, and for the triggers that punctuate growth accelerations, slowdowns, and sudden reversals, has attracted the interest of economists for centuries. Considerable attention has been paid to the interplay between the accumulation of physical and human capital, and population change; improvements in the efficiency with which inputs are transformed to outputs; policy and institutional choices; technological advances; resource endowments, climate, location, and geography; and opportunities for learning and economic 'catch-up'. The roles of some of these factors and their relevance to the experience of colonial Malaya and post-independence Malaysia are explored in Chapters 5 and 7.

This chapter is more concerned with issues of measurement. It sets out the record of Malaysia's economic growth for the period 1960–2017 and analyses the correlates of that growth: principally, factor accumulation and productivity change. It looks at the components of factor accumulation, and identifies the separate roles played by investments in physical capital and investments in human capital, as well as by the growth of the labour force. It compares Malaysia's track record on growth with that of a variety of benchmark countries, some regional, some resource-rich. The contributions of important demographic changes, as well as changes in the structure of output compared with past economic performance, are also quantified.

Finally, the chapter turns its attention to the critical question of the longer-term sustainability of Malaysia's development trajectory. While some of the extractive activities on which the economy still depends are renewable, others entail the exploitation of natural resources that are non-renewable. New advances in the measurement of 'genuine wealth' and 'adjusted net saving' are explained, and the measurements for Malaysia are presented. To a significant extent, Malaysia's high gross domestic savings rate has been eroded by the exploitation of natural capital. Overall, however, Malaysia has added to its stock of 'genuine wealth'.

The analysis begins with a review of the record of economic growth since independence, and returns to the question of economic 'catch-up' between 1970 and 2017. To provide continuity with Chapter 5, the data and analysis start with the 1960s. At the global income frontier, the trajectory of Malaysia's GDP per capita is compared with that of the US. Malaysia's economic performance is also gauged against countries that had similar income gaps with the US around 1960, and with other relevant benchmarks.

In an accounting sense, economic growth occurs either because of more intense application of inputs (capital, human capital, and labour) or because of advances in total factor productivity or TFP (the efficiency with which inputs are combined to produce outputs). The second section estimates the contributions of input accumulation and TFP to Malaysia's growth and explores the factors underlying both.

Labour productivity, or output per worker, is an important metric and is directly linked to changes in standards of living and in welfare levels. Output per worker is generally higher in more advanced countries. The third section reviews the trajectory of labour productivity in Malaysia and identifies the contributions to its growth from capital investment, investment in human capital, and TFP growth.

Although much can be learned from aggregate information, it can also mask important underlying structural features of growth. Even if there are no gains in labour productivity at the sectoral level, if workers migrate from lower- to higher-productivity activities, gains in aggregate labour productivity will be registered (the Baumol 'structural bonus'). The fourth section assesses these changes in economic structure, the extent of this structural bonus, and sector-level productivity.

As discussed in Chapter 2, Malaysia has undergone a demographic transition since independence which has had a marked impact on the country's age structure, including on the share of the population of working age. The fifth section assesses how demographic changes have contributed to Malaysia's economic growth through the resulting 'demographic dividend'.

Malaysia's natural resources have played an important role in its economic development. Rubber, tin, palm oil, and timber, as well as crude oil and natural gas, have all made significant contributions to GDP. While some of these natural assets are renewable (rubber, palm oil, and, potentially, tropical timber resources and products), tin and hydrocarbon resources are not. Counting their depletion as income rather than depreciation—the prevalent modality—gives a misleading impression of the extent to which economic growth is sustainable. The final section of this chapter looks to the future, assessing issues of sustainability using the concept of 'genuine wealth'—a measure of the value of a nation's physical, human, natural, financial, and institutional capital. The conclusions then draw out some of the key themes of the chapter.

The broad contours of the post-independence phases of development are set out in Table 6.1, providing context for this chapter. The detailed institutional and policy responses are discussed in Chapter 7.

Table 6.1 Post-independence phases of development

1957–1969 Building of the nation state
This phase was marked by moves to unify and build the apparatus and institutions of the new nation state; the assertion of Malay political power and the design of new political institutions; a continuation of colonial economic policies and commodity dependence; widening inequalities, endemic rural poverty, and continuing ethnic tensions; land divisions and agricultural schemes; and the formation of the national planning architecture.
1969 Political crisis
This year saw racial riots and consequent political redirection.
1971–1990 The New Economic Policy (NEP)
This era saw the crystallization of the NEP and the emergence of a redistributive and interventionist state; formation of government-linked companies (GLCs); extension of agricultural schemes and greater use of subsidized investment vehicles; diversification within agriculture (into palm oil); the initial stages of structural transformation; a demographic transition and dividend; a switch from being a net energy importer to a net energy exporter; a broadening of the export base, export-oriented industrialization, and economic diversification; a 'Look East' policy; economic experimentation and the Heavy Industries Corporation; input-intensive growth alongside growing inefficiencies; and the onset of internal and external imbalances.
1985–1986 Commodity price crisis
Halfway through the 1980s, the economy suffered a commodity price collapse, accompanied by domestic economic stresses and asset destruction, which included a property market collapse, a stock market meltdown, and a nascent banking and financial sector crisis. There followed fiscal policy retrenchment with expansionary monetary policy.
1987–1997 Economic redirection
After the Plaza Accord of 1985, foreign direct investment liberalization and exchange rate realignments stimulated investment interest. Other features of this period were privatization policies, fiscal consolidation, and deregulation of markets, which contributed to a stock market boom; a concerted focus on exports and export performance; rapid manufacturing and industrial growth; weakening checks and balances in private and public sectors; and looming vulnerabilities in the corporate and financial sectors and in other asset markets.

1997–1999 Asian financial crisis

The crisis was externally triggered, but exposed domestic vulnerabilities in the financial and corporate sectors. This phase saw a systemic crisis in the banking sector, as well as corporate bankruptcies, a sharp recession, and asset market dislocation. The government imposed controls on capital flows and pegged the exchange rate to provide latitude for independent monetary policy actions.

1999–2003 Recovery and weak accumulation of manufactured capital

Per capita incomes remained below the peak of 1997 until 2002. This phase also witnessed a sharp decline of private sector investment; a decline in TFP; the onset of early deindustrialization; and stiffer competition for investment from China and elsewhere. Manufacturing exports and high-tech exports as a share of total exports started to taper, and were then dented by the bursting of the dot-com bubble in 2002.

2004–2008 Solid growth

This phase recorded robust economic advances; a recovery in TFP growth; continuing gains in the share of services in employment and output; and terms-of-trade gains as oil prices started to rise.

2008–2009 Global financial crisis and Great Recession

The global financial market meltdown led to deflation and demand compression. The downdraft was felt in Malaysia in exports, the terms of trade, and the financial sector. A strong counter-cyclical fiscal and monetary stimulus package was launched.

2009–2017 Growth recovery and moderation

Growth recovered but fell short of planning targets in a period of fiscal consolidation. Deficits widened in human capital, productivity, governance, and intangible assets. Despite divestment of some GLC assets, ties between government and business remained close and, in some cases, deepened. The rationalization of subsidies contributed to fiscal consolidation. Deindustrialization, the rise of the service economy, and a renewed dependence on commodities continued.

The Record on GDP Growth

This section charts Malaysia's economic ascent from 1960 to 2017. The starting point of 1960 has been selected based on data availability, and because it pre-dates by a decade the introduction of the NEP. More probing questions about the changing conditions that influenced the trajectory of economic growth and structural change are discussed in Chapter 7, where Malaysia's development experience is considered in the context of the episodic crises and reversals that triggered important institutional and policy shifts.

A hallmark of Malaysia's experience is the way in which disruptive events have elicited pragmatic adjustments, becoming windows of opportunity for policy change. While the country has traversed distinctive (if not discrete) stages of development, its experience has been unique and non-linear. It is helpful analytically to think of Malaysia's development as having passed through a number of phases or stages.[1] Within each phase, the character of development has differed. The colonial period—from about 1870 until unification and independence in 1957—saw important economic and institutional developments that left their imprint on the newly independent nation. In subsequent years, new institutional structures began to take shape, although many colonial economic policies and structures remained in place. Widening inequalities and a legacy of ethnic segmentation erupted into violence in 1969.

The period from 1970, beginning with the NEP in 1971, then witnessed institutional and policy redirection. Despite some failures, this was a period of catch-up growth and poverty reduction (Figures 6.1 and 6.2). This phase ended with the Asian financial crisis which exposed weaknesses in the underlying structure of the economy, in particular its lagging financial infrastructure, narrow economic base, and reliance on input-intensive growth.

As Malaysia entered the new millennium, competition from China and weaker investment performance tempered growth. Inequalities again started to widen. To sustain momentum, Malaysia began focusing on productivity advances and innovation to promote continued growth. This strategy required greater attention to investments in the nation's intangible capital—essentially, institutions and human capital—and to the value placed on its natural and environmental resources.

Between 1960 and 2017, Malaysia achieved an annual average rate of growth of real GDP per capita of 3.9 per cent, generating real per capita incomes in 2017 that were over 9.3 times larger than in 1960.[2] Average living standards, as captured by the growth of per capita real consumption

1 Rostow (1962) describes a process in which development proceeds linearly from less advanced to more advanced states: from traditional societies, to 'take-off', to the stage of 'high mass consumption'. Rostow's description of development as an evolutionary process resembles the experience of northern Europe. One key criticism of the model, however, is that it fails to explain why development occurred where and when it did. Numerous other criticisms of Rostow's model have been made (Acemoglu and Robinson, 2012). More generally, other scholars argue against the imposition of fixed models, that no two nations' pathways to development can ever be the same, as one nation's development alters the context in which others seek to progress. Some scholars subscribe to the view that every time and place is unique (see, for example, Woolcock et al., 2009).

2 For the analysis of Malaysia's growth, all estimates are based on the PWT9.1 variable 'RGDP NA', which Feenstra et al. (2015) expressly recommend for analysis of the growth of GDP over time in a single country. This variable is measured in 2011 US$ and applies GDP growth rates calculated in constant national prices to the PWT9.1 level estimate of output-side real GDP in 2011—that is, the variable 'CGDP O', which is expressed in purchasing power parity (PPP) prices. 'RGDP NA' is also used for productivity calculations and comparisons. All cross-country income and growth comparisons use expenditure estimates of GDP in PPP prices (the PWT9.1 variable 'RGDP E'), which include the effects of changes in the terms of trade, and better reflect underlying changes in the standard of living. Growth rates calculated over intervals of greater than one year are cumulative annual averages.

expenditure, grew at a cumulative average rate of 3.8 per cent. In contrast to the colonial period, it would seem that the benefits of per capita income growth were felt more directly in the rising levels of private consumption, although there is marked variation in consumption growth rates over time. Table 6.2 shows per capita growth by decadal averages before, during, and after the period of the NEP.

Table 6.2 Malaysian standards of living have continued to rise in the 57 years since 1960

Period	Real GDP growth per capita (%)	Real consumption growth per capita (%)	Difference
1960–1969	3.4	2.0	1.4
1970–1979	6.8	6.3	0.5
1980–1989	2.7	1.4	1.4
1990–1999	4.2	2.3	1.8
2000–2009	2.3	4.8	–2.5
2010–2017	3.4	4.8	–1.4
1960–2017	*3.9*	*3.8*	*0.1*
1971–1989 (NEP)	*4.0*	*3.5*	*0.5*
1990–2017 (Post NEP)	*3.5*	*4.1*	*–0.6*

Sources of data: PWT9.1; Feenstra et al. (2015).

Figure 6.1 shows the trajectory of GDP per capita and consumption per capita. The measure of consumption from PWT9.1 combines private and government consumption, as both are considered as contributing to the standard of living of the general population. Over the period 1960–2017, the speed of per capita income doubling slowed gradually,[3] a trend that is consistent with the predictions of Solow-type models of convergence. Figure 6.2 shows growth rates of real GDP per capita over the period 1955–2017, with their ten-year moving average (or trend) values. The moving average accelerated in the 1970s and 1990s, decelerated in the 1980s, and drifted lower after the Asian financial crisis.

The diamonds in Figure 6.1 identify six years in which per capita income contracted (recessions), and the grey shaded bars identify intervals during which income was lower than its immediately preceding peak level. There was a short one-year recession in 1975, a more protracted one in the mid 1980s, the reversals triggered by the Asian financial crisis of the late 1990s and the dot-com crash of 2000–2001, and finally the downdraft precipitated by

3 Per capita income doubled from 1960 to 1974, again from 1974 to 1992, and again from 1992 to 2013.

the global financial crisis and the Great Recession of 2008. Output reversals have had a frequency of about one per decade since 1970.

The trajectory of consumption per capita appears closely correlated with that of income per capita. Although not immediately visible from Figure 6.1, consumption per capita has been somewhat more volatile than income, with income shocks generating amplified consumption responses.[4] While there are periods in which both GDP per capita and consumption per capita exhibit high levels of volatility, there is no apparent trend to volatility. GDP growth was just as volatile in the first decade of the new millennium as it was in the 1970s. The diversification of economic activity over the past 60 years and the gradual shift of resources out of agriculture and into industry, and later into services, has thus not been associated with a decline in the volatility of GDP growth (Chapter 8).[5] However, as Sultan Nazrin Shah (2017) shows, volatility during the pre-war colonial period was extreme, and, if only by comparison, the post-independence period has been relatively tranquil.

Figure 6.1 **Malaysia has experienced 57 years of growth in income and living standards**

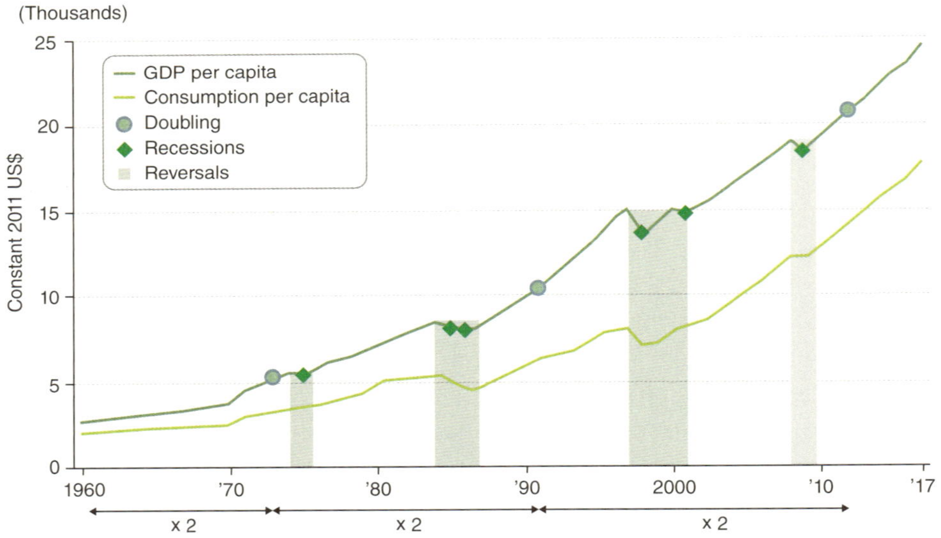

Sources of data: See Chapter 5, Box 5.1.

4 This is consistent with the 'Deaton Paradox', which postulates that if forward-looking consumers perceive income shocks to be more permanent than transient, there will be disproportionate changes to consumption. An investigation of the consumption–income relationship is beyond the scope of this inquiry, however.

5 This observation seems not to be affected by the frequency of the data. Volatility appears to cycle whether growth is measured annually or as ten-year cumulative averages.

Figure 6.2 **Malaysia's trend in real GDP per capita growth has gradually slowed since the late 1990s**

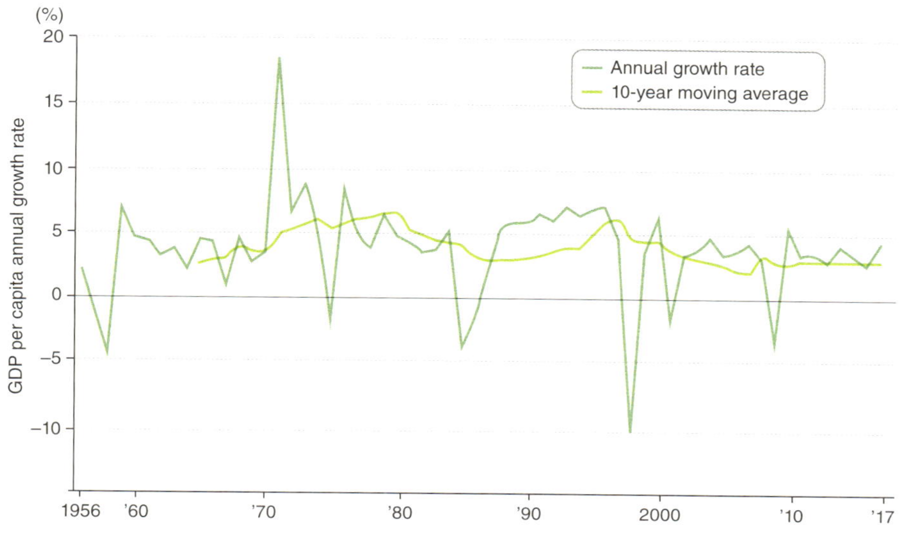

Sources of data: PWT9.1; Feenstra et al. (2015).

Income Convergence and Catch-up

Figure 6.3 shows the degree to which Malaysia has narrowed the gap in per capita GDP with the US, which is used throughout this analysis as the frontier.[6] In 1960, Malaysia's per capita GDP was just 15 per cent of that of the US. By 2017, it was a little above 46 per cent. The trajectory of catch-up has not been monotonic, however, with the gap widening in the mid 1980s and again after the Asian financial crisis. Nevertheless, the convergence since 1970 offers a striking contrast to the pre-independence experience.

The convergence of per capita income of the kind shown in Figure 6.3 is sometimes termed 'relative' convergence, as it is measured in terms of an income ratio. An increasing ratio suggests that the rate of growth of per capita income in Malaysia is faster than that in the frontier economy. However, relative convergence (a rising ratio) does not necessarily imply that the simple difference, or the absolute gap in per capita incomes (US income per capita less Malaysian income per capita), is narrowing.[7] Indeed, despite

6 Per capita GDP here is measured in PPP terms using the expenditure estimates from PWT9.1, which capture the effects of terms-of-trade changes.

7 Relative convergence requires that $g^M > g^{US}$, where g is the rate of growth and the superscripts label Malaysia and the US values. Absolute income convergence requires that $(Y^M/Y^{US}).g^M - g^{US} > 0$, where g is the rate of growth and Y is the level of GDP.

relative convergence, there was non-convergence of absolute per capita income levels (a widening gap in *levels*) through to about 2002. Since then, Malaysia has seen both relative and absolute convergence with the US. If the so-called 'middle-income trap' is defined in terms of *stalled* convergence, there is not yet any evidence that Malaysia has succumbed.

Figure 6.3 Malaysia is catching up with the income frontier—the US—but the gap remains wide

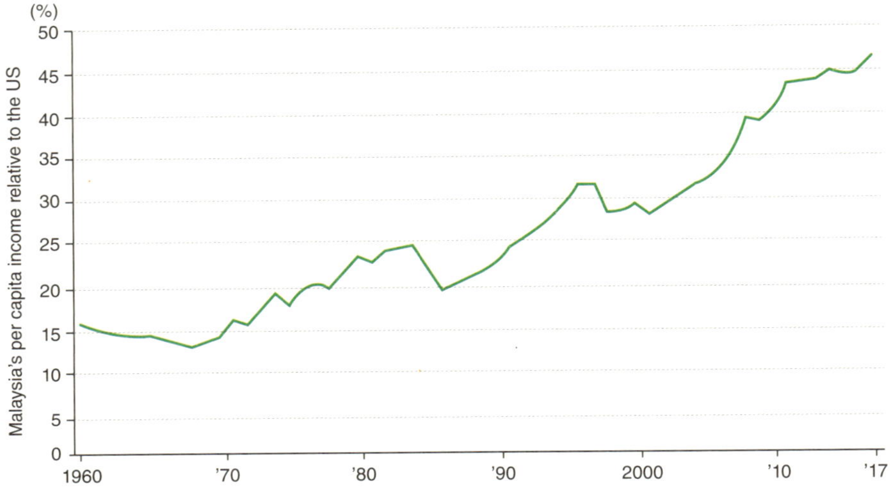

Sources of data: PWT9.1; Feenstra et al. (2015).

As well as comparing Malaysia with the frontier economy, it is also useful to examine how Malaysia's performance in closing the income gap with the US has fared against those of other countries. Three sets of benchmarks are used in this exercise. First, comparisons are made with the newly industrialized economies (NIEs) of East Asia: Hong Kong, the Republic of Korea, Singapore, and Taiwan. In 1960, per capita GDP in both the Republic of Korea and Taiwan was somewhat lower than in Malaysia, while per capita incomes in Hong Kong and Singapore were somewhat higher.

A second group of benchmark countries comprises some of Malaysia's partners in ASEAN: Indonesia, the Philippines, and Thailand. In 1960, Malaysia already had a level of per capita GDP that was higher than all three of these neighbouring countries.[8] The transitional economies of the Lao People's Democratic Republic, Myanmar, and Viet Nam are excluded, as their transition to becoming market economies only began in the 1990s. Brunei is also excluded because its very high oil income, which lifts its per capita GDP above that of the US, renders comparison meaningless. China, which is not

8 Singapore is excluded from the ASEAN benchmark group as it is grouped with the NIEs.

a member of ASEAN, is added to this group because of its importance to the global and East Asian economies.

A third benchmark is provided by natural-resource-rich countries considered to have avoided the 'resource curse'. Although the empirical evidence is ambiguous, there are some arguments that suggest that an abundance of natural resources can be a hindrance rather than a boon to economic development. One argument is that natural resources and the rents they generate can weaken political institutions, which in turn leads to poor economic choices. Another maintains that a dependence on natural resources exposes an economy to volatility and impairs development of the dynamic manufacturing sector (Dawe, 1996). For our purposes, Botswana (a sparsely populated country with just over 2 million people and heavily dependent on diamond exports) and Chile (a country heavily dependent on copper exports) are both considered natural-resource success stories. While other countries such as Australia, Canada, and Norway could be added to the list of natural-resource-based successes, as already advanced countries they are not relevant examples for benchmarking catch-up.

Figure 6.4 (left panel) shows the same data on catch-up given in earlier figures, but now plotted alongside NIE data. From 1960 to 2017, all NIEs demonstrated rapid catch-up with the US and have considerably narrowed their income gaps. Indeed, per capita GDP in Singapore is now higher than in the US, while in Hong Kong it is broadly equal.

The experiences of the Republic of Korea and Taiwan are of particular interest. In 1960, the former had a per capita income lower than Malaysia's, but by the 1980s their positions were reversed, and Malaysia subsequently continued to fall further behind. Taiwan, which had a comparable income gap in 1960, has consistently outperformed Malaysia ever since, and by 2017 had a per capita GDP of about 85 per cent of that in the US compared with Malaysia's roughly 46 per cent.

Figure 6.4 (right panel) shows Malaysia's performance against the three selected ASEAN neighbours and China. In 1960, Malaysia began with a higher per capita GDP than these ASEAN neighbours and China, and has maintained that lead ever since. The Philippines has made barely any inroads on US income levels over the past five decades. Thailand, which had seen the gap with the US narrow quickly until the mid 1990s, then lost considerable ground as a result of the Asian financial crisis. It was not until 2007 that Thailand returned to the position it had been in in 1996. Income in Indonesia, the lowest of the group in 1960, made slow gains on the US frontier until the Asian financial crisis,[9]

9 The Solow model predicts that convergence should occur more quickly from lower initial income levels, all other things being equal. The observation that convergence has been slower in Indonesia thus suggests that all other factors were *not* equal.

and then abruptly regressed. As with Thailand, it took more than a decade for Indonesia to regain its 1996 position. While the crisis also seriously interrupted catch-up in Malaysia, the retreat from the frontier was less marked than in Thailand, Indonesia, or the Philippines, and the recovery of lost ground was somewhat quicker. Compared with the Republic of Korea, however, the impact on Malaysia was more severe and the subsequent recovery more drawn out.

China's situation was somewhat different in that there is no evidence of catch-up before the end of the 1970s. At about this time, China abandoned the disastrous policies of its Cultural Revolution and embarked on an experimental path towards the phased liberalization of its economy. As reform momentum built in the 1980s and 1990s, China slowly closed the income gap with the US. An inflection point was reached around 2000, after which the rate of catch-up accelerated.

Figure 6.4 **Malaysia's per capita income is losing ground against the NIEs, but compares favourably with three ASEAN countries and China**

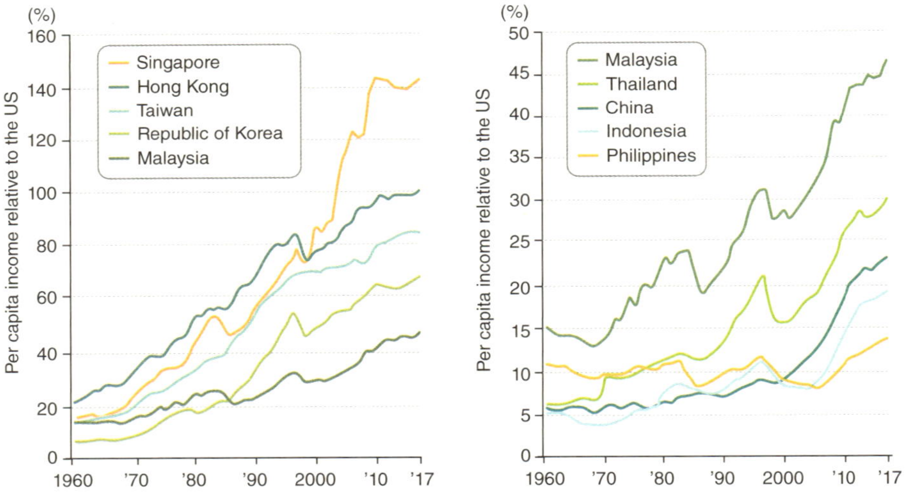

Sources of data: PWT9.1; Feenstra et al. (2015).

Figure 6.5 summarizes Malaysia's performance relative to that of Chile and Botswana. In 1960, Chile had a higher per capita income than Malaysia, but it regressed relative to the US in the 1970s during a period of political and institutional upheaval. While renewed catch-up began in the 1980s, progress was followed by another reversal in the 1990s. By 2017, the gap between GDP per capita in Chile and in the US was slightly wider than that between Malaysia and the US. Botswana, on the other hand, has seen steadier gains, albeit from lower initial levels of per capita income.

Figure 6.5 **Malaysia has outperformed successful resource-rich nations**

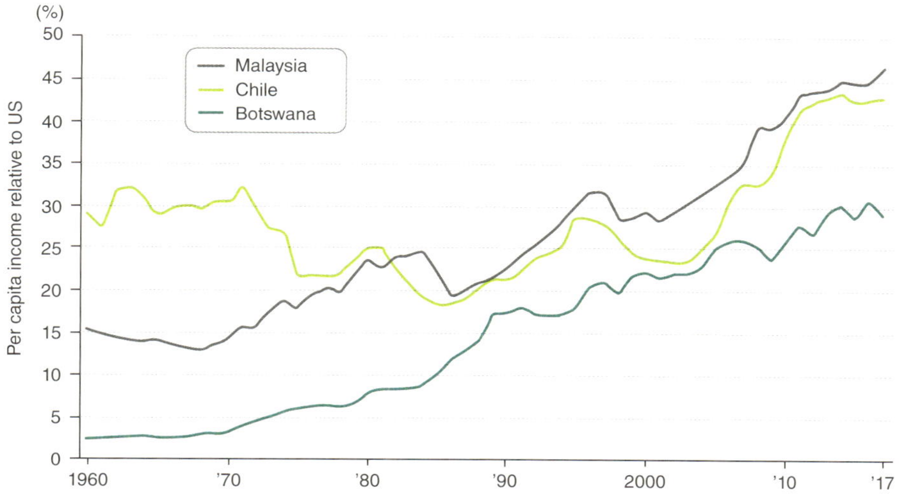

Sources of data: PWT9.1; Feenstra et al. (2015).

In summary, since the 1970s Malaysia has gradually closed the gap with US income levels. It has outperformed its peers in ASEAN (other than Singapore), and its performance compares favourably with that of Botswana and Chile, two resource-rich nations.

Measured against the NIEs, however, Malaysia's track record has been less impressive. The Republic of Korea and Taiwan, which had similar income levels in 1960, have left Malaysia behind and have moved to close the income gap with the US much more rapidly. This suggests that although Malaysia has had reasonably positive economic outcomes, its political and economic choices since independence may have failed to exploit its full potential. However, the experiences of the NIEs point to the opportunities that still exist to sustain growth and raise living standards—a topic taken up in the next chapter.

Total Factor Productivity Growth and Input Growth

From an accounting perspective, aggregate economic growth can occur either through the more intensive application of inputs—such as physical capital, labour, and human capital—or through gains in TFP, although it is challenging to measure this effectively (Box 6.1). For advanced countries, TFP growth is usually interpreted as reflecting costless gains in the efficiency with which inputs are converted into outputs, and is associated with innovation and improvements in technology, production, and management processes. For countries that are still some way behind the income frontier, however, in addition to these factors TFP is likely to encompass a wide array of other variables as well, including shifts in economic structure, demand and supply shocks, demographic change, policy and regulatory changes, and underlying institutional conditions.

Box 6.1 Some shortcomings of TFP calculations

At the microeconomic level, if all the assumptions that underpin TFP calculations were met, TFP would be a measure of costless improvements in the efficiency with which inputs are transformed into output, or of technological advances in those processes, capturing an important facet of development. However, TFP measures have a number of limitations for assessing an economy's productivity, as discussed, for example, by Bosworth and Collins (2003).

First, TFP is measured as a residual. Consequently, anything that has an impact on output that is not registered in input intensity will be attributed to TFP. Such influences go beyond changes in efficiency or technological changes, and may include institutional and policy changes, a variety of demand and supply shocks, and political events.

Second, measurement errors will also be reflected in TFP estimates. If improvements in the quality of output are not adequately captured, TFP measures will understate improvements in welfare. On the input side, aggregate TFP measures may fail to capture how changes in the composition of capital affect output. For example, the impact on output of large, costly investments in infrastructure may be less immediate than the impact of investments in machinery. In addition, measured inputs should capture variations in the time intensity of their use, but where stock measures are used, and where stock–flow relationships vary over time, changes in utilization will register instead in measured TFP.

Third, the assumptions that underlie TFP measurement may not be met. For example, aggregation bias is likely to occur during periods in which resources migrate from low- to higher-productivity activities (for instance, from agriculture to industry), or from high- to lower-productivity activities (for example, from industry to services). And when markets are imperfect, prices will not be equated with marginal productivity, an assumption that is needed to equate factor shares with output elasticities, and hence to allocate the productivity of specific inputs to output growth.

Fourth, as an accounting concept, TFP measures on their own reveal little about the underlying causes of growth, and neither do they allow the identification of what might underlie the observed changes in measured TFP.

Finally, as TFP metrics deploy conventional national accounting metrics, they necessarily give an incomplete picture of 'genuine development'. For example, rapid TFP growth could be accompanied by environmental degradation or the destruction of natural capital, both of which would indicate that growth is unsustainable.

The calculations for Malaysia for the period 1960–2017 are described in Box 6.2. Results can also be derived from a decomposition of standard national income accounting identities. TFP *growth* rates are reported over consecutive five-year periods using cumulative five-year averages for all years from 1960.[10] Consecutive averages help to remove the biases that may occur when data are presented for pre-selected intervals, such as calendar decades or planning periods. TFP *levels* are reported annually.

Box 6.2 PWT9.1 enhancements and TFP calculations

The calculation of the level and growth of TFP follows the methodology set out in Inklaar and Timmer (2013). An identical methodology is used by the OECD in its annual productivity comparisons. The annual levels of TFP presented here employ real GDP measured in constant national prices. The cumulative averages have been calculated using annual observations of real GDP and PWT9.1 values for capital, labour, human capital, and the labour share in value added.

Cumulative average TFP growth between period *t* and *t–n* is calculated as:

$$TFP_{t,t-n} = \frac{1}{n} ln\left(\frac{Y_t}{Y_{t-n}}\right) - ln\,Q_{t,t-n}$$

where *Y* is real GDP measured in national prices, *ln Q* is the Tornqvist quantity index[11] of the growth of factor inputs, and *n* is the number of years over which TFP is being measured. The Tornqvist quantity index is measured as:

$$ln\,Q_{t,t-n} = \frac{1}{n}\left(\frac{1}{2}\cdot(\alpha_t + \alpha_{t-n})\cdot ln\left(\frac{K_t}{K_{t-n}}\right) + \left(1 - \frac{1}{2}\cdot(\alpha_t + \alpha_{t-n})\right)\cdot ln\left(\frac{N_t}{N_{t-n}}\right)\right)$$

where *K* is the flow of capital services, *N* is quality-adjusted labour, and α is the time-varying elasticity of output with respect to capital, which is approximated using the observed share of capital in value added in each period.

Finally, the quality-adjusted measure of labour is calculated as the product of the number of people employed, and an index of human capital, measured as the average years of schooling adjusted for the rate of return to schooling.

Enhancements in PWT9.1 include small revisions in PPP data and the incorporation of revised and extended national accounts data, covering the period up to 2017. PWT9.1 also features an important change in the methodology of capital measurement, with

10 Annual estimates have also been calculated. These are somewhat 'noisier' than the cumulative five-year averages. The PWT9.1 annual observations underlying these calculations draw on UN national accounts estimates. There are some differences between the UN estimates of real GDP and those of other agencies, such as the World Bank's World Development Indicators. These differences will show up in differences in estimates of TFP growth for some years.

11 The main feature of the Tornqvist Index is that the weight used is an average of the weights in the current and base periods. It differs from the Laspeyres and Paasche indices, which use base-year and current-year weights respectively.

a detailed measure of the *flow* of capital services replacing earlier capital-stock-based measures (Inklaar and Woltjer, 2019). While improved measures of factor productivity result from such enhancements, these still depend on assumptions of perfect competition in product and factor markets, and the presence of translog production functions. Feenstra et al. (2015) suggest that their proposed TFP measures may, however, still be applicable in contexts where these restrictive assumptions do not hold.

Figure 6.6 presents a decomposition of real GDP growth into input growth and TFP growth for 1960–2017 (measured in 2011 domestic prices). The light yellow and light green bars, which occur at five-year intervals, coincide with the end of each five-year Malaysian planning period. Three main observations emerge.

Figure 6.6 **TFP's contribution to Malaysia's GDP growth has been low and highly pro-cyclical**

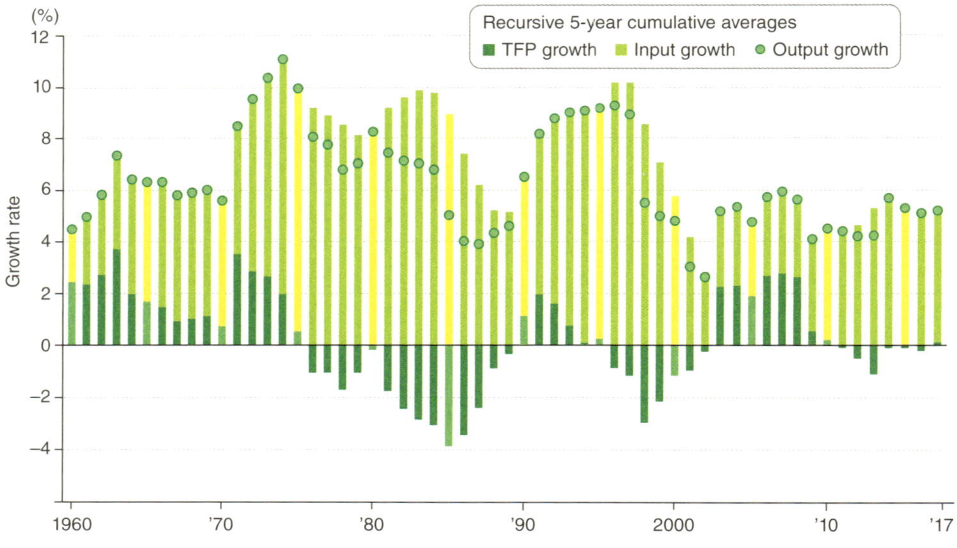

Sources of data: PWT9.1; Feenstra et al. (2015).

First, as other studies have noted, factor *accumulation* rather than total factor *productivity* has accounted for most of Malaysia's growth since 1960 (Box 6.3). TFP growth from 1960 to 2017 averaged 0.3 per cent annually (Table 6.3), whereas inputs grew at an annual average rate of 6.1 per cent. However, these average estimates are heavily influenced by large, negative estimates of TFP in years adjacent to those when GDP contracted. Median (or representative) TFP growth, which is less affected by extreme negative or positive values, has been somewhat higher, at 1.1 per cent, compared with median input growth of 5.0 per cent. Thus, while the contribution of TFP to economic growth has certainly been subordinate to that of input growth, it has not been negligible, accounting for about 17 per cent of median growth between 1960 and 2017.

Box 6.3 TFP estimates for Malaysia

The PWT9.1-based estimates of TFP growth for Malaysia—built on an improved methodology and richer information—do not always correspond with other estimates. The presence of differences is not unexpected given the enhancements of the PWT9.1 estimates. Indeed, these estimates show some distinctive differences from those of PWT9.0, underlining the susceptibility of TFP estimates to differences in the methods of calculation of inputs, outputs, prices, and factor shares.

The PWT9.1 long-run average of 0.3 per cent is lower than the estimate of 1 per cent that Bosworth and Collins (2003) report for East Asia (excluding China) for the shorter interval of 1960–2000. The PWT9.1 estimates for the 1960s and 1970s are also lower than those cited for Malaysia by Drabble (2000), although both agree that TFP regressed in the 1980s.

For the first part of the 1990s, PWT9.1 and World Bank (2016) estimates both suggest a return to positive TFP growth, with the World Bank reporting a somewhat faster expansion. For 1996–2000, these sources again agree, although PWT9.1 suggests larger reversals in TFP than the World Bank.

The PWT9.1 estimate for 2001–2005 of 1.2 per cent is lower than the estimate of the Malaysia Productivity Corporation (2016) for the same period, and both are lower than the estimate of the World Bank (2016). There is, nevertheless, agreement among sources that TFP slowed in 2006–2010. The PWT9.1 estimates suggest that TFP was 0.3 per cent for this period, while the Malaysia Productivity Corporation (2016) suggests marginally higher growth of 0.5 per cent, with the World Bank (2016) giving an estimate of 1 per cent. The Malaysia Productivity Corporation (2016) reports that in 2011–2014 TFP grew at an annual rate of 0.7 per cent, while the PWT9.1 estimate for this period is 0.6 per cent. For 2011–2017, the PWT9.1 estimate is close to one per cent. Malaysia Productivity Corporation's (2017) estimate for 2012–2016 is 1.1 per cent.

A new method of calculating TFP developed by Go et al. (2016) and employing new data yields yet another set of estimates for Malaysia for 1965–2010. These estimates bear a strong similarity to those reported here in terms of overall levels, the pattern of cyclicality, and the latter's phasing.

Perkins et al. (2017, Table 3) summarize the results of a large number of other estimates for Malaysia. While these exercises have often produced different estimates, they conclude that the rates have been low over a protracted period, a finding consistent with the evidence presented in this chapter.

Table 6.3 Malaysian TFP growth has rebounded since the 1990s, but remains low

Period	Annual average TFP growth (%)
1960–1969	1.5
1970–1979	–1.1
1980–1989	–0.9
1990–1999	0.3
2000–2009	1.1
2010–2017	1.0
1960–2017	*0.3*
1971–1989 (NEP)	*–1.1*
1990–2017 (Post NEP)	*0.8*

Sources of data: PWT9.1; Feenstra et al. (2015).

The second observation is that, viewed over a longer time frame, Malaysia's productivity performance has been highly uneven. Periods demonstrating solid advances have been followed by lengthy periods of decline. This feature of the data comes through clearly in Figure 6.7, which shows the trajectory of TFP *levels*, now measured annually. Malaysia registered advances in TFP levels in the early years of independence through to 1971, with average annual growth of 2.0 per cent. These years witnessed significant institutional development and structural change in the Malaysian economy, including growing urbanization, and the start of a longer-term movement of resources out of low-income agricultural activities and into industry and, to a lesser extent, services. In this period, Malaysia was the world's top producer of rubber, and palm oil was also beginning to make its mark. The Rubber Research Institute's R&D helped to raise productivity, as did huge efforts in the replanting of higher-yielding trees. There were also innovations in the processing and marketing of rubber (Chapter 8).

Perhaps equally important was the modernization and diversification of agriculture into palm oil and other commercial crops. It is possible, therefore, that rising TFP levels and elevated growth during this period are the result of a combination of institutional advances, efficiency gains from inter-sectoral resource reallocation, and productivity gains within agriculture.[12] Another factor that might explain the apparent gains witnessed, at least towards the end of this period, is the rapid development of crude oil extraction activities, which are often misrepresented as technologically static.

12 High rates of TFP growth were also observed in China between 2000 and 2010, when it too was undergoing large structural and institutional changes (Malaysia Productivity Corporation, 2017). Martin and Mitra (2001) have shown that agricultural activities often exhibit faster rates of TFP growth than either manufacturing or services.

Figure 6.7 **Malaysia's TFP has improved since the late 1990s, but has yet to exceed the peak of the early 1970s**

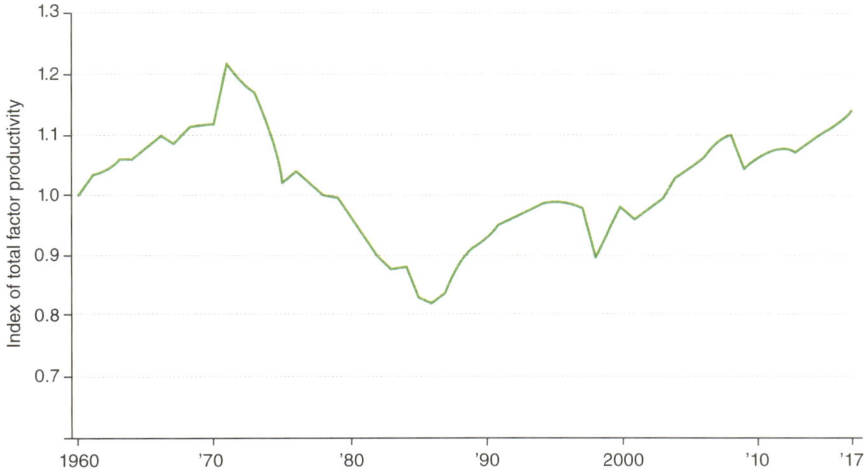

Sources of data: PWT9.1; Feenstra et al. (2015).

Having made considerable progress in the 1960s, productivity then slowed significantly between 1972 and 1987. This period spans the era of Malaysia's NEP (Chapter 7). Economic growth, especially in the 1970s, was largely a consequence of the rapid growth of inputs. In the second decade of the NEP period, there was also a global recession in 1982 and a sizeable negative commodity price shock in 1984–1985, as well as a number of costly domestic policy experiments. In particular, the government's Heavy Industries Corporation of Malaysia (HICOM) programme—part of the Look East policy introduced in the early 1980s[13]—entailed large investments in areas in which Malaysia faced significant cost disadvantages in global markets. It fell to the state to fund these investments and to absorb the consequent operating losses. When commodity prices fell in 1984–1985, Malaysia's fiscal space quickly narrowed, and austerity measures were introduced.[14] It would seem that the productivity setbacks experienced during the first half of the 1980s were closely tied to excessive investments in assets with low rates of return and to a subsequent commodity price shock, the negative income effects of which were amplified by fiscal retrenchment.

13 Malaysia's Look East policy was initiated by then prime minister Dr Mahathir Mohamad and sought to model the country's economic growth on the successful development of East Asian countries, especially Japan, and the rapidly industrializing Republic of Korea. Among several initiatives arising from the policy were investments in heavy industries, including automobiles through the Proton project and the Malaysia Incorporated concept designed to increase public–private partnerships (Jomo and Wee, 2014). The policy also aimed to raise labour productivity by adopting a Japanese work ethic (loyalty, discipline, and commitment) and management practices, with training programmes for young Malaysians at Japanese universities and institutes.

14 The public sector was unable to counteract the trend as its overborrowing and spending severely constrained its capacity to act.

TFP levels began to recover in the late 1980s as Malaysia implemented a more aggressive strategy to promote and liberalize export-oriented foreign direct investment. A privatization programme was also initiated at this time, which gathered momentum in the early 1990s (Chapter 7). During this period there was an upswing in TFP, although TFP levels remained below those seen in 1960–1970. The first part of the 1990s, in particular, saw rapid economic growth and solid gains in TFP. However, Malaysia's institutional capabilities eventually had difficulty in keeping pace with the rapid economic growth: credit and debt denominated in foreign currencies grew exponentially, asset prices ballooned, and the corporate sector became highly leveraged.

In 1996—before the Asian financial crisis—TFP began to reverse, perhaps signalling emerging stresses within the domestic economy. Much sharper falls in TFP then occurred during the depth of the crisis in 1997 and 1998. The subsequent recovery in productivity levels was temporarily interrupted in 2001 by the recessionary impact of the bursting of the dot-com bubble. By this time, Malaysia had developed a dynamic electronics export sector. Thereafter, productivity levels again began to register gradual growth before being dented yet again by the 2008 Great Recession. The pattern of post-recession recovery then repeated itself. Even so, by 2017, productivity levels in Malaysia were still no higher than they had been in 1971. It is also of interest that the five-year moving average data suggest that the largely homegrown economic setbacks of the mid 1980s and the Asian financial crisis were *preceded* by a trend of decline in TFP. By contrast, trend declines in TFP *followed* the externally triggered recessions of 1975 and 2008.

The third notable feature of Malaysia's TFP growth is that it is moderately pro-cyclical. A simple correlation of annual real GDP growth and TFP *growth* yields r=0.7.[15] This behaviour (which is also apparent in calculations based on annual data) has been observed in other countries and over long periods of time (for example, in the US data). A possible explanation for the pro-cyclical pattern lies in the hoarding of labour during economic downturns and in factors that constrain the adjustment of capital services in response to demand shocks. Other explanations focus on the endogeneity of investment, noting that faster economic growth may stimulate productivity-improving investments.[16] But it is possible, too, that the pro-cyclical pattern of Malaysian

15 'New classical economists' assert that the direction of causation is from exogenous productivity shocks to changes in output rather than from demand shocks to productivity.

16 However, there is little evidence of such an effect in the Malaysian data. TFP correlates negatively with lagged growth of the capital stock (and with the quality index for human capital). This may reflect the inefficient investments in heavy industries during this period, a policy now regarded as having been a costly failure. Park (2015) finds a more general correlation between slumps in TFP and excessive investment rates (see https://blogs.adb.org/blog/global-productivity-slump-common-and-country-specific-factors).

TFP growth may be a statistical artefact. Measures of capital services, in particular, may not fully capture adjustments in utilization rates or, indeed, the destruction of capital that can occur in the face of severe economic shocks.

Turning to input growth, Figure 6.8 identifies the separate contributions of capital and labour. The labour component of input growth in turn comprises changes in the numbers of people employed and in the quality of labour (human capital). The data reveal that both capital services and quality-adjusted labour have made significant contributions to Malaysia's input growth.

Capital services grew at an annual average rate of 2.9 per cent from 1960 to 2017, with quality-adjusted labour growing at an average rate of 2.5 per cent. However, the growth of capital services has shown considerably greater variation than that of labour. Major pushes in the capital investment component of capital services occurred after the introduction of the NEP in the early 1970s, during the HICOM period of the early 1980s, and in the 1990s, as foreign direct investment in export manufacturing and the property market boomed. Investment rates have generally dipped after recessions, recovering shortly afterwards, but following the Asian financial crisis investment languished until 2003. Underlying capital utilization and rates of return on capital are also likely to have been pro-cyclical. Although capital accumulation, which has a decisive influence on measured capital services, has picked up since, the elevated investment rates seen in the second half of the 1980s and the first half of the 1990s have not returned.

Figure 6.8 Malaysia's input growth has been fast but cyclical

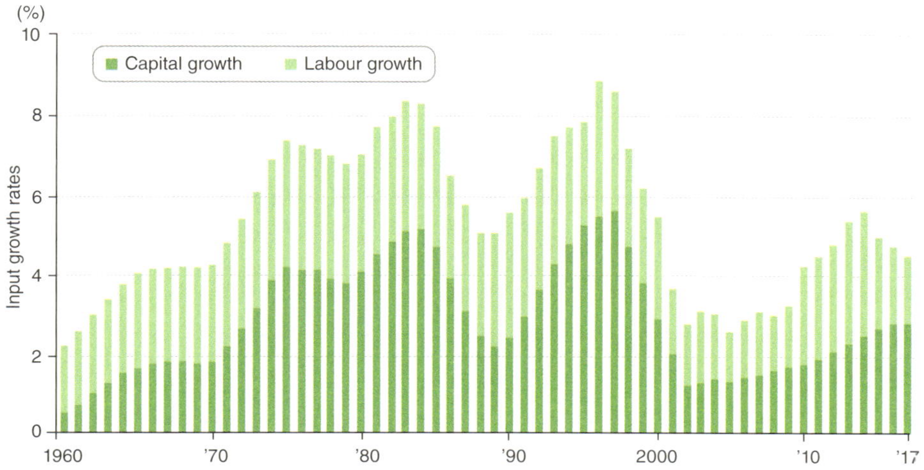

Sources of data: PWT9.1; Feenstra et al. (2015).

Factor Productivity Benchmarks

Figure 6.9 (left panel) plots the trajectory of Malaysian TFP *levels* alongside those of the Republic of Korea, Singapore, and Taiwan.[17] The measures in this figure are computed from national accounts estimates of output at common national prices. It was observed above (Figure 6.4) that these economies have all outperformed Malaysia in terms of the speed at which they have narrowed the gaps between their per capita GDPs and that of the US. Since the early 1980s, all three of these countries have outperformed Malaysia in their TFP gains, with the gap in performance widening for most of the period. Is it, then, faster TFP growth that has led to faster income convergence in these three economies?

One way to approach this question is to compare growth of per capita GDP with growth of TFP over the same interval in each country. From such comparisons, it is apparent that although TFP growth has been faster in the NIEs, it cannot arithmetically account for much of the faster growth of GDP per capita. In the Republic of Korea, Singapore, and Taiwan, as in Malaysia, the growth of GDP per capita has been predominantly input-intensive. In the Republic of Korea, for example, there was a staggering 48-fold increase in real GDP from 1960 to 2017. Over this period, the country's level of TFP more than doubled, but its capital stock soared an astonishing 57 times. Moreover, the number of quality-adjusted workers increased nine-fold. In the Republic of Korea, and in the other NIEs, factor accumulation dwarfs TFP in accounting for growth.

While faster convergence with advanced income levels in the NIEs is not, therefore, a simple consequence of their faster TFP growth rates, De Long (1996) observes that TFP growth and the rate of factor accumulation are unlikely to be independent of each other. He notes that faster TFP growth—triggered by any number of technological, institutional, policy, or regulatory factors—may, in stimulating the growth of output, encourage investment in physical capital, thereby accelerating factor accumulation. Moreover, since the real cost of capital declines as per capita income rises, productivity growth, which lifts income, will transform a set amount of saving into additional investment, resulting in both a higher capital–output ratio and a higher per capita income. Any sustained advantage in TFP growth may thus also boost per capita income through other channels. The higher incomes generated by even a small TFP premium may, for instance, increase the demand for literacy, in turn lowering female fertility rates and accelerating a demographic transition in which lower population growth then raises the capital–output ratio and per capita income.

These possibilities are intriguing, but the question of whether comparatively modest TFP differentials have amplified impacts on factor accumulation, and thereby on the speed of convergence of per capita incomes across countries, requires deeper investigation than is possible here. Within

17 TFP levels are all scaled to unity in 1960 to allow a comparison of relative performance.

the small sample of NIEs and Malaysia, the differences in TFP growth rates do not obviously correlate with rates of input accumulation and per capita income growth. As Krugman (1994) observes, the real growth 'miracle' in East Asia is more likely to lie in *how* these countries were able successfully to accumulate savings and convert them, with relative efficiency, into productive investments, including in infrastructure.

Feenstra et al. (2015) recommend that in comparing productivity performance across countries, the measures of output used should be those that apply common (as opposed to national) prices.[18] Figure 6.9 (right panel) shows the trajectory of TFP using PPP estimates of GDP.[19] These trajectories are akin to the catch-up data presented above (Figure 6.4) for GDP per capita, but now the variable of interest is TFP. Productivity growth at the US frontier has slowed notably since 2000, with TFP rates exhibiting a downward trend from a growth rate of 1.0 per cent a year in 2001–2012 to about 0.6 per cent in 2017 (OECD, 2019).

Figure 6.9 Compared with the Republic of Korea and Taiwan, Malaysia's TFP has changed only moderately since 1960; it is slowly closing the gap with the US frontier

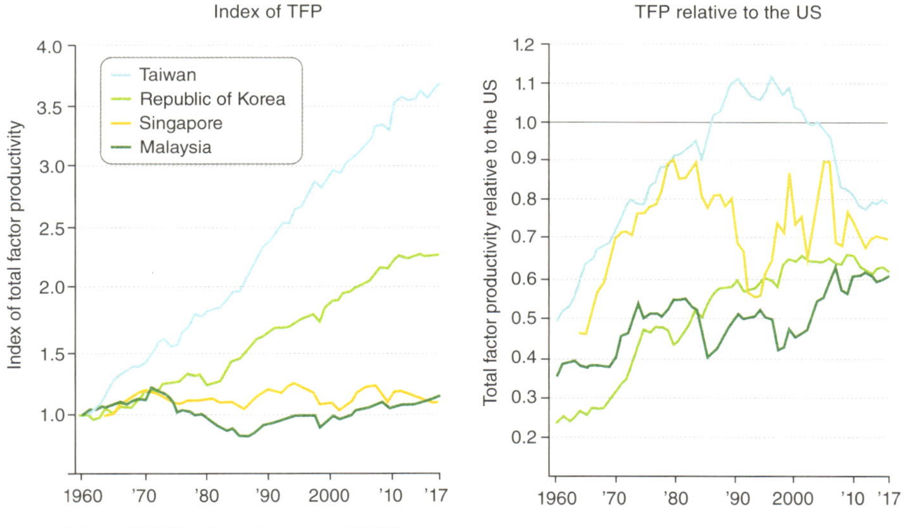

Sources of data: PWT9.1; Feenstra et al. (2015).
Note: For Singapore, TFP data are only available from 1964.

18 Feenstra et al. (2015) describe two such measures: 'C' metrics and 'R' metrics. 'C' metrics hold prices fixed across countries in a common year. 'R' metrics hold prices fixed across countries and across years. Productivity measures based on 'C' metrics are recommended for cross-country comparisons at a point in time, with productivity in the US indexed to 100 in all years. Accordingly, when viewed over time, these measures are akin to catch-up or gap measures and do not take account of productivity improvements at the frontier. Feenstra et al. (2015) caution that for different years, these measures may employ different prices. However, a comparison of GDP (output) between 'C' and 'R' metrics reveals series that are almost perfectly correlated: for Malaysia and benchmark NIEs, Pearson's correlation coefficient is greater than 0.99.

19 A 'welfare-relevant' PPP TFP measure, which replaces GDP with a PPP measure of domestic absorption, exhibits similar trajectories to those shown for the GDP measure, although Singapore displays a sharper fall in the ratio towards the end of the sample period.

At one level, these PPP metrics present a rather more subdued assessment of catch-up for Malaysia. Whereas per capita GDP measured in PPP units is gaining ground on per capita income in the US (in both relative and absolute terms), the PPP-based measure of Malaysian productivity up to 2017 has made up only about five per cent of the gap since the late 1970s. In large measure, the upward trend in the productivity ratio between the Asian financial crisis and the Great Recession served only to regain ground that had already been lost in the 1980s and in the midst of the crisis, although there was some modest progress. Observed gains in per capita income (measured in PPP units) have occurred because of faster rates of capital deepening[20] in Malaysia (which is comparatively labour intensive) than in the US (which is comparatively capital intensive).

In terms of the NIE benchmarks, TFP *levels* in Singapore and Taiwan are closer to the US than TFP levels in Malaysia, which are broadly comparable with those seen in the Republic of Korea. However, in terms of underlying TFP *growth*, the Republic of Korea has posted larger gains. Measured in PPP units, Malaysia's TFP has grown at an average rate of 1.0 per cent from 1960 to 2017 compared with 1.6 per cent for the Republic of Korea. Over the period up to 2017, TFP growth in both Singapore and Taiwan averaged 0.8 per cent.

Bosworth and Collins (2003) observe that the use of PPP estimates in measuring TFP introduces a strong positive correlation between investment rates and per capita incomes. To the extent that this does happen, it will tend to increase investment shares and capital stock estimates in higher-income countries, which could be reflected in lower TFP growth rates if multiple PPP conversion factors are used. Bosworth and Collins (2003) also argue that estimates of outputs and inputs expressed in national rather than PPP units should be used in productivity comparisons, as it is national prices that guide firms' decisions on the mix of factors used in production. The national-accounts-based measures of TFP (left panel of Figure 6.9) present a more sombre account of Malaysia's productivity advances as compared with the Republic of Korea and Taiwan.

Components of Labour Productivity Growth

The rate at which labour productivity advances is an important metric of development. The growth of labour productivity provides an indication of the extent to which there is scope for growth of real wages, and therefore of how standards of living for the general population may be changing. As

20 That is, an increase in the ratio of capital to people employed.

countries develop, their labour productivity levels tend to rise towards those of advanced countries.

From an accounting perspective, changes in labour productivity (the ratio of GDP to employment) can be attributed to increases in the capital intensity of production, to improvements in the quality of labour as human capital accumulates, and to TFP growth. Figure 6.10 shows the trajectory of labour productivity growth in Malaysia for the period 1960–2017. Over these years, labour productivity grew at an annual average rate of 3.3 per cent. Three-quarters of this growth was accounted for by capital deepening, with TFP growth accounting for about 9 per cent. The cumulative five-year average estimates exhibit the same strong pro-cyclical pattern as the TFP data, although only in one of the 57 years is labour productivity growth negative. Again, as with the TFP estimates above, labour productivity declined prior to the setback of the mid 1980s and before the Asian financial crisis, but after any externally induced output reversals.

Figure 6.10 **Malaysia's labour productivity gains have been largely driven by capital investment, except in the early 1960s and the mid 2000s**

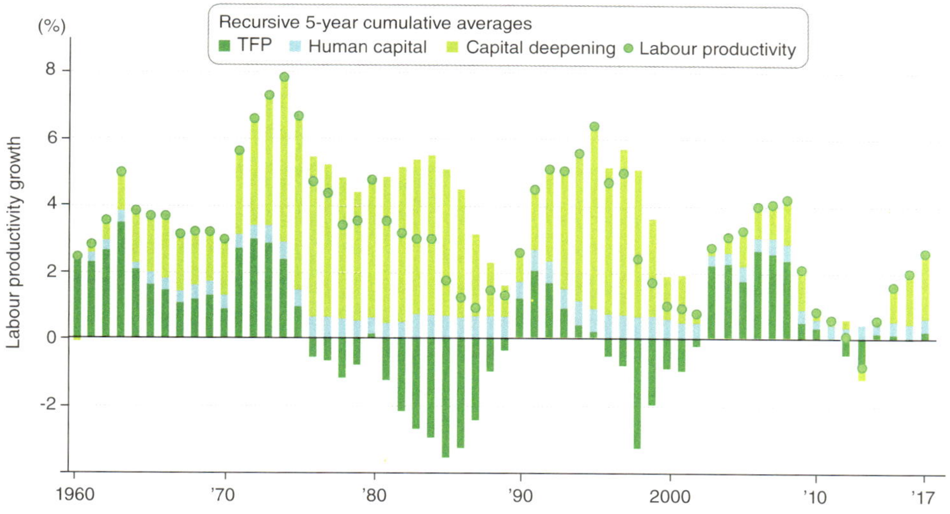

Sources of data: PWT9.1; Feenstra et al. (2015).

In this standard decomposition of labour productivity growth, it is implicitly assumed that increases in capital occur independently of TFP growth and of other factors that might stimulate investment, such as a higher-quality labour force. Bosworth and Collins (2003) discuss an alternative decomposition in which the contribution of TFP growth to labour productivity gains is calculated on the basis that the contribution of capital to increased labour productivity is limited to the impact of investment on increases in the capital–output ratio. Effectively, the strong assumption is made that

TFP growth (or growth in human capital), in addition to raising output, lifts investment to maintain a constant capital–output ratio. This is similar to the perspective offered by De Long (1996). Application of this formulation increases the portion of labour productivity growth that is 'explained' by TFP growth to 31 per cent for the period 1960–2017. The contribution of capital is then correspondingly diluted.[21]

As Bosworth and Collins (2003) note, the assumptions that lead to this interpretation of the influence of TFP on labour productivity seem extreme, especially in circumstances where advances in TFP may themselves be embodied in investment in new physical capital. Consequently, while conventional estimates of the contributions of TFP that take no account of induced capital deepening may understate the true contribution of TFP to labour productivity growth, the alternative formulation, which limits the capital contribution to what occurs through an increase in the capital–output ratio, is likely to exaggerate the impact of TFP. The upshot is that, while the contributions of TFP and investment to physical capital are both likely to be important for promoting labour productivity advances, and are perhaps mutually reinforcing, the range within which their 'true' contributions to gains in labour productivity lie may be wide. In Malaysia, TFP may have contributed to anywhere between 9 and 31 per cent of the gains in labour productivity over the period in question, depending on how much investment is considered to have been induced by productivity gains.

Turning to the quality of labour, PWT9.1 equates the stock of human capital with the average years of schooling, adjusted by an assumed rate of return of 9.4 per cent for each additional year (Psacharopoulos, 1994). Measured in this way, Malaysia's index of human capital roughly doubled between 1960 and 2017, whereas labour productivity grew by a factor of 6.3. By applying the labour share in total value added to the increase in the stock of human capital, the conventional decomposition implies that the accumulation of human capital has accounted for about 13 per cent of the gains in Malaysian labour productivity over this period.

By way of comparison, the PWT9.1 estimates show little difference between the rate of human capital accumulation in the Republic of Korea and Singapore, and in Malaysia, but show a faster rate of accumulation in Malaysia than in Taiwan. When considering levels rather than rates of accumulation, however, the NIEs all had higher levels of human capital than Malaysia in 1960, an advantage which they have sustained throughout the period of study.

21 It is equal to the product of the growth of the capital–output ratio and the quotient of the share of labour in value added to the capital share: see Bosworth and Collins, 2003, p. 131.

An alternative set of measurements of human capital based on the lifetime earnings of workers is considered below.

It was noted above that GDP per capita grew at a cumulative average rate of 3.9 per cent and consumption per capita at an average rate of 3.8 per cent between 1960 and 2017. By comparison, labour productivity grew at 3.3 per cent over the same period. The gap between the growth of GDP per capita and the growth of labour productivity reflects the fact that the labour force increased faster than the overall population over this interval (resulting in a lower dependency ratio). The rising share of labour in Malaysian factor income recorded by PWT9.1 may help explain the faster rate of growth of consumption per capita.

Ng et al. (2017) explain the rising share of labour in factor income as a consequence of the labour intensity of services and of the increased share of services in total employment. Malaysia's service sector has a larger labour share than industry, and the economy's reliance—particularly in the traditional SME sector—on low-wage migrant workers is likely to have biased economic discovery and technological choices against capital and skill intensity, thereby contributing to the rising labour share. The authors suggest that while these trends promote greater equality in the distribution of income, they are likely to be detrimental to productivity advances and sustained economic growth.

A comparison of Malaysia's advances in labour productivity with those of benchmark countries facilitates broader judgements about its achievements. Figure 6.11 (left panel) shows the trajectories of GDP per person employed in constant PPP units for Malaysia, the Republic of Korea, Singapore, and Taiwan, all measured relative to the US. These data suggest that while Malaysia has made some inroads on US productivity levels, it is catching up at a slower rate than the NIEs, whose relative productivities in 1960 were broadly similar to Malaysia's. The rate of catch-up in Malaysia also appears to have slowed after the recession of 2008–2009 despite a slowdown in US productivity growth over the same period. A similar slowdown can be seen in the data for the Republic of Korea and Taiwan, but not for Singapore.

Figure 6.11 (right panel) presents analogous measures of productivity, but with labour input now measured by total hours per year. Data on hours are generally preferred for productivity measurement, but the relevant PWT9.1 data for Malaysia only go back to 1970 and so the sample period is shorter. The hours data show uniformly larger gaps with the levels of US labour productivity, indicating that annual hours worked are greater on average in Malaysia and the NIEs than in the US. Measured by hours, aggregate labour productivity in Malaysia in 2017 was just 33 per cent of that in the US, although it had increased from 16 per cent in 1970. In 2017, output per hour in Singapore was 74 per cent of that in the US, with the figures for the Republic of Korea and Taiwan at 52 per cent and 66 per cent respectively. On the basis of these metrics, it is reasonable to conclude that Malaysia's productivity gains since independence have been modest, and that it has performed poorly relative to the NIEs.

Figure 6.11 **Malaysia's output per person is slowly closing the gap with the US, but trails NIE benchmarks, while output per hour worked shows only small gains on US levels**

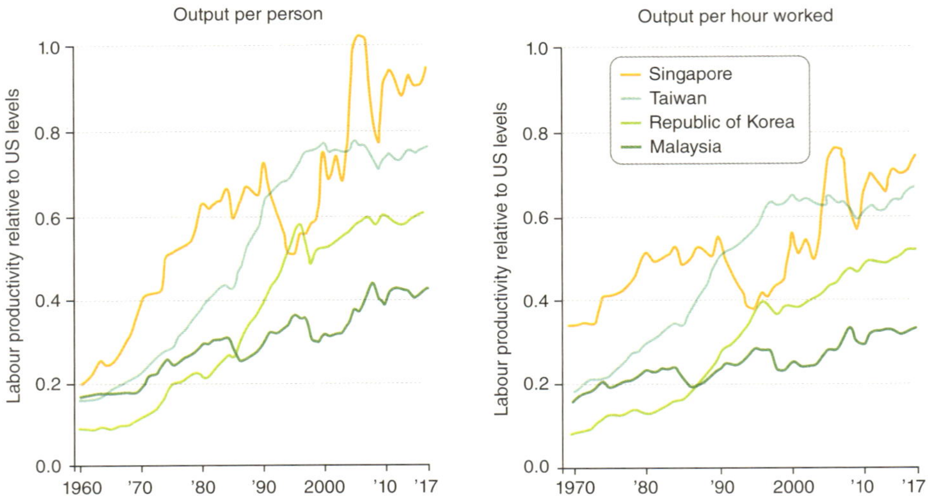

Sources of data: PWT9.1; Feenstra et al. (2015).
Note: Productivity is output measured in 2011 international PPP prices per person engaged.

Structural Change, the Structural Bonus, and Sector Productivity

Structural Change

So far, the analysis of income, input, and productivity growth has been conducted at the level of the aggregate economy. However, the contemporary profile of economic activity in Malaysia bears little resemblance to its profile in 1960 (Chapter 8). Figure 6.12 shows the changing structure of output and employment in the post-independence economy, highlighting the country's remarkable transformation from a primary-commodity-producing country in 1960 to one in which industry and services were contributing the lion's share of output and employment by 2017. The economy in 2017 was more diversified in output and employment than it was in 1960, when agriculture and mainly low-productivity services accounted for just under 90 per cent of employment and about 80 per cent of output.

The patterns and dynamics of structural change differ among sectors. The service sector, which contributed most to GDP in 2017 and is the largest sector for employment, increased its share of GDP from around 42 per cent in 1960 to 55 per cent by 2017, while its share of employment doubled over approximately the same period, from about 29 per cent in 1957 to 62 per cent in 2017. The manufacturing sector has seen a smaller increase in its employment than its output share. In 1960, it contributed 8.6 per cent of output, and in 1957 about 6.4 per cent of employment. At its peak in around 2000, manufacturing's share of output had risen to 31 per cent and its share of employment to about 23 per cent. Agriculture, on the other hand, has seen its output share contract from 40 per cent in 1960 to 8.2 per cent in 2017, while its employment share shrank from 59 per cent in 1957 to 11.3 per cent in 2017.

Figure 6.12 Malaysia has diversified output and employment, with jobs in services, especially government services, growing rapidly[a]

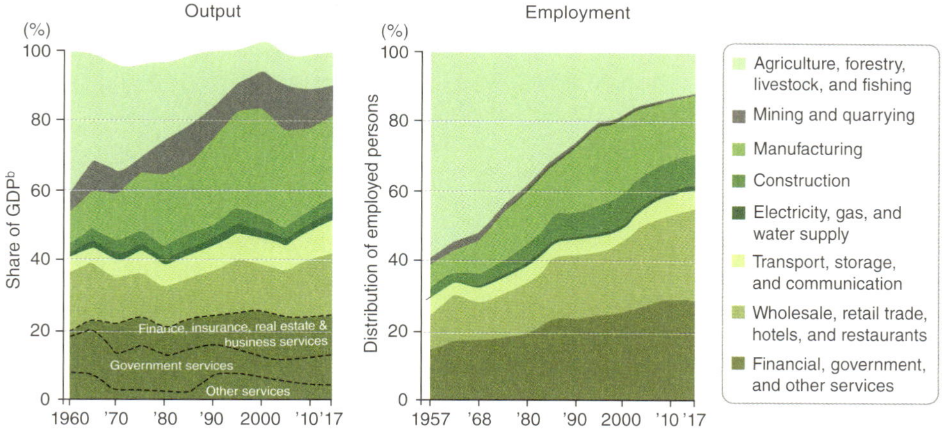

Sources of data: For GDP by sector, 1960 and 1965, Department of Statistics–Malaysia (1975); for GDP by sector, 1970 to 2000, Economic Planning Unit–Malaysia, Malaysia Plans (various years); for GDP by sector, 2005 and 2017, Economic Planning Unit–Malaysia (2018d). For employment 1957, Department of Statistics–Malaysia (1960); for employment 1962, 1967, and 1968, Department of Statistics–Malaysia (1968); for employment 1975 to 2016, Department of Statistics–Malaysia, Labour Force Survey Malaysia (various years).

Notes:

[a] Data for GDP by sector for 1960 and 1965 relate to Peninsular Malaysia; data for employment for 1975 and earlier are for Peninsular Malaysia.

[b] The component output data do not total 100 per cent, as imputed bank service charges have not been deducted and import duties have not been included.

Structural Bonus

Shifts in the structure of output reflect both differential sectoral investment rates and a reallocation across the economy of mobile resources. But how do these structural shifts register in aggregate outcomes? If resources move from lower- to higher-productivity activities, for example, this will generate income gains and stimulate growth during the time it takes for the reallocation to be completed—the Baumol 'structural bonus' (Box 6.4).

Box 6.4 Structural shifts and economic growth: The Baumol structural bonus

The most famous structural model is perhaps Lewis's (1954) dual-sector model of 'surplus labour'. Given access to an unlimited supply of labour in the 'traditional' (low-productivity) sector, the Lewis model describes a process in which the 'modern' (high-productivity) sector expands through the absorption of increasing quantities of labour from the traditional sector (this is discussed further in Chapter 8). The movement of workers from low- to higher-productivity activities, by itself, generates growth. Moreover, as workers from the traditional sector are absorbed into modern-sector jobs—at wages kept low by the large reserve pool of labour in the agricultural sector—profits are then used for investment and expansion of the modern sector.

This process of labour migration, changes in the profile of economic activity, rising investment, and economic growth continues until the marginal product of labour remaining in the traditional sector begins to rise, pushing wages up in the modern sector and reducing investible surpluses. Although the growth generated by the reallocation of labour from low-productivity agriculture to higher-productivity industry and services is transitory—it lasts only as long as there is an available pool of agricultural labour—allocative gains can continue, as workers within the industrial and service sectors migrate to activities higher up the value-added chain.

The growth rate of aggregate labour productivity can be decomposed into the growth rates of labour productivity *within* sectors (weighted by the sector's share in output) and the effect of labour reallocation *between* sectors with different productivity levels. The relevant calculation is:

$$\hat{p} = \sum_i \hat{p}_i \cdot x_i + \sum_{i \neq j} \hat{n}_i \cdot \left(\frac{p_i - p_j}{p} \right)$$

where $\hat{p}$ is the aggregate time rate of change of labour productivity, $\hat{p}_i$ is the rate of change in sector i, p the initial aggregate level of labour productivity, p_i and p_j the initial levels of productivity in sector i and j, x_i the share of sector i in aggregate output, and $\hat{n}_i$ the rate of change in the share of employment of sector i over time. In this calculation, the reference sector (say, agriculture) is sector j, and the Baumol bonus is the second term on the right side, equal to the sum (across all non-agricultural sectors) of the product of sector changes in labour share and the sector productivity differential with agriculture.

If, in the initial stages of development and diversification, workers move from low-productivity agriculture into higher-productivity industry, the bonus will be positive. As resources eventually move out of industry into lower-skilled and lower-productivity service activities, the bonus will become a productivity 'burden' and will slow aggregate productivity advances.

Source: Asian Development Bank (2007).

Figure 6.13 summarizes calculations of Malaysia's structural bonus over the period 1980–2011; the PWT9.1 database provides information only for this narrower window. Calculations of the bonus are sensitive to sector definitions and disaggregation.

Estimates are shown at three levels of sector aggregation: two sectors (agriculture and non-agriculture); three sectors (agriculture, industry, and services); and nine sectors in which industry and services are further disaggregated. In all cases, the mining sector is excluded, so the bonus is measured for the non-oil, non-gas, and non-tin economy, as its inclusion would distort the results. Mining has the highest level of labour productivity due to its high capital intensity and its employment share has shrunk over time, which would indicate a dynamic productivity penalty rather than a bonus. As non-mining activities employed around 98 per cent of workers in 1970 and over 99 per cent of workers by 2011, the calculations are therefore more meaningfully undertaken for the non-mining sector.

The estimates are five-year moving averages, which allow trends to be more clearly differentiated from high-frequency movements. Observations at each point in time summarize the average outcome over the current and previous four years. These smoothed measures of the structural bonus are highly correlated at the two-, three-, and nine-sector levels.

At its peak, the structural bonus equates to a 2 per cent improvement in labour productivity (using the three-sector calculations). This peak contribution is an outlier, however, and disguises the fact that, when viewed over the entire sample period, the bulk of gains in aggregate productivity growth occurs through productivity improvements *within* sectors. In the two-sector calculations, the Baumol bonus is 8 per cent of total labour productivity gains, increasing to nearly 12 per cent in the nine-sector calculation.

Although it is difficult to attribute causality, it appears that the positive bonus at the start of the sample period occurred as workers were still moving out of agriculture into industry; this continued through to the second half of the 1970s. The retreat in the bonus in the first half of the 1980s is associated with declining employment shares of high-productivity industry (during the capital-intensive HICOM period) and rising employment shares in lower-productivity agriculture and services. Only when employment in industry (export manufacturing) began to grow quickly in the late 1980s and 1990s did the bonus rebound as the industrial share in aggregate employment rose. The bonus then remained in positive territory until the start of the millennium. By this time, the share of industrial employment had peaked, reaching its highest point in 1997. Thereafter, a declining share of industry and a rising share of services in total employment resulted in a dynamic productivity 'penalty'.

This penalty does not surface in the two-sector configuration of the economy, where the higher-productivity, non-agricultural share in employment continued to rise until the end of the period.

Figure 6.13 **Sector shifts created a productivity bonus but the subsequent shift to services created a penalty**[a]

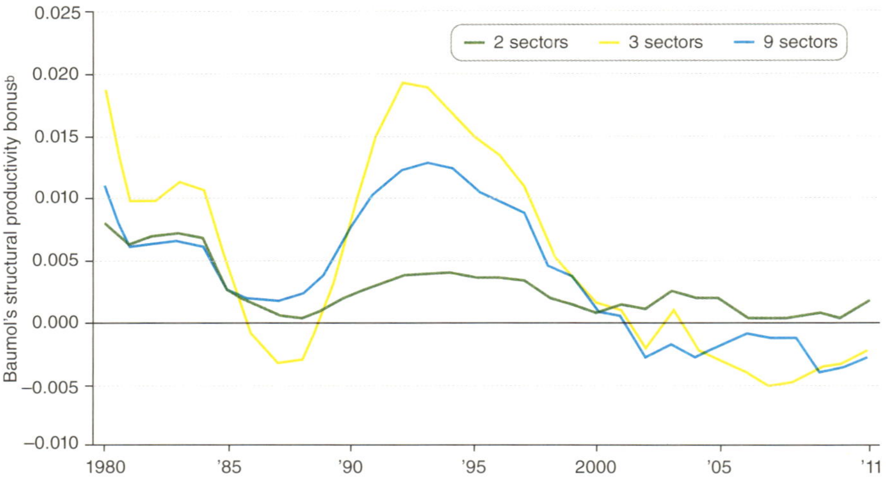

Sources of data: University of Groningen, GGDC (2019); Timmer et al. (2015).
Notes:
[a] While there is high productivity in financial services, this sector accounts for only a very small proportion of overall employment in services, most of which is in low-productivity activities.
[b] Five-year moving averages.

Sector Productivity

What, then, was happening to labour productivity at the sectoral level? The panels of Figure 6.14 show the trajectory of labour productivity in five sectors from 1975 to 2011. Real value added per worker (in 2005 national prices) is measured on the vertical axis of each scatterplot, and the sector's share in non-oil GDP is measured on the horizontal axis. The ranges on the vertical and horizontal scales differ from panel to panel depending on the data points. The labels identify the initial (1975) and terminal (2011) observations, and other years as appropriate. Labour productivity levels are highest in manufacturing and financial services, and lowest in construction.

Figure 6.14 Within-sector improvements in productivity generally dominate for 1975–2011

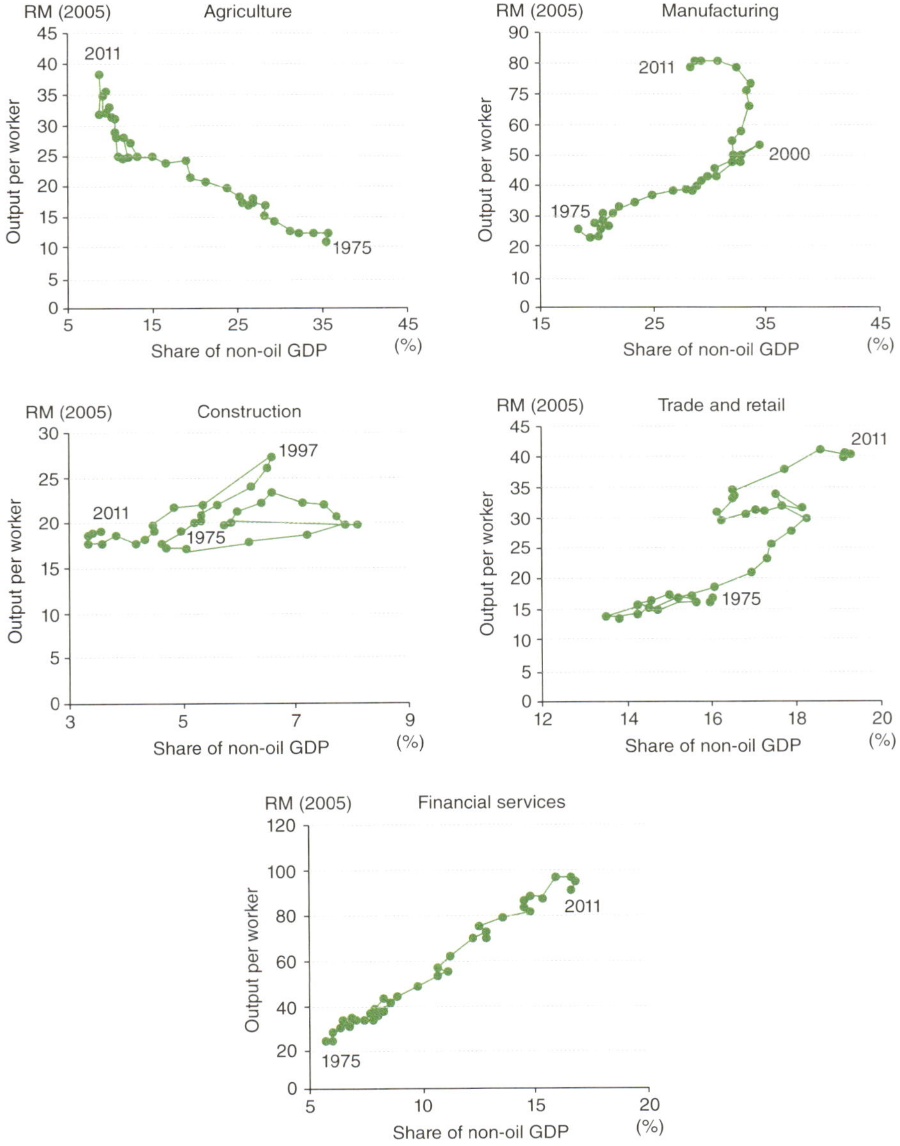

Sources of data: University of Groningen, GGDC (2019); Timmer et al. (2015).

In all activities other than construction, labour productivity increased from 1975 to 2011, indicating that within-sector productivity gains (as well as the reallocation of labour between sectors) were contributing to the growth of aggregate labour productivity. Indeed, after 2000, within-sector productivity gains accounted for all of the aggregate productivity growth, and compensated for the 'burden' that occurred as workers moved out of high-productivity industrial activities into service activities characterized by lower levels of productivity.[22]

Demographic Dividend

GDP per capita can also be affected by the impacts of the demographic dividend. Bloom and Williamson (1998) and Bloom et al. (2001) have explained how lower fertility rates and the changing age structure of a population during the 'demographic transition' may accelerate economic growth. Historically, changes in the age structure of a population have been triggered initially by falling child mortality rates, which have then encouraged falling fertility rates (Chapter 4). These demographic changes have had potentially far-reaching effects not just on a population's structure, but also on its social and economic organization, and on the values placed on education, work, and the economic role of women.

From a demographic accounting perspective, successively smaller cohorts of children translate into a reduced support ratio: a smaller number of consumers relative to the size of the working-age population. Other things being equal, the reduced support ratio lifts output (income) relative to the total population. This positive income effect will be increased if lower fertility rates encourage expanded female participation in the labour force, widening the gap between the labour force and population growth rates. If, as family size declines, parents decide to invest more resources in each child, healthier and better-educated cohorts will raise labour productivity in future years, with additional positive impacts on income. These positive income effects are not guaranteed, however, and require an economy that creates productive jobs to absorb workers. The demographic dividend, although long-lasting (estimated to be around 60 years for Asia), is also transitory. As the bulge in

22 Unfortunately, the PWT9.1 database does not provide sufficient information to allow sector-by-sector comparisons of productivity with that at the US frontier, nor with benchmark NIEs.

the population begins to age, positive impacts taper and may eventually be reversed as older retired cohorts increase the support ratio.

Mason et al. (2017) identify an additional channel through which changes in age structure can influence potential income and growth. This 'second demographic dividend' occurs if, with the prospect of longer lives, older workers increase their savings in order to provide for additional years in retirement, and their higher savings translate into productive investments in the domestic economy. Higher capital per worker then raises income levels, and, over an extended adjustment period (around 50 years), contributes to accelerated economic growth. Again, there is nothing guaranteed about this second dividend, and its presence and size are contingent on family and social arrangements for retirement support and saving, as well as on enabling policy and institutional factors that influence the allocation of, and returns to, capital investments. Although chronologically the second dividend follows the first, and the first tapers before the second begins, they may operate contemporaneously for a time.

There have been numerous efforts to quantify the impact of the demographic transition on income and growth, often within the framework of cross-country growth regressions. They face numerous challenges, however, particularly in sample selection, specification, and measurement. The difficulties of separating cause and effect from the direct effects of a changing age structure have led to different estimates of the impact and its attribution to induced changes in investment in produced and human capital.

An alternative approach relies on demographic accounting methods as explained by Mason et al. (2017), who provide estimates of the demographic growth dividends for Malaysia (Figure 6.15). These calculations suggest that Malaysia began to benefit from the 'first demographic dividend' from around 1970, and that by the 1980s the falling support ratio was adding as much as 1 percentage point a year to GDP growth. The dividend then increased further from the late 1980s as the second dividend (a savings-induced rise in the capital–output ratio) supplemented the first. At its peak—from around 2000 to 2015—the dividend added approximately 1.7 percentage points to growth, exceeding the contribution of TFP growth. After about 2016, the calculations of Mason et al. (2017) suggest that the first dividend tapered more quickly than the second dividend grew, and the overall impact on growth started gradually to recede.

Figure 6.15 **Malaysia's changing age structure has supported growth**

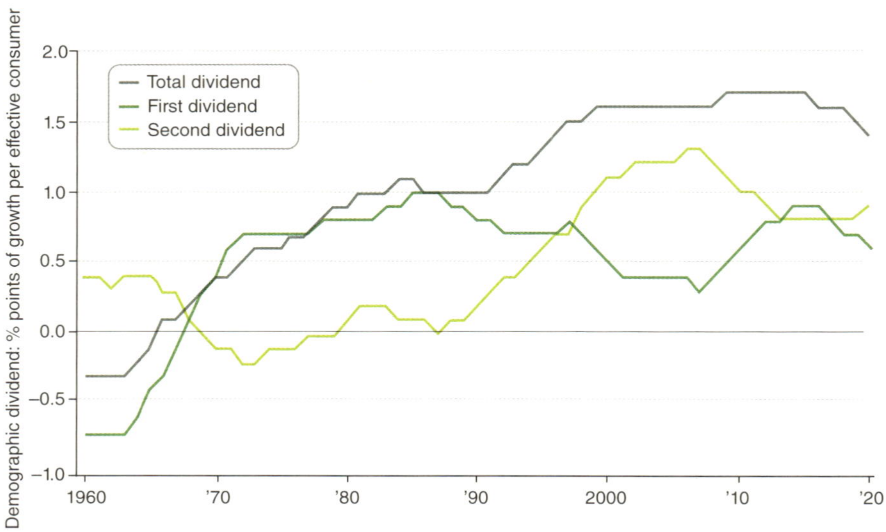

Source of data: Mason et al. (2017).

Genuine Wealth

All the metrics of economic growth and productivity analysed above rely on the measurement of GDP as their empirical foundation. But while such metrics provide useful summary indicators of historical economic income and performance, they have limitations for evaluating whether a nation is on a *sustainable* development path. For example, the exploitation of a non-renewable resource adds to conventionally measured GDP, but if there is no offset for the loss of natural capital,[23] the resulting contraction of the natural asset base will be at the cost of future generations. Just because a nation has experienced growth does not mean that it will continue to do so in the future. While GDP provides an insight into a country's income over a period of time, it is the assets and liabilities on its balance sheet that will determine its potential to *sustain* that income into the future.

23 The 'Hartwick rule' states that in order to preserve future consumption levels, the rents (the difference between price and the marginal user cost) from the exploitation of non-renewable resources must be invested in reproducible capital (manufactured and human capital) or foreign assets.

Contributions by the World Bank (2011b), Lange et al. (2018), and Arrow et al. (2012) provide frameworks for measuring sustainability.[24] Box 6.5 introduces the concept of 'genuine wealth' and the closely related concept of 'inclusive wealth' (or 'comprehensive wealth'), both of which are pivotal to these frameworks.

Box 6.5 Genuine wealth and inclusive (or comprehensive) wealth

Wealth (broadly defined to include all assets) is both a better barometer of a nation's development and a better indicator of the sustainability of that development than GDP. In theory, GDP should represent the return on a nation's wealth, but in practice it turns out to be a poor proxy. A puzzle arises when measures of GDP are compared with estimates of accumulated investments in physical capital ('manufactured capital'). Typically, GDP is outsized relative to the estimated stock of manufactured capital—often about one-third of such capital (World Bank, 2011b), suggesting either that returns on assets are very high, or that national wealth is significantly underestimated.

The World Bank (2011b) initially proposed that this apparent puzzle could be resolved by recognizing that the wealth of a nation includes much more than its manufactured capital. The 'genuine wealth' of a nation should instead be equated with the value of all of its assets: its ownership of manufactured capital, natural capital, and intangible capital (primarily human and institutional capital, as well as knowledge). The World Bank's (2011b) operational approach to estimating genuine wealth made direct estimates for manufactured capital and for important (but not all) elements of natural capital. The value of a nation's intangible capital was then derived residually, having deducted the direct estimates of manufactured and natural capital from an imputation of the present discounted value of intergenerational consumption, which was equated with total wealth.

In a subsequent major departure from this approach, the World Bank, through the work of Lange et al. (2018), has provided a bottom-up measure of wealth that now includes direct measurement of the value of human capital. Following a logic similar to that in Arrow et al. (2012), the revised method treats improvements in institutions, governance, social capital, and knowledge in terms of the impact that they have on how productively other assets are used. In particular, the World Bank sees improvements in these dimensions as enhancing the lifetime earnings of workers, which in turn is equated with an increase in the value of their human capital.

24 A large number of indicators have been proposed to measure sustainability; Neumayer (2004) provides a review of earlier measures. In more recent years, indicators such as the Legatum Prosperity Index and the World Economic Forum's Inclusive Development Index seek to blend multidimensional information (economic, social, environmental, physical, and governance) to arrive at key conclusions about a nation's development and its sustainability. Despite their creativity, these exercises lack a structure which links measurement to an analytical framework that clarifies exactly what sustainability is, or defines the conditions under which it occurs.

The flow counterpart of genuine wealth is genuine saving—genuine wealth in the last period plus genuine saving in the last period being equal to genuine wealth in the current period. If genuine saving, evaluated at relevant shadow prices for the component assets, is positive, this means that the nation's aggregate wealth is increasing.[25] If the rate of growth of genuine wealth is at least as fast as population growth, then genuine wealth per capita is at least being sustained from one period to the next. However, a positive value for genuine saving per capita does not necessarily mean that the economy is moving along an 'optimal path' in which the welfare of citizens, now and in the future, is being maximized. Indeed, Arrow et al. (2012) demonstrate that 'optimal' may not always be 'sustainable'.

A concept closely related to genuine wealth is the 'productive base' of an economy, or its 'inclusive wealth' (also called 'comprehensive wealth') (Arrow et al., 2012). Inclusive wealth is defined as the value of a nation's manufactured, human, health, and natural capital. In this approach, too, technology, knowledge, and institutions are considered as 'enabling' assets that influence the shadow prices of the capital assets of the productive base. For example, where institutions are efficient and promote inclusive development, the shadow price of (or social return on) capital investment is high (lifting inclusive wealth), while if institutions are dysfunctional, the shadow price of capital is low (lowering inclusive wealth).

In the underlying conceptual framework of Arrow et al. (2012), sustainable development is defined in terms of a sequence of values for intergenerational welfare (adjusted for population size). If this sequence of values is non-decreasing, development is considered sustainable. In an important set of results, Dasgupta and Maler (2000), Dasgupta (2001), and Arrow et al. (2013) demonstrate that intergenerational welfare has the potential to increase *only* if the productive base of the economy is expanding relative to its population. Shrinking genuine wealth (negative genuine saving), or a shrinking productive base relative to population, are therefore inconsistent with sustainability. This definition allows for substitutability between the different components of capital, so that expanding manufactured capital, for example, can substitute for declining natural capital. This definition of sustainability ignores, however, possible limits on substitution, which could occur, for example, if depletion of a natural asset reaches a catastrophic tipping point.

While these wealth metrics possess conceptual clarity, their measurement presents enormous challenges. Information on asset stocks (particularly natural capital) is incomplete and often missing. Where there are no markets for the underlying assets, or where there are significant externalities, estimating shadow prices (or social value) is notoriously difficult. As experimentation and improvements within this ambitious research programme are ongoing, current measures of genuine wealth need to be interpreted with caution. Still, they provide a useful forward-looking complement to GDP-based measures of historical performance.

---

25 Shadow prices capture the social value associated with the flow of services generated by an asset, which may not equate with the market value of those services. In the presence of market failures or taxes and subsidies, social values will generally diverge from market values. For example, the market value of felled Malaysian timber will reflect contemporaneous demand and supply conditions in the market for timber, but will not internalize the values for carbon sequestration, or for the ecological services provided by tropical hardwood trees.

Estimates of genuine wealth for Malaysia for 1995, 2000, 2005, 2010, and 2014 are reported by Lange et al. (2018), using the World Bank's latest valuation and imputation methods.[26] These latest estimates feature improvements and extended asset coverage, notably to include human capital and a wider range of natural assets. The valuations are in constant local prices converted to US dollars using market exchange rates. PPP estimates are not yet available. Not all relevant assets are included in this exercise, as there was a requirement that data be available on a consistent basis across all 141 study countries. For some assets, markets are missing. For example, some ecosystem assets—such as the soil retention services of forests—are not included, although the value of forest timber and other forest products are. The definitions and methods of valuation used by the World Bank adhere closely to the System of National Accounts (SNA) guidelines, and by extension to the SNA in the Standards for Environmental-Economic Accounting.

Table 6.4 shows estimates of genuine wealth per capita for Malaysia over the two decades from 1995 to 2014. These data show that genuine wealth per capita grew at a cumulative average rate of 3.2 per cent. By comparison, the PWT9.1 estimate of growth of real GDP per capita income over the same period, measured in national prices, was 2.8 per cent. Taken at face value, these estimates of genuine wealth suggest that Malaysia has been on a sustainable development path—one in which it is able to sustain future standards of living—with the growth of produced capital and human capital more than compensating for the erosion that has occurred in the value of its natural capital.[27] Over this period, the value of Malaysia's sub-soil assets, primarily gas and oil, has increased due to new discoveries and rising prices, which add to capital gains. The value of Malaysia's agricultural croplands has also increased. The major loss in the value of natural capital has occurred through the loss of timber and non-timber values of Malaysia's tropical forests.

Lange et al.'s (2018) estimates show that human capital was the fastest-growing component of Malaysia's genuine wealth from 1995 to 2014, with a cumulative average growth rate of 4.2 per cent.[28] Their estimates of the

26 Arrow et al. (2012) observe that the earlier World Bank (2011b) calculations of total wealth, and therefore the earlier imputations of intangible wealth, are built on assumptions that presuppose the very sustainability that they are seeking to evaluate. While the World Bank no longer imputes the present value of lifetime consumption, it does make similar projections for lifetime earnings, and this too seems to make presuppositions about sustainability. However, this circularity seems unavoidable in any exercise that requires the projection of asset valuations into the future.

27 Vincent and Rozali Mohamed Ali (2005) report a similar exercise covering the period 1970–1990, and also arrive at the conclusion that Malaysia was more than replacing any reductions in natural capital with manufactured capital. Human capital and net foreign assets were not included in these calculations. Lange et al.'s (2018) estimates benefit from better data and methodological improvements.

28 This is a much faster rate of accumulation than suggested by the estimates of PWT9.1, which yield human capital growth of just 1 per cent. The methodologies employed in PWT9.1 and by Lange et al. (2018) differ, and these factors and measurement issues explain some of the differences. As some elements of what the World Bank defines as human capital would be included in the TFP residual of PWT9.1, different values are to be expected, but the divergence is wide and points to the need to be mindful of both conceptual differences and measurement problems.

value of human capital are based on estimates of the net present discounted value of the lifetime earnings of the Malaysian workforce, and differ from conventional measures of human capital, which are based on the adjusted returns to average years of schooling. The World Bank makes the case that its measure, built up from micro-survey data, better reflects the economic benefits created by investments in an educated and healthy workforce. The value of human capital in this approach is also influenced by improvements in the quality of enabling assets, such as institutions, which raise the earnings of the workforce. Although the World Bank's estimates suggest that growth in the value of human capital in Malaysia has, since 1995, been faster than in benchmark countries such as the Republic of Korea and Singapore, they also show the persistence of Malaysia's large absolute deficits in the per capita level of human capital. Only since 2005 has Malaysia begun to close the gap in the absolute value of this deficit with the Republic of Korea, as well as with the US, but the gap with Singapore has widened. In the terms employed earlier, there has been *relative* but not *absolute* catch-up with the value of human capital embodied in Singapore's workers.

Table 6.4 **Malaysia's human capital is the fastest-growing component of its genuine wealth**

Per capita in constant 2014 US$	1995	2000	2005	2010	2014	Annual average growth (%) 1995–2014
Human capital	81,113	88,778	96,978	159,716	180,729	4.2
Natural capital	29,432	21,129	23,251	29,965	28,657	–0.1
Net foreign assets	–3,094	–2,488	–1,129	96	–173	–15.2
Produced capital	22,155	23,831	22,225	24,638	29,989	1.6
Total wealth	*129,606*	*131,249*	*141,325*	*214,415*	*239,203*	*3.2*

Source of data: Lange et al. (2018).

Figure 6.16 (left panel) compares the trajectory of genuine wealth per capita in Malaysia with that in the Republic of Korea and Singapore, all measured against the level of per capita genuine wealth at the US frontier. These comparisons employ market exchange rates, not PPP conversion factors.

These estimates suggest that Malaysia is on a sustainable development path because its total wealth per capita is increasing and converging with US levels. However, the rate of convergence is so slow that if past rates are a reliable guide to future ones, it will take Malaysia 63 years to close half of the gap with the US. In addition, the estimates suggest that Malaysia's rate of accumulation has fallen behind those of the Republic of Korea and Singapore.[29]

Figure 6.16 (right panel) shows the same information for human capital per capita. The gap with the frontier in this measure is larger than the gap for total wealth. The gap is also wider for the Republic of Korea and Singapore, reflecting the intensive investments that these countries have made in manufactured capital. However, the deficits in human capital accumulation between Malaysia and the Republic of Korea and Singapore are larger than the corresponding deficits in genuine wealth per capita, suggesting that this is an area in which Malaysia lags behind and which may be limiting its potential. Possible reasons for this deficit in human capital include the quality and relevance of education, an exodus of disillusioned graduates—particularly from among the Chinese community—looking for expanded opportunities and improved status elsewhere, and other policy and institutional factors that may diminish potential lifetime earnings (Chapters 2 and 3).

Figure 6.16 **Malaysia is more than replacing its depleted natural assets with produced assets, but its accumulation of human capital is slower than in the Republic of Korea and Singapore, and deficits are wide**

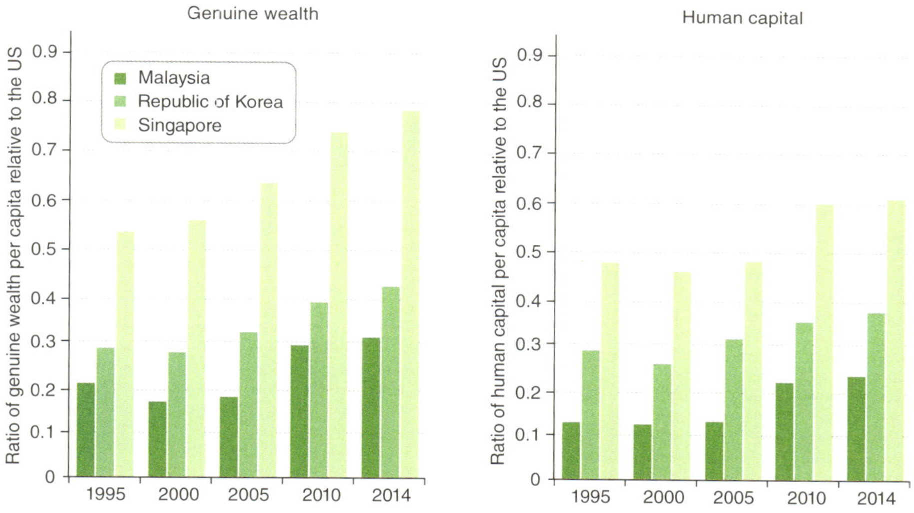

Source of data: Lange et al. (2018).

Estimates of 'adjusted net saving', which adjusts annual estimates of gross domestic saving for depreciation of physical capital, investments in education, depletion of minerals, and changes in the value of natural capital and the environment, are reported annually by the World Bank, dating back

29 Taiwan is not a member of the World Bank, and the World Bank does not provide estimates for it.

to 1974 for Malaysia. While providing a high frequency and perhaps a more policy-relevant metric of sustainability, measures of adjusted net saving differ from genuine wealth in important ways. Adjusted net saving estimates, unlike estimates of genuine wealth, do not allow for capital gains and discovery of resources. Nor do they account for increases in the value of human capital—as distinct from education spending—in the same way as Lange et al.'s (2018) estimates of genuine wealth. Indeed, as Lange et al. (2018) observe, it is possible for estimates of genuine wealth to increase and yet for adjusted net saving to be observed as negative, as sometimes happens in some natural-resource-rich African countries.

Figure 6.17 shows the trajectory of gross national saving as a percentage of gross national income and the corresponding ratio for adjusted net saving. In each year for which data are available, adjusted net saving has been positive, suggesting that Malaysia has set aside enough resources to add to its wealth. Yet the large gap between the gross and adjusted net savings rates still suggests that substantial claims on wealth are being made in the form of the depreciation of manufactured capital and the depletion of natural capital, and that these require large compensatory saving. The close correlation between the adjusted net savings rate and the gross savings rate suggests that movements in the former are largely driven by changes in gross saving (as per the national accounts), with a reasonably stable relationship between the adjustments and movements of underlying gross national income. Note that no allowances are made in these estimates for particulate emissions or for other sources of damage to the environment.

Figure 6.17 Adjusted net saving is positive, but high gross saving masks loss of natural assets

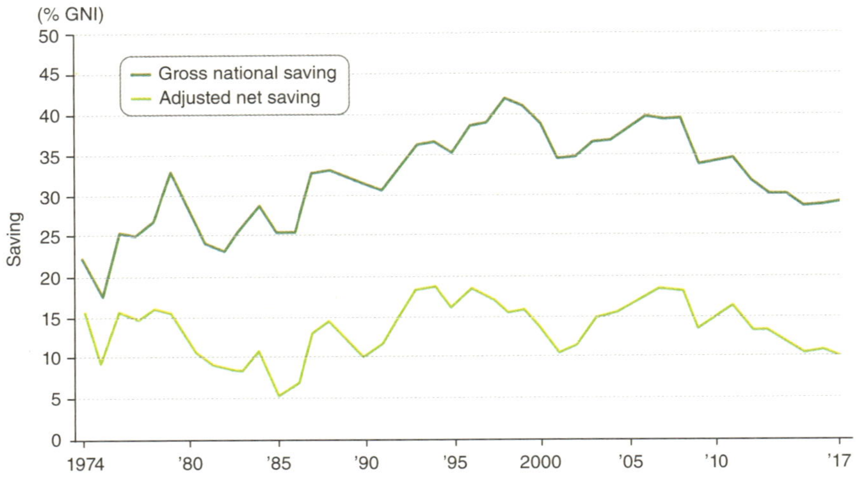

Source of data: World Bank (2018a).

To complete the discussion of genuine wealth, Table 6.5 provides earlier estimates of the changes in Malaysia's inclusive wealth reported by the United Nations and by Mumford (2016), based on the methodology of Arrow et al. (2012) (Box 6.5). While these estimates indicate that Malaysia's inclusive wealth per capita rose overall from 1990 to 2010, they show that it did not increase in all periods. They also suggest that the claims on natural capital throughout the period have been larger than the increases in produced capital.

Of particular interest is the interval 2000–2005. For this period, the United Nations Environment Programme and United Nations University (2014) calculate that, although GDP per capita increased, there was an erosion of inclusive wealth or the productive base of the Malaysian economy. The main reason appears to be the collapse of investment in manufactured capital that followed the Asian financial crisis, in circumstances in which the natural capital of the nation continued to contract. The data also suggest that human capital accumulation suffered a sharp slowdown following the crisis.[30]

Table 6.5 How Malaysia's inclusive wealth and GDP per capita have changed

	Changes in values (2005 US$)			
	1990–1995	1995–2000	2000–2005	2005–2010
Produced capital	3,474	2,717	1,241	1,829
Natural capital	–3,937	–3,439	–3,014	–2,314
Human capital	4,183	2,223	791	2,546
Inclusive wealth	3,720	1,447	–981	2,060
GDP	1,155	494	612	764

Sources of data: Mumford (2016); United Nations Environment Programme and United Nations University (2014).

A comparison of this 2014 study's results with benchmarks broadly confirms other findings. Measures of inclusive wealth are generally highly correlated with conventionally measured GDP per capita. Malaysia performs significantly better in accumulation on a per capita basis than either Indonesia or the Philippines; estimates suggest that wealth contracted in resource-rich Indonesia. Yet accumulation in the Republic of Korea and Singapore has outpaced that in Malaysia.

Thus, assessed according to a range of metrics, the country's development appears 'sustainable'. Malaysia's investments in produced and human capital more than compensate for the depletion of its mineral resources, and in this sense the country has successfully diversified its asset base.

30 For the same period, Lange et al. (2018) show an increase in genuine wealth. In these estimates (Table 6.4 above), the value of produced capital falls in 2000–2005, but there is an increase in the value of natural capital, probably attributable to rising oil prices in these years.

Conclusions

This chapter has analysed the nature and origins of Malaysia's economic growth from the time of independence to the present. The headline figures are encouraging: between 1960 and 2017, real GDP per capita grew on average by 3.9 per cent a year, such that per capita income in 2017 was over nine times that in 1960. There were periods in which growth faltered—for instance, during the mid 1980s and in the years following the Asian financial crisis and the Great Recession. Nevertheless, the gap with GDP per capita in the US—the frontier country—has narrowed in relative terms. The NIEs—Hong Kong, the Republic of Korea, Singapore, and Taiwan—are closing this gap faster than Malaysia, however, even if other countries are lagging behind.

Per capita GDP can increase through several channels. Capital accumulation through investment in physical capital can raise output, as can investment in human capital. Output can also increase through TFP. This can occur through a composition effect: economy-wide output per capita can rise if workers migrate from low-productivity sectors (such as agriculture) to those with higher productivity (such as manufacturing), raising GDP and GDP per capita. TFP can also rise because of innovations or improved efficiency in production. TFP was an important source of economic growth up to the early 1970s, a period when the economy was benefiting from improvements in agricultural productivity, more general economic modernization, and growing urbanization. During the period of the NEP, TFP regressed. While TFP growth has been positive during the post-NEP period (1990–2017), it has been comparatively modest, averaging just 0.8 per cent annually.

On average over the period 1960–2017, labour productivity grew at an annual rate of 3.3 per cent. Three-quarters of this was due to capital deepening (an increase in capital per worker), one-eleventh due to TFP growth, and almost one-eighth due to investment in human capital. Although the index of human capital in Malaysia grew at a rate comparable with those in the Republic of Korea and Singapore, the *level* of human capital in Malaysia was below that of these two countries and Taiwan in 2017. Output per hour worked was 33 per cent of that in the US in 2017 compared with 74 per cent in Singapore, 66 per cent in Taiwan, and 52 per cent in the Republic of Korea. Using this measure of labour productivity, Malaysia's productivity gains since independence have been modest and compare unfavourably with those of the NIEs.

After 1980, the Baumol bonus was most pronounced in Malaysia in the late 1980s and the 1990s when the industrial share in aggregate employment rose significantly. Following the peak in the industrial share in 1997, the bonus weakened and became a penalty—registering a negative value—when the share of services in total employment rose.

GDP per capita can also rise through impacts of the demographic dividend. In the first impact, successively smaller cohorts of children reduce the rise in the denominator (population) without affecting the numerator (GDP). If lower fertility rates encourage female labour force participation, the demographic transition can even boost GDP, further raising GDP per capita. The demographic dividend can work through other channels, too. If, as family size declines, parents decide to invest more resources in each child, healthier and better-educated cohorts will raise labour productivity in future years. A second demographic impact occurs if the increased cohort of working individuals then chooses to save more for their extended retirement, thus boosting capital accumulation and productivity. From around 1970, Malaysia began to benefit from the first impact. By the 1980s, the falling ratio of dependants to workers was adding as much as 1 percentage point a year to GDP growth. At its peak between 2000 and 2015, the combined demographic dividend added about 1.7 percentage points to growth.

Malaysia is a country with rich natural resources, some of which are renewable—such as rubber, palm oil, and tropical timber—while others are not—such as tin and hydrocarbons. Future growth in an economy reliant on non-renewable resources may be far weaker than current and past rates if the natural resources are being rapidly exhausted. The World Bank has proposed an indicator of future growth potential, which it calls genuine wealth. This includes the stocks of manufactured capital, natural capital, human capital, and intangible assets. Malaysia's genuine wealth grew at a cumulative average rate of 3.2 per cent for the period 1995–2014. Human capital was its fastest-growing component, although the gap in its level with Singapore was widening. Crucially, the World Bank's estimates suggest that Malaysia is on a sustainable development path because its total wealth per capita is increasing and converging with US levels. However, the rate of convergence is so slow that, all else being equal, it could take Malaysia 63 years to close half of the gap with the US.

At the macroeconomic level, the Malaysian economy has been fairly well managed, even if it has been prone to periodic setbacks occurring about once a decade. While some of these have been the result of external shocks, the deeper and more protracted reversals of the mid 1980s and the Asian financial crisis were more a consequence of ill-fated domestic policy choices, which will be discussed in the next chapter.

Chapter 7

Advances, Reversals, and Changes, 1970–2017

Building on Chapter 6, this chapter looks at the major policy developments that have framed Malaysia's economic transformation since 1970. Key reference points are the national five-year plans and the three Outline Perspective Plans (OPPs) that cover intervals of varying lengths spanning the period 1970–2010. These documents—products of extensive consultation within government, across states, and involving the private sector, civil society, and international organizations—distil national economic objectives, and identify the programmes to achieve goals and the means to support their attainment.[1]

These decades have also seen a plethora of subsidiary plans, strategies, and policies, which drill down into the various sectors, and highlight thematic dimensions of the nation's efforts to align development outcomes with aspirations. These plans and policies target aggregate or economy-wide performance, with reference to sector and thematic issues aligned with the period of each OPP.

OPP1 (1971–1990) fleshed out the New Economic Policy (NEP) of 1971, this being the government's response to the riots in 1969 (Chapter 2). The NEP was not so much a set of policies as a politically crafted statement of intent, drafted by the National Operations Council during the Emergency period when parliament was temporarily suspended. It outlined the imperatives of redressing ethnic inequalities, rebalancing society, and reducing absolute poverty as essential means for ensuring national unity and security. OPP1 concretized the NEP, which was seen to have moved beyond its political

1 Until November 2018, the Economic Planning Unit (EPU), established in 1962 out of the Planning Secretariat, coordinated the preparation of Malaysia's various perspective and development plans. The EPU, which was under the Prime Minister's Department, took its direction from the prime minister and worked closely with the Ministry of Finance and the central bank on macroeconomic matters, and with various other ministries and agencies, as well as with civil society on social issues. In November 2018, the EPU was integrated into the newly created Ministry of Economic Affairs as part of the new government's reorganization.

aspirations to become a national development policy in terms of long-term targets for the ethnic distribution of income, for the equity ownership of corporate assets, for jobs and occupations, and for economic growth.

OPP2 (1991–2000) introduced the National Development Policy. In many ways a continuation of the NEP, it emphasized the need for accelerated poverty reduction and for 'balanced' development.

OPP3 (2001–2010) launched the National Vision Policy, which sought to internalize the lessons learned from the Asian financial crisis of the late 1990s, with the goal of building a resilient and competitive economy, while ensuring continuity with the distributional policies of OPP1 and OPP2.

In July 2010, the government unveiled the Tenth Malaysia Plan (MP10), 2011–2015, and in 2016 the Eleventh Malaysia Plan (MP11), 2016–2020, was announced. Both of these incorporated selected elements of the New Economic Model formulated by the National Economic Advisory Council (NEAC) in 2010, which aimed for Malaysia to become a high-income nation by 2020.

Needless to say, reality does not always conform to the plan. Over the period 1970–2016, Malaysia made many advances and witnessed episodes of fast growth, but also experienced costly economic reversals. The economy suffered a severe recession in 1985–1986 during OPP1. The Asian financial crisis flared up in 1997–1999 as OPP2 was drawing to a close. During OPP3, the economy was affected by the downdraft caused by the bursting of the dot-com bubble in 2002, and just six years later was hit by the global financial crisis and Great Recession of 2008–2009. This chapter considers the factors behind these crises, and examines their economic and wider impacts, along with Malaysia's responses.

Despite these challenges and setbacks, over the past few decades Malaysia has become a vastly more affluent and—according to income metrics—more equal society (Chapter 9). It has graduated to join the ranks of upper-middle-income countries.[2] With the national aspiration to become a high-income country, the question now is whether the economy is caught—or risks becoming caught—in a 'middle-income trap'. What are the factors that might thwart the nation's ambitions?

This chapter is organized chronologically around the OPP periods and MP10. Each section sets out the economic background and context; describes the

2 According to the World Bank's classification for the fiscal year beginning July 2018, upper-middle-income economies are those with per capita gross national income (GNI) of between US$3,896 and US$12,055, measured using its Atlas conversion factor. In 2017, Malaysia had a per capita income of US$9,650 according to this metric, down from a high of US$11,010 in 2014.

major goals and policies articulated in the plans and their rationale; evaluates outcomes against stated objectives; and offers some brief conclusions on achievements and missed opportunities. The chapter also highlights some of the policy and institutional challenges that will need to be overcome if Malaysia is to complete its transformative economic agenda.

Outline Perspective Plan 1, 1971–1990

From independence to the end of the 1960s Malaysia's economy had moved up a gear in terms of both faster GDP growth and the diversification of its productive base. Agricultural productivity saw gains from FELDA's land settlement programmes (Box 8.2 in Chapter 8) and the expansion of palm oil production. Investments were also made in rubber cultivation through the planting of higher-yielding trees. Improved *padi* irrigation and drainage allowed many farmers to double their crops. The quality of rural life improved due to investments in rural infrastructure, including electrification and sanitation. In the urban centres, the public sector was creating jobs, as was an emerging manufacturing sector incubated by the Pioneer Industries Programme of the 1960s. Malaysian women increasingly participated in these new modern-sector employment opportunities.

Yet ethnic imbalances—a legacy of the colonial economic model—remained stubbornly embedded in the structure of the economy and in the wider society. Although the country posted healthy GDP growth, poverty rates stayed high and remained concentrated largely in rural areas (Chapter 8). The economy was not creating jobs at a rate that could absorb the additions to the labour force. Inequalities persisted: many rural Malays and low-skilled workers in the urban informal sector were cut off from the benefits of an expanding modern economy, and youth unemployment rates in urban centres soared, pushed higher by the migration of young unskilled workers from rural areas.

New Economic Policy: Rationale and Scope

The 1969 political crisis was the proximate cause of the fundamental reorientation of Malaysia's economic policies, as marked by the adoption of the NEP. But deep divisions were long-standing, and the threat to national unity and security was not new. While ostensibly a plural society, the contours of Malaysia's economy, politics, and geography were drawn along ethnic lines. Promoting national cohesion, the logic ran, would require a narrowing of these ethnic divisions, which in turn would compel a fundamental restructuring of Malaysia's society and economy.

The NEP outlined broad directions and guiding principles, and OPP1 was formulated to direct the transformations. It signalled a decisive break from the past: the end of the 'essentially liberal' economic regime that had, in essence, been carried over from the colonial era into the first decade of independence; and the creation of a state-led developmental apparatus that would spearhead economic rebalancing. The orthodox formula of 'growth first, redistribution later' was replaced with 'redistribution with growth'. Primacy was now to be given to redistributive goals, with economic growth targeted at a rate consistent with redistribution and with the overarching aim of national unity (Faaland et al., 2003, p. 33).

The purpose here is not so much to assess whether the strategy underpinning the NEP was 'correct', or whether it was relevant and responsive to the problems confronting Malaysia at the time. These issues have been written about extensively elsewhere (Faaland et al., 2003; Gomez et al., 2018), and consensus among the various commentators will prove elusive, as the counterfactual is unknowable. Rather, the main objective in this chapter is to seek an understanding of the driving forces behind economic growth and other important economic trends over the NEP period.

Targets and Policies in OPP1

OPP1 encompassed the second to the fifth of Malaysia's five-year economic plans (MP2 to MP5), from 1971–1975 to 1986–1990. Each plan contained a set of diagnostics, a statement of development objectives, and a description of the actions intended to realize its goals. Each also had an economic framework setting out the expected trajectory of the overall economy, including a summary of its main economic accounts, an investment plan, and a financing plan. Around the midpoint of each plan, a review was conducted, which then set out major adjustments to targets and programmes based on the progress so far. Annual refinements and resource allocations were coordinated through the national budget process.

Notwithstanding the emphasis on ethnicity-focused distributional aims (Box 7.1), MP2 set its sights on accelerated economic growth, targeting an average annual growth rate for GDP of 6.7 per cent, with GDP per capita growth of 4.2 per cent. These initial targets exceeded the strong performance of the 1960s (Chapters 5 and 6). Coupled with fast output growth, the plan aimed to reduce unemployment to a maximum of 7.3 per cent (from 8 per cent in 1970) by generating job growth of more than 3 per cent a year. The plan also contained targets for the growth of exports (6.7 per cent annually) and for major sectors of the economy. It targeted manufacturing growth of 11.7 per cent a year, signalling an intention to diversify the productive base. Nevertheless, the plan also set targets for agriculture, envisaging that agricultural extension, modernization, and diversification would make it possible to achieve growth of 8.4 per cent per year for the sector.

Box 7.1 Initiatives for ethnic distribution in MP2

Perhaps the single most important target of MP2 was the ethnic distribution of equity ownership in corporations: 30 per cent by *Bumiputera* and a minimum of 40 per cent by all Malaysians by 1990. In 1970, *Bumiputera* owned less than 2 per cent of such equity. While the goal of redistributing equity ownership was long term, it had a profound impact on the institutional development of the modern Malaysian state.

Other measures to advance the aims of MP2 included state support for *Bumiputera* business incubation and development; ethnic quotas for jobs in government and the private sector; preferred placements of young *Bumiputera* (essentially Malays) in schools; reservation of university places; favourable contract bidding and procurement terms for *Bumiputera* businesses on government contracts; and discounts and reservations on housing and commercial property. Other initiatives—including land development programmes, investments to facilitate the transformation from peasant to commercial agriculture, and expanded access for disadvantaged communities to social services—aimed to add to the productive base of the economy, in addition to serving ethnic distributional goals.

Although ethnic disparities were of pre-eminent concern, OPP1 recognized that poverty crossed racial lines, and it identified target groups that included the predominantly Chinese communities of the New Villages and the *Orang Asli* (Chapters 1, 2, and 5).[3]

Even before the introduction of the NEP, the government, through the Ministry of Finance Incorporated—a public holding company created in 1958 and wholly owned by the Ministry of Finance—had established public enterprises to pursue important goals (Gomez et al., 2018). Bank Bumiputera was established in 1965 to facilitate wider access to credit for Malays, and the trust agency Perbadanan Nasional Berhad (PERNAS) was set up in 1969 to acquire equity in foreign-owned companies (for example, London Tin). In 1966, Majlis Amanah Rakyat (MARA), a government agency, was established to help nurture industrial ventures with the intention of their later transfer to Malay ownership and management. Other entities had already been created to focus on rural development, including the Federal Land Consolidation and Rehabilitation Authority (FELCRA), the Federal Agricultural Marketing Authority (FAMA), and the Rubber Industry Smallholders Development Authority (RISDA). Specialized entities were also established, such as Bank Pertanian to support *padi* cultivation in Kedah and Perlis, and the

3 This early recognition of the fact that poverty crossed racial lines diminished in MP2, and it is not until MP3 that there is any further mention of the situation of the communities in the New Villages. Idrus (2013) makes the case that the *Orang Asli* (Chapter 2) were left behind by the NEP.

Urban Development Authority to advance Malay property ownership. OPP1 used these and other government-linked companies (GLCs) as vehicles to implement its diverse programmes.[4]

MP2 emphasized that production in the industrial sector should be for exports, and that foreign direct investment (FDI) would be required to support this goal. Accordingly, legislation was passed in 1971 that created free trade zones offering incentives to foreign investors. This new strategy recognized that import-substituting activities had limited potential for job creation, given Malaysia's small domestic market. This was in contrast to the Pioneer Industries Programme which, although it did not directly discriminate against exports, had placed an emphasis on investment in activities that would replace imports.

This eclectic recipe for an outward-looking, pro-growth economic diversification strategy, combined with affirmative action on education, jobs, asset ownership, and support for developing *Bumiputera* productive capabilities, continued into the period of the Third Malaysia Plan (MP3), 1976–1980. Perhaps encouraged by positive growth outcomes between 1971 and 1975—and possibly also because of concerns about the challenges of making rapid inroads into poverty—MP3 revised upwards the growth target for the OPP1 period (1971–1990) to an annual average rate of 8 per cent, and set a target of 8.5 per cent for GDP growth for 1976–1980. MP3 also aimed for faster manufacturing growth (12.2 per cent a year), and an increase in the economy-wide investment rate (up to about 25 per cent by 1990 from 21 per cent in 1970).

MP3 featured new affirmative actions, including subsidized credit schemes. The Industrial Coordination Act of 1975 set out quotas for public and private sector *Bumiputera* employment.[5] As low incomes constrained savings and asset accumulation by the *Bumiputera*, the government also established specialized trust institutions to accumulate wealth on behalf of the *Bumiputera* community. In particular, Permodalan Nasional Berhad (the investment trust agency), established in 1979, acquired equity of domestically listed companies, which it then consolidated into trust fund assets, selling units at a discount to eligible *Bumiputera*. The trust fund structure, which only permitted sales back to the fund, was designed to prevent *Bumiputera* beneficiaries from taking profits from equity that had been parcelled out to them at a discount through onselling to non-*Bumiputera*, which would then frustrate NEP asset-ownership targets (Gomez et al., 2018).

4 GLCs are companies that have a primary commercial objective and in which the federal government has a direct controlling stake—that is, the ability to appoint board members and senior management, and to make major decisions, such as in relation to contract awards, restructuring and financing, and acquisitions and divestments (Gomez et al., 2018).

5 According to Jomo (2018), the Act strengthened government control of the manufacturing sector and led to large capital outflows.

The Fourth Malaysia Plan (MP4), 1981–1985, underscored the priority to be given to the economic and social rebalancing goals of the NEP, but foreshadowed a new emphasis on the development of heavy industry. From the development budget, the allocation for industry rose to 27.3 per cent from 15.3 per cent in MP3 (Drabble, 2000, Table 10.8). Inspired by the economic experience of the Republic of Korea, as well as the Japanese *zaibatsu* industrial model, the objective was to support further economic diversification through the development of capital and intermediate goods industries such as steel, cement, shipbuilding, and motor vehicles. Investments in these projects were structured as joint ventures between the Heavy Industries Corporation of Malaysia (HICOM), set up as a government holding company in 1980, and Japanese industrial partners.

At one level, this emphasis on heavy industry was aimed at acquiring the industrial technology and know-how that FDI in labour-intensive export activities had not delivered. At another, the policy aimed to create a class of elite *Bumiputera* capitalists. Other intended outcomes included the strengthening of domestic economic linkages, and support for *Bumiputera* small- and medium-sized enterprises (SMEs) through vendor development programmes, which were introduced later. However, as these capital-intensive industries would not create a significant number of jobs, the earlier stress on labour-intensive exports—namely, textiles and electronics—remained firmly in place, with the targeted annual growth for manufacturing exports raised to 24.2 per cent during MP4.

MP5 (1986–1990) was the final plan of the OPP1 period. The preceding five years had been challenging for Malaysia, with slow global growth owing to restrictive monetary measures and high global interest rates to combat spiralling inflation, and a sharp deterioration in the terms of trade as the price of the country's primary commodity basket tumbled.

With the prospect of missed OPP1 targets for 1990, MP5 modified the earlier heavy industry investment initiatives, emphasizing the need for rationalization of the public sector, fiscal consolidation, disciplined investment, and acceleration of the privatization programme, which had been introduced in 1983. Privatization was seen not just as a way of promoting greater economic efficiency and reducing financial burdens, but also of advancing *Bumiputera* asset ownership. The target for GDP growth was lowered during MP5 to 5 per cent, and spending targets were framed to finance the resource gap, drawing on domestic resources, including the pension resources of the Employees Provident Fund. Even with these more modest economic targets, however, MP5 maintained broad continuity in the redistributive and poverty alleviation goals.

Outcomes, 1971–1980

Figure 7.1 shows the trajectory of gross national income (GNI) per capita over the period of OPP1, with gross capital formation measured as a share of GDP. By any standards, the first decade of the NEP saw solid economic expansion, with real GNI per capita posting average growth of 4.9 per cent[6] during the decade. This was achieved despite a brief recession in 1974–1975 triggered by the elevated interest rates that high-income countries had pursued to neutralize the inflationary impacts of the oil price hikes of late 1973. The downdraft from the resulting compression of global demand and declining commodity prices briefly rocked the Malaysian economy.[7] Exports of goods and services, still dominated by primary products and accounting for over 50 per cent of GDP, fell by 3 per cent. GNI per capita declined by just over 1 per cent in 1975. Incomes were also compressed by terms-of-trade losses. This brief setback in the early years of the NEP was essentially a consequence of the continuing primary commodity dependence that had left the economy vulnerable to global demand shocks.

Figure 7.1 Strong income gains were recorded up to 1989, despite recessions

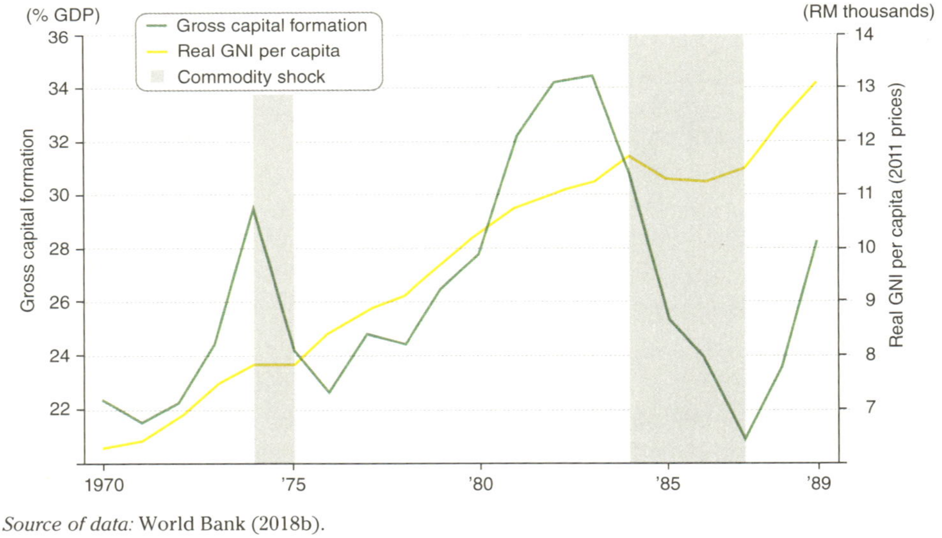

Source of data: World Bank (2018b).

In line with global demand, economic recovery followed quickly in Malaysia, with per capita growth of GNI soaring to 8 per cent in 1976. Measured from the trough of 1975, per capita GNI grew at an average rate of 5.5 per cent until the end of the decade. During this period, there was strong input growth and, after a dip in 1974–1975, a rebound in levels of total factor

6 Unless otherwise indicated, all growth rates represent cumulative annual averages over the relevant interval.

7 In 1975, crude oil exports accounted for less than 10 per cent of Malaysia's merchandise export basket, and the country was still a net importer of oil.

productivity (TFP; Chapter 6). Manufacturing output, stimulated by exports, posted double-digit growth, and its share in total GDP rose by 4 percentage points to 20 per cent by 1980.[8] Although agriculture continued to grow, its share in GDP was declining over time.

Measured both against benchmark developing economies and against Malaysia's own economic performance in the 1960s, it would appear that the NEP did little to dampen economic growth during the 1970s. Indeed, the priority given to labour-intensive, export-oriented manufacturing, alongside strong investment performance, stimulated economic gains. Poverty reduction and societal rebalancing were also making headway. Solid growth of employment[9] and per capita income saw the headcount poverty rate fall from 49.3 per cent in 1970 to 29.2 per cent in 1980 (MP4, p. 4), with sharp reductions in poverty among both rural and urban populations (MP4, Table 3.2, p. 34). Malay average monthly income had risen to 50.1 per cent of the Chinese level by 1980, up from 41.8 per cent in 1970. By 1980, the equity ownership of Malay and other *Bumiputera* individuals and trust agencies had risen to 12.4 per cent from 4.3 per cent in 1970 (MP4, Table 3.14, p. 62). The NEP appeared to be on track.

The NEP increased the state's involvement in the economy. State resources were applied in a raft of schemes intended to reduce poverty, upgrade physical and social infrastructure, and create opportunities for Malays and other *Bumiputera*. The share of government consumption in GDP rose from 15.6 per cent in 1970 to 20.2 per cent by 1980. Public sector capital and other development spending also climbed and by 1980 stood at 8.8 per cent of GDP, up from 5.7 per cent in 1970. The share of employment in government services increased from 11.7 per cent to 13.9 per cent over the decade (MP4, Table 4.6, p. 81).

The rising profile of the state in the economy also manifested itself in other important ways. Notably, the creation and growth of government-linked financial and industrial entities such as Permodalan Nasional Berhad and Petroliam Nasional Berhad (the national oil company, usually shortened to Petronas) was rapidly transforming Malaysia's institutional and economic landscape. Snodgrass (1995) notes that the government invested in over 1,000 financial and industrial entities during the 1970s and 1980s. Drabble (2000, p. 199) cites a figure of 1,188 government-linked entities with paid-up capital of RM24 billion. Through the control of these entities by the Ministry of Finance Incorporated, the government vastly extended its influence over the financial and productive spheres of the economy. These investments were outside the government budget, largely financed by growing oil revenues (Box 7.2).

---

8 See MP3, Table 2.1, p. 11. Note that MP3 reports figures for 1975–1980 rather than the plan period of 1976–1980. Output-based estimates of GDP from the Malaysian Statistics Department do not start until 1988.

9 Unemployment had fallen to 5.3 per cent by 1980 from 7.8 per cent in 1970 (MP4).

Box 7.2 Malaysia's hydrocarbon industry

Onshore oil was first discovered in Miri, Sarawak, and North Borneo (Worth, 1940) more than a century ago, but the modern growth of Malaysia's hydrocarbon industry only began after the first offshore oil discoveries were made in Sarawak in 1963 and in Sabah in 1971. Since then, the country's hydrocarbon industry has boomed, such that by 2016 Malaysia had become the second-largest oil and natural gas producer in Southeast Asia after Indonesia, and the world's tenth-largest exporter of natural gas and third-largest exporter of liquefied natural gas.

1974 Petroleum Development Act and creation of Petronas

From late 1973 to early 1974, there was a six-month-long oil crisis when the Organization of the Petroleum Exporting Countries (OPEC) imposed an embargo on the US, and the oil price more than tripled. Against the backdrop of this crisis, and recognizing the importance of having centralized control over the hydrocarbon industry for national development, the Malaysian government enacted the Petroleum Development Act 1974 (Nasarudin Md Idris, 2006). This legislation vested ownership of petroleum, as well as exclusive rights for exploring, exploiting, and obtaining it, in Petronas. The industry had previously been governed by the Petroleum Mining Act 1966, which implemented a system of long-term concessions for upstream activities, whereby multinational corporations were given exclusive rights to explore and produce resources in return for the payment of royalties and taxes. Petronas signed its first two petroleum-sharing contracts in 1976 for offshore exploration in Sarawak and Sabah. Under the new arrangements, contractors provided all of the financing and bore the risks of exploration, development, and production activities in exchange for a share of total production.

Production and exports

Malaysia's oil and gas production has surged since the early 1980s (Box Figure 7.1, left panel). In 2016, crude oil production stood at around 741,000 barrels per day, of which 390,000 barrels were exported; production had peaked in 2003 at 829,000 barrels per day, of which 426,000 barrels were exported. Almost all of the country's crude oil exports are shipped within Asia and the Pacific, the majority to Australia, Thailand, India, and Singapore. Production of natural gas soared from just 1,000 million standard cubic metres in 1980 to 41,000 million in 2000, and 64,000 million in 2016.

The value of Malaysia's hydrocarbon exports rose rapidly between the early 1970s and 1985, and then again from the late 1990s, and since 2000 has consistently been above 50 per cent of the total value of major primary commodity exports, while accounting for about 10 per cent of all exports (Box Figure 7.1, right panel).

Hydrocarbon revenues

Hydrocarbon revenues—levies, taxes, duties, and dividends from Petronas—have been extremely important in financing Malaysia's general budget, including providing subsidies to energy producers and consumers, and supporting economic growth. Without these revenues, government expenditure might not have been sustainable.

In 2015, oil and gas revenues accounted for around 20 per cent of government revenue compared with 12 per cent in 1995 and 8 per cent in 1975 (Ministry of Finance–Malaysia, various years). Yet the intense volatility of hydrocarbon prices has caused major swings in government revenues. For example, between 2000 and 2016, government revenues from petroleum ranged from a high of 39 per cent in 2009 to a low of 13 per cent in 2016.

Box Figure 7.1 Malaysia's oil and gas production soared from the early 1980s, with hydrocarbons accounting for an increasing share of primary commodity exports

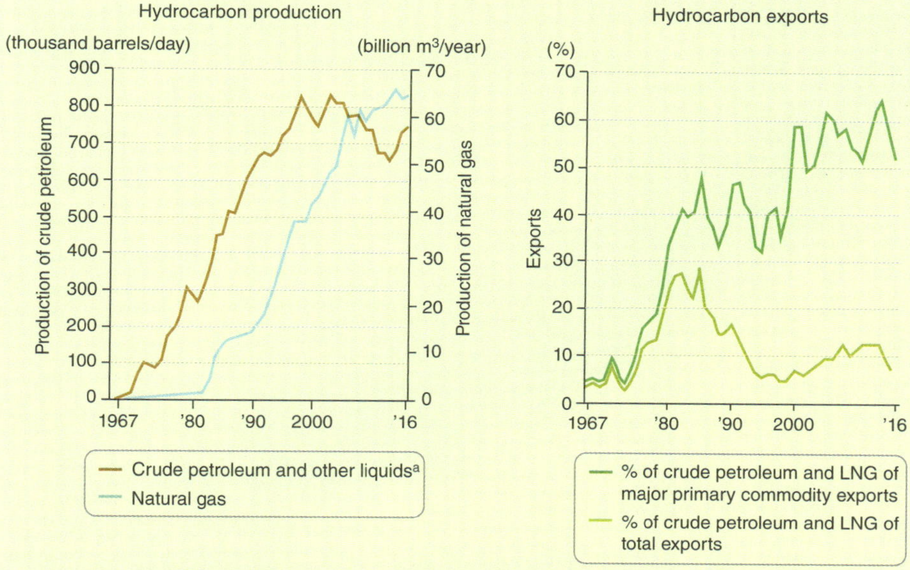

Sources of data: For exports, Ministry of Finance–Malaysia (various years). For production, U.S. Energy Information Administration (2018) and Organisation for Economic Co-operation and Development (2018b).

Note: [a] Including crude oil, condensate, and other liquids.

The sharing of rights over Malaysia's oil and gas resources between the federal government and the state governments of the oil-producing states of Sabah, Sarawak, and Terengganu has long been a contentious issue (Zainal Aznam Yusof, 2011). Based on the 1974 Petroleum Development Act, Petronas makes fixed percentage income payments to the federal and state governments, while the federal government also receives substantial dividends and royalties. In 2014, Sarawak's legislative assembly passed a motion seeking to increase the payments it receives from oil (the state has 29 per cent of the country's known oil reserves and more than half its known gas reserves). It is currently challenging the Petroleum Development Act and pursuing its rights under the Malaysia Agreement 1963, including the reinstatement of its territorial waters to 12 nautical miles from the shoreline.

Outcomes, 1981–1990

In 1980, a period of high and accelerating US inflation was brought to an abrupt halt by a radical tightening of monetary policy—the so-called 'Volcker shock'. Even with the taming of inflation and a return to economic growth in the US, however, high real (US dollar) interest rates of more than 5 per cent were sustained until the end of the decade. Following a well-established pattern, these elevated interest rates dented the demand for commodities, raising the opportunity costs of investing in them, as well as the costs of storage. When economic growth slowed in high-income countries in 1984–1985, commodity prices tumbled (Figure 7.2).

Figure 7.2 **Primary commodity prices sank in the mid 1980s**

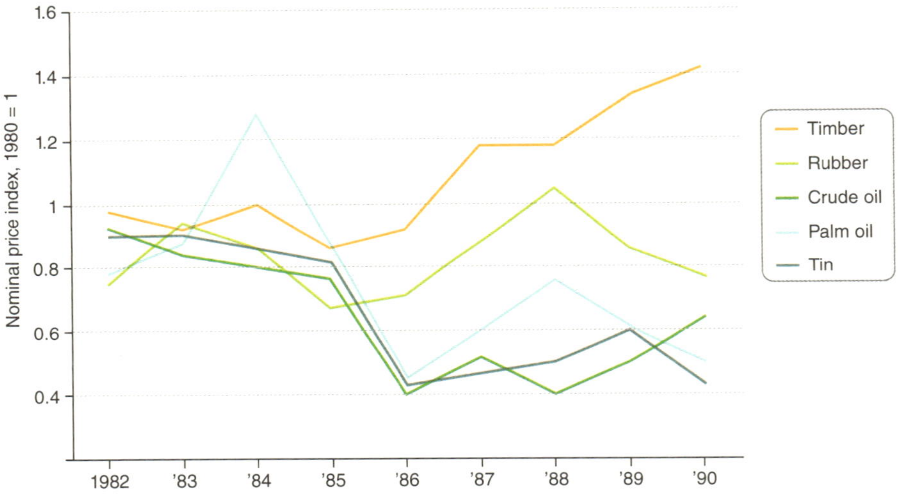

Source of data: World Bank (2018a).

As noted above, the redistributive and affirmative interventions of the NEP had led to a departure from the colonial tradition of fiscal conservatism that marked the first dozen years of independence. To a large extent, the rising tide of government spending was a concomitant of programmes intended to achieve the goals of the NEP.[10] The short-term trajectory of spending was also influenced by efforts to stabilize the economy. In particular, a budgetary stimulus in 1981—intended to boost domestic demand in circumstances of flagging global growth—added to spending. That year, the headline fiscal deficit ballooned to over 20 per cent of GDP. Thereafter, recurrent outlays

10 In 1980, the final year of MP3, there was an astonishing 74 per cent increase in nominal development spending outlays by the federal government, followed by a further 52 per cent increase in 1981. Although the overall level of development spending then began to taper, by 1985 accumulated outlays during MP4 were 230 per cent larger than they had been during MP3 and, as a share of nominal GDP, they rose from 11 per cent during MP3 to 14 per cent during MP4. Likewise, recurrent budgetary outlays as a percentage of GDP rose moderately over this period.

continued to grow, although development expenditure tapered. Nevertheless, development expenditure remained at historically high levels, and fiscal deficits, although narrowing, had become the new norm. By 1985, the federal deficit was still 4.5 per cent of GDP (MP6, Table 2–7, p. 71), and claims on the public sector were continuing to accumulate, especially with the sharp drop in commodity prices. To meet its financing needs, the government borrowed heavily from the Employees Provident Fund, which required safe long-term domestic currency assets in which to invest members' contributions.

After a run of current account surpluses in the second half of the 1970s that had kept external debt at modest levels, deficits surfaced in the early 1980s for a short period. The Malaysian ringgit was pegged to an overvalued US dollar, lowering the domestic costs of imports for Malaysian consumers and industries, but raising the foreign currency costs of Malaysia's non-primary exports.[11] Investments in heavy industries also required substantial imports of capital equipment. Double-digit current account deficits, expressed as a percentage of GNI, occurred in 1982 and 1983, and while there was some subsequent narrowing, external debt was set on a steep upward path. External debt as a share of GNI more than doubled between 1980 and 1984, from 28 per cent to 59 per cent. Much of the external debt was long term and over 70 per cent was public or publicly guaranteed, up from 61 per cent in 1980.

Still, business was booming. Industrial activity, including construction, was growing at a feverish pace of 12 per cent a year, spurred by investment in property, new infrastructure projects, and the capital assets needed for heavy industry. Bank credit as a share of GDP was also growing quickly, and new loosely regulated non-banking financial institutions were proliferating. Domestic credit provided by the financial sector was fast outstripping nominal GDP, rising from just under 69 per cent of GDP in 1980 to nearly 118 per cent in 1985 (World Bank, 2018b).

Large twin deficits, high and rising levels of external debt, and rapidly growing domestic credit narrowed the space in which Malaysia could respond to adverse shocks. And in the mid 1980s, an adverse shock did hit: in 1984–1985, global demand sagged and the prices of Malaysia's major primary export commodities sank. By March 1986, crude oil prices had fallen by 67 per cent compared with their level in October 1985. Palm oil prices also crashed, and by 1986 were only 20 per cent of their peak at the start of 1984.[12] Rubber and tin prices fell, and were mired well below their levels at the start of the decade (Figure 7.2). Although the volume of exports increased for some categories, merchandise export revenue contracted by 6.9 per cent in 1985

11 Primary exports, including oil, rubber, palm oil, and tin, were usually priced in US dollars.

12 These peak prices at the start of 1984 were themselves significantly elevated compared with the prices in the early 1980s.

and by a further 11 per cent in 1986. Manufactured goods exports were also affected by the downdraft from weakened global demand, falling in nominal terms by 4.7 per cent in 1985 (World Bank, 2018b).

As the share of exports in GDP and of primary exports in merchandise exports were both still large, at 54 per cent and 63 per cent respectively, the substantial negative commodity price shock of 1985–1986, as tin and palm oil prices collapsed, reverberated throughout the domestic economy, precipitating a recession. The net barter terms of trade declined by 7 per cent in 1985, and a further 12.9 per cent in 1986. Aggregate GDP shrank in 1985 by 1 per cent, and per capita GDP declined by 1.5 per cent. Oversupply in the property market curtailed construction activity, and real estate asset prices weakened. Cash-flow problems surfaced in the corporate sector. Investment crashed as the private sector reassessed future earnings prospects, and was hit again in 1987 as the government slashed development outlays.

In the financial system, the quality of loan portfolios deteriorated as distressed borrowing and non-performing loans increased, and the need for greater provisioning eroded banks' profits. Those financial institutions with high levels of exposure to real estate were particularly badly affected. High domestic real interest rates—which rose to over 10 per cent—coupled with a credit squeeze aggravated deflationary pressures. By end-1986, the market capitalization of the Kuala Lumpur Stock Exchange, in which trust agencies had acquired an increasing interest, had fallen by 44 per cent compared with end-1984. There were also sporadic runs on non-banking financial institutions, and 24 cooperative deposit-taking institutions had to be wound up (Sheng, 1989).

While the first decade of the NEP had seen strong job creation and falling unemployment, these trends were now reversed. By 1986, unemployment had climbed to 7.6 per cent, a rate higher than that seen at the height of the political crisis in 1969. With falling incomes and rising unemployment, poverty reduction efforts suffered a setback, although unlike during the colonial period, safety nets had by this time been established to provide welfare support to targeted groups.[13]

The impact of the recession on living standards was pronounced. Real household consumption per capita contracted by 2.3 per cent in 1985, by 12.5 per cent in 1986, and again by a little under 1 per cent in 1987. It was not until 1989 that this measure inched back up to above the pre-recession level seen in 1984 (Figure 7.3). Persistent unemployment and pressures on

13 In 1984, the year immediately preceding the recession, MP5 reported a headcount poverty index in Peninsular Malaysia of 18.4 per cent (MP5, Table 3–1, p. 86). MP6 cited a poverty incidence of 20.7 per cent in Malaysia in 1985 (Table 1.8, p. 32). It is difficult to judge how reliable these estimates are or the extent to which they might be linked.

household income explain some of this slow recovery of consumption. It is also possible that the recession may have disproportionately and negatively influenced expectations of future income growth, thereby encouraging higher levels of saving.[14]

Figure 7.3 **Consumption per capita dipped sharply during the 1985–1986 recession**

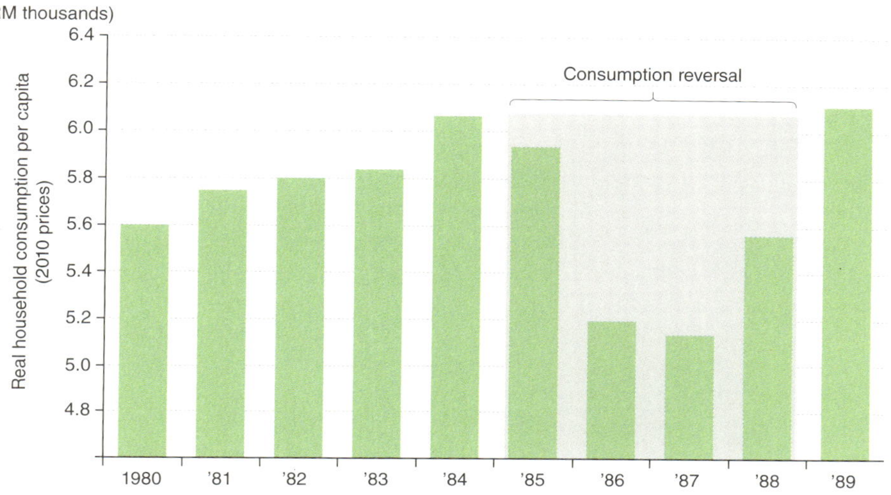

Source of data: World Bank (2018b).

At the macro level, the response to the country's first economic crisis entailed a combination of fiscal tightening—with steep declines in government expenditure as a share of GDP—and a loosening of monetary policy. Bank Negara relaxed its management of the exchange rate, and the ringgit depreciated by 13.5 per cent against the US dollar between 1984 and 1989 in response to forces in the foreign exchange market. Monetary easing was also facilitated by reduced liquidity and statutory reserve requirements for banks, which lowered their costs of funding. Deposit rates were liberalized.

Apart from allowing the ringgit to depreciate, several other structural adjustment measures were implemented, including expenditure retrenchments, tax rate reductions, and a push for privatization. Expenditure-reduction measures focused largely on development expenditure, mainly because state investments in industry had proven costly and disappointing (Box 7.3). In nominal terms, development expenditure in the MP5 period (1986–1990) was 75 per cent of that in the previous period (1981–1985). In 1987 alone, development expenditure was slashed by 37 per cent. Government

14 The permanent income hypothesis and other theories link consumption expenditure to the future value of earnings rather than to current income, as in Keynesian-type models. The gross domestic savings rate rose by 6 percentage points between 1986 and 1989. Part of this rise may have been due to households' downward revisions of the value of their future earnings. It is not possible here, however, to disaggregate the savings rate in order to identify the response of household saving to the recession.

final consumption in the second half of the 1980s averaged 15 per cent of GDP compared with 16.4 per cent in the first (World Bank, 2018b).

Box 7.3 Industrial policy misadventures

In Malaysia, investment in heavy industries in the early 1980s was initially motivated by the possibilities for import substitution and by the potential to deepen domestic backward and forward industrial linkages. However, the preparation, discipline, and expertise that had guided similar investment strategies in Japan and the Republic of Korea were, in general, lacking.

Chee (1994) describes a raft of problems that beset government investments. The list is long and includes management failures created by the secondment of inexperienced government bureaucrats to large industrial companies; operational failures caused by the lack of essential industrial expertise and skills; financial burdens created by over-optimistic assessments of demand and resulting excess capacity; risks created by high levels of foreign currency borrowing for projects whose revenue streams were almost wholly in local currency; and poor investment decisions, for example, about the location of industrial plants and the procurement of plant and equipment. Although one or two ventures did attain profitability—Malaysia Shipbuilding and Engineering, for instance, reported a profit in 1990—most did not. By 1988, HICOM had invested RM2 billion in a portfolio of projects that had generated fewer than 5,000 direct jobs, had made a negligible contribution to exports, and had drained fiscal resources (Chee, 1994).

Although the fiscal costs of early failures of large HICOM investment demanded a tactical retreat, government support for 'strategic' ventures continued. Over a protracted period, subsidies and protection stifled competition and enterprise, penalized consumers on quality as well as price, and diluted incentives for efficiency and innovation (Nehru, 2012). Although state-directed investment in heavy industries can be seen as part of efforts to diversify and rebalance Malaysia's economy, the opportunity costs have been high, and the outcomes in the 1980s ill served the redistributive and growth objectives of the NEP.

Critically, the crisis triggered a re-evaluation of the NEP and of some major economic policies. The private sector in particular received new emphasis. The state sought to limit its exposure to loss-making heavy industries and began to ramp up its privatization programme. By mid 1992, 13 state enterprises (including Telekom Malaysia and Malaysia Airlines) with a capital value of RM213 billion had been fully or partially privatized (Drabble, 2000, p. 201). But the efficiency gains that might have been expected from a transparent and well-conceived privatization programme were probably blunted. New owners were selected from among the ranks of the politically well-connected, who then benefited from low asset valuations. Gomez and Jomo (1997) note that large proportions of the rents created in this way were then invested in unproductive and speculative real estate and other ventures. In cases of partial privatization, the Ministry of Finance retained influence over governance and management.

Regulations on investment—particularly on requirements for *Bumiputera* participation in equity—were also relaxed. With a particular focus on its ownership targets, the NEP was reviewed to ensure that its implementation would be more realistic so as not to sacrifice growth. Exemptions were introduced for foreign investors who exported more than 50 per cent of their output or sold to free trade zones, and the thresholds at which the *Bumiputera* equity and employment quotas cut in (set out in the 1975 Industrial Coordination Act) were lowered. The requirement for licences for manufacturing investments below RM2.5 million was waived. The Promotion of Investment Act 1985 provided additional incentives, including tax breaks and credit facilities targeted at exporting companies.

This shift in policy direction proved timely. The yen had appreciated sharply following the Plaza Accord in 1985,[15] eroding Japanese competitiveness. Moreover, with high and rising wage costs in the Republic of Korea and Taiwan, Malaysia, along with China and other nations, benefited from the relocation of export-oriented firms looking for cheaper production platforms. A recovery in investment had started as early as 1986, and FDI inflows to Malaysia more than tripled between 1986 and 1989. With a cheaper exchange rate and compression of domestic demand, the current account deficit began to narrow. The recovery gathered pace as commodity prices improved, and by 1988 the economy was once more in full swing.

Bank Negara had taken several steps to bolster the financial system. It successfully headed off the risk of systemic financial failure (Sheng, 1989). In 1986, it tightened regulations on loss recognition and provisioning. It also injected capital into three vulnerable banks and took control of four licensed finance companies (a sector with large exposure to the deteriorating property sector). Almost all cooperative banks ran into trouble and came under investigation or supervision by the central bank. The largest cooperative bank, the Cooperative Central Bank, was placed under receivership. Problems in the insurance sector (of undercapitalization) saw it also brought under Bank Negara's regulatory net. In 1989, new prudential measures were introduced under the Banking and Financial Institutions Act (BAFIA), which were intended to limit private sector borrowing from banks, and, in particular, foreign currency borrowing.

---

15 The 1985 Plaza Accord was an agreement between the five leading economies of the time—France, Japan, the US, the UK, and West Germany—to bring down the dollar against mainly the Japanese and West German currencies, and to reduce the US trade deficit. The Accord succeeded in these aims, but also led to an effective depreciation of the ringgit against Malaysia's East Asian trading competitors.

OPP1 Summary

The main aims of the NEP were in essence political, but the development of a vibrant and modern economy and material self-improvement were, from the outset, seen by the government as integral to providing the resources and creating the new opportunities necessary for redistribution. So, to what extent did Malaysia experience economic progress between 1971 and 1990?

The NEP's goals for economic growth were ambitious, especially considering the primacy given to redistributive aims and the rebalancing of society. OPP1 set a modified target for annual average growth of real GDP of 8 per cent for 1971–1990. Only a handful of developing economies have been able to sustain this level of performance over two decades, and these countries are ethnically much more homogeneous than Malaysia (Box 7.4).

Box 7.4 Ethnic diversity and economic growth

Snodgrass (1995) notes, using simple historical cross-tabulated observations, that ethnic diversity is *associated* with poorer growth outcomes, but does not necessarily *cause* them, as ethnic diversity may be correlated with other fundamental forces that influence the potential of an economy to advance.

Easterly and Levine (1997) provide evidence to show that the rate of per capita GDP growth among countries is negatively related to ethnic fractionalization, but that this relationship weakens when other factors are taken into account, such as differences in human capital. In a large sample of countries, ethnic fractionalization was associated with poorer outcomes in terms of infrastructure quality, financial depth, and educational achievements. Other studies have observed that ethnic fractionalization tends to undermine the quality of governance and institutions, and through this channel weakens growth.

Montalvo and Reynal-Querol (2005 and 2017) distinguish between fractionalization and polarization. Polarization exists where there is an ethnically dominant group and a number of ethnically subordinate groups, whereas fractionalization occurs where there are a number of ethnic groups, but none dominates. Montalvo and Reynal-Querol argue that, empirically, polarization has damaging effects on growth, which operate through higher risks of civil unrest, reduced investment, and higher levels of government consumption (to channel resources to the dominant group). Fractionalization also affects growth negatively, but through other channels (for example, by inhibiting the diffusion of ideas). Extending this work, Goran (2014) finds that ethnic fractionalization has a direct negative effect on growth, whereas ethnic polarization negatively influences growth of per capita income, operating indirectly through channels such as reduced investment and greater instability.

Other evidence points to positive development benefits of ethnic diversity. Perhaps most relevant to the NEP and its affirmative action programmes are the findings of Alesina et al. (2016). These authors look not just at the effects of ethnic diversity, but at the intersection of ethnic diversity and ethnic inequality and their joint impacts on development. They find that the unequal distribution of wealth between ethnic groups has a negative effect on income, and that it is this inequality rather than diversity per se that adversely affects outcomes. Ethnic inequality is bad for investment and the authors find that the unequal distribution of resources across 'ethnic homelands' has a strong negative effect on income. This finding appears to resonate with the NEP's concern over the post-colonial legacy of an association between ethnicity and economic function. These empirical results, along with earlier findings by Kyriacou (2013), imply that policies which bring about greater ethnic equality have the potential to be growth-promoting.

To the extent that this recent evidence proves robust, it seems ironic that more than four decades after the NEP, these findings provide an evidentiary basis to validate, on economic grounds, affirmative action and redistributive interventions in ethnically unequal societies. However, these findings do not, in themselves, vindicate some aspects of the NEP's implementation, which are discussed later in this chapter.

During the two decades of OPP1, the economy became larger, more industrialized and service-oriented, more open to trade, less dependent on primary commodities, more urbanized, and with fewer people trapped in poverty (Figure 7.4). The societal rebalancing sought by the NEP was also witnessed in the shifts in equity ownership towards *Bumiputera*, and in the growing representation of *Bumiputera* in targeted occupations.

In terms of annual GDP growth (Figure 7.4, top-left panel), Malaysia averaged a highly respectable 6.7 per cent cumulative growth from 1970 to 1990.[16] In per capita terms, cumulative growth averaged 4.1 per cent, placing Malaysia among the top ten best-performing developing countries during this period. Still, the reversal in the mid 1980s somewhat blemished this scorecard: per capita GDP growth was 5.1 per cent in 1970–1980, but averaged just 2.5 per cent in 1980–1990.

During the period 1970–1990, Malaysia transformed itself from a primary commodity producing and exporting economy to a newly industrializing nation (Figure 7.4, top-right panel). The share of manufacturing in total GDP increased from 13 per cent to 24 per cent, and the share of agriculture shrank from 33 per cent to 15 per cent. The share of services also rose, partly reflecting a larger state presence in the economy and the expanded delivery of public services.

Malaysia had always been an open trading economy. Nevertheless, the share of trade in GDP multiplied during OPP1, to the extent that the value of exports and imports combined had reached over 150 per cent of nominal GDP by 1990. Primary commodity exports continued to be an important source of income over the period 1970–1990, with revenues from rubber, tin, palm oil,

16 Although the precise growth rates reported are influenced by the selection of start and end points, the choice of 1970 and 1990 as years for comparison does not materially affect the interpretation of development achievements.

Figure 7.4 Malaysia's economic transformation, 1970–2000

Sources of data: World Bank (2018b); Economic Planning Unit–Malaysia (2018b).
Note: Poverty estimates for 2000 are based on 2002 data.

and timber supplemented by oil exports, but their importance receded as manufacturing exports boomed (Figure 7.4, two middle panels).

The growth and structural transformation of the economy was accompanied by rapid urbanization (Figure 7.4, bottom-left panel), and by significant reductions in the incidence of poverty in both rural and urban areas (Figure 7.4, bottom-right panel).[17] Other social indicators, such as life expectancy at birth, showed marked progress (Chapter 4).

The societal rebalancing efforts of the NEP made headway. In 1970, foreigners held 63.3 per cent of corporate equity in Malaysia. By 1990, Malaysians held 74.6 per cent, with Malays (including trust organizations) having increased their share from just 2.4 per cent in 1970 to 19.3 per cent. While still under-represented in the private sector, Malay participation in the modern economy increased, as did their representation in professional and technical occupations, owing largely to the expansion of government employment.

If the NEP had costs—for instance, in terms of rent-seeking and the allocative inefficiencies and distortions it created—these costs seem to have been more than counterbalanced by policies that successfully lifted investment rates, diversified and raised productivity in agriculture, improved human development, attracted FDI, and supported vigorous exporting activity. Malaysia also had its share of good luck during OPP1. It benefited from a booming oil sector and, for the most part, favourable commodity prices, which helped to finance redistributive programmes. Even in the depths of the 1985–1986 recession, external developments moved decisively in the country's favour. Finally, economic policy was, overall, characterized by pragmatism. There was a willingness to change course when desired outcomes failed to materialize, as witnessed in the successive easing of the regulations of the Industrial Coordination Act—to assuage the anxieties of Chinese entrepreneurs and to attract FDI—and in the adoption of privatization policies in the late 1980s.

As Malaysia entered the 1990s it had justifiable cause for optimism, but it also had to confront difficult challenges, including balancing the tensions between equity and growth, and navigating its way in a rapidly globalizing and highly competitive world economy.

17 The data shown are for Peninsular Malaysia only, as data for 1970 are not available for Sabah and Sarawak. Their inclusion in the figures reported for 1990 increases the poverty rate to 17.1 per cent from 15 per cent on the peninsula alone.

Outline Perspective Plan 2, 1991–2000

The National Development Policy: Rationale and Scope

By 1990, considerable progress had been made in modernizing the economy and in reducing poverty. Efforts to attract export-oriented FDI, and the willingness to regulate this sector outside the scope of the NEP, had underpinned the country's strong economic performance. But while FDI was creating decent jobs for workers, its enclave status, with few backward linkages to the domestic economy and little transfer of either knowledge or technology, was a growing cause for concern.

Of equal concern to the political leadership was the modest progress that had been made in nurturing a *Bumiputera* commercial and entrepreneurial class, and the still limited *Bumiputera* engagement in the private sector. *Bumiputera* participation in commerce and business was often passive, and was based on their transfer of ethnicity-based entitlements to non-*Bumiputera* concerns in return for the rents that these exclusive advantages created—the so-called *Ali Baba* partnerships. In this context, OPP2 (EPU, 1991) introduced the National Development Policy (NDP) to guide the nation's development until 2000. Like the NEP, the NDP outlined a set of broad aspirations and principles that would frame more detailed five-year development plans and other initiatives.[18]

The NDP foreshadowed a shift in strategy. It emphasized 'balanced development', which it defined as the pursuit of economic growth *with equity*. Growth was now given primacy, and the state would orchestrate efforts to deliver the aspirations of *Wawasan 2020*.[19] Consistent with this focus on economic modernization and industrialization, the NDP emphasized the importance of maintaining macroeconomic discipline and promoting advances in productivity and efficiency. It stressed the vital role that the private sector would play in delivering the desired outcomes, with state guidance and coordination. The liberalization initiatives adopted in response to the economic setbacks of the mid 1980s would remain. Societal rebalancing objectives were carried over from the NEP, including targeted programmes for poverty reduction and support for the '*Bumiputera* Commercial and Industrial Community'. Although the target of 30 per cent *Bumiputera* equity ownership

18 A National Economic Consultative Committee (NECC) was formed in 1989 to guide the formulation of the NDP in five key areas: the national economy, poverty reduction, rebalancing society, human resource development, and data standardization. The NECC embraced a wide cross-section of stakeholders and at times considered the successes and failures of the NEP. Ultimately, however, many of the NECC proposals were set aside and the strategic priorities of the NDP were crafted directly by the Prime Minister's Office (Kyle, 2017).

19 Formulated in 1990, *Wawasan* (Vision) *2020* was not so much a plan as a statement of aspirations that accompanied MP6. *Wawasan 2020* established the principles that the state would then embed in the economy and in wider society so that the nation would become a self-sufficient and 'advanced' economy by 2020.

in the domestic economy was retained, OPP2 no longer identified a date for its attainment.

Targets and Policies in OPP2

By 1990, the Malaysian economy had fully recovered from the recession of the mid 1980s and was expanding faster than at any time since 1976. Per capita GNI grew at a cumulative average rate of 6.6 per cent in 1987–1990. This period of flourishing growth—the product of the normal bounce that occurs in the recovery from a deep recession, combined with the fruits of investment liberalization and an export boom—set the scene for the ambitious economic targets of MP6 (1991–1995). MP6 set its sights on annual GDP growth of 7.5 per cent and manufacturing growth of 11.5 per cent. It presented industrialization and industrial restructuring as the mechanisms to advance productivity and efficiency, rather than the promotion of heavy industry. Nevertheless, planned allocations for non-financial public enterprises increased four-fold relative to MP5 targets, and an ambitious target of 17 per cent growth was set for manufactured exports.

As in earlier periods, a significant contribution was anticipated from investment, with the investment rate targeted at 34.9 per cent of GDP. But the MP6 targets were also predicated on exceptional productivity gains. Aggregate TFP growth was expected to contribute over 40 per cent to aggregate output expansion, a target that, if achieved, would have marked a distinct break from what had been attained in the past (Chapter 6). From this point on, TFP targets were to become a preoccupation of Malaysia's plans. Given the nebulous nature of TFP—with the Solow residual deemed 'a measure of our ignorance about the causes of economic growth' by Abramovitz (1956, p. 11)—the use of such a target in focusing programmes, guiding resource allocation, and galvanizing efforts, as opposed to more specific micro-based targets for productivity and efficiency, seemed operationally remote.

In line with the new emphasis of OPP2, MP6 highlighted the need for programmes to restructure and privatize industry, to upgrade technology and enhance productivity, to expand the capabilities of the labour force, and to accelerate capital market development. It was thought that measures to assist the development of high-value service activities in areas such as tourism and consultancy would contribute to economic diversification and job creation. The government regarded a strengthened financial sector and capital markets as essential to enabling the private sector to play a bigger role in mobilizing resources.

Although the main focus of MP6 was on creating the conditions for rapid and sustained growth, it also retained the emphasis of earlier plans on reducing poverty through targeted assistance. The aim was to reduce the overall incidence of poverty to 11 per cent by 1995. As the profile of poverty had a distinctive spatial pattern—with poverty largely concentrated in Kelantan, Kedah, Pahang, Perlis, and Terengganu on the peninsula, and in Sabah and Sarawak in East Malaysia—programmes to promote greater spatial equality were also emphasized, including through the allocation of development expenditure.

MP7 (1996–2000) was formulated on the cusp of the Asian financial crisis. MP6 had easily beaten its aggregate targets for the economy, which had grown at a cumulative average rate of 9.1 per cent and at a per capita average rate of 6.5 per cent over the period 1991–1995. Against this background, and with East Asia's newly industrialized economies (NIEs) demonstrating an ability to sustain rapid growth, the growth target for GDP during MP7 was increased to 8 per cent a year, up from 7.5 per cent in MP6. Targeted sector growth rates envisaged continued modernization and industrialization supported by a vibrant service sector, along with high rates of investment and rapid productivity gains.

The focus on export-oriented manufacturing growth remained, as did the privatization programme that had built momentum during MP6. These strategic thrusts were to be complemented by state-led activities in a narrower range of heavy industries (in particular, car making, cement, and steel). The goal was to internationalize production through support for the development of 'competitive industry clusters'. The overall aim was to create conditions conducive to accelerated growth at the macroeconomic and micro-industrial levels. Although poverty reduction and redistributive programmes remained in place, they were a supplement to the state-led economic modernization agenda rather than the plan's core. Measures such as the vendor development programme to support the *Bumiputera* commercial and industrial community also continued.

Outcomes for OPP2

Figure 7.5 (left panel) shows the trajectory of GNI per capita and the ratio of gross capital formation to GDP. Over the period 1991–2000, the economy grew at a cumulative average rate of 6.2 per cent, or 3.7 per cent per capita. However, the contrast between the outcomes of MP6 and MP7 could not have been more dramatic: in 1991–1995, per capita GNI grew at a cumulative average rate of 6.6 per cent, a rate of growth that almost entirely evaporated during MP7, when per capita incomes rose by just 0.1 per cent (an increase that was due only to growth in 1996–1997). At the close of OPP2 in 2000, GNI per capita was still below the peak recorded in 1997. It would take until

2003 for real GNI per capita to exceed its 1997 level. Against the 1997 peak in GNI per capita, cumulative per capita output losses between 1998 and 2002 amounted to 25.8 per cent of the 1997 level (area 'A' in the left panel, bounded from below by GNI per capita). The shock to income caused by the Asian financial crisis was far deeper and more persistent than that triggered by the 1985–1986 recession, when per capita incomes had climbed back to above pre-crisis levels within four years.

Figure 7.5 Legacies of the Asian financial crisis included large output losses, languid investment, and large declines in real household per capita consumption

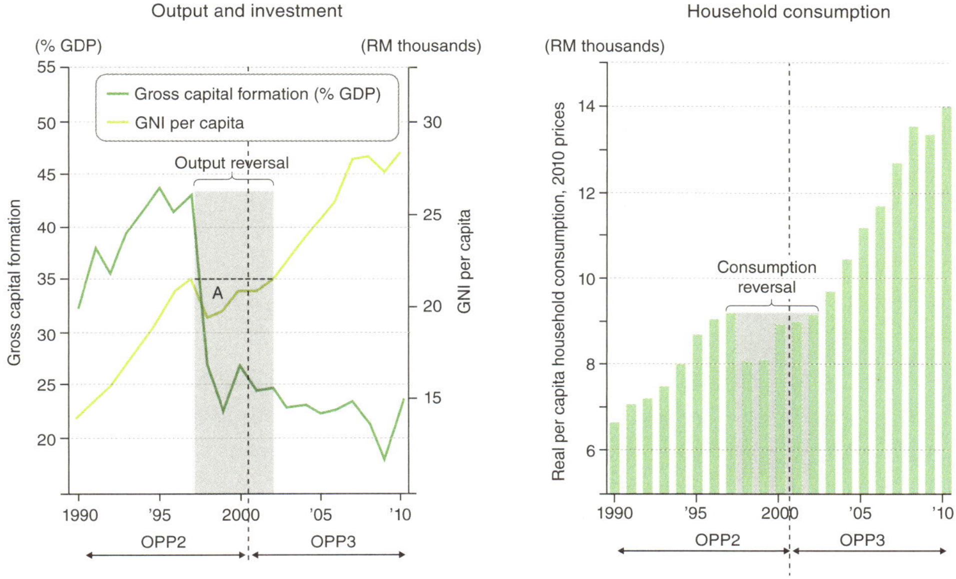

Source of data: World Bank (2018a).

The collapse of investment precipitated by the crisis was reminiscent of the 1985–1986 recession. But unlike in the earlier reversal, investment rates did not rebound even well into the OPP3 period. The steepness of the collapse was in part a function of the unprecedented heady investment rates of the mid 1990s, which were among the world's highest at the time. For a protracted period after the Asian financial crisis, investment then languished at rates below those spanning MP2 to MP6.

The right panel of Figure 7.5 shows the trajectory of real household consumption in the OPP2 and OPP3 periods. The impact of the Asian financial crisis on household consumption broadly paralleled its impact on output. Measured relative to the 1997 pre-crisis peak, real household consumption per capita was, on average, 6 per cent below its 1997 level until 2002, yielding accumulated losses of 30.1 per cent relative to the 1997 level.

Viewed from the vantage point of 1996, the MP6 period had been characterized by a remarkable spell of economic expansion, which seemed to vindicate the reforms and the change in strategic direction that began in the second half of the 1980s and were then embedded in OPP2. Strong growth brought overall unemployment down to just 2.5 per cent by 1996. Gross domestic savings rates were approaching 40 per cent of GDP, and there were surpluses on the federal government's budget. Although current account deficits had surfaced in the first part of the 1990s (in part owing to high levels of capital imports), the total external debt service ratio was a healthy 9.1 per cent of total export revenue in 1996, and the ratio of the total stock of debt relative to export earnings and external income was 41.8 per cent that year (World Bank, 2018b). The real effective exchange rate of the Malaysian ringgit was appreciating (China Economic and Industry Data, 2018). Reported non-performing loans were low, at 3.5 per cent (National Economic Action Council, 1998). Consumer and producer price inflation was modest despite low and falling unemployment and output levels that were almost certainly greater than the potential that the economy could sustain (National Economic Action Council, 1998). Migrant labour provided a flexible buffer against cost pressures: the headcount of migrant workers in the economy increased by nearly 250,000 between 1990 and 1995 (World Bank, 2018b).

Although a variety of indicators gave little warning of the convulsions ahead, some alarm bells were ringing. Credit growth was breaking all speed limits, and had more than doubled from 73.8 per cent of nominal GDP in 1991 to 158.3 per cent in 1997. Linked to this explosion in credit, equity and property prices had ballooned. Corporate Malaysia was also becoming more highly leveraged. In 1995, capitalization of the Kuala Lumpur Stock Exchange stood at 300 per cent of GDP, the highest ratio globally (Athukorala, 2012), and by 1996 the valuation of the Kuala Lumpur Composite Index was approximately double that of 1991. Although external debt levels gave no cause for concern when measured according to conventional thresholds, the maturity structure of external debt had shortened. Short-term external debt as a share of foreign exchange earnings from goods, services, and primary income had risen from 5.3 per cent in 1991 to 15.6 per cent in 1997. The ratio of the stock of short-term debt to total foreign exchange reserves had risen to 79 per cent in 1997 from just 17.7 per cent in 1991.

There were also doubts about the sustainability of the accelerated growth seen in the MP6 period. Although output price pressures were muted, wages were running ahead of labour productivity growth, and the hoped-for advances in TFP were not being realized (Chapter 6). Before the crisis, growth of TFP had started to taper, and any continuing growth in labour productivity was being propelled almost entirely by ever greater capital input intensity. Incremental investment per unit of output had risen from 3 in 1988 to 6.5 in 1997, suggesting that capital spending was becoming increasingly inefficient under OPP2. Largely owing to bloated investment spending and an extraordinarily high investment rate, current account deficits had been created.

The counterfactual—of how events might have panned out had the Asian financial crisis not occurred—is unknowable. But growing economic imbalances and asset price bubbles would eventually have required resolution. Much of what was invested during the early 1990s and was fuelling input-led growth would ultimately have delivered low rates of return. The credit growth that fed into inflated stock and property prices presented acute risks. Asset price corrections, when they occurred, would have weakened bank balance sheets and the wider financial system. Even if the crisis had not occurred, the idea that the heady growth of the late 1980s and the first half of the 1990s would have been sustained, as MP7 and several distinguished economists and international organizations had assumed, seems implausible.[20]

Although the Asian financial crisis is generally viewed as a consequence of private sector, banking, and corporate failures, some aspects of Malaysia's state-directed redistributive policies added to the country's vulnerabilities. The state, through the Ministry of Finance Incorporated and other GLCs, had acquired considerable interests in domestic banks and in the equity market through the operation of its trust fund vehicles. By the mid 1990s, state interests were also highly visible in the corporate business sector. The state used this influence to pursue its redistributive agenda. The provision of easy and subsidized access to credit for the well-connected, along with forbearance on their debt obligations, served to weaken the financial system. The state's influence on business strategy, finances, hiring policies, and operations subordinated the pursuit of shareholder value to redistributive goals.

At the same time, state-managed trust funds, which by the early 1990s had a significant presence in the domestic equity market, exercised market power and managed their portfolios to ensure large dividends rather than to impose discipline on the companies they owned. These practices and the culture of rent-seeking which they incubated were inimical to competition and market discipline. They weakened the fabric of the financial system,[21] damaging business development and growth, deterring investment by the

---

20 Even as the Asian financial crisis was unfolding, the Asian Development Bank (1997) and the World Bank foresaw in their economic outlooks that East Asian countries would continue to enjoy a rapid pace of economic growth.

21 Although reported non-performing loans of the banking system were modest, at 3.6 per cent in 1996 (one year before the 1997 crisis), the practice of lending into arrears and a lenient classification system meant that actual non-performing loans were probably hugely under-reported. On 1 January 1998, the period in arrears for classifying a loan as non-performing by banking institutions was reduced from six months to three months (BNM, 1997).

non-*Bumiputera* business community, and distorting incentives. Ultimately, they served to undermine the economic growth to which OPP2 sought to give precedence. Box 7.5 describes the impact of the Asian financial crisis on Malaysia, as well as the responses to the crisis.

Box 7.5 Asian financial crisis, 1997–1999

The crisis was triggered in July 1997 when the central bank of Thailand ran down its foreign exchange reserves as it defended the baht from speculative attacks. The large short-term capital outflows that followed caused Asian currencies, including the Malaysian ringgit, to depreciate sharply.

The crisis had a profound effect on Malaysia's macroeconomic conditions. Real GDP per capita contracted by 9.7 per cent in 1998 in the steepest decline since independence, and it took six quarters for the economy to return to growth. The ringgit depreciated by 36 per cent against the US dollar between 1996 and 1998. By August 1998, the market capitalization of the Kuala Lumpur Stock Exchange had dived by 74 per cent relative to its previous peak in 1997. US dollar international reserves also declined, and by end-1997 were 25 per cent below the level they had been at 12 months before, owing to a large reversal of capital flows. Interest rates spiked, with the base lending rate rising to nearly 14 per cent for a brief period in 1997.

In 1998, unemployment climbed to 3.2 per cent, at which time retrenched workers numbered 84,000. Lay-offs continued until 2001, with manufacturing the worst affected sector. Consumer price inflation accelerated to average 5.3 per cent in 1998, double the level in 1997.

In July 1998, the National Economic Recovery Plan was launched, and by September of that year Malaysia had begun to implement a regime of pegging its currency and instituting selective capital controls, thereby creating space for independent monetary policy to support recovery and stability. Whereas other crisis-hit economies elected to participate in the International Monetary Fund (IMF)-led assistance plans, Malaysia chose not to, because its external account remained in surplus, and because the government considered that IMF conditions could delay the recovery of the domestic economy (Radelet and Sachs, 1998). Malaysia fared much better than Indonesia, for example.

With this latitude on monetary management, interest rates were lowered, and by 1999 had come down from the earlier peaks and reverted to pre-crisis levels, helping to reduce the burden on borrowers. Fiscal support was also provided. In particular, government social spending increased after the crisis, and cyclical deficits surfaced as revenues narrowed.

To rehabilitate the financial system, special-purpose agencies were established to restructure and strengthen domestic banking institutions, and to help corporations restructure their debts (BNM, 1998). Banks were consolidated, and prudential regulations and supervision upgraded (Villanueva and Lim, 2008; Siregar and Lim, 2010). The system of corporate governance that had allowed excessive risk-taking and leverage was also subjected to major legislative and regulatory reform after the crisis.

Malaysia's policy response to the crisis was unique, and even ran counter to standard IMF recommendations for other East Asian nations. In the country's own approach to crisis resolution, capital control measures and pegging of the ringgit were undertaken to stabilize the exchange rate, banks were recapitalized using domestic resources, and safeguarding of the country's social safety net was prioritized. These measures proved effective in supporting the economy while also protecting national economic sovereignty, and were even emulated by a number of countries some years later.

The crisis led to the sidelining of the OPP2 agenda, and caused the government to prioritize restoring confidence and growth. Still, the OPP2 period witnessed some tangible achievements: by 2000, the economy was 50 per cent larger than it had been in 1990; it was more diversified and industrialized; and it was more closely integrated with the global trading system. Despite the hardships of the crisis, poverty had all but been eradicated in the expanding urban areas, and was also continuing to fall steadily in rural areas (Figure 7.4).

Outline Perspective Plan 3, 2001–2010

The National Vision Policy: Rationale and Scope

The National Vision Policy (NVP), 2001–2010, succeeded the NDP and its predecessor, the NEP. It sought to consolidate and advance the strategic ambitions of those earlier agendas by honing Malaysia's strategy to accommodate changing global economic realities. Poverty eradication remained at the centre of the NVP. The redistributive aims of the NVP were expressed in terms of the goal of 'reducing imbalances among and *within* ethnic groups'. The NVP emphasized the need to build both a resilient and competitive economy, and an equitable society to ensure unity and social stability.

In the economic sphere, and responding to the experience of the Asian financial crisis, the NVP stressed the need for sound economic management; improved efficiency and productivity; strengthened financial and corporate institutions; enhanced competitiveness; and boosted investments in a 'productive and knowledgeable workforce'. The NVP introduced a new theme to support economic diversification and growth: the development of a 'knowledge economy'.[22]

Despite differences in phrasing, the NVP provided continuity with the NDP on an agenda that would give primacy to economic growth and that, when

22 Although not of primary concern in this chapter, the NVP also elevated the importance of environmental considerations.

growth occurred, would create outcomes in which the benefits of improved prosperity would be distributed to reduce imbalances.

Targets and Policies in OPP3

The concrete goals of OPP3 (EPU, 2001) were articulated through MP8 and MP9. The overriding aim was still to make Malaysia a fully developed nation ('in its own mould') by 2020. Given the setback of the Asian financial crisis, MP8 (2001–2005) estimated that this would require an average of 7 per cent growth in real GDP over the first two decades of the new millennium. For the MP8 period, the goal was 7.5 per cent. MP8 recognized that in order to sustain accelerated growth without risking macroeconomic and financial imbalances, or running into other binding constraints, rapid productivity growth would be required. Equally, it emphasized that economic resilience would require strengthened fiscal and monetary management, and tighter financial market development and regulation.

Themes from earlier plans were echoed in MP8. A more active *Bumiputera* commercial and industrial community was to be nurtured through outsourcing by multinational corporations to local businesses (through vendor programmes), privatization of state entities, and financial and non-financial assistance to SMEs. A target of absolute poverty incidence of 0.5 per cent was set for 2005, and emphasis was given to consolidating, rationalizing, and integrating poverty-eradication initiatives under the umbrella of the *Skim Pembangunan Kesejahteraan Rakyat* (People's Welfare Development Scheme). FDI would continue to be encouraged, but with a focus now on quality, specifically in high-technology manufacturing and in areas that would facilitate technology transfer, R&D, human resource development, and market access for domestic enterprises.

To foster the knowledge economy, MP8 referred to the need to invest in R&D and science and technology, to expand information and communications technology (ICT) infrastructure, and to upgrade human resources. Areas for attention included a more attuned education system supporting lifelong learning, incentives to encourage R&D, and public sector investment in an upgraded ICT backbone. The wider use of the English language in education, more residential schools to teach maths and science, and greater private sector investment in tertiary education were identified as important components of an 'efficient and responsive' education system. New funding mechanisms, including venture capital, were to support the start up and incubation of new knowledge-based businesses.

A variety of sector masterplans supported MP8. The (Second) Industrial Masterplan, 1996–2005, set out a blueprint for industry to move up the value-added chain and into science- and technology-based commercial activities. The Financial Masterplan, 2001–2010, provided a roadmap for a resilient banking sector, built around core banks and modern market infrastructure that could safeguard depositors' funds and ensure the efficient allocation of credit. The plan singled out support for developing Islamic institutions and instruments. The linked Capital Markets Masterplan explained how Malaysia would take steps to deepen its domestic bond and derivatives markets, and support the growth, for example, of investment funds.

Consistent with moving up the value-added chain, and with initiatives promoting greater efficiency, MP8 sought annual average growth of TFP of 2.8 per cent (or 37.2 per cent of the total growth target of 7.5 per cent). Manufacturing was again to be the main engine of growth, with expansion targeted at 8.9 per cent; if realized, this would take its share in total value added close to 36 per cent by 2005, up from 33.4 per cent in 2000. Services, however, would remain the largest sector, contributing over 50 per cent of GDP, and were targeted to grow at 7.7 per cent. Although the share of agricultural output in GDP would continue to recede, the sector was still expected to grow by 3 per cent (later revised to 2 per cent), as was the mining industry. The budgetary allocations for non-financial public enterprises as a share of GDP, and for planned cumulative spending relative to MP7, were reduced.

At the midpoint of the NVP, MP9 (2006–2010) introduced the National Mission. In terms of its core economic and social objectives, there was little difference between the National Mission and the NVP, but important nuances were apparent. Economic growth ambitions were moderated in the National Mission, and there was a renewed emphasis on agricultural development in MP9 under the New Agricultural Programme. Sustained productivity improvements—rather than large capital spending and mega projects—were emphasized as the driver of economic growth.[23] The National Mission stressed the need for educational reforms to support the development of productive capabilities, as well as for improvements in governance and public service delivery. The formation of a National Integrity Council in 2004, and the transformation plan for GLCs formulated in the same year, had foreshadowed these new priorities.

---

23 While allocations to mega projects were cut in response to the Asian financial crisis, they were subsequently increased as the crisis passed. However, the prime minister, Abdullah Badawi, had, early in his term, signalled his intention to scale back on large capital projects (including the planned North–South electric railway, and an aluminium smelter in Sarawak), and soon began to cancel or defer projects.

MP9 aimed for GDP growth of 6 per cent, with TFP targeted to contribute 2.2 per cent, or about 36 per cent of the overall growth. Growth of 6.7 per cent was planned for manufacturing, and 6.5 per cent for services, with government services projected to grow at a more modest 4.5 per cent. The target for agricultural growth was raised from the 2 per cent of MP8 to 5 per cent. The New Agricultural Programme emphasized the development of large-scale commercial agriculture centred on food cultivation, alongside palm oil and rubber. Investments downstream would aid diversification in manufacturing. On poverty, the goals were to eliminate hardcore poverty by 2010 and to reduce the national poverty incidence to 2.8 per cent by that year. Inequality targets were also reframed: by 2010, the ratio of *Bumiputera* to Chinese income was to rise to 66.6 per cent from about 61.1 per cent in 2004; and the gap between rural and urban incomes was to narrow to 50 per cent from 47.4 per cent in 2004.

The Global Financial Crisis and Great Recession, 2008–2009

MP9 was thrown out of kilter by the global financial crisis and the Great Recession, which began with the bankruptcy of Lehman Brothers in September 2008, the biggest corporate bankruptcy in US history. US investors lost confidence in the value of sub-prime mortgages, triggering a credit and liquidity crunch. The unprecedented escalation of credit and liquidity risks later developed into a vicious circle, effectively drying up liquidity of the US dollar. An underlying cause was the deregulation of the US financial system and the apparent lack of supervision over derivative products, as well as the highly interconnected nature of the financial system (Wheelock, 2012).[24]

Globally, this crisis was the worst since the Great Depression in terms of its duration and depth. Global economic output did not sink to the lows of the Great Depression only because developed nations' central banks worked together to prevent the collapse of the financial system, and to provide enough liquidity to avoid a prolonged crunch (Piketty, 2014; Eichengreen, 2016). The Great Recession also saw some advanced economies introduce negative interest rates and inject massive amounts of money into their countries' finances through the creation of new money (quantitative easing) by central banks, to buy (back) financial assets such as government bonds.

---

24 Another perspective is that the cause was the failure to regulate rather than deregulation (Calabria, 2009).

Impact and Responses

In 2009, a year after the onset of the Great Recession, Malaysia's real GDP contracted by 2.4 per cent. However, it took only three quarters for the economy to return to growth compared with six quarters following the Asian financial crisis. Exchange rate flexibility and expansionary monetary policies helped to lessen the impact of the Great Recession (Elekdag et al., 2012). The direct impact was also minimized because Malaysia's banking sector was robust and not significantly linked to sub-prime loans in the US. Since the Asian financial crisis, the country had undertaken several structural reforms, accumulated large foreign reserves, continued to register current account surpluses, and taken steps to ward off speculators. The banking system was sound. Non-performing loans of commercial banks accounted for only 2.2 per cent of overall loans, and the ratio of total provisions/impairment provisions to net non-performing loans/impaired loans was 385.4 per cent (BNM, 2008). In 2007, the banking system's leverage position recorded a risk-weighted capital ratio of 13.2 per cent, well above the minimum 8 per cent capital requirement (BNM, 2008). However, tight global liquidity saw a reduction in capital inflows, particularly FDI (Goh and Lim, 2010).

The impact on Malaysia was felt primarily through the contraction of exports as the world's major economies went into recession. Higher inflation occurred not at the onset of the crisis in late 2008, but in the first half of 2008 when there were intense inflationary pressures owing to sharp increases in the prices of oil, food, and other commodities. By the time the crisis erupted in the US in the second half of 2008, inflation in Malaysia had subsided, reflecting lower aggregate demand.

The Great Recession, like the Asian financial crisis, led to unemployment: 16,500 workers were retrenched in 2008 and 25,000 in 2009, although these numbers were not large relative to the size of the labour force.[25] The two crises affected some groups more than others: youth unemployment had always been relatively high, but it increased by 1.9 per cent in 1997 to reach 8.9 per cent, and by 1.0 per cent in 2008 to reach 10.6 per cent. Before the crises, women were disproportionately represented among the unemployed, but on average, employment losses were larger for men than for women. The growth rate of real wages declined at the onset of the Great Recession, but recovered strongly the following year, unlike during the Asian financial crisis (Figure 7.6).

25 In both crises, the impact on unemployment was mitigated by the large number of foreign workers who were repatriated, as was also the case during the Great Depression of the 1930s.

Figure 7.6 **Growth of real wage rates fell in both crises, but at different points during their progression**

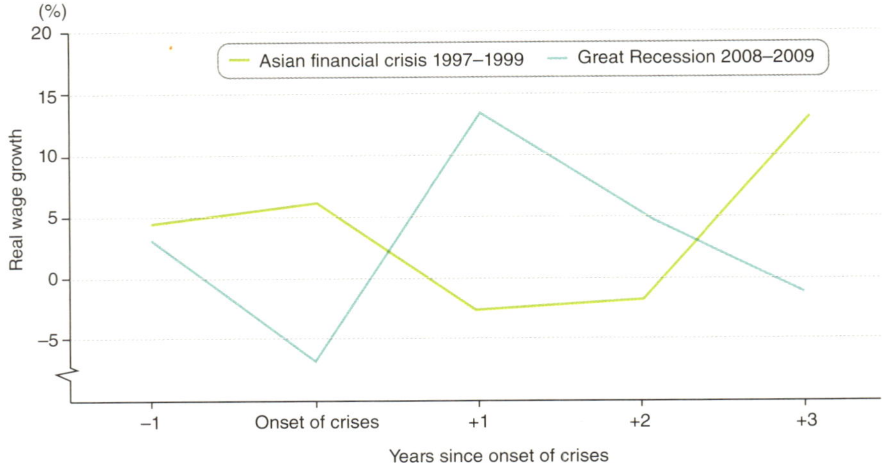

Source of data: Ministry of Finance–Malaysia (various years).

The Great Recession, like the Asian financial crisis, highlighted the importance of fiscal stimulus packages to offset external shocks. Two stimulus packages were implemented to boost the domestic economy. The first, announced in November 2008, was a RM67 billion stimulus amounting to 9.6 per cent of GDP, and the second, announced in March 2009, totalled RM60 billion (BNM, 2009). Despite the decline in government revenue, overall expenditure increased owing to the fiscal stimulus packages (Figure 7.7). Some differences and similarities between these two crises and the Great Depression are highlighted in Box 7.6.

Figure 7.7 **Government development and social expenditure rose during the Asian financial crisis and the Great Recession**

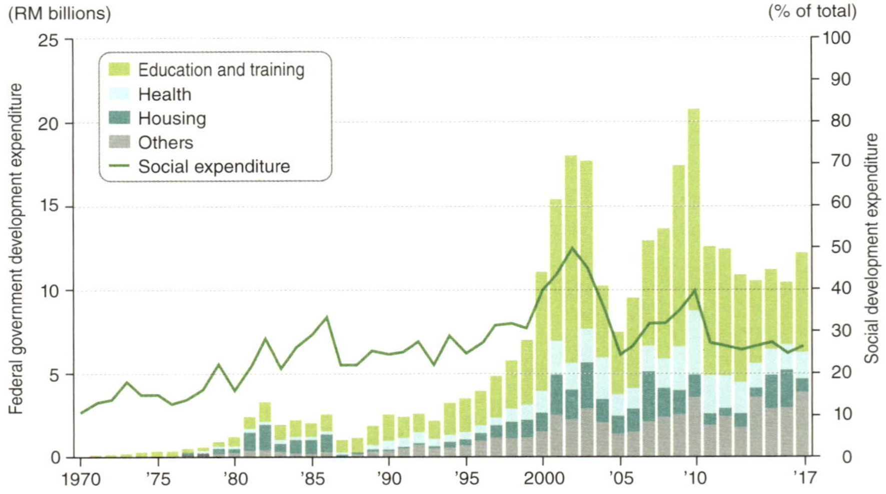

Sources of data: Lim (1977); Ministry of Finance–Malaysia (various years).

Box 7.6 Some similarities and differences between the three crises: the Great Depression, the Asian financial crisis, and the Great Recession

Two of these great crises—the 1929 Great Depression and the 2008–2009 Great Recession—originated in the US, while the 1997–1999 Asian financial crisis arose in Thailand. Despite the gap of 80 years separating the first and last, there are important parallels to be drawn between the three crises. All started as external financial crises, but the shocks were eventually transmitted through the export sector, which in turn affected the real economy through reduced private investment and private consumption activities.

There are, however, crucial differences. The Great Depression and Great Recession were mainly crises of exports, while the Asian financial crisis started off as a currency crisis and eventually ended up affecting Malaysia's real economy. Four years after the Great Depression, Malaya was still experiencing a recession, whereas within one and a half years of the Asian financial crisis and of the Great Recession, Malaysia had recovered in terms of both economic growth and exports (Box Figure 7.2).

Box Figure 7.2 Economic and export recoveries were swift and V-shaped after the Asian financial crisis and the Great Recession, unlike during the Great Depression

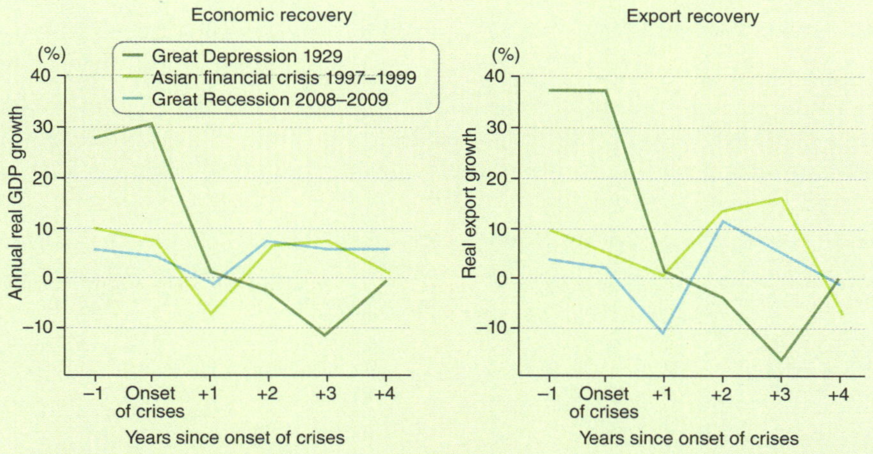

Sources of data: Sultan Nazrin Shah (2017); Department of Statistics–Malaysia (various years).

During the colonial period, economic recovery was slow, hampered as it was by the absence of both external and domestic demand. The authorities lacked effective mechanisms to determine what was going wrong and what action to take. There was no domestic central bank to implement monetary policy, and the colonial government did not have the benefit of hindsight to allow it to implement Keynesian fiscal policies to boost the domestic economy. Moreover, the colonial government had maintained a tradition of pursuing balanced fiscal budgets, except during recession years, whereas by the time of the Asian financial crisis and the Great Recession, the Malaysian government's expenditure was on an increasing trend during the crisis years (Box Figure 7.3).

Box Figure 7.3 Since the Asian financial crisis, the fiscal position has been in prolonged deficit

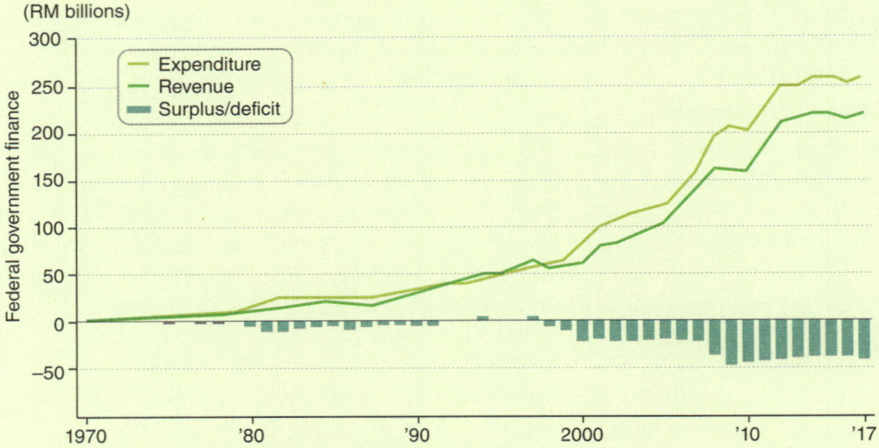

Source of data: Ministry of Finance–Malaysia (various years).

During the Asian financial crisis and the Great Recession, Malaysia's fiscal and monetary authorities responded vigorously to stabilize the economy. Interest rates were cut to encourage consumption and investment. In addition, funds were set aside to boost private investment through public–private partnership initiatives in education, health, and tourism.

In view of the openness of the economy, one lesson from all three crises is that there is a need for Malaysia to rebalance its growth strategy away from dependence on the external sector, and to focus more on domestic demand, particularly investment, to reduce its vulnerability to external shocks.

Outcomes for OPP3

The OPP3 period (2001–2010) started just as Malaysia's recovery from the Asian financial crisis was interrupted by the bursting of the dot-com bubble. Turmoil in the global electronics sector dented demand for Malaysia's manufactured exports, which were heavily concentrated in electrical and electronic goods. In US dollar terms, Malaysia's merchandise exports declined by 10.5 per cent between 2000 and 2001. Recovery was swift, however. By 2003, real GDP was growing rapidly, surpassing, in this year, the pre-crisis peak level of per capita income attained in 1997.

Over the OPP3 period, real GDP growth averaged 4.9 per cent, and in per capita terms real GNI grew at 3.5 per cent (Figure 7.8), outcomes far short of what had been envisaged in OPP3 and targeted in MP8 and MP9. OPP3 initially set a target of 7.5 per cent growth for 2001–2010. Although the global financial crisis of 2008 put a dent in Malaysia's plans and hindered the country's aspiration to become a fully developed nation by 2020, the period between the bursting of the dot-com bubble and the global financial crisis saw respectable real GDP growth of 5.8 per cent, although this was still some way short of the targets.

Despite the shortfall in aggregate growth outcomes, there were increasing indications that growth was depending less and less on input growth and more on productivity improvements. During OPP3, the incremental capital–output ratio fell to less than 4.5 from the unprecedented heights seen before the Asian financial crisis, and there were solid advances in TFP from 2003 to 2008 (Chapter 6). However, the TFP reversals that coincided with the shocks of 2001–2002 and with the global financial crisis meant that, overall, the productivity targets of MP8 and MP9 were not met. PWT9.1 data show that peak TFP annualized growth was a little over 3 per cent in 2004, but the average for the period 2001–2010 was just 0.8 per cent. As a proportion of realized GDP growth, this was less than 20 per cent, falling far short of the targets set in MP8 and MP9 of 37 per cent and 36 per cent respectively. As well as the forces that tend to reduce TFP in cyclical downswings, TFP growth may also have been held in check by falling investment rates (to the extent that productivity gains are embodied in new capital), low rates of innovation, inefficiencies in output markets, and slow progress in upgrading the capabilities of the labour force (Chapter 3).

The sharp decline in investment rates and their failure to revert to pre-crisis levels is shown in Figure 7.8. While investment rates appeared to have faltered during the OPP3 period, this was, in part, an illusion created by the investment bubble and the heavy government spending on mega projects that preceded the Asian financial crisis. Lower investment rates after the crisis and throughout OPP3 probably reflected the capacity overhang from the excessive investment of the pre-crisis years. Inspection of the composition of investment shows that the main downward adjustments were to private rather than public sector capital formation (Table 7.1). The sharp decline in private investment most likely reflected the more difficult funding conditions that were being faced as a result of the tightening of bank credit and depressed equity values, as well as heightened risk aversion and a reassessment of long-term earnings prospects.

Figure 7.8 **Incomes climbed during OPP3 despite two recessions, and efficiency improved**

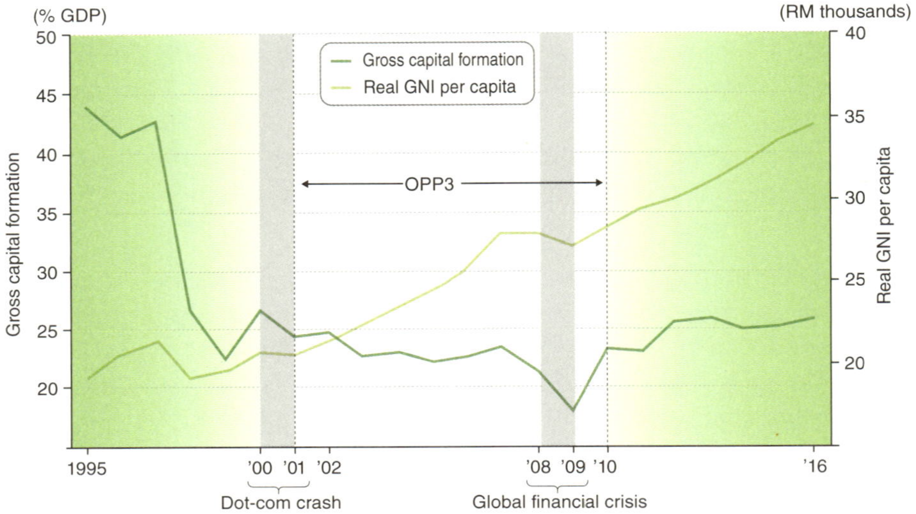

Source of data: World Bank (2018a).

Table 7.1 **Private investment collapsed after the Asian financial crisis**

Gross fixed capital formation (% GDP)	1995	2000	2005	2010
Public sector	12.4	11.9	10.1	10.1
Private sector	31.2	13.4	12.2	12.3
Total	43.6	25.3	22.3	22.4

Sources of data: Economic Planning Unit–Malaysia (2001) MP8, Table 2.2, p. 26; Department of Statistics–Malaysia (various years), Annual National Accounts Gross Domestic Product.

Note: GLC investment is included under 'private'. As of 2013, government entities controlled 455 companies, either in terms of majority ownership of shares or through being the single largest shareholder (Gomez et al., 2018).

Other factors were also in play. FDI ratcheted up through the mid 1980s and into the early 1990s, peaking in 1992 at close to 9 per cent of GDP (Figure 7.9). On the eve of the Asian financial crisis, inflows were a more modest 5.1 per cent of GDP. After the crisis and throughout the OPP3 period, FDI was more muted. The emergence of China, India, and the transitional economies of Southeast Asia (Cambodia, Lao People's Democratic Republic, and Viet Nam) as viable lower-cost production platforms in Asia meant that Malaysia faced stiffer competition for the available pool of FDI funds. Increasingly, too, the country faced competition from more distant nations in South America and Eastern Europe. The decline in FDI accounts for some of the reduction of investment rates during the OPP3 period. Subdued FDI also suggests that Malaysia had only limited success in attracting the 'higher-quality'—high value-added, R&D-oriented, and technologically sophisticated—FDI that it had sought.[26]

Figure 7.9 **FDI inflows were volatile and lower during OPP3**

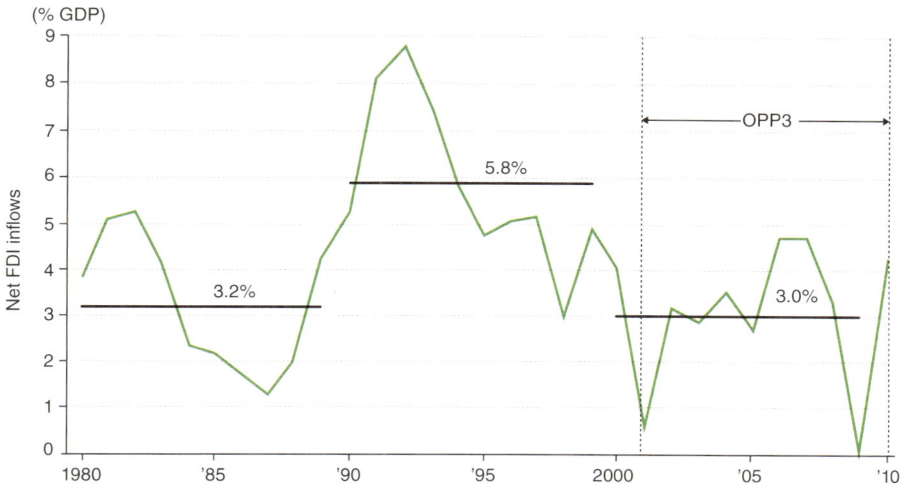

Source of data: World Bank (2018a).
Note: Decade averages are shown by horizontal bars (1980–1989, 1990–1999, and 2000–2009).

Three other possible explanations for the decline in private investment have been suggested.

First, as a consequence of weaknesses in the implementation of the NEP, 'rent-seeking, patronage and often opaque procurement' may have deterred domestic investment (NEAC, 2010, p. 7). Some investors may have perceived elevated risks concerning the security of their investments, as policy and regulation could be capricious (Gomez, 2018).

A second and related conjecture is that the heavy presence in parts of the economy of GLCs, which benefited from favourable regulatory treatment and access to government contracts, may have discouraged private sector investment (NEAC, 2010). Menon and Ng (2013) provide empirical evidence for 2007–2011 which shows that where GLC presence in an industry crossed a size threshold (60 per cent of industry revenues), it had a negative effect on private sector investment in that industry. The fact that the total assets

26 It can be argued that FDI—particularly that which focused on the assembly of electronics—found Malaysia attractive because of favourable investment incentives as well as the availability of land and relatively cheap labour. FDI itself is sometimes seen as a contributory factor in keeping Malaysia dependent on low-skilled foreign labour and hindering its progress up the technological chain. But this dependence on low-skilled, labour-intensive industries was a consequence of conditions in which there was a surplus of labour of the right kind, and this continued to make labour cheap. FDI simply responded to the incentive structures that Malaysian policy and institutional frameworks had created. If Malaysia had built competitive advantages further up the value chain, FDI would have leveraged these and invested; but Malaysia did not.

of GLCs were growing rapidly during OPP3, and much more quickly than those of non-GLCs, suggests that this crowding-out effect may have been substantial. Crowding out may also have occurred through the fiscal strain that loss-making GLCs placed on the government. Menon (2017) estimates that GLCs accumulated losses of RM85 billion over a 35-year period (spanning the period before and after OPP3). Demands of this scale on the national budget could be expected to have raised interest rates and the cost of capital.

Third, GLC investment languished after the global financial crisis. At the end of 2015, GLC assets amounted to 51 per cent of GDP (Menon, 2017). Although some researchers have suggested that GLCs had outperformed other entities, Menon (2017) points out that these performance metrics are inflated by the preferential treatment that GLCs received from the state. The poor performance of GLCs such as Proton Holdings and Malaysia Airlines is well documented, but more generally Wan Mardyatul Miza Wan Tahir and Sinnasamy (2012) have demonstrated that GLCs did less well in creating shareholder value than non-GLCs such as IOI, Public Bank, or Tan Chong Motors. The pursuit of non-commercial objectives by GLCs at the behest of the state, and weaknesses in the governance and operational management of many, are likely to have taken a toll on profitability and investment.

Figure 7.10 summarizes performance during the OPP3 period, as well as during the MP10 and earlier OPP periods. The top-left panel shows per capita income and per capita household consumption in the terminal year of each perspective plan. It should be borne in mind that OPP1 spans 20 years, whereas OPP2 and OPP3 each span ten years. By the close of OPP3, per capita GDP was 29 per cent higher than at the close of OPP2, and per capita household consumption was 57.3 per cent higher. The growth of per capita GDP in OPP3 was considerably lower than that during OPP2, however. Part of the explanation for this may lie in the higher initial levels of income at the start of OPP3. As countries become more prosperous, it is usual for income growth to decelerate (Figure 6.2 in Chapter 6, and Box 5.2 in Chapter 5). As discussed below, a shift of resources from higher-productivity industry into lower-productivity services slowed growth. Comparatively tepid growth during OPP3 was also a function of the impact of the Great Recession. Cumulative average growth of GDP per capita from 2000 to 2007, prior to the onset of the crisis, was almost 2 percentage points higher than from 2000 to 2010.

The period of OPP3 differs from OPP1 and OPP2 insofar as it saw larger improvements in the average standard of living, as measured by real consumption per capita, than in the expansion of GDP per capita. This difference appears to be attributable to a structural decline in savings rates

Figure 7.10 Malaysia's economic transformation, 1970–2015

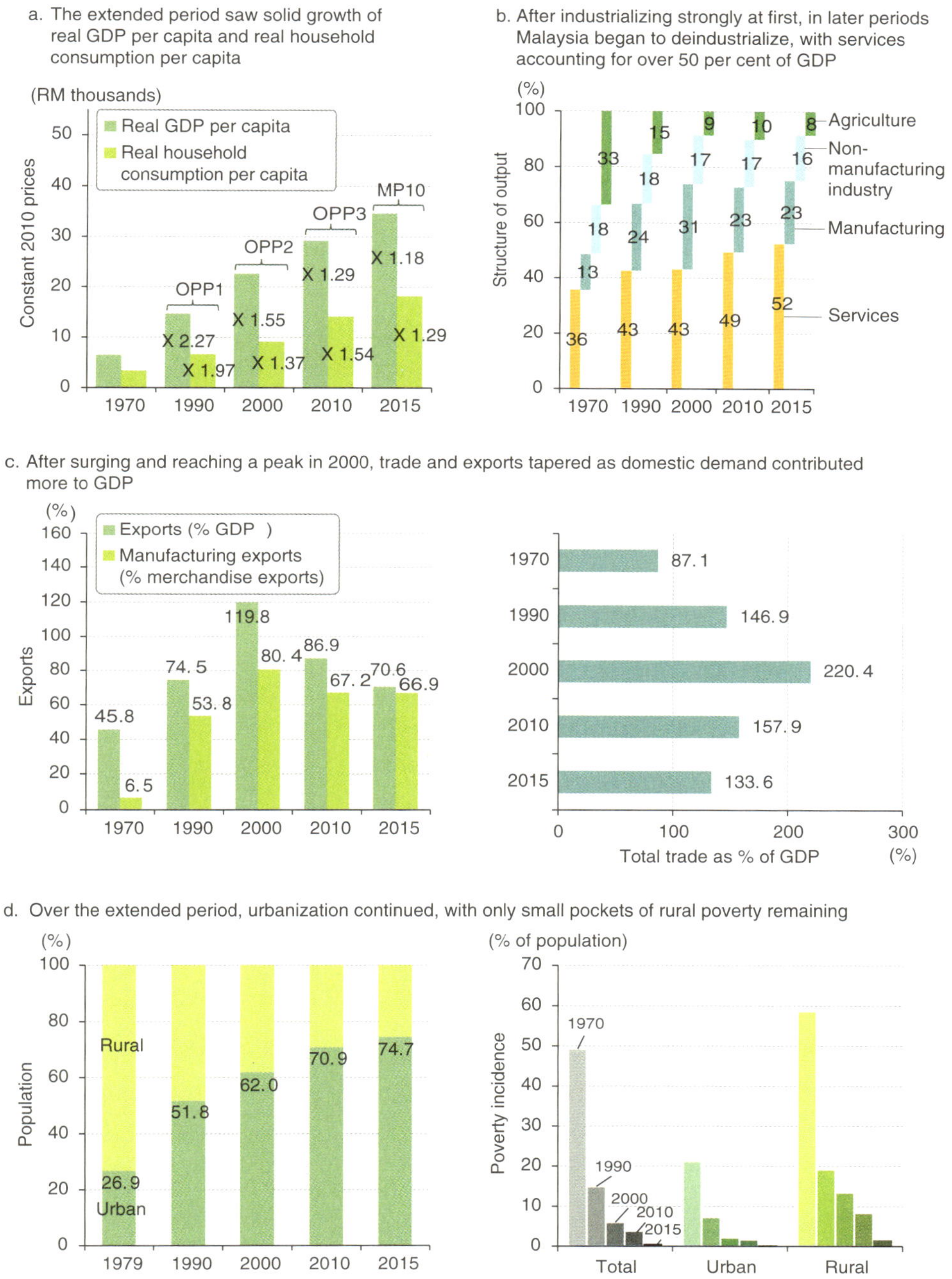

Sources of data: World Bank (2018b); Economic Planning Unit–Malaysia (2018b).

Note: Poverty estimates for 2000 are based on 2002 data; those for 2010 and 2015 relate to data from 2008 and 2014, respectively.

during the OPP3 period. At the end of OPP2, in 2000, the gross domestic savings rate was a remarkably high 46 per cent of GDP. By 2010, this ratio had declined to 39 per cent. While separate data on household saving are unavailable, it seems likely that households may have begun to save a smaller fraction of their disposable income. Although savings rates are affected by transitory factors, including temporary shocks to income (as occurred in 2008–2010), the observed decline in the savings rates continued beyond OPP3, suggesting that the underlying factors at work were structural rather than transitory. Subsidies and other price controls may also have encouraged consumption spending (NEAC, 2010).

The top-right panel in Figure 7.10 shows the evolving structure of output during OPP3. Both MP8 and MP9 were predicated on the continuing industrialization of the economy, but the profile of industry and manufacturing output peaked in 1999 and then began to retreat in the early years of OPP3. Critically, a similar pattern is seen in the share of manufacturing employment in total employment. The GGDC data show that the employment share of manufacturing peaked in 1997 at 24.9 per cent, and then followed a sharp downward trend during the OPP3 period, falling to a trough of 17.5 per cent in 2009 (University of Groningen, GGDC, 2019).

Rodrik (2015) explains how patterns in the structure of output and employment are influenced by the structural demand and supply characteristics of an economy, and by its participation in global trade (in conditions in which there is limited substitution in demand between manufactured goods and services). If labour productivity in manufacturing grows faster than that in services (Chapter 6), the employment share of manufacturing will eventually fall.[27] But differential productivity growth alone cannot explain falling output shares. For this to occur, there has to be a secular demand shift away from manufacturing, or, in the case of a small open economy like Malaysia's—which is a price taker for manufactured goods—a relative decline in the price of manufactured goods.[28]

In comparison with the income levels at which the shares of manufacturing output and employment declined in high-income countries (or in the NIEs), deindustrialization in Malaysia (as indicated by declining shares of industrial output in GDP) would appear to have arrived early. This was not an indication

27 This is true provided that the elasticity of substitution of demand between manufactured goods and services is less than one. If the elasticity of substitution is greater than one, falling manufacturing prices will stimulate demand for manufacturing output, which will offset the impact of productivity gains on employment.

28 When output shares are calculated in nominal terms, as here, an increase in the price of services relative to manufactures will have the effect of increasing the share of services in total output, all other things being equal. This explains part of the shift observed in Malaysia, but real output (and employment) shares were also moving in favour of services.

of the maturity of the country's economy, however. The question of why Malaysia deindustrialized early is a difficult one to answer.

To the extent that industrialization had been propelled by FDI, lower levels of FDI during OPP3 are a proximate cause of declining manufacturing shares in output and employment. Declining real prices for manufactured goods in global markets, and the emergence of lower-cost production platforms elsewhere, may have placed Malaysia at a growing competitive disadvantage, with manufacturing output prices falling faster than Malaysia could improve its productivity.[29] The rise of China as a low-cost supplier of many manufactured goods to the global economy may have been a contributory factor in muted FDI, but Malaysia's exports of manufactured components to China also grew during this period. These trends raise the question of why Malaysia was largely unable to move up the global value-added supply chain. Had this occurred, specialization in higher-productivity manufacturing activities could have allowed the manufacturing output share to continue to grow. But as many advanced countries have experienced, rapid labour productivity advances alone may not be enough to reverse a declining manufacturing employment share.

Malaysia's deindustrialization during OPP3, as indicated by lower levels of FDI, was at odds with the general trend among its ASEAN peers (excluding Singapore), particularly that of the ASEAN manufacturing hubs—Thailand, Viet Nam, and Indonesia. In fact, throughout the first part of OPP2, Malaysia had been ahead of the pack, and was attracting higher FDI than these other ASEAN economies. Its stock of FDI as a percentage of GDP far surpassed that of most ASEAN countries (excluding Singapore) between 1998 and 2000. The tide turned, however, with the Asian financial crisis, which saw FDI favouring Thailand over Malaysia. This was especially apparent over the period 1998–2002, when FDI (measured in US dollars) in Thailand rose to a high in 1998, fluctuated, then rebounded in 2001, while FDI in Malaysia fell in 1998 and kept falling to a low in 2001.

For all the years of OPP3, FDI in Thailand exceeded that in Malaysia, and its cumulative FDI was 1.5 times Malaysia's during the ten-year period compared with 0.7 times in the preceding decade. Between 1998 and 2002, FDI in Thailand was 1.8 times that in Malaysia compared with 0.5 times in the preceding five years. It would seem that, following the Asian financial crisis, Thailand had a comparative advantage in certain sectors. By the close of OPP3 in 2010, Thailand's stock of FDI to GDP had reached parity with Malaysia's compared with 24.7 per cent against Malaysia's 54.1 per cent in 2000.

29 Data from the World Bank Enterprise Survey (2016) show declining labour productivity in export manufacturing, where productivity is measured as sales revenue per worker, confirming the likelihood of falling prices. The same report also show rising labour productivity, but declining employment in the sector.

Already in the early 1990s, Malaysia had launched an Action Plan for Industrial Technology Development. Organizations and mechanisms were created to support leading-edge industries, including through the creation of science and technology parks. Although these initiatives were modelled on the successful experiences of the Republic of Korea, Singapore, and Taiwan, Perkins et al. (2017) note that their effectiveness in Malaysia was blunted by political considerations, especially the appointment of unqualified and inexperienced managers. The upshot was that the vision, discipline, and operational conditions required for success were missing. The same authors conclude that subsequent initiatives by the government to encourage investments in R&D appear to have met with equally disappointing results for technological upgrading. Only a handful of Malaysian firms, such as United Engineers Malaysia and Petronas, have been able to expand their international operations. Other successful businesses which started as Malaysia-domiciled companies, such as the Kerry Group, have since moved their headquarters elsewhere (Perkins et al., 2017).

The Tenth Malaysia Plan, 2011–2015[30]

The 'Growth Report' (World Bank, 2008) lauded Malaysia as one of only 13 nations globally that had managed to sustain an average growth rate of 7 per cent or more over a 25-year period since 1950. Viewed through this lens, Malaysia's economic development has undoubtedly been a success. By the close of OPP3 in 2010, Malaysia was a highly urbanized nation with modern physical and social infrastructure, a large industrial base, and with the vast bulk of its population free of poverty (Figure 7.10).

But despite these considerable achievements, doubts were growing as to whether Malaysia could, by 2020, attain the high-income status that successive plans had targeted. Several worrying trends had emerged: premature deindustrialization; a brain drain; lagging productivity; low investment rates; and persistent fiscal deficits and rising public debt. 'Pervasive corruption' (NEAC, 2010, p. 7) and the state's conflicting functions as regulator, business owner, and business operator, meanwhile, were among the issues hobbling private enterprise.

Concerned that Malaysia's vision was in jeopardy, in 2009 the prime minister convened the NEAC as an independent body to formulate a New Economic Model for the country. The NEAC's evidence-based diagnostics and

30 This period also saw the launching of the Second Financial Masterplan, 2011–2020, which included aims to strengthen financial sector linkages and intra-regional integration.

broad stakeholder consultations were crystallized into eight key strategic initiatives, with a recommendation for a 'big push' on reforms to tackle interlocking constraints. Removing barriers and distortions that discouraged competitive market behaviour, whether in the labour market or at the business and government levels, was an imperative throughout these initiatives. The expectation was that the NEAC's recommendations would provide inputs to the MP10 planning process, which was by this time under way.

Targets and Policies in MP10

MP10 (2011–2015) retained the primacy given to economic growth in OPP3, but in a departure from previous plans, it construed distributional goals in terms of equality of opportunity for all Malaysians rather than just through ethnicity-based outcomes. MP10 was framed around ten 'big ideas' embracing economic, social, and environmental dimensions, of which the following six referred specifically to economic action areas:[31]

- *Internally driven, externally aware*—essentially, this entailed promoting competitiveness and efficiency;
- *Leveraging on diversity internationally*—deepening regional integration and connectivity;
- *Unleashing productivity-led growth and innovation*—investing in skills and R&D, and attracting high-quality FDI;
- *Nurturing and retaining top talent*—including encouraging the return of the diaspora;
- *Concentrated growth, inclusive development*—investing in clusters, economic corridors, cities, and public transport systems;
- *Supporting effective and smart partnerships*—seeing government as a facilitator and enabler of private sector development and as a collaborator with private sector partners in the delivery of public services.

MP10 set out a large array of policies, programmes, and projects aimed at addressing the critical challenges involved in promoting a more efficient and innovative private-sector-driven economy. For example, it outlined commitments on liberalizing the service sector within the framework of World Trade Organization obligations and ASEAN agreements; it identified initiatives to provide improved financial and non-financial services to SMEs, promising greater deregulation to reduce the time and monetary costs of starting and operating a business; and it committed to 'rationalizing' the role

31 The remaining 'big ideas' included the need to properly value Malaysia's precious environmental endowments; to foster responsive and efficient government (government as a 'competitive corporation'); to transform to a high-income economy; and to ensure equality of opportunity.

of GLCs in the economy by gradually divesting non-core and non-competitive assets, and introducing new competition legislation to create a level playing field between GLCs and other actors.

Recognizing the limits of input-driven growth and observing that productivity growth had fallen short of ambitions, MP10 echoed earlier plans in presenting the strategic theme of boosting productivity levels to sustain economic growth. It set out a multipronged approach to improving productivity, entailing investments in education, skills development, and talent retention; critical infrastructure (for example, expanded broadband connectivity, and upgraded utilities and industrial parks); innovation capabilities (R&D support in 11 'national key economic areas'); and economic efficiency (the use of market-based incentives rather than subsidies).

Because economic growth during MP9 had fallen short of its target, MP10 aimed for accelerated growth to enable Malaysia to achieve high-income status by 2020. It programmed a growth rate for real GDP of 6 per cent, with services at 7.2 per cent, manufacturing at 5.7 per cent, and agriculture at 3.3 per cent. As in earlier plans, the expectation was that advances in TFP would generate more than one-third of this growth (38 per cent). MP10 assigned a major role to the private sector as the catalyst for the desired economic transformations, and envisaged growth of 12.8 per cent for real private sector investment, with FDI as a major component.

Finally, having injected substantial fiscal resources into the economy to shield it from the downdraft of the global financial crisis, MP10 recognized the need for fiscal consolidation and set modest targets for growth of real public consumption and investment of 4.8 per cent and 5 per cent respectively. It also emphasized the importance of continued efforts to improve public sector efficiency through leveraging the Government Transformation Programme, as well as public–private initiatives to support funding for major planned investments, such as toll roads and university branch campuses.

Outcomes for MP10

After the global financial crisis, GDP growth resumed quickly during the MP10 period. Although falling short of the plan target of 6 per cent, it averaged a solid 5.1 per cent during 2011–2015, while GNI per capita expanded at an average rate of 3.4 per cent (Figure 7.11). Expansion of domestic demand led the way, with vigorous growth of both investment and consumption. Over the plan period, gross fixed capital formation rose by 7.9 per cent in real terms, with the private sector accounting for the bulk of the expansion. The aggregate investment rate drifted up above 25 per cent of GDP, its highest level in over a decade. Private investment climbed as a share of GDP from 12.3 per cent in 2010 to 17.3 per cent in 2015 (MP11, p. 2–6). Growth of the capital stock accelerated and, from the supply side, accounted for the largest portion of realized growth, contributing an annual average of 3.3 percentage points to headline GDP growth from 2010 to 2015 (PWT9.1).

Figure 7.11 **The MP10 period saw solid growth and some investment recovery**

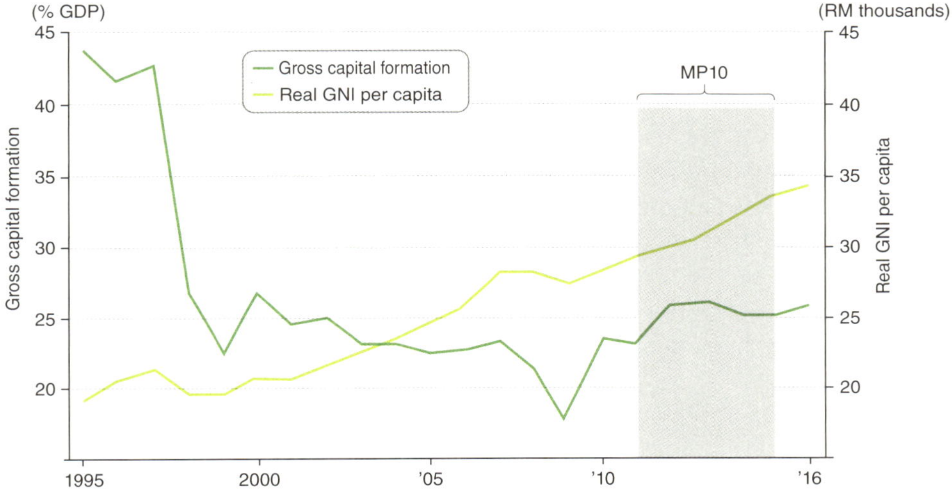

Source of data: World Bank (2018a).

As in OPP3, standards of living improved faster than GNI per capita. During MP10, household consumption per capita expanded at an annual average rate of 5.1 per cent. Again, as in OPP3, accelerated consumption growth was accompanied by a declining trend in the gross domestic savings rate, which by 2015 had fallen to 32.8 per cent of GDP, some 6.5 percentage points lower than it had been at the end of OPP3. To the extent that the lower domestic savings rate was reflected in reduced household saving, it could easily explain the gap between the growth of real income and the growth of household consumption. However, household gross debt also saw a sharp increase during MP10, rising from 76.1 per cent of GDP in 2011 to 89.1 per cent by 2015. On the other side of the household balance sheet, asset growth was even faster, rising by about 15 percentage points of GDP.

Solid growth during MP10 was accompanied by modest consumer price inflation, which averaged 2.4 per cent in 2011–2015. The fiscal consolidation promised by the plan materialized, and the overall federal budget deficit as a percentage of GDP trended downwards from –4.7 per cent in 2011 to –3.2

per cent in 2015. So, too, did the non-oil primary deficit (IMF, 2016). This was despite lower oil prices and declining dividends paid to the government by Petronas in 2015. The introduction of a 6 per cent goods and services tax in 2015 increased revenues.[32] By the end of June 2015, government debt as a share of GDP had slowed, having peaked at 54 per cent (the government-imposed debt ceiling was 55 per cent of GDP). However, the finances of the consolidated public sector[33] saw a widening gap between revenues and outlays as a consequence of the deficits of non-financial public enterprises, whose revenues were hit by adverse commodity price movements and whose outlays remained high due to continued large investment spending. Solid, although declining, merchandise trade surpluses offset persistent external services deficits, supporting a current account surplus in each year of MP10.

During MP10, longer-term trends towards urbanization and the reduction of absolute poverty continued. By 2015, the service sector accounted for more than one-half of GDP. The trend towards a smaller industrial and manufacturing sector, which had taken hold during OPP3, continued. And, in parallel with the shift towards services, the share of exports in GDP continued to decline. In fact, during the MP10 period, exports of goods and services only inched up in volume terms by an annual average rate of 1.8 per cent. In US dollar terms, the annual growth of merchandise exports averaged a mere 0.5 per cent. However, the rationalization of the role of the state in business that MP10 promised appears not to have materialized (Box 7.7).

Box 7.7 Rationalization of government-linked companies

Echoing the recommendations of the NEAC's New Economic Model, MP10 promised to rationalize the role of GLCs in the economy, and to separate more clearly the state's regulatory functions from its operational engagement in business.

In July 2011, the government launched its Economic Transformation Programme. One of its key initiatives was to reduce the government's role in business. As part of this wider initiative, 33 GLCs were identified either for outright sale (21), or listing (7), or a paring down of the government's stake (5). Wan Saiful Wan Jan (2016, p. 4) reports that by end-2015, 32 of the 33 companies had been divested, and that government-linked investment companies (GLICs) had reduced their aggregate shareholdings in 30 of the 33 large GLCs.

32 It was eventually zero-rated in 2018 following the general elections, which brought in a change of government for the first time since independence. A sales and service tax was reinstated.

33 The consolidated public sector includes the accounts of non-financial public enterprises, encompassing 28 major companies as well as many minor companies. Among these are Telekom Malaysia Berhad, Tenaga Nasional Berhad, Petronas, Boustead Holdings Berhad, Malaysia Airlines, and United Engineering Malaysia Holdings Berhad.

However, Wan Saiful Wan Jan (2016, p. 8) also presents data showing that the government had, at the same time, actually increased its holdings in the 30 firms that comprise the Kuala Lumpur Composite Index from 43.7 per cent in 2011 to 47.1 per cent in 2015. Acquisitions by GLCs during the period amounted to RM51.7 billion against disposals of RM29.5 billion. The government's promise to reduce its role in business appears not to have been met. Indeed, the creation of yet another GLC in 2009 under the control of the Ministry of Finance, 1Malaysia Development Berhad (1MDB), happened during the MP10 period.

The challenge of divestment of GLCs and the persistence of patronage have continued to the present, with new forms of government–business networks emerging (Gomez, 2019).

Productivity

Figure 7.12 presents annual estimates of TFP growth calculated from PWT9.1. These are (raw) year-on-year calculations with no smoothing, and are thus more susceptible to transient shocks and events.[34] During MP10, Malaysia had little success in reversing the trend of declining productivity growth that had taken hold over an extended period prior to MP10. In fact, average TFP growth during the MP10 period was lower than it had been during the OPP3 period. Independent estimates of TFP presented by the IMF (2017) corroborate this observation, although exact estimates of TFP growth differ from year to year. Part of the reason for this slowing average productivity growth during MP10 may have been the coincident trend of slowing global productivity growth. However, TFP levels had stagnated in Malaysia well before the global slowdown (Chapter 6).

Drawing on data from its Enterprise Surveys, the World Bank (2016) looks at productivity trends in Malaysian manufacturing, differentiating between firms that export and those that serve the domestic market, and between large and small firms. These firm-level findings suggest that during MP10 the slowing of labour productivity was concentrated mainly in larger firms that exported. The World Bank attributes the slowdown to the more difficult global demand conditions which followed the global financial crisis. As the numerator in the Enterprise Survey measure of labour productivity is sales revenue, and as global manufacturing export prices had been on a declining

34 Chapter 6 describes the data and methodological innovations incorporated in these estimates, and, in examining longer-term trends, presents TFP estimates averaged over successive five-year intervals. Among innovations that would tend to lower the PWT9.1 estimates of TFP is the explicit allowance made for human capital accumulation in the measure of labour inputs. Improved measures of manufactured capital may also account for some of the differences. Estimates of TFP by the EPU, reported in various plans, are consistently higher than those by PWT9.1.

trend, the World Bank's findings also suggest that larger manufacturing firms were having difficulty in moving up the value chain during the MP10 period.

Figure 7.12 **TFP growth showed virtually no improvement during MP10**

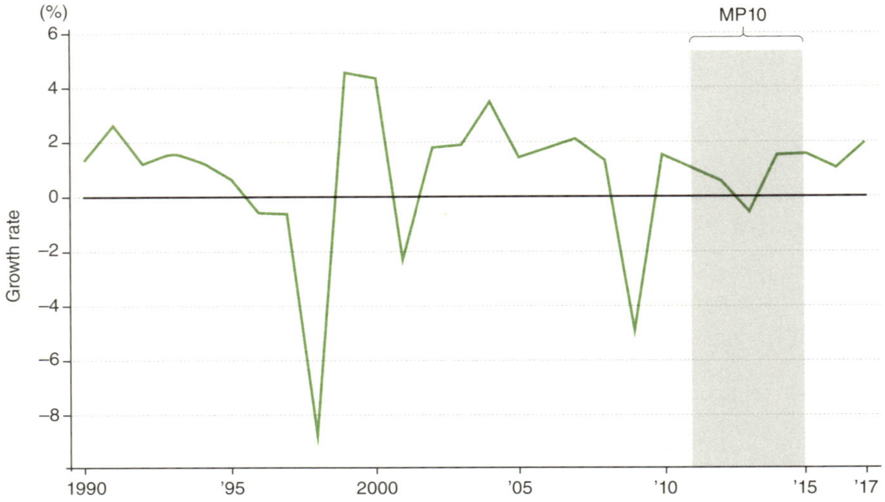

Source of data: PWT 9.1; Feenstra et al. (2015).

More generally, MP10 identified the need to boost productivity in manufacturing, pointing to mechanisms to promote innovation and skills development, and to ease the constraints faced by SMEs. That the World Bank Enterprise Survey data show labour productivity declining between 2010 and 2015 suggests that MP10 efforts did not pay off in quick productivity advances. Using the World Bank's metrics, labour productivity declined by 2.1 per cent between 2010 and 2015 after an increase of 4.6 per cent between 2005 and 2010. The gaps between high- and low-productivity manufacturing firms widened during MP10, highlighting the potential for sizeable output gains if resources could be transferred from the least efficient companies to those firms operating at the efficiency frontier.

Productivity declined in all manufacturing subsectors during MP10, pointing to the existence of some unidentified systemic cause. Labour productivity also declined in resource-based sectors such as petroleum and chemical products. Of note is the performance of small firms as compared with larger ones. Small firms in traditional sectors such as wood, furniture-making, and paper products showed the strongest gains in labour productivity. Firms serving the domestic market experienced smaller declines in labour productivity than exporting firms.

Finally, the Enterprise Survey data suggest that the most productive manufacturing firms in Malaysia faced the largest distortions in output markets, and that if these distortions had been corrected, productivity gains would have followed. Among the causes of these distortions, the World Bank suggests that the preferential treatment of GLCs, weak market regulation, and pervasive subsidies may have shifted the allocation of resources towards less efficient firms.

Export Diversification

Since independence, Malaysia has had considerable success in diversifying its economy. Manufacturing exports, particularly of electrical and electronic goods and of machinery, have played an important part. However, there were indications during OPP3 that manufacturing export performance had begun to weaken.

Figure 7.13 summarizes how Malaysia's export basket has evolved over the period spanning MP7 to MP10. This is the longest period for which data based on the Standard International Trade Classification (SITC) are available.

These data show that the combined share of manufacturing SITC categories in the total merchandise export basket started to decline during OPP3, and that this decline continued through MP10. Notably, more recent data for 2016 and 2017 show a limited reversal of this trend. This retreat is offset by a growing share of natural-resource-based products in the export basket. The combined share of crude materials, minerals and fuels, animal and vegetable oils, and chemicals began to show an upward trend from around 2002–2003. Although opportunities for innovation and productivity gains are usually present across the entire economy, and although oil and gas, palm oil, and agriculture are all designated as national key economic areas (NKEAs) in MP10,[35] primary and primary processing activities are not typically at the cutting edge of technological change and economic transformation.[36]

---

35 Eleven activities were designated as NKEAs in MP10, encompassing primary, secondary, and tertiary activities, as well as one geographical area, Kuala Lumpur. These NKEAs cover much of the country's existing economic activity, and together account for a large portion of its GDP. Notable exclusions were construction, utilities, and public administration.

36 Several service activities are designated as NKEAs, but service exports, measured in US dollar terms, barely grew at all during MP10, posting annual average growth of just 0.1 per cent. A World Bank (2016) study also found that service sector firms in Malaysia were much less productive than their manufacturing counterparts, confirming one concern about the consequences of premature deindustrialization on overall productivity.

Figure 7.13 **Manufactured exports are in retreat**

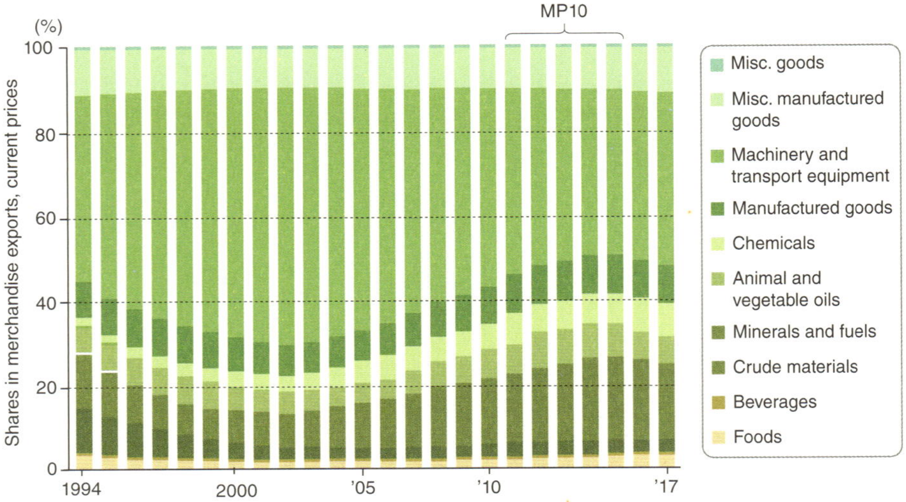

Source of data: Economic Planning Unit–Malaysia (2018c).

Note: The data are expressed in terms of nominal (ringgit) shares of total merchandise exports. The length of the bars measures shares in total merchandise exports, with those coloured in shades of green combining the SITC categories that are considered 'manufacturing'. These cover 'manufactured goods', 'machinery and transport equipment', and 'miscellaneous manufactured goods'.

A nation's ability to export more technologically sophisticated goods provides a strong indication of its potential for economic catch-up and its progress to high-income status. Figure 7.14 shows how Malaysia's manufactured goods export basket is moving in the wrong direction technologically.

Paralleling the declining trend of manufactured goods' export shares, it would appear that the high-technology content of manufacturing exports also drifted down during the OPP3 period. While the share of high-tech exports showed little change during MP10, by 2015 they represented a considerably smaller share of manufactured exports than they had in 2000. The share of high-tech exports in total merchandise exports fell by even more, as the share of manufactured exports in total merchandise exports had also fallen by 2015. The more modest contribution of medium- and high-tech activities to manufacturing value added shown in Figure 7.14 reflects the fact that these firms were more likely to export than other manufacturing entities. Firms that were not exporting would have included many SMEs and local firms that were part of vertically integrated supply chains, and that supported larger assembly operations based in Malaysia.

Figure 7.14 Manufactured exports are becoming less technologically sophisticated

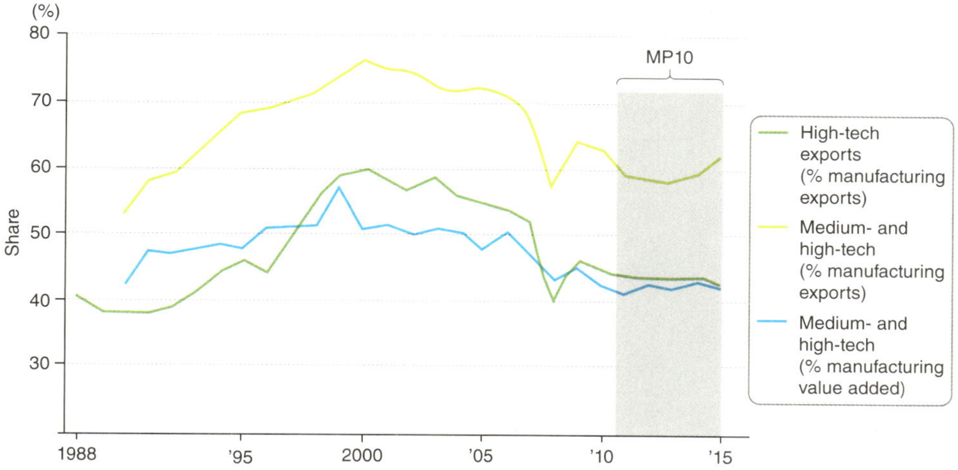

Source of data: World Bank (2018a).

Innovation-led Growth

A key strategic thrust of MP10 was a framework for 'supporting innovation-led growth'.[37] More time will have to pass before the outcome of Malaysia's efforts to foster innovation on multiple fronts and embed knowledge in the domestic economy can be assessed, as there are long gestation lags before such investments and initiatives bear fruit. The benefits of these targeted actions will ultimately depend on the success of the government in developing the connective tissue that holds innovation ecosystems together.

At the heart of an innovative economy are citizens with the relevant skill sets and mindsets that are required for participation in activities that use and create knowledge. The wider society must also be open to new ideas and value talent. And while a country's innovation ecosystem may be geographically and culturally localized, its actors must be connected to global networks and systems in order to thrive. By end-2015, Malaysia still had significant deficits in these areas.

In response to the 'brain drain',[38] a cornerstone of MP10 was the creation in 2011 of TalentCorp to drive Malaysia's talent strategy (Chapter 2). Under

37 A Knowledge Economy Masterplan had been prepared as early as 2002.

38 As of 2015 at the close of MP10, the number of Malaysians living overseas was estimated to be 1.8 million (Stefanidou, 2016) out of a population of around 31.2 million. An earlier World Bank (2011a) study suggested that the working-age diaspora was composed of a substantial proportion of educated and skilled Malaysian citizens, especially ethnic Chinese. The same study also showed a steady fall in the number of skilled and professional expatriates working in Malaysia.

TalentCorp's direction, programmes were set up to attract returning experts, such as the revised Returning Expert Programme, as well as to retain highly qualified expatriates in Malaysia and to encourage increased female participation in the labour force. However, by 2017, the programme to attract returning Malaysians, which offers tax relief and other inducements, had processed fewer than 5,000 successful applications (TalentCorp, 2018), a tiny number relative to the stock of educated and skilled workers who had left Malaysia by this time.

The production and nurturing of talent among young citizens rests on the development of an education system that is responsive to the nation's evolving economic and social needs. Although Malaysia had spent heavily on education, at the close of MP10 this was yet to be reflected in commensurate improvement in outcomes (as measured in TIMSS and PISA scores) in key areas such as science and maths (Chapter 3). At the post-secondary level, affirmative action policies had put inclusiveness and entitlements in conflict with merit and excellence in both the selection of students and the appointment of faculty. The standards of Malaysian universities and their low rankings on research output pointed to the need for strengthened networks to facilitate the development, exchange, and transfer of knowledge (Perkins et al., 2017). Furthermore, a lack of proficiency in the English language among school and university students may have put Malaysia at a disadvantage, particularly in the fields of science and technology where English is the dominant medium of research and communication.[39]

The report card in other areas important for innovation is more positive. By the close of MP10, Malaysia had created the institutional framework to support investment in innovation-intensive economic activities, and had built much of the required infrastructure backbone. Malaysian firms had also been spending more on R&D as a share of GDP than their ASEAN partners. However, Malaysia's spending on R&D is predominantly undertaken by public sector institutions (such as the Malaysian Palm Oil Board and universities), and by GLCs (such as Petronas and Telekom Malaysia), while foreign-based companies invest very little; the country's spending is, moreover, still some way short of that in the NIEs (Figure 7.15). Although there has also been an improvement in the volume of research publications emanating from Malaysian universities, these have yet to translate into a greater number of patent applications, as has occurred in the Republic of Korea and Taiwan (Perkins et al., 2017).

39 However, MP11 (2016–2020) has signalled a change in direction and features goals to ensure that students are proficient in *Bahasa Malaysia* and English, and are also encouraged to learn a third language.

Figure 7.15 **Investments in R&D have risen as a share of GDP, but are still at moderate levels compared with the NIEs and China**

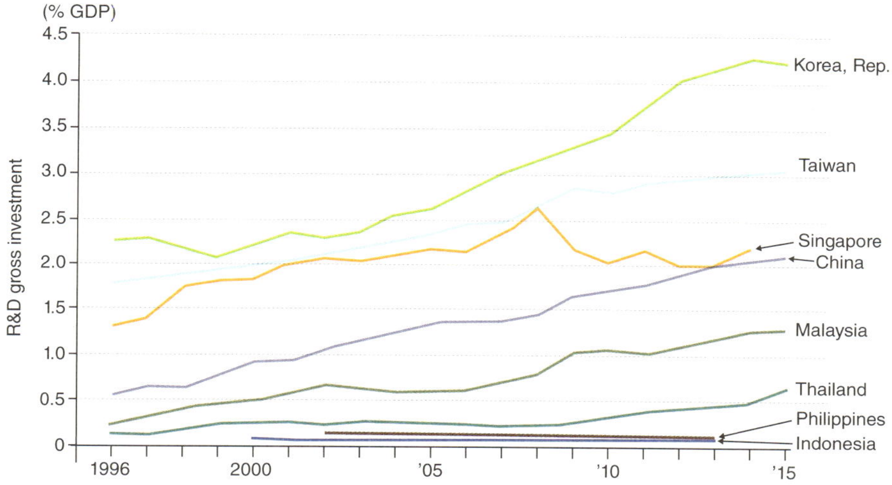

Source of data: World Bank (2018a).

The wider economic environment in which innovation systems evolve is critical. In the absence of an efficient and flexible economy, innovation is unlikely to prosper. Where new enterprises are shut out from markets, or put at a competitive disadvantage, or face the threat of expropriation of their assets, the high-risk investments needed to bring ideas from the laboratory to the market are unlikely to be made.

Building an economy in which innovation is the engine of growth places high demands on government. As MP10 emphasized, public financial support for R&D is critical, and the government must invest in education, infrastructure, and public goods. The government should also share risks with the private sector and support collaboration in strategic areas where markets are unable to respond to opportunities. In all these efforts, success is likely to hinge on the application of principles of sound governance, the presence of relevant competencies, incentives that encourage desired behaviour, and the disciplined application of appropriate performance criteria.

MP11 and the New Directions Set in Its Mid-term Review

By the end of MP10, increasing concerns were being expressed that the quality of education and human capital, as well as lagging productivity and the lack of an innovation culture, could derail efforts to achieve advanced nation status by 2020. MP11 (2016–2020) (EPU, 2018e) was formulated with a focus on accelerating human capital development and productivity, enhancing inclusiveness, and strengthening infrastructure and innovation for more robust economic growth.

Two years into the plan, Malaysia underwent a change of government following the May 2018 general election. In October 2018, the new government issued the Mid-term Review of MP11, which realigned socio-economic policies and strategies for 2018–2020. The balance of emphasis shifted from economic growth to institutional reforms, reflecting the government's aspirations for more sustainable and inclusive growth. Developing human capital and raising productivity, enhancing inclusive and green development, and strengthening growth were maintained as goals, while the push for good governance and the pursuit of more balanced regional development became new priorities. With a renewed emphasis on governance reforms and fiscal consolidation, the target of achieving high-income status was pushed back to 2024.

Another important component of the review was the articulation of strategies to address the challenges and opportunities of the fourth industrial revolution. In an age of the internet of things, 5G, 3D printing, cloud computing, advanced robotics, and artificial intelligence, among other technological advances, the way that businesses design, produce, commercialize, and distribute products and services is changing rapidly on a global scale (ESCAP and ADB, 2018). While Malaysia is classified as one of the top ten economies with the largest ICT to GDP ratio, its adoption of enabling technologies has been slow. The country's manufacturing sector as a whole still straddles Industry 2.0 (mass production) and Industry 3.0 (automation), although the electrical and electronics, aerospace, and automotive sectors are already venturing into Industry 4.0.

The MP11 review introduced the National Industry 4.0 Policy Framework, 2018–2025, and highlighted the broad strategies to be pursued under this framework to accelerate adoption of Industry 4.0–related technologies across sectors. Measures to improve funding, infrastructure, the regulatory environment, and the upskilling of talent were recognized as key enablers. Initiatives to improve the coordination, management, and governance of R&D and commercialization activities were also identified.

Conclusions

The NEP marked a turning point in Malaysia's development, and outcomes in the following decade demonstrated that economic growth with greater equity was possible. There is little doubt that during the first decade of the NEP, the country made remarkable headway in rebalancing its economy and society. The eclectic mix of policies succeeded in stimulating accelerated economic growth, while actively sponsoring fairer ethnic representation in the fruits of economic modernization. The country reaped a dividend from greater agricultural productivity, from the movement of resources out of agriculture into more productive industry and services, and from lower young-age dependency rates.

In the first half of the 1980s, Malaysia's efforts to leapfrog to a highly industrialized economy floundered, creating heavy fiscal burdens. A commodity price collapse in 1985 triggered reforms and redirection. A new emphasis on manufacturing exports met with tremendous success, boosted by attractions bestowed on Malaysia by the Plaza Accord and by a pragmatic approach to the treatment of foreign direct equity investment outside the net of the NEP. The second half of the 1980s also saw the start of a privatization programme and the consolidation of investments in heavy industries.

The first half of the 1990s saw torrid economic growth, propelled by booming investment, rapid credit growth, and receptive global economic conditions. But lax financial regulation, weak corporate governance, market exuberance, and growing inefficiencies left the country vulnerable to risks. In July 1997, these vulnerabilities were exposed following a collapse of confidence in the Thai baht, which triggered the Asian financial crisis. Malaysia navigated its own course out of the crisis, but it took until 2003 for per capita income to regain the level achieved in 1997. Nevertheless, progress on poverty reduction continued, and by the end of the millennium Malaysia had become an urbanized and industrial society.

Despite the bursting of the dot-com bubble in 2001, which dented Malaysia's electronic exports sector, solid growth once again resumed in the 2000s. But Malaysia was slowly losing its edge in export manufacturing activities, and this period saw the onset of premature deindustrialization, with declining shares of employment and output in the industrial sector. Efforts to upgrade the manufacturing and industrial base towards less labour-intensive and higher value-added activities experienced limited success in the face of growing competition from low-cost export platforms elsewhere in Asia and the wider global economy. Policy efforts aimed at creating deeper value through the agro-industry complex also saw mixed results.

The Great Recession of 2008 set Malaysia back. Unlike at the time of the Asian financial crisis, however, Malaysia was by this point far less exposed to risk. Aided by a large fiscal stimulus programme, economic growth quickly resumed in 2009. Still, deeper questions lingered about the ability of the Malaysian economy to navigate difficult transitions and to achieve the high-income status to which it aspires.

The NEAC (2010) observed that Malaysia had reached a defining point in its development at the end of OPP3 and the start of MP10. The rhetoric of MP10 signalled clarity on the challenges facing the economy and on the need for redirection. After the dislocation caused by the global financial crisis in 2008–2009, the economy performed solidly at the macroeconomic level despite weakening commodity prices. At a deeper level, however, little changed. By 2015, the country had yet to make significant progress on the new course it had charted. Over the MP10 period, the main structural and institutional challenges remained entrenched, and the economy was continuing to gravitate towards a situation in which natural resources were increasingly important.

The aspiration for growth to be led by productivity and innovation was hardly realized, and MP10's promise to rationalize the role of the state and its GLCs remains largely unfulfilled. Ultimately, the concentration of ownership and control of businesses in the hands of the state, and the use of these businesses to serve wider political goals, is inimical to the development of a vibrant and innovative economy.

The headway made in addressing this vexed issue will largely shape the nation's longer-term economic prospects, as well as its success in promoting continued growth with equity (Part 4). Although the battle against absolute—if not relative—poverty is all but over, initially as a result of agriculture's key role in the economy, and subsequently as a product of the country's structural transformation (Chapter 8), income inequality remains a continuing concern (Chapter 9).

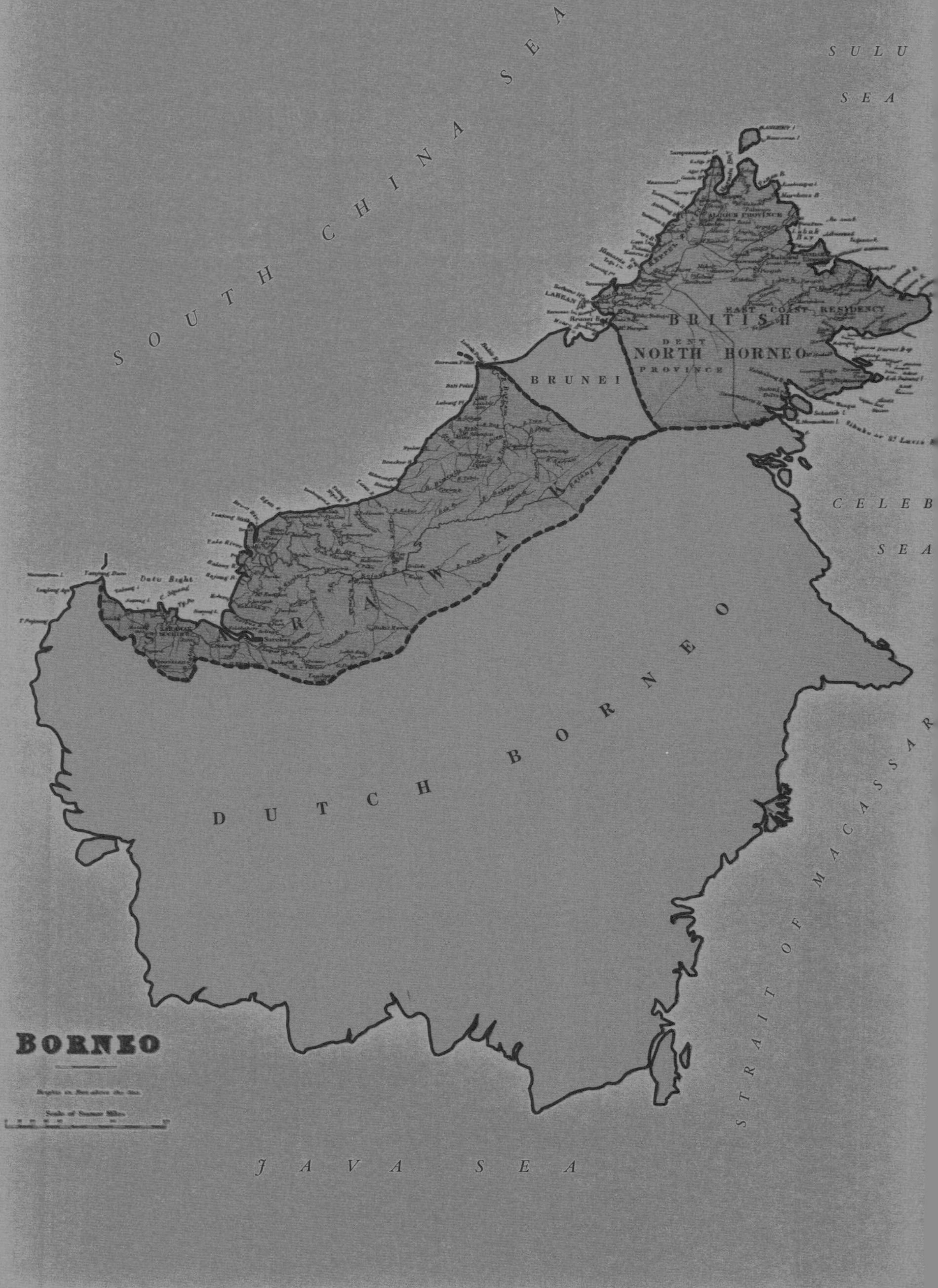
SOUTH CHINA SEA
SULU SEA
CELEB
SEA
BRITISH NORTH BORNEO
EAST COAST RESIDENCY
DENT PROVINCE
BRUNEI
LABUAN
Datu Bight
DUTCH BORNEO
STRAIT OF MACASSAR
JAVA SEA
BORNEO

Adapted from:
Edward Stanford,
Borneo, London, 1885

Courtesy of:
HRH Sultan Sharafuddin Idris Shah
and Dato' Richard Curtis

PART 4

ACHIEVING GROWTH WITH EQUITY

Chapter 8

Agricultural Development and Poverty Reduction

Colonial imbalances in economic and social development perpetuated—even increased—absolute poverty and inequality in Malaya during the first half of the 20th century (Chapter 9). Real wages of the many migrants working on estates and in mines were kept low by the seemingly inexhaustible supply of workers from impoverished, densely populated areas in China, India, and the Dutch East Indies (Chapter 2). Most of those engaged in traditional agriculture were subsistence peasant Malay farmers outside the wage economy, many of whom were indebted and existed on the margins of society.[1] Extreme poverty and the associated problems of inadequate nutrition, susceptibility to infectious diseases, landlessness, and insecurity were widespread, and, in rural areas, endemic. The poor lacked the education and the means to escape the poverty trap.

In the immediate post–World War II period, there were concerted efforts to improve the livelihood of the rural poor, to strengthen rural infrastructure, and to diversify and invigorate the rural economy, for instance through the programmes of the Rural Industrial Development Authority (RIDA) (Chapter 5, Box 5.7), and later, after its establishment in 1956, the Federal Land Development Authority (FELDA).[2] Despite these efforts, at least half of Malaysians were still living below the poverty line in 1970 (Anand, 1983).[3] Poverty was overwhelmingly a rural phenomenon, and was particularly

1 Many of the rural poor were exploited either by their Malay landlords or by Chinese traders, and there was no legal framework to protect them (Ungku Abdul Aziz, 1964 and 1965).

2 During the 1950s and 1960s, high budgetary priority was given by the government to rural economic and social development, especially through the RIDA and FELDA programmes which were brought together under the Ministry of Rural Development headed by Tun Abdul Razak—who also served as the country's first deputy prime minister.

3 Anand cites a poverty rate of 49.3 per cent, based on a poverty line of RM33, in connection with Peninsular Malaysia. Given that development was lagging in Sabah and Sarawak, the Malaysian figure is likely to have been higher. Among the ethnic groups in the peninsula, the poverty rates were 64.8 per cent for Malays, 39.2 per cent for Indians, and 26 per cent for Chinese in 1970 (Anand, 1983, p. 139).

acute in the northern and east coast states of Kedah, Perlis, Kelantan, and Terengganu, which had benefited little from the strong economic growth elsewhere in the peninsula.

Among the poorest population groups were those working as *padi* farmers, farm labourers, rubber smallholders and estate workers, and fishermen, most of whom were Malays. In addition, Chinese residents of the New Villages numbering around 1 million, the bulk of the indigenous communities living in Sabah and Sarawak, as well as the *Orang Asli* were also living in absolute poverty—that is, with insufficient income to meet minimum nutritional needs and to purchase the essential non-food items required to sustain a decent standard of living (EPU, 1976). Widespread poverty and inequality, and unbalanced development, eventually contributed to the emergence of ethnic conflicts and to the consequent formulation of the NEP in 1971. A central objective of the NEP was 'to eradicate poverty among all races' and to ensure more balanced development, as well as to encourage urban-sector employment (Chapters 2 and 7).

How did Malaysia's transition from rural agricultural employment to modern urban-sector employment contribute to poverty reduction? The question is easier to pose than to answer. Rising agricultural productivity creates a food surplus that can feed a growing urban population. Productivity in urban-based industries is generally higher than in agriculture, and the attractive wages offered in these industries will encourage workers to migrate from rural areas. Overall, poverty is reduced through both mechanisms: migrating workers will enjoy higher incomes in the modern urban sector, while the incomes of those who remain in rural employment will benefit from rising agricultural productivity. These two-way linkages between agricultural productivity and poverty reduction constitute an important but poorly understood aspect of long-run economic development. They operate, moreover, within the framework of the structural transformation of the economy, which historically has been a sustainable pathway out of poverty for both rural and urban households.

Agricultural productivity in Malaysia is often analysed from a 'dualistic' perspective: large-scale, efficient estate agriculture producing mainly rubber and palm oil versus smallholder, often impoverished, farm households operating especially in the *padi* sector, but also engaged on the margins of the rubber and oil palm estates. This chapter expands on this approach to analyse the role of agriculture in the country's structural transformation and rapid escape from absolute poverty from a multi-commodity (rice, rubber, and palm oil) perspective. However, it does not focus in any depth on the historical development of individual commodities,[4] and touches only briefly on the policy and institutional drivers that stimulated the changes in agricultural productivity, and on the programmes that aimed directly to reduce poverty.

This chapter has four sections. The first begins by briefly reviewing the colonial context of agriculture up to independence. The second describes the process of structural transformation away from traditional peasant agriculture to modern agriculture, using a set of macroeconomic variables. The third presents a state-level analysis of the linkages between Malaysia's agricultural development and poverty reduction from 1970 up to, in general, 2015. It also assesses trends in the three most important agricultural commodities—rice, rubber, and palm oil—as a basis for understanding the transformation within the agricultural sector.

The final section analyses the linkages between agricultural growth and poverty reduction, using econometric analysis that entails a sequence of increasingly complex steps. For each of Malaysia's 13 states, key time series variables—GDP per capita, poverty rates, the share of agriculture in GDP, the share of the agricultural labour force in total employment, and the main agricultural commodities produced—are analysed. This section aims to answer the following two questions: does agricultural productivity have a significant impact on state-level poverty reduction? And are some commodities more 'pro-poor' than others? From the analysis, conclusions can be drawn about the role of agriculture in raising welfare levels.

Historical Context: The Horns of a Dilemma[5]

Tin had brought the British Empire to the Malay peninsula in the late 19th century. Despite the obvious importance of keeping tin operations profitable, British colonial administrators—with their need for labour, capital, and skilled management expertise, and encouraged by capitalist entrepreneurs in the Straits Settlements—were also contemplating the vast agricultural potential of what they saw as a largely empty but verdant tropical rainforest on the peninsula. When tin prices faltered at the turn of the century and the growing automobile industry massively increased the demand for rubber, the

4 A summary of all of Malaysia's agricultural commodity systems as they developed in the 50 years after independence is contained in the two-volume study by Fatimah Mohamed Arshad et al. (2007). There are important studies on the rice sector by Goldman (1975), Taylor (1981), and Davidson (2018). A useful comparative study of palm oil production can be found in Byerlee et al. (2017), and of the rubber industry in Barlow (1978).

5 This title is taken from the heading to Chapter 6 of Lim's classic analysis of colonial influence on Malaya's agricultural development (Lim, 1977). His volume provides the standard perspective on the dilemmas faced by a newly independent Malaysian government as it grappled with the colonial legacy of export-oriented agriculture, while trying to meet insistent domestic demands from an expectant population.

opportunity to capitalize on this agricultural potential was taken. By 1912, the value of rubber exports had overtaken tin, previously Malaya's leading export, and by 1915 rubber exports were nearly double the value of tin (Chapter 5). In North Borneo and Sarawak, rubber had also become the main cash crop by the beginning of the 20th century.

Supporting the tin industry had presented colonial administrators with a trade-off. Workers were needed for mining operations and ancillary activities, and some of these came from the Malay population that was otherwise engaged in subsistence rice production, which generated occasional surpluses that found their way to the market. At the same time, the migrant workers entering the peninsula in increasing numbers (Chapter 2) needed to be fed and most of them regarded rice as their staple food. Thus, rice demand was increasing, while local production was either stagnant or decreasing. But resources devoted to increasing domestic rice production came at a high opportunity cost of forgone investments in supporting the tin industry. Colonial administrators were well aware of this problem, with rising rice imports from Burma, Thailand, and Cochin China filling the gap between increasing rice demand and lagging domestic rice supplies. As Lim (1977) writes of this dependence on foreign rice imports:

> As the war in Europe dragged on, there appears to have been an increased consciousness of the dangers in the country's dependence on imported food. Such an awareness was long overdue. Between 1911 and 1916, the Federated Malay States imported an average of 190,000 tons of rice annually, or approximately 82 percent of annual rice consumption, a figure of such magnitude that it was obvious there would be serious consequences should there be any breakdown in the import supplies. (Lim, 1977, p. 120)

The development of the rubber industry sharpened the trade-off, as rubber plantations required good agricultural land and access to roads and communications. Many smallholder farmers who might otherwise have been growing *padi* found lucrative wage employment on rubber plantations, and very quickly learned that growing rubber on the fringes of the commercial estates was a profitable sideline to growing *padi* and other subsistence crops. Colonial administrators were trapped. They could continue to support the rubber plantations but face large and often expensive rice imports (as well as unchanging standards of living for the Malay population); or they could devote substantial resources, at high opportunity cost, to raising rice yields among traditional cultivators. This trade-off was not resolved until after independence, and even now dominates debates on agricultural policy.

Subsistence agriculture, which had been the basis of the Malay economy, was overshadowed by mining, plantation, and other commercial activities associated with a developing colonial-type capitalist economy (Lim, 1977). In the traditional Malay economy, labour was self-employed, unspecialized, and directed at satisfying the basic wants of the peasant household. In the colonial economy, labour took a different form, consisting of wage workers, many of whom were migrant labourers working for money wages. Living standards in the traditional economy were poor and were only marginally better for most workers in the colonial economy. Poverty remained pervasive. This was also the situation in North Borneo and Sarawak.

The form of capital in this colonial economy was also different, consisting of roads, railways, machinery, and other products of new technology. Monetization of the economy stimulated development. Land had traditionally been used in small amounts by groups of peasants, but now it was rapidly being taken and opened up for large-scale mineral and agricultural exploitation. New centres of settlement emerged and old ones were revitalized, leading to new settlement patterns vastly different from those encouraged by traditional subsistence agriculture.

These two forms of economic structure—the traditional and the colonial capitalist—remained much the same throughout the colonial period. It was only after independence that a gradual convergence began.

Structural Transformation

The structural transformation of poor agrarian economies into rich industrial- and service-based ones centred on predominantly urban areas has been a subject of great historical interest (Clark, 1940; Chenery and Taylor, 1968; Lin and Monga, 2018). This transformation is arguably the only sustainable pathway out of poverty for poor societies (Timmer and Akkus, 2008). Baumol (1967) argues that structural imbalances in labour productivity can only be solved by movements of labour from low- to high-productivity employment, which in the early stages of development means workers moving from agriculture to industry and from rural to urban jobs. Average labour productivity for the whole economy increases in the process—the Baumol 'structural bonus' (Chapter 6, Box 6.4).

The standard approach to understanding this transformation has been some variant of the 'dual-sector' development model associated with Arthur Lewis (1954). Surplus labour from agricultural households migrates to more productive employment in the industrial sector in cities, generating economic growth. The need for productivity growth in the agricultural sector is also sometimes stressed as a means of feeding workers in the cities while keeping labour productivity in agriculture from falling too far behind that in industry (Lewis, 1954; Johnston and Mellor, 1961; C.P. Timmer, 1988; M.P. Timmer et al., 2015). But the literature has paid very little attention to the *details* of these changes in agricultural productivity (Chenery and Syrquin, 1975;

Johnston and Kilby, 1975), because gains in agricultural productivity tend to be commodity-specific. Investments in agricultural research, in programmes to intensify agriculture and deliver higher yields, and in agricultural price policies to support farm incomes, all require a focus on specific commodities.

Structural transformation is usually depicted as the result of four interacting forces:

- Declining share of agriculture in a country's aggregate GDP;
- Declining share of the national labour force employed in agriculture;
- Movement of surplus agricultural labour to urban jobs in industry or modern services, leading to rapid growth of these sectors; and
- Demographic transition that accompanies these sectoral changes, with death rates falling faster than birth rates resulting in a period of rapid population growth (Chapters 4 and 6).

This structural transformation is remarkably uniform: poor countries have relatively large rural economies; rich countries have relatively small agricultural sectors. Yet, within agriculture the process entails great diversity. The question here is whether that diversity—specifically, the commodity composition of agricultural output—is potentially a source of faster structural transformation, or, is, conversely, an impediment.

Because structural transformation has proven to be a sustainable pathway out of poverty, and because raising labour productivity in agriculture has been an essential component of that pathway, knowing more about the nature of the links between the commodity composition of agricultural output and the resulting impact on poverty rates is key to understanding the long-run dynamics of poverty reduction. For example, are some commodities more 'pro-poor' than others? And is there a connection between commodity production and poverty reduction? The Malaysian historical record provides a fertile field for addressing these issues.

Although this is primarily an empirical account focused on Malaysia, some straightforward analytics can be employed. Changes to two variables drive structural transformation: the share of agriculture in GDP (measured in constant prices), defined as AgGDPshr; and the equivalent share of the agricultural labour force in total employment, defined as AgEMPshr. The difference between these two shares measures the gap in labour productivity between the agricultural and non-agricultural sectors—AgGAPshr.[6] AgEMPshr is nearly always larger than AgGDPshr, and thus labour productivity within agriculture is lower than that outside agriculture. At the margin, moving a worker from agricultural employment to industrial or modern service employment will be a source of economic growth: economy-wide output per worker will rise.

6 As defined, AgGAPshr is also the negative of the Gini coefficient measuring inequality in incomes (proxied by labour productivity) between the two sectors. For a proof and discussion of the intuition behind this relationship, see Timmer and Akkus (2008).

Consider, however, that labour productivity in agriculture has two components: the physical yield of commodities on the land at the disposal of the farm household (AgYield); and the unit value of that output in home consumption or on the market (AgPrice). For simplicity, assume that AgGDP = AgYield * AgPrice. AgGDP thus depends on productivity (yields) and output prices.[7] This then explains why commodity composition is so important, because both AgYield and AgPrice are commodity-specific. These commodity totals can be aggregated into an overall output term—AgGDP—but the real action is at the commodity level.

Agricultural labour productivity and farm incomes can be raised by policies affecting output prices as well as by investments that raise the physical yields of crops and livestock. Innovation in the agricultural sector which results in an increase in output leads to a rise in labour and capital productivity. For example, following research, manual pollination of oil palm was replaced in the 1980s by the use of the weevil beetle. Another area of innovation is the expansion and growing sophistication of downstream activities. This is illustrated by the creation of a wide range of oleochemicals, biodiesel, and a variety of food and non-food products in the oil palm industry. The number of palm oil refineries also increased from just 15 in 1976 to around 50 by 2000.

In the following discussion, the price and quantity dimensions of agricultural labour productivity (and incomes) are kept analytically separate, although it is recognized that market equilibrium and disequilibrium adjustments will entail co-determination of prices and quantities that will condition the extent to which these can be made independent variables. Large subsidies—of which Malaysia has extensive experience—are often needed to keep them separate.

It is possible to assemble a rough measure of all three structural transformation variables—AgGDPshr, AgEMPshr, and AgGAPshr—for relatively long historical periods for Malaysia by decade, and these can be compared with equivalent measures for Indonesia and Japan from 1880 to 2010 (Figure 8.1 and Box 8.1).

The similarity of Malaysia's structural transformation path to those of Japan and Indonesia is striking, yet so are the differences in development outcomes between the three countries.[8] It is the *nature* of the agricultural transformation that helped to drive each country's structural transformation—

7 The value of the produce is equal to the quantity of output produced multiplied by its market price per unit.

8 The sharp difference in the path of AgGAPshr for Indonesia compared with the very similar paths of Malaysia and Japan stems from the importance of petroleum exports from Indonesia after the 1880s. Indonesia has only recently become a net oil importer. Petroleum exports add significantly to GDP but have very little direct impact on employment. Thus, Indonesia's AgEMPshr is similar to that in the other two countries, but its AgGDPshr is much lower, implying that AgGAPshr is larger (in absolute terms).

and that was simultaneously driven by it—that helps to explain both the commonalities and the sharp differences in economic performance over more than a century.

Figure 8.1 **Malaysia, Indonesia, and Japan showed similar patterns of agricultural transformation over 1880–2010**

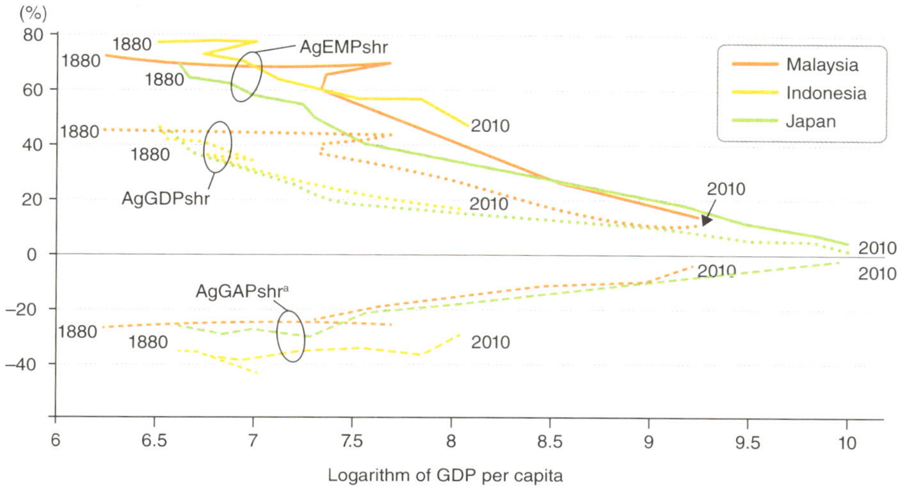

Source of data: Timmer (2017).

Note: [a] Positive values of AgGAPshr (AgGDPshr – AgEMPshr) denote higher labour productivity in agriculture relative to non-agricultural sectors.

Box 8.1 Measuring structural transformation in Malaysia, Indonesia, and Japan

Box Table 8.1 presents a summary of the basic aggregate data used in Figure 8.1 for measuring structural transformation. Three of the four variables are:

- AgGDPshr—percentage share of agricultural GDP in total GDP;
- AgEMPshr—percentage share of agricultural employment in total employment;
- AgGAPshr—percentage share of agricultural GDP in total GDP minus the percentage share of agricultural employment in total employment (AgGDPshr – AgEMPshr).

Values for the third variable are typically negative because the share of the labour force working in agriculture is nearly always larger than the contribution of those workers to GDP.

Closing this gap in labour productivity between agriculture and manufacturing is one of the main drivers of economic growth (Lewis, 1954). However, in many countries the gap has tended to widen in the early stages of rapid economic growth because gains in labour productivity in manufacturing tend to outpace those on farms. Only better-integrated labour markets and significant movements of surplus labour from rural to urban areas have narrowed this gap.

The fourth variable is the logarithm of per capita GDP for each decade—lnGDPpc. The data for this variable draw heavily on the Maddison project database (University of Groningen, 2018) and Sultan Nazrin Shah (2017).

The income data from the Maddison project database are real GDP per capita expressed in 2011 US$ (Bolt et al., 2018). The Malaysian data for 1900–1939 use the series developed by the author, and for 1950–2016 are taken from the Maddison project, but both are re-scaled to the Maddison benchmarks. In principle, the income data should be comparable among countries and over time. In fact, there is much guesswork in the data before 1920 for all three countries, although the margin of error is significantly wider for Malaya and Indonesia. The data for 1880 are estimates.

Box Table 8.1 Historical data on agricultural transformation for Malaysia, Indonesia, and Japan

		1880	1900	1920	1950	1970	1990	2000	2010
Malaysia	AgGDPshr	44	44	44	40	32.6	15.2	8.6	10.1
	AgEMPshr	72	70	68	65	52.0	26.0	18.4	13.3
	AgGAPshr	−28	−26	−24	−25	−19.4	−10.9	−9.8	−3.2
	lnGDPpc	6.635	6.742	7.573	7.782	8.117	9.076	9.538	9.823
Indonesia	AgGDPshr	44.1	41.4	36.7	35.5	27.8	18.5	15.6	13.2
	AgEMPshr	76.3	76.4	76.8	72.2	64.7	55.9	45.3	38.3
	AgGAPshr	−32.2	−35.5	−40.1	−36.7	−36.9	−37.4	−29.7	−25.1
	lnGDPpc	6.890	6.981	7.176	7.070	7.213	8.065	8.152	8.906
Japan	AgGDPshr	41.4	31.6	23.9	17.8	7.7	3.5	2.3	1.2
	AgEMPshr	68.9	61.0	54.1	39.4	17.3	7.2	5.1	3.7
	AgGAPshr	−27.5	−29.4	−30.2	−21.6	−9.6	−3.7	−2.8	−2.5
	lnGDPpc	6.705	7.362	7.725	7.837	9.465	10.179	10.413	10.477

Sources of data: Sultan Nazrin Shah (2017); University of Groningen (2018).

State-level Agricultural Development and Poverty Reduction, 1970–2015

Poverty and Economic Data

Tables 8.1, 8.2, and 8.3 show poverty rates and key economic and agricultural variables for each of the 13 Malaysian states.[9] To simplify the results, most data are shown at ten-year intervals only, but for the econometric analysis employed later, annual data spanning 46 years are used.

9 To produce a balanced data set for panel estimation of econometric models, missing data for each variable were filled in using exponential interpolation. The interpolated values are shown in *italics* so as to distinguish 'actual' from 'estimated' values. Virtually all the econometric results discussed below were first obtained using only actual data, and were then re-estimated with the full balanced data set. The results were generally very similar.

Table 8.1 **Poverty rates and GDP per capita still differ markedly among states, despite substantial progress**

State	1970	1980	1990	2000	2010	2015
	Poverty rate (%)					
Johor	45.7	*16.8*	*8.1*	*2.9*	*1.2*	*0.0*
Kedah	*63.2*	*49.8*	*26.7*	*12.5*	*3.6*	*0.2*
Kelantan	76.1	*51.4*	*29.6*	*22.4*	*4.0*	*0.6*
Melaka	44.9	*19.4*	*10.9*	*2.5*	*0.3*	*0.0*
Negeri Sembilan	*44.8*	*22.8*	*8.8*	*3.5*	*0.6*	*0.3*
Pahang	43.2	*24.2*	*8.8*	*9.7*	*1.8*	*0.4*
Penang	43.7	*18.2*	*6.7*	*0.8*	*1.0*	*0.2*
Perak	48.6	*28.1*	*15.6*	*6.6*	*2.6*	*0.4*
Perlis	73.9	*55.7*	*18.2*	*11.8*	*4.1*	*0.1*
Selangor	29.2	*13.1*	*6.3*	*1.6*	*0.6*	*0.1*
Terengganu	68.9	*47.0*	*29.3*	*19.7*	*3.0*	*0.5*
Sabah	*58.3*[a]	*39.1*	*29.1*	*20.6*	*14.2*	*3.3*
Sarawak	*56.5*[a]	*44.1*	*20.4*	*11.0*	*4.1*	*0.7*
Malaysia	49.3[b]	*34.1*	*15.1*	*7.7*	*3.1*	*0.5*
	Real GDP per capita (RM)					
Johor	901	2,914	4,008	8,480	22,035	27,391
Kedah	751	2,103	2,597	5,435	14,034	17,175
Kelantan	466	1,493	1,706	3,718	9,806	11,200
Melaka	798	2,296	3,669	9,508	29,367	35,672
Negeri Sembilan	979	3,435	3,709	7,824	29,363	34,458
Pahang	978	3,183	3,626	6,367	23,884	28,547
Penang	983	3,639	5,176	12,992	33,597	41,119
Perak	980	2,861	3,476	8,201	18,206	23,529
Perlis	n/a	2,266	2,909	6,561	17,409	19,787
Selangor	1,613	4,602	6,242	10,673	32,300	38,855
Terengganu	595	3,714	6,973	14,121	21,574	23,895
Sabah	1,103	3,066	3,720	5,741	17,830	18,940
Sarawak	829	2,292	3,881	7,880	35,033	39,351
Malaysia	1,087	3,207	4,389	8,962	28,733	36,640

Sources of data: Department of Statistics–Malaysia (various years); Economic Planning Unit–Malaysia (various years).

Notes:

GDP per capita (RM) for 1970 are in 1970 prices; for 1980 and 1990 are in 1978 prices; for 2000 are in 1987 prices; and for 2010 and 2015 are in 2010 prices.

[a] 1976.

[b] Data are for Peninsular Malaysia.

Figures in italics are interpolated from the nearest years to which they relate: see footnote 9.

A dramatic reduction in absolute poverty levels is revealed. Overall, Malaysia's poverty rate fell from 49.3 per cent in 1970 to just 7.7 per cent in 2000, and to less than 0.5 per cent in 2015 (Table 8.1). In 1970, absolute poverty rates were high in all states (Map 8.1).[10] In six of the 13 states—four of the former Unfederated Malay States, plus Sabah and Sarawak—more than half the population was still living in poverty in 1970. FELDA (Box 8.2) and other rural development programmes introduced during the late colonial period and in the decade after independence had not yet had a significant impact. However, in successive decades poverty rates began to decline appreciably in all states, such that by 2015, in 12 of the 13 states, less than 1 per cent of the population was living in poverty. Only in Sabah was the figure higher than this, at 3.3 per cent; this state is also characterized by a high level of income inequality (Chapter 9).

10 In population terms, 12 of Malaysia's 13 states more than doubled in size between 1970 and 2015, although growth rates differed; Sabah's population, for example, grew five-fold. Only in Perak did the population size less than double; this state had the slowest growth of just 0.9 per cent a year. Differential population growth rates are only loosely associated with differential incomes and poverty rates, and reflect the effects of both net international and internal migration (Chapter 2).

Map 8.1 **Poverty rates fell dramatically in Malaysia's states over 1970–2015**

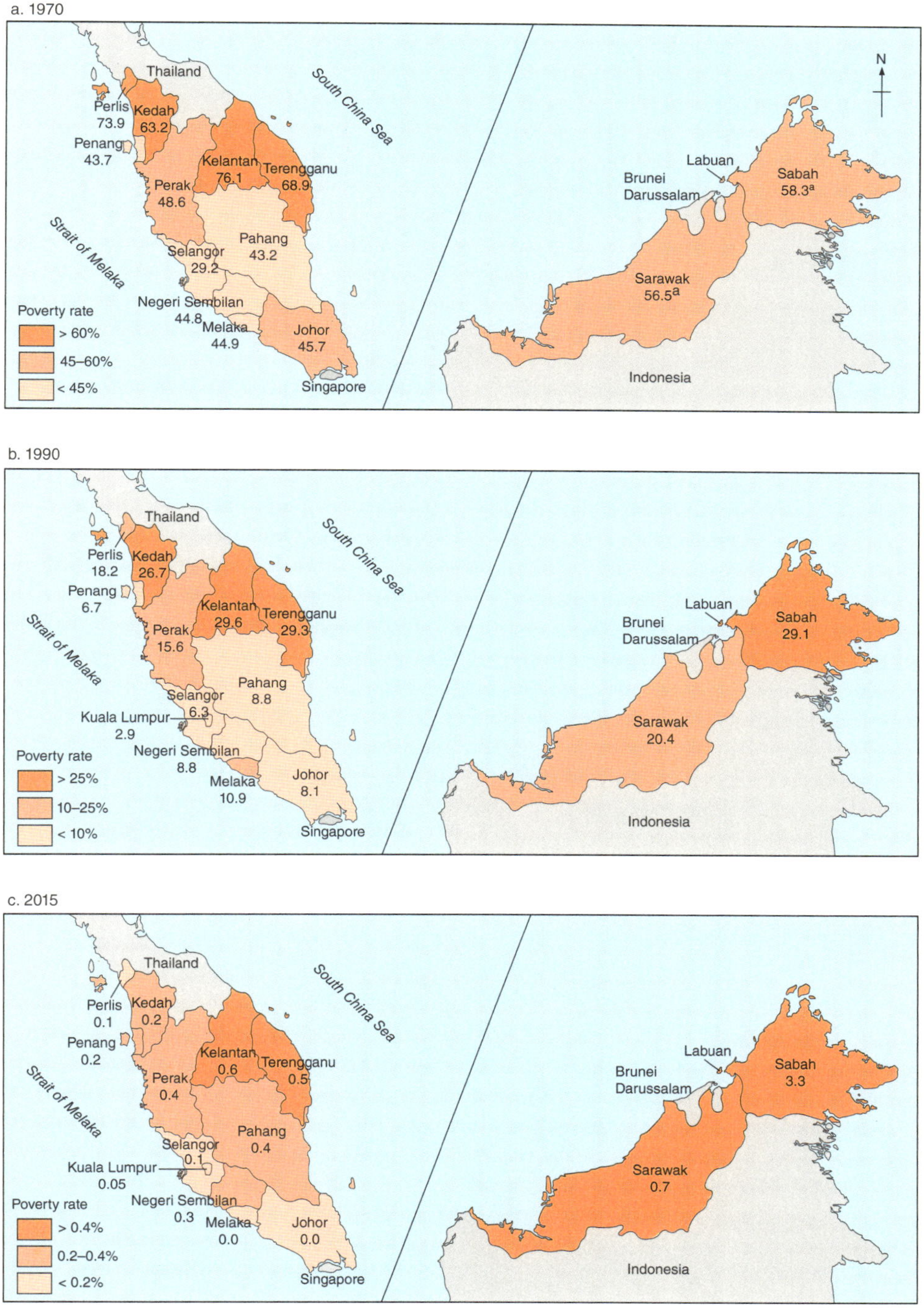

Source of data: Table 8.1.
Note: [a] Data are for 1976.

Box 8.2 The Federal Land Development Authority and poverty reduction

As the sun set on the colonial period, problems of rural poverty, landlessness, small and fragmentary holdings, and inequitable landownership were crying out for agrarian reforms.[11] These problems were especially acute in the predominantly Malay east coast and northern states, which were also experiencing high rates of population growth. In 1955, a government working party recommended the establishment of the Federal Land Development Authority (FELDA), an organization which would aim to resettle some of the landless poor and those with uneconomic holdings in new commercial land development schemes, with the eventual goal of them owning their own smallholdings. On 1 July 1956, FELDA was formally established as a statutory body to channel large amounts of federal development funding into state governments for land schemes, with an initial capital of RM10 million.[12]

FELDA settlements were established in virgin jungles provided by state governments and cleared by contractors. Settler households were allocated four hectares of land. The costs of providing the supporting infrastructure, including roads, water supply, public amenities, schools, and clinics were met by the government. In 1956, five initial projects were identified, with the *Ayer Lanas* scheme in Kelantan becoming the pilot. In 1957, ten more projects were funded in six states, with four located in traditionally low-income areas of Kelantan, Pahang, Terengganu, and Kedah. By 1959, 11 projects had been established, covering 31,000 acres and benefiting 3,000 settler families.

Settlers were supposed to be selected according to a points system, based on a combination of social need and experience in agriculture, although in practice political patronage played a part (Pletcher, 1990; Ishak Shari, 1994). The choice of crop depended on the export price outlook and soil suitability. Some two-thirds of the settlers were in estates that cultivated oil palm, which increasingly became the preferred crop because it entailed lower investment costs than rubber, and also had faster payback periods. FELDA accelerated this diversification into oil palm, with the shorter maturation periods in comparison with rubber proving attractive to poor cultivators with little capital or access to credit.

The recovery of loans provided to settlers was expected to begin once crops reached maturity. Repayments would be deducted from settlers' monthly incomes over 15 years, after which they were promised rights to the land that they worked on, which would then become an intergenerational asset. Land rights incentivized settlers to make long-term capital investments and to increase productivity.

By 1960, FELDA had increased the number of schemes to 14, and the number of settlers (with their families) to 4,662. But this was far short of the target set by the First Five-Year Plan of the Federation of Malaya, of 36 schemes and 14,400 settlers,

11 The Islamic inheritance system practised by Malays, which divides land equally among eligible heirs, had contributed to the fragmentation and subdivision of cultivable areas, making them less economically viable, especially where there were no arrangements for co-ownership or common cultivation. Under FELDA arrangements, it was proposed that there should be one single proprietor for each holding and that subdivision should be prohibited (Archive document DO 35/9778, 1958–1960).

12 Some of the funds for FELDA were provided by the Colonial Development Corporation, and later by the international financial institutions, in the form of loans.

due to capacity constraints at state level (Federation of Malaya, 1961). During the Second Plan, 1961–1965, 114,735 acres of land were developed, but only 6,083 out of a targeted 24,000 families were settled (MacAndrews, 1977). In later plans, however, momentum increased and higher settler targets were met.

In 1979, the FELDA scheme was extended to Sabah, but its presence in Sarawak was delayed due to concerns over land titles, and although FELDA did become established in this state, local villagers were only hired to work on the plantations and were not given land.

In 1990, there was a major policy change as the federal government stopped the recruitment of new settlers, and FELDA's role as a land settlement authority ceased (although successive governments still provided support for settlers). FELDA subsequently functioned as an agribusiness land development agency—a plantation company with commercial objectives—rather than as a state organization with social development objectives. This change resulted from a scarcity of new land for development and the high cost of resettling families (Sutton and Buang, 1995). In 2012, FELDA Global Ventures Holdings (later renamed FGV Holdings Berhad) was formed as a private investment vehicle, a group company with subsidiaries involved in upstream and downstream activities, including 355,000 hectares of plantations, oil palm and rubber processing mills, palm oil and sugar cane refineries, bulking installations, logistics, and R&D in agriculture. Following a successful public listing, FGV's cash-rich financial position rapidly deteriorated due to poor corporate governance, and eventually required a substantial government bailout.

The FELDA scheme undoubtedly helped in diversifying the country's agricultural sector and improving its productivity. It also helped to transform some of the landless peasantry into landowning, modern cash-crop producers. Many settlers' children gained access to higher education and achieved upward social mobility. But there were problems, including long delays in securing land titles, lax debt management, and the out-migration of the second and third generations as the original settlers retired and their trees became unproductive. Although the full costs and benefits of the FELDA programme are uncertain, Ragayah Haji Mat Zin (2013) estimates that it may have lifted some 100,000 families—overwhelmingly Malay but also of some other communities—out of poverty. Yet the FELDA communities' lack of self-sustainability, individual accountability, and personal responsibility for their own future have led to a continued dependence on government assistance. Conversely, the government appears to have encouraged this relationship so as to try to ensure the vote of FELDA communities, rather than empowering them to be self-reliant.

Poverty rates are closely associated with per capita incomes, and changes in each follow different well-defined curves. Figure 8.2 shows these trends for Negeri Sembilan, Pahang, Perak, and Selangor—the former Federated Malay States. Poverty initially falls extremely quickly from 40–50 per cent of the population at GDP per capita levels of just over RM5,000, to about 10 per cent of the population at GDP per capita levels of about RM15,000. After that, the rate of poverty decline slows significantly in relation to rises in GDP per capita.

Throughout the 46-year period, while Sabah's per capita income was never the lowest, its poverty rate was consistently among the highest; evidently, other factors than GDP per capita are important for poverty reduction.

Figure 8.2 **Poverty rates declined with rising per capita incomes over 1970–2016**

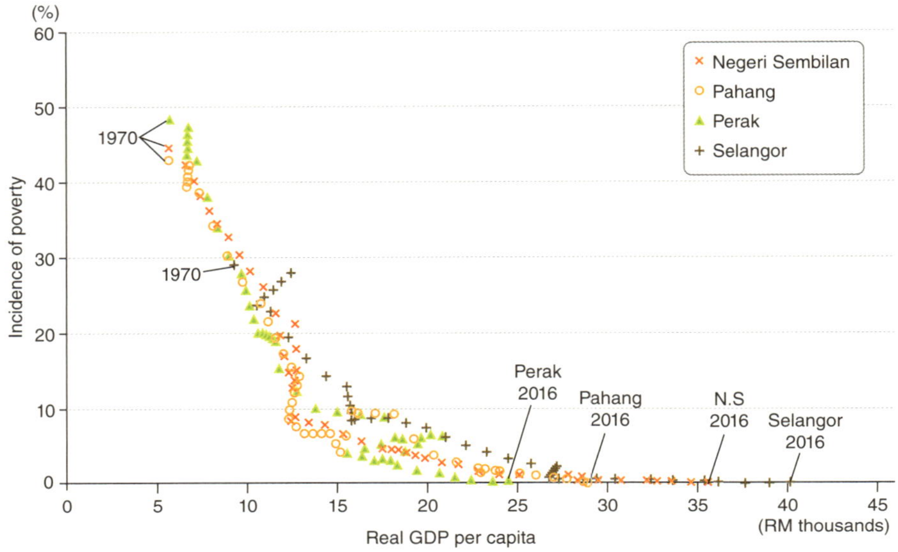

Sources of data: Department of Statistics–Malaysia (various years); Economic Planning Unit–Malaysia (2018a).

Measures of Structural Transformation at State Level

The three basic macroeconomic measures of structural transformation—AgEMPshr, AgGDPshr, and AgGAPshr—for each period and for each state are given in Table 8.2. Many values had to be interpolated, especially for the earlier years. AgEMPshr was reported quite regularly from 1970 onwards, usually at three-year intervals up to 2005, when annual data became available. The data on AgGDPshr are much sparser and the interpolation therefore occurs over longer intervals, but these data also became available annually after 2005. The AgEMPshr data are more reliable.

In 1970, only four states had *less* than half of their labour force engaged in agriculture: Melaka, Penang, Perak, and Selangor. They had all urbanized faster than the other states during the early 20th century. By 2015, on the other hand, only three states were left with *more* than 20 per cent of their labour force engaged in agriculture: Pahang, Sabah, and Sarawak. By any historical standards, this has been an extraordinarily quick structural transformation.[13]

13 For a discussion of which sectors the workers moved to after leaving agriculture, see Chapter 6.

Table 8.2 **Shares of agricultural employment and agricultural GDP in states' GDP have declined steeply in all 13 states**

		1970	1980	1990	2000	2010	2015
Johor	AgEMPshr	0.54	0.43	0.26	0.13	0.08	0.09
	AgGDPshr	0.41	0.34	*0.22*	*0.15*	0.17	0.15
	AgGAPshr	–0.13	–0.09	–0.04	0.02	0.09	0.06
Kedah	AgEMPshr	0.70	0.59	0.34	0.19	0.16	0.13
	AgGDPshr	0.57	0.52	*0.32*	*0.16*	0.16	0.14
	AgGAPshr	–0.13	–0.07	–0.02	–0.03	0.00	0.00
Kelantan	AgEMPshr	0.70	0.55	0.38	0.25	0.21	0.15
	AgGDPshr	0.42	0.42	*0.35*	*0.28*	0.29	0.25
	AgGAPshr	–0.28	–0.13	–0.03	0.03	0.08	0.10
Melaka	AgEMPshr	0.45	0.30	0.17	0.09	0.05	0.04
	AgGDPshr	0.32	0.22	*0.13*	*0.07*	0.11	0.13
	AgGAPshr	–0.14	–0.08	–0.04	–0.02	0.06	0.09
Negeri Sembilan	AgEMPshr	0.55	0.44	0.34	0.18	0.13	0.11
	AgGDPshr	0.37	0.28	*0.19*	*0.11*	0.11	0.09
	AgGAPshr	–0.17	–0.15	–0.15	–0.08	–0.02	–0.02
Pahang	AgEMPshr	0.60	0.50	0.42	0.34	0.26	0.23
	AgGDPshr	0.44	0.45	*0.37*	*0.27*	0.28	0.24
	AgGAPshr	–0.16	–0.05	–0.05	–0.06	0.02	0.00
Penang	AgEMPshr	0.25	0.13	0.05	0.03	0.02	0.01
	AgGDPshr	0.20	0.06	*0.03*	*0.02*	0.02	0.02
	AgGAPshr	–0.05	–0.07	–0.02	–0.01	0.01	0.01
Perak	AgEMPshr	0.46	0.38	0.28	0.17	0.15	0.12
	AgGDPshr	0.30	0.23	*0.20*	*0.18*	0.20	0.16
	AgGAPshr	–0.16	–0.14	–0.07	0.01	0.05	0.04
Perlis	AgEMPshr	0.73	0.55	0.33	0.21	0.15	0.13
	AgGDPshr	n/a	0.44	*0.37*	*0.29*	0.27	0.23
	AgGAPshr	n/a	–0.11	0.04	0.07	0.12	0.10
Selangor	AgEMPshr	0.24	0.23	0.09	0.03	0.02	0.02
	AgGDPshr	0.15	0.11	*0.05*	*0.02*	0.02	0.02
	AgGAPshr	–0.09	–0.12	–0.04	–0.01	0.00	0.00
Terengganu	AgEMPshr	0.63	0.46	0.36	0.20	0.14	0.10
	AgGDPshr	0.40	0.23	*0.16*	*0.12*	0.12	0.08
	AgGAPshr	–0.23	–0.23	–0.2	–0.08	–0.02	–0.02
Sabah	AgEMPshr	0.57	0.56	0.41	0.36	0.35	0.35
	AgGDPshr	0.53	0.37	*0.32*	*0.30*	0.27	0.21
	AgGAPshr	–0.05	–0.19	–0.09	–0.06	–0.08	–0.15
Sarawak	AgEMPshr	0.64	0.60	0.47	0.35	0.29	0.25
	AgGDPshr	0.37	0.27	*0.18*	*0.14*	0.14	0.14
	AgGAPshr	–0.27	–0.33	–0.29	–0.21	–0.15	–0.11

Sources of data: Department of Statistics–Malaysia (various years).
Notes: AgGAPshr = AgGDPshr – AgEMPshr.
Figures in italics are interpolated from the nearest years to which they relate: see footnote 9.

The evidence suggests that most agricultural labourers were 'pulled' out of the sector by better earning opportunities elsewhere, rather than 'pushed' out by rural poverty.[14] The distinction is important in determining the welfare consequences of structural transformation. A 'pull' transformation, the most common form in East and Southeast Asia, tends to raise labour productivity in both the agricultural and non-agricultural sectors, and leads to significantly rising incomes. A 'push' transformation, characteristic of many countries in South Asia and Sub-Saharan Africa, by contrast, tends simply to relocate rural poverty to urban slums, with no gains in labour productivity in either sector.[15]

Unusually, Table 8.2 shows that a number of states—and, most distinctively, Perak—had *positive* values of AgGAPshr for 2000, 2010, and 2015. Figure 8.3 shows the complete annual time series data for Perak for the same variables, and reveals 18 observations with a positive AgGAPshr, with one value of nearly 0.1 (or nearly 10 per cent in the figure's notation). The large number of positive observations for AgGAPshr is important because these reflect a local economy where labour productivity within agriculture is higher than that outside agriculture. While atypical compared with global historical trends, this pattern occurs to varying degrees in seven Malaysian states, several of which retain important agricultural sectors. Box 8.3 examines the possibility that commodity prices, both on international markets and due to domestic policy interventions, can account for this pattern. The example focuses on Perak, but the price effect illustrated is likely to be a significant factor in all seven states with positive values for AgGAPshr.

Box 8.3 An example from Perak of the potential impact of prices on agricultural GDP

Measured agricultural productivity depends on the physical production per hectare on the farm and on the prices the farmer receives for that output. The variable AgGDPshr depends on both production and prices. For a given level of AgEMPshr, a higher AgGDPshr can result from a production or a price effect. Either way, the gap variable AgGAPshr is still the difference between AgGDPshr and AgEMPshr.

Normally the gap variable is negative, reflecting the higher labour productivity in non-agricultural than in agricultural employment. However, a number of Malaysian states have shown higher labour productivity in agriculture since the turn of the century, and the question is whether this is because physical productivity in agriculture has accelerated, or whether it is due to higher commodity prices (either temporary or

14 For a discussion of the policy measures that stimulated this rural-to-urban migration, see Chapter 7.

15 See Badiane (2011) and Losch et al. (2012) for details of structural transformation in Africa. India's mixed experience is described by Binswanger-Mkhize (2012).

permanent). The data are largely insufficient to settle this question across multiple states, but it is possible to illuminate the argument using data from Perak, where the reversal of the normal patterns of structural transformation stands out (Figure 8.3).

Only nationwide commodity prices are available (Box Table 8.2), but these should serve as a rough approximation given that Malaysian commodity markets are reasonably well integrated. Note that these are individual commodity prices, not a general measure of the agricultural terms of trade with the non-agricultural economy. The price of rice, which is policy determined, has risen sharply since 2005, but there is no clear trend for rubber or palm oil, the prices of which are determined on international markets.

Box Table 8.2 Prices of agricultural products[a]

	Average price of 'Standard Malaysian Rubber 20', free on board	Crude palm oil local delivered price	*Padi* monthly price of producers
1975	1,316	1,055	467
1980	2,737	919	468
1985	1,735	1,046	450
1990	2,046	701	460
1995	3,826	1,473	477
2000	2,425	997	538
2005	5,231	1,394	620
2010	10,581	2,701	750
2015	5,219	2,154	1,200

Sources of data: For rubber, Department of Statistics–Malaysia (2016b). For palm oil, Malaysian Palm Oil Board (various years). For rice, Food and Agriculture Organization of the United Nations (various years).

Note: [a] Average monthly producer price (RM per metric ton) for Kedah/Perlis, medium grade, 1995–2015.

Annual agricultural GDP data by state are only available from 2005, which corresponds to the time period of interest. Ideally, the contribution of *each* commodity to a state's value added (to GDP) is required, but such data are not yet available. As an approximation, the value added by each commodity can be calculated by multiplying the state's production of each commodity (which is known with considerable accuracy) by the national average price. The calculations are carried out for Perak for 2010.

Using commodity production quantities (Table 8.3) and commodity prices (Box Table 8.2), the production values (in current prices) of rice, rubber, and palm oil production are obtained (Box Table 8.3). These values are then adjusted using commodity prices from the year 2000. The difference between the two series is the impact of commodity prices, as opposed to production, on AgGDP.

Box Table 8.3 Value added to rice, rubber, and palm oil in Perak

	2010
AgGDP (millions)	8,599
Approximate value added using current commodity prices, in RM millions	
Rice	143.7
Palm oil	4,883.4
Rubber	939.7
Total	5,966.8
Total as share of AgGDP (%)	69.4
Total, using 2000 commodity prices	2,121.1
AgGDP at 2000 commodity prices [8,599 – (5,966.8 – 2,121.1)]	4,753.3
AgGDPshr using current prices	0.20
AgEMPshr	0.15
AgGAPshr (the difference between the two rows above)	0.05
AgGAPshr at commodity prices prevailing in 2000	–0.04

The results are clear. Higher prices for the three commodities account for the positive value of AgGAPshr in 2010. Removing the contribution of higher commodity prices restores a negative value for AgGAPshr. Physical productivity per worker in agriculture is not higher than that in non-agriculture. The 'post-structural-transformation' patterns observed in Perak and in several other states with important agricultural sectors, however, may well be welfare-enhancing, and might reflect how agriculture can be made both sustainable and attractive to a new generation of farmers.

Figure 8.3 Perak saw a dramatic agricultural transformation over 1970–2016

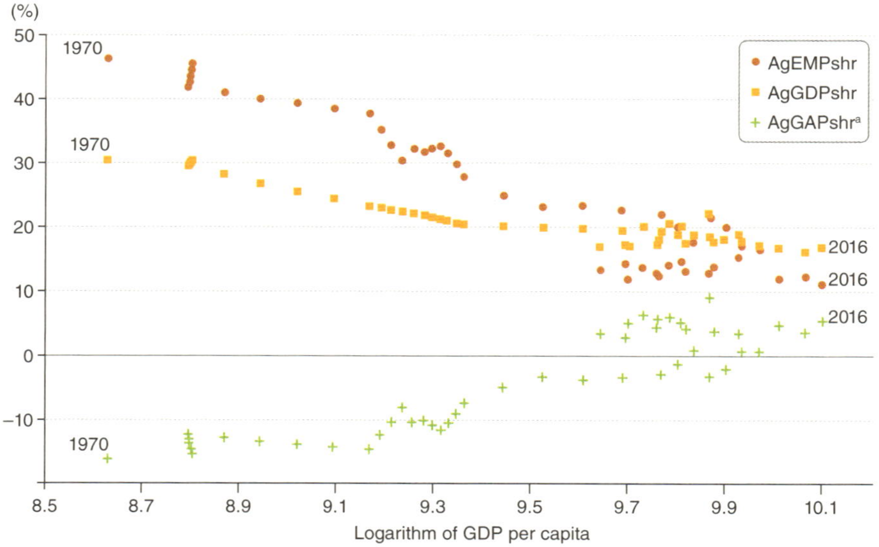

Note: [a] Positive values of AgGAPshr (AgGDPshr – AgEMPshr) denote higher labour productivity in agriculture than in non-agricultural sectors.

Agricultural Commodities

Evolving Agricultural Policies

Agricultural policies and programmes have long been an integral component of Malaysia's national economic planning frameworks. Over the period 1984–2011, three separate National Agricultural Policies (NAP1–3) were launched, as well as a ten-year National Agro-food Policy (NAP4).[16] The key objectives of the early policies were to raise the incomes of farmers in the non-estate sectors and on smallholdings, by lifting productivity and by increasing the value of agricultural produce.

Efforts to enhance the efficiency of *padi* production so as to achieve self-sufficiency were promoted by encouraging the development of large-scale commercial operations, in order to create larger and more viable production units. The private sector became increasingly involved in large-scale production and support industries.

Rubber was a continuing theme within national policies, but with an increasing emphasis on stimulating the downstream processing and manufacturing of higher value-added rubber-based products. Smallholdings too minor to be economically viable were consolidated into estate-type production units to achieve economies of scale. R&D efforts were directed towards developing new forms and uses of rubber and rubber products, propagating high-yielding clones, and mechanization.

With the aim of moving towards commercialization of the palm oil industry, vast new land areas were opened up by government agencies. Land was also made available for other agro-food crops to support further diversification in agriculture (Indrani, 2001). R&D was again promoted, especially on the use of new technologies and on downstream activities, such as high-quality hybrids and varieties, better packaging, and food processing into value-added products (Zaharah A. Rahman, 2012).

By the early 1990s, major structural changes were taking place in the agricultural sector, resulting in acute labour shortages, increasing costs, and growing competition for land and water resources. NAP3's response was to deepen links with other sectors, to enhance food security, and to encourage human resource development in order to raise agricultural land and labour productivity. NAP4, launched in 2011, aims to promote high-value-added, sustainable agricultural development and private sector investment, while seeking to overcome some of the multiple challenges that the sector faces. These include the increasing reliance on foreign workers, the existence of inefficient smallholdings of an uneconomic size, volatile price fluctuations, a

16 Ministry of Agriculture–Malaysia, 1984, 1992, 1998; Ministry of Agriculture and Agro-Based Industry, 2011.

widening food trade deficit, climate change, and intense global competition resulting from international trade agreements.

Commodity Prices

Commodity prices are critical to understanding Malaysia's structural transformation and the gap between labour productivity within and outside agriculture. The three most important agricultural commodities in the majority of states are rice, rubber, and palm oil (Table 8.3). Accounting for about half of the total agricultural GDP for all states in 2015, their production trajectories are quite different. Other food sectors are expanding rapidly as consumer demand grows for fruits and vegetables, livestock and dairy products, and fish.

Table 8.3 States' shares of total production of rice, rubber, and crude palm oil vary greatly

	1970	1980	1990	2000	2010	2015
Rice						
Johor	0.8	*0.6*	*0.3*	0.4	0.5	*0.5*
Kedah	34.0	*47.6*	*40.1*	35.7	34.2	*39.6*
Kelantan	13.1	*12.9*	*9.6*	11.9	11.1	*11.5*
Melaka	2.2	*1.3*	*0.6*	0.3	0.2	*0.4*
Negeri Sembilan	3.0	*0.9*	*0.5*	0.3	0.4	*0.3*
Pahang	2.7	*1.0*	*0.8*	1.0	1.0	*1.2*
Penang	7.2	*4.2*	*3.3*	4.9	5.8	n/a
Perak	15.6	*11.4*	*11.9*	11.8	12.1	*12.6*
Perlis	8.3	*9.7*	*9.3*	*8.8*	*9.1*	*9.8*
Selangor	8.2	*6.1*	*7.8*	8.3	8.6	*9.0*
Terengganu	5.0	*4.3*	*3.5*	3.8	3.1	*2.9*
Sabah	n/a	n/a	*6.0*	7.1	5.9	*4.5*
Sarawak	n/a	n/a	*6.0*	5.9	8.1	*7.7*
Total	100	100	100	100	100	100
Malaysia (tonnes 000s)	914.6	1,140.5	1,251.3	1,381.7	1,588.5	1,681.7
Rubber						
Johor	25.9	28.1	19.2	*14.3*	*16.0*	*18.8*
Kedah	12.5	15.2	15.4	*16.5*	*17.3*	*18.4*
Kelantan	4.1	2.7	4.0	*7.0*	*6.7*	*9.6*
Melaka	7.4	6.1	6.9	*2.3*	n/a	n/a
Negeri Sembilan	12.6	13.2	15.0	*17.7*	*17.3*	*18.9*
Pahang	6.9	9.0	14.1	*16.0*	*13.3*	*14.4*
Penang	2.5	2.7	1.1	*2.7*	*7.3*	*5.4*
Perak	14.6	14.1	12.6	*12.9*	*10.2*	*7.0*

	1970	1980	1990	2000	2010	2015
Selangor	11.8	7.6	5.7	*2.4*	*0.0*	n/a
Terengganu	1.5	1.3	2.2	*3.4*	*3.4*	*1.6*
Sabah	n/a	n/a	2.4	*3.7*	*5.4*	*4.7*
Sarawak	n/a	n/a	1.2	*1.3*	*3.0*	*1.1*
Total	100	100	100	100	100	100
Malaysia (tonnes 000s)	1,196.5	1,463.9	1,291.0	1,118.3	870.7	663.8
Crude palm oil						
Johor	n/a	30.8	27.6	18.5	16.5	15.8
Kedah	n/a	n/a	1.3	1.0	1.6	1.6
Kelantan	n/a	1.0	2.1	1.5	1.4	1.4
Melaka	n/a	n/a	0.6	0.6	0.7	n/a
Negeri Sembilan	n/a	6.3	5.5	3.0	3.2	3.4
Pahang	n/a	17.6	20.7	14.5	15.0	14.9
Penang	n/a	n/a	1.2	0.4	0.5	n/a
Perak	n/a	14.6	12.8	11.4	10.6	10.1
Selangor	n/a	17.8	10.3	4.3	3.5	2.5
Terengganu	n/a	4.4	4.9	2.8	2.9	2.5
Sabah	n/a	6.4	11.1	34.1	31.3	29.0
Sarawak	n/a	1.0	1.8	8.0	12.8	18.7
Total		100	100	100	100	100
Malaysia (tonnes 000s)		2,486.8	6,094.6	13,976.2	16,993.7	19,760.1

Sources of data: Department of Statistics–Malaysia (various years); Malaysian Palm Oil Board (various years).
Note: Figures in italics are interpolated from the nearest years to which they relate: see footnote 9.

Rice

Rice is the staple food of Malaysians. For much of the colonial era, rice was produced on a subsistence basis and there were few efforts to promote commercial cultivation. *Padi* growing was a traditional occupation of Malays, and colonial policy had sought to preserve this by restricting non-Malay access to rice-growing lands (Tan, 1963; Kratoska, 1982). Productivity was low, and about two-thirds of Malaya's rice consumption was imported from Siam and Burma (Overton, 1994). Given the widespread poverty among Malay *padi* farmers, measures to increase their incomes became imperative after independence: the agricultural sector became a top priority in the national development plans, and later in a sequence of national agricultural policies.

Key policy initiatives to raise rice productivity included the modernization of traditional agricultural methods, *in situ* infrastructural development, and the use of high-yielding varieties of rice, as well as double cropping (Jackson, 1972). To support double cropping, substantial investments were made in large-scale irrigation schemes, including the *Muda* irrigation scheme in Kedah and Perlis (262,500 acres), the *Kemburu* scheme in Kelantan (47,000 acres), and the upgrading of the *Krian* irrigation scheme in northern Perak. In 1969, the Malaysia Agricultural Research and Development Institute was established. The Guaranteed Minimum Price, introduced in 1949 for *padi* purchased by the government, was adjusted upwards several times, as price support was seen as a means of reducing poverty among *padi* farmers, who were concentrated in the poorest states. These various measures led to substantial increases in rice production in the 1960s and 1970s.

Kedah, the leading producer in 1970 and currently, more than doubled its production between 1970 and 2015, from 311,000 to 667,000 metric tons. Sharp increases also occurred in Perak, Perlis, Selangor, and Sarawak, all states which made substantial early investments in irrigation (Taylor, 1981). However, over the longer term rice production has only increased moderately, growing at an average rate of around 1.3 per cent per year between 1970 and 2015 (Table 8.3). Despite the increased production, Malaysia has not yet achieved self-sufficiency. In 2016, it was still importing almost 30 per cent of its rice consumption.

Rubber

Rubber trees—*Hevea brasiliensis*—were introduced into Malaya in the 1870s, with the first seedlings planted in the Residency gardens in Kuala Kangsar, Perak (Loadman, 2005). By the early decades of the 20th century the large-scale commercial planting of rubber had propelled the economy to unprecedented prosperity, as the mass production of automobiles in the US spurred huge growth in estate rubber planting by European companies (Chapter 5).

Rubber output and exports surged during this period and Malaya became the world's leading producer, a position it maintained for much of the century. The industry enjoyed buoyant—albeit volatile—growth before demand and prices plunged with the impact of the Great Depression. Rubber exports virtually ceased during the Japanese occupation. In these periods, and especially when supplies were disrupted, the synthetic rubber industry began to advance, at first in Germany and Russia, and then in North America, Europe, and Japan (Barlow et al., 1994). By the time Malaya achieved independence, petroleum-based synthetic rubber was beginning to challenge the dominance of natural rubber.

After independence, Malaya's rubber industry thus found itself in fierce competition with synthetic rubber. Prices were generally low, although still volatile at times. The federal and state governments supported new planting activities by opening up new land areas through FELDA and other schemes, and through research programmes to develop higher-yielding trees, led by the Rubber Research Institute. Output of natural rubber increased from 0.8 million tonnes in 1960 to 1.2 million tonnes in 1970, representing 40 per cent of global production and accounting for half of global growth in natural rubber production over the decade. In 1970, rubber production was concentrated almost entirely in the peninsula, with the main rubber-producing states being Johor (26 per cent) and Perak (15 per cent), and with Negeri Sembilan, Kedah, and Selangor close behind (Table 8.3).

Between 1970 and 1990, growth in the natural rubber industry was interrupted by price shocks precipitated first by the surge in oil prices in the 1970s, which reduced demand for fuel and consequently for automotive products, and then by the global recession of the early 1980s. To curtail these steep price declines in natural rubber, supply adjustment mechanisms were adopted, including the Malaysia Crash Programme, 1974–1976,[17] and the International Natural Rubber Agreements, which ran from 1979 to 1999 (Barlow et al., 1994). Rising labour and land costs contributed to the challenging operating environment, however, driving many rubber producers to switch to oil palm cultivation, which was increasingly seen as the more profitable sector and was less labour intensive. Malaysia's natural rubber output, once the mainstay of the economy, began a secular decline, with production in 2015 at just 45 per cent of its 1980 peak (Table 8.3). In Johor, the leading rubber-producing state until 2000, the value of production in 2015 was less than half of that in 1970. Other leading rubber-producing states have witnessed similar declines. Overall, during 1970–2015, rubber production decreased by an average of 1.3 per cent per year.

Amid increasing industrialization and diversification of exports, the share of natural rubber in total exports fell from over half in 1960 to less than 4 per cent in 1990, and to a negligible share in the first 16 years of the 21st century (Figure 8.4). Its share in major primary commodity exports also collapsed over the same period, from more than 70 per cent to less than 5 per cent. Malaysia's share of global natural rubber output has also shrunk, with Thailand and Indonesia now the world's largest producers. With palm oil far surpassing the natural rubber industry in terms of both earnings and share of exports, the importance of unprocessed natural rubber to the economy has diminished. However, since the mid 1980s, Malaysia has become a major manufacturer and exporter of a range of rubber goods, including tyres, medical products, and footwear. Rubber-product manufacturing contributes significantly to employment and export earnings (Goldthorpe, 2015).

---

17 The Crash Programme, which lasted for 18 months, aimed to reduce rubber supply and to raise long-term productivity in order to stabilize prices.

Figure 8.4 **The share of rubber in Malaysia's exports has tumbled to insignificance, as has its share in exports of primary commodities**

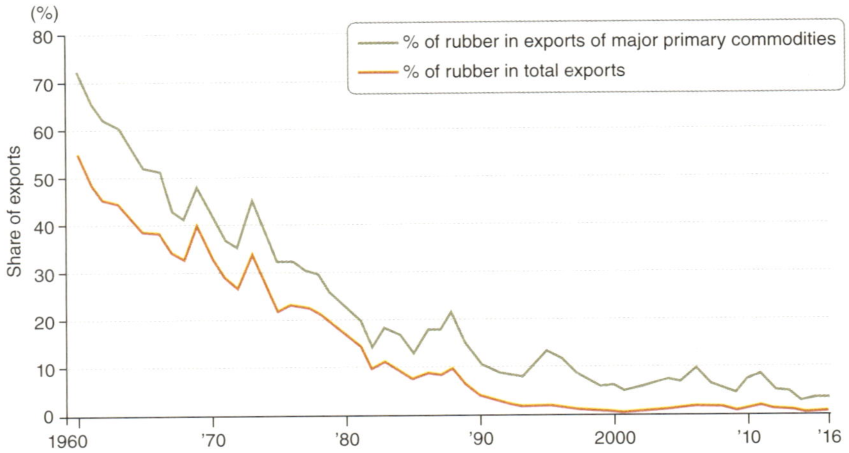

Source of data: Bank Negara Malaysia (various issues).

Palm Oil

The growth of Malaysia's palm oil industry has been spectacular. Commercial interest in oil palm—*Elaeis guineensis*—began to expand from around 1935 due in part to highly volatile rubber prices, although small quantities of palm oil were being exported a decade earlier. Recognizing that Malaya had optimal growing conditions for oil palm, that the trees yield fruit just three years after planting compared with five to seven years for rubber, and that they continue to bear fruit for 20 years or more, large European agency houses began to invest in the crop. Selangor, Perak, and Johor were the main areas of cultivation initially, and many rubber and coconut estates were converted to the more profitable and less labour-intensive oil palm (Jackson, 1967; Bissonnette and De Koninck, 2017).

Oil palm cultivation greatly expanded in the 1960s as the government's agricultural diversification policy incentivized private production in order to reduce dependence on natural rubber, which was facing declining prices and growing competition from synthetic rubber (Tate, 1996). Oil palm cultivation was remunerative for both estates and smallholders, with the FELDA scheme a key driver in relation to the latter (Box 8.2). Settlers on oil palm schemes earned incomes 1.6 times higher than those on rubber estates, and five times higher than the average rice farmer (Pletcher, 1990). FELDA's share of total oil palm cultivation had risen to one-third by 1984, up from 11.4 per cent in 1965, and it had become the country's largest single producer and exporter of palm oil.

From the late 1970s, as part of the NEP, the government bought out or negotiated the transfer of plantation ownership from foreign-domiciled companies to national ones through its investment vehicle Permodalan Nasional Berhad. By the start of the 21st century, the equity of the large plantation companies was largely nationally owned. The palm oil industry, supported by R&D and promoted internationally by the Malaysian Palm Oil Council, had evolved in a similar manner to the rubber industry some 50 years earlier. Plantation companies expanded into downstream production and manufacturing of palm-based products, mainly edible oils and basic oleochemicals (Teoh, 2002). As production of crude palm oil increased, manufacturers switched from petrochemicals to the cheaper oleochemicals, notably palm kernel lauric oils and other derivatives, used in the production of laundry detergent, toothpaste, soap, and shampoo.

In the early 1980s, Malaysia accounted for more than half of global palm oil production and 70 per cent of global exports. At that time, the big palm-oil-producing states were Johor (31 per cent), Selangor (18 per cent), Pahang (18 per cent), and Perak (15 per cent); Sabah and Sarawak were smaller players, producing 6 per cent and 1 per cent respectively. Malaysia was also the world's most efficient palm oil refiner at that time, owing to government support (Jomo, 2018).

Figure 8.5 **The share of palm oil in Malaysia's total exports has trended fairly steadily over the last 25 years, unlike the rising but volatile trend in its share in major primary commodity exports**

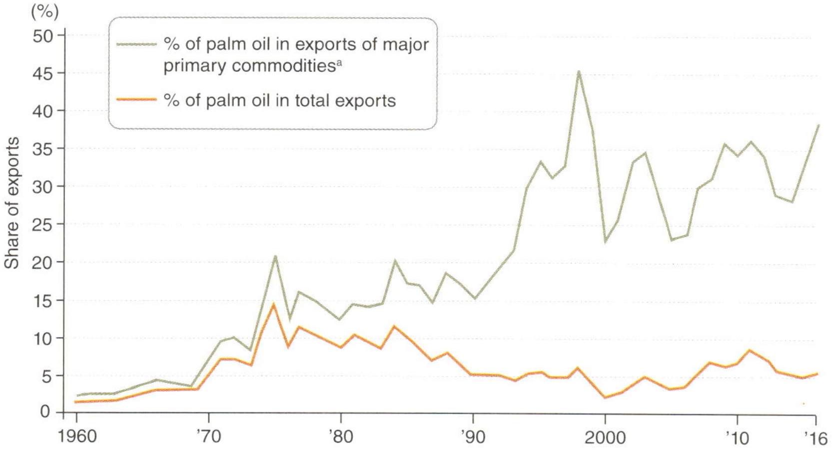

Sources of data: Department of Statistics–Malaysia (various years); Ministry of Finance (various years).
Note: [a] Major primary commodities are rubber, tin, palm oil, saw logs and sawn timber, petroleum, and liquefied natural gas.

Between 1980 and 2015, production of palm oil increased at an average rate of 5.9 per cent per year, with higher growth in the two decades after 1980. As the industry expanded, there was large-scale planting in Sabah and Sarawak on converted forest land. By 2015, the shares in total production of Sabah and Sarawak had increased to 29 per cent and 19 per cent respectively. The share of Johor, previously the leading producer, fell to 16 per cent, that of Perak to 10 per cent, and that of Selangor to only 2.5 per cent, while Pahang accounted for 15 per cent (Table 8.3).

The palm oil industry remains important for Malaysia's economy, although its growth has not been entirely uncontroversial.[18] Its products have taken an increasing share of the country's exports of primary commodities, accounting for around one-third in the 2010s, and about 5 per cent of total exports (Figure 8.5). Almost all palm oil products (crude, processed, and palm stearin) are exported, with India, the EU, China, Pakistan, and the US as the main importers. The industry contributes significantly to federal and state government revenues, and has been highly resilient, withstanding multiple price recessions over the past half-century or so. The palm oil revolution is critical to understanding the role of agriculture in Malaysia's poverty reduction and its structural transformation. There are two basic analytical approaches, bottom-up and top-down, although these can be mixed. The first builds on field research and observations linked to interviews with key participants in the palm oil sector (for example, Byerlee et al., 2017). The second employs disaggregated data—at state level over the several decades that witnessed the rapid expansion of palm oil—linked to econometric analysis using panel data procedures. This second approach is described in the next section, which first sets out the modelling analysis, and then examines the linkages that it reveals between agricultural growth and poverty reduction. The experience of rubber and rice are analysed along with palm oil.

Structural Transformation at State Level

A striking illustration of Malaysia's structural transformation at state level can be seen in Figure 8.6: to my knowledge, this is the first time that the structural transformation has been disaggregated to this level over an extended period. Two features stand out. First, the employment share in agriculture (AgEMPshr) and the agricultural share in GDP (AgGDPshr) decline as state-level real GDP per capita increases. The contribution of the agricultural sector to GDP has

18 Oil palm cultivation has been subject to growing criticism over its impact on the environment and on local communities. As part of efforts to reduce their carbon dioxide emissions from fossil fuel consumption, the US and EU both promoted the use of vegetable oils as biofuels in the second half of the 2000s, contributing to a surge in demand for the crop. But increased production has resulted in extensive deforestation and the burning of peatland soil in Malaysia and Indonesia, the two largest palm oil producers.

fallen markedly in all 13 states. Second, as real GDP per capita increases, AgGAPshr becomes positive: that is, there are fewer observations that are negative. Over time, agricultural productivity has surged, with less labour being used in almost all states.

The figure bears a close resemblance to the pattern observed in similar cross plots over countries, rather than states within the same country (Timmer and Akkus, 2008). This resemblance provides reassurance that attempting to understand the role of agriculture in economic growth and poverty reduction in Malaysia by examining the changing relative structure of agricultural employment and contribution to GDP is a productive line of enquiry.

Figure 8.6 All states in Malaysia saw dramatic agricultural transformation over 1970–2016

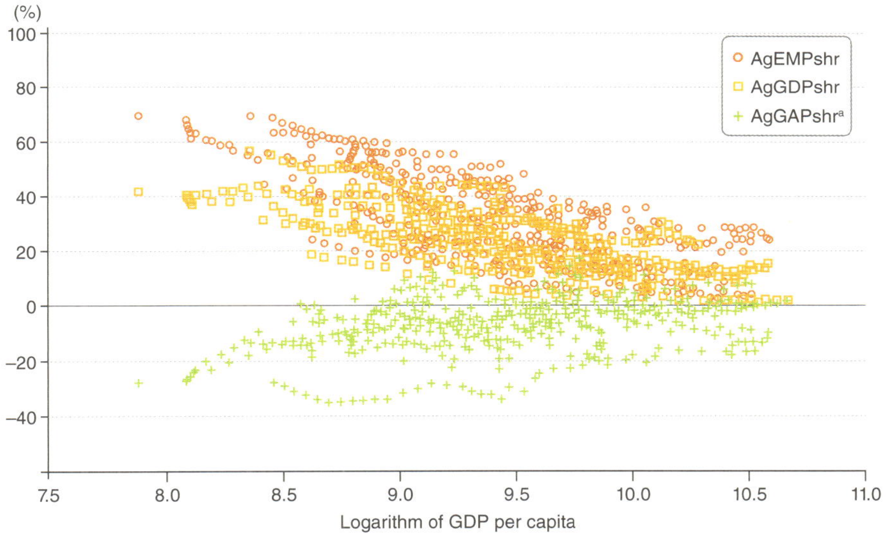

Note: [a]Positive values of AgGAPshr (AgGDPshr – AgEMPshr) denote higher labour productivity in agriculture than in non-agricultural sectors.

Linkages between Agricultural Growth and Poverty Reduction

An econometric analysis was undertaken to help to explain the trends in poverty rates at state level, in which the variable to be explained in all the regression equations is the poverty rate in each year for each state (Box 8.4). This section is necessarily technical, and the reader may wish to skip to the subsection 'Results' at its end.

Box 8.4 The econometric strategy for analysing the Malaysian data

The data available for analysis are:

Box Table 8.4 Definitions of variables for analysing Malaysian data

Variable	Definition	Transformation
POVX	Natural log of incidence of poverty (actual and interpolated)	Natural log
Time	Trend (1, 2, 3…)	
GDPPC	Real GDP per capita (actual and interpolated)	Natural log
AgEMPshr	Share of agricultural employment in total state employment (actual and interpolated)	Range [0,1]
AgGDPshr	Share of agricultural GDP in total state GDP (actual and interpolated)	
AgGAPshr	AgGDPshr – AgEMPshr (typically a negative value)	
RICEX	Production of rice (actual and interpolated)	Natural log
POX	Production of palm oil (actual and interpolated)	Natural log
RUBX	Production of rubber (actual and interpolated)	Natural log

For most variables, the observations start in 1970 and annual observations go up to 2016. Most variables have some, but not many, missing values for which interpolated values are used, but this is unlikely to affect the general conclusions of the econometric analysis. It is, of course, recognized that the set of independent variables included in the models is not exhaustive.

A modified step-wise regression technique is used, starting with very simple specifications that often have only time trend variables. This provides a baseline before 'real' variables are added to see their additional contribution. The dependent variable in all regressions is POVX, the natural logarithm of the poverty rate in each state for each year. As shown in Table 8.1, this variable varies across states and over time. The econometric models specified below attempt to explain this variation. Several models were specified and estimated, of which six are reported here; all the regressions include fixed-effect coefficients (different intercepts) for each state:

1. $POVX = a + b*Time + c*Time^2$ (used as a base regression to see how much variance in poverty rates is explained simply by the time trend and its square)
2. $POVX = a + b*Time + c*Time^2 + d*GDPPC$
3. $POVX = a + b*Time + c*Time^2 + d*GDPPC + e*AgEMPshr$
4. $POVX = a + b*Time + c*Time^2 + d*GDPPC + e*AgEMPshr + f*RICEX$
5. $POVX = a + b*Time + c*Time^2 + d*GDPPC + e*AgEMPshr + f*POX$
6. $POVX = a + b*Time + c*Time^2 + d*GDPPC + e*AgEMPshr + f*RUBX$

Variations on these models are tried with alternative variables, time periods, and specifications, and these are discussed in the text. These six models, however, provide the core framework for the statistical analysis.

Explaining the results from the many different specifications is complex. Fortunately, the panel structure of the data offers an easy starting point. Annex Table 8.1 presents the simplest specification: fixed-effect coefficients for each state and for each year from 1970 to 2016. No 'real' variables are included: the table simply reports how much of the total variation among states and over time can be accounted for by the unique and constant characteristics of each state and each year. The coefficients for each state are assumed to hold for all time periods and the coefficients for each year are assumed to hold for all states. The result is that this fixed-effect specification accounts for 92 per cent of the total variation in POVX (Annex Table 8.1). Obviously, some very fundamental structural aspects of each state—for instance, history, culture, institutions, and natural ecology—are important in explaining changes in poverty over time. The state-specific coefficients show wide variation, reflecting the significant variations in the poverty conditions in each state. The poorest state is Sabah and the richest is Selangor. The structural difference in poverty rates between these two states is large: the rate in Sabah is nearly four times as large as that in Selangor.

Similarly, broad nationwide forces must explain the power of the year fixed-effects variables to explain changes in poverty. These nationwide forces must be at least partly driven by macroeconomic forces that affect all states more or less equally. Some confirmation of this can be seen by examining the coefficients for 1998 to 2001 (Annex Table 8.1). The steady progress in reducing poverty stopped abruptly in 1998, and poverty increased again in 1999. Indeed, using the anti-logs of the coefficients reveals that the national poverty rate increased by 24 per cent between 1997 and 1999. The low rate of poverty achieved in 1997 was not attained again until 2002. This episode, of course, corresponds to the Asian financial crisis, which severely affected the economy (Chapter 7).

As important as the year fixed-effect coefficients are, they behave in a very regular pattern, mirroring the accelerating decline in poverty from 1970 to 2016. More than 95 per cent of the variation in the yearly coefficients from the fixed-effect specification can be explained by a very simple model, using only time and time squared as independent variables (Annex Table 8.2). Because the yearly fixed-effect coefficients take up so many degrees of freedom, and mask the impact of 'real' variables such as income per capita, share of employment in agriculture, and composition of commodity production in each state over time, the time/time-squared specification is used in all regression analysis in the rest of the chapter (as explained in Box 8.4.).

The first step in using 'real' variables to explain poverty is shown in Annex Table 8.3, which introduces the level of GDP per capita (GDPPC) for each state for each year as an explanatory variable (keeping the time and time-squared variables in the regression, as is the case in all subsequent regressions). The results are quite dramatic. Indeed, GDPPC is almost uniformly an important determinant of poverty rates, with only Sabah and Sarawak not having highly significant negative coefficients.[19] Because both POVX and GDPPC are in natural logarithms, the coefficients can roughly be interpreted as elasticities: a 10 per cent *increase* in GDPPC in Johor, for example, leads to a *decrease* in the poverty rate of 18.5 per cent. By international standards, this is a relatively large response to income changes, and reflects a reasonably strong connection between economic growth (GDPPC) and incomes of the poor.[20]

The results for Sabah and Sarawak run counter to the trends for Peninsular Malaysia. In fact, Sabah has a significant *positive* coefficient on GDPPC, indicating that higher average incomes in the state lead to a higher poverty rate. The coefficient for Sarawak is insignificant. Further analysis using expanded models with additional explanatory variables sheds some light on these rather perplexing results.

Table 8.4 adds the share of employment in agriculture as an additional explanatory variable (AgEMPshr). This specification keeps the time variables and GDPPC, thus controlling for the time-related structural changes in the economy and the level of per capita incomes. The results are both complicated and intriguing. For example, although AgEMPshr and GDPPC are closely correlated, there is enough independent variation for a large number of significant coefficients for each variable. Seven states continue to have significant negative coefficients on GDPPC, while Kelantan, Negeri Sembilan, Pahang, Penang, Terengganu, and Sarawak lose significance.

Five states have significantly negative coefficients on AgEMPshr, while Penang and Negeri Sembilan have a significant positive coefficient. Does this set of mixed results conform with expectations? AgEMPshr is the most reliable marker of the structural transformation; AgGDPshr would be preferable, but the data are patchy. Therefore, all other things being equal, a small value for AgEMPshr should also be associated with a low poverty rate. The coefficient would thus be positive, as it is for Penang.[21] But this specification also includes the time and time-squared variables, which capture much of the gradual transformation of the Malaysian economy, as well as the GDPPC variable, which captures the impact of state-level incomes directly.

Taking these considerations into account, the negative coefficients do conform with expectations; similar effects have been seen in other countries.

19 With a declining value in the poverty rate, a negative coefficient implies that an increase in real GDP per capita (GDPPC) leads to a reduction in poverty rates, thus having a pro-poor effect.

20 See Timmer (2018) for a review of the literature on this for Asia.

21 With only AgEMPshr and fixed effect, all the states have highly significant positive coefficients when only AgEMPshr is included, along with a constant term. Penang has by far the largest coefficient.

With incomes held constant, and the structural effects largely captured by the time and time-squared trends, a larger AgEMPshr reflects the fact that comparatively more economic activity in the state is concentrated in agriculture, and that this has a pro-poor effect. In short, in some states raising labour productivity in agriculture has been a pro-poor activity.

Table 8.4 The agricultural employment share has positive and negative impacts on poverty

Independent variable (GDPPC)	Coefficient	Independent variable (AgEMPshr)	Coefficient
Johor	–7.534 ***	Johor	–17.879 ***
Kedah	–2.366 ***	Kedah	–3.315 **
Kelantan	–0.490	Kelantan	0.647
Melaka	–2.289 ***	Melaka	–5.586 **
Negeri Sembilan	0.098	Negeri Sembilan	3.454 *
Pahang	–1.068 *	Pahang	–2.774
Penang	–0.291	Penang	7.010 **
Perak	–1.800 ***	Perak	–4.800 **
Perlis	–1.771 **	Perlis	–4.014 **
Selangor	–2.364 ***	Selangor	–3.427
Terengganu	0.047	Terengganu	0.781
Sabah	1.739 **	Sabah	–1.753
Sarawak	0.390	Sarawak	1.753
C	17.104 ***		
Time	0.036 **		
$Time^2$	–0.002 ***		

Fixed effects (Cross)	Coefficient	Effects specification: cross-section and period fixed	
Johor	61.813	R-squared	0.937
Kedah	9.357	Adjusted R-squared	0.933
Kelantan	–8.664	Akaike info criterion	1.230
Melaka	8.260	Schwarz criterion	1.537
Negeri Sembilan	–16.371	Hannan-Quinn criterion	1.350
Pahang	–2.836	Durbin-Watson statistic	0.380
Penang	–12.428	S.E. of regression	0.433
Perak	4.389	Sum squared residual	101.678
Perlis	4.114	Log likelihood	–318.219
Selangor	8.795	Probability (F-statistic)	0.000
Terengganu	–13.996		
Sabah	–29.051		
Sarawak	–18.087		

Notes: Level of statistical significance: * 10 per cent; ** 5 per cent; *** 1 per cent.
The dependent variable is the state poverty rate.

Commodity Production and Poverty Reduction

Many farmers specialize in growing a single crop, but at the state and national level agriculture is a remarkably heterogeneous activity. An important question is whether the commodity composition of that agricultural activity contributes to, or detracts from, its pro-poor character. For example, price support and subsidized inputs for poor rice farmers might boost their incomes and lift them out of poverty, but if the resultant high farm prices for rice are passed on to rice prices in urban areas, these could hurt poor consumers.[22] Smallholder rubber farmers might be poor when rubber prices are low. Similarly, unskilled labourers on corporate-owned palm oil estates might make too little to live above the poverty line.

Understanding the net effect on poverty of changes in the production of Malaysia's important agricultural commodities is complex. Nonetheless, it is a worthwhile endeavour because even a rough estimate of how the production of different commodities affects poverty may provide useful insights with important policy implications. With the data already presented in this chapter, it is possible to take a first step towards producing such estimates. To do so, state-level production of rice, rubber, and palm oil are added, in separate regressions, to the specification presented in Table 8.4. A summary of the commodity coefficients for each of the three specifications is presented in Table 8.5, along with the effect that inclusion has on the GDPPC coefficient. That is, all the coefficients in Table 8.4 are free to change with the introduction of the new commodity-specific variables, and the *interaction* between commodity production and the impact of incomes (GDPPC) on poverty is captured by the change in the GDPPC coefficient.[23]

Results

The results show that the kinds of commodities, as well as the states in which they are produced, matter considerably for poverty reduction. The impact is not uniform, however, and local circumstances matter at least as much as the type of commodity production. From the findings presented above, three key observations emerge.

---

22 Price supports for farmers do not necessarily raise the price for consumers if marketing subsidies are used.

23 The actual regression results of rice and palm oil, the two main commodities in this analysis, are reported in Annex Tables 8.4 and 8.5. The summary results in Table 8.5 are taken from these tables. No attempt has been made to assess the statistical significance of the change in the GDPPC coefficients. What is important is the strong difference in the signs of the changes for the rice and palm oil regressions.

Table 8.5 Commodity composition matters for poverty reduction[a]

State	Rice		Rubber		Palm Oil	
	Coefficient[b]	Change in GDPPC coefficient[c]	Coefficient[b]	Change in GDPPC coefficient[c]	Coefficient[b]	Change in GDPPC coefficient[c]
Johor	0.09	0.26	1.02 ***	0.30	0.33	1.20
Kedah	–1.07 *	–0.56	1.03 **	0.08	0.11	0.61
Kelantan	0.09	0.34	1.08 ***	0.61	–0.01	–0.01
Melaka	–0.74 ***	–0.25	0.07	–2.34	0.11	–1.10
Negeri Sembilan	0.29 **	0.30	–0.15	0.32	–0.4	–0.56
Pahang	0.70 ***	0.43	–0.44 **	0.26	–0.69 **	–1.21
Penang	0.84 *	1.51	0.19 **	0.58	1.99 ***	–1.10
Perak	1.33 **	0.52	0.04	–0.08	0.87 *	0.13
Perlis	–2.51 ***	–0.38	-	-	-	-
Selangor	1.52 **	0.84	–0.11 **	–1.04	2.78 ***	–1.10
Terengganu	–2.12 ***	0.24	0.88 ***	0.12	–0.29	–0.29
Sabah	–0.54	–0.41	0.58 *	0.19	–0.05	–0.19
Sarawak	0.61	0.39	0.56 ***	0.61	0.2	0.53

Notes: Level of statistical significance: * 10 per cent; ** 5 per cent; *** 1 per cent.
[a] Based on equations 4, 5, and 6 in Box 8.4. The dependent variable is the state poverty rate.
[b] Positive coefficients imply no poverty-reducing impacts, and negative coefficients imply a reduction in poverty rates.
[c] The change in GDPPC coefficient is the difference between its value in Table 8.4 and its value when commodity production levels are added.

First, each commodity has a significantly *different* direct impact on poverty, with some states demonstrating positive linkages for individual commodities and other states negative ones. For example, the direct impact of increasing rice production *reduces* poverty (holding all other factors constant) in four states—Kedah, Melaka, Perlis, and Terengganu. However, it raises poverty in five states—Negeri Sembilan, Pahang, Penang, Perak, and Selangor. As noted, the relative importance of smallholder rice production in each state is a major driver of this result, as is the prevalence of urban poverty in states where rice production is not so significant.

For rubber, increasing production tends not to reduce poverty in most states; only in Pahang and Selangor does it have a significant impact on reducing poverty. Rubber production has been falling in most states, and the remaining producers may not have the resources to diversify out of low-return rubber production. In states where the shift out of rubber has been slower, like Kedah and Kelantan, poverty rates have remained higher.

For palm oil, increasing production directly reduces poverty only in Pahang, and increases it in Penang, Perak, and Selangor. As discussed below, the major impact of palm oil production seems to be on income distribution in a state. These results need to be interpreted with caution, however. One reason is because prices and production of palm oil may not be positively correlated. Increases in commodity prices improve the economic livelihood of all farmers within the sector, but when prices fall, smallholders are most at risk of a decline in income (Abdul Aziz Abdul Rahman, 1996; Faisal M. Mohd Noor et al., 2017). Another reason is that the high start-up costs and the need for expensive fertilizers limit the suitability of oil palm as a poverty-reducing measure for the poorest rural households (Ayat K. A. Rahman et al., 2008). A distinction should thus be made between the differential effects of production of palm oil and prices on large plantation owners, smallholders, and general workers, including migrants. These impacts can only be disentangled through further study using microdata and other approaches.

Second, adding separately the three commodity systems to the regression specification in Table 8.4 has a notable impact on the elasticity of poverty reduction from the growth in per capita incomes (the coefficients on GDPPC). Including rice and rubber production in the equation *increases* the impact of GDPPC on POVX in nine states (Annex Table 8.4 for rice), thus making economic growth more pro-poor in these states. This result is almost certainly driven by the important role of smallholder producers in rice and rubber cultivation.

Including palm oil, however, has exactly the opposite effect, with the GDP per capita coefficient *falling* in eight states (Annex Table 8.5). The contrast with including rice in a similar specification is striking: rice increases the impact of income growth on poverty reduction, while palm oil reduces the impact. More specifically, for rice, none of the coefficient changes in Table 8.5 eliminates the beneficial impact of income growth on poverty reduction. However, increases in rice production tend to make income growth more equal, and increases in palm oil production tend to make income growth less equal. This result is likely due to the dominance of corporate organizations in palm oil production, with most of the profits flowing to owners outside the state of production, and labourers, many of them migrants, receiving relatively low wages.

Third, the actual coefficients estimated for each state for each commodity have low correlations with plausible explanatory variables that are easy to measure. For example, the size of commodity production in the state, or the degree of urbanization, is only weakly associated with the estimated impact of the commodity on poverty rates. It is easy to imagine, for instance, that efforts to increase rice production using increased financial incentives and higher prices will reduce poverty among rice growers, but will hurt the poor in rural and urban areas. Figure 8.7 illustrates this relationship by plotting the rice coefficients against the urbanization rates in each state in 1980 and 2010.[24] The fitted trend lines reveal a modest positive relationship in both periods: rice production has less of a poverty-reducing impact the more highly urbanized the state. Indeed, rice production actually increases poverty in the most urbanized states, almost certainly because price incentives to farmers are passed on to consumers as higher rice prices in urban markets. This would particularly affect low-income consumers below the urban poverty line, because this group typically consumes large quantities of rice.

Figure 8.7 **Rice production has less of a poverty-reducing impact the more highly urbanized the state, 1980 and 2010**

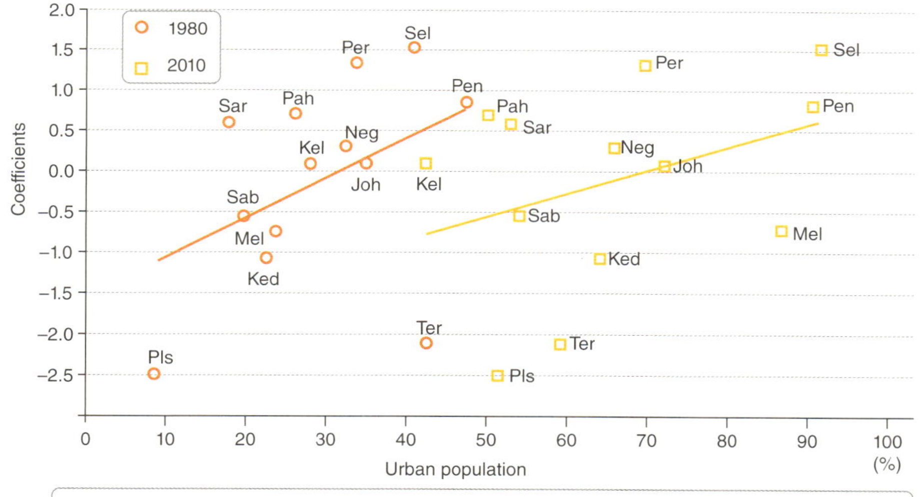

Joh	=	Johor	Mel	=	Melaka	Pen	=	Penang	Sel	= Selangor
Ked	=	Kedah	Neg	=	Negeri Sembilan	Per	=	Perak	Ter	= Terengganu
Kel	=	Kelantan	Pah	=	Pahang	Pls	=	Perlis	Sab	= Sabah
									Sar	= Sarawak

Note: Positive coefficients imply higher poverty rates; negative coefficients imply lower poverty rates.

24 See equation 7 defined in Box 8.4.

Conclusions

At independence, alongside many daunting and complex multi-dimensional challenges—especially unbalanced development, economic and social segmentation, and widespread poverty—Malaysia also inherited some substantial advantages from British colonial investments and policies. These included a developed communications and transportation infrastructure, a functioning civil service staffed largely with nationals, and well-developed commodity systems with efficient links to international markets. But some of these advantages also posed serious impediments to the new government. One such impediment has been the tension between the needs of the estate-based export crop sector and the costs of promoting domestic food production, largely based on rice.

This issue had an ethnic dimension because of the differing ownership and employment patterns of estate agriculture and smallholder *padi* producers. But it was also an economic issue because domestic rice production was quite expensive relative to the cost of imports. Keeping Malay rice producers in business through protection against imports and extensive subsidies for water and fertilizer slowed Malaysia's structural transformation in the early years after independence, but it also helped to reduce the deep poverty endemic to the rural Malay community. The rationale for government subsidies for rice, including a guaranteed minimum price, may be understood from the fact that the largest rice-producing states—Kedah, Kelantan, and Perlis—were also the poorest.

After 1970, structural transformation accelerated in nearly all states, including those where the share of agriculture in GDP was over 60 per cent—Kedah, Kelantan, Pahang, Perlis, Terengganu, Sabah, and Sarawak. Rural Malays found higher-paid jobs in urban areas: in the civil service, the military, and the national police in particular, as well as in manufacturing and a broad range of other occupations. Many Malays also became entrepreneurs and benefited from the NEP's affirmative action measures. The labour productivity of farmers who remained behind rose nearly as quickly as that of workers in urban areas, so the gap between rural and urban labour productivity started to narrow. Fast-rising incomes in rural and urban areas led to a rapid decrease in poverty, so that by the turn of the millennium absolute poverty had been almost eliminated, although income inequality still remained relatively high.

Rubber and palm oil production have vastly different impacts from *padi* production on the reduction of poverty, probably because of the distinction between corporate agriculture (rubber and oil palm) and smallholder agriculture (mostly *padi*).[25] The analysis cannot definitively determine the reasons for this difference, but the ownership patterns are one possible explanation. From the 1970s and even earlier, many large rubber estates were converted for oil palm cultivation, especially in Johor, Selangor, and Perak, as palm oil production became much more profitable than rubber production. The potential of palm oil production to reduce poverty by generating growth and increasing incomes has been noted by the World Bank (2011c). To realize this potential requires large-scale land acquisition for agriculture to be carried out with proper compensation and without loss of livelihood, especially for indigenous communities (Deininger et al., 2011).

Relatively little is known about the impact of agricultural commodity prices on poverty and its rate of decline. The analysis presented here has shown that higher commodity prices tend to lead to poverty reduction, but not in a uniform manner. Tantalizing evidence was adduced which indicated that much of the apparent 'reversal' of structural transformation in Perak (and probably in several other states) was caused by sharply increased prices for rubber, palm oil, and rice from 2005 to 2015 relative to prices in 2000. The producer price of rice is set politically and defended with a host of trade and price support measures. The prices for rubber and palm oil, however, are determined on international markets over which Malaysia has hardly any control. Thus, the country is at the mercy of international price movements with respect to continued high incomes from commodity production.

The growth and diversification of Malaysia's agriculture were key drivers in dramatically reducing poverty. A rapid and relatively efficient structural transformation has left the agricultural sector in the shadows compared with the more vibrant service and industrial sectors. Corporate agriculture, especially the cultivation of oil palm, remains dynamic. But food-oriented agriculture, especially rice farming, faces a more difficult future unless its focus changes to high-value foods. Labour productivity in agriculture has increased rapidly over the past 40 years, as it has in other non-agricultural

---

25 The divide between plantations and smallholders has become increasingly blurred with the emergence of organized smallholders under the management of agencies like FELDA, run along the lines of plantations, as well as with the development of private plantations and unorganized smallholders. While privately owned estates are still predominant in the cultivation of oil palm, rubber is increasingly being dominated by largely unorganized smallholders due to the conversion of rubber plantations to oil palm. And although poverty has declined substantially over time, inequality between smallholders and commercial farmers has widened (Fatimah Mohamed Arshad, 2013).

sectors, although from a lower base (Chapter 6). Rural-to-urban migration has played a major role in this convergence.

Malaysia's food security depends on a healthy agricultural sector connected to modern supply chains, efficient agro-processing, and competitive retail outlets. But food security no longer depends on the degree of rice self-sufficiency. More nutritious foods—vegetables, fruits, animal protein, and fish products—have greater value added at the farm level, as well as along the entire domestic food supply chain. These foods will have a much more important role in ensuring food security in the future.[26]

This chapter's analysis has provided several insights into the linkages between Malaysia's agricultural commodities and poverty reduction, but has left unanswered questions that can only be resolved with further in-depth fieldwork, and more detailed data on agricultural GDP at the state level and its individual commodity composition.

Beyond the substantial reduction in absolute poverty, Chapter 9—the last historical chapter—assesses Malaysia's steps and missteps on the long journey towards more widely shared national prosperity.

26 While the health consequences of Malaysia's changing dietary patterns are not fully understood, diet is implicated in the upsurge in the rates of obesity and diabetes. A nutrition-oriented food policy is needed, consistent with consumer preferences, market forces, and public health realities, but strong behavioural resistance to dietary changes would need to be overcome. Reducing the intake of unhealthy fats, sugars and ultra-processed food, increasing the intake of fresh fruits and vegetables, and adding regular exercise to a mostly sedentary urban lifestyle would all contribute to a healthier future and to higher labour force productivity.

Annex Table 8.1 Steady progress in poverty reduction halted during the Asian financial crisis but resumed in year 2000

Fixed effects (Cross)	Coefficient	Effects specification: cross-section and period fixed	
Johor	–0.802	R-squared	0.929
Kedah	0.442	Adjusted R-squared	0.922
Kelantan	0.767	Akaike info criterion	1.418
Melaka	–0.744	Schwarz criterion	1.851
Negeri Sembilan	–0.451	Hannan-Quinn criterion	1.587
Pahang	–0.122	Durbin-Watson statistic	0.208
Penang	–0.814	S.E. of regression	0.469
Perak	0.071	Sum squared residual	118.938
Perlis	0.421	Log likelihood	–365.756
Selangor	–1.104	Probability (F-statistic)	0.000
Terengganu	0.666		
Sabah	1.156		
Sarawak	0.512		
Intercept	**Coefficient**		
C	2.088***		

Fixed effects (Year)	Coefficient	Fixed effects (Year)	Coefficient	Fixed effects (Year)	Coefficient
1970	1.995	1986	0.914	2002	–0.392
1971	1.960	1987	0.897	2003	–0.570
1972	1.924	1988	0.789	2004	–0.747
1973	1.888	1989	0.680	2005	–0.832
1974	1.852	1990	0.578	2006	–0.917
1975	1.816	1991	0.476	2007	–1.001
1976	1.680	1992	0.374	2008	–1.080
1977	1.584	1993	0.256	2009	–1.159
1978	1.488	1994	0.136	2010	–1.423
1979	1.392	1995	0.017	2011	–1.687
1980	1.303	1996	–0.171	2012	–1.952
1981	1.214	1997	–0.360	2013	–2.540
1982	1.125	1998	–0.253	2014	–3.128
1983	1.036	1999	–0.145	2015	–3.730
1984	0.947	2000	–0.228	2016	–4.100
1985	0.930	2001	–0.310		

Notes: Level of statistical significance: *** 1 per cent.
Fixed-effect coefficients for each state and across the year measure variation across states and over time. These coefficients account for unique characteristics of each state and year. The dependent variable is the state poverty rate. A decline in the value of the coefficient from the previous year represents a decline in poverty.

Annex Table 8.2 Controlling for time-related structural changes in the economy, 95 per cent of variation in poverty is explained

Independent variable	Coefficient
C	1.793***
Time	–0.010
Time^2	–0.002***
R-squared	0.953
Adjusted R-squared	0.951
Akaike info criterion	0.703
Schwarz criterion	0.821
Hannan-Quinn criterion	0.747
Durbin-Watson statistic	0.153
S.E. of regression	0.333
Sum squared residual	4.891
Log likelihood	–13.515
Probability (F-statistic)	0.000

Notes: Level of statistical significance: *** 1 per cent.
The dependent variable is the coefficient from the year fixed-effect regression given in Table 8.1.

Annex Table 8.3 An increase in real GDP per capita lowers poverty rates

Independent variable (GDPPC)	Coefficient	Independent variable (GDPPC)	Coefficient
Johor	–1.855 ***	Perak	–0.874 ***
Kedah	–1.120 ***	Perlis	–0.703 *
Kelantan	–0.583 **	Selangor	–2.000 ***
Melaka	–1.410 ***	Terengganu	–0.311 **
Negeri Sembilan	–1.160 ***	Sabah	1.653 *
Pahang	–0.692 ***	Sarawak	–0.155
Penang	–1.301 ***		
Independent variable	**Coefficient**		
C	10.830 ***		
Time	0.058 ***		
$Time^2$	–0.003 ***		

Fixed effects (Cross)	Coefficient	Effects specification: cross-section and period fixed	
Johor	8.910	R-squared	0.927
Kedah	2.683	Adjusted R-squared	0.923
Kelantan	–2.151	Akaike info criterion	1.336
Melaka	4.750	Schwarz criterion	1.546
Negeri Sembilan	2.725	Hannan-Quinn criterion	1.418
Pahang	–1.564	Durbin-Watson statistic	0.284
Penang	3.970	S.E. of regression	0.461
Perak	0.315	Sum squared residual	118.177
Perlis	–1.166	Log likelihood	–362.127
Selangor	10.758	Probability (F-statistic)	0.000
Terengganu	–4.360		
Sabah	–22.766		
Sarawak	–6.168		

Notes: Level of statistical significance: * 10 per cent; ** 5 per cent; *** 1 per cent.
The dependent variable is the state poverty rate.

Annex Table 8.4 Rice production has different impacts on poverty at state level

Independent variable (GDPPC)	Coefficient	Independent variable (AgEMPshr)	Coefficient	Independent variable (RICX)	Coefficient
Johor	–7.790***	Johor	–16.581***	Johor	0.087
Kedah	–1.804**	Kedah	–1.185	Kedah	–1.067*
Kelantan	–0.834	Kelantan	0.532	Kelantan	0.085
Melaka	–2.042***	Melaka	1.523	Melaka	–0.739***
Negeri Sembilan	–0.198	Negeri Sembilan	3.566*	Negeri Sembilan	0.287**
Pahang	–1.501***	Pahang	–1.898	Pahang	0.700***
Penang	–1.800**	Penang	0.530	Penang	0.843*
Perak	–2.320***	Perak	–2.299	Perak	1.329***
Perlis	–1.392**	Perlis	–4.479**	Perlis	–2.508***
Selangor	–3.208***	Selangor	0.476	Selangor	1.521**
Terengganu	–0.197	Terengganu	1.782*	Terengganu	–2.123***
Sabah	2.150**	Sabah	–2.603	Sabah	–0.543
Sarawak	–0.003	Sarawak	0.569	Sarawak	0.606

Independent variable	Coefficient
C	20.375***
Time	0.099***
$Time^2$	–0.003***

Fixed effects (Cross)	Coefficient	Effects specification: cross-section and period fixed	
Johor	59.047	R-squared	0.947
Kedah	13.324	Adjusted R-squared	0.942
Kelantan	–11.228	Akaike info criterion	1.105
Melaka	6.998	Schwarz criterion	1.521
Negeri Sembilan	–20.177	Hannan-Quinn criterion	1.268
Pahang	–9.782	Durbin-Watson statistic	0.531
Penang	–10.472	S.E. of regression	0.402
Perak	–11.373	Sum squared residual	81.988
Perlis	25.760	Log likelihood	–256.538
Selangor	–4.853	Probability (F-statistic)	0.000
Terengganu	6.636		
Sabah	–30.729		
Sarawak	–25.136		

Notes: Level of statistical significance: * 10 per cent; ** 5 per cent; *** 1 per cent.
The dependent variable is the state poverty rate.

Annex Table 8.5 Palm oil production has different impacts on poverty at state level

Independent variable (GDPPC)	Coefficient	Independent variable (AgEMPshr)	Coefficient	Independent variable (RICX)	Coefficient
Johor	–8.731***	Johor	–18.135***	Johor	0.326
Kedah	–2.973***	Kedah	–3.177**	Kedah	0.114
Kelantan	–0.477	Kelantan	0.168	Kelantan	–0.013
Melaka	–1.188	Melaka	–0.943	Melaka	0.112
Negeri Sembilan	0.659	Negeri Sembilan	4.555**	Negeri Sembilan	–0.404
Pahang	0.138	Pahang	–2.771	Pahang	–0.693**
Penang	0.813	Penang	26.082**	Penang	1.992***
Perak	–1.934***	Perak	1.447	Perak	0.874*
Perlis	-	Perlis	-	Perlis	-
Selangor	–1.265*	Selangor	6.911**	Selangor	2.780***
Terengganu	0.335	Terengganu	1.034	Terengganu	–0.290
Sabah	1.930	Sabah	–0.807	Sabah	–0.046
Sarawak	–0.141	Sarawak	3.220	Sarawak	0.203

Independent variable	Coefficient
C	7.740**
Time	0.103***
$Time^2$	–0.003***

Fixed effects (Cross)	Coefficient	Effects specification: cross-section and period fixed	
Johor	77.118	R-squared	0.942
Kedah	21.930	Adjusted R-squared	0.935
Kelantan	–0.586	Akaike info criterion	1.047
Melaka	4.123	Schwarz criterion	1.515
Negeri Sembilan	–8.694	Hannan-Quinn criterion	1.232
Pahang	3.535	Durbin-Watson statistic	0.618
Penang	–37.939	S.E. of regression	0.387
Perak	0.521	Sum squared residual	57.664
Perlis	-	Log likelihood	–177.733
Selangor	–31.522	Probability (F-statistic)	0.000
Terengganu	–4.981		
Sabah	–22.066		
Sarawak	–7.717		

Notes: Level of statistical significance: * 10 per cent; ** 5 per cent; *** 1 per cent.
The dependent variable is the state poverty rate.

Chapter 9

Inequality: A Century of Change

The huge differences in average living standards among countries, and between the rich and poor within countries, have made the subject of inequality the central focus of many leading economists (Krugman, 1994; Sachs, 2011; Stiglitz, 2012; Deaton, 2013; Piketty, 2014). Vast inequality in income and wealth has led some to contend that the rich of today are living through a new Gilded Age, or 'Belle Époque', exceeding even the excesses of the 1870s and 1920s, with enormous riches concentrated at the top of the income and wealth distributions.[1] The argument is often made that wide inequality inhibits social inclusion, weakens social cohesion, and can ignite social conflict.

Policy success in minimizing inequality and promoting fairness requires the right balance between government intervention and the free market. This involves determining what levels of social services, such as education, health, and income transfers, should be provided; what regulations should be adopted to protect the rights of workers; and what type of tax system should be put in place. With an awareness that the dividends from economic growth should not be skewed towards the rich, and that in a multi-ethnic country social conflict can result from the unfettered operation of markets, since independence and especially after the tragic events of 1969, the Malaysian government has consistently sought to ensure that prosperity is widely shared.

Income can be viewed from three perspectives: growth, poverty, and inequality. Growth is about how average incomes change (Chapters 5, 6, and 7); poverty is about the bottom of the income distribution (Chapter 8); and

1 The income and wealth shares of the top 1 per cent are the headline in rising inequality. Before World War I, this 1 per cent received about a fifth of total income in the UK and US. By 1950, that share had been cut by more than half. In the post–World War II period, industrial economies were relatively egalitarian and income differences were modest, as the cost of war, inflation, and progressive taxation eroded differentials. However, since 1980 the 1 per cent has seen its income share surge again (Krugman, 1994).

inequality, the focus of this chapter, is about how widely incomes are spread among households. This chapter explores how economic policies and institutional arrangements have affected the levels and patterns of inequality in Malaysia over the past 11 decades or so.

An assessment of income differentials and inequality in colonial Malaya has been held back by the limited direct evidence on income or consumption before World War II. The earliest surveys giving insights into income inequality were analysed by Anand (1983), providing a baseline for poverty and inequality in post-independence Malaysia. With the recent availability of national income accounts for the first four decades of the 20th century (Sultan Nazrin Shah, 2017) and related databases from the Economic History of Malaya Project (www.ehm.my), it has now become possible to use indirect approaches to estimate inequality in colonial Malaya, and to track how it has changed over time. Although it is not possible to determine *income* inequality from this data set, it is possible to assess inequality in *expenditure* by analysing consumption differentials.

Estimates are made of the per capita expenditures of six 'consumption standards', broadly defined in terms of ethnicity and occupation. The standards of living vary substantially across these six consumption standards, and a conspicuously high level of consumption inequality is observed, reflecting the structure of economic production, vast differentials in wages, and lack of workers' protection.

This chapter begins with an analysis of inequality during the British colonial period, using indirect estimation methods applied to consumption expenditure. The sequence of steps in the estimation process is necessarily technical and readers may choose to skip to the summary at the end of this section. The next section assesses trends in income growth and inequality in post-independence Malaysia, especially the half-century since 1970. The following section considers the challenges of measuring income inequality from the available data sources, and the types of indices applied. An evaluation is then made of the impact of two recent financial and economic crises on income inequality in Malaysia: the Asian financial crisis and the Great Recession.

The chapter goes on to analyse differentials in income inequality by ethnic community, urban versus rural residence, education, household size, and state. The final section moves beyond simple two-way relationships to further explore the factors responsible for unequal incomes, using multiple regression techniques. Throughout, extensive use is made of the Gini coefficient (among other indicators) as a summary measure of inequality (Box 9.1).

Box 9.1 The Gini coefficient and the Lorenz curve

A widely used measure of inequality is the Gini coefficient, which is based on the Lorenz curve, an example of which is presented in Box Figure 9.1. The Lorenz curve—notationally *L*(*p*)—plots the share of total income received by the poorest *p* individuals in the population. The curve shown is that for Malaysia in 2016, which is examined in more detail later in the chapter.

Box Figure 9.1 The Lorenz curve, 2016

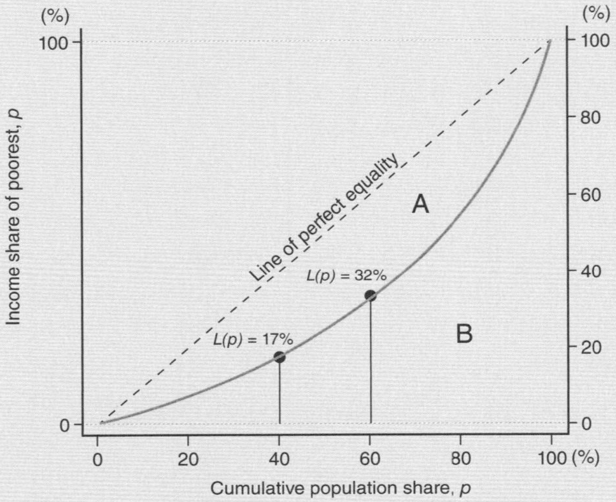

The graph shows that the poorest 40 per cent of the population in this year received just 17 per cent of total income. If incomes had been equally distributed over the whole population, the 'poorest' 40 per cent would have received 40 per cent of total income. This is shown by the line of perfect equality—the dashed line in the figure. The poorest 60 per cent of the population received just 32 per cent of total income compared with 60 per cent under perfect equality. When income is unequally distributed, the Lorenz curve is 'bowed' beneath the line of perfect equality: the more unequally distributed the income, the more bowed the Lorenz curve.

The Gini coefficient measures the area between the Lorenz curve and the hypothetical line of perfect equality, expressed as a proportion or percentage of the area under the equality line. Graphically, it is defined as the area A divided by the sum of the areas A and B. If incomes were perfectly equally distributed, the Lorenz 'curve' would lie along the dashed line of perfect equality and the area A would collapse to zero.

Hence a Gini of 0 represents perfect income equality. If all individuals except one earned zero income, the Lorenz curve would hug the horizontal axis for all but the final individual. In this case the area B would be zero and the Gini coefficient would be equal to 1 (or 100 per cent if the Gini is expressed as a percentage). The Gini coefficient for the Lorenz curve shown is 0.396. Although the Gini is based on the incomes of all sampled individuals, it tends to be most sensitive to changes in income distribution around the median (Atkinson, 1970).

Inequality and Consumption in Malaya, 1900–1939

There is little direct evidence on inequality in income or consumption in Malaya before World War II. Still, estimates made by Sultan Nazrin Shah (2017) reveal wide differences in expenditure per capita across six 'consumption standards'—Malay labour, Indian labour, Chinese labour, Asiatic clerical, Eurasian clerical, and European—conceptualized on the basis of ethnicity and occupation (Figure 9.1).[2] The standards of living varied greatly across these six standards. In 1900, per capita consumption in the Malay labour standard was slightly less than 4 per cent of that in the European standard. Although the differential had narrowed marginally by 1920, it then widened again so that by 1939 the consumption level of those in the Malay labour standard was only about 3 per cent of that in the European standard.

Differentials between the three poorer standards—comprising some 97 per cent of the population—were more modest, albeit still significant. For example, per capita consumption of the Chinese labour standard was 1.5 times that of the Malay labour standard in 1900, and 1.3 times that of the Malay labour standard in 1939. This finding is consistent with the higher wages earned by the Chinese who were generally employed in the relatively higher-paid skilled and semi-skilled occupations.[3] Most Malays were engaged in subsistence rice farming and fishing (Parmer, 1960; Ramasamy, 1994; Kaur, 2004).

2 These consumption standard differentials were based on indirectly estimated expenditures, and excluded directly estimated expenditures on opium/chandu, education and medical fees, utilities, rail and ferry transport, and miscellaneous items. The differentials reported here are based on total expenditures, that is, indirectly and directly estimated expenditures. Sultan Nazrin Shah (forthcoming) provides the details.

3 Because Indian workers accepted lower wages than Chinese workers, plantation companies that initially employed Chinese labourers replaced them with Tamils in the early decades of the 20th century (Labour Research Department, 1926).

Figure 9.1 **Malay labour consumption per capita never exceeded 5 per cent of the European consumption standard during 1900–1939**

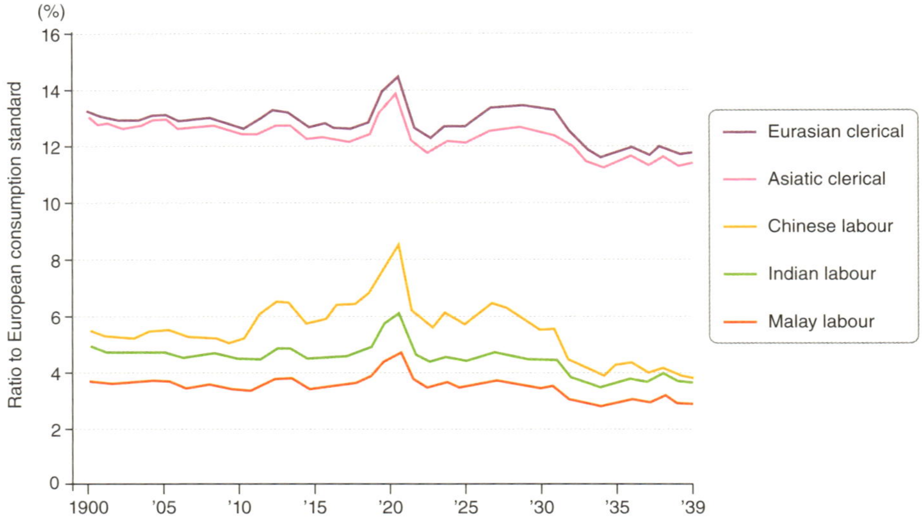

Source of data: Sultan Nazrin Shah (forthcoming).
Note: European consumption standard = 100.

Savings and remittances abroad would have varied across the six standards, so it is highly probable that variations in per capita *consumption* underestimate per capita *income* differences across standards. For example, savings and remittances of individuals in the four highest consumption standards are likely to have been proportionately greater than those of individuals in the Malay and Indian standards.

In short, inequality in consumption during this period was staggering, and there were no redistribution mechanisms under British colonial laissez-faire economic policy (Chapter 5).[4]

Piece-wise Linear Lorenz Curves

Although there are no individual-level observations, it is possible to construct 'piece-wise linear' Lorenz curves and obtain Gini coefficients based on these estimates of the per capita consumption levels of each standard. These assume no intra-standard variation in per capita consumption: all those within a standard are assumed to have the same consumption level. Milanovic et al. (2011, p. 260) refer to these as 'lower-bound Ginis'. The 'true' Gini coefficients will obviously be far higher, given expected intra-standard variation in per capita consumption.

4 Income tax was introduced only in 1948 to support post-war reconstruction efforts and as the movement towards decolonization began.

By way of example, a piece-wise linear Lorenz curve using consumption per capita for the six standards in 1920 is shown in Figure 9.2. The first point along the Lorenz curve is labelled 'Poorest standard: Malay labour'. The first segment of the curve assumes that all Malay labour individuals enjoyed the same consumption of Straits$90.2 in 1920, and that there were no poorer individuals in this standard. In that year, individuals in the Malay labour standard accounted for 55 per cent of the population, but only 36 per cent of total consumption. Hence the Lorenz curve lies below the line of perfect equality. If all individuals in each of the six standards had enjoyed the same consumption levels, Malay labour individuals would also have enjoyed a 55 per cent share of total consumption.

Figure 9.2 **Poorest three labour standards accounted for 95 per cent of the population but only 79 per cent of Malaya's consumption in 1920**

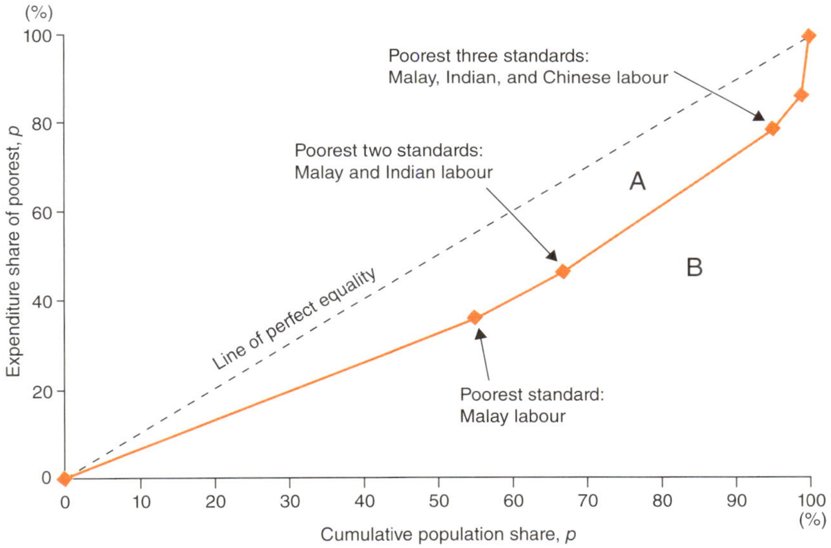

The second point along the curve is labelled 'Poorest two standards: Malay and Indian labour'. Indian labour individuals enjoyed a consumption level of Straits$119 in 1920. Indian labour and Malay labour individuals accounted for 67 per cent of the population, but only 46 per cent of total consumption. Hence the Lorenz curve is still well below the line of perfect equality. Because Indian labour individuals enjoyed a slightly higher standard of living than Malay labour individuals, this second linear segment of the Lorenz curve is slightly steeper than the first.

The third point along the curve is labelled 'Poorest three standards: Malay, Indian, and Chinese labour'. Chinese labour individuals enjoyed a consumption level of Straits$161 in 1920. These three poorest standards accounted for 95 per cent of the population, but only 79 per cent of total consumption. Once again, because Chinese labour individuals enjoyed a higher level of consumption than the other two labour standards, the Lorenz curve between the second and third points is steeper than in the first two segments.

The remaining segments of the Lorenz curve become progressively steeper as the three richer standards are included. The segment linking the Asiatic and Eurasian clerical standards is too small to detect in the graph, as only 0.1 per cent of the population were in the Eurasian clerical standard in 1920. The per capita consumption of the European standard in 1920 was Straits$1,909. All other standards earned less than this, so the final segment of the Lorenz curve passes through values of 100 per cent on both axes.

Lower-bound Gini

The lower-bound Gini coefficients, based on the piece-wise linear Lorenz curve, are shown in Table 9.1.[5] They indicate significantly higher levels of inequality over the period, especially after 1910. Consumption inequality is likely to be lower than income inequality because of variations in savings and remittances across standards, as mentioned above. Furthermore, since these Gini coefficients are based on the assumption that there is no variation in per capita consumption *within* the standards, they will understate the true degree of inequality among Malayan individuals.

Table 9.1 Lower-bound Gini coefficients for Malaya increased over time

1900	1905	1910	1915	1920	1925	1930	1935	1939
0.217	0.223	0.231	0.304	0.271	0.301	0.299	0.295	0.295

Intra-standard Consumption Variance

Consumption Gini coefficients that do allow for intra-standard variations can also be estimated to give a sharper picture of consumption inequality in the colonial period. However, as these are based on untested assumptions, they should be interpreted with caution. The two key assumptions are that:

- The distribution of per capita *income* within standards can be used to inform the distribution of per capita *consumption*. This is a strong assumption: richer households are likely to save or repatriate more

5 When there is no intra-standard variation in consumption, the Gini coefficient is given by:

$$G_1 = \sum_i^N \sum_j^N \frac{\omega_i \omega_j c_i}{c} \operatorname{sign}(c_i - c_j)$$

where N is the number of standards (six in our case), ω_i and ω_j are the population shares of standards i and j respectively, c_i and c_j are the average per capita consumption of standards i and j respectively, and c is the aggregate per capita consumption (Young, 2011).

of their income, so inequality in income is likely to exceed that in consumption. This bias is minimized through the choice of the income subsample used.

- The intra-standard distributions of per capita income and consumption are log normal.[6]

The log-normal distribution has been used to estimate Gini coefficients when data sources are scarce (Box 9.2). For example, Modalsli (2011) uses this distribution to analyse income inequality with limited data from a collection of 25 'social tables' from the Roman Empire to British India in 1947.

Box 9.2 Estimating intra-standard consumption variance

The assumption of the log-normal distribution for intra-standard variations in consumption has one very helpful feature: the distribution's Gini coefficient has the following closed form:

$$G_i = 2\phi\left(\frac{\sigma_i}{\sqrt{2}}\right) - 1 \qquad (1)$$

where G_i is the Gini coefficient for the *i*th standard, σ_i is the standard deviation of log per capita consumption of individuals within standard *i*, and ϕ is the cumulative standard normal distribution function. With knowledge of a consumption standard's Gini coefficient, the standard deviation of log consumption per capita is obtained simply by inverting equation (1):

$$\sigma_i = \sqrt{2}\phi^{-1}\left(\frac{1+G_i}{2}\right) \qquad (2)$$

where ϕ^{-1} is the inverse of the cumulative standard normal distribution. Within each consumption standard *i*, mean consumption is $c_i = exp\left(\mu_i + 0.5\sigma_i^2\right)$ where μ_i is the mean of log consumption among those in the *i*th consumption standard. And $\sigma_i^2 = ln\left(1 + cv_i^2\right)$, where $cv_i (= s_i/c_i)$ is the coefficient of variation, that is, the ratio of the standard deviation of consumption per capita (s_i) to the mean level of consumption per capita (c_i) in standard *i*. This means that the assumption of a constant variance of log consumption (σ_i^2) implies that the coefficient of variation (s_i/c_i) would also be constant. The standard deviations of consumption per capita within standards are proportional to their means.

Given each standard's σ_i^2, the national Gini is then obtained by:[7]

$$G = \sum_j^N \sum_j^N \frac{\omega_i \omega_j c_i}{c}\left[2\phi\left(\frac{\ln(c_i) - \ln(c_j) + 0.5(\sigma_i^2 + \sigma_j^2)}{\sqrt{\sigma_i^2 + \sigma_j^2}}\right) - 1\right] \qquad (3)$$

6 Log-normality assumes that the logarithm of income is normally distributed, rather than income itself. The standard reference is Aitchison and Brown (1957).

7 For the derivation of equation (3), see Modalsli (2011) and Young (2011).

Intra-standard Dispersion

In estimating Malaya's pre-1940 consumption Gini, the challenge is to find reasonable estimates of the variance of each consumption standard σ_i^2. Because there are no income or expenditure surveys available for the pre-war period, assumptions about intra-standard variation are based on post-war surveys. Anand (1983) analyses several household surveys that could provide a guide to per capita consumption inequality within standards. These are the 1957–1958 Household Budget Survey, the 1967–1968 Malaysian Socio-Economic Sample Survey of Households, and the 1970 Post-enumeration Survey (PES).

Anand reports significant differences in income Gini coefficients for Peninsular Malaysia based on these three surveys: 0.371 for the Household Budget Survey, 0.562 for the Malaysian Socio-Economic Sample Survey of Households, and 0.513 for the PES. After a detailed investigation of the three data sets, he concludes that the 'differences are not indicative of actual changes in inequality over time, and might be wholly due to differences between the surveys in income concept and coverage' (Anand, 1983, p. 42). His preferred survey is the 1970 PES, and per capita income inequalities from this survey are used to inform likely intra-standard variations in per capita consumption in the colonial period.

The PES was conducted around the start of the NEP period, and while it provides the closest guide to calibrating the intra-standard consumption variations in the colonial era, changes had already taken place by this time. For example, the Malay, Indian, and Chinese populations in pre-war Malaya were predominantly rural, whereas by 1970 the urban shares of the three ethnic groups had grown considerably, especially those of Chinese and Indians (Chapter 2).

According to the 1970 PES, 29 per cent of the population of Peninsular Malaysia was urban. Some 14 per cent of Malays, 36 per cent of Indians, and 49 per cent of Chinese lived in metropolitan areas or towns.[8] The national Gini coefficients by ethnicity reported by Anand are thus unlikely to capture consumption inequality in predominantly rural colonial populations. For this reason, the intra-standard dispersions in per capita consumption are assumed to be best based on the Gini coefficients reported by Anand for the rural populations of Malays, Indians, and Chinese in 1970. Among these individuals, savings are likely to have been sufficiently small for subgroup income variations to provide reasonable estimates of σ_i^2.

8 See Anand (1983), Table 3.11. The proportion of Chinese living in urban areas had grown significantly by 1970 because of the resettlement of many rural Chinese to New Villages during the Emergency (Box 1.2 in Chapter 1 and Box 5.8 in Chapter 5).

The Gini coefficients based on the dispersion of per capita incomes among rural Malays, Indians, and Chinese in 1970 are given in Table 9.2. Collectively, these three consumption standards accounted for around 95 per cent of the population of Malaya over the period 1900–1939, so the overall Gini will largely be determined by assumptions made about the intra-standard variations for these low-income groups. For simplicity, it is assumed that there was no intra-standard variation in consumption per capita for the richest three standards (Asiatic clerical, Eurasian clerical, and European), which together accounted for only 5 per cent of the population.[9]

Table 9.2 Subgroup rural Gini coefficients and log-normal standard deviations, 1970

Consumption standard	G_i	σ_i
Malay labour	0.427	0.798
Indian labour	0.412	0.765
Chinese labour	0.404	0.751

Source of data: Anand (1983), Table 3.11.
Note: The standard deviations are derived using equation (2) in Box 9.2.

Using equation (3) in Box 9.2, per capita consumption Gini coefficients for Malaya are estimated using the intra-standard standard deviations (σ_i) given in Table 9.2. The results are presented in Table 9.3, where G_1 values—Gini coefficients estimated assuming no intra-standard variation in consumption from Table 9.1—are also shown. Using similarly sparse data, Milanovic et al. (2011) estimate Gini coefficients of 0.485 for Siam in 1929, and 0.497 for British India in 1947. The Malayan Gini coefficients are similar, but they reveal a high and rising level of inequality over the first four decades of the 20th century, with a distinct worsening after the Great Depression.

Table 9.3 Consumption inequality increased in colonial Malaya between 1900 and 1939

	1900	1910	1920	1930	1939
G_1	0.217	0.231	0.271	0.299	0.295
G	0.484	0.490	0.502	0.528	0.547
P90/P10	9.140	9.290	9.163	10.058	8.567
P90/P50	3.166	3.192	3.056	3.448	3.042

Notes: See above text for details of G_1. See following text for details of P90/P10 and of P90/P50.

Simulated Indicators of Inequality

The distribution of per capita consumption in a mixed log-normal distribution is not itself log normal, and closed-form expressions for other indicators of

9 Anand's (1983) reported Gini coefficient of 0.707 for 'Other' ethnic groups captures the substantial differences in per capita consumption of the richest three standards.

inequality cannot be derived. Simulation methods can be used instead to obtain these indicators and to facilitate graphical techniques such as the Lorenz curve. Simulated log-normal observations for each of the six consumption standards are created for the four decennial years. The simulated data are based on a sample size of ten million, distributed among the six standards to reflect their shares in the population. The simulated observations are based on the mean per capita consumption levels, the log-normal distribution, and the standard deviations given in Table 9.2.

Two widely used indicators of inequality are P90/P10 and P90/P50. The numerator of these ratios, P90, is the lowest income earned by the richest 10 per cent of the population; the denominator, P10, is the highest income earned by the poorest 10 per cent of individuals; and P50 is the median income, the income of an individual halfway through the distribution. If incomes were equally distributed, these numbers would be 1. In 1900, the ratio of mean per capita consumption of Malay labour to that of Europeans was 27, while the P90/P10 ratio, for simulated data with intra-standard variability, was 9.14. Furthermore, although the estimated Gini coefficient rose to its highest level in 1939, the P90/P10 and P90/P50 ratios for that year fell from the levels they had been at a decade earlier (Table 9.3).

The simulated data can also be used for graphical presentations of the dispersion of per capita consumption (Figure 9.3). The first Lorenz curve (the solid black line in the figure) is based simply on the 1900 mean per

Figure 9.3 **Lorenz curves for colonial Malaya bow more with intra-standard inequality**

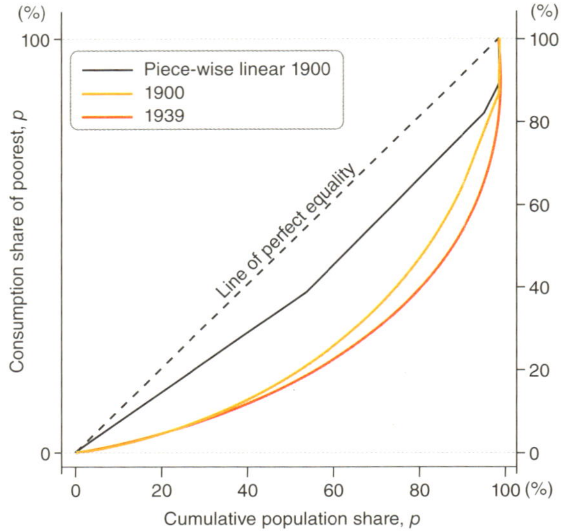

capita consumption estimates. It allows for no intra-standard variations in per capita consumption. The second (yellow) and third (orange) curves are based on simulated data for 1900 and 1939, and both allow for intra-standard dispersion, as described above.

The graph clearly illustrates the increasing inequality in the colonial period: the Lorenz curve for 1939 is everywhere further from the line of equality than that for 1900; the respective Gini coefficients are 0.547 and 0.484.

Summary of Inequality in the Colonial Era

Colonial Malaya was a highly unequal society. Imbalances in economic and social development perpetuated and increased consumption inequality during the first half of the 20th century.[10] The Europeans and a small minority of Malays, Chinese, and Indians who were living according to the European standard were far better off than the vast majority. As Myrdal (1968) observes in his seminal book *Asian Drama*, written around a decade after the country achieved independence in 1957, although Malaya was one of the richest countries in 'South Asia', there was vast inequality 'between the several ethnic groups and, especially, between the different classes within them' (Myrdal, 1968, p. 383).

Ownership of plantation and mining assets, as well as control of the lucrative export and import trade, were in the hands of British agency houses and, to a much lesser extent, a small group of wealthy Chinese businessmen located mainly in the Straits Settlements. Laissez-faire economic policies ensured that the rewards from substantial economic growth were largely expatriated by these agency houses. Real wages of the estate and mining labourers were kept low by the seemingly unlimited supply of new migrants, and there was no safety net for those who lost their jobs at times of depressed rubber and tin prices.[11] Many among the working population were engaged in subsistence farming—predominantly Malays, but also a significant share of the Chinese—outside the monetized wage economy. Most farmlands were owned by the Malay aristocracy. Poverty, illiteracy, insecurity, and indebtedness were endemic.

10 In one of the most thorough studies of income inequality and poverty in post-colonial Malaysia, Anand estimates that for 1957–1958 the mean household incomes per month for the Malays, Indians, and Chinese were M$144, M$217, and M$272 respectively (Anand, 1983, p. 36). An earlier analysis of ethnic income differentials for 1947, based on the national income accounts estimated by Benham, is given in Silcock and Fisk (1963, p. 276–281).

11 Myrdal (1968) further notes that a portion of the income accruing to low-paid migrant workers on the estates was remitted to their families. Plantation wages, although low, were usually higher than earnings in subsistence farming.

Measuring Income Inequality in Malaysia, 1970–2016

The previous section analysed *consumption* inequality. This section analyses *income* inequality,[12] using data from a series of six Household Income Surveys (HISs) conducted in 1995, 1999, 2004, 2009, 2014, and 2016 by the Department of Statistics–Malaysia. Together they provide a perspective on changing trends in household income and in its distribution over these two decades. Comparing the HIS results with Anand's (1983) baseline estimates for 1970 helps to illuminate longer-term trends.

Income inequality has received growing worldwide attention from economists, politicians, and the media, especially in the US and Europe, where the focus is on the rising share of the top 1 per cent of the income distribution. French economist Thomas Piketty (2014) has expressed concern that modern market economies are returning to something like the Gilded Age in the US, or the 'Belle Époque' in France, periods in which income differentials widened considerably. He demonstrates that if the rate of return on capital exceeds the growth rate of the economy, income inequality will worsen, with top earners enjoying a rising share of total income. Atkinson et al. (2011) find evidence supporting Piketty's concerns: top income shares have increased hugely in English-speaking countries and in India and China. Markets by themselves have proved inadequate in helping the poorest, with the result that growing prosperity has been accompanied by growing inequality.

In Malaysia, a more equitable income distribution has been a central policy objective, especially since the 1969 ethnic riots.[13] The NEP sought to decouple the association of ethnic group with occupation so as to achieve a fairer distribution of income among the different ethnic communities, as well as spatially between different states and between rural and urban areas (Chapters 2 and 7). The National Development Policy, which replaced the NEP in 1990, continued affirmative action for Malays and other *Bumiputera*, although with an increased focus on intra-ethnic income inequality. Economic policies have been designed to promote growth while ensuring that the benefits of that growth are widely shared. Social policies have focused on increasing access to education at all levels, and on providing government transfers and other benefits to the most disadvantaged.

12 By focusing on income, this chapter analyses inequality of outcomes rather than inequality of opportunity.

13 In the period between independence and 1970, the continuation of laissez-faire policy perpetuated the urban bias in the distribution of the benefits of economic growth, and it appears that income inequality widened, although differences in the methodologies used to collect income data during this period make the magnitude of change uncertain (Snodgrass, 1980; Shireen Mardziah Hashim, 1998).

Limitations of Income Survey Data

Income surveys, based as they are on population sampling frames, often fail to fully capture the incomes of the very top earners.[14] This group represents an extremely small share of the population, but an extremely significant share of total income. Inequality indices are very sensitive to the exclusion or inclusion of top incomes, so the probable absence of these individuals and their households from income surveys is a major weakness. For this reason, much of the recent international research on top income shares is based instead on tax return data, as these tend to provide far better coverage of the top earners. According to Piketty et al. (2016), the income share of the top 1 per cent in China in recent years was about 7 per cent according to surveys, but around 13 per cent according to income tax data.[15]

For their part, tax data have two shortcomings: low-income earners are not covered if they pay no tax; and tax returns are for individuals rather than households. If households have more than one taxpayer, inequality measures based only on tax data will be biased upwards. Larrimore et al. (2017) calculate measures of inequality in the US, based firstly only on household survey data (Current Population Survey), and secondly only on tax data where the unit is the household rather than the individual. The Gini coefficient in March 2010 was estimated at 0.483 using the former measure, and was around 8 per cent higher for the latter, at 0.524. Burkhauser et al. (2017) also find that survey data underestimate top income shares relative to tax data, particularly between the mid 1990s and the late 2000s.

The likely under-representation of the highest income earners needs to be kept in mind when interpreting the income-inequality measures based on HIS data. This under-representation will probably have less bearing on the interpretation of *trends* unless the omission of the highest income earners is increasing. But if the incomes of the highest earners are under-reported, the *level* of inequality will be underestimated.

The HIS data presented below are subject to another limitation. The universe of the data analysed relates only to Malaysian citizens. It excludes migrant workers, who tend to be the lowest skilled and lowest paid. This will have the effect of underestimating inequality, and although it may not markedly

---

14 Greater efforts are needed to carefully evaluate the HIS-estimated mean incomes compared with those obtained through the national accounts and other sources, so that any weaknesses can be identified and corrections made. Similarly, including legally employed migrant workers in the sample and making these data available would improve low-income profiles.

15 Using tabulations of income tax data classified in broad income groups, Atkinson (2015) has estimated the distribution of top incomes in Peninsular Malaysia from 1947 to 1988, and in Malaysia from 1992 to 2012. While the estimates are sensitive to different assumptions about income control groups and about adjustments for different income definitions, his data show that the share of income of the top 5 per cent of income earners has declined over time from around 19 per cent in 1995 to 18 per cent in 2012 (Atkinson, 2015, p. 13). This trend is broadly consistent with the decline in income inequality shown in Table 9.7 of this chapter using HIS data.

affect the Gini coefficient, it could affect other inequality measures (Box 9.3). There are thus potential biases in indicators of inequality arising from missing income earners at both tails of the distribution.

Box 9.3 The impact of inclusion of non-Malaysian citizens on inequality measures is small

The 2004 HIS covered both Malaysian and non-Malaysian citizens. In that year, of Malaysia's population of 25.5 million, around 7 per cent were non-Malaysian citizens. Of the 173,000 individuals surveyed for the 2004 HIS, however, just 4 per cent were non-Malaysian citizens. This under-representation of non-Malaysian citizens in the 2004 HIS may be partly because some foreign workers live in collective households, and partly because they are heavily clustered in particular states, such as Sabah, Selangor, and Penang, which could result in their being under-represented in a national sample.

Some non-Malaysian citizens may live in their own households, while others live as members of the households where they work—as maids, for example. Houseworkers are considered to be independent one-person households. Their incomes consist of payments received in cash and those given in kind as goods and services, and will therefore include food and accommodation provided by the household that employs them.

The effects on inequality of the inclusion of non-Malaysian citizens are set out in Box Table 9.1, where the indices are calculated across individuals in the 2004 HIS. The measures (defined below) consistently indicate a higher level of inequality when non-Malaysian citizens are included, although the differences are very small.

Box Table 9.1 Inequality is marginally higher in 2004 when non-Malaysian citizens are included

		Malaysian citizens	Citizens and non-Malaysian citizens
Per capita income	Gini coefficient	0.482	0.485
	Lowest quintile share (%)	4.30	4.25
Equivalized income[a]	Gini coefficient	0.458	0.461
	Lowest quintile share (%)	4.84	4.81

Note: [a] See Box 9.4 for a definition of equivalized income.

Income Surveys and the National Accounts

Mean income estimated from surveys is often lower than per capita income or consumption obtained through national accounts (Deaton, 2005). This phenomenon has been linked with the under-reporting of very high incomes in surveys. Banerjee and Piketty (2010) find that in India the discrepancy between estimates of household final consumption expenditure in the national accounts and in household surveys stems from this issue of missing or under-reported top-level incomes. Lakner and Milanovic (2015) also attribute the difference between national accounts and survey incomes entirely to the top decile, but only when the survey income estimate is lower than the national accounts estimate. They smooth the top decile using a Pareto distribution, following the procedure described in Atkinson (2007).

Anand and Segal (2008, 2015, and 2017) give reasons to question this use of national accounts to adjust survey data at the top end. Although national accounts data are based on a wide range of sources (generally including tax return data), they are often substantially revised and can provide unreliable benchmarks, especially in low-income countries (Jerven, 2013). Attributing the mismatch of survey data and national accounts entirely to the top end of the distribution is therefore questionable. For example, Lakner and Milanovic (2013 and 2015) find that in 2008 in India, the survey mean was only 53 per cent of the national accounts target, and they attribute the remaining 47 per cent of the mismatch to the top decile.

Ng (2018) adjusts the Gini coefficient for Malaysia by stretching the top incomes to match the national accounts controls. He bases the correction on the divergence between aggregate income in the HIS for 2012, 2014, and 2016, and aggregate consumption for these years from the national accounts. Ng reports 'corrected' Gini coefficients for 2012, 2014, and 2016 of 0.498, 0.437, and 0.435 respectively, compared with the 'official' estimates of 0.431, 0.401, and 0.399. Stretching the upper tail to match the national accounts controls raises the Gini by around 10 per cent. Ng also corrects for omitted low-income households (non-citizens are excluded), but the impact of this on the Gini coefficient is marginal (Box 9.3).[16]

The possible omission of the very rich from surveys may be one reason why survey aggregates fail to match national accounts totals. But the assumption that this is the only factor accounting for the difference is unsupportable. There is very little direct evidence to indicate that the survey/national accounts mismatch is entirely due to top-end under-reporting. Furthermore, the national accounts income estimates are themselves subject to a wide range of possible measurement errors.

In stretching the top end of the distribution with 'synthetic' observations, moreover, details of the original households' characteristics are lost. This then precludes an analysis of the factors responsible for income inequality, conducted by linking the characteristics of households with their position in the income hierarchy. This kind of analysis, using HIS data not adjusted to cover the highest income earners, is presented here. To the extent that the

16 Ng's Gini coefficients corrected for under-reporting at both ends of the distribution are 0.499, 0.443, and 0.441 for 2012, 2014, and 2016 respectively. In a recent innovative study of trends in income inequality in Malaysia, Muhammed Abdul Khalid and Li (2019) use income tax data to adjust the HIS at the top end of the distribution, and then scale the distribution to ensure it agrees with the national accounts. In 2014, the income shares of the top 1 per cent of adults rose from 8 per cent based on the HIS alone to 15 per cent when both adjustments are made.

HISs fail to fully capture the very top end of the distribution, the measures of inequality reported here can be viewed as representing the lower bounds of the true degree of inequality.

Malaysian Household Income Surveys

The HISs contain detailed information on individuals and households,[17] including household income (by source) and the characteristics of household members, such as their age, sex, education, health, and marital status. The surveys cover individuals living in private residences, but exclude those living in an institutional setting—for example, hotels, hospitals, and military barracks—as well as non-Malaysian citizens. The sampling frames for the surveys are based on the most recent population census.[18]

Table 9.4 **Household characteristics have changed markedly over time**

				Households (%) with:		
	Sample	Average household size	Average no. of children[a]	1–2 members	3–4 members	5 or more members
1970[b]	25,023	5.36	2.23	9.23	12.36	78.40
1995	37,351	4.63	1.71	19.97	30.62	49.41
1999	36,495	4.47	1.44	20.64	32.75	46.60
2004	36,482	4.47	1.35	20.42	32.73	46.85
2009	43,026	4.16	1.14	23.32	36.99	39.68
2014	81,137	4.24	1.04	19.56	39.54	40.90
2016	78,297	4.05	0.94	23.19	39.71	37.10

Source of data: Derived from unpublished data from the Household Income Surveys of 1995, 1999, 2004, 2009, 2014, and 2016, supplied by the Department of Statistics–Malaysia.

Notes:

[a] For 1970, children are classified as persons aged below 15; for other years, they are classified as persons aged below 14.

[b] 1970 figures are for Peninsular Malaysia and are estimated from Anand (1983).

HIS sampling weights are applied for means and percentage shares.

The sample sizes—the numbers of households covered—are given in Table 9.4, along with trends in household composition.[19] Both the average household size and the average number of children in the household have fallen markedly. In the latest survey, the mean number of children fell below 1.

17 A household is defined as a person or group of persons who usually live together and make common provision for food and 'other essentials of living'.

18 A two-stage stratified sampling design was adopted: the primary stratum consists of the states of Malaysia, including the Federal Territories of Kuala Lumpur and Labuan; the second, of the urban-rural strata. An urban area is defined as a built-up area with a population of 10,000 or above; other areas are defined as rural. The term 'rural' thus covers small urban communities with populations of between 1,000 and 9,999.

19 The household characteristics in Table 9.4 and all other statistics reported in this section are weighted by 'sampling weights' in the HIS. These are used to weight the sample back to the population from which it was drawn. By definition, these weights are the inverse of the probabilities of being included in the sample due to the sampling design. A very small number of households were dropped when the identity of the household head was not recorded.

The proportion of households with one or two members has remained roughly constant over the last two decades, at around one-fifth. The proportion of 'large' households—that is, households with five members or more—has generally fallen over the last two decades, while that of households with three or four members has risen. In summary, there have been significant changes in both household size and composition.

Type of Income

In the HISs, household income is defined as the total income accruing to household members in cash and in kind 'on a regular basis in one year or more often'. The concept of gross income includes income from four sources: paid employment, self-employment (including imputed rent for owner-occupied houses), asset income (such as from shares and property), and transfers (including from the government) in cash, goods, and services. This definition of income has not changed over the period analysed.

The weighted mean household income from each source, expressed as a percentage of total income, is given in Table 9.5. Paid employment is the main source of income, accounting for around two-thirds of the total, but has been declining over time. Around a quarter of income comes from self-employment. Asset income and transfers account for a small fraction of income, but both have increased significantly over the past decade.

Table 9.5 **Paid employment is the main source of Malaysian household income**

	Shares in total income (%)			
	Paid employment	Self-employment	Assets	Transfers
1995	66.7	26.2	1.6	5.5
1999	65.7	26.5	1.4	6.4
2004	67.9	25.4	1.5	5.2
2009	68.2	22.0	3.6	6.2
2014	65.0	24.1	3.3	7.6
2016	63.0	24.1	4.4	8.5

Source of data: Derived from unpublished data from the Household Income Surveys of 1995, 1999, 2004, 2009, 2014, and 2016, supplied by the Department of Statistics–Malaysia.

In his assessment of the income data taken from the 1970 PES covering Peninsular Malaysia, Anand (1983, p. 22) notes that 'since the PES was not an income survey as such, it is possible that the usual errors associated with responses on income may have been aggravated'. As with the HISs, the interview unit was the household, defined as 'a group of people who live together with a common budget for food and other essentials of living'. The PES definition of income was similar to that used in the HISs, including the imputation of owner-occupation of dwellings. However, the income data were coded into 23 intervals, with the top interval open ended.

National Trends in Inequality

Mean and Median Incomes

Table 9.6 sets out a time series of real gross mean and median income—nominal income deflated by the consumer price index (2000 = 100). It eliminates the effects on incomes of increases in the general price level, and measures the purchasing power of the incomes received. The top panel shows the mean, median, and coefficient of variation (CV) of real incomes at the household level.[20]

Table 9.6 Malaysian real income has more than doubled since 1995

	Mean	Growth	Median	Growth	CV	Median/Mean
Household annual real income (RM, 2000 prices)						
1995	28,218	-	19,113	-	1.194	0.677
1999	30,099	1.7	20,721	2.1	1.105	0.688
2004	36,578	4.3	24,716	3.9	1.529	0.676
2009	39,500	1.6	27,774	2.5	1.067	0.703
2014	53,607	7.1	40,023	8.8	0.992	0.747
2016	58,259	4.3	43,779	4.7	0.991	0.751
Per capita annual real income (RM, 2000 prices)						
1995	6,090	-	3,930	-	1.299	0.645
1999	6,732	2.6	4,439	3.2	1.225	0.659
2004	8,178	4.3	5,315	3.9	1.619	0.650
2009	9,498	3.2	6,316	3.8	1.214	0.665
2014	12,654	6.6	9,057	8.7	1.116	0.716
2016	14,400	6.9	10,425	7.6	1.105	0.724
Equivalized annual real income (RM, 2000 prices)						
1995	10,955	-	7,524	-	1.184	0.687
1999	11,905	2.2	8,240	2.4	1.112	0.692
2004	14,384	4.2	9,758	3.7	1.451	0.678
2009	16,258	2.6	11,193	2.9	1.092	0.688
2014	21,676	6.7	16,043	8.7	1.005	0.740
2016	24,328	6.1	18,169	6.6	0.997	0.747

Source of data: Derived from unpublished data from the Household Income Surveys of 1995, 1999, 2004, 2009, 2014, and 2016, supplied by the Department of Statistics–Malaysia.
Notes: 'Growth' refers to the average annual growth rate since the previous HIS.
Means and medians are based on weighted observations.

20 The CV is the 'normalized' standard deviation—the ratio of the standard deviation to the mean. Lower CV values imply that incomes are less dispersed around the mean. The CV has generally fallen since 1995.

Real average annual household income (in 2000 prices) more than doubled between 1995 and 2016, from RM28,218 to RM58,259 (top panel). The real income of the median household was substantially below that of the mean, indicating that the distribution of household income has a long upper tail.[21] However, the median household income is gradually getting closer to the mean. In 1995, the median household's income was 68 per cent of the mean. By 2016, it had risen to 75 per cent. When the median closes in on the mean in this manner, it is a sign that the upper tail of the distribution has shortened: in other words, it shows that incomes are converging.

Two features of these data stand out: the slow growth in mean household income in 1999 after the Asian financial crisis, and the slow growth in 2009 following the Great Recession in the US and Europe. The effects on median household income were less pronounced, reflecting the disproportionate impact that these two macroeconomic crises had on richer Malaysian households; this is discussed in the next section. Nevertheless, real household income recovered quickly after both crises: between 1999 and 2004 it rose on average by around 4 per cent a year, and between 2009 and 2014 by over 7 per cent a year. These favourable growth rates in real income continued between 2014 and 2016.

Because the needs of households vary depending on their size and demographic composition, the total income and spending of a household is likely to give a misleading picture of the welfare of its members. A one-person household requires income and spending sufficient to meet only one person's needs. A larger household naturally requires more income to reach the same level of welfare for its members as the single-member household.

Rather than simply analysing household income, the central panel of Table 9.6 contains details of household income divided by the number of household members: per capita income. The mean, median, and CV in this panel are for individuals, not households. Thus, in 2016 the average individual lived in a household with an annual income of RM14,400 per household member (in 2000 prices). If all individuals in the survey are ordered by their household's income per member, the individual halfway along—the median—would be in a household with an income of RM10,425 per member. Median income per capita is again closing in on the mean: it was 65 per cent of the mean in 1995, and 72 per cent in 2016. The weakest growth rates in mean and median income per capita were again experienced in the crisis years of 1999 and 2009.

The bottom panel of Table 9.6 shows the key statistics using 'equivalized' income. The use of indices of inequality based on equivalized income is

21 Very high incomes raise the mean but have no effect on the median.

necessary to take into account variations over time in household size and in the demographic composition of households (Box 9.4). Equivalized income indices are preferred for making comparisons over time and for analysing subgroup or spatial differentials. As with the middle per capita panel, the mean, median, and CV are for individuals in the surveys, not households.

Box 9.4 Equivalized income

Households vary in their size (number of members) and in age-sex composition. They also vary in the extent of income sharing among members. Younger household members typically require fewer resources than adults. Economies of scale mean that some fixed costs, such as housing and household durables, can be shared among more members in large households. A widely employed means of comparing living standards among households is the use of equivalized household income, which is derived in three steps:

- Incomes received by all household members are aggregated into household income.
- Total income is divided by the number of 'adult equivalents', using an appropriate equivalence scale. A weight is given to each member of the household and these are summed to arrive at the 'equivalized household size'. A widely used scale that is applied in this chapter is the modified scale from the Organisation for Economic Co-operation and Development (OECD, p. 157).[22] This attaches a weight of 1.0 to the first adult, 0.5 to the second and to each additional member aged 14 and over, and 0.3 to each child aged under 14.
- The resulting figure is called 'equivalized income' and is attributed equally to each member of the household.

By contrast, household income per capita simply divides total household income by the number of its members, regardless of their age.

All three measures—household, per capita, and equivalized annual real income—show the same general features: there is reduced growth in the crisis years (1999 and 2009); the relative gap between the mean and the median has fallen over time, indicating a shortening upper tail; and the dispersion around the mean measured by the CV has fallen.

Lorenz Curves

Figure 9.4 shows the cumulative proportions of equivalized income in 1995 and 2016 through two Lorenz curves. The Lorenz curve for 2016 lies everywhere

22 The 'OECD-modified equivalence scale' was adopted by the Statistical Office of the European Union in the late 1990s for income analysis in the bloc (Eurostat, 2003). This scale was first proposed by Hagenaars et al. (1994). The original 1982 OECD scale had assigned a weight of 1 to the first adult, 0.7 to the second, and 0.5 to each child below 17 years.

to the northwest of that for 1995, indicating that equivalized incomes were more equitably distributed in 2016 than they were two decades earlier. The Gini coefficient fell from 0.448 in 1995 to 0.396 in 2016. This is a substantial improvement comparable to the decline in poverty (Chapter 8).

What proportion of total income would need to be reallocated among households to achieve perfect income equality? The Schutz coefficient, sometimes called the 'Robin Hood Index', answers this question (Schutz, 1951; Kondor, 1971). The coefficient is shown in Figure 9.4 as the maximum distance between the line of equality and the Lorenz curve, $L(p)$. The maximum value of $p - L(p)$ is attained where the slope of $L(p)$ is 1, and this is true when $p = p_m$, where p_m is the proportion of individuals earning less than the mean. In 2016, the proportion of individuals earning less than the mean equivalized income was 65.8 per cent, and $L(65.8)$ was 37.0 per cent—that is, the poorest 65.8 per cent of individuals received 37 per cent of total income. The Robin Hood Index for 2016 is therefore 28.8 per cent (65.8 per cent less 37.0 per cent). This is the amount of total income that would have to be transferred from richer households to poorer ones to achieve complete income equality. In 1995, the Robin Hood Index was 33.2 per cent, requiring a greater proportion of income to be redistributed to give equal shares.

Figure 9.4 **Malaysia's inequality in equivalized income was lower in 2016 than in 1995**

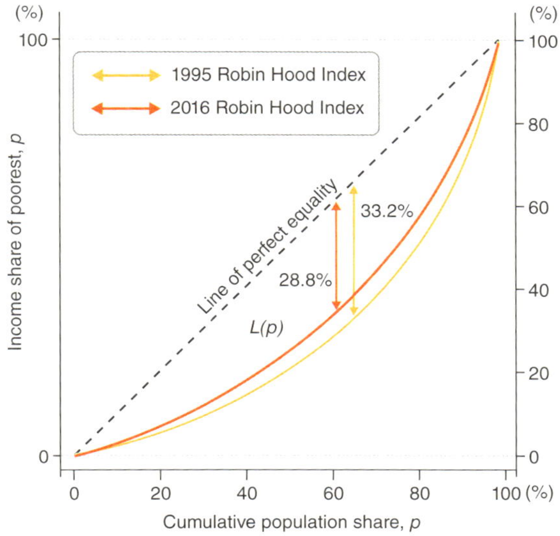

Gini

Trends in inequality can be assessed by comparing the Gini coefficients from all the HISs, along with those reported in the PES for Peninsular Malaysia in 1970. The left-hand panel of Figure 9.5 shows the Gini among households for both income per capita and equivalized income. The panel on the right presents Gini coefficients among individuals, matching the Lorenz curves shown in Figure 9.4. Gini coefficients for equivalized income are lower than those in per capita terms, indicating that inequality is less pronounced when account is taken of household size and composition. Poorer households are likely to be the larger ones and the ones with more children. For these reasons, per capita income will be lower than equivalized income for these households, and the Gini coefficient based on per capita income will be higher.[23]

Figure 9.5 **Malaysia's income is becoming more equal as measured by the Gini coefficient**

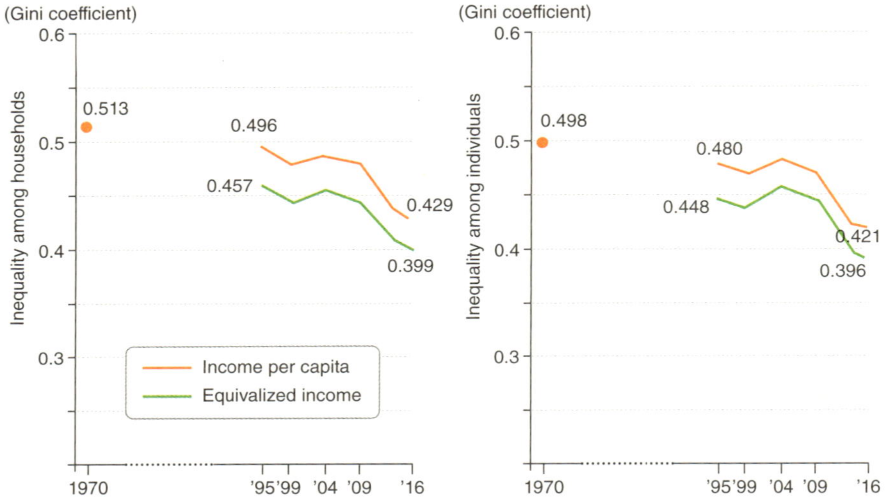

Source of data: Derived from unpublished data from the Household Income Surveys of 1995, 1999, 2004, 2009, 2014, and 2016, supplied by the Department of Statistics–Malaysia.
Note: The 1970 Gini coefficients from Anand (1983) are for Peninsular Malaysia.

Income inequality among Malaysian citizens has narrowed sharply since 1995, with the Gini coefficients falling steadily and showing pronounced declines in 1999 and 2009. Comparisons with other Asian economies are revealing (Figure 9.6). The Gini coefficients for Japan, the Republic of Korea, and Taiwan are substantially lower than those for Singapore and Malaysia, but with the exception of Japan's, have remained largely unchanged, unlike Malaysia's, which is on a downward trend. The Gini coefficients for 23 OECD countries averaged 0.317 in 2015, compared with 0.421 for Malaysia in 2016.[24]

23 The Gini coefficient for total household income is expected to be higher than those for per capita and equivalized income in Figure 9.5, as it would capture not only variations in household income but also variations in household size.

24 The OECD Gini coefficients and percentile ratios are based on income per capita (OECD, 2018a).

Although Malaysia still has some way to go in catching up with these newly industrialized economies (NIEs) and OECD countries, the trend over the past two decades is encouraging.

Figure 9.6 **Gini coefficients for Malaysia are substantially higher than those for Japan and the NIEs, with the exception of Singapore[a]**

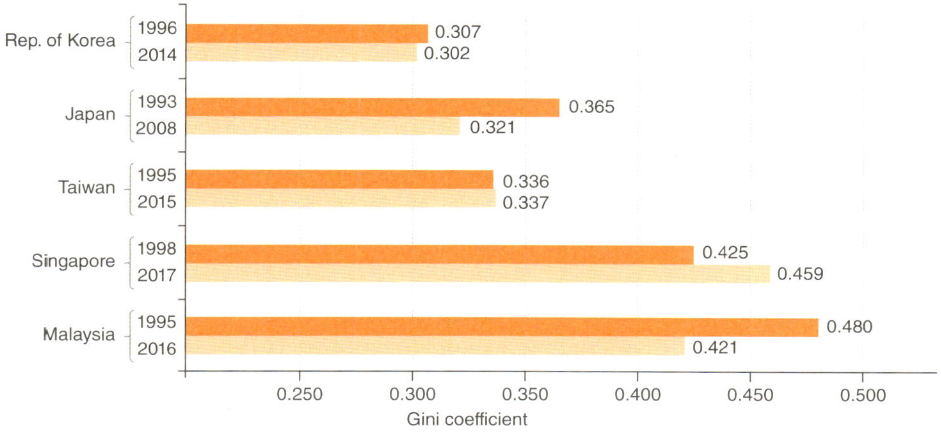

Sources of data: Asian Development Bank (2009); Department of Statistics–Singapore (2018).
Note: [a] The Gini coefficients are based on household income per capita, with the exception of Japan in 1993, which is based on equivalized disposable household income.

Percentile Ratios and Shares

Table 9.7 sets out the percentile income ratios, P90/P10 and P90/P50, as defined above. Both income ratios have fallen over time, with significant declines in 2014 and 2016. In the most recent HIS, the poorest of the top 10 per cent of individuals enjoyed an income of around 2.5 times the median, and around six times the highest income of the poorest 10 per cent. For 23 OECD countries in 2015, the average P90/P10 and P90/P50 ratios for per capita income were 4.3 and 2.0 respectively, both lower than those for Malaysia in 2016, which were 6.6 and 2.6.

An alternative perspective on trends in inequality is given by the percentile shares in total income (Table 9.7). If incomes were equally distributed among individuals, the bottom 20 per cent of individuals would receive 20 per cent of total income. With unequal shares, the bottom 20 per cent of individuals would receive far less than 20 per cent of income. The shares are calculated for both equivalized and per capita income to allow for comparison with Anand's 1970 figures.

Table 9.7 **Income share of the top 5 per cent has declined, while that of the bottom 40 per cent has increased**

	Bottom quintile	Lowest 40%	Top quintile	Top 5%	P90/P10	P90/P50
			Income per capita			
1970[a]	4.3	12.3	54.8	28.5	-	-
1995	4.5	13.0	53.4	25.2	8.8	3.1
1999	4.6	13.3	52.4	24.0	8.5	3.1
2004	4.3	12.6	53.2	24.7	9.3	3.2
2009	4.5	12.9	52.2	23.6	8.9	3.0
2014	5.6	15.4	48.8	21.8	6.7	2.7
2016	5.6	15.5	48.1	21.1	6.6	2.6
			Equivalized income			
1995	5.1	14.5	50.7	23.3	7.4	2.9
1999	5.2	14.6	50.1	22.6	7.3	2.8
2004	4.8	13.8	51.2	23.4	8.0	2.9
2009	5.1	14.1	50.1	22.0	7.7	2.9
2014	6.1	16.6	46.8	20.4	5.9	2.5
2016	6.2	16.7	46.2	19.6	5.8	2.5

Source of data: Derived from unpublished data from the Household Income Surveys of 1995, 1999, 2004, 2009, 2014, and 2016, supplied by the Department of Statistics–Malaysia.
Note: [a] The 1970 shares from Anand (1983) are for Peninsular Malaysia.

Measured by per capita income, the poorest 20 per cent of individuals received between 4 and 6 per cent of the total income over the 46-year period, with their share increasing over time. By contrast, the share of the top 5 per cent ranged from 29 to 21 per cent over the same period on a significant declining trend. There was little change in the income share of the poorest quintile between 1970 and 2009. Of course, this quintile would still have experienced improving standards of living, but their *relative* position did not improve. There was a marginal and modest improvement in their share between 2009 and 2016.

In terms of income shares for three broad percentile groups—the bottom 40 per cent, the middle 40 per cent, and the top 20 per cent—the poorest 40 per cent have increased their share over time at the expense of the richest 20 per cent (Figure 9.7). In 2016, the bottom 40 per cent of income earners received just 16 per cent of total income, but this was still larger than two decades previously when their share had been 13 per cent. The income share of the middle 40 per cent increased from 33 per cent in 1970 to over 36 per cent in 2016. While not a dramatic change, this was again a movement in the right direction. Both the bottom 40 per cent and the middle 40 per cent have increased their income shares relative to the top 20 per cent of earners (right panel of Figure 9.7).

Figure 9.7 **The income share of Malaysia's middle 40 per cent has risen**

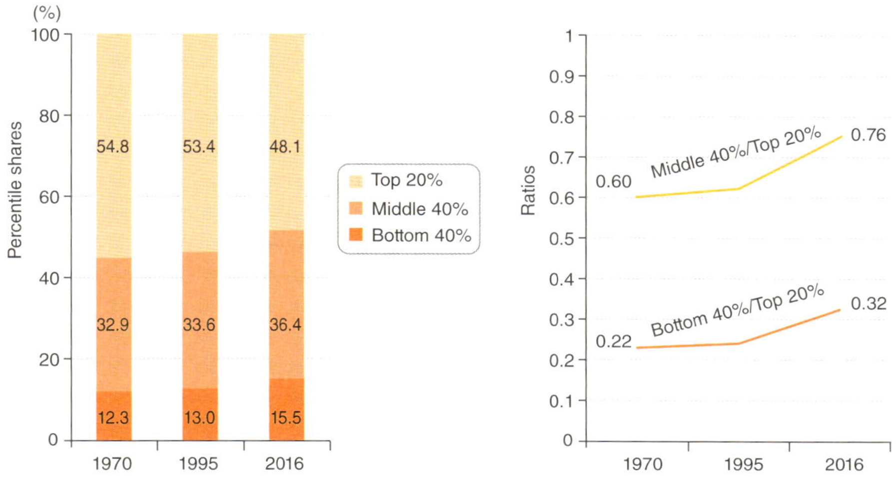

Source of data: Department of Statistics–Malaysia (2019). Derived from unpublished data from the Household Income Surveys of 1995 and 2016, supplied by the Department of Statistics–Malaysia.

Note: The 1970 shares from Anand (1983) are for Peninsular Malaysia.

Impact of Financial Crises on Income Inequality

The Malaysian economy was hit hard by the Asian financial crisis that began in mid 1997, and, to a lesser extent, by the Great Recession that started in late 2007 (Chapters 7 and 8). How did these two crises affect income inequality in developed countries and in Malaysia?[25]

International Experience

The effects of the Great Recession on income inequality in developed countries have been extensively documented. Jenkins et al. (2013) examine 21 high-income OECD countries, among which the experience of European countries is typical. Table 9.8 shows data on the percentage point changes in

25 Some analysts consider income inequality to be one of the contributory factors to financial crises. Excess borrowing by low-income households may, for example, lead to financial turbulence. Kirschenmann et al. (2016, p. 171) analyse data from 14 developed countries for 1870–2008, and find that income inequality is 'a relevant predictor of financial crises especially when it is at a relatively high level'. Bordo and Meissner (2012) come to a different conclusion. Analysing data from 14 advanced countries for 1920–2000, they find that inequality does not lead to financial crises.

the Gini coefficient and S80:S20—the share of total income of the richest fifth relative to that of the poorest fifth—for 15 European countries. It also gives the percentage point change in relative poverty, defined as the proportion of the population with an equivalized net household income of less than 60 per cent of the median income.

As the Great Recession took effect, reductions in Gini coefficients indicate that incomes became more equally distributed in ten of 15 European countries, and typically the S80:S20 ratios and relative poverty rates also fell. Cribb et al. (2017) contrast this with earlier UK recessions in the 1980s and 1990s when income inequality rose sharply. Muriel and Sibieta (2009), however, after reviewing three UK recessions (1973–1975, 1979–1981, and 1990–1992) conclude that, 'Having fallen, risen and stayed constant during these recessions, income inequality has clearly not moved in one single direction during recessions in the past' (p. 23). Meyer and Sullivan (2013) find that income inequality in the US continued to rise throughout 2000–2011, including in the years of the Great Recession. Similarly, the US Census Bureau reports that Gini coefficients for all households rose from 0.432 in 2007 to 0.438 in 2008, and to 0.443 in 2009. The international evidence is therefore mixed, but for the majority of countries affected by the Great Recession, inequality declined.

Table 9.8 Inequality fell in many OECD countries following the Great Recession

	Percentage point changes in inequality indices, 2007–2009		
	Gini	**S80:S20**	**Poverty rate**[a]
Austria	–0.1	0.0	–0.3
Belgium	–0.9	–0.2	–0.1
Denmark	1.8	0.8	1.5
Finland	–0.9	–0.2	–0.5
France	0.7	0.2	0.8
Germany	–0.9	–0.3	0.4
Greece	–0.5	–0.3	–0.2
Ireland	–2.5	–0.6	–2.2
Italy	0.2	0.1	–0.5
Netherlands	–2.1	–0.3	–0.2
Norway	–1.5	–0.3	–0.2
Portugal	–2.1	–0.5	–0.6
Spain	2.6	1.5	1.1
Sweden	0.1	0.0	0.7
UK	–0.2	0.0	–1.3

Source of data: Jenkins et al. (2013), Table 4.
Note: [a] Proportion of the population living in a household with an equivalized net household income of less than 60 per cent of the median income.

The Macroeconomic Impact on Malaysia

The Asian financial crisis started in Thailand in July 1997 and spread rapidly across Southeast Asia. It had a profound impact on the Malaysian economy over the next few years. The start of the Great Recession is commonly identified as September 2007, although the National Bureau of Economic Research dates its beginning as December of that year. Its impact on Malaysia was similarly spread over the following two years. Real aggregate GDP fell by more than 7 per cent in 1998 (Table 9.9). A year later, its level was still below that of 1997. Real per capita GDP did not exceed its 1997 level until 2003. The effect on Malaysia of the Great Recession was unsurprisingly weaker, but still strong enough for both real aggregate GDP and real GDP per capita to fall in 2009.

It is to be expected that the average household was affected by these two crises. But the interesting question addressed in the next section is whether the effects were distributed evenly throughout all households, rich and poor.

Table 9.9 Malaysia's GDP was affected by the two financial crises

Asian financial crisis	Real aggregate GDP, 1997=100	Change (%)	Real per capita GDP, 1997=100	Change (%)
1997	100.0	7.3	100.0	4.6
1998	92.6	–7.4	90.3	–9.7
1999	98.3	6.1	93.4	3.5
2000	107.0	8.9	99.2	6.1
2001	107.4	0.3	97.3	–1.9
2002	112.1	4.3	99.4	2.2
2003	118.2	5.5	102.8	3.4
2004	126.7	7.2	108.0	5.1
Great Recession	**Real aggregate GDP, 2007=100**	**Change (%)**	**Real per capita GDP, 2007=100**	**Change (%)**
2007	100.0	6.3	100.0	4.3
2008	104.8	4.8	102.9	2.9
2009	103.3	–1.5	99.5	–3.3
2010	110.9	7.4	105.0	5.5
2011	116.8	5.3	108.7	3.6
2012	123.2	5.5	112.9	3.9
2013	129.0	4.7	115.5	2.3
2014	136.7	6.0	120.9	4.7

Source of data: Economic Planning Unit–Malaysia (2018d).

Malaysian Inequality in Crisis Years

The HISs of 1999 and 2009 are conveniently close enough to the two crises to allow fairly accurate assessments to be made of their impact on income inequality. The 'crisis years' referred to here are 1999 and 2009. The Gini coefficients and CVs for these years are given in Table 9.10. For comparative purposes, figures are also given for the earlier non-crisis years of 1995 and 2004. The indices measure inequality among individuals in the surveys, and all individuals in the household are assumed to share equally its per capita or equivalized income.

The CV measure is always far lower in the crisis years, with the reduction particularly pronounced in 2009, probably because the survey date almost overlapped with the Great Recession. The Gini coefficients in the two crisis years were also lower than those in the earlier years. In 2009, the Gini coefficients based on income per capita and equivalized income fell substantially below their values in the previous HIS.

Table 9.10 Inequality in crisis years narrowed relative to pre-crisis years in Malaysia

	Income per capita		Equivalized income	
	Gini	CV	Gini	CV
1995	0.480	1.299	0.448	1.184
1999	0.470	1.225	0.443	1.112
2004	0.481	1.619	0.458	1.451
2009	0.471	1.214	0.446	1.092

Source of data: Derived from unpublished data from the Household Income Surveys of 1995, 1999, 2004, and 2009, supplied by the Department of Statistics–Malaysia.

With less inequality in crisis years, it appears that the gap between Malaysia's rich and poor narrowed, mainly because richer households were hit harder by the crises. In 1995, the bottom 20 per cent of individuals accounted for only 4.5 per cent of total income per capita, the bottom 40 per cent for 13 per cent, and the top 10 per cent for 37 per cent (Table 9.11). The shares of the bottom 20 per cent and 40 per cent rose in 1999 and 2009, while the share of the top 10 per cent fell, with almost identical trends observed for equivalized incomes. The decline in the share of the top 10 per cent was particularly pronounced in 2009.

The S80:S20 ratio also fell in recession years. Both financial crises appear to have hit richer individuals harder than poorer ones, but relative poverty changed only marginally in the crisis years (Box 9.5). The relative poverty line income is linked with the median, which, unlike the mean, is unaffected by reductions in the incomes of the rich. So although the income shares of the poor increased in crisis years, the fraction of relatively poor individuals was largely unchanged.

Table 9.11 Income shares of the top 10 per cent declined in recessions

	S80:S20	Bottom 20%	Bottom 40%	Top 10%
		Income per capita		
1995	11.8	4.51	13.02	37.11
1999	11.3	4.63	13.30	35.99
2004	12.4	4.30	12.63	36.58
2009	11.7	4.47	12.93	35.53
		Income per adult equivalent		
1995	9.9	5.10	14.50	34.70
1999	9.6	5.20	14.60	34.00
2004	10.6	4.80	13.80	34.80
2009	9.9	5.10	14.10	33.50

Source of data: Derived from unpublished data from the Household Income Surveys of 1995, 1999, 2004, and 2009, supplied by the Department of Statistics–Malaysia.

Box 9.5 Malaysia's relative poverty in crisis years, 1999 and 2009

Malaysia's poverty rate rose from 6.1 per cent to 8.5 per cent from 1997 to 1999, and from 3.6 per cent to 3.8 per cent from 2007 to 2009 (Chapters 7 and 8).[26] An alternative illustration of how low-income households fared in the crisis years is given by the proportion of individuals in 'relative poverty', where the poverty line income moves in line with the median income. Relative poverty rates generally fell in European countries in the aftermath of the Great Recession (Table 9.8).

An individual is defined as relatively poor if he or she lives in a household with income per capita, or equivalized income, that is below 60 per cent of the median income (the OECD definition). When this measure is applied to Malaysian per capita income and equivalized income, it shows that relative poverty rates tended to increase marginally in crisis years compared with their values four to five years earlier (Box Table 9.2).

Box Table 9.2 Malaysian relative poverty rates increased marginally in recession years

	Income per capita	Equivalized income
	60% of median	60% of median
1995	26.17	24.39
1999	26.36	24.73
2004	27.53	26.18
2009	27.81	26.11

Source of data: Derived from unpublished data from the Household Income Surveys of 1995, 1999, 2004, and 2009, supplied by the Department of Statistics–Malaysia.

26 Official poverty rates for 1999 were based on a revised methodology (EPU, 2018b). The United Nations Development Programme–Malaysia (2007) reports an increase in the poverty rate between 1997 and 1999 using the revised methodology for both years: the proportion of poor households rose from 6.67 per cent to 8.14 per cent over this interval.

Differentials in Income Inequality

Income inequality in Malaysia has historically had ethnic and spatial dimensions, inherited as part of the legacy of the colonial era. Policies that seek to create a more equitable income distribution, like the NEP, have attempted to do so through affirmative action programmes targeting education, employment, rural development, and housing. In this section, the different dimensions of income inequality are analysed: ethnicity, strata (urban–rural), household size, education, and state.

Ethnicity, Strata, and Household Size

Ethnic income differentials have narrowed considerably over time, although a sizeable gap remains (Figure 9.8). In the left panel, mean equivalized incomes (among individuals) for Chinese and for Indians are expressed as ratios of the mean incomes of Malays and other *Bumiputera* (which are set to 100). The mean income differentials between Malays and other *Bumiputera* on the one hand, and Chinese or Indians on the other, have narrowed appreciably over the last two decades. For example, in 1995 the Chinese mean equivalized income was 87.9 per cent higher than that of Malays and other *Bumiputera*, and this had declined to 59.4 per cent by 2016.

Figure 9.8 **Ethnic income ratios have tended to converge over time**

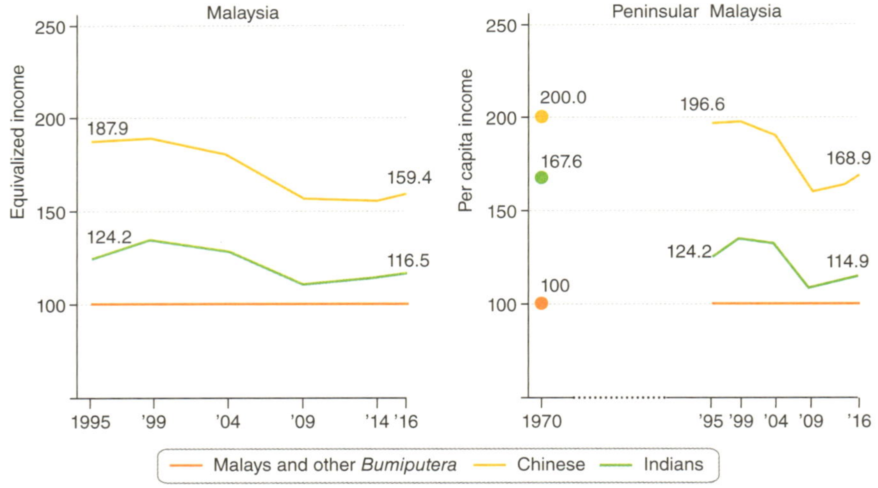

Source of data: Derived from unpublished data from the Household Income Surveys of 1995, 1999, 2004, 2009, 2014, and 2016, supplied by the Department of Statistics–Malaysia.
Note: Income of Malays and other *Bumiputera* = 100.

The right panel shows the ethnic differentials for per capita income in Peninsular Malaysia, to allow for comparison with the 1970 PES estimates. Although there is still a notable gap in mean income between the Chinese on the one hand, and the Malays and other *Bumiputera* on the other, it has narrowed significantly since the NEP was launched.

The Gini coefficient is not decomposable into the subgroup contributions of the ethnic groups, but variations in the Gini by ethnicity can shed light on intra-ethnic inequality; that is, they show how income inequality differs within each group. The Gini coefficients for equivalized income and income per capita—the latter for Peninsular Malaysia to allow for comparison with 1970—are shown in Table 9.12. As with trends in the national Gini coefficients described above, these figures show that intra-group inequality has narrowed impressively since 1995 for all three major ethnic communities.

The Gini coefficient based on equivalized income for Malays and other *Bumiputera* declined from 0.427 to 0.379 between 1995 and 2016; for Chinese over the same period from 0.422 to 0.389; and for Indians from 0.391 to 0.382. By 2016, the income inequality within each of the three communities was much the same.

Table 9.12 Levels of inequality within each community are declining

	Malays and other *Bumiputera*	Chinese	Indians	All ethnic groups[a]
	Equivalized income Gini coefficients: Malaysia			
1995	0.427	0.422	0.391	0.448
1999	0.419	0.412	0.407	0.443
2004	0.444	0.428	0.421	0.458
2009	0.444	0.413	0.427	0.446
2014	0.388	0.391	0.398	0.402
2016	0.379	0.389	0.382	0.396
	Per capita income Gini coefficients: Peninsular Malaysia			
1970[b]	0.455	0.454	0.500	0.498
1995	0.457	0.455	0.428	0.479
1999	0.444	0.433	0.441	0.468
2004	0.467	0.446	0.445	0.481
2009	0.457	0.434	0.455	0.463
2014	0.404	0.412	0.421	0.422
2016	0.393	0.403	0.406	0.414

Source of data: Derived from unpublished data from the Household Income Surveys of 1995, 1999, 2004, 2009, 2014, and 2016, supplied by the Department of Statistics–Malaysia.

Notes: [a] The national Gini for 'all ethnic groups' is not an average of the ethnic Gini coefficients, as it includes inequalities both *between* ethnic groups and *within* them.

[b] 1970 figures are from Anand (1983).

Figure 9.9 explores intra-ethnic income inequality through the percentile shares and ratios within ethnic groups, based on per capita income. The national trends described above also apply to the three main ethnic communities. For all three, the share of the lowest quintile rose from 4.5 per cent to 5.6 per cent from 1995 to 2016; among *Bumiputera*, the bottom quintile share rose from 4.9 per cent to 6.0 per cent over the same period, a change very similar to that shown in the figures for 'all ethnic groups'.

As well as comparing intra-ethnic distributions of income, the ethnic composition of individuals *within the percentile groups* can also be analysed. This indicates if there is a relationship, whether direct or indirect, between ethnic group and income inequality. If ethnicity played no direct or indirect role in income inequality, the ethnic shares in each percentile group would match their shares in the broader population. For example, it would be expected that the share of Malays and other *Bumiputera* individuals in the bottom quintile would be the same as the share of individuals in this ethnic group in the population as a whole. The ethnic shares of the population in each percentile group are given in Table 9.13, where the percentiles are based on equivalized income.

In the 1995 HIS, Malays and other *Bumiputera* constituted 62 per cent of the total population, but 85 per cent of individuals in the lowest income quintile. In 2016, the corresponding figures were 68 per cent and 83 per cent respectively (Table 9.13). Conversely, they increased their shares in the top income quintile from 41.5 per cent in 1995 to 52.8 per cent in 2016. For the Chinese, their share in the top income quintile has declined from 50.2 per cent in 1995 to 37.8 per cent in 2016, consistent with their declining share in the population. The Indian share in the bottom quintile has risen from 4.5 per cent in 1995 to 7 per cent in 2016 for a population share of 8–9 per cent. Their share of the top income quintile also rose from 7.7 per cent to 8.8 per cent. In summary, the ethnic dimension of income inequality has diminished somewhat over time, but it still persists and may largely be explained by differentials in location, educational attainment, and employment patterns.

Figure 9.9 **Share of income of the bottom quintile is rising while that of the top quintile is falling among all communities**

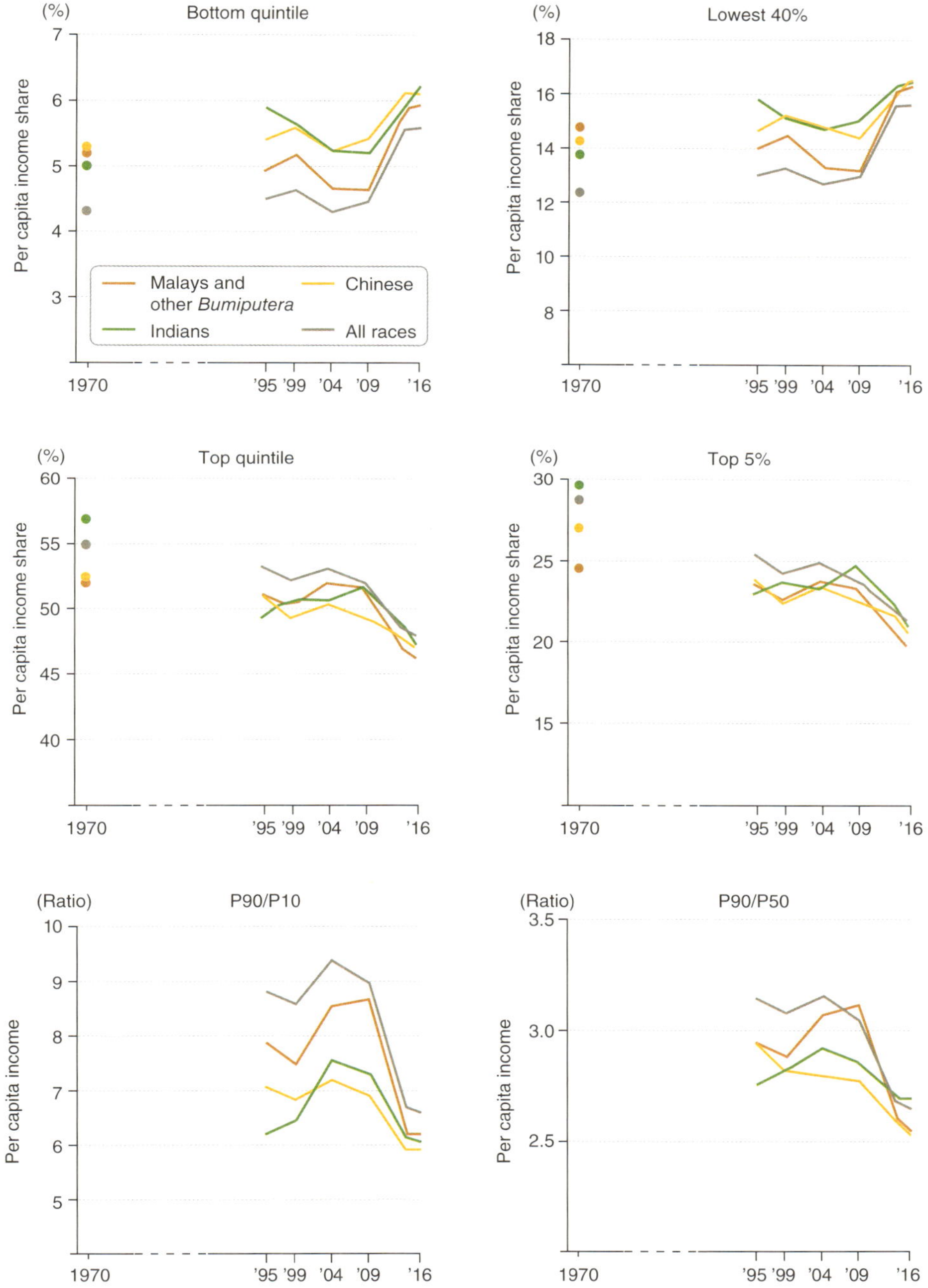

Source of data: Derived from unpublished data from the Household Income Surveys of 1995, 1999, 2004, 2009, 2014, and 2016, supplied by the Department of Statistics–Malaysia.
Note: The 1970 shares from Anand (1983) are for Peninsular Malaysia.

Table 9.13 Malays and other *Bumiputera*, rural, and large households are more likely to be in the bottom income quintile and less likely to be in the top 5 per cent

		Shares in equivalized income groups (%)				
		Population share	Bottom quintile	Lowest 40%	Top quintile	Top 5%
	Ethnicity					
1995	Malays and other *Bumiputera*	62.0	85.3	77.3	41.5	33.4
	Chinese	27.4	5.9	11.7	50.2	59.4
	Indians	8.3	4.5	7.0	7.7	6.8
	Others	2.3	4.3	4.0	0.6	0.4
2004	Malays and other *Bumiputera*	65.5	87.1	80.7	46.4	37.6
	Chinese	24.9	6.3	11.2	44.5	51.7
	Indians	8.6	5.4	7.0	8.3	9.4
	Others	0.9	1.2	1.1	0.8	1.3
2016	Malays and other *Bumiputera*	68.1	82.7	78.2	52.8	42.3
	Chinese	21.8	7.8	11.6	37.8	47.0
	Indians	8.8	7.0	8.2	8.8	10.2
	Others	1.3	2.5	2.1	0.6	0.5
	Location[a]					
1995	Urban	53.1	21.4	30.7	82.4	88.0
	Rural	46.9	78.6	69.3	17.6	12.0
2004	Urban	64.0	32.1	41.7	90.4	95.6
	Rural	36.0	67.9	58.3	9.6	4.4
2016	Urban	77.4	52.8	62.2	93.6	96.6
	Rural	22.6	47.2	37.8	6.4	3.4
	Household size					
1995	1 or 2	6.6	5.2	5.2	10.4	13.2
	3 or 4	23.5	14.6	17.1	34.5	38.8
	5 or more	69.9	80.2	77.8	55.1	47.9
2004	1 or 2	7.3	4.2	5.3	10.4	12.3
	3 or 4	26.0	14.6	18.3	37.4	40.3
	5 or more	66.8	81.2	76.4	52.2	47.4
2016	1 or 2	9.8	6.7	7.0	14.3	18.2
	3 or 4	34.6	21.0	25.3	46.1	49.6
	5 or more	55.6	72.3	67.7	39.6	32.3

Source of data: Derived from unpublished data from the Household Income Surveys of 1995, 2004, and 2016, supplied by the Department of Statistics–Malaysia.

Note: [a] The urban and rural population proportions are obtained from the HIS surveys, and may differ from estimates made by the Department of Statistics–Malaysia from other data sources.

The population shares of urban and rural households have changed over time: urban living has become far more common in recent years due to migration from rural areas. Those in rural households are disproportionately numerous in the lowest income quintile (Table 9.13). In 2016, nearly half of individuals with equivalized incomes in the lowest quintile lived in rural areas compared with around one-fifth in the population as a whole. In the 21st century, fewer than 4 per cent of Malaysia's richest individuals are resident in rural areas. Location clearly plays a role, whether directly or indirectly, in income inequality and in poverty.

The mean equivalized income of individuals living in rural areas is about half that of urban individuals, a ratio that has narrowed only a little since 1995 (left panel of Figure 9.10). The distributions of income within urban and rural areas are similar, with the Gini coefficients being reasonably close (right panel of Figure 9.10). The intra-rural income distribution remains more equal than that in urban areas.

Figure 9.10 **Inequality is declining for rural and urban households**

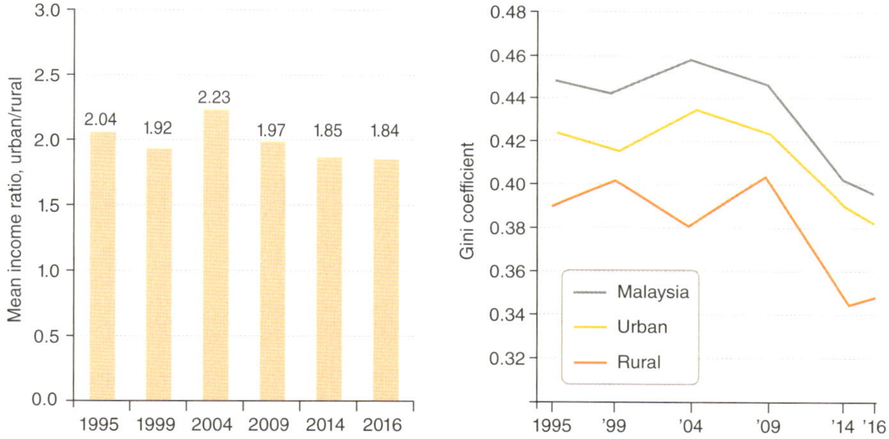

Source of data: Derived from unpublished data from the Household Income Surveys of 1995, 1999, 2004, 2009, 2014, and 2016, supplied by the Department of Statistics–Malaysia.

The inequality measures described in this chapter are based on money incomes and take no account of spatial variations in the cost of living. Housing and transportation costs are substantially higher in some urban areas. A household living in Kuala Lumpur, the nation's capital, will face housing costs of 2.4 times the average in Malaysia's states. Moreover, the capital's residents face transportation costs roughly three times those in other states.[27] Individuals living in Kuala Lumpur are likely to be earning more

27 This figure is based on unpublished data supplied by the Department of Statistics–Malaysia for 2014 on prices by state and stratum.

than those in rural locations, but they do face a significantly higher cost of living.

Larger households generally have more child members. Because of both their size and composition, the per capita and equivalized incomes of larger households are lower than those of smaller households (Table 9.13).

Malaysian households have become progressively smaller, partly because of the lower fertility levels among all ethnic groups (Chapter 4), and partly because of a preference for nuclear families. The mean number of household members has fallen from close to five in 1995 to just over four in 2016 (Table 9.4). In 1995, 70 per cent of individuals lived in large households with five or more members; by 2016 this share had fallen to 56 per cent. Such households accounted for 80 per cent of the poorest individuals in 1995, and 72.3 per cent in 2016. Poorer individuals generally lived in large households, while individuals living in small households were much more likely to be in the top quintile and the top 5 per cent.

Education

The education dimension of income inequality is assessed according to the schooling level of the head of household. Education plays a large part in explaining income inequality because it is highly correlated with occupation, with the most educated individuals concentrated in the highest-paid occupational groups (Chapter 3). Figure 9.11 confirms the importance of the association between education and income inequality.

In 1995, 54 per cent of all individuals lived in households where the head had primary schooling or less,[28] but 77 per cent of individuals with equivalized income in the lowest quintile lived in such households. By 2016, educational attainment had improved so that only 15 per cent of individuals lived in less-educated households. Yet around one-third of the poorest individuals lived in households in which the head had only primary schooling or no schooling at all. At the other end of the distribution, close to 80 per cent of the top 5 per cent of income earners had tertiary schooling, whereas only 27 per cent of the population as a whole had schooling beyond secondary level.[29]

28 The category 'none' also includes a small proportion of households where the schooling of the head of household was not known.

29 A separate cross tabulation of educational attainment for individuals living in rural and urban areas showed that relative poverty rates of individuals with equivalized income below half of the median were much higher in rural than in urban areas for any given level of education. However, care is necessary in interpreting such data, since the cost of living in rural areas—especially housing and food costs—is often far lower than in urban areas.

Figure 9.11 Educational attainment and income group are closely associated

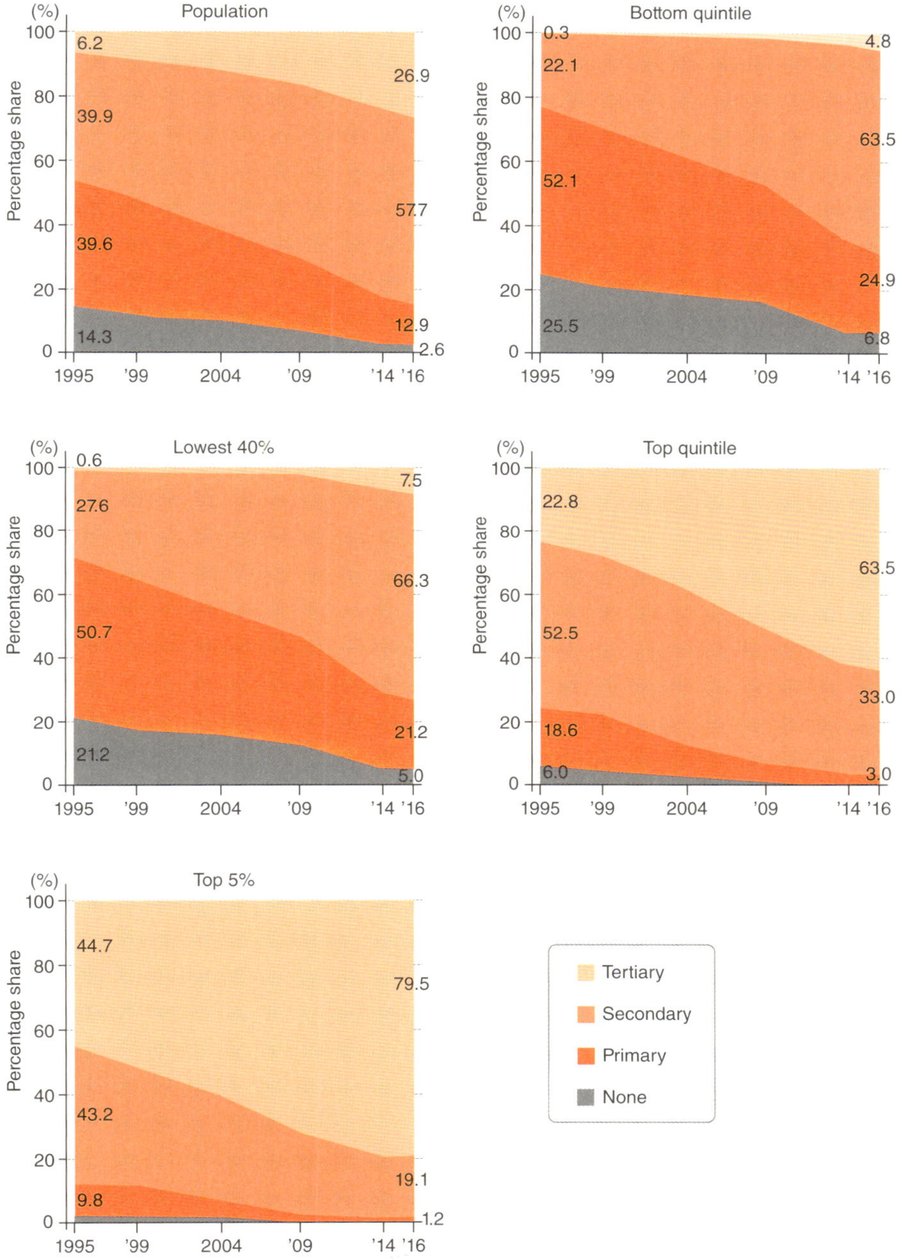

Source of data: Derived from unpublished data from the Household Income Surveys of 1995, 1999, 2004, 2009, 2014, and 2016, supplied by the Department of Statistics–Malaysia.

Note: The figure shows the proportions of individuals in each of the broad percentiles by schooling of household head.

State

Income inequality between individuals varies by state, as shown in Map 9.1. Measured by the equivalized income Gini coefficients, inequality in 1995 was highest in Selangor, Kelantan, Terengganu, Sabah, Sarawak, and Kuala Lumpur. However, variations in the Gini coefficients across states were far lower in the 2016 HIS, when Sabah was the only state with a coefficient above 0.4.

Map 9.1 Income inequality fell in Malaysian states over 1995–2016, but differentials remain

a. 1995

b. 2016

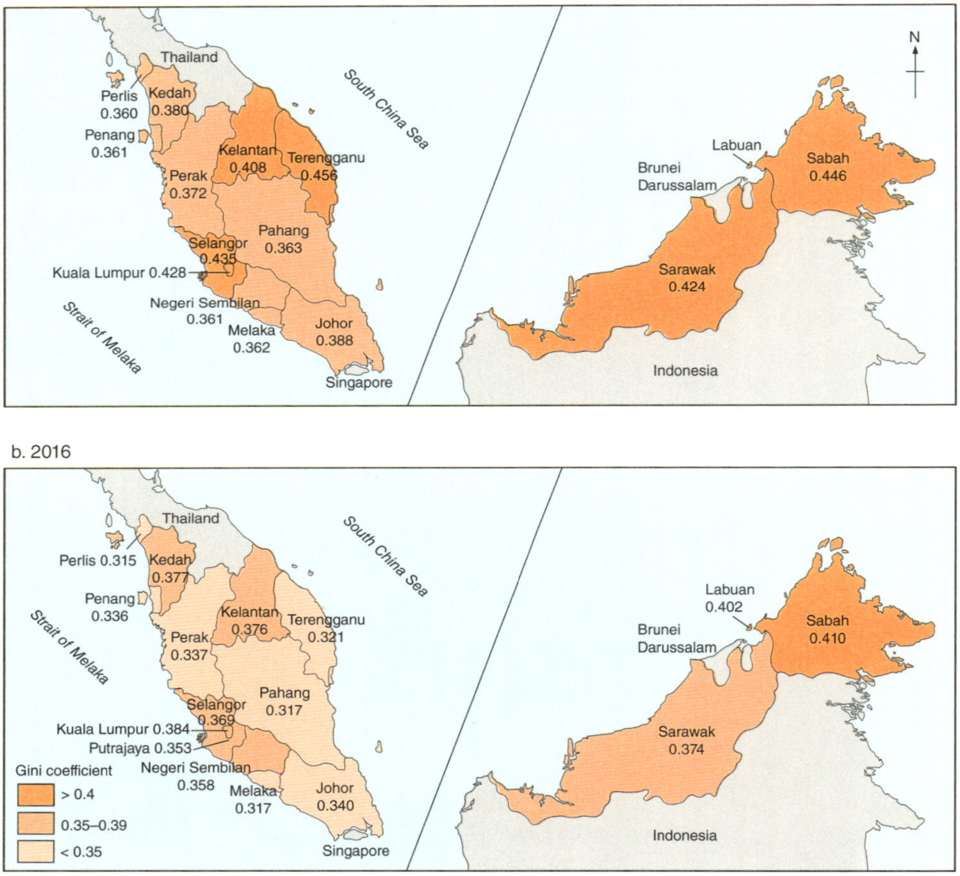

Source of data: Economic Planning Unit–Malaysia (2018b).

Individuals living in Selangor are far more likely to be among those with an equivalized income above the 95th percentile. Of all Malaysians in this percentile group, 40 per cent or more live in Selangor. Likewise, individuals in Selangor are far less likely to be in the bottom income quintile; only 4 per cent of those in the bottom quintile lived in Selangor in 1995, and only 6 per cent in 2016. In 1995, over half of the lowest income quintile were concentrated in four states: Kedah, Kelantan, Terengganu, and Sabah. By 2016, the spatial distribution had changed somewhat, but low incomes were still heavily concentrated in four states: over half of the lowest income quintile individuals lived in Kedah, Kelantan, Sabah, and Sarawak in this year.

Determinants of Income Inequality

Modelling Determinants

The analysis in the previous section suggests that income inequality is strongly influenced by the covariates covered: ethnicity, strata (urban–rural), household size, education, and state. However, the tables are 'two-dimensional' and possibly misleading. For example, ethnicity may influence incomes for several reasons. Malays and other *Bumiputera* may be over-represented in the lowest quintile because they have lower schooling levels, reside in states or rural communities with limited modern-sector employment opportunities, and generally live in larger households. Policies aimed at reducing inequality need to look beyond the simple two-way relationships to establish which mechanisms are largely responsible for unequal incomes. One approach is to use multiple regression, where the effect of any one factor is measured by holding other possible influences constant (Box 9.6).

Box 9.6 **Modelling income inequality determinants**

Econometric techniques are applied to analyse the probability of any individual being in the lowest and highest income percentiles through the use of a logit model. For the bottom quintile case, the dependent variable takes the value 1 if the individual's equivalized income puts him or her in the bottom quintile, and 0 otherwise. Similar dichotomous variables are defined for other percentile groups. The logit model is written as:

$$\text{Prob}(Y = 1 \mid x) = e^{x'\beta} / (1 + e^{x'\beta})$$

where $Y = 1$ indicates that the individual is in the percentile group, x is a vector of variables that influence Y, and β is a vector of parameters to be estimated. The variable *Low-quintile* takes the value 1 if the individual's equivalized income is below the 20th percentile, and 0 otherwise. The variable *Top-quintile* takes the value 1 if the individual's equivalized income is above the 80th percentile, and 0 otherwise. Finally, the variable *Top 5pc* takes the value 1 if the individual's equivalized income is above the 95th percentile, and 0 otherwise. The logit model is estimated for each of these three dependent variables separately for 1995, 2004, and 2016.

Model Results

The results for *Low-quintile* are set out in Table 9.14; those for *Top-quintile* and *Top 5pc* are in Annexes 9.1 and 9.2. Dummy variables are defined for strata (urban = 1) and each state, ethnicity, sex of head of household (female = 1), and schooling level.

Table 9.14 Ethnicity influences the probability of low income—logistic regressions: *Low-quintile*

	Coefficient		
	1995	**2004**	**2016**
Age	–0.012 ***	–0.017 ***	–0.017 ***
Secondary	–1.020 ***	–0.954 ***	–0.790 ***
Tertiary	–3.603 ***	–3.488 ***	–2.685 ***
Household size	0.085 ***	0.154 ***	0.196 ***
Kedah	1.160 ***	0.809 ***	1.128 ***
Kelantan	1.897 ***	1.484 ***	1.806
Melaka	0.280 **	0.092	–0.031 ***
Negeri Sembilan	0.224 *	–0.338 **	0.537 ***
Pahang	0.715 ***	0.272 **	0.676 **
Penang	–0.154	–0.840 ***	0.179 ***
Perak	1.140 ***	0.859 ***	0.847 ***
Perlis	1.234 ***	0.817 ***	0.840 ***
Selangor	–0.146	–0.570 ***	–0.586 ***
Terengganu	2.112 ***	1.396 ***	0.520 ***
Sabah	1.100 ***	1.482 ***	1.256 ***
Sarawak	0.602 ***	0.407 ***	0.952 ***
Kuala Lumpur	–0.648 ***	–0.382 **	–1.037
Labuan	n/a	0.206	0.179 *
Strata	–1.043 ***	–0.919 ***	–0.694 ***
Chinese	–1.398 ***	–1.209 ***	–0.833 ***
Indian	–0.488 ***	–0.134	0.188 ***
Other	0.097	–0.315	–0.107
Female head of household	0.206 ***	0.265 ***	0.418 ***
Constant	–1.109 ***	–0.784 ***	–0.741 ***
Pseudo R^2	0.2621	0.2794	0.2547

Notes: Level of statistical significance: * 10 per cent; ** 5 per cent; *** 1 per cent.
There were no households in the lowest quintile in Putrajaya.

The models include a constant term, and this describes a household with the following baseline characteristics: a rural *Bumiputera* household headed by a male with primary schooling (or less) and living in Johor. The signs on the coefficients in Table 9.14 indicate whether the corresponding departure from the baseline has a positive or negative effect on the probability of the individual being in the relevant percentile group. For example, a negative coefficient for 'Tertiary' in the model for *Low-quintile* indicates that individuals in households where the head has tertiary education (and with all other characteristics unchanged) are far less likely than the baseline household to be in the bottom quintile.

The results for the three years were generally very similar.[30] For the *Low-quintile* logit there were two interesting differences (Table 9.14). First, the sign on the coefficients of some states varied. In 1995 and 2004, individuals living in Penang were *less* likely than those in Johor (the benchmark) to be in the bottom quintile. By 2016, however, they were *more* likely to be in the low-income group. The reverse applies to Melaka. In both 1995 and 2004, individuals living in this state were more likely than those in Johor to be in the bottom quintile, whereas the reverse applies to 2016, where the sign in Table 9.14 is negative. The second notable change between the years is that the results indicated a shift in the relationship between ethnicity and income over time. Indian individuals were *less* likely to be in the low-income quintile in 1995 and 2004 than Malays and other *Bumiputera*, such that the sign of the Indian coefficient for these years was negative. In 2016, the sign of this coefficient switched to positive: Indian individuals were *more* likely than Malays and other *Bumiputera* to be in the bottom quintile, and the coefficient is statistically significant.

Individuals living in households headed by a female are more likely than those living in households headed by a male to be in the bottom quintile, and are generally less likely to be in the top percentiles.[31] There are a number of possible reasons for this. This may be because females are likely to earn less than males with similar characteristics, or because their head of household status is due to widowhood or divorce, and they are balancing part-time work with caring for children.

Most of the variables included in the logit model have the expected signs and are statistically significant, confirming the associations indicated in the 'two-dimensional' tables in the last section, while now also controlling for the effects of other possible determinants. Even when the household head's age, schooling, strata, state, and household size are controlled for, ethnicity remains a significant factor for the likelihood of being in the low and high percentile groups. Chinese individuals are less likely than Malays and other

30 There are also some interesting changes over time. For example, the urban coefficient in the low-income quintile regression has become much less negative, suggesting that the locus of poverty could be moving to urban areas.

31 The proportion of households headed by a female in the population was around 15 per cent over the two decades.

Bumiputera to be in the bottom quintile, and are more likely to be in the top quintile or top 5 per cent (Annex Tables 9.1 and 9.2).

Of course, ethnicity may be playing an independent role because of omitted or unobservable characteristics correlated with race. The 'Pseudo R^2' statistics reported in the logit regressions are low enough to suggest that there may well be a number of key characteristics not covered in this analysis or in the HIS. Prominent among these is the occupation and employment sector of the household head. If many Malays and other *Bumiputera* are employed in the public sector, and if incomes in the public sector are lower than in the private sector, then ethnicity is picking up the effect of occupational choice. The HIS did not provide this information, and it is clearly an important area for future research.

In summary, these results show that a variety of factors have effects, independent of one another, on income levels in Malaysia. These factors include the sex and level of education of the household head, the state of residence, strata (urban–rural), household size, and ethnicity. Even after controlling for other important explanatory variables, ethnicity has an independent effect on income distribution.

Conclusions

At independence, Malaysia was bequeathed a highly segmented, unequal, and economically unbalanced society. Differentials in private consumption patterns between the richest and poorest groups were vast. An analysis of six consumption standards, defined on the basis of ethnicity and occupation, shows that in 1900 consumption expenditure per head by individuals in the European standard—the highest—was some 27 times greater than that of individuals in the Malay labour standard—the lowest—and that four decades later the differential, far from diminishing, had widened.

There was a high and rising level of inequality over the first four decades of the 20th century, with a distinct worsening after the Great Depression. Using indirect techniques and based on limited data, the Gini coefficient is estimated to have risen substantially between 1900 and 1939. Despite sustained growth in GDP, wages for the bulk of the population grew only modestly in real terms over this period: this is reflected in the much lower growth rate of private consumption expenditure than GDP. After the Japanese occupation and in the period up to independence, inequality continued and may even have worsened, as the colonial legacy of laissez-faire economic policy and segmented social policy was sustained.

'Growth with equity', or 'redistribution through growth', became the primary policy objective of the independent Malaysian government. Starting with the NEP in 1971, this approach continued through subsequent policies and programmes in the following decades, with the government playing a more interventionist role in managing economic policy and blending it with affirmative social objectives. A key aim was to maintain unity by decoupling the association of race with occupation, essentially by incentivizing Malays and other *Bumiputera* to transition from low-productivity agricultural employment into the modern urban economy, and to higher occupational levels in both the public and private sectors. Efforts were also made to achieve a fairer spatial distribution of employment across all states. A battery of affirmative action policies favouring Malays and other *Bumiputera*—in education, access to scholarships, employment, business licences, share ownership, and housing—were vigorously implemented, aiming to ensure that the benefits of growth were broadly shared.

Malaysian standards of living have improved markedly since the 1970s, and between 1995 and 2016 the real average household income more than doubled. Malaysia has also become a more equitable country. Based on per capita income, the Gini coefficient of Malaysian citizens improved from 0.498 in 1970 to 0.421 in 2016. When making comparisons over time, inequality indices based on equivalized income are used in order to take account of temporal variations in household size and in the demographic composition of households, both of which have changed markedly. Data necessary to calculate equivalized income Gini coefficients are only available from 1995, and these show the Gini coefficients falling from 0.448 in 1995 to 0.396 in 2016. In 2015, by comparison, the Gini coefficients for 23 OECD countries, based on per capita income, averaged 0.317. Malaysia still has some way to go, but the trend is encouraging.

Malaysia has also achieved a somewhat fairer income distribution among ethnic groups, especially for Malays and other *Bumiputera,* but there remains a sizeable gap, with the Chinese having the highest mean income. Intra-ethnic income inequality has fallen sharply for all three main ethnic communities, and by 2016 the Gini coefficient was much the same for each of them. Still, inequalities in income are conspicuous between urban and rural areas, among states, among households of different sizes, and especially by educational level. These patterns are similar to those seen in most countries. The role played by ethnicity, however, remains one important key to understanding income inequality in Malaysia.

Although income inequality is strongly influenced by factors such as ethnicity, urban versus rural residence, and education, it is necessary to look beyond the simple two-way relationships to establish the mechanisms that are responsible for unequal incomes. Using multiple regression analysis, where the effect of any one factor is measured while holding other possible influences constant, it was found that ethnicity has an independent effect on income distribution.

In its focus on income, this chapter misses what is likely to be the large inequality in the distribution of *wealth* in Malaysia, which can be expected to be much greater than that of income. Inequality of wealth can have a profound effect on the ability of individuals to manage at times of unemployment or economic stress (Muhammed Abdul Khalid, 2016). It can also affect life-course opportunities and limit options for upward social mobility. Data on the distribution of wealth, such as shareholdings, property, and various other assets, are not readily available. But, as Piketty (2014) has shown, if the rate of return on capital exceeds the growth rate of the economy, the accumulated wealth of rich individuals will increase faster than average incomes, and wealth will be increasingly owned by a smaller group of individuals. Over time, the distribution of wealth will become increasingly unequal even when the distribution of income is unchanged.

Still, Malaysia's development has been reasonably equitable, as evidenced by improved income equality and the rise of a sizeable middle class—those with incomes in the middle 40 per cent of the income distribution—which includes members of all communities. With sustained high levels of economic growth, accompanied by rapid urbanization, higher educational attainment, and increased modern-sector employment, a multi-ethnic middle class has emerged. This is reflected in the representation of all communities across a wide spectrum of professional and managerial occupations in the private and public sectors (Abdul Rahman Embong, 2002).

At the same time, pro-poor growth policies and programmes (including rural development programmes such as land schemes under FELDA), increased access to education at all levels, and improved access to medical and health services have helped to almost eradicate absolute poverty. Supportive policies, including affirmative action measures, have played an important part in bringing about these changes. Even so, while the income share of the bottom 20 per cent of individuals has improved in recent years, it remains unacceptably low. In 2016, their share was just over 6 per cent, whereas the top quintile received close to half of total income. Raising the living standards of Malaysia's poorest households remains a public policy challenge, especially in a rapidly evolving globalized environment where technological changes and robotics are affecting employment and earnings. This will require continuing government intervention, including through the more inclusive targeting of low-income households. It is this subject to which we turn in Part 5, and the final chapter.

Annex Table 9.1 Residents of Kuala Lumpur are more likely to be in the top quintile—logistic regressions: *Top-quintile*

	Coefficient		
	1995	2004	2016
Age	0.002 **	0.017 ***	0.026 ***
Secondary	1.180 ***	1.320 ***	1.117 ***
Tertiary	3.467 ***	3.538 ***	3.121 ***
Household size	–0.161 ***	–0.210 ***	–0.240 ***
Kedah	–0.954 ***	–0.720 ***	–0.589 ***
Kelantan	–1.097 ***	–0.830 ***	–0.921 ***
Melaka	–0.413 ***	–0.388 ***	–0.224 ***
Negeri Sembilan	–0.391 ***	0.076	–0.425 ***
Pahang	–0.841 ***	–0.395 ***	–0.845 ***
Penang	–0.184 ***	–0.116	–0.634 ***
Perak	–1.150 ***	–0.801 ***	–0.767 ***
Perlis	–1.155 ***	–0.611 ***	–0.980 ***
Selangor	0.560 ***	0.748 ***	0.394 ***
Terengganu	–1.018 ***	–0.795 ***	–0.555 ***
Sabah	0.084	–0.303 ***	–0.328 ***
Sarawak	–0.095	–0.153 *	–0.427 ***
Kuala Lumpur	0.366 ***	0.568 ***	0.662 ***
Labuan	n/a	–0.039	0.317 ***
Putrajaya	n/a	n/a	0.790 ***
Strata	0.926 ***	0.949 ***	0.670 ***
Chinese	1.129 ***	1.155 ***	0.854 ***
Indian	0.011	0.025	0.011
Others	–0.753 ***	0.125	0.074
Female head of household	0.004	–0.180 **	–0.539 ***
Constant	–2.929 ***	–3.530 ***	–3.899 ***
Pseudo R^2	0.290	0.314	0.272

Note: Level of statistical significance: * 10 per cent; ** 5 per cent; *** 1 per cent.

Annex Table 9.2 Tertiary education raises the likelihood of high income—logistic regressions: *Top 5%*

	Coefficient		
	1995	**2004**	**2016**
Age	0.025***	0.032***	0.041***
Secondary	1.511***	1.432***	1.492***
Tertiary	3.899***	3.755***	3.815***
Household size	–0.213***	–0.195***	–0.283***
Kedah	–1.089***	–1.105***	–0.375***
Kelantan	–1.288***	–1.104***	–1.218***
Melaka	–0.604***	–1.168***	–0.354**
Negeri Sembilan	–0.575***	–0.257	–0.261*
Pahang	–0.584***	–0.550***	–1.049***
Penang	–0.365**	–0.246	–0.605***
Perak	–1.206***	–1.401***	–1.050***
Perlis	–1.138***	–0.687**	–1.354***
Selangor	0.769***	0.894***	0.645***
Terengganu	–0.656***	–0.595**	–0.720***
Sabah	0.101	–0.478***	–0.302***
Sarawak	–0.080	–0.048	–0.457***
Kuala Lumpur	0.801***	0.648***	0.826***
Labuan	n/a	0.669**	0.841***
Putrajaya	n/a	n/a	1.266***
Strata	0.716***	1.061***	0.673***
Chinese	1.321***	1.239***	0.945***
Indian	0.057	0.327**	0.291***
Others	–0.624**	0.853**	0.300
Female head of household	–0.319***	–0.555***	–0.716***
Constant	–5.534***	–6.808***	–7.177***
Pseudo R^2	0.345	0.344	0.296

Note: Level of statistical significance: * 10 per cent; ** 5 per cent; *** 1 per cent.

MALAYSIA
SOUTH CHINA SEA
STRAIT OF MELAKA
Kangar
PERLIS
Alor Setar
KEDAH
Georgetown
P. PINANG
Kota Bharu
KELANTAN
Kuala Terengganu
TERENGGANU
PERAK
Ipoh
PAHANG
Kuantan
Kuala Lumpur
Shah Alam
SELANGOR
N. SEMBILAN
Seremban
MELAKA
Bandaraya Melaka
JOHOR
Johor Bahru
Kuching
Simanggang
Sibu
Bintulu
SARAWAK
Miri
Batang Baram
Batang Rajang
Batang Baleh
Labuan
Kudat
Kota Kinabalu
Sungai Sugut
SABAH
Keningau
Tenom
Sungai Kinabatangan
Sandakan
Lahad Datu
Kalabakan
Tawau
Semporna

PART 5

CREATING AN INCLUSIVE AND SUSTAINABLE FUTURE

Chapter 10

Working Towards an Inclusive and Sustainable Future

It is an observation from earlier chapters which bears repeating: Malaysia has made impressive progress in the more than six decades since the end of colonial rule. These achievements are all the more remarkable given that the new democratic nation has made them while simultaneously contending with a legacy of marked economic and social stratification, ethnic segmentation, and geographical imbalances, as well as internal and external threats.

Malaysians today are far better educated and more highly skilled than their forebears, live much longer and healthier lives, and enjoy a level of affluence that would once have been unimaginable. The benefits of progress have been widely felt among all communities, with the extreme poverty that affected more than half of the population at independence now virtually eliminated, and income inequalities narrowed. The fact that many Malaysians now live in their own homes in and around vibrant modern cities reflects a highly successful structural transformation from dominance by agriculture to the rise of the more dynamic service and industrial sectors. By 2015, Malaysia had either met or exceeded most of the United Nations Millennium Development Goals set in 2000, including those on poverty and hunger, education, disease, and child and maternal mortality, thereby attaining levels characteristic of high-income countries.

Malaysia's development policies and plans have generally been pragmatic, and have successfully promoted macroeconomic stability, structural economic diversification, and beneficial integration with the global economic community. These advances would not have been made without purposeful investment in the capacity of the state: the role of the state in guiding and driving the transition from a low- to a middle-income economy has been fundamental.[1] Growth with equity became the primary policy

1 Malaysia did have the advantage of the institutions it inherited from the British (including a functioning civil service with well-trained personnel). It also benefited from the physical infrastructure built during the colonial era, albeit infrastructure that was funded by the exploitation of the country's natural resources.

objective, beginning with the 1971 NEP and continuing through subsequent policies and programmes in the following decades, as the government played an interventionist role in managing macroeconomic policy and blending it with social objectives.

Malaysia's economic and social accomplishments have differentiated it from many of its developing-country peers of the 1950s (World Bank, 2008). The ingredients of the country's success include the efficient transformation of its natural capital into financial wealth, and the extensive investments in economic and social infrastructure that this wealth has supported. All communities have played an important role in this transformation and have contributed to economic growth and development. The country's distinctive ethnicity-based affirmative action policies and programmes, which began in the colonial era, were embodied in the federal constitution, and were greatly expanded under the NEP, initially worked well in levelling up economic and social opportunities.

Malaysia's development scorecard is not without blemish, however. Achievements in human capital accumulation, productivity, and innovation are lacklustre, and in recent years the country has fallen further behind the more dynamic economies of East Asia (Perkins et al., 2017). Despite redistributive efforts, gaps between the rich and poor remain too wide. Development remains spatially uneven, with Sabah and Sarawak, and the peninsular states of Kedah, Kelantan, Pahang, and Terengganu, still lagging behind the more prosperous west coast states of the peninsula.

It is *institutional* weaknesses, however, which have come to pose the greatest challenge to continued development progress and have aggravated Malaysia's vulnerabilities. The paramount challenge facing the country is that of becoming a cohesive society which offers all of its citizens a voice, respects and celebrates diversity, and places effective checks on those entrusted with power. To these ends, institutions must build trust, operate for the benefit of the people, and be accountable to the whole nation. Political power must be more widely distributed and decentralized so as to reduce the chances of malfeasance and abuse.

What sets advanced nations apart is the quality of their institutions: institutions which secure property rights, promote fair competition, and raise the productivity and value of the assets that these nations create and possess. In this sense, what is important for economic outcomes is the character of political and economic governance, and the standards and policies that frame incentives, facilitate exchange, distribute rewards, and influence levels of social trust and cooperation.[2]

2 A wealth of empirical evidence demonstrates that there is a positive relationship between the quality of institutions and economic outcomes; see, for example, Rodrik et al. (2004). Chapter 7 has cited evidence that the low levels of trust engendered by ethnic polarization and fragmentation can present multiple obstacles to efficiency and economic growth.

The larger goal of affirmative action—as a means to unify the nation by addressing the sharp imbalances in income, wealth, and opportunity inherited at independence—has yet to be met. Far more Malays, natives of Sabah and Sarawak, and other *Bumiputera*[3] are now at the forefront of the modern economy, but affirmative action programmes have created new forms of ethnic segmentation, which are particularly pronounced in the education system, public sector employment, and support for business. In many instances, inducements offered in these areas have created a sense of entitlement among target beneficiaries. As a consequence, they have thwarted performance, productivity, and innovation, and have contributed to an exodus of higher-educated Malaysian citizens seeking improved social status and economic prospects abroad—a 'brain drain'.[4]

Malaysia's strong focus on economic growth, meanwhile, has taken its toll on the environment. Economic advances and a dependence on fossil fuels have harmed the country's natural environment, intensifying carbon emissions and lowering air quality. Voracious logging and the conversion of tropical forestland for plantation agriculture and human settlement have at times threatened precious ecosystems, and hurt the livelihoods of indigenous forest dwellers (Yeo, 2013). Efforts are being made to promote green growth, and to ensure that the palm oil industry is sustainable through the Malaysian Sustainable Palm Oil certification scheme. The United Nations Sustainable Development Goals (SDGs), a blueprint for a more sustainable future, provide an appropriate framework for addressing Malaysia's environmental challenges.

This concluding chapter makes the case for a genuinely inclusive model of development in which all Malaysians count.[5] But the process of forging a consensus on the country's future path and ensuring that agreed commitments are scrupulously adhered to will be challenging, given the strong ethnic and religious undercurrents in society. Political mobilizations that have

3 The term '*Bumiputera*' is not found in the federal constitution and is of political coinage. It broadly refers to persons and groups eligible for affirmative action schemes. However, there is some controversy as to who qualifies within its protective remit. Foremost in the list of those included would be 'Malays' of the peninsula and 'natives of Sabah and Sarawak'. The *Orang Asli* are not included in Article 153 of the federal constitution, but their 'protection, well-being or advancement' is mentioned in Article 8(5)(c). Some commentators define *Bumiputera* even more broadly to include native Indonesians, Malaysians of Siamese extract, Malaysian-Muslim Indians, Peranakan, and the Kristang people of Portuguese-Eurasian descent.

4 A significant contributor to Malaysia's brain drain is skill selectivity: higher-skilled Malaysian citizens seeking employment abroad more suited to their skill levels. The World Bank (2011a, p. 106) identifies skill selectivity as the main driver of emigration in Malaysia, since the skilled are 'much more than proportionally represented in the migrant population'.

5 An inclusive model of development is consistent with Agenda 2030—adopted by all United Nations member states in 2015—which integrates the economic, social, and environmental pillars of sustainable development through the 17 SDGs and related targets. This framework supports economic and social policies that focus on promoting economic growth, decent jobs, social fairness, well-being, and environmental sustainability (Sachs, 2015 and 2017).

contributed to a social environment that favours cleavages and segmentation further sharpen the challenges.

A more inclusive society also requires a more decentralized model of governance, one which tolerates differences and dissent as intrinsic to any healthy democracy. Top-down models of governance are inappropriate in our increasingly complex, globally connected, and fast-paced world. The state will continue to have an important convening and coordinating role, of course. Increasingly, however, the private sector, the scientific and academic communities, non-governmental organizations, and civil society more broadly construed must also become meaningfully engaged in formulating policy, designing strategy, and finding, implementing, and taking ownership of agreed solutions to the issues that face the nation.[6]

The political and economic institutions established during the colonial era were extractive, exclusive, and built primarily to serve the interests of the ruling British elite.[7] Malaysia has come a long way since then and the development of more inclusive institutions has led to the nation's prosperity becoming much more equitably shared. In order to maintain and sustain social progress in the 21st century, however, these institutions must continue to respond to existing and new national challenges, and to the evolving international environment.

The human rights of all Malaysians, embedded in the United Nations Charter of 1945, must continue to be safeguarded, and laws protecting other rights and freedoms need to be fairly and dispassionately implemented at all times. The rule of law must prevail over the rule of individuals or elites. Public policy space must increasingly accommodate and mobilize new channels of participatory democracy, including via online platforms and social media in order for diverse voices to be heard. These new channels for democracy will help to ensure that Malaysia more cohesively embraces all stakeholders and communities in keeping with the spirit of the federal constitution and with the *Rukunegara*—the national value system.

The following ideas—framed as 'five challenges for the future'—are intended as a contribution to the wider discussion among stakeholders about how to realize the vision of transforming Malaysia into a more prosperous, resilient, and cohesive nation: a nation that cares for the welfare and well-being of all of its citizens.

---

6 Goldsmith and Eggers (2004) refer to this model of government as 'governing by network'. They argue that this form of decentralized, engaged government is better suited to the post-modern society, and observe that the transformation is already under way in some countries, with the role of government executives shifting from the direct delivery of services to the orchestration of networks of public, private, and non-profit organizations which deliver the services instead.

7 For a detailed historical account of the operations of extractive political and economic institutions and their links with European colonialism, see Acemoglu and Robinson (2012).

One: Affirmative Action

Affirmative action policies have rightly been credited with achievements in the 'restructuring' of Malaysian society, as well as with contributing to huge reductions in absolute poverty (Lee et al., 2013). These policies have undoubtedly helped to ensure that all communities are represented within the country's middle class (those with incomes in the middle 40 per cent of the income distribution). Affirmative action policies have also lifted *Bumiputera* representation in management occupations, with their share rising from 22.4 per cent in 1970 to 36.8 per cent in 1995, and reaching 42.4 per cent in 2018.

There is also evidence that affirmative action policies may have helped to weaken the inter-generational persistence of exclusion and poverty. According to Abdul Rahman Embong (2006, p. 133), the parents of over half of the new Malaysian middle class were 'mostly farmers, workers or lower-rung white collar employees'. A recent World Bank cross-country study on intergenerational mobility found that economies with a higher share of adults who are more educated than their parents (*absolute* upward intergenerational mobility) appear to correspond with those in which the educational attainment of individuals is less dependent on the educational attainment of their parents (*relative* intergenerational mobility). Malaysia stood out as one of the outliers to this trend, as it has very high absolute mobility as compared with other countries.

Relative intergenerational mobility in Malaysia was similar to that in Japan, suggesting low inequality of opportunity. However, Malaysia's absolute intergenerational mobility was higher than that in Japan, and 'among the greatest in the world' (Narayan et al., 2018, p. 105). Malaysia's rise in education levels has been more rapid than in economies that developed earlier, with more than 80 per cent of Malaysians born in the 1980s achieving higher education levels than their parents.[8] Evidence produced by the Khazanah Research Institute (KRI) (2016) suggests that, irrespective of ethnicity, the link between parental income and a child's earning prospects is much weaker in Malaysia than in many other countries.[9]

While affirmative action has enabled more equitable sharing in the country's prosperity, there have also been notable shortcomings, due in part

---

8 Intergenerational mobility in income is generally higher in rich countries than it is in developing countries (Narayan et al., 2018). Intergenerational mobility is particularly high in some northern European countries like Denmark, Norway, and Finland, but perhaps unexpectedly it is low in the US and the UK (Corak, 2016).

9 This study relies on parent recall of income earned three decades earlier, however, and the expected respondent errors may result in a downward bias in this measure of intergenerational mobility.

to poorly designed programmes and in part to weaknesses in implementation. With the benefit of hindsight, several questions could be asked:

- One of the thrusts of the NEP is the eradication of poverty irrespective of ethnicity. In the implementation of programmes to end absolute poverty, were all communities treated equally? Should we expand our definition of poverty to encompass other factors including access to opportunities?
- Did affirmative action require that the public sector become largely mono-ethnic to the virtual exclusion of other communities? Would greater diversity in the public services, married with policies ensuring the healthy representation of Malays and other *Bumiputera*, have better served national unity?
- Could affirmative action have been implemented more inclusively, so that all communities had equitable access to opportunities in an expanding economy?

Affirmative action has in many areas created a culture of patronage, while helping to concentrate wealth in the hands of the well connected (Gomez, 2009 and 2013). Increasingly, the focus of such policies has shifted from being pro-poor to being pro-business. The political bargain that was struck—in which elites consolidated their political power in exchange for privileges and resources—bred 'pervasive' rent-seeking and corruption (National Economic Advisory Council [NEAC], 2010, p. 11). The negative impacts of this corruption and of the increasingly unhealthy relationship between the state and business were far-reaching: they eroded the quality of government services, undermined the rule of law and regulation in the public interest, damaged social trust, harmed the environment, and subordinated legitimate development concerns to the interests of political and economic elites.

This malaise became deeply embedded in business and commerce. In particular, government-linked investment vehicles and companies, which were initially conceived as mechanisms to acquire wealth on behalf of the Malays and other *Bumiputera*, were sometimes diverted to pursue political ends and to enrich those with connected interests (Gomez et al., 2018). The costs went beyond the vast subsidies and fiscal bailouts required to cover the debts of bad state investments and inefficient business operations. Increasingly, the control exercised by government-linked entities (GLEs) over the commanding heights of the economy created insecurity for private investors and stifled competition.

It has to be appreciated that the pursuit and application of the principle of inclusion must take place in the context of the political and constitutional parameters fashioned in the course of Malaysia's unique history and evolution as a nation. The point has been made in earlier chapters that the constitution paved the way for affirmative action based on ethnicity. In fact, affirmative action policies for Malays—including land reservation, provision of free education, scholarships, and appointments to the civil service—were introduced during British colonial rule. They were later protected through the provision for 'safeguarding the special position of Malays and of the legitimate interests of other communities' in the Federation of Malaya Agreement 1948 (Archive document CO 537/2143, 1947, p. 5), and then made explicit in the 1957 Constitution of the Federation of Malaya. Article 153 (2) of the constitution pointedly contains phrases such as 'reservation for ... such proportion as [the *Yang di-Pertuan Agong*] may deem reasonable of positions in the public service ... and of scholarships ... permits or licenses' (Commissioner of Law Revision–Malaysia, 2010, p. 145).

The special position accorded to Malays, natives of Sabah and Sarawak, and other *Bumiputera* in the constitution, however, is not exclusive of the interests and welfare of the other communities. In fact, the first clause of Article 153 states that the *Yang di-Pertuan Agong* has an equal responsibility to safeguard 'the legitimate interests of other communities'. Hence, affirmative action for *Bumiputera* is to be pursued with due regard for the legitimate interests of the other communities in the spirit of inclusion.

The future design of affirmative action policies and programmes needs to be based on firm and fair observance of the balance of interests among all communities as provided for in the constitution. More than ever, such policies must be geared towards the creation of pathways to opportunity for all those who are disadvantaged, irrespective of their ethnicity.[10] All communities must be involved and must share in the benefits of the nation's development in order to achieve the creation of a just society. To realize this aim, 'it is important for the weak and less fortunate to be given assistance in order for them to compete on par with other parties' (Department of Information–Malaysia, 2004, p. 21). Promoting a fairer distribution of income must remain a key policy objective, consistent with SDG 10, which aims for reduced inequalities (Box 10.1).[11]

---

10 In 2012, the government introduced a cash-transfer mechanism targeted at low-income groups, using criteria based on household and individual earnings.

11 Inequality is a complex and multidimensional concept. Chapter 9 focuses on inequality of *outcomes* rather than inequality of *opportunities*. Gender, ethnicity, and cultural group membership, as well as geographical location, can all affect individuals' abilities to participate in society on equal terms. In addition, children of poor parents will often lack the opportunities available to children born in richer families. Observed inequalities of income and wealth—material inequalities—are likely to reflect the deeper inequalities of opportunity, where circumstances, not just efforts, count. For an interesting discussion of economic inequality, see International Panel on Social Progress (2018).

Box 10.1 Aiming for the 'Reduced inequalities' of SDG 10 via low-income households

Public policy must continue to focus on the distribution of income, especially at its lower tail, in order to reduce inequality and increase social well-being. Reflecting favourable economic growth, Malaysia's mean real household income in 2016 was double what it had been in 1995, and real GDP per capita was 76 per cent higher. The very poorest households across all of Malaysia's states have undoubtedly benefited from rising standards of living, with *absolute* poverty, where individuals have insufficient income to meet their basic needs, all but eradicated. Still, people may consider themselves to be poor not because they lack the basic necessities of life, but because they do not enjoy the standards of living that others enjoy—*relative* poverty.

The impact of Malaysia's economic growth on relative poverty—the share of individuals receiving less than 60 per cent of the median equivalized income (in the OECD's definition)—has been far less dramatic. The proportion of the population in relative poverty remained stubbornly high up to 2009, and in 2016 around 22 per cent of individuals still lived in households with an equivalized income of less than 60 per cent of the median (Box Figure 10.1). The figure for children aged under 14 is even higher, at 27 per cent; in other words, more than one-quarter of Malaysian children are in households living in relative poverty.

Many developed countries also struggle to reduce relative poverty. In the UK, for example, 18 per cent of individuals received an income of less than 60 per cent of the median at the beginning of the 21st century, and this figure was only marginally lower, at 16 per cent, in 2016–2017.

Malaysia's high relative poverty rates may well be due, in part, to demographic factors. The average household size in the UK is 2.4, while in Malaysia it is just above 4. The Malaysian poor tend to live in larger households, with several children, and this may partly explain why relative poverty is higher, as larger numbers of dependants at home will inevitably depress per capita, or equivalized, income.

Box Figure 10.1 About one-fifth of Malaysian adults, and one-quarter of all children, live in relative poverty, although the differential has narrowed with declining fertility levels

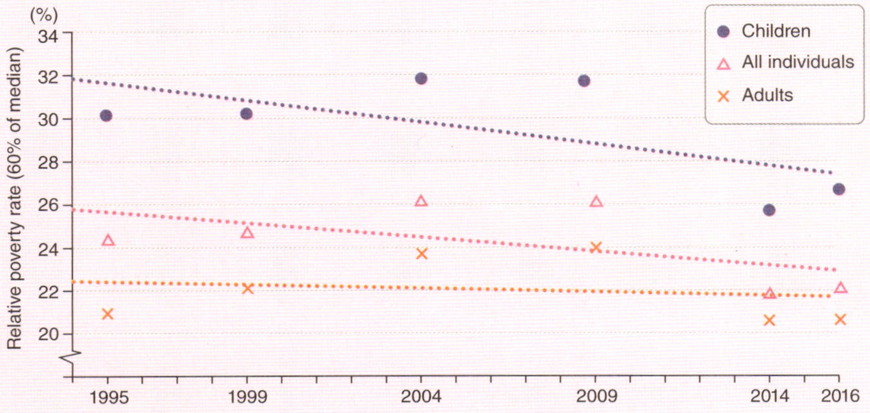

Source of data: Household Income Surveys, 1995, 1999, 2004, 2009, 2014, and 2016.

Raising the income of large, poor households will help to improve economic and social inclusion. One way of achieving this is to raise government transfers to these households and strengthen the social safety net; the increased government spending this entails could possibly be financed through a more progressive income tax system. As employment income constitutes the largest share of household income, the provision of employable skills to low-income groups must be part of the menu of support, as must better job opportunities for mothers.

In large Malaysian households, where the heads typically also have low levels of education, there are likely to be fewer income earners because child-care responsibilities prevent mothers from working. The provision of affordable child care may thus help to encourage mothers to work. Helping mothers to engage in full-time work in this way has two advantages: it avoids the adverse effects on incomes of prolonged part-time work, and it further raises family income. In Denmark and Sweden, policy priorities have shifted from enabling part-time work for working mothers to encouraging full-time work. Mothers in these countries typically work, and work full-time, out of preference (Rasmussen et al., 2004).

With the growing use of increasingly advanced technology, including artificial intelligence, the relative demand for higher-skilled and higher-paid workers is likely to rise, while the incomes of lower-skilled and lower-paid workers will remain depressed. This trend makes it imperative for Malaysia's education system to ensure that both women and men from low-income families receive a quality education, especially a thorough grounding in science, technology, engineering, and mathematics (STEM), and that there are second-chance opportunities for those who drop out, or who want to return to education at a later stage.

The locus of need and of poverty has changed markedly since the formulation of the NEP in 1971. Today, poverty is no longer confined to rural areas. Malaysia is predominantly urban and more than half of those with low incomes live in urban areas, facing higher costs than those in rural areas.[12] Poor urban households will need targeted assistance. However, as poverty remains most persistent among Malays and other *Bumiputera*, interventions will naturally be targeted more towards the disadvantaged sections of this community.

The imperative of reorienting affirmative action programmes echoes earlier recommendations made by the NEAC (2010), which also emphasized the importance of developing programmes focused on need rather than on ethnicity *per se*.[13] Affirmative action programmes should increasingly concentrate on building capacities and capabilities which enable, rather than create a sense of entitlement, so as to ensure positive outcomes.

---

12 Some 56 per cent of individuals with 'equivalized' income (the total income of their household divided by the number of equivalent adults in the household—Box 9.4) of less than half of the median now live in urban locations.

13 The NEAC identifies those in need as the bottom 40 per cent of households. Ultimately, budgetary resources and the scale of assistance may influence the definition of the target group.

Critical design elements of new programmes would include the transparent definition of needs; interventions that are disciplined by accountability and hard budgets; and exit clauses triggered either when goals are met, or if failures persist.[14] It is precisely those disadvantaged Malays, the indigenous communities of Sabah and Sarawak, and other *Bumiputera* such as the *Orang Asli* and the new urban poor of other communities, who would be among the major beneficiaries of such new arrangements. Affirmative action should also be used as a vehicle to cultivate inter-ethnic cohesion among disadvantaged communities rather than to widen cleavages.

Two: Diversified Development

The diagnostics of earlier chapters set out the manifold challenges that have emerged as Malaysia has navigated its way from being a poor, newly independent nation towards becoming a more complex and prosperous economy that aspires to high-income status and high human development. Following the setback of the 2008 Great Recession, the NEAC (2010) report, which advocated a 'New Economic Model' for Malaysia, identified a set of core challenges for the country to address. The authors of that report concluded that Malaysia was caught in a 'middle-income trap'.

The core challenges identified by the NEAC included slowing economic growth; wide income disparities; labour market distortions and a reliance on low-skilled and low-wage foreign labour; a 'disastrous exodus of human capital' (NEAC, 2010, p. 42); poor educational outcomes; stagnant productivity growth; depressed levels of investment and the crowding out of the private sector through excessive state involvement in the economy; and the heavy costs of doing business. In the NEAC's view, Malaysia was snared from below by low-cost emerging market economies eroding its competitive advantages in export markets, and from above by its inability to move up the value chain, out of simple assembly operations and into the more innovative and complex activities in which advanced economies specialize.

To address this worrying set of circumstances, the NEAC recommended a raft of measures to invigorate the private sector, upgrade human capital, bolster markets and competition, streamline bureaucracy, level opportunities, advance inclusion, encourage value creation, stimulate innovation, and preserve Malaysia's precious natural resources. The NEAC's report stressed the interconnectedness of challenges and solutions, and, above all, the importance of political leadership in championing and pushing for the implementation of these deep reforms.

14 The instruments used to deliver support must not distort incentives or otherwise impede the efficient operation of markets. The use of vouchers, unconditional cash transfers, and other market-friendly mechanisms should be considered as appropriate.

Nearly ten years later, there is still much that is relevant in the NEAC's assessment and in its vision for a brighter future for Malaysia.[15] However, the underlying premise of the NEAC's proposed strategy—that the political will for radical institutional change and reform was genuine (in around 2009)—proved to be overly optimistic. Ultimately, the logic and integrity of the NEAC's agenda drifted, as its recommendations were parsed and reinterpreted in subsequent planning frameworks (MP10, 2011–2015 and MP11, 2016–2020), and in the Government Transformation Programme, which was also launched in 2009.

Prosperity and graduation to high-income status remain important aspirations for Malaysia (Box 10.2). However, a broader focus on truly inclusive and sustainable development is vital. In technical terms, a new focus on the 'genuine wealth' of the nation is called for. Genuine wealth is the combined *value* to society of the nation's ownership of natural capital, human capital, and built manufactured capital, plus its net foreign assets. For development to be sustainable, the nation's genuine wealth (per capita) must expand. As the NEAC report highlights, and as successive national plans also recognize, Malaysia can no longer develop and prosper through the exploitation of its natural capital and the more intensive application of inputs (physical inputs of capital and labour) alone.

Box 10.2 Transitioning to a high-income economy

Malaysia's past economic growth has, to a large extent, depended on factor accumulation—capital and labour. Significant gains were also made through moving low-productivity labour out of agriculture and into higher-productivity jobs in the urban economy. It helped that foreign investment was readily available for import-substituting industries in the early phase, and later for export-oriented industrialization. Foreign investment brought its own specific product-related technology and markets. Given higher fertility rates during this period of economic expansion and a continuous stream of better-educated entrants into the labour market from the schooling system, the supply of labour was assured. Any gaps could be met with foreign labour.

These conditions have changed, however. Foreign direct investment has slowed, and as a result of fertility declines, the growth of domestic labour supply has decelerated. Agriculture is no longer the primary source of economic growth or poverty reduction,

15 The analysis in earlier chapters indicates that there had been few improvements by the end of the 10th Malaysian Plan period (2015). Perkins et al. (2017) concur, and point in particular to the way in which disappointing educational outcomes have contributed to lacklustre performance in productivity and innovation.

although its role in Malaysia's food system and the nutritional well-being of the population remains crucial. Additionally, competition for foreign direct investment and market share has intensified, both with countries in Asia—such as China, India, Viet Nam, Indonesia, and Thailand—and with emerging market economies on other continents. If Malaysia is to succeed in becoming a high-income economy, sustained advances in productivity will thus be essential.

The keys to accelerating productivity gains are threefold: eliminating market distortions and reducing inefficiency; making up ground in human capital accumulation; and creating a climate for private investment and business that enables enterprise, competition, and innovation. In 2009, the University of Malaya launched an initiative to enhance innovation by expanding high-quality research through the establishment of eight interdisciplinary research clusters, reduced to four in 2018 so as to achieve greater impact. The success of these clusters will depend on whether government supports an enabling environment by providing local infrastructure and increasing its levels of R&D expenditure, and on whether there is collaboration with high-quality researchers as well as with innovative private sector partners.

In many ways, market distortions are a by-product of earlier policies and of the close nexus that these have engendered between government and business. A credible divestment programme for GLEs—one that ensures fair market value for the privatized assets—is essential for creating space for the private sector to grow and compete on a level playing field. The NEAC (2010), among others, has set out principles to guide divestment, including the phasing out of GLE activities in areas where the private sector is operating efficiently, the expanded use of partnerships with private sector companies, and the imposition of strict commercial operating principles on remaining GLEs operating in areas deemed to be of strategic national interest. If the country is to transition to a high-income economy, the government's new role should be as a facilitator and regulator of business, not as an owner and operator.

Malaysia's education system has struggled to keep up with the demands created by unrelenting technological change and by related changes in the international division of labour due to intensified international competition for investment. Human capital accumulation has lagged behind that in the Republic of Korea, Singapore, and many other countries. In the World Bank's Human Capital Index 2018, Malaysia ranked just 55th out of 157 countries (World Bank, 2019).[16] Students who enter universities should be well grounded in STEM subjects, but outcomes suggest that primary and secondary school systems are falling short. Meanwhile, universities are struggling to produce graduates with the skills that the market demands. Talented students who face ethnic barriers to entry to universities are being lost to overseas institutions and to emigration. Educational priorities and policies require a radical rethink.

16 The World Bank's Human Capital Index 2018 measures the expected future productivity of a child born in that year relative to the benchmark of complete education and full health. It seeks to quantify the amount of human capital that a child born in 2018 can expect to achieve at age 18, based on current education and health outcomes (World Bank, 2019).

While the private sector must be the engine that powers Malaysia's future economic growth, the state will still have an important role to play. Government must provide direction and coordination, and must regulate in the public interest. It will continue to have responsibility for providing and financing the delivery of public goods, including fiscal and financial stability, in an efficient and equitable manner. It will also retain its important custodial role of ensuring that national assets are managed and invested wisely.

Within these boundaries, government must strive to minimize the time and monetary costs to the private sector of doing business. It also has the responsibility to ensure a climate that encourages private investment and that protects the legitimate interests of investors. Beyond these functions, however, the question of how government can best support the private sector is more vexed.

From a classical economics perspective, a case for government intervention and support for the private sector can be made in circumstances where there are information, coordination, or other forms of market failure. This is certainly the situation with R&D, and with the start up of completely new activities. In these areas, investors are susceptible to the risk that they may be unable to appropriate the benefits of their investments due to spillovers or the presence of copycats. In such cases, measured subsidies and other forms of support are likely to be needed to stimulate innovation and new enterprise. Rodrik (2009) sets out design principles that help to ensure beneficial outcomes, but also to discipline interventions. More activist government-led approaches involving the selection of 'winning sectors' or strategic clusters, for example, need to be subject to exacting tests. Malaysia's own experience, and the experience of other countries, suggests that such approaches have often failed to deliver the anticipated benefits.

The size and quality of future economic growth will also be influenced by the structure of incentives that businesses and investors face. For example, policies that compress wages or raise the costs of capital investment will have the effect of retarding productivity growth. Meanwhile, inducements to foreign investors should be linked to the spillover benefits that they promise in the form of knowledge, know-how, and technology transfer.

Under the umbrella of inclusion and sustainability, four areas deserve priority attention: accelerating human capital accumulation; halting and reversing Malaysia's brain drain by expanding the talents of, and the opportunities open to, those who face barriers to inclusion; stimulating private enterprise and supporting 'economic discovery' (that is, encouraging investment in new viable activities); and creating a natural and physical environment that is both safe and sustainable, while managing the country's natural resources for the benefit of all.

Within each of these four areas, the enunciation of a new set of high-level policy principles or protocols, along with the identification of desired outcomes (a description of changed conditions), would help to provide concordance and guide more detailed planning.[17] For example, within the area of stimulating private enterprise and supporting 'economic discovery', alongside the articulation of principles that would delimit the nature of the state's direct investment in business, the government could lead in the preparation of a credible divestment programme for government-owned companies. A successful programme would not only help to expand future fiscal space, it would also have the potential (through lowering barriers to entry) to stimulate private investment, create new and decent jobs, and generate benefits for consumers through expanded choice and/or lower prices.[18]

Three: Immigration and Labour Market Regulations

Malaya's economic achievements during the colonial era were, in no small measure, made possible by the hard work of its migrant workers. Many of these have settled, raised families, and become valued members of Malaysia's multicultural population.

After independence, Malaysia initially maintained the strict immigration controls which had been put in place during the late colonial era, driven by political considerations about ethnic balance. But as labour shortages began to emerge in the early 1980s, and as the country's ethnic composition became less finely balanced, regulations were loosened and large migrant inflows were once again permitted. Private employers began recruiting lower-skilled foreign workers, both legally and illegally, which helped to sustain high economic growth.[19]

Today, Malaysia once again relies on low-cost migrant labour from Asia's seemingly inexhaustible supply, in much the same way that businesses used

17 For example, one such principle might be that the full social opportunity costs of the consumption of non-renewable minerals and other non-renewable resources that are owned by the state must be more than offset by the benefits that derive from the investment of the fiscal resources that they create. This principle would, in turn, require that the state seek to maximize its take of the rents generated by non-renewable resources (a principle of fiscal neutrality). Other principles that might be followed could cover the issues of how rents are to be used and invested for the benefit of this and future generations. These might then frame fiscal and other rules. Other principles might, for example, define the goals and nature of affirmative action, and determine the criteria to be applied, or set out guidelines to govern education policy.

18 Given the scale of Malaysia's government-linked financial investment companies and government-linked businesses in the economy, divestment will need to be carefully phased to ensure that assets attract a fair value and that the new ownership structures are consistent with broader development ambitions. In these circumstances, and in preparation for eventual divestment, the rationalization and restructuring of inefficient but viable government-linked companies should be given priority, and where they are moribund and insolvent, these firms could be wound up.

19 The country's fairly porous borders make illegal migration difficult to control.

cheap migrant labour in colonial Malaya. Many of the low-paid unskilled jobs, especially in agriculture, assembly-based industries, construction, and low-end services, are undertaken by non-Malaysians. This exerts a downward pressure on the skill composition of the country's human capital base. The transition to skill-intensive, higher-value-added employment has not occurred at a pace sufficient to enable a significant reduction in the dependence on foreign workers.

Increasingly, the presence of relatively low-cost, low-skilled foreign labour has become a major impediment to Malaysia's ambition to become a high-income economy. The problem is that the flow of workers depresses real wages, and imparts a bias towards labour-intensive technologies and low-cost business models. The large available pool of low-cost labour blunts incentives to invest in skills upgrading and the acquisition of knowledge. To the extent that new capital investment facilitates the development and use of improved technologies, the availability of low-cost labour also impedes the rate of technological change.

A further challenge lies in the fact that migrant workers provide competition for the country's poorest and most disadvantaged Malays and other *Bumiputera*, who have been the primary intended beneficiaries of affirmative action programmes. Although the counterfactual cannot be observed, more controlled immigration could have lifted the real wages and incomes of Malays and other *Bumiputera*, narrowing income disparities among Malaysian citizens and thereby contributing to broader distributional goals.

There are policy guidelines governing the entry of migrant workers, including annual levies on foreign workers differing by sectoral and skill level, which aim to control the size of the inflows. But these have failed to have a significant impact on recruitment, partly because of cost differentials between local and foreign workers in terms of wages and benefits, and partly because of sizeable inflows of illegal migrants.

As part of an agenda which emphasizes inclusion, the rights of today's non-Malaysian workers will need to be strengthened through measures including regular reviews of national minimum wage legislation, in order to ensure that these workers benefit from national prosperity, as well as to help reduce inequality. Denying social benefits to lower-wage migrant workers will only give rise to pockets of poverty and ill health, and will exacerbate other social issues. On the other hand, the provision of social benefits to migrants can be unsustainable and lead to fiscal strains. The costs of core social benefits for migrants—for their health and shelter, for example—should be covered by employers as part of recruitment conditions, to ensure that these private sector costs are not passed on to the government.

Poverty has always been a key force driving international migration, and this will continue to be the case. Economic migrants from lower-income countries are motivated by the promise of higher wages and better lives. With the large cross-border movements of lower-skilled workers, economic migration has become a major public policy issue globally. Malaysia, like other prosperous countries, needs to develop a migration policy that balances its economic aspirations with the desired levels of foreign workers, while taking into account their rights and well-being.

Four: Environmental Management for Sustainability

Natural capital has been a vitally important component of Malaysia's genuine wealth. As the country moves towards high-income status, other components of genuine wealth—particularly human capital—will increase in importance. But in the face of looming threats to the environment, and the potentially devastating consequences of environmental damage for human well-being, the management and custodianship of Malaysia's natural capital will require even closer attention. Placing inclusion at the centre of national development policy forces a sharper focus than ever before on sustainability and sustainable environmental management. Inclusive development, by definition, must embrace the needs of both current and future generations. Choices made now will leave an indelible mark on the country's future.

Malaysia today faces multiple environmental onslaughts, including high rates of carbon dioxide emissions, deforestation, and air and river pollution from unregulated industries. Deforestation is also responsible for the displacement of marginalized communities. The country's ecological footprint far exceeds the capacity of its ecosystem to replenish its rich natural resources. The risk is that unregulated lifestyle choices will further threaten natural resources, and will entail the increasing production of waste and pollution. However, if the trends suggested by broader international experience also play out in Malaysia, the demand for environment-friendly goods and services (including clean air, better water quality, and improved biodiversity) should increase with increases in real incomes. Adapting the SDGs' environmental agenda to Malaysia's circumstances would help to redirect behaviour towards a sustainable future.

SDG 13, for example, calls for combating climate change and global warming through reduced greenhouse gas emissions (mitigation), and adaptation measures to increase climate resilience. Malaysia is a signatory to the United Nations 2015 Paris Climate Agreement to keep human-caused global warming to below 2 degrees Celsius compared with the pre-industrial era. Malaysia's economy is fossil-fuel-based in an era when fossil fuels are increasingly giving way to low-carbon energy sources such as wind, solar, hydro, and nuclear power. The country's high carbon emissions are also aggravated by deforestation, as trees are an important source of carbon storage. Policies must be introduced to encourage a staged transition from fossil fuels to a cleaner national energy system.

Malaysia shares international concerns about the conservation and sustainable use of the oceans, seas, and marine resources, as articulated in SDG 14. Malaysia's coastal communities, which include many low-income households, are highly dependent on the marine environment for their sustenance and livelihoods. Overfishing to supply the seafood export industry and local consumption, along with the depletion of fish stocks, is threatening the social and economic well-being of these coastal communities. Massive coastal development is destroying sensitive marine habitats, including coral reefs, seagrass beds, and mangroves. Ecosystem-based management that considers the interactions of land, water, and living resources must instead ensure better management and protection of the marine environment.

Similarly, protecting and restoring terrestrial ecosystems by sustainably managing forests and halting biodiversity loss is critical for Malaysia; this aim is set out in SDG 15. The country has already used much of its virgin rainforest for large-scale commercial monocrop plantations that produce high-demand exports like palm oil and, in earlier years, rubber. There is a pressing need to recognize that Malaysia's unique terrestrial ecosystem provides many valuable services, including clean water and air, food, medicines, carbon sequestration, biodiversity, and other invaluable benefits. Today's choices for the future must carefully balance the expected returns from continued investment in monocrops with the as yet considerably undervalued benefits of sustainably managed and biodiverse forests.

Working towards sustainability demands improved environmental governance. Better regulatory and administrative coordination between the federal and state agencies involved in the planning, management, and enforcement of environmental matters is required (Vincent and Rozali Mohamed Ali, 2005). An ecosystem-based approach and multi-stakeholder processes should be put in place, along with more engagement among the public and private sectors, as well as civil society, in managing Malaysia's environmental and natural resources.

Five: Implementation

Implementation is often the stumbling block in translating development priorities into effective action. This final section offers some suggestions on how to manage the transition.

Administrative Alignment and Configuration

An important but neglected issue is the size and structure of the executive branch of government—how it is organized, what it does, how it spends, and how it is resourced—and why this matters for development outcomes. An effective government is one that delivers beneficial outcomes in an efficient, cost-disciplined way. At one level, effectiveness will depend on how ministries and other entities perform. But effectiveness will also be influenced by how functions are defined and configured among different government entities. A lack of clarity about functions, and multiple overlapping mandates across different government entities, are likely to elevate expenditure and transaction costs, and exacerbate coordination problems. Even where mandates are clear, as in the case of federal, state, and local levels of government, the presence of effective coordination mechanisms is still essential to ensure that the implementation of programmes is unimpeded.[20]

The public interest is also likely to be ill served when government entities act in conflicting capacities, say, as policymaker and regulator, or as regulator and investor. State ownership and control of the corporate sector through government-linked investment companies raises the crucial question of whether government should function mainly as a facilitator of business, or as a direct and powerful investor. If state ownership and involvement in business are deemed to be in the public interest, as might be the case for strategic assets, it is important that independent oversight and regulation of state-owned businesses exist.

Other structural issues also need attention, including the question of how to ensure that cross-cutting development issues receive adequate attention and are appropriately resourced. Is it better to centralize responsibility—for instance, on environmental matters—in a stand-alone ministry, or to distribute the function across ministries to ensure that cross-cutting

20 Coordination issues have long been recognized and addressed through a variety of mechanisms, including the Implementation and Coordination Unit of the Prime Minister's Department, underlining the importance of sound implementation (Hunter, 2013; World Bank, 2017). The creation of a performance and service delivery culture in government is essential to budgetary discipline and improved social outcomes.

concerns are mainstreamed in the business of all government entities? Are both approaches needed? Or, in seeking to align resources with priorities and drive performance, can Malaysia learn from the Republic of Korea's model in which intertwined strategy, planning, and budgetary issues are the responsibility of its unified Ministry of Strategy and Finance? To take another example, if science and innovation are now to be a high national priority, is there a case for establishing a Ministry of Science and Innovation as in Canada, or a Ministry of the Knowledge Economy as in the Republic of Korea? These are huge questions to address, but the alternative option of working within inert administrative structures designed many decades ago may not be 'fit for the future'.

Human Resources

Effective human resource capacities will also be vital for the focused pursuit of improved development outcomes. Government, and the public sector more broadly, will need to attract, retain, and promote talent on the basis of qualifications, merit, and performance. Public sector employment must be perceived as rewarding, and as a viable career path for all citizens. The ethics and values that employees in this sector must uphold should be integral to human resource training, processes, and policies. Citizens need to have confidence in the integrity of all public officials.

Data for Evidence-based Policy

This book's final subsection ends where the Economic History of Malaya Project began some two decades ago: with the crucial importance of data for evidence-based analysis and policy. As the popular phrase goes, 'what gets measured and monitored, gets managed'.

National income accounts, which focus largely on market transactions and on flows and stocks in the formal economy, must urgently be expanded to encompass wider concepts of sustainability. In particular, the implementation of the System of Environmental-Economic Accounting and the System of Experimental Ecosystem Accounting (both offshoots of the original System of National Accounts) should be given priority. Progress in measuring and reporting on sustainable development is imperative (United Nations, 2013), and Malaysia should be in the vanguard. The roadmap set out by the Department of Statistics–Malaysia (2018b) to guide the transition to a system of environmental-economic accounts by 2020 is an excellent starting point and needs to be adequately resourced.

Improved and expanded statistical data are also required to allow the tracking of Malaysia's progress on other critical development outcomes. Measuring progress on inclusivity requires high-quality data on the dynamics of poverty and on the distribution of income and wealth, as well as on the changing conditions that influence citizens' quality of life. Longitudinal data that chart the circumstances of different cohorts of Malaysians as they move through life would allow policymakers to gain improved insights into the impact of their policies at grass-roots level. A well-functioning labour market information system that tracks sectoral and firm-level information on labour needs, supply, and mobility would lead to improved labour market monitoring and decision-making. The collection of such information requires long-term human and financial investments.

The new digital ecosystem is expanding exponentially. It needs to be managed in the interests of society, with the privacy rights of individuals respected and with safeguards on the curation, security, and use of data. The challenges of regulation and education should not be underestimated, but if these can be satisfactorily addressed, digital technology offers tremendous opportunities. These opportunities are already being leveraged, and are contributing to improvements in the efficient delivery of government services.

Big Data also offers intriguing opportunities for designing and monitoring development policies. Providing real-time maps of economic activity is no longer merely a fantasy. Already, the Billion Prices Project run out of the Massachusetts Institute of Technology gives *daily* inflation updates for 22 economies, helping to keep governments better informed, and providing the opportunity to fine-tune policies (Cavallo and Rigobon, 2016). Furthermore, satellite data are now being used to provide high-frequency metrics of Chinese manufacturing activity, and can also be used to monitor everything from the quality of roads to the logging of forests (Wigglesworth, 2018). In the future, bank balance sheets audited in real time, made available by blockchain technology, may present the prospect of much better early-warning systems and enhanced macro-prudential stabilization policies.

In other ways, too, digitized data is opening up previously undreamed-of possibilities. The 'internet of things' can, for example, provide granular consumption data to inform policies for improved energy management and resource conservation. In terms of inclusion, meanwhile, social media feeds can help not only to identify stakeholders, but also to provide them with an effective voice in matters that affect their futures—although it should be recognized that the honesty and quality of data derived from social media can be problematic. The possibilities for tapping into real-time sources of information to assist policy design, interventions, and monitoring are expansive. Ultimately, however, beneficial economic and social outcomes for Malaysians will hinge on the relevance and reliability of the information captured, and on the balance between legitimate interests in protecting individual privacy and a public interest in improved and expanded information to guide development policy and regulatory design.

Looking ahead, Malaysia must confront a number of serious and interrelated challenges which, if not addressed, could thwart its ambition of becoming a high-income nation. Increasingly, future prosperity and inclusiveness will be co-dependent. Prosperity will be required to provide the resources needed to support all Malaysians, especially the disadvantaged. Without more inclusive policies, meanwhile, the country may continue to squander valuable resources, talent, and opportunities, thereby putting at risk the cohesion essential for social progress and the well-being of all Malaysians. This final chapter has identified some of the obstacles still to be faced on the journey to high-income status and to the more equitable sharing of wealth. Based on the country's inspiring progress over the last six decades, Malaysia is certainly well placed to overcome these challenges as it strives for inclusive development.

REFERENCES
INDEX

References

Abdul Aziz Abdul Rahman (1996), 'Smallholder Agriculture', in K. S. Jomo and S. K. Ng (eds.), *Malaysia's Economic Development, Policy and Reform* (Selangor: Pelanduk Publications).

Abdul Halim Tamuri and Che Pee Saad (2008), 'The Development of Islamic Education in Malaysia: An Analysis', in Ibrahim Ahmad Bajunid (ed.), *Malaysia, From Traditional to Smart Schools: The Malaysian Educational Odyssey* (Shah Alam: Oxford Fajar).

Abdul Hamid Omar (1994), *The Judiciary in Malaysia* (Kuala Lumpur: Asia Pacific Publications).

Abdul Karim Bagoo (1962), 'The Origins and Development of the Malay State Guides', *Journal of the Malayan Branch of the Royal Asiatic Society*, 35/1, 51–94.

Abdul Majid Ismail (1974), *The History of Early Medical and Health Services in Malaysia* (Kuala Lumpur: Malaysian Historical Society).

Abdul Rahim Ramli (2018), *Johor Darul Ta'zim, An Abode of Dignity* (Johor Bahru: UTM Press).

Abdul Rahman Embong (2002), *State-led Modernization and the New Middle Class in Malaysia* (New York: Palgrave).

—— (2006), 'Between Optimism, Contestation and Caution: The Second Generation Middle Classes in Malaysia', in Hsin-Huang Michael Hsiao (ed.), *The Changing Faces of the Middle Classes in Asia-Pacific* (Taipei: Center for Asia-Pacific Area Studies, Academia Sinica), 133–154.

Abdul Rahman Hasan and Nair, P. L. (2014), 'Urbanisation and Growth of Metropolitan Centres in Malaysia', *Malaysian Journal of Economic Studies*, 51/1, 87–101.

Abramovitz, M. (1956), 'Resource and Output Trends in the United States since 1870', *American Economic Review* (May), p. 11.

Acemoglu, D., and Robinson, J. A. (2012), *Why Nations Fail: The Origins of Power, Prosperity, and Poverty* (New York: Crown Publishers).

Ahmad Fauzi Abdul Hamid (2010), *Islamic Education in Malaysia*, RSIS Monograph No. 18 (Singapore: Nanyang Technological University).

Ahmad Ibrahim (1965), *Islamic Law in Malaya* (Singapore: Malaysian Sociological Research Institute).

Aitchison, J., and Brown, J. A. C. (1957), *The Lognormal Distribution, with Special Reference to Its Uses in Economics* (Cambridge: Cambridge University Press).

Alesina, A., Michalopoulos, S., and Papaioannou, E. (2016), 'Ethnic Inequality', *Journal of Political Economy*, 124/2, 428–488.

Allen, J. De V., Stockwell, A. J., and Wright, L. R. (1981), *A Collection of Treaties and Other Documents Affecting the States of Malaysia, 1761–1963*, vol. 1 (London: Oceana Publication), 390–392.

Amrith, S. S. (2014), 'The Art of Medicine: Migration and Health in Southeast Asian History', *The Lancet*, 384, 1569–1570.

Anand, S. (1983), *Inequality and Poverty in Malaysia: Measurement and Decomposition* (New York: Oxford University Press).

Anand, S., and Segal, P. (2008), 'What Do We Know about Global Income Inequality?' *Journal of Economic Literature*, 46/11, 57–94.

—— (2015), 'The Global Distribution of Income', in A. B. Atkinson and F. Bourguignon (eds.), *Handbook of Income Distribution*, vol. 2A (Amsterdam: North-Holland), 937–979.

—— (2017), 'Who are the Global Top 1%?', Working Paper 8, International Inequalities Institute (London School of Economics and Political Science).

Andaya, B. W., and Andaya, L. Y. (2017), *A History of Malaysia* (3rd edn., Basingstoke: Palgrave Macmillan).

Arrow, K. J., et al. (2012), 'Sustainability and the Measure of Wealth', *Environment and Development Economics*, 17/3, 317–353.

—— (2013), 'Sustainability and the Measure of Wealth: Further Reflections', *Environment and Development Economics*, 18/4, 504–516.

Asian Development Bank (1997), *Emerging Asia: Changes and Challenges* (Manila: Asian Development Bank).

—— (2007), *Asian Development Outlook 2007* (Manila: ADB), https://www.adb.org/publications/asian-development-outlook-2007-growth-amid-change, accessed 8 August 2018.

—— (2009), *Key Indicators for Asia and the Pacific 2009* (Manila: ADB), https://www.adb.org/sites/default/files/publication/27727/key-indicators-2009.pdf, accessed 27 November 2018.

—— (2018), *Key Indicators for Asia and the Pacific 2018* (Manila: ADB), https//www.adb.org/sites/default/files/publication/443671/ki2018.pdf, accessed 27 November 2018.

Athukorala, P. C. (2012), 'Malaysian Economy in Three Crises', *Departmental Working Paper, 2010–2012* (Australian National University).

Atkinson, A. B. (1970), 'On the Measurement of Inequality', *Journal of Economic Theory*, 2/3, 244–263.

—— (2007), 'The Distribution of Earnings in OECD Countries', *International Labour Review*, 146/1–2, 41–60.

—— (2015), 'Top Incomes in Malaysia 1947 to the Present (with a Note on the Straits Settlements 1916 to 1921)', *World Wealth and Income Database*, https://wid.world/document/wid_methodology_notes_2013_5_malaysia/, accessed 2 April 2019.

Atkinson, A. B., Piketty, T., and Saez, E. (2011), 'Top Incomes in the Long Run of History', *Journal of Economic Literature*, 49/1, 3–71.

Awang Had Salleh (1994), 'Phases of Development of Modern Education in Malaysia', in Shamsul Amri Baharuddin and Institut Tadbiran Awam Negara (Malaysia), *Malaysian Development Experience: Changes and Challenges* (Kuala Lumpur: National Institute of Public Administration).

Ayat K. A. Rahman, et al. (2008), 'The Malaysian Palm Oil Supply Chain: The Role of the Independent Smallholders', *Oil Palm Industry Economic Journal*, 8/2, 7–27.

Azizah Kassim (2014), 'Foreign Workers in Malaysia in the Post-Independence Era: Race Paradigm in State Policy, Academic Writings and Public Discourse', in A. Milner, Abdul Rahman Embong, and S. Y. Tham (eds.), *Transforming Malaysia: Dominant and Competing Paradigms* (Singapore: ISEAS Publishing), 143–177.

Azizah Kassim, Too, T., and Mahani Zainal Abidin (2014), 'The Management of Foreign Workers in Malaysia: Institutions and Governance Regime', in R. H. Adams Jr. and Ahmad Ahsan (eds.), *Managing International Migration for Development in East Asia* (Washington, DC: World Bank Group).

Azlan Tajuddin (2012), *Malaysia in the World Economy (1824–2011): Capitalism, Ethnic Divisions, and 'Managed' Democracy* (Maryland: Lexington Books).

Badiane, O. (2011), 'Agriculture and Structural Transformation in Africa', *Stanford Symposium Series on Global Food Policy and Food Security in the 21st Century*, 7 April 2011 (California: Stanford University).

Baker, D., Jayadev, A., and Stiglitz, J. (2017), 'Innovation, Intellectual Property, and Development: A Better Set of Approaches for the 21st Century', paper presented as part of a series of arguments from AccessIBSA, a project supported by Shuttleworth Foundation (Washington, DC: Center for Economic and Policy Research), http://cepr.net/images/stories/reports/baker-jayadev-stiglitz-innovation-ip-development-2017-07.pdf, accessed on 18 September 2018.

Banerjee, A., and Piketty, T. (2010), 'Top Indian Incomes, 1922–2000', in A. B. Atkinson and T. Piketty (eds.), *Top Incomes: A Global Perspective* (Oxford: Oxford University Press).

Bank Negara Malaysia [BNM] (1997), *Bank Negara Annual Report 1997* (Kuala Lumpur).

—— (1998), *Bank Negara Annual Report 1998* (Kuala Lumpur).

—— (2008), *Financial Stability and Payment Systems Report* (Kuala Lumpur).

—— (2009), *Bank Negara Annual Report 2009* (Kuala Lumpur).

—— (various issues), *Quarterly Statistics Bulletin* (Kuala Lumpur).

Barber, A. (2008), *Malaya: The Making of a Nation, 1510–1957* (Kuala Lumpur: AB & A).

Barlow, C. (1978), *The Natural Rubber Industry: Its Development, Technology, and Economy* (Kuala Lumpur: Oxford University Press).

Barlow, C., Jayasuriya, S., and Tan, C. S. (1994), *The World Rubber Industry* (London: Routledge).

Barro, R. J. (2001), 'Human Capital and Growth', *The American Economic Review*, 91/2, 12–17.

Barro, R. J., and Lee, J. W. (1994), 'Sources of Economic Growth', *Carnegie-Rochester Conference Series on Public Policy*, 40/1, 1–46.

Baumol, W. J. (1967), 'Macroeconomics of Unbalanced Growth: The Anatomy of Urban Crisis', *The American Economic Review*, 57/3, 415–426.

Beaglehole, J. H. (1969), 'Malay Participation in Commerce and Industry: The Role of RIDA and MARA', *Journal of Commonwealth Political Studies*, 7/3, 216–245.

Becker, G. S. (1993), *Human Capital: A Theoretical and Empirical Analysis with Special Reference to Education* (3rd edn., Chicago: University of Chicago Press).

Benham, F. C. (1951), *The National Income of Malaya: 1947–1949* (Singapore: Government Printers).

Bernanke, B. S. (2004), 'Money, Gold, and the Great Depression', remarks at the H. Parker Willis Lecture in Economic Policy, 2 March 2004, Washington and Lee University, Lexington, VA, https://www.federalreserve.gov/boarddocs/speeches/2004/200403022/default.htm, accessed 8 August 2018.

Bernanke, B. S., and James, H. (1990), 'The Gold Standard, Deflation, and Financial Crisis in the Great Depression: An International Comparison', NBER Working Paper No. 3488 (National Bureau of Economic Research).

Bhanoji Rao, V. V. (1976), *National Accounts of West Malaysia, 1947–1971* (Singapore: Heinemann Educational Books).

—— (1980), *Malaysia, Development Pattern and Policy, 1947–1971* (Singapore: Singapore University Press).

Bhattacharya, J., and Kripalani, C. (2015), *Indian and Chinese Immigrant Communities: Comparative Perspectives* (London: Anthem Press).

Binswanger-Mkhize, H. P. (2012), 'India 1960–2010: Structural Change, the Rural Non-farm Sector, and the Prospects for Agriculture', paper prepared for the Stanford Symposium Series on Global Food Policy and Food Security in the 21st Century, 10 May, Stanford University.

Bissonnette, J-F., and De Koninck, R. (2017), *Social and Environmental Implications of Plantation Agriculture in Malaysia and Indonesia*, Oxford Research Encyclopaedias, Environmental Science (New York: Oxford University Press), environmentalscience.oxfordre.com, accessed 26 February 2018.

Blake, C. (1990), *A View from Within: The Last Years of British Rule in South-East Asia* (Somerset: Castle Cary Press).

Bloom, D. E., Canning, D., and Sevilla, J. (2001), 'Economic Growth and the Demographic Transition', NBER Working Paper No. 8685 (National Bureau of Economic Research).

Bloom, D. E., and Williamson, J. G. (1998), 'Demographic Transitions and Economic Miracles in Emerging Asia', *The World Bank Economic Review*, 12/3, 419–455.

Blythe, W. L. (1947), 'Historical Sketch of Chinese Labour in Malaya', *Journal of the Malayan Branch of the Royal Asiatic Society*, 20/1, 64–125.

Bolt, J., et al. (2018), 'Rebasing "Maddison": New Income Comparisons and the Shape of Long-run Economic Development', GGDC Research Memorandum GD-174 (Groningen Growth and Development Centre, University of Groningen).

Booth, A. (2016), *Economic Change in Modern Indonesia: Colonial and Post-Colonial Comparisons* (Cambridge: Cambridge University Press).

Bordo, M. D., and Meissner, C. M. (2012), 'Does Inequality Lead to a Financial Crisis?', *Journal of International Money and Finance*, 31/8, 2147–2161.

Bosworth, B. P., and Collins, S. M. (2003), 'The Empirics of Growth: An Update', Brookings Papers on Economic Activity, no. 2, 113–206.

British Information Services (1960), *The UK Colonial Development and Welfare Acts*.

Broaderick, E. G. (1919), *Administration Report for the Year 1918* (Selangor), p. 13.

Burkhauser, R. V., et al. (2017), 'Top Incomes and Inequality in the UK: Reconciling Estimates from Household Survey and Tax Return Data', *Oxford Economic Papers*, 70/2, 301–326.

Butcher, J. G. (1979), *The British in Malaya, 1880–1941: The Social History of a European Community in Colonial South-East Asia* (Kuala Lumpur: Oxford University Press).

Byerlee, D., Falcon, W. P., and Naylor, R. L. (2017), *The Tropical Oil Crop Revolution: Food, Feed, Fuel and Forests* (London: Oxford University Press).

Calabria, M. A. (2009), 'Did Deregulation Cause the Financial Crisis?', *Cato Policy Report*, 31/4, 5–8.

Cameron, J. (1865), *Our Tropical Possessions in Malayan India* (London: Smith Elder).

Campbell, P. C. (1923), *Chinese Coolie Emigration to Countries Within the British Empire* (London: Routledge).

Carr-Saunders, A. M. (1948), 'Report of the Commission on University Education in Malaya' (Kuala Lumpur: Government Press).

Cavallo, A., and Rigobon, R. (2016), 'The Billion Prices Project: Using Online Prices for Measurement and Research', *Journal of Economic Perspectives*, 30/2, 151–178, http://www.thebillionpricesproject.com/, accessed 3 April 2019.

Cavendish, A. (1911), *Report on the Census of Kedah and Perlis, 1911* (Penang: The Criterion Press Ltd).

Chan, S. (1965), 'Kelantan and Trengganu, 1909–1939', *Journal of Malaysian Branch of the Royal Asiatic Society*, 38/1, 159–198.

Chander, R. (1977), *General Report, 1970 Population Census of Malaysia* (Kuala Lumpur: Department of Statistics–Malaysia).

Chang, J. H. (2001), 'Planning Rubber Plantations: Tropical Production, Malaria and the Management of Labor in British Malaya, 1900–1942', paper for the 15th International Planning History Society Conference, 15–18 July 2012, Sao Paulo.

Chapman, D., and Chien, C. L. (2014), 'Expanding Out and Up: What are the System-Level Dynamics? A Case Study of Malaysia and Thailand', in *Higher Education in Asia: Expanding Out, Expanding Up: The Rise of Graduate Education and University Research* (Montreal: UNESCO Institute for Statistics).

Cheah, J. S., and Ong, H. T. (2005), 'Book Review: The History of Medicine in Malaysia —The Foundation Years', *Annals of the Academy of Medicine*, http://www.annals.edu.sg/pdf/35VolNo1200601/V35N1p60.pdf, accessed 20 December 2017.

Chee, P. L. (1994), 'Heavy Industrialisation: A Second Round of Import Substitution', in K. Jomo (ed.), *Japan and Malaysian Development in the Shadow of the Rising Sun* (London: Routledge), 244–262.

Chenery, H. B., and Syrquin, M. (1975), *Patterns of Development, 1950–1970* (London: Oxford University Press).

Chenery, H. B., and Taylor, L. (1968), 'Development Patterns among Countries and Over Time', *Review of Economics and Statistics*, 50/3, 391–416.

China Economic and Industry Data (2018), *Malaysia Real Effective Exchange Rate*, https://www.ceicdata.com/en/indicator/malaysia/real-effective-exchange-rate, accessed 8 August 2018.

Clark, C. (1940), *The Conditions of Economic Progress* (London: Macmillan).

Coale, A. J., and Watkins, S. C. (1986), *The Decline of Fertility in Europe* (New Jersey: Princeton University Press).

Cobbold Commission (1962), *Report of the Commission of Enquiry, North Borneo and Sarawak* (London: Her Majesty's Stationery Office), ch. 4, General Matters, p. 46.

Collier, P. (2018), *The Future of Capitalism: Facing the New Anxieties* (UK: Allen Lane).

Comber, L. (1955), 'Chinese Secret Societies in Malaya: An Introduction', *Journal of the Malayan Branch of the Royal Asiatic Society*, 29/1, 146–147.

—— (1957), *An Introduction to Chinese Secret Societies in Malaya* (Singapore: D. Moore).

—— (2003), 'The Malayan Security Service (1945–1948)', *Intelligence and National Security*, 18/3, 128–153.

Commissioner of Law Revision–Malaysia (2010), *Federal Constitution* (repr., Kuala Lumpur: Percetakan Nasional Malaysia).

Corak, M. (2016), 'Inequality from Generation to Generation: The United States in Comparison', Discussion Paper No (9929), The Institute for the Study of Labor, Bonn.

Cowan, C. D. (1951) (ed.), 'Sir Frank Swettenham's Perak Journals, 1874–1876, Introduction', *Journal of the Malayan Branch of the Royal Asiatic Society*, 24/4, 7–32.

Cribb, J., Hood, A., and Joyce, R. (2017), 'Recessions, Income Inequality and the Role of the Tax and Benefit System', Report R137, Institute for Fiscal Studies.

Dasgupta, P. (2001), *Human Well-being and the Natural Environment* (Oxford: Oxford University Press).

Dasgupta, P., and Maler, K-G. (2000), 'Net National Production, Wealth and Social Well-being', *Environment and Development Economics*, 5/1, 69–93.

Da Vanzo, J., and Kusnic, M. W. (1980), *Income Inequality and the Definition of Income: The Case of Malaysia* (California: The Rand Corporation).

Davidson, J. S. (2018), 'Stagnating Yields, Unyielding Profits: The Political Economy of Malaysia's Rice Sector', *Journal of Southeast Asian Studies*, 49/1, 105–128.

Davis, K. (1945), 'The World Demographic Transition', *Annals of the American Academy of Political and Social Science*, no. 273, 1–11.

Dawe, D. (1996), 'A New Look at the Effects of Export Instability on Investment and Growth', *World Development*, 24/12, 1905–1914.

Deaton, A. (2005), 'Measuring Poverty in a Growing World (or Measuring Growth in a Poor World)', *The Review of Economics and Statistics*, 87/1, 1–19.

—— (2013), *The Great Escape: Health, Wealth, and the Origins of Inequality* (New Jersey: Princeton University Press).

De Long, J. B. (1996), 'Cross-Country Variations in National Economic Growth Rates: The Role of "Technology"', prepared for the Federal Reserve Bank of Boston Conference on Technology and Economic Growth, 5–7 June 1996, http://www.j-bradford-delong.net/Econ_Articles/Growth_and_Technology/Role_of_Technology_.pdf, accessed 12 March 2018.

De Micheaux, E. L. (2017), *The Development of Malaysian Capitalism from British Rule to the Present Day* (Petaling Jaya: Strategic Information and Research Development Centre).

Deininger, K., et al. (2011), 'Rising Global Interest in Farmland: Can It Yield Sustainable and Equitable Benefits?', *The International Bank for Reconstruction and Development* (Washington, DC: IBRD).

Del Tufo, M. V. (1949), *A Report on the 1947 Census of Population, Malaya (Comprising the Federation of Malaya and the Colony of Singapore)* (London: Crown Agents for the Colonies).

Department of Information–Malaysia (2004), *Rukunegara, Siri Pengetahuan Am*, ed. Beh Ah Fat (2nd edn., Kuala Lumpur: Jabatan Perkhidmatan Penerangan Malaysia).

Department of Orang Asli Affairs (1972), *A Brief Note on the Orang Asli of West Malaysia and Their Administration* (Malaysia: Ministry of National and Rural Development).

Department of Statistics–Malaysia (1968), *Social-Economic Sample Survey of Malaysia, 1968.*

—— (1975), *National Accounts of Peninsular Malaysia, 1960–1971.*

—— (1991), *Vital Statistics Time Series Malaysia, 1911–1985.*

—— (2001), *Vital Statistics Time Series Malaysia, 1963–1998.*

—— (2005–2010), *Annual National Accounts, Gross Domestic Product.*

—— (2012), *Vital Statistics Malaysia 2011.*

—— (2013), *Vital Statistics Malaysia 2012.*

—— (2014), *Intercensal Mid-year Population Estimates, Malaysia and States, 2001–2009.*

—— (2015a), *Vital Statistics Malaysia 2013.*

—— (2015b), *Vital Statistics Malaysia 2014.*

—— (2015c), *Vital Statistics Time Series Malaysia, 2000–2009.*

—— (2016a), *Vital Statistics Malaysia 2015.*

—— (2016b), *Rubber, Malaysia Economics Statistics–Time Series 2016*, www.dosm.gov.my, accessed 8 June 2018.

—— (2016c), *Employed Persons by State, 2016*, www.dosm.gov.my, accessed 8 June 2018.

—— (2017a), *Statistics Yearbook Malaysia, 2016.*

—— (2017*b*), *Vital Statistics Malaysia 2017.*

—— (2017c), *Social Statistics Bulletin Malaysia, 2017.*

—— (2018a), *Current Population Estimates Malaysia*, 2018.

—— (2018b), *Green Economy Indicators Malaysia*, https://www.dosm.gov.my/v1/index.php?r=column/cone&menu_id=ZDU2TmFuYzYzMTVpa2R5YzI1citFZz09, accessed 21 May 2019.

—— (various years between 1957 and 2018), Social Statistics Bulletin.

—— (various years), *GDP by State*, www.dosm.my, accessed 8 June 2018.

—— (various years), *GDP by State and Kind of Economic Activity*, www.dosm.my, accessed 8 June 2018.

—— (various years), *Gross Export by Major Agricultural and Mining Commodities*, www.dosm.gov.my, accessed 8 June 2018.

—— (various years), *Labour Force Survey Report Malaysia.*

—— (various years), *Annual National Accounts.*

Department of Statistics–Singapore (2018), *Key Household Income Trends, 2017, Singapore*, https://www.singstat.gov.sg/-/media/files/publications/households/pp-s24.pdf, accessed 27 November 2018.

Dhu Renick Jnr, R. (1965), 'The Emergency Regulations of Malaya Causes and Effect', *Journal of Southeast Asian History*, 6/2, 1–39.

Dodge, N. N. (1980), 'Population Estimates for the Malay Peninsula in the Nineteenth Century, with Special Reference to the East Coast States', *A Journal of Demography*, 34/3, 437–475.

Dol Ramli (1963), *History of the Malay Regiment, 1933–1942* (Kuala Lumpur: Regimental Committee of the Royal Malay Regiment).

Drabble, J. H. (1989), *The Emergence of the Modern Malayan Economy: The Impact of Foreign Trade in the Nineteenth Century* (Clayton: Monash University, Centre of Southeast Asian Studies).

—— (2000), *An Economic History of Malaysia, c. 1800–1990: The Transition to Modern Economic Growth* (London: Macmillan Press).

Drake, P. J. (1969), *Financial Development in Malaya and Singapore* (Canberra: Australian National University Press).

—— (1979), 'The Economic Development of British Malaya to 1914: An Essay in Historiography with Some Questions for Historians', *Journal of Southeast Asian Studies*, 10/2, 262–290.

—— (2018), *Merchants, Bankers, Governors: British Enterprise in Singapore and Malaya, 1786–1920* (Singapore: World Scientific Publishing).

Dumanig, F. P., David, M. K., and Symaco, L. P. (2012), 'Competing Roles of the National Language and English in Malaysia and the Philippines: Planning, Policy and Use', *Journal of International and Comparative Education*, 1/2, 104–115.

Durand, F., and Curtis, R. (2013), *Maps of Malaya and Borneo: Discovery, Statehood, and Progress* (Kuala Lumpur: Jurga Publications).

Dzulkifli Abdul Razak, Morshidi Sirat, and Chang, D. W. (2019), 'Falsafah Pendidikan Kebangsaan in a "W.E.I.R.D." World of Education', in Dzulkifli Abdul Razak, Morshidi Sirat, and D. W. Chang (eds.), *Higher Education in Malaysia, A Critical Review of the Past and Present for the Future* (Penang: University Sains Malaysia and University Sains Islam Malaysia), 11–22.

Easterly, W., and Levine, R. (1997), 'Africa's Growth Tragedy: Policies and Ethnic Divisions', *Quarterly Journal of Economics*, 112/4, 1203–1250.

Economic Planning Unit–Malaysia [EPU] (1966), *First Malaysia Plan, 1966–1970* (Kuala Lumpur: Government Printers).

—— (1971), *The First Outline Perspective Plan, 1971–1990.*

—— (1971), *Second Malaysia Plan, 1971–1975.*

—— (1976), *Third Malaysia Plan, 1976–1980.*

—— (1981), *Fourth Malaysia Plan, 1981–1985.*

—— (1986), *Fifth Malaysia Plan, 1986–1990.*

—— (1991), *The Second Outline Perspective Plan, 1991–2000.*

—— (1991), *Sixth Malaysia Plan, 1991–1995.*

—— (1996), *Seventh Malaysia Plan, 1996–2000.*

—— (2001), *The Third Outline Perspective Plan, 2001–2010.*

—— (2001), *Eighth Malaysia Plan, 2001–2005.*

—— (2006), *Ninth Malaysia Plan, 2006–2010.*

—— (2007), *50 Years of Charting Malaysia's Development* (Kuala Lumpur: Percetakan Nasional Malaysia Berhad).

—— (2011), *Tenth Malaysia Plan, 2011–2015.*

—— (2016), *Eleventh Malaysia Plan, 2016–2020.*

—— (2018a), *Development Plans, 2018*, http://www.epu.gov.my, accessed 8 August 2018.

—— (2018b), *Household Income and Poverty*, http://www.epu.gov.my/en/socio-economic/household-income-poverty, accessed 8 August 2018.

—— (2018c), *External Trade*, http://epu.gov.my/en/economic-statistics/external-trade, accessed 8 August 2018.

—— (2018d), *Social Economy Statistics, National Accounts*, http://epu.gov.my/en/economic-statistics/national-accounts, accessed 8 August 2018.

—— (2018e), *Mid-Term Review of the Eleventh Malaysia Plan, 2016–2020.*

Eichengreen, B. (2016), *Hall of Mirrors: The Great Depression, The Great Recession and the Uses—and Misuses—of History* (New York: Oxford University Press).

Eichengreen, B., and Temin, P. (1997), 'The Gold Standard and the Great Depression', NBER Working Paper No. (6060), National Bureau of Economic Research, https://ideas.repec.org/p/nbr/nberwo/6060.html, accessed 8 August 2018.

Elekdag, S., Lall, S., and Alp, H. (2012), 'An Assessment of Malaysian Monetary Policy During the Global Financial Crisis of 2008–09', IMF Working Paper, 1 January 2012, International Monetary Fund.

Eng, L. A. (1986), 'Peasants, Proletarians and Prostitutes: A Preliminary Investigation into the Work of Chinese Women in Colonial Malaya', Research Notes and Discussions Paper No. 59 (Singapore: Institute of Southeast Asian Studies).

Eurostat (2003), *European Social Statistics—Income, Poverty and Social Exclusion: 2nd Report* (Luxembourg: Office for Official Publications of the European Communities).

Faaland, J., Parkinson, J. R., and Rais Saniman (2003), *Growth and Ethnic Inequality: Malaysia's New Economic Policy* (Kuala Lumpur: Utusan Publications and Distributors).

Faisal M. Mohd Noor, et al. (2017), 'Beyond Sustainability Criteria and Principles in Palm Oil Production: Addressing Consumer Concerns Through Insetting', *Ecology and Society*, 22/2.

Faridah Abdul Rashid (2012), *Research on the Early Malay Doctors 1900–1957 Malaya and Singapore* (Bloomington: Xlibris Corporation).

Fatimah Mohamed Arshad (2013), 'Agriculture in Malaysia: Evolution and Issues', in Ahmad Fauzi Puasa, Sulaiman Mahbob, and Zakariah Abdul Rashid (eds.), *Malaysian Economy: Economic Transformation Programme: Next Economic Experience* (Kuala Lumpur: Malaysian Institute of Economic Research).

Fatimah Mohamed Arshad, et al. (2007), *50 Years of Malaysian Agriculture: Transformational Issues, Challenges and Direction* (Serdang: Universiti Putra Malaysia Press).

Federation of Malaya (1948), *Federation of Malaya Agreement* (Kuala Lumpur: Government Printer).

Feenstra, R. C., Inklaar, R., and Timmer, M. P. (2015), 'The Next Generation of the Penn World Table', *American Economic Review*, 105/10, 3150–3182, https://www. rug.nl/ggdc/productivity/pwt/related-research, accessed 8 August 2018.

Fell, H. (1960), *1957 Population Census of the Federation of Malaya, Report No. 14* (Kuala Lumpur: Department of Statistics–Federation of Malaya).

Ferguson, N. (2002), *Empire, the Rise and Demise of the British World Order and the Lessons for Global Power* (London: Allen Lane).

Fisk, E. K. (1959), 'The Economics of the Handloom Industry of the East Coast of Malaya', *Journal of the Malayan Branch of the Asiatic Society*, 32/4, 5–72.

Foo, G. (2011), 'Quantifying the Malaysian Brain Drain and an Investigation of Its Key Determinants', *Malaysian Journal of Economic Studies*, 48/2, 93–116.

Food and Agriculture Organization of the United Nations (various years), 'Rice Statistics', http://www.fao.org/statistics/en/, accessed 8 August 2018.

Glass, D. V. (1973), *Numbering the People: The Eighteenth-century Population Controversy and the Development of Census and Vital Statistics in Britain* (Farnborough: Saxon House).

Go, D. S., Kurlat, S., and Lim, J. J. (2016), 'A Cross-Country Database of Total Factor Productivity and Potential Output', paper presented at SEM Conference, July 2015, http://repository.cmu.edu/cgi/viewcontent.cgi?article=1123&context=sem_conf, accessed 8 August 2018.

Goh, S. K., and Lim, M. H. (2010), *The Impact of the Global Financial Crisis: The Case of Malaysia*, TWN Global Economy Series 26, Financial Crisis and Asian Developing Countries (Penang: Third World Network).

Goldman, R. H. (1975), 'Staple Food Self-Sufficiency and the Distributive Impact of Malaysian Rice Policy', *Food Research Institute Studies*, 14/3, 251–293.

Goldsmith, S., and Eggers, W. D. (2004), *Governing by Network: The New Shape of the Public Sector* (Washington, DC: Brookings Institution Press).

Goldthorpe, C. C. (2015), *Rubber Manufacturing in Malaysia: Resource-based Industrialization in Practice* (Singapore: NUS Press).

Gomes, A. G. (2015), 'Marginalisation of the Orang Asli of Peninsular Malaysia', in M. L. Weiss (ed.), *Routledge Handbook of Contemporary Malaysia* (Oxford: Routledge), 279–289.

Gomez, E. T. (2009), 'The Rise and Fall of Capital: Corporate Malaysia in Historical Perspective', *Journal of Contemporary Asia*, 39/3, 345–381.

—— (2013), 'Nurturing Bumiputera Capital: SMEs, Entrepreneurship and the New Economic Policy', in E. T. Gomez and J. Saravanamuttu (eds.), *The New Economic Policy in Malaysia: Affirmative Action, Ethnic Inequalities and Social Justice* (Singapore: NUS Press).

—— (2019), 'Business as Usual: Regime Change and Government-Linked Companies in Malaysia', *Global Asia*, 14/1, 98–103.

Gomez, E. T., and Jomo, K. S. (1997), *Malaysia's Political Economy: Politics, Patronage and Profits* (Cambridge: Cambridge University Press).

Gomez, E. T., et al. (2018), *Minister of Finance Incorporated, Ownership and Control of Corporate Malaysia* (IDEAS, Kuala Lumpur: Palgrave Macmillan).

Goran, E. (2014), 'How Ethnic Diversity Affects Economic Growth', *World Development*, vol. 59C, 275–297.

Greenhalgh, C., and Rogers, M. (2010), *Innovation, Intellectual Property and Economic Growth* (New Jersey: Princeton University Press).

Gullick, J. M. (1981), *Malaysia: Economic Expansion and National Unity* (London: Ernest Benn Limited).

—— (1987), *Malay Society in the Late 19th Century: The Beginnings of Change* (Singapore: Oxford University Press).

—— (1992), *Rulers and Residents: Influence and Power in the Malay States, 1870–1920* (Singapore: Oxford University Press).

—— (2001), 'Sultans and Residents', in B. K. Cheah (ed.), *The Encyclopedia of Malaysia, vol. 7: Early Modern History, 1800–1940* (Kuala Lumpur: Archipelago Press).

—— (2004), *Indigenous Political Systems of Western Malaya* (rev. edn., London: The Athlone Press).

Hagan, J., and Wells, A. (2005), *The British and Rubber in Malaya, c. 1890–1940* (Australia: University of Wollongong).

Hagenaars, A. J. M., de Vos, K., and Asghar Zaidi, M. (1994), *Poverty Statistics in the Late 1980s: Research Based on Micro-data* (Luxembourg: Office for Official Publications of the European Communities).

Hairudin Harun (1990), 'Medicine and Imperialism: A Study of the British Colonial Medical Establishment, Health Policy and Medical Research in the Malay Peninsula, 1786–1918', PhD thesis, University of London.

—— (2017), *Medicine and Imperialism, vol. 2: A History of Colonial Health Policy in the British Malaya, 1784–1918* (n.p.).

Haji Abdul Rahman bin Hasan (2013), *Education and Social Characteristics of the Population, 2010 Population and Housing Census of Malaysia* (Putrajaya: Department of Statistics–Malaysia).

Hanushek, E. A. (2013), 'Economic Growth in Developing Countries: The Role of Human Capital', *Economics of Education Review*, 37, 204–202.

Hanushek, E. A., and Woessmann, L. (2007), *The Role of Education Quality in Economic Growth*, World Bank Policy Research Working Paper 4122.

Hare, G. T. (1902), *Census of the Population, Federated Malay States, 1901* (Kuala Lumpur: Government Printers).

Harper, T. N. (1999), *The End of Empire and the Making of Malaya* (Cambridge: Cambridge University Press).

—— (2017), 'The Tools of Transition: Education and Development in Modern Southeast Asian History', in C. A. Bayly et al. (eds.), *History, Historians and Development Policy: A Necessary Dialogue* (Manchester: Manchester University Press).

Harvie, C. H. (1960), *National Accounts of the Federation of Malaya 1955–1960* (Kuala Lumpur: Department of Statistics–Federation of Malaya).

Heckman, J. (1979), 'Sample Selection Bias as a Specification Error', *Econometrica*, 47, 153–161.

Heussler, R. (1981), *British Rule in Malaya: The Malayan Civil Service and Its Predecessors, 1867–1942* (Oxford: Clio Press).

Hirschman, C. (1971), 'Ownership and Control in the Manufacturing Sector of West Malaysia', *UMBC Economic Review*, 7/1, 21–30.

—— (1974), 'Economic Progress in Malaysia: How Widely Has It Been Shared?', *UMBC Economic Review*, 10/2, 35–44.

—— (1975), 'Net External Migration from Peninsular Malaysia, 1957 to 1970', *Malayan Economic Review*, 20, 38–54.

—— (1979), 'Political Independence and Educational Opportunities in Peninsular Malaysia', *Sociology of Education*, 52, 67–83.

—— (1980), 'Data and Perspectives: Demographic Trends in Peninsular Malaysia, 1947–75', *Population and Development Review*, 6/1, 103–122.

—— (1987), 'The Meaning and Measurement of Ethnicity in Malaysia: An Analysis of Census Classifications', *Journal of Asian Studies*, 46/3, 555–582.

Ho, H. L. (2006), 'The Rubber and Tin Industries in Malaya During the Emergency, 1948–1960', paper presented at the *19th IAHA Conference*, 22–25 November 2006, Manila, Philippines.

Hood Salleh (2006) (ed.), *The Encyclopedia of Malaysia, vol. 12: Peoples and Traditions* (Kuala Lumpur: Archipelago Press).

Hooker, M. B. (1984), *Islamic Law in South East Asia* (Singapore: Oxford University Press).

Huff, W. G. (2002), 'Boom-or-Bust Commodities and Industrialization in Pre–World War II Malaya', *The Journal of Economic History*, 62/4, 1074–1115.

Hunter, M. (2013), 'Who Makes Public Policy in Malaysia?', *New Mandala*, 19 February 2013, http://asiapacific.anu.edu.au/newmandala/2013/02/19/who-makes-public-policy-in-malaysia/, accessed 21 August 2018.

Idrus, R. (2013), 'Left Behind: Orang Asli Under the New Economic Policy', in E. T. Gomez and J. Saravanamuttu (eds.), *The New Economic Policy in Malaysia: Affirmative Action, Ethnic Inequality and Social Justice* (Singapore: NUS Press and ISEAS Publishing).

Indrani, T. (2001), 'Agriculture and Food Security: Developments in Malaysia', in *Situation of Agriculture in Malaysia—A Cause for Concern* (Petaling Jaya: Education and Research Association for Consumers, Malaysia), Ch. 1.

Inklaar, R., and Timmer, M. P. (2013), *Capital, Labour and TFP in PWT8.0* (The Netherlands: Growth and Development Centre, University of Groningen).

Inklaar, R., and Woltjer, P. (2019), 'What is new in PWT9.1?', https://www.rug.nl/ggdc/docs/pwt91_whatsnew.pdf, accessed 3 May 2019.

Innes, J. R. (1901), *Report on the Census of the Straits Settlements taken on 1st March, 1901* (Singapore: Government Printing Office).

Institute for Medical Research (2018), 'History: Founding and Development of the Institute', http://www.imr.gov.my/index.php/en/corporate-info/about-imr, accessed 9 August 2018.

International Association for the Evaluation of Educational Achievement (2018), 'TIMSS and PIRLS', https://timssandpirls.bc.edu/, accessed 8 August 2018.

International Bank for Reconstruction and Development [IBRD] (1955), *The Economic Development of Malaya: Report of a Mission Organized by the IBRD at the request of the Federation of Malaya, the Crown Colony of Singapore and the United Kingdom* (Washington, DC: IBRD).

International Monetary Fund [IMF] (2016), 'Malaysia 2016 Article IV Consultation—Press Release; Staff Report; and Statement by the Executive Director for Malaysia', *IMF Country Report*, No. 16/110, May 2016, Washington, DC: International Monetary Fund.

—— (2017), 'Malaysia 2017 Article IV Consultation—Press Release; Staff Report; and Statement by the Executive Director for Malaysia', *IMF Country Report*, No. 17/101, April 2017, Washington, DC: International Monetary Fund.

—— (2018), *Malaysia: Selected Issues* (Washington, DC: IMF).

International Panel on Social Progress (2018), *Rethinking Society for the 21st Century, vol. 1, Socio-Economic Transformations* (Cambridge: Cambridge University Press).

International Rubber Study Group (various years), 'Rubber Statistical Bulletin', http://www.rubberstudy.com/pub-stats-bulletin.aspx, accessed 10 September 2018.

IPSOS Business Consulting (2012), 'E&E Sector Study on the Supply–Demand of Talent in Malaysia: Final Report', https://www.talentcorp.com.my, accessed 8 August 2018.

Isahak Haron (2015), 'Kesan Program Dwi-Bahasa [Dual-Language Program DLP]? Indikator dari Ujian TIMSS 2007, 2011 and PISA 2012 akibat dasar PPSMI', MS.

Ishak Shari (1994), 'Rural Development and Rural Poverty in Malaysia: The Experience During the New Economic Policy, 1971–1990', in Jamilah Arrifin (ed.), *Research Findings and the Gender Dimension in Malaysia: Poverty Amidst Plenty* (Petaling Jaya: Pelanduk Publications).

Ismail Mohd Salleh, and Meyanathan, S. D. (1993), *Malaysia: Growth, Equity, and Structural Transformation* (Washington, DC: World Bank).

Jackson, J. C. (1967), 'Oil Palm: Malaya's Post-Independence Boom Crop', *Geography*, 52/3, 319–321.

—— (1972), 'Rice Cultivation in West Malaysia: Relationships Between Culture History, Customary Practices and Recent Developments', *Journal of the Malaysian Branch of the Royal Asiatic Society*, 45/2, 76–96.

Jackson, R. N. (1961), *Immigrant Labour and the Development of Malaya, 1786–1920* (Federation of Malaya: Government Press).

Jain, R. K. (1970), *South Indians on the Plantation Frontier in Malaya* (Kuala Lumpur: University of Malaya Press).

Jeffries, C. (2015), *The Colonial Empire and Its Civil Service* (Cambridge: Cambridge University Press).

Jefferies, J., Conroy, D. W., and Clark, H. (2015) (eds.), *The Handbook of Textile Culture* (London: Bloomsbury Academic).

Jenkins, S. P., et al. (2013), *The Great Recession and the Distribution of Household Income* (Oxford: Oxford University Press).

Jerven, M. (2013), 'Comparability of GDP Estimates in Sub-Saharan Africa: The Effect of Revisions in Sources and Methods Since Structural Adjustment', *Review of Income and Wealth*, vol. 59, supplement S1, pp. S16–S36.

Jesudason, J. V. (1989), *Ethnicity and the Economy: The State, Chinese Business and Multinationals in Malaysia* (Singapore: Oxford University Press).

Johnston, B. F., and Kilby, P. (1975), *Agriculture and Structural Transformation: Economic Strategies in Late Developing Countries* (New York: Oxford University Press).

Johnston, B. F., and Mellor, J. W. (1961), 'The Role of Agriculture in Economic Development', *American Economic Review*, 51/4, 566–593.

Jomo, K. S. (1986), *A Question of Class: Capital, the State, and Uneven Development in Malaysia* (Singapore: Oxford University Press).

—— (1990) (ed.), *Undermining Tin: The Decline of Malaysian Pre-eminence* (Sydney: Transnational Corporations Research Project).

—— (2018), *Economic Growth Environment and Privatisation: Essays by Dr Jomo K. Sundaram, Third Holder of the Tun Hussein Onn Chair* (Kuala Lumpur: Institute of Strategic and International Studies (ISIS) Malaysia).

Jomo, K. S., and Wee, C. H. (2014), *Malaysia @ 50: Economic Development, Distribution, Disparities* (Selangor: Strategic Information and Research Development Centre).

Jones, G. W. (1984), *Demographic Transition in Asia* (Singapore: Maruzen Asia).

Jones, L. W. (1962a), *Population Census of North Borneo, 1960* (Kuching: F. W. Goodwin).

—— (1962b), *Population Census of Sarawak, 1960* (Kuching: F. W. Goodwin).

—— (1966), *The Population of Borneo: A Study of the Peoples of Sarawak, Sabah and Brunei* (London: Athlone Press).

Kahin, G. M. (1947), 'The State of North Borneo 1881–1946', *The Far Eastern Quarterly*, 7/1, 43–65.

Kaur, A. (1995), 'The Babbling Brookes: Economic Change in Sarawak 1841–1941', *Modern Asian Studies*, 29/1, 65–109.

—— (2001), *Historical Dictionary of Malaysia* (2nd edn., London: Scarecrow Press).

—— (2004), *Wage Labour in Southeast Asia Since 1840: Globalisation, the International Division of Labour and Labour Transformations* (Basingstoke: Palgrave Macmillan).

Kennedy, J. (1962), *A History of Malaya* (London: Oxford University Press).

Keynes, J. M. (2009), *The End of Laissez-Faire: The Economic Consequences of the Peace* (New York: Prometheus Books; first published as *The Economic Consequences of the Peace*, 1926).

Khasnor Johan (1984), *The Emergence of the Modern Malay Administrative Elite* (Singapore: Oxford University Press).

Khazanah Research Institute (2016), *Climbing the Ladder: Socio-economic Mobility in Malaysia* (Kuala Lumpur: Khazanah Research Institute).

—— (2018), *The School-to-Work Transition of Young Malaysians* (Kuala Lumpur: Khazanah Research Institute).

Khoo, K. K. (1972), *The Western Malay States 1850–1873: The Effects of Commercial Development on Malay Politics* (Kuala Lumpur: Oxford University Press).

—— (1999), 'Japan's Economic Activities in Malaya: The Inter-War Years', MS.

—— (2017), *The Autobiography of a Historian* (Kuala Lumpur: Kala Publishers).

Khoo, K. K., and Mohd Taib Osman (2011) (eds.), *The Encyclopedia of Malaysia, vol. 16: The Rulers of Malaysia* (Kuala Lumpur: Archipelago Press).

Khoo, S. G. (1995), *General Report of the Population Census, vol. 2, Population and Housing Census of Malaysia 1991* (Kuala Lumpur: Department of Statistics–Malaysia).

Khoo, S. N., and Abdur-Razzaq Lubis (2005), *Kinta Valley: Pioneering Malaysia's Modern Development* (Penang: Perak Academy).

Khoo, T. H. (1983), *General Report of the Population Census, 1980 Population and Housing Census of Malaysia* (Kuala Lumpur: Department of Statistics–Malaysia).

Kim, Y. E., and Loayza, N. V. (2018), 'The Drive toward Universal Health Coverage', Research & Policy Briefs from the World Bank Malaysia Hub, No. 13, World Bank Group, http://documents.worldbank.org/curated/en/989061521813294877/pdf/124552-REVISED-The-Drive-Toward-Universal-Health-Coverage-final.pdf, accessed 15 November 2018.

King, F. H. H. (1957), *Money in British East Asia* (London: H.M.S.O).

Kirschenmann, K., Malinen, T., and Nyberg, H. (2016), 'The Risk of Financial Crises: Is There a Role for Income Inequality?', *Journal of International Money and Finance*, 68, 161–180.

Kitingan, J. G., and Ongkili, M. J. (1989) (eds.), *Sabah 25 Years Later, 1963–1988* (Kota Kinabalu: Institute for Development Studies).

Klein, I. (1969), 'Britain, Siam and the Malay Peninsula, 1906–1909', *The Historical Journal*, 12/1, 119–136.

Koay, S. L. (2017), 'The Dawn of Higher Education in Malaysia', *Penang Monthly*, February 2017 (Penang Institute).

—— (2018), *The Genesis of Higher Education in Colonial Malaya*, https://www.ehm.my/publications/articles/the-genesis-of-higher-education-in-colonial-malaya, accessed 8 August 2018.

Kobkua, S-P. (1984), 'The 1902 Siamese-Kelantan Treaty: An End to the Traditional Relations', *Journal of the Siam Society*, 72, 97–101.

Koh, D. S. J., and Kyoko, T. (1984), 'Japanese Competition in the Trade of Malaya in the 1930s', *Southeast Asian Studies*, 21/4, 374–399.

Koike, K. (2017), 'Managing Agency Capitalism and Malayan Rubber: Harrisons & Crosfield Ltd. (1900–1940)', *Journal of the Malaysian Branch of the Royal Asiatic Society*, 90/312, 73–100.

Kondor, Y. (1971), 'An Old-New Measure of Income Inequality', *Econometrica*, 39/6, 1041–1042.

Kratoska, P. H. (1982), 'Rice Cultivation and the Ethnic Division of Labour in British Malaya', *Comparative Studies in Society and History*, 24/2, 280–314.

—— (1988), 'The Post-1945 Food Shortage in British Malaya', *Journal of Southeast Asian Studies*, 19/1, 27–47.

—— (2018), *The Japanese Occupation of Malaya and Singapore, 1941–45: A Social and Economic History* (2nd edn., Singapore: NUS Press).

Krugman, P. (1994), 'The Myth of Asia's Miracle', *Foreign Affairs*, 73/6, 62–78.

Kyle, J. (2017), 'Perspectives on the Role of the State in Economic Development: Taking Stock of the "Developmental State" After 35 Years', Discussion Paper 01597, January 2017, International Food Policy Research Institute.

Kyriacou, A. P. (2013), 'Ethnic Group Inequalities and Governance: Evidence from Developing Countries', *Kyklos*, 66/1, 78–101.

Labour Research Department (1926), *British Imperialism in Malaya*, Colonial Series No. 2 (London: The Labour Research Department).

Lakner, C., and Milanovic, B. (2013), 'Global Income Distribution: From the Fall of the Berlin Wall to the Great Recession', *World Bank Policy Research Working Paper 6719*, World Bank.

—— (2015), 'Global Income Distribution: From the Fall of the Berlin Wall to the Great Recession', *The World Bank Economic Review*, 30/2, 203–232.

Lange, G. M., Wodon, Q., and Carey, K. (2018) (eds.), *The Changing Wealth of Nations 2018: Building a Sustainable Future* (Washington, DC: World Bank).

Langelett, G. (2002), 'Human Capital: A Summary of the 20th Century Research', *Journal of Education Finance*, 28/1, 1–23.

Larrimore, J., Mortenson, J., and Splinter, D. (2017), 'Household Incomes in Tax Data: Using Addresses to Move from Tax Unit to Household Income Distributions', *Finance and Economics Discussion Series 2017–002*, Board of Governors of the Federal Reserve System, https://doi.org/10.17016/FEDS.2017.002, accessed 8 August 2018.

Lau, A. (1991), *The Malayan Union Controversy 1942–1948* (Singapore: Oxford University Press).

Leary, J. (1989), *The Importance of the Orang Asli in the Malayan Emergency 1948–1960* (Victoria: Monash University).

Lee, H. A., Gomez, E. T., and Yacob, S. (2013), 'Ethnicity, Economy, and Affirmative Action in Malaysia', in E. T. Gomez and R. Premdas (eds.), *Affirmative Action, Ethnicity, and Conflict* (Abingdon: Routledge), 67–94.

Lee, H. G. (2013), 'Racial Citizenship and Higher Education in Malaysia', in E. T. Gomez and J. Saravanamuttu (eds.), *The New Economic Policy in Malaysia: Affirmative Action, Ethnic Inequalities and Social Justice* (Singapore: ISEAS Publishing).

Lee, K. H., and Nagaraj, S. (2012), 'The Crisis in Education', in H. Hill, S. Y. Tham, and Ragayah Haji Mat Zin (eds.), *Malaysia's Development Challenges* (Kuala Lumpur: Routledge Malaysian Studies Series).

Lee, K. H., and Tan, C. B (2000) (eds.), *The Chinese in Malaysia* (Shah Alam: Oxford University Press).

Lee, K. Y. (2011), *Lee Kuan Yew: Hard Truths to Keep Singapore Going* (Singapore: Straits Times Press).

Lee, M. N. N., and Thah, S. S. (2017), 'Lessons from Malaysia (Smart Schools Initiative)', in M. Trucano and G. Dykes (eds.), *Building and Sustaining National Educational Technology Agencies: Lessons, Models and Case Studies from Around the World* (Washington, DC: The World Bank).

Lee, S. A. (1974), *Economic Growth and the Public Sector in Malaya and Singapore, 1948–1960* (London: Oxford University Press).

—— (1990), *The Monetary and Banking Development of Singapore and Malaysia* (3rd edn., Singapore: Singapore University Press).

Lee, V. J., et al. (2009), 'Economic Analysis of Pandemic Influenza Vaccination Strategies in Singapore', *PLOS ONE*, 4/9, https://doi.org/10.1371/journal.pone.0007108, accessed 10 June 2019.

Leete, R. (1996), *Malaysia's Demographic Transition: Rapid Development, Culture, and Politics* (Kuala Lumpur: Oxford University Press).

—— (2007), *Malaysia: From Kampung to Twin Towers, Fifty Years of Economic and Social Development* (Kuala Lumpur: Oxford University Press).

—— (2011), 'The Politics of Population', in *Malaysia Policies & Issues in Economic Development* (Kuala Lumpur: Institute of Strategic and International Studies), 57–68.

Leigh, M. B. (1974), *The Rising Moon: Political Change in Sarawak 1959–1972* (2nd edn., Sydney: Sydney University Press).

—— (2018), *Deals, Datus, and Dayaks: Sarawak and Brunei in the Making of Malaysia* (Petaling Jaya: Strategic Information and Research Development Centre, Malaysia).

Lemon, A. H. (1919), *Administration Report for the Year 1918, Negeri Sembilan*, p. 14.

Leong, Y. F. (1999), *Labour and Trade Unionism in Colonial Malaya: A Study of the Socio-Economic and Political Bases of the Malayan Labour Movement, 1930–1957* (Penang: Universiti Sains Malaysia).

Lewis, W. A. (1954), 'Economic Development with Unlimited Supplies of Labour', *The Manchester School*, 22, 3–42.

Li, D. J. (1982), *British Malaya: An Economic Analysis* (2nd edn., rev., Kuala Lumpur: Institute for Social Analysis).

Liew, K. K. (2010), 'Planters, Estate Health and Malaria in British Malaya (1900–1940)', *Journal of the Malaysian Branch of the Royal Asiatic Society*, 83, 91–115.

Lim, C. Y. (1967), *Economic Development of Modern Malaya* (Kuala Lumpur: Oxford University Press).

Lim, T. G. (1977), *Peasants and Their Agricultural Economy in Colonial Malaya, 1874–1941* (Kuala Lumpur: Oxford University Press).

Lin, J. Y., and Monga, C. (2018) (eds.), *The Handbook of Structural Transformation* (London: Oxford University Press).

Linehan, W. (1936), 'A History of Pahang', *Journal of the Malayan Branch of the Royal Asiatic Society*, 14/2, 125.

Loadman, J. (2005), *Tears of the Tree: The Story of Rubber—A Modern Marvel* (Oxford: Oxford University Press).

Loh, F. K. W. (1988), *Beyond the Tin Mines: Coolies, Squatters and New Villages in the Kinta Valley* (Singapore: Oxford University Press).

Loo, E. C., and McKerchar, M. (2014), 'The Impact of British Colonial Rule on the Malaysian Income Tax System', *Journal of Tax Research*, 12/1, 238–252.

Losch, B., Freguin-Gresh, S., and White, E. T. (2012), *Structural Transformation and Rural Change Revisited: Challenges for Late Developing Countries in a Globalizing World* (Washington, DC: AFP and the World Bank).

MacAndrews, C. (1977), *Mobility and Modernisation: The Federal Land Development Authority and Its Role in Modernising the Rural Malay* (Yogyakarta: Gadjah Mada University Press).

Macintyre, D. (1961), 'Britain's Intervention in Malaya: The Origin of Lord Kimberley's Instructions to Sir Andrew Clarke in 1873', *Journal of Southeast Asian History*, 2/3, 47–69.

MacMichael, H. A. (1946), *Report on a Mission to Malaya* (London: His Majesty's Stationery Office).

Mahathir Mohamad (1970), *The Malay Dilemma* (Singapore: Donald Moore).

Makepeace, W., Brooke, G. E., and Braddell, R. (1921), *One Hundred Years of Singapore*, vol. 2 (London: John Murray).

Malaysian Palm Oil Board (various years), 'Malaysia Palm Oil Statistics', http://www.mpob.gov.my/faqs/804-malaysian-oil-palm-statistics, accessed 8 August 2018.

Malaysia Population and Family Development Board (2016), *Report on Key Findings: Fifth Malaysian Population and Family Survey 2014* (Kuala Lumpur: LPPKN).

Malaysia Productivity Corporation (2016 and 2017), 'Productivity Report 2015/2016 and 2016/2017', http://www.mpc.gov.my/productivity-performance/, accessed 8 August 2018.

Manderson, L. (1996), *Sickness and the State: Health and Illness in Colonial Malaya, 1870–1940* (Melbourne: Oxford University Press).

Mankiw, N. G., Romer, D., and Weil, D. N. (1992), 'A Contribution to the Empirics of Economic Growth', *Quarterly Journal of Economics*, 107/2, 407–437.

Marriott, H. (1911a), *Report on the Census of the State of Johore taken on the 10th March, 1911* (Singapore: Singapore Government Printing Press).

—— (1911b), *Report on the Census of the Straits Settlements taken on the 10th March, 1911* (Singapore: Government Printing Press).

Martin, W., and Mitra, D. (2001), 'Productivity Growth and Convergence in Agriculture versus Manufacturing', *Economic Development and Cultural Change*, 49/2, 403–422.

Mason, A., et al. (2017), 'Support Ratios and Demographic Dividends: Estimates for the World', Technical Paper No. 2017/1 (United Nations Department of Economic and Social Affairs, Population Division).

Maznah Mohamad (1996), *The Malay Handloom Weavers: A Study of the Rise and Decline of Traditional Manufacture* (Singapore: Institute of Southeast Asian Studies).

McDonald, E. M. (1956), *Report of the Registrar-General on Population, Births, Deaths, Marriages and Adoptions for the Year 1955* (Kuala Lumpur: National Registration Dept).

McFadyean, A. (1944) (ed.), *The History of Rubber Regulation, 1934–1943* (London: George Allen & Unwin Ltd).

Mehmet, O. (2011), 'A Revisiting Cultural Transformation: Education System in Malaya During the Colonial Era', *World Journal of Islamic History and Civilization*, 1/1, 37–48.

Menon, J. (2017), 'Government-linked Companies: Impacts on the Malaysian Economy', *Policy IDEAS*, No. 45 (Institute for Democracy and Economic Affairs–Malaysia).

Menon, J., and Ng, T. H. (2013), 'Are Government-Linked Corporations Crowding Out Private Investment in Malaysia?', Working Papers in Trade and Development No. 2013/03 (Australian College of Asia and the Pacific).

Meyer, B. D., and Sullivan, J. X. (2013), 'Consumption and Income Inequality and the Great Recession', *American Economic Review: Papers & Proceedings*, 103/3, 178–183.

Milanovic, B., Lindert, P. H., and Williamson, J. G. (2011), 'Pre-Industrial Inequality', *The Economic Journal*, 121/551, 255–272.

Milner, A. (1982), *Kerajaan: Malay Political Culture on the Eve of Colonial Rule* (Tucson: University of Arizona Press).

Milner, A., Abdul Rahman Embong, and Tham, S. Y. (2014) (eds.), *Transforming Malaysia: Dominant and Competing Paradigms* (Singapore: Institute of Southeast Asian Studies).

Ministry of Agriculture–Malaysia (1984), *National Agricultural Policy 1984–1991* (Kuala Lumpur: Government Printers).

—— (1992), *National Agricultural Policy 1992–1997* (Kuala Lumpur: Government Printers).

—— (1998), *National Agricultural Policy 1998–2010* (Kuala Lumpur: Government Printers).

Ministry of Agriculture and Agro-Based Industry (2011), *National Agro-Food Policy 2011–2020* (Putrajaya: Government Printers).

Ministry of Education–Malaysia (2013), *Malaysia Education Blueprint 2013–2025 (Preschool to Post-Secondary Education)* (Putrajaya: Ministry of Education, Malaysia).

—— (2015), *Malaysia Education Blueprint 2015–2025 (Higher Education)* (Putrajaya: Ministry of Education, Malaysia).

—— (various years between 1970 and 2017), *Malaysia Educational Statistics* (Putrajaya: Ministry of Education, Malaysia).

Ministry of Education–Taiwan (2018), 'Gender Statistics', https://english.moe.gov.tw/cp-28-14508-95005-1.html, accessed 22 October 2018.

Ministry of Finance–Malaysia (1972, 1973, and various years), *Economic Reports* (Kuala Lumpur: Ministry of Finance).

Ministry of Home Affairs–Malaysia (2019), http://www.data.gov.my, accessed 30 May 2019.

Modalsli, J. (2011), 'Inequality and Growth in the Very Long Run: Inferring Inequality from Data on Social Groups', Memorandum No. 11/2011 (Department of Economics, University of Oslo).

Mohamed Noordin Sopiee (1974), *From Malayan Union to Singapore Separation, 1945–1965* (Kuala Lumpur: Penerbit Universiti Malaya).

Mohammad Bakri Musa (2003), *An Education System Worthy of Malaysia* (Michigan: Strategic Information Research Development, University of Michigan).

Mohd Zahirwan Halim Zainal Abidin, et al. (2017), 'Survival of the Pondok Learning Institution in Malaysia', *International Journal of Academic Research in Business and Social Sciences*, 7/3, 822–830.

Montalvo, J. G., and Reynal-Querol, M. (2005), 'Ethnic Polarization, Potential Conflict and Civil Wars', Economics Working Papers 770 (Department of Economics and Business, Universitat Pompeu Fabra).

Montalvo, J. G., and Reynal-Querol, M. (2017), 'Ethnic Diversity and Growth: Revisiting the Evidence', Economics Working Papers 1585 (Department of Economics and Business, Universitat Pompeu Fabra).

Morrah, P. (1963), 'The History of the Malayan Police', *Journal of the Malayan Branch, Royal Asiatic Society*, vol. 36, pt. 2, no. 202, 46–79.

Mudeliar, V., Nair, C. R. S., and Norris, R. P. (1983) (eds.), *Development of Hospital Care and Nursing in Singapore* (Singapore: Ministry of Health).

Muhamad Ali (2016), *Islam and Colonialism: Becoming Modern in Indonesia and Malaya* (Edinburgh: Edinburgh University Press).

Muhammed Abdul Khalid (2016), *The Colour of Inequality, Ethnicity, Class, Income and Wealth in Malaysia* (Petaling Jaya: MPH Group Publishing Sdn. Bhd).

Muhammed Abdul Khalid, and Li, Y. (2019), 'Income Inequality and Ethnic Cleavages in Malaysia: Evidence from Distributional National Accounts (1984–2014)', World Inequality Database, https://wid.world/document/9231/, accessed 11 October 2019.

Mukherjee, H., and Wong, P. K. (2011), 'The National University of Singapore and University Malaya: Common Roots and Different Paths', in P. Atlbach and J. Salmi (eds.), *The Road to Academic Excellence: The Making of World-Class Research Universities* (Washington, DC: The IBRD/The World Bank), http://elibrary.worldbank.org, accessed 8 August 2018.

Mumford, K. J. (2016), 'Prosperity, Sustainability and the Measurement of Wealth', *Asia and the Pacific Policy Studies*, 3/2, 226–234.

Muriel, A., and Sibieta, L. (2009), 'Living Standards During Previous Recessions', IFS Briefing Note BN85 (Institute for Fiscal Studies), http://www.ifs.org.uk/bns/bn85.pdf, accessed 8 August 2018.

Myrdal, G. (1968), *Asian Drama, An Inquiry into the Poverty of Nations*, vol. 1 and vol. 2 (New York: The Twentieth Century Fund).

Nadaraja, K. (2016), 'Malay Reaction to the 1930s Economic Depression in Malaya', *Malaysian Journal of History, Politics & Strategic Studies*, 42/1, 46–64.

Nadzan Haron (1990), 'Colonial Defence and the British Approach to Problems in Malaya 1874–1918', *Modern Asian Studies*, 24/2, 275–295.

Narayan, A., et al. (2018), *Fair Progress? Economic Mobility Across Generations Around the World* (Washington, DC: World Bank).

Nasarudin Md Idris (2006), 'Oil for Development: The Experience of Malaysia', presented at the Third OPEC International Seminar, 12–13 September 2006, Vienna, http://www.opec.org/opec_web/static_files_project/media/downloads/press_room/Nasruddin_Idris.pdf, accessed 5 March 2018.

Nathan, J. E. (1922), *The Census of British Malaya (The Straits Settlements, Federated Malay States and Protected States of Johore, Kedah, Perlis, Kelantan, Trengganu and Brunei), 1921* (London: Waterlow & Sons Limited).

National Economic Action Council (1998), 'The National Economic Recovery Plan, Agenda for Action', The National Economic Action Council, http://mir.com.my/lb/econ_ plan/, accessed 8 August 2018.

National Economic Advisory Council [NEAC] (2010), *New Economic Model for Malaysia, Part 1* (Kuala Lumpur: Percetakan Nasional Sdn. Bhd).

National Population and Family Development Board–Malaysia (2016), *Report on Key Findings, Fifth Malaysian Population and Family Survey (MPFS-5) 2014* (Kuala Lumpur: National Population and Family Development Board).

Nehru, V. (2012), 'Modern Industrial Policy: Lessons from Malaysia's Auto Industry', Carnegie Endowment for International Peace, http://carnegieendowment.org/2012/03/22/modern-industrial-policy-lessons-from-malaysia-s-auto-industry-pub-47625, accessed 8 August 2018.

Ness, G. D. (1962), 'Planning for Economic Development in Malaysia', MS (Institute of World Current Affairs, Washington DC).

Neumayer, E. (2004), 'Sustainability and Well-being Indicators', WIDER research papers, 2004/23 (UNU–WIDER).

Ng, A. (2018), 'Inequality in Malaysia: The Changing Contour of Income Distribution since the 1970s', paper presented at Khazanah Research Institute Seminar on Malaysia Income Distribution in a Global Context, 18 January 2018, Kuala Lumpur.

Ng, A., Tan, Z. G., and Tan, T. T. (2017), 'What Explains the Increase of Labour Income Share in Malaysia? Between Productivity, Technology, and Foreign Workers', draft paper for the 5th Annual Bank Negara Malaysia Economics Research Workshop, November 2017, Kuala Lumpur.

Nik Haslinda Nik Hussain (2007), 'Writing on Orang Asli into Malaysian History', in B. K. Cheah (ed.), *New Perspectives and Research on Malaysian History: Essays on Malaysian Historiography (MBRAS Monograph 41)* (Kuala Lumpur: Malaysian Branch of the Royal Asiatic Society), 211–228.

Nonini, D. M. (1992), *British Colonial Rule and the Resistance of the Malay Peasantry, 1900–1957* (New Haven, CT: Yale University Southeast Asia Studies).

Notestein, F. W. (1953), 'Economic Problems of Population Change', in *Proceedings of the Eighth International Conference of Agricultural Economists* (London: Oxford University Press).

Ong P. L., et al. (2014), 'The Making of Malaysian Solidarity: A Historical Look at Education and Social Cohesion in Sarawak', *Malaysian Journal of Society and Space*, 10/1, 36–48.

Ongkili, J. P. (1985), *Nation Building in Malaysia, 1946–1974* (Singapore: Oxford University Press).

Ooi, K. G. (1990), 'Sarawak Malay Attitudes Towards Education During the Period of Brooke Rule, 1841–1946', *Journal of Southeast Asian Studies*, 21/2, 340–359.

—— (1997), *Of Free Trade and Native Interests: The Brookes and the Economic Development of Sarawak 1841–1941* (Kuala Lumpur: Oxford University Press).

—— (2012), 'Torn Between Economics, Public Health and Chinese Nationalism: The Anti-Opium Campaign of Colonial Malaya, c. 1890s–1941', in L. Monnais and H. J. Cook (eds.), *Global Movements, Local Concerns: Medicine and Health in Southeast Asia* (Singapore: NUS Press).

—— (2018), *Historical Dictionary of Malaysia* (2nd edn., London: Rowman and Littlefield).

Organisation for Economic Co-operation and Development [OECD] (2013), *Southeast Asian Economic Outlook 2013: With Perspectives on China and India* (Paris: OECD Publishing), http://dx.doi.org/10.1787/saeo-2013-en, accessed 8 August 2018.

—— (2014), 'PISA 2012 Results in Focus: What 15-year-olds Know and What They Can Do With What They Know', https://www.oecd.org/pisa/keyfindings/pisa-2012-results-overview.pdf, accessed 8 August 2018.

—— (2015), *The Innovation Imperative: Contributing to Productivity, Growth and Well-being* (Paris: OECD Publishing), http://dx.doi.org/10.1787/9789264239814-en, accessed 18 September 2018.

—— (2016), *PISA 2015 Results, vol. 1: Excellence and Equity in Education* (Paris: OECD Publishing).

—— (2017), *Organisation for Economic Co-operation and Development Reviews of Innovation Policy: Malaysia 2016 Report* (Paris: OECD Publishing).

—— (2018a), 'Income Inequality', https://data.oecd.org/inequality/income-inequality.htm, accessed 8 August 2018.

—— (2018b), 'Crude Oil Production', https://data.oecd.org/energy/crude-oil-production.htm, accessed 20 May 2019.

—— (2019), 'GDP Per Capita and Productivity Growth', OECD Productivity Statistics, https://doi.org/10.1787/data-00685-en, accessed 12 May 2019.

Organisation for Economic Co-operation and Development/Eurostat (2005), *Oslo Manual: Guidelines for Collecting and Interpreting Innovation Data, 3rd Edition, The Measurement of Scientific and Technological Activities* (Paris: OECD Publishing), https://doi.org/10.1787/9789264013100-en, accessed 18 September 2018.

Overton, J. (1994), *Colonial Green Revolution? Food, Irrigation and the State of Colonial Malaya* (Oxon, UK: CAB International).

Park, D. (2015), 'The Global Productivity Slump: Common and Country-specific Factors', https://blogs.adb.org/blog/global-productivity-slump-common-and-country- specific-factors, accessed 8 August 2018.

Parkinson, C. N. (1964), *British Intervention in Malaya, 1867–1877* (Kuala Lumpur: University of Malaya Press).

Parmer, J. N. (1960), *Colonial Labor Policy and Administration: A History of Labor in the Rubber Plantation Industry in Malaya* (Locust Valley, NY: Published for the Association for Asian Studies by J. J. Augustin).

—— (1990), 'Estate Workers' Health in the Federated Malay States in the 1920s', in P. J. Rimmer and L. M. Allen (eds.), *The Underside of Malaysian History: Pullers, Prostitutes, Plantation Workers* (Singapore: Singapore University Press).

Perkins, D. H., Rasiah, R., and Woo, T. W. (2017), 'Explaining Malaysia's Past Economic Growth and Future Prospects', Working Papers Series WP No. 1 (Jeffrey Cheah Institute on Southeast Asia, Sunway University).

Phua, K. H. (1990), 'The Development of Health Services in Malaya and Singapore 1867–1960', PhD thesis, University of London.

Piketty, T. (2014), *Capital in the Twenty-First Century* (Cambridge, MA: Harvard University Press).

Piketty, T., Li Yang, and Zucman, G. (2016), 'Capital Accumulation, Private Property and Rising Inequality in China, 1978–2015', NBER Working Paper No. 23368, April 2017 (National Bureau of Economic Research).

Pletcher, J. (1990), 'Public Interventions in Agricultural Markets in Malaysia: Rice and Palm Oil', *Modern Asian Studies*, 24/2, 323–340.

Pountney, A. M. (1911), *The Census of the Federated Malay States: Review of the Census Operations and Results, 1911* (London: Darling & Son Limited).

Pridmore, F. (1975), *Coins and Coinages of the Straits Settlements and British Malaya, 1786 to 1951* (California: National Museum).

Psacharopoulos, G. (1994), 'Returns to Investment in Education: A Global Update', *World Development*, 22/9, 1325–1343.

Purcell, V. (1965), *The Chinese in Modern Malaya* (2nd edn., Kuala Lumpur: Oxford University Press).

Puthucheary, J. J. (1960), *Ownership and Control in the Malayan Economy* (Singapore: Donald Moore).

—— (1978), *The Politics of Administration: The Malaysian Experience* (Kuala Lumpur: Oxford University Press).

Radelet, S., and Sachs, J. (1998), 'The Onset of the East Asian Financial Crisis', NBER Working Paper No. 6680, August 1998 (National Bureau of Economic Research).

Ragayah Haji Mat Zin (2013), 'The New Economic Policy and Poverty Eradication in Malaysia', in E. T. Gomez and J. Saravanamuttu (eds.), *The New Economic Policy in Malaysia: Affirmative Action, Ethnic Inequalities and Social Justice* (Singapore: NUS Press).

Rais Yatim (2007), 'The Road to Merdeka', in A. Harding and H. P. Lee (eds.), *Constitutional Landmarks in Malaysia, the First 50 Years 1957–2007* (Singapore: LexisNexis), 1–24.

Ramasamy, P. (1994), *Plantation Labour, Unions, Capital, and the State in Peninsular Malaysia* (Kuala Lumpur: Oxford University Press).

Rasiah, R. (2018), 'Innovation Policy, Inputs, and Outputs in ASEAN', in Ambashi, M. (ed.), *Innovation Policy in ASEAN* (Jakarta: Economic Research Institute for ASEAN and East Asia), 277–320.

Rasiah, R. (2019), 'Building Networks to Harness Innovation Synergies: Towards an Open Systems Approach to Sustainable Development', *Journal of Open Innovation: Technology, Market, and Complexity*, 5/3, 70, https://doi.org/10.3390/joitmc5030070, accessed 5 February 2020.

Rasiah, R., and Yap, X. S. (2015), 'Innovation Performance of the Malaysian Economy', in *The Global Innovation Index, 2015: Effective Innovation Policies for Development* (Geneva: WIPO; Ithaca, NY: Cornell University; Fontainebleau, France: INSEAD), 139–146.

Rasmussen, E., Lind, L., and Visser, J. (2004), 'Divergence in Part-time Work in New Zealand, the Netherlands and Denmark', *British Journal of Industrial Relations*, 42/4, 637–658.

Reece, B. (2011) (ed.), *End of an Era: The Borneo Reminiscences of C.F.C. Macaskie, C.M.G.* (Kota Kinabalu: Opus Publications Sdn. Bhd).

Reinhardt, J. M. (1970), 'Administrative Policy and Practice in Sarawak: Continuity and Change Under the Brookes', *The Journal of Asian Studies*, 29/4, 851–862.

Ricardo, D. (1911), *On the Principles of Political Economy & Taxation* (London: J. M. Dent).

Robert, L. R. (1972), 'The Duff Syndicate in Kelantan 1900–1902', *Journal of the Malayan Branch of the Royal Asiatic Society*, 45/1.

Robson, J. H. M. (2001), *Records and Recollections (1889–1934)*, MBRAS Reprint 21 (Kuala Lumpur: Malaysian Branch of the Royal Asiatic Society).

Rodrik, D. (2009), *One Economics, Many Recipes: Globalization, Institutions and Economic Growth* (New Jersey: Princeton University Press).

—— (2015), 'Premature Deindustrialization', NBER Working Paper No. 20935, February 2015 (National Bureau of Economic Research).

Rodrik, D., Subramaniam, A., and Trebbi, F. (2004), 'Institutions Rule: The Primacy of Institutions over Geography and Integration in Economic Development', *Journal of Economic Growth*, 9/2, 131–165.

Rosnani Hashim (1994), 'Educational Dualism in Malaysia: Implications for Theory and Practice', PhD thesis, University of Florida.

Ross-Larson, B. (1980), 'Social and Political Setting', in K. Young, W. C. F. Bussink, and P. Hasan (eds.), *Malaysia: Growth and Equity in a Multiracial Society* (Baltimore: Johns Hopkins University Press).

Rostow, W. W. (1962), *The Stages of Economic Growth* (London: Cambridge University Press).

Rudner, M. (1972), 'The Draft Development Plan of the Federation of Malaya, 1950–1955', *Journal of Southeast Asian Studies*, 3/1, 63–96.

—— (1975), 'Financial Policies in Post-War Malaya: The Fiscal and Monetary Measures of Liberation and Reconstruction', *The Journal of Imperial Commonwealth History*, 3, 323–348.

—— (1976), 'The Structure of Government in the Colonial Federation of Malaya', *Southeast Asian Studies, Kyoto University*, 13/4, 495–512.

—— (1977), 'Education, Development and Change in Malaysia', *Southeast Asian Studies*, 15, 23–62.

—— (1994), *Malaysian Development: A Retrospective* (Ottawa: Carlton University Press).

Runciman, S. (1992), *The White Rajahs: A History of Sarawak from 1841–1946* (Kuala Lumpur: S. Abdul Majeed & Co).

Ruslan Khalid (2013), *Quest for Architectural Excellence, A Malaysian Experience* (Marshall Cavendish: Singapore).

Rutter, O. (1922), *British North Borneo: An Account of its History, Resources and Native Tribes* (Kota Kinabalu: Opus Publications Sdn. Bhd).

Sachs, J. D. (2005), *The End of Poverty: Economic Possibilities for Our Time* (New York: The Penguin Press).

—— (2011), *The Price of Civilization: Reawakening American Virtue and Prosperity* (New York: Random House).

—— (2015), *The Age of Sustainable Development* (New York: Columbia University Press).

—— (2017), *Building the New American Economy: Smart, Fair, and Sustainable* (New York: Columbia University Press).

Sadka, E. (1954) (ed.), 'The Journal of Sir Hugh Low, Perak, 1877', *Journal of the Malayan Branch Royal Asiatic Society*, 27/4, 11.

—— (1968), *The Protected Malay States, 1874–1895* (Kuala Lumpur: University Malaya Press).

Sandhu, K. S. (1969), *Indians in Malaya: Some Aspects of Their Immigration and Settlement (1786–1957)* (Cambridge: Cambridge University Press).

Sandhu, K. S., and Wheatley, P. (1989), *Management of Success: The Moulding of Modern Singapore* (Singapore: Institute of Southeast Asian Studies).

Santasombat, Y. (2017) (ed.), *Chinese Capitalism in Southeast Asia: Cultures and Practices* (Singapore: Palgrave Macmillan).

Saw, S. H. (1988), *The Population of Peninsular Malaysia* (Singapore: Singapore University Press).

Schutz, R. R. (1951), 'On the Measurement of Income Inequality', *American Economic Review*, 41, 107–122.

Schultz, T. W. (1960), 'Capital Formation by Education', *Journal of Political Economy*, 68/6, 571–583.

—— (1961), 'Investment in Human Capital', *The American Economic Review*, 51/1, 1–17.

Secretary of State for the Colonies (1946), *Malayan Union and Singapore: Statement of Policy on Future Constitution*, Cmd (6724) (London: His Majesty's Stationery Office).

Shaari Abdul Rahman (2001), *Population Distribution and Basic Demographic Characteristics, 2000 Population and Housing Census of Malaysia* (Putrajaya: Department of Statistics–Malaysia).

—— (2002), *Education and Social Characteristics of the Population, 2000 Population and Housing Census of Malaysia* (Putrajaya: Department of Statistics–Malaysia).

Shad Saleem Faruqi (2019), *Our Constitution* (Selangor Darul Ehsan: Thomson Reuters Asia).

Shaharil Talib (1984), *After Its Own Image: The Trengganu Experience, 1881–1941* (Singapore: Oxford University Press).

—— (1995), *History of Kelantan 1890–1940* (Selangor: The Malaysian Branch of the Royal Asiatic Society).

—— (1996), 'Twentieth Century Capitalism in Southeast Asia: The Balance Sheet', *JATI—Journal of Southeast Asian Studies*, 2, 53–63.

Shamsul, A. B., and Athi, S. M. (2015), 'Ethnicity and Identity Formation: Colonial Knowledge, Colonial Structures and Transition', in M. L. Weiss (ed.), *Routledge Handbook of Contemporary Malaysia* (Oxford: Routledge), 267–278.

Sheng, A. (1989), 'Bank Restructuring in Malaysia: 1985–88', Policy, Planning and Research Department working papers, No. WPS 54 (World Bank), http://documents.worldbank.org/curated/en/215951468758685508/Bank-restructuring-in-Malaysia-1985–88, accessed 8 August 2018.

Shireen Mardziah Hashim (1998), *Income Inequality and Poverty in Malaysia* (Maryland: Rowman and Littlefield).

Silcock, T. H., and Fisk, E. K. (1963) (eds.), *The Political Economy of Independent Malaya: A Case-Study in Development* (Singapore: Eastern Universities Press).

Sinnadurai, V. (1990), *The Privy Council Cases: Malaysia, Singapore, Brunei* (Kuala Lumpur: Professional Law Books and London: Sweet and Maxwell).

Siregar, R. Y., and Lim, C. S. (2010), 'The Role of Central Banks in Sustaining Economic Recovery and in Achieving Financial Stability', *Journal of Advanced Studies in Finance*, 1/1, 83–99.

Siti Rohani Yahaya (2009), 'The Development Process and Women's Labour Force Participation: A Macro Level Analysis of Patterns and Trends from the 1980s', in Jamilah Ariffin (ed.), *Readings on Women and Development in Malaysia: A Sequel Tracing Four Decades of Change* (Selangor: MPH).

Smith, A. (1910), *The Wealth of Nations* (London: J. M. Dent).

Smith, T. E. (1952), *Population Growth in Malaya: An Analysis of Recent Trends* (London: Royal Institute of International Affairs).

Snodgrass, D. R. (1980), *Inequality and Economic Development in Malaysia* (Kuala Lumpur: Oxford University Press).

—— (1995), 'Successful Economic Development in a Multi-Ethnic Society: The Malaysian Case', Development Discussion Paper, Issue 503 (Harvard Institute for International Development, Harvard University).

Solomon, J. (1988), *The Development of Bilingual Education in Malaysia* (Kuala Lumpur: Pelanduk).

South, F. W. (1946), 'British Administration in Malaya', *Australian Journal of Public Administration*, 6/2, 83–100.

Stefanidou, D. (2016), 'Can Singapore and Malaysia Keep Their Talents Home?', *ASEAN Today*, http://www.aseantoday.com/2016/09/can-singapore-and-malaysia-keep-their-talents-home/, accessed 8 August 2018.

Stevenson, R. (1975), *Cultivators and Administrators: British Educational Policy Towards the Malays, 1875–1906* (Kuala Lumpur: Oxford University Press).

Stiglitz, J. E. (2006), *Making Globalization Work* (New York: W. W. Norton & Company Ltd.).

—— (2012), *The Price of Inequality: How Today's Divided Society Endangers Our Future* (New York: W. W. Norton & Company Ltd).

Stiglitz, J. E., and Greenwald, B. C. (2015), *Creating a Learning Society: A New Approach to Growth, Development and Social Progress* (New York: Columbia University Press).

Stiglitz, J., Sen, A., and Fitoussi, J-P. (2010), *Mismeasuring Our Lives: Why GDP Doesn't Add Up (The Report by the Commission on the Measurement of Economic Performance and Social Progress)* (New York, NY: The New Press).

Stockwell, A. J. (1984), 'British Imperial Policy and Decolonization in Malaya, 1942–52', *The Journal of Imperial and Commonwealth History*, 13/1, 68–87, DOI: 10.1080/03086538408582679.

Stubbs, R. (1974), 'Counter-Insurgency and the Economic Factor: The Impact of the Korean War Prices Boom on the Malayan Emergency', Occasional Paper No. 19 (Institute of Southeast Asian Studies, ISEAS).

Sultan Nazrin Shah (2017), *Charting the Economy: Early 20th Century Malaya and Contemporary Malaysian Contrasts* (Kuala Lumpur: Oxford University Press).

—— (forthcoming), *Charting the Economy: Estimating Malaya's Historical Gross Domestic Product 1900–1939* (Kuala Lumpur: Oxford University Press).

Sunderland, R. (1964), *Winning the Hearts and Minds of the People: Malaya, 1948–1960* (Santa Monica: RAND).

Suppiah, U., and Raja, S. S. (2016), *The Chettiar Role in Malaysia's Economic History* (Kuala Lumpur: University of Malaya Press).

Sutton, K., and Buang, A. (1995), 'A New Role for Malaysia's FELDA: From Land Settlement Agency to Plantation Company', *Geography*, 80/2, 125–137.

Swettenham, F. (1906), *British Malaya: An Account of the Origin and Progress of British Influence in Malaya* (London: John Lane).

Tai Yuen, W. (2013), *Chinese Capitalism in Colonial Malaya, 1900–1941* (Selangor: Universiti Kebangsaan Malaysia).

TalentCorp (2018), 'Returning Expert Programme', https://www.talentcorp.com.my/rep, accessed 8 August 2018.

Tan, C. B. (2000), 'Socio-Cultural Diversities and Identities', in K. H. Lee and C. B. Tan (eds.), *The Chinese in Malaysia* (Shah Alam: Oxford University Press), 37–70.

Tan, L. E. (2000), 'Chinese Schools in Malaysia: A Case of Cultural Resilience', in K. H. Lee and C. B. Tan (eds.), *The Chinese in Malaysia* (Shah Alam: Oxford University Press), 228–254.

—— (2001), 'Multiple School Systems in a Plural Society', in *The Encyclopaedia of Malaysia, vol. 7: Early Modern History (1800–1940)* (Kuala Lumpur: Archipelago Press).

Tan, S. H. D. E. (1963), *The Rice Industry in Malaya, 1920–1940* (Singapore: Malaya Publishing House).

Tate, D. J. M. (1996), *The RGA History of the Plantation Industry in the Malay Peninsula* (Kuala Lumpur: Oxford University Press).

Taylor, D. C. (1981), *The Economics of Malaysian Paddy Production and Irrigation* (Bangkok: The Agricultural Development Council).

Teh, N. P., and Chor, F. T. (2017), 'Low Fertility in Malaysia. Can It Be Explained?', *Journal of Population Research*, 34/2, 101–118.

Teoh, C. H. (2002), *The Palm Oil Industry in Malaysia: From Seed to Frying Pan* (Selangor: WWF Switzerland).

The Commissioner of Law Revision–Malaysia. 2010. *Federal Constitution* (Reprint). Kuala Lumpur: Percetakan Nasional Malaysia.

Thillainathan, R. (2007), 'Economic Planning in Malaysia—Its Origin, Functions and Process', MS.

Thio, E. (1969), *British Policy in the Malay Peninsula, 1880–1910, vol. 1: The Southern and Central States* (Kuala Lumpur: University of Malaya Press).

Thoburn, J. T. (1977), *Primary Commodity Exports and Economic Development: Theory, Evidence and a Study of Malaysia* (London: John Wiley & Sons).

—— (1994), *Tin in the World Economy* (Edinburgh: Edinburgh University Press).

Thompson, V. (1943), *Postmortem on Malaya* (New York: The Macmillan Company).

Tilman, R. O. (1968), *Education and Political Development in Malaysia*, repr. series 27 (New Haven: Yale University).

Timmer, C. P. (1988), 'The Agricultural Transformation', in H. Chenery and T. N. Srinivasan (eds.), *Handbook of Development Economics*, vol. 1 (Amsterdam: North-Holland), 275–331.

—— (2015), *Food Security and Scarcity: Why Ending Hunger Is So Hard* (University of Pennsylvania Press and the Center for Global Development).

—— (2017), 'The Structural Transformation in Japan, Indonesia and Malaysia from 1880 to 2010: Part 1—Data and Trends', https://www.ehm.my, accessed 8 August 2018.

—— (2018), 'Reflections of Indonesia's Progress 50 years after Myrdal's *Asian Drama*', in D. Nayyar (ed.), *Asian Transformations: An Inquiry into the Development of Nations*, vol. 2 (Helsinki: United Nations University–WIDER).

Timmer, C. P., and Akkus, S. (2008), 'The Structural Transformation as a Pathway Out of Poverty: Analytics, Empirics and Politics', Working Paper 150 (Center for Global Development).

Timmer, M. P., de Vries, G. J., and de Vries, K. (2015), 'Patterns of Structural Change in Developing Countries', in J. Weiss and M. Tribe (eds.), *Routledge Handbook of Industry and Development* (London: Routledge), 65–83.

Too, C. C. (1990), *Notes on History of the Communist Party of Malaya* (Kuala Lumpur: University of Malaya).

Tregonning, K. G. (1964), *A History of Modern Malaya* (Singapore: Eastern Universities Press for University of London Press).

—— (1965), *A History of Modern Sabah (North Borneo, 1881–1953)* (Singapore: University of Malaya Press).

Trocki, C. A. (2002), 'Opium and the Beginnings of Chinese Capitalism in Southeast Asia', *Journal of Southeast Asian Studies*, 33/2, 297–314.

Tunku Shahriman Tunku Sulaiman (2004), 'The Johore Military Forces: The Oldest Army of Malaysia Regulars in the Peninsula', *Journal of the Malaysian Branch of the Royal Asiatic Society*, 77/2, 95–105.

Tunku Shamsul Bahrin (1967), 'The Pattern of Indonesian Migration and Settlement in Malaya', *Asian Studies*, 5/2, 233–257.

Turnbull, C. M. (1974), 'British Planning for Post-war Malaya', *Journal of Southeast Asian Studies*, 5/2, 239–254.

Tzannatos, Z., and Johnes, G. (1997), 'Training and Skills Development in the East Asian Newly Industrialised Countries: A Comparison and Lessons for Developing Countries', *Journal of Vocational Education and Training*, 49/3, 431–453.

Ul Haque, I. (1972), 'Analysis of Natural Rubber Market', Economic Staff Working Paper No. 133, August 1972, Trade Policies and Projections Division, Economics Department, World Bank.

Ungku Abdul Aziz (1964), 'Poverty and Rural Development in Malaysia', in *Kajian Ekonomi Malaysia (Malaysian Economic Studies)*, 1/1, 75–105.

Ungku Abdul Aziz (1965), 'Poverty Proteins and Disguised Starvation', in *Kajian Ekonomi Malaysia (Malaysian Economic Studies)*, 2/1, 7–48.

United Nations (1970), *Treaty Series: Treaties and International Agreements Registered or Filed and Recorded with the Secretariat of the United Nations*, vol. 750, nos. 10760 and 10761, https://treaties.un.org/doc/Publication/UNTS/Volume%20750/v750.pdf, accessed 19 September 2018.

—— (2013), *A New Global Partnership: Eradicate Poverty and Transform Economies Through Sustainable Development—The Report of the High-Level Panel of Eminent Persons on the Post-2015 Development Agenda* (New York: United Nations Publications).

—— (2019), *Charter of the United Nations*, https://www.un.org/en/charter-united-nations/, accessed 29 May 2019.

United Nations Department of Economic and Social Affairs (2005), 'Malaysia, Public Administration Country Profile', http://unpan1.un.org/intradoc/groups/public/documents/un/unpan023317.pdf, accessed 8 August 2018.

—— (2018), 'Global Migration Database (UNGMD)', http://www.un.org/en/development/desa/population/migration/data/, accessed 1 November 2018.

United Nations Department of Economic and Social Affairs, Statistics Division (2017), *Principles and Recommendations for Population and Housing Censuses* (ST/ESA/STAT/SER.M/67/Rev.3) (New York: United Nations Publications).

United Nations Development Programme (2015), *Human Development Report 2015: Work for Human Development* (New York: United Nations Development Programme).

United Nations Development Programme (2018), *Human Development Indices and Indicators: 2018 Statistical Update* (New York: United Nations Development Programme), http://hdr.undp.org/en/content/human-development-indices-indicators-2018-statistical-update, accessed 19 September 2018.

United Nations Development Programme–Malaysia (2007), *Measuring and Monitoring Poverty and Inequality* (Kuala Lumpur: United Nations Development Programme).

United Nations Economic and Social Commission for Asia and the Pacific [ESCAP] and Asian Development Bank [ADB] (2018), *Embracing the E-Commerce Revolution in Asia and the Pacific* (Manila: Asian Development Bank), http://dx.doi.org/10.22617/TCS189409-2, accessed 20 November 2018.

United Nations Educational, Scientific and Cultural Organization [UNESCO] (2018a), 'Inbound Internationally Mobile Students by Country of Origin', http://data.uis.unesco.org/Index.aspx?queryid=171, accessed 22 July 2018.

—— (2018b), 'Distribution of Tertiary Graduates by Field of Study', http://data.uis.unesco.org/index.aspx?queryid=163, accessed 8 August 2018.

—— (2018c), 'Gross Enrolment Ratio by Level of Education', http://data.uis.unesco.org/#, accessed 22 October 2018.

United Nations Environment Programme and United Nations University (2014), *Inclusive Wealth Report: Measuring Progress Towards Sustainability: Summary for Decision Makers* (Delhi: United Nations University–IHDP).

University of Groningen (2018), 'Maddison Historical Statistics', https://www.rug.nl/ggdc/ historicaldevelopment/maddison/, accessed 8 August 2018.

University of Groningen, Groningen Growth and Development Centre [GGDC] (2019), '10 Sector Database', https://www.rug.nl/ggdc/productivity/10-sector/, accessed 5 May 2019.

University of Malaya Editorial Board (1955), *Fifty Years of Education in Malaya* (Singapore: University of Malaya).

U.S. Energy Information Administration (2018), 'International Energy Statistics', https://www.eia.gov/, accessed 8 August 2018.

Villanueva, D. P., and Lim, C. S. (2008), 'Managing Capital Flow', in D. Villanueva (ed.), *Macroeconomic Policies for Stable Growth* (Singapore: World Scientific Publishing).

Vincent, J., and Rozali Mohamed Ali (2005), *Managing Natural Wealth: Environment and Development in Malaysia* (Washington, DC: RFF Press).

Vlieland, C. A. (1932), *A Report on the 1931 Census and on Certain Problems of Vital Statistics, British Malaya (The Colony of The Straits Settlements and the Malay States under British Protection, namely The Federated Malay States of Perak, Selangor, Negri Sembilan and Pahang and the States of Johore, Kedah, Kelantan, Trengganu, Perlis and Brunei)* (London: The Crown Agents for the Colonies).

Voon, P. K. (1977), 'Rural Land Ownership and Development in the Malay Reservations of Peninsular Malaysia', *South East Asian Studies*, 14/4, 496–512.

—— (1978), 'Evolution of Ethnic Patterns of Rural Land Ownership in Peninsular Malaysia: A Case Study', *South East Asian Studies*, 15/4, 510–529.

Wad, P. (2012), 'Revitalizing the Malaysian Trade Union Movement: The Case of the Electronics Industry', *Journal of Industrial Relations*, 54/4, 494–509.

Wan Arfah Hamzah and Ramy Bulan. 2003. *An Introduction to the Malaysian Legal System*. Shah Alam: Penerbit Fajar Bakti.

Wan Mardyatul Miza Wan Tahir and Sinnasamy, G. (2012), 'Dividend Policy: Evidence of Government-Linked Companies (GLCs)', Proceedings of the 2012 International Conference on Innovation Management and Technology Research, 21–22 May 2012, Malacca, Malaysia, 280–284.

Wan Ramlah Wan Abdul Raof (2011), *Population Distribution and Basic Demographic Characteristics, 2010 Population and Housing Census of Malaysia* (Putrajaya: Department of Statistics–Malaysia).

Wan Saiful Wan Jan (2016), 'Lesser Government in Business: An Unfulfilled Promise?', Policy IDEAS 27, Institute for Democracy and Economic Affairs, http://ideas.org.my/wp-content/uploads/2016/04/FINAL-lesser-government-in-business.pdf, accessed 8 August 2018.

Watson, M. (1921), *The Prevention of Malaria in the Federated Malay States: A Record of Twenty Years' Progress* (2nd edn., New York: E. P. Dutton and Company).

Watson, R. G. (1919), *Administration Report for the Year 1918*, pp. 15 and 17.

Webster, A. (1998), *Gentlemen Capitalists: British Imperialism in South East Asia 1770–1890* (London: Tauris Academic Studies).

Wellington, A. R. (1926), 'The Ways and Means Adopted by Government for the Control of Malaria in the Federated Malay States', *The Malayan Medical Journal and Estate Sanitation*, 1/3, 16–20.

Wheelock, D. C. (2012), 'Too Big to Fail: The Pros and Cons of Breaking Up Big Banks', *The Regional Economist, Federal Reserve Bank of St. Louis*, October issue, pp. 10–11.

White, N. J. (2013), *The International Order of Asia in the 1930s and 1950s* (London: Routledge).

Wigglesworth, R. (2018), 'Can Big Data Revolutionise Policymaking by Governments?', *Financial Times*, 31 January 2018.

Wilkinson, R. J. (1912), 'Census of the Wild Tribes', in A. M. Pountney (ed.), *The Census of the Federated Malay States: Review of the Census Operations and Results* (London: Darling & Son Ltd).

Winstedt, R. O. (1922), 'The Aboriginal Races', in J. E. Nathan (eds.), *The Census of British Malaya (The Straits Settlements, Federated Malay States and Protected States of Johore, Kedah, Perlis, Kelantan, Trengganu and Brunei)* (London: Waterlow & Sons Limited).

Winstedt, R. O. (1962), *A History of Malaya (Revised)* (Singapore: Marican and Sons).

Wong, D. (2004), *HSBC: Its Malaysian Story* (Singapore: Editions Didier Millet).

Wong, L. K. (1965), *The Malayan Tin Industry to 1914, with Special Reference to the States of Perak, Selangor, Negri Sembilan, and Pahang (Association for Asian Studies, Monographs and Papers, No. 14)* (Tucson: University of Arizona Press).

Woolcock, M., Szreter, S., and Rao, V. (2009), 'How and Why Does History Matter for Development Policy?', Working Paper 68 (Brooks World Poverty Institute, University of Manchester).

World Bank (1995), 'The Economic Development of Malaya', http://documents.worldbank.org/curated/en/172531468774650530/The-economic-development-of-Malaya, accessed 8 August 2018.

—— (1997), *Global Economic Prospects and the Developing Countries* (Washington, DC: The World Bank).

—— (2008), *Commission on Growth and Development—The Growth Report: Strategies for Sustained Growth and Inclusive Development* (Washington, DC: IBRD/World Bank), http://siteresources.worldbank.org/EXTPREMNET/Resources/489960-1338997241035/Growth_Commission_Final_Report.pdf, accessed 8 August 2018.

—— (2010), *Malaysia Economic Monitor: Growth Through Innovation* (Bangkok: World Bank).

—— (2011a), *Malaysia Economic Monitor: Brain Drain* (Bangkok: World Bank).

—— (2011b), *The Changing Wealth of Nations: Measuring Sustainable Development in the New Millennium* (Washington, DC: World Bank).

—— (2011c), 'The World Bank Group Framework and IFC Strategy for Engagement in the Palm Oil Sector', www.ifc.org/palmoilstrategy, accessed 5 May 2019.

—— (2013), *Malaysia Economic Monitor: High-Performing Education* (Bangkok: World Bank).

—— (2016) *Malaysia Economic Monitor: The Quest for Productivity Growth* (Kuala Lumpur: World Bank).

—— (2017), *Driving Performance from the Center: Malaysia's Experience with PEMANDU* (Kuala Lumpur: World Bank Group), http://documents.worldbank.org/curated/en/318041492513503891/Driving-performance-from-the-center-Malaysia-s-experience-with-PEMANDU, accessed 6 June 2019.

—— (2018a), 'Data Bank', http://databank.worldbank.org/data/home.aspx.

—— (2018b), 'World Development Indicators', http://wdi.worldbank.org/tables.

—— (2018c), *Improving Education Sector Performance in Malaysia: Lessons from a Delivery Unit Approach* (Kuala Lumpur: World Bank).

—— (2019), *World Bank Development Report 2019: The Changing Nature of Work* (Washington, DC: IBRD/World Bank).

Worth, W. J. (1940), 'Notes on Mineral Research in North Borneo', *The Asiatic Review (London)*, 36/126, 359–371.

Wu M. A. 1999. *The Malaysian Legal System*. 2nd edn. Kuala Lumpur: Pearson Education.

Yen, C. H. (2000), 'Historical Background', in K. H. Lee and C. B. Tan (eds.), *The Chinese in Malaysia* (Shah Alam: Oxford University Press).

Yeo, S. (2013), '80% of Malaysian Borneo's Rainforests Destroyed by Logging', *Climate Home News*, 18 July 2013, http://www.climatechangenews.com/2013/07/18/80-of-malaysian-borneos-rainforests-destroyed-by-logging/, accessed 4 September 2018.

Yeoh, B. S. A. (1993), 'Urban Sanitation, Health and Water Supply in Late Nineteenth and Early Twentieth Century Colonial Singapore', *South East Asia Research*, 1/2, 143–172.

Yip, Y. H. (1969), *The Development of the Tin Mining Industry of Malaya* (Kuala Lumpur: University of Malaya Press).

Yoshimura, M. (2002), 'Japanese Occupation and Economic Policy in Malaya', *Sejarah: Journal of the Department of History*, 10/10, 21–51.

Young, A. (2011), 'The Gini Coefficient for a Mixture of Ln-Normal Populations', MS (London School of Economics and Political Science).

Yuen, C. L. (1974), 'Japanese Rubber and Iron Investments in Malaya, 1900–1941', *Journal of Southeast Asian Studies*, 5/1, 18–36.

—— (1978), 'The Japanese Community in Malaya before the Pacific War: Its Genesis and Growth', *Journal of Southeast Asian Studies*, 9/2, 163–179.

Zaharah A. Rahman, 2012. 'Agricultural Research and Development in Malaysia', *The International Society for Southeast Asian Agricultural Sciences*, 18/2, 22–33.

Zainal Aznam Yusof (2011), 'The Developmental State: Malaysia', in P. Collier and A. J. Venables (eds.), *Plundered Nations? Successes and Failures in Natural Resource Extraction* (Hampshire: Palgrave Macmillan).

Zakaria Haji Ahmad (1977), 'The Police and Political Development in Malaysia: Change, Continuity and Institution-building of a Coercive Apparatus in a Developing, Ethnically Divided Society', PhD thesis, Massachusetts Institute of Technology.

—— (2006), *The Encyclopaedia of Malaysia, vol. 11: Government and Politics (1940–2006)* (Singapore: Archipelago Press).

Zaki Tun Azmi (2011), 'The Common Law of Malaysia in the 21st Century', paper presented at the Singapore Academy of Law Annual Lecture 2011, Singapore, http://journalsonline.academypublishing.org.sg/Journals/Singapore-Academy-of-Law-Journal/eArchive/ctl/eFirstSALPDFJournalView/mid/495/ArticleId/544/Citation/JournalsOnlinePDF, accessed 16 March 2018.

Archive Documents

Colonial Office (CO)

— (1925), CO 874/1012: *Borneo Administration Enquiry* (The National Archives–UK).

— (1926), CO 717/53/14: *Education Policy in Malaya.*

— (1927–1930), CO 531/21/4: *Defence of Sarawak Oil Fields.*

— (1928), CO 717/60/15: *Chinese Vernacular Education in Malaya.*

— (1928), CO 717/61/6: *Federated Malay States Annual Report on Education for the Year 1927.*

— (1931), CO 717/84/5: *Hospitals Kuala Lumpur.*

— (1931), CO 273/574/8: *Education in Malaya—Address by Sir George Maxwell on Education in Malaya at the Intercolonial Congress on Education in the Colonies, Paris, September 1931.*

— (1931), CO 273/576/16: *Memorandum on The Sultan Idris Training College and Malay Vernacular Education.*

— (1932), CO 273/579/1: *Annual Report on the Social and Economic Progress of the People of the Straits Settlements for 1931.*

— (1933), CO 717/101/1: *Federated Malay States Annual Report of the Education Department for the Year 1932.*

— (1936–1938), CO 717/119/1: *Federated Malay States Annual Report of the Education Department for the Year 1935.*

— (1937), CO 852/95/6: *Economic Survey of the Colonial Empire, Unfederated Malay States.*

— (1940), CO 273/662/5: *Report on State of Public Health in Malaya and Work of Medical Departments, 1939.*

— (1943–1944), CO 865/54: *Administration Departmental Organisation Medical.*

— (1945), CO 273/675/11: *Future Constitution for Malay Peninsula.*

— (1945), CO 273/675/12: *Future Policy New Constitution: Initial Relations with Malay Sultans on the Liberation of Malaya.*

— (1946), CO 273/676/6: *Malayan Education: A Post-war Programme by H. R. Cheeseman (1946).*

— (1946), CO 537/1565: *Views of Chinese in Malacca on the Malayan Union Constitution.*

— (1946), CO 717/149/14: *Financial Policy in the Malayan Union.*

— (1947), CO 537/2143: *Malayan Union: Policy.*

— (1947), CO 717/164/5: *Malay Economic Affairs.*

— (1947), CO 927/43/4: *Development of Malayan Union.*

— (1950), CO 717/192/7: *Draft Development Plan: Federation of Malaya.*

— (1950), CO 825/90: *Economic and Social Policy in Malaya.*

— (1950), CO 825/90: *Economic and Social Policy in the Borneo Territories: Sarawak, North Borneo and Brunei.*

— (1951), CO 717/202/1: *Law and Order: Economic Effects.*

— (1951 and 1952), CO 717/208/8 and 9: *Rural Industrial Development Authority (RIDA): Federal Government Press Statement.*

— (1951), CO 825/86: *Regional Cooperation; Economic Development; Preparation of Plans by S.E.A. Territories; Federation of Malaya.*

— (1955–1957), CO 889/8: *1957 Constitutional Commission and Representations to Lord Reid.*

Dominions Office (DO)

— (1957–1960), DO 35/9990: *Federation of Malaya: Economic Policy* (The National Archives–UK).
— (1958–1960), DO 35/9778: *Federal Land Development Authority.*

Foreign and Commonwealth Office (FCO)

— (1960), FCO 141/17151: *Singapore Colonial Policy, the Grand Design Part A* (The National Archives–UK).
— (1960), FCO 141/17151-2: *Singapore Colonial Policy, the Grand Design, Proposed Closer Association/Federation of the Federation of Malaya, Singapore and the Borneo Territories.*
— (1961), FCO 141/17152: *Singapore Colonial Policy, the Grand Design Part B.*
— (1969), FCO 24/485: *Civil Disturbances in Malaysia Following General Election.*

Foreign Office (FO)

— (1900), FO 69/224: *Correspondence from Duff Syndicate Limited* (The National Archives–UK).
— (1902), FO 93/95/16: *Declaration, Draft Agreement, and Note Relative to Kelantan and Trengganu.*
— (1904), FO 881/8305: *Correspondence of the Report of Affairs in the State Kelantan for the Year August 1903.*

Historical Administrative and Annual Reports

Federated Malay States

— (1911, 1927–1935), *Annual Report of the Federated Malay States, 1911, 1927–1935.*
— (1913, 1925, 1932), *Report on the Working of the Labour Department for the Year 1912, 1924, 1931, Supplement to the Federated Malay States Government Gazette* (Kuala Lumpur).
— (1927), *Annual Report of the Medical Department, Federated Malay States, 1927 by Dr. R. Dowden, pp. 4–5.*
— (1937), *Annual Report on the Social and Economic Progress of the People of the Federated Malay States for 1937 by C. D. Ahearne* (Kuala Lumpur: Federated Malay States Government Press).
— (various years), *Federated Malay States Census Reports.*

Federation of Malaya

— (1950a), *Malayan Statistics: General Section, April 1950* (Singapore).

— (1950b), *Draft Development Plan of the Federation of Malaya* (Kuala Lumpur, Government Press).

— (1952), *Report of the Registrar-General on Population, Births and Deaths for the Year 1950* (Kuala Lumpur).

— (1953–1955), *Annual Report on the Federation of Malaya for the Year 1952–1954* (Kuala Lumpur).

— 1956. *A Plan of Development for Malaya*, 1956–1960. Kuala Lumpur: Government Press.

— (1960), *'Immigration Ordinances, 1959', No. 12 of 1959, Ordinances and Acts passed during the year 1959* (Kuala Lumpur).

— (1961), *Second Five-Year Plan, 1961–1965* (Federation of Malaya: Government Press).

Malayan Union

— (1948), *Report on the Registration of Births and Deaths for the Years 1946* (Kuala Lumpur. Singapore).

Singapore

— (1946–1947), *Annual Report of the Medical Department* (Singapore).

— (1954), *Report of the Joint Committee on the Future of the University of Singapore*, Command Paper No. 36 of 1954.

— (1959), *Report of the Ministry of Health* (Singapore).

Straits Settlements

— (1881–1932), *Report of the Protector of Chinese* (Singapore).

— (1926–1927), *Annual Colonial Report on the Colony of Straits Settlements* (London).

— (1931), *Annual Report of the Secretary for Chinese Affairs* (Singapore).

— (1933), *Annual Departmental Reports of the Straits Settlements for the Year 1931* (Singapore).

— (1937), *Annual Report on the Social and Economic Progress of the People of the Straits Settlements, 1937.*

— (1946), *Annual Report of the Medical Department 1946* (Colony of Singapore).

— (various years), *Straits Settlements Census Reports.*

Straits Settlements and Federated Malay States

— (1933–1938), *Report on the Immigration Department* (Singapore).

— (1939), *Malayan Year Book 1939, Statistics Department of the Straits Settlements and Federated Malay States* (Singapore).

Index

Page numbers in bold indicate reference to map or figure

D

F

G

J

P

Q

R

S

T

U